Studies in the ...   ...es
...u Construction

The Proceedings of the Fifth Annual
Construction History Society
Conference

Queens' College, University of Cambridge, 6-8th April 2018

Edited by

James W.P. Campbell

Nina Baker

Amy Boyington

Michael Driver

Michael Heaton

Yiting Pan

Henrik Schoenefeldt

Michael Tutton

David Yeomans

Published by The Construction History Society
1 Scroope Terrace
Cambridge
CB2 1PX

www.construction.co.uk

© 2018, First Edition
ISBN 978-0-9928751-4-5

Formatting and layout by Yiting Pan
First printed by Lulu print on demand for the Construction History Society

Proceedings of the Fifth Construction History Society Conference
edited by James W P Campbell, Nina Baker, Amy Boyington, Michael Driver, Michael Heaton, Yiting Pan,
Henrik Schoenefeldt, Michael Tutton, and David Yeomans

The Fifth Annual Construction History Society Conference

Organised by:

The Construction History Society
in association with CIBSE

Hosted by:

Queens' College, University of Cambridge &
The Department of Architecture, University of Cambridge

Organising Committee

Chair: James W P Campbell
Secretary: Amy Boyington
Treasurer: Jonathan Lee
Exhibitions: Michael Heaton

Scientific Committee

Chair: David Yeomans
Antonio Becchi
James Campbell
Nina Baker
Michael Driver
Mike Heaton
Will McClean
Henrik Schoenefeldt
Michael Tutton
Christine Wall

Editorial Committee

Chair: James W P Campbell
Secretary: Amy Boyington
Nina Baker
Michael Driver
Michael Heaton
Yiting Pan
Henrik Schoenefeldt
Michael Tutton,
David Yeomans

Acknowledgements

The preparation of any conference takes an enormous amount of time and effort on behalf of a large number of people. I am hugely grateful to all those who have assisted in the planning of this, Fifth Annual Construction History Society Conference. In particular I would like to thank Dr Amy Boyington and Dr Yiting Pan who have worked so hard to put these proceedings together. David Yeomans as chair of the Scientific Committee took on the unenviable task again of collecting all the abstracts together and distributing them to the various members of the scientific committee for review. I am as always grateful for his sage advice and I would like to thank him and all the other members of that committee for their efforts in reviewing all these proposals. Once the papers were in the editorial committee took over and went painstakingly through every paper. Any errors remaining are my fault not theirs.

I would like to thank all those staff of the Architecture Department and Queens' College, in the University of Cambridge for hosting this conference, without whose aid none of this would be possible. I would like to thank all those members of the Committee of the Construction History Society who give their time so generously to the society without any form of remuneration. They are Antonio Becchi, Michael Driver, Michael Heaton, Niall Bird, Will Maclean, Alan Palmer, Michael Tutton, Nina Baker, Andrew Jackson, Jonathan Lee, and the journal editors Christine Wall, Hermann Schlimme and Will Maclean, ably assisted by Wendy Andrews (Editorial Secretary) and Karey Draper (Book Reviews). Without their support the Society would not function. This year we tragically lost an important member of the committee and a great friend to us all, Treve Rosoman. He will be sadly missed.

James W P Campbell
2018

Contents

Preliminaries

History of Building Services

Contents

The Ancient World

The Middle Ages

The Seventeenth and Eighteenth Centuries

The Nineteenth Century

The Twentieth Century

Contents

The Twenty-First Century

Preliminaries

Introduction

The current volume contains the proceedings of the two-day conference held at Queens' College, Cambridge from 6-8 April 2018. This year the first day of the conference is entirely devoted to the history of building services, which is chaired by Dr Henrik Schoenefeldt, Senior Lecturer in Sustainable Architecture at the University of Kent, Member of the CIBSE Heritage Group and National Teaching Fellow. In this conference Building Services were always conceived in the widest terms to encompass not only plumbing, artificial lighting and ventilation, but also the ways that buildings were adapted to provide these without recourse to external sources of power. Historically this was, of course, often the case by necessity. In his Keynote talk, *Towards a History of Building Services*, Dr Schoenefeldt is exploring some of the boundaries between the history of environment design and construction history. This talks draws, amongst others, on his current research project within the Palace of Westminster Restoration and Renewal Programme. The project comprises the first study to systematically reconstruct the Houses of Parliament's nineteenth-century ventilation system, combining site surveys with archival research. This project has revealed the great extent to which its construction had been shaped by the design of the historic ventilation system.[1]

The second day of the conference followed the format of previous years with a more general call for papers on all aspects of the history of construction. We were delighted to receive many papers in the second category that cover a wide range of fields and periods from the ancient world to the present day.

This volume is thus divided into two parts. The first section deals with the first day and the history of the built environment and the papers are arranged alphabetically by authors, while the rest of the volume is divided into sections chronologically following the previous volumes in the series.

Preliminaries

This book is timely: Reyner Banham's ground-breaking history of building services, *The Architecture of the Well-tempered Environment,* published in 1969, celebrates its fiftieth anniversary next year in 2019. It thus seems to be a pertinent moment to be holding a conference looking at what has happened since it first appeared. As an area of construction history, despite the increasing literature on the subject outside the field, it seems fair to say that it still remains underdeveloped within it, with comparatively few papers in conferences and journals looking at aspects of building services. This leads naturally to the question of what such a study might contain. Banham's claim in *The Architecture of the Well-tempered Environment* that mechanical approaches only began in the eighteenth and nineteenth century is surely incorrect unless we take a very narrow definition of "mechanical". Plumbing and drainage was an integral part of construction since Antiquity, as were methods for heating and the removal of fumes. Roman hypocaust systems were every bit as complicated as the air-based heating systems that reappeared in the nineteenth century and were of course inspired by, and based on, those earlier precedents. Nonetheless the changes in approach and understanding are just as important to note. The mathematisation of science saw the development of workable theories of fluid dynamics that would later influence plumbing and ventilation. Arguably, however, such influences were minor compared to the introduction of steam power and then electricity which had more immediate and profound effects.

The main argument of the Banham's book is that the development of the building services was marked by a transition from largely structural to mechanical approaches to environmental control. Whilst structural solutions relied on the intelligent use of built form, methods of construction and materials to achieve an adequate indoor climate, acoustics, lighting or ventilation, the development of mechanical services allowed environmental control to become less dependent on structural solutions. The latter climaxed in the mid-twentieth century in tall buildings combining the hermetically-sealed glass-curtain walls with mechanical ventilation and air-conditioning. SOM's Lever House in New York represents one prominent early example.

Although Banham saw this transition as the outward expression of technological progress, his book illustrates that the history of construction and the history of building services are closely intertwined, inseperable. The link between the two, however, is rarely explored. The premise underlying this year's Construction History Conference is that a focus on the interrelationship between questions of construction, materials, environmental design and services has the potential of yielding new insights and a more comprehensive history of building technology.

The development of mechanical services, including modern concepts of central heating and ducted air, had an increasingly strong influence on the development of architecture from the early nineteenth century onwards. Two important journal articles in the history of building services that builds directly on Benham's narrative were published in the 1970s. The first was '*19th Century Mechanical System Designs*,' by Donald Prowler and Robert Bruceman in 1977, and '*Central Heating and Forced Ventilation: Origins and Effects on Architectural Design*' by Robert Bruegmann in 1978.[2] Covering pioneering developments in the late 18th to mid-19th century these papers have addressed significant gaps in Banham's work with its strong focus on later nineteenth-century and the modern movement. Moreover, some of the most significant buildings within the history of nineteenth-century environmental design were not covered in his book. The first is the Palace of Westminster, which, created after the fire of 1834 as a purpose built parliament. It was the earliest building where the principles of warm air central heating and stack-ventilation were applied on a large scale, providing a precedent for the servicing of many public building from 1850 until the early 20th century before the introduction of electrically-powered fans. These included, amongst others, the Natural History Museum (1873), the Royal Albert Hall (1871) and Glasgow University (1870). Individual building case studies looking at the integration of building services have been published since. Significant studies, include, amongst others, Jeffrey Cook and Tanis Hinchcliffe, 'Designing the well-tempered institution of 1873' (1995) and 'Delivering the well-tempered institution of 1873' (1996) are significant as they also critical review the performance of the historic system [3]. Todd Willmert's article 'Heating Methods and Their Impact on Soane's Work: Lincoln's Inn Fields and Dulwich Picture Gallery' (1993) explores the role of technical experimentation within the work of the architect John Soane.[4]

Another significant pair of buildings excluded from Banham's book was Joseph Paxton's Crystal Palace in Hyde Park (1851) and Sydenham (1854), which are significant as they illustrate how innovative principles of environmental control, initially developed at a much smaller scale within the context of glasshouse horticulture, were exploited to adapt fully-glazed structures climatically for human, non-horticultural purposes. In his book 'The Glasshouse' John Hix has explored how the challenge of cultivating rare non-native plants in Britain's temperate climate was driving extensive experimentation with central heating and solar design principles.[5] The application of these principles to the Crystal Palace, however, has only been examined more recently in two articles, 'The Crystal Palace Environmentally Considered' (2008) and 'Adapting Glasshouses for Human Use: Environmental Experimentation in Paxton's Designs for the 1851 Great Exhibition Building and the Crystal Palace, Sydenham'(2011).[6] The work of John McCean, Henry Russel-Hitchcock, and Bill Addis have illuminated its significance within the history of production engineering and structural design, but it also exemplified a synthesis of structural and environmental thinking in Victorian engineering.[7] The idea of using glass covered public spaces to create microclimates with no or little mechanical heating became widely deployed in the second half of the nineteenth-century. A notable examples are Horace Jones's design for the Smithfield Market, completed in 1868. Its climate was regulated following similar process of environmental monitoring and control. It operated on a principle that Dean Hawkes described as the 'Selective mode' of environmental control. The horticultural glasshouse, and its later adaptations, represented a site where both structural and mechanical engineering approaches could co-evolve as two major traditions of environmental design.

Our opening paper in this volume, the keynote lecture by Professor Dean Hawkes on day one, examines how Banham's *The Architecture of the Well-tempered Environment* was somewhat biased in its treatment of services and their relation to architecture, championing an approach that brought the mechanical to the foreground and expressed it visually. This he compares to the approach of Louis Kahn and others where the architecture is no less dependent and determined by the services but where (unlike for instance Richard Roger's Pompidou) the services are concealed rather than exposed.

Section One: Services

The first section of the book takes the papers from the first day of the conference. They are arranged here alphabetically, rather than in the sessions that were used in the conference itself, simply for clarity. The book thus opens with Jørgen Burchhardt's paper, *The Hidden System: how District Heating came to Town* which examines the development of district heating systems in Denmark. District hearting systems are becoming popular once again in Northern Europe, where they are now being championed as a more sustainable solution than local heating systems. This paper shows how such systems were first installed in Denmark in the 19th century and how the country now has a very extensive network of district heating systems from which much can be learned.

Some of the same problems of producing extensive heating systems are explored in Jozefien Feyaert's paper, *Building Services in Nineteenth-Century Belgian Cellular Prison Architecture*. As Feyaerts shows in this well-illustrated paper, the wish to have single occupancy of cells in large prisons in the 19th century created considerable challenges in terms of plumbing, heating and ventilation. The results were systems of considerable complexity that aimed to keep cells warm but adequately ventilated and free from smells, which were an obvious problem when the water closet was housed within the cell itself.

By contrast, John Gelder's paper, *Roman Building Services and Architectural Manuals* provides a survey of the treatment of building services in Roman treatises, covering not only aqueducts and water supply, but also hypocausts, sounding vessels in theatres, water clocks and sundials. His useful tables show that the authors were far from accurate in their descriptions of Roman practice and not even consistent amongst themselves.

The next paper Silvia Groaz's, *Ducts and Moldings: the Ambiguous Inventions of Franco Albini and Franca Helg* could hardly be more different. It looks again at the expressive facades of the period 1957-1972 of La Rinascente store in Rome (described briefly in Banham's *The Architecture of the Well-tempered Environment*) and the SNAM offices at San Donato Milanese both of which incorporated elaborate ventilation systems within their façades. This paper relates directly to the one that follows. Again following on from Banham, Boris Hamzean's *The Evolution of the Pompidou Centre's Air-Conditioning System: Towards a new Figure of Architecture* discusses directly how Renzo Piano and Richard Roger's designs were influenced by La Rinascente. It tells the fascinating story of the interaction between the engineers and the architects over the final forms of the system which so dominates the façade.

Over the past six years Dr Schoenefeldt has developed and delivered a specialist module in the history of environmental design and technology, 'AR828: *Rediscovery: Understanding historic buildings and past environmental technologies,*' which forms part of the MSc in Architecture and Sustainable Environment. At this conference seven students are presenting the findings of research undertaken within the context of this module during Michaelmas 2017. Hala Roshdy Hegazy's paper, *The Open air School as a Typology [in the] 20th century*, is the first of the student papers from Kent. It traces the extraordinary development of Open Air schools. These have been studied in the English and German context, but Hegazy looks at those in the USA. Within the context of the modern movement the Open Air Schools movement can be interpreted as a counterpart to the hermetically sealed and mechanical serviced environments. Composed of lightweight structures, capable of being opened to the open air to a point where their function was reduced to no more than simple shelters against rain, represented an alternative environmental architecture. These structures were not created to immerse the human body within an artificial climate, but to expose it to the outside air and the sun. This practice of exposing the body was part of a historic methods of tuberculosis treatment, which, alongside its architecture, became obsolete and superseed by drug-based treatments of TB, following the discovery of streptomycin in the 1940s. The particularly notable features of this paper are the extraordinary photographs of children sitting in outside classrooms, wrapped up against the freezing temperatures of the northern US winter.. The photograph of the Open Air School sit in sharp contrast to the sun shining down on Steve Baer's strange Zome house in Albuquerque, New Mexico with its water drum solar collecting wall. This is the subject of Mariam Itani's appropriately titled paper, *Case Study Analysis on the Baer House*, a building that is introduced in the second edition of Banham's *The Architecture of the Well-tempered Environmen*, published in 1984. The last of this first group of papers from the Kent school is Alisa Kahn's *Sanatoria for treatment of tuberculosis and the aftercare colonies*, which looks at three 20th century tuberculosis hospitals: Dr Varrier Jones's Papworth Village Settlement (1916-1920), Jan Duiker's Sanatorium Zonnestraal, Netherlands (1925-31) and Alvar Aalto's Paimio Sanatorium, Finland (1929-33). The paper includes some delightful hand drawn explanatory sketches by the author. Similar to Hegazy's study of Open Air schools, this paper explores a strand of environmental design that was concerned with therapeutic use of natural light and air, yet it also challenges the modern movement's claimed association of transparency with heliotherapeutic treatment. As the glass of Duiker's transparent patient wings intercepted ultraviolet light, patients still had to be stationed on open balconies in order to gain access to fresh air and direct sunlight.

Dr Ranald Lawrence paper, *The environmental role of transition spaces in Victorian architecture*, uses three examples, the lobbies of the Houses of Commons (1852), the Natural History Museum (1873) and the Glasgow School of Art (1910), to explore the use of intermediate spaces inside nineteenth-century public buildings, displaying interiors with climatic diversity. The latter co-existing with early attempts to create spaces with uniform artificially conditioned spaces. The next two papers return to the twentieth century. The first, Samuel Leatt's *Owen Williams's Boots' "Wets" factory [1930-1932] - a case study on the daylight factory typology* provides a fascinating insight not only into the environmental design of this extraordinary building, which is still in use, but also shows how its construction and form was influenced by the work of Albert and Mortiz Kahn, with whom Williams had worked in the United States. It stresses how, before the widespread use of the electric light, daylight was an essential aspect of factory design. Kan Liang's *Case Study: The Norris Cotton Federal Office Building [1970-1976]* looks at another concrete building, this time one which is deep plan and lit by artificial light. Liang's paper looks at the early computer control and solar collection systems for this HVAC-dependent building, which attempted to make it state-of-the-art for the time. Designed and built between 1973 and 1976, it was built within the same political context as Steve Baer's experimental solar house, but instead of aiming to achieve full autonomy from oil through the use of renewal energy and passive solar design, the *Norris Cotton Federal* aimed to demonstrate how far mechanically serviced buildings could become more energy efficient. It performance was also monitored by the National Bureau of Standard, addressing questions of energy efficiency addressed as well as user satisfaction.

Dermott O'Dywer's paper *The Drainage of the Fucine Lake in Antiquity and in the Nineteenth Century* tells the fascinating story of how the Romans tried, and nineteenth century engineers succeeded, in draining a completely landlocked lake in central southern Italy. The Lake used to fill a hollow in the mountains about 100km East of Rome. As a piece of water it was a breeding ground for mosquitos and malaria. O'Dywer's paper explains the extraordinary lengths the Romans went to under the Emperor Claudius to construct a tunnel 5.6 km long under a mountain. Although the Romans succeeded in building the tunnel, it failed to drain the lake. He goes on to show how nineteenth-century engineers then followed the Roman tunnel, making a much larger tunnel between 1824 and 1835, when the lake was particularly low. This tunnel succeeded in draining it entirely, creating the flat area of arable land which still exists today.

Libraries, before the widespread availability of electric light, had to deal with the conflicting problems of providing windows large enough to read by with a source of heating to allow readers to work while avoiding any of risks associated with naked flames in buildings full of highly flammable materials. Most early examples in Northern Europe just ignored the heating problem entirely. Surabhi Pandurangi's, *Understanding Preservation and Comfort in the British Museum Reading Room*, discusses how the architect Sydney Smirke and the head librarian Antonio Panizzi transformed the central courtyard of the old British Museum into a magnificent new reading room, surrounded by top lit iron book stacks and a hot air heating system installed to provide comfort for the readers. This scheme was significant in that the architect had taken the lead in designing the defining features of the ventilation and warm air central heating system. They were determined prior to engaging Phipson as contractor and specialist building services consultant. The plans, submitted for competitive tender in 1855, provided the contractors with exceptionally detailed specifications for the design of the system, including precise specification of the temperature range, ventilation rate and air velocities to be maintained within reading room. Having introduced the services into his architectural plans from an early stage, Smike succeed in delivering a scheme in which the construction, architectural plan and building service infrastructure were closely intertwined. This contrasts with many other public buildings constructed in the mid and late nineteenth century. In buildings such as the Royal Courts of Justice, the Natural History Museum, the Royal Albert Hall or the Palace of Westminster the challenge of integrating modern building services within the architectural fabric only received serious consideration at a relative late stage.[8] This resulted in architectural plans having to be altered or the design of the building services being constrained.

The penultimate paper in this section, Fiona Smyth's *"Symphony for Full Orchestra and Asbestos": Tuning Albert Hall during WWII* tells the ususual story of the move of the Proms from the now largely forgotten Queen's Hall to the Albert Hall after the former was bombed in the Blitz in the Second World War, and the subsequent modifications to improve the acoustics of the Albert Hall.

The section ends with Qian Wang's *Case Study: The Temperate House at Kew—Controlling the climate under a glass sky.* The Temperate House's construction was plagued with problems and completed in 1899, 30 years after construction began. This paper examines how its design integrated central heating and natural ventilation to maintain, both in summer and winter, the climate conditions required to sustain an extensice collection of temperate plants. It also shows that the adoption of a timber-frame glass envelope was a conscious departure from the sophisticated wrought-iron technology adopted for the construction of the Palm House in the 1840s.

This collection of papers is interesting not only in showing how much work remains to be done on building services but also in how much of what can be learned from past projects is still applicable to day. In many ways the current interest is the very opposite of Banham's. Banham reveled in the expression of modern mechanical engineering and promoted an architecture that not only incorporated as much plant as possible but positively celebrated that plant. In the second edition of *The Architecture of the Well-tempered Environment* the Pompidou is thus very much an example for Banham of good practice. In a world where conspicuous celebration of energy profligacy is no longer appropriate such an approach seems outmoded, but what is striking is how relevant Banham's book still remains. Many of the papers in this volume used his examples as a striking off point and in highlighting the importance of so many early technical solutions he was a undoubtedly a pioneer in the field. What these papers have also revealed is how by digging deeper there is so much more left to be discovered and that current research has barely scratched the surface of the fascinating field.

Section Two: General Studies in Construction History

The second half of this volume is devoted to studies in the general field of construction history. As past volumes of this series have shown, construction history is a broad field. It is not just the history of building technology or the history of civil, mechanical and structural engineering, although it includes these, and they remain a dominating area. It also encompasses archaeology and economic and social history, as it examines how those building in the past thought about building problems and the factors that influenced them. The flow of money into building projects, for instance, had a profound influence on the physical form of the results as did the supply of labour. The richness of the subject of construction history lies in its ability to bring together radically different approaches in the analysis of building projects to draw new insights. Just as there are many ways in which buildings can be analysed so there are many in ways in which the papers collected together here could be arranged. Again they were arranged thematically in the conference itself. Here, however, they are arranged for simplicity, chronologically, as in previous volumes.

Ancient World

Despite its huge importance in construction history, archaeology remains underrepresented in these volumes. Only three papers look at the world before the Middle Ages. Two are in the first section and both look at Roman technology: John Gelder's paper *Roman Building Services and Architectural Manuals,* and Dermott O'Dywer's *The Drainage of the Fucine Lake in Antiquity and in the Nineteenth Century.* The only paper in this section is Alessandro Pierattini's *The beginnings of stone construction in archaic Greece* looks at the technical problems of stonemasonry in early Corinth in ancient Greece, which provides important new evidence from stone markings on the ways stone was cut and lifted into position.

Middle Ages

The six papers in this volume that cover the period broadly termed the Middle Ages look at surveying, stonemasonry and carpentry. The first of the three papers on stonework, entitled *The Vault over the Crossing Tower in Lincoln Cathedral in the Context of European Gothic Architecture* uses digital photogrammetry. This new process shows great promise for recording historic buildings. A series of standard photographs are taken and fed into a computer programme (in this case Agisoft PhotoScan Professional) which works out the geometry of the surfaces photographed and then stitches the images back onto a computer model of the photographed surfaces. The result is a fully-coloured 3D scan of the vault. Here the process is used to show that Lincoln's vault is similar but not the same as examples elsewhere. The process of influence was the visible rather than by movement of craftsmen.

Michael Wood's *King's College Chapel Vault: Movement, Restraint and Foundation Loading* looks at the interesting question of whether the various iron straps and reinforcements added above the vault of King's College Chapel are necessary. Structural calculations showing that existing buildings stand up are not normally accepted in Construction History journals or conferences. The emphasis should always be on how the builders understood what they were doing. Here they are justified in exploring whether Scott's interventions are necessary and suggest that they were, or at least (thanks to recent movement) now are.

Karl-Magnus Melin's *Medieval Counter-Rebated Doors: a Door from the Diocese of Lund compared with English examples* is a brilliant investigation of a very peculiar type of timber door construction, previously thought to have been confined to 11th and 12th century England but shown here to have also existed in Southern Sweden in the early 15th century and thus presumably also used elsewhere.

In *Trace Methods of the Romanesque Churches of Val D'Aran*, Mónica López Piquer and Josep Lluis I Gionovart, looks at the fascinating problem of orientation of churches. Roman basilicas were orientated with the throne in an apse at the West end. Christianity chose the reverse. The apse was moved to the East end, the church orientated to the sun rise or supposedly to the date of the martyrdom of the relevant saint. This has always been difficult to establish. This paper uses new survey data to explore this issue.

Churches also form the subject of Mattias Hallgren and Robin Gullbrandsson's paper. They tell the fascinating story of the discovery of a decorative 12/13th century timber roof concealed by a 15th century vault. Lastly, Shirley Markley's, *Earth-Mortared Masonry Construction – its Symbolism and Functionality – an Irish and United Kingdom Perspective* shows how earth mortar, too easily assumed to be the poor-person's alternative to lime mortar, used only for houses, was also used for ecclesiastical architecture.

Seventeenth and Eighteenth Centuries

Lee Prosser's *The Roofs of Inigo Jones Revisited* provides a hugely important survey of Jones's surviving roof structures in the light of the roof Prosser has himself discovered and surveyed in Hampton Court Palace. The introduction of the King Post Truss into England by Jones had already been noted by David Yeomans in his book *The Trussed Roof,* and my own PhD studied Wren's use of the structure, surveying a great many of his roofs in the later seventeenth century, but here Prosser adds significantly to what was previously known, establishing that Jones was responsible for popularising the form. Carpentry is also the theme of Aikaterine Maria Chalvatzi's *Theatre Construction in Eighteenth Century France* which looks specifically at the influence of the Palais-Royal and goes on to show how the wooden structures gave way to iron ones in the 19th century.

Mark Samuel's paper, *The Dry Dock at Ramsgate: Smeaton or Rennie* grew out of archaeological examinations of the surviving remains which forced a search of the documentary sources. As this paper shows the dock had a much longer history. A new dry dock had been constructed by John Smeaton in the 18th century and then a John Rennie had carried out extensive works and the question is whether Rennie's works entirely replaced Smeaton's or were simply repairs. This question provides the answer.

Nineteenth Century

The nineteenth century usually proves to be an abundant source of papers for the CHS conference and this year was no different. Six papers cover diverse subjects. The first, by Chris How, looks at the *First Wire Nail machines and their origins* traces the development. How's story starts in the eighteenth century with pin and needle making. He goes on to show that the headed nail was patented in the early years of the 19th century in Paris, thirty years earlier than previously believed. Beatrice Lampariello, *Cells and Epines-Contreforts for a New kind of Vaulted Roofing: the Church of Saint-Jean-de-Montmartre in Paris* looks at innovative brick and reinforced concrete vaulting system developed for the church at the end of the 19th century. Iva Stoyanova's paper, *Scaffolds for the Iron Glass Roof of the Gallery Vittorio Emanuele II: challenges, design and evolution* discusses the various scaffolding systems that have been used to construct and later repair this remarkable structure. The gallery will remind many of the Crystal Palace, built for the Great Exhibition but sadly later destroyed in a fire after it was moved to Sydenham. Although most people associate Joseph Paxton's name with the building of the Crystal

Palace, the firm in charge of its construction and its subsequent move was Fox Henderson. As Robert Thorne's *The Rise and Fall of Fox Henderson 1840-1856* shows, this made the engineering firm famous. What was surprising is that the practice then lasted only 16 years. This paper traces the reason for its rise and subsequent dramatic fall.

Ignacio-Janvier Gil-Crespo's *Military Reports about the wall and fortification projects in Havana, 19ᵗʰ century,* tackles a very different rise and fall, that of a large fortification. It follows the marvellous trail of maps and drawings tracing Havana's now almost entirely demolished fortifications. In his paper *From the drawing to the wall: the operational chain of building stone on the restoration worksite of St Martin's church in Liège during the nineteenth century,* Antoine Baudry tells the story of the supply of stone for the restoration of a medieval gothic church in the then newly-formed kingdom of Belgium.

Twentieth Century

The division between nineteenth and twentieth centuries is an entirely artificial one and many of the papers in the previous section cover developments in this period, just as many papers in this section start by looking backwards to earlier changes. Matthijs Degraeve and Frederik Vandyck's paper, *Spatial analysis of timber construction SMEs in Brussels (1880-1980)* is a case in point. It maps the prevalence of timber fabrication companies in the period in question in Belgium, focusing in on a narrower area to look at surviving buildings. This is an unusual piece of construction history. The study of the changing form of building industry and its economic and social background has always been an important part of construction history and an important counter-balance to studies which all too easily concentrate on the technology used to construct buildings. A building site can only be understood properly by looking at both aspects and indeed also drawing in wider factors such as political and legislative structures and problems of material supply. What is interesting here is that the study of the businesses turns back to a study of the buildings in which they operated.

Continuing the theme of studies that look at how building sites operated, Michael Mulvey's paper, *'Once Hard men were heroes': Masculinity Cultural Herosim and Performative Irishness in the Post War British Construction Industry* represents a refreshingly new approach which draws on literary sources to explore the mindset of post-war Irish economic migrants workers in the building industry and in particular their "tough-guy" self-image. In a political environment today where the reliance on cheap migrant labour in the building industry is a critical point of discussion in the United Kingdom, these issues could hardly seem more relevant.

Mario Rinke and Roshanak Haddadi's paper, *The Riding Arena in St Moritz and the locomotive depot in Bern – a comparative study of early glulam construction in Switzerland,* returns to more traditional construction history territory, exploring the development of new materials, here glue laminated roof structures in the first few decades of the twentieth century. New materials became critical in war time and the two World Wars in the twentieth century drive technical innovation in many areas including building materials. This is immediately apparent in the supply of temporary war time buildings. Karey Draper's research *Armstrong Huts in the Great War (1914-1918)* grows out of her pioneering PhD (which I supervised) which identified over 60 temporary hut types in the First and Second World War in Britain. Here she focuses on one of the best known but least understood: the Armstrong Hut in the First World War. Draper's work has been strongly dependent on archival research, which for Government works is thankfully abundant, although a surprising quantity of material has been lost.

Archives form the subject of the next paper. This looks at the archives of Cecil Hewett (1926-1998). This conference marks the twentieth anniversary of Hewett's death. Hewett dominated the study of Medieval structural carpentry in the 1970s and 1980s in Britain, producing a series of beautifully illustrated volumes on the many aspects of structural carpentry but particularly of church and cathedral roofs. He had a woodworking background and a sharp eye for details, particularly the forms of joints and he became known for his theories of dating buildings by these joints, before dendrochronology became common or indeed viable. Trained as an artist, his drawings were works of art in their own right. This year's conference is accompanied by an exhibition of previously unseen drawings. Ming [Charmaine] Shan Ng's paper provides an insight into the contents of the substantial archives of his drawings and papers that he left to the Essex Record Office in Chelmsford. These include many drawings of structures for books that were never published and in some cases form the only record of now lost structures. Hewett's work remains controversial and was debated at the conference. The chief problem is that his drawings were not based on accurate measurements and are thus beguiling but unreliable and in many cases potentially misleading. As his work becomes accessible to a new generation of researchers a proper study of what he produced and its limitations is overdue.

Valdimir Ladinski's *Immediate Housing Construction Following the 1963 Skopje Earthquake* shows the problems of lack of archival material. Here he identifies prefabricated houses erected after the 1963 earthquake as temporary accommodation after the 1963 earthquake in Macedonia, at the time part of Communist Yugoslavia. The scale and speed of reconstruction is impressive but it would be interesting to know more about the types of prefabricated buildings, where they came from, who designed them and what were they originally designed for. Ladinski's paper provides the groundwork for such further research. The next paper, Joel Audefroy's *History of Early Twentieth Century Anglo-Carribbean Wooden Houses in Chetumal City, Quintana Roo, Mexico* traces similar low-rise construction, here focusing more on techniques than any notion of prefabrication. As reinforced concrete becomes all too prevalent across the globe, the question here is how far to document this vernacular construction and protect it despite the fact that it is not very old.

In Roberta Lucente and Laura Greco's *The Montreal Stock Exchange Tower by Luigi Morretti and Pier Luigi Nervi (1961-1965* continues Greco's studies of Nervi buildings which have appeared in previous volumes in this series, using sketches and drawings from the archives to show how Nervi and Moretti thought through the design of this high rise concrete structure.

Twenty-First Century

Luciano Cardellicchio's *The Italian engineering contribution in the technical development of the new Hertziana Library by Juan Navarro Baldeweg,* draws on documents of the time to trace the role of the engineer in the decision-making process. Studying such decision-making processes forms the back-bone of construction history and in documenting this process for a building built within living memory Luciano is able to call upon the direct recollections of the individuals involved. This paper is thus not only a useful contribution in terms of recording process for future historians but also poses a very useful question: how recent can a building be for it to be considered history? Can studies of contemporary buildings such as this be considered construction history at all? When is a building historical? This introduction is probably not the place to discuss any of these issues in detail. Perhaps the most obvious response is that it is a question of approach: it is possible to analyse any completed project in a number of ways, and it is construction history if approached from that point of view.

Concluding Remarks

In a year that could have easily been short of papers the devotion of the first day of the conference entirely to the History of Building Services has led to what we hope our readers will agree is a substantial volume. At over 550 pages it is the largest volume in the series so far. The forty-one papers summarized here thus provide an overview of the broad range of just some of the research being carried out in the growing field of construction history, while the papers on building services show how fruitful this area of research is and how much — as in every area of construction history —there remains to be done. We hope you will enjoy this volume and find in its varied contents material that is both useful and interesting in stimulating further debate and research in the growing field of construction history.

James W.P. Campbell
Conference Chairman

Henrik Shoenefeldt
Chairman of Day One
(History of Buildings Services)

Construction History Society
April 2018

References

[1] The project was subject of a feature article: Liza Young, 'Uncovering the secret of Parliament's lost building services,' *CIBSE Journal*, November 2017, pp. 24-28.

[2] R. Brucemann and D. Prowler, '19th Century Mechanical System Designs', *Journal of Architectural Education*, vol. 30, 1977, pp. 11-15; R. Bruegmann, 'Central Heating and Forced Ventilation: Origins and Effects on Architectural Design', *JSAH*, vol. 37, 1978, pp. 143-160.

[3] J. Cook, T. Hinchcliffe, 'Delivering the well-tempered institution of 1873', *Architectural Research Quarterly*, vol. 2, no. 1, September 1996, pp. 66-75; J. Cook, T. Hinchcliffe, 'Designing the well-tempered institution of 1873', *Architectural Research Quarterly*, vol. 1, no. 2, December 1995, pp. 70-78.

[4] T. Willmert, 'Heating Methods and Their Impact on Soane's Work: Lincoln's Inn Fields and Dulwich Picture Gallery', *Journal of the Society of Architectural Historians*, vol. 52, no. 1, March 1993, pp. 26-58.

[5] J. Hix, *The glasshouse*. London: Phaidon, 1996.

[6] H. Schoenefeldt, 'The Crystal Palace – Environmentally Considered', *Architectural Research Quarterly*, vol. 12, 2008, pp. 283–94; H. Schoenefeldt, 'Adapting Glasshouses for Human Use: Environmental Experimentation in Paxton's Designs for the 1851 Great Exhibition Building and the Crystal Palace, Sydenham', *Architectural History*, vol. 54, 2011, pp. 233–73.

[7] J. McKean, *Crystal Palace: Joseph Paxton and Charles Fox*. London: Phaidon, 1994; H-R. Hitchcock, *Architecture: Nineteenth and Twentieth Centuries*. Harmondsworth: Penguin, 1977; B. Addis, 'The Crystal Palace and its Place in Structural History', *International Journal of Space Structures*, vol. 21, no. 1, 2006, pp. 11-36.

[8] H. Schoenefeldt and M. Köhler, 'The Royal Standard', *CIBSE Journal*, April 2017, pp. 36-8. The challenges of integrating a complex system of building services into Charles Barry's existing architectural scheme has been explored in, H. Schoenefeldt, 'The Lost (First) Chamber of the House of Commons', *AA Files*, vol. 72, June 2016, pp.44-56; H. Schoenefeldt, *Architectural and scientific principles in the design of the Houses of Parliament, in Gothic Revival Worldwide*. Leuven: Leuven University Press, 2016, pp. 174-99.

After Banham: "I do not like pipes, I do not like ducts

Dean Hawkes

Darwin College, University of Cambridge, UK

Introduction: an 'Unwarranted apology'

At the turn of the eighteenth and nineteenth centuries a profound change occurred in the nature of architecture. For the first time the environmental function of the form and construction of a building came to be assisted by mechanical devices – systems for warming, ventilation and, soon afterwards, artificial lighting. In the standard histories of architecture this transformative moment passes without mention. This changed with the publication in 1969 of Reyner Banham's *The Architecture of the Well-tempered Environment*.[1] In the first paragraph of the opening chapter that he entitled, *Unwarranted apology*, Banham wrote,

> In a world more humanely disposed and more conscious of where the prime humane responsibilities of architects lie, the chapters that follow would need no apology, and would probably never need to be written. It would have been apparent long ago the art and business of creating buildings is not divisible into two intellectually separate parts – *structures* on the one hand, and on the other *mechanical services*.[2]

Banham set in motion the now substantial field of environmental history in architecture. With the passage of almost half a century, this history has evolved and deepened beyond Banham's inevitably broad-brush treatment.[3]

In this paper I wish to develop a particular critique of Banham by exploring one of the central questions in environmental architecture, the relation of structure and services. In a key passage Banham quoted Louis Kahn's now famous statement,

> I do not like pipes, I do not like ducts. I hate them really thoroughly, but because I hate them so thoroughly, I feel that they have to be given their place. If I just hated them and took no care, I think they would invade the building and completely destroy it. *I want to correct any notion you may have that I am in love with that kind of thing*. (my italics).[4]

Speaking in 1964, Kahn was responding to the pressure he felt as modern services systems seemed to demand ever more space within buildings. This was exactly the time when he was engaged with two major science laboratory projects, the Richards Medical Research Building, Philadelphia, 1957-65 and the Salk Institute for Biological Studies, San Diego, 1959-65. In both the specialised requirements for servicing laboratories added to the conventional requirements for environmental services, thus increasing the spatial demands of the mechanical systems. This was the origin of the distinction that Kahn drew between 'served' and 'servant' spaces that became a key strategy in all of his subsequent buildings, investing them with a specific and coherent topography. Peter Blundell Jones went so far as to suggest that this was Kahn's "main contribution to the history of architecture".[5]

After Banham: "I do not like pipes, I do not like ducts"

For Banham the idea of 'served' and 'servant' played an essential part in the development of the categories of 'concealed' and 'exposed' power that became a central element in his analysis of environmental strategies in the architecture of the second half of the 20th century. The key building was the Richards Laboratories, with its clusters of service towers surrounding the square laboratory floor plates and soaring high above the roof, as shown in Mary Banham's axonometric drawing (Fig. 1).

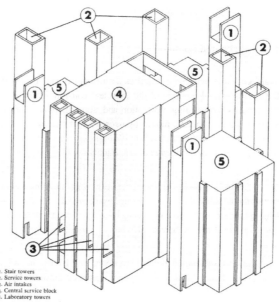

1. Stair towers
2. Service towers
3. Air intakes
4. Central service block
5. Laboratory towers

Fig. 1 Richards Laboratories, Philadelphia. Architect, Louis Kahn. Axonometric drawing. After Reyner Banham.

This explicit differentiation of *human – served* and *mechanical – servant* territories became one of the principal themes in Banham's analysis. A significant antecedent to Richards that Banham proposed was Frank Lloyd Wright's Larkin Building at Buffalo, NY, completed in 1906. Here we have an office building whose striking originality drives quite fundamentally from its environmental setting. Wright himself wrote,

> The Larkin administration building was a simple cliff of brick hermetically sealed to keep the interior space clear of the poisonous gases in the smoke from the New York Central trains that puffed along beside it.[6]

Once again, an axonometric drawing illustrates the environmental discipline of the building (Fig. 2) and reveals its similarities with the Richards Laboratories, although here disciplined by the bi-axial symmetries of its Beaux Arts conventions. The central, atrium-like office block is 'served' by clusters of ducts and staircases at all four corners. For Wright, as for Kahn, human circulation was deemed to be a 'service'. The Larkin Building was demolished in 1950 and it is improbable that it was a conscious precedent for Kahn's building since, as Banham suggests, its environmental topography went unnoticed by earlier historians.

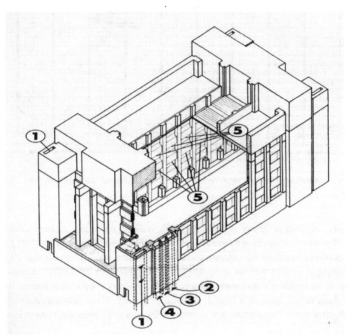

Fig. 2   Larkin Building, Buffalo.   Architect, Frank Lloyd Wright.   Axonometric drawing.   After Reyner Banham.

In the 2nd edition of *The Architecture of the Well-tempered Environment*, published in 1984, Banham identified Renzo Piano and Richard Rogers' Centre Pompidou as one of the significant demonstrations of 'served' and 'servant', or in his favoured term, 'exposed power'.   The plan (Fig. 3) show the affinity between this building and both Richards and Larkin, with the body of the building embraced between the exposed mechanical services, pipes and ducts, that cover the entire east façade and the glass-enclosed escalators – one again people circulation expressed as 'service' – that weave across the west facade.

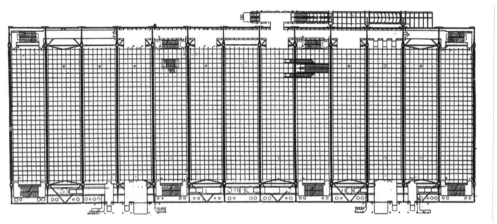

Fig. 3   Centre Pompidou, Paris.   Architects: Renzo Piano and Richard Rogers. Typical Floor Plan.
©RSHP/Fondazione Renzo Piano.

Writing of Rogers' later Inmos factory at Newport, South Wales, with its take on exposed services, he declared that, "... here was a set of architectural temperaments who, unlike Louis Kahn, did not 'hate pipes', but saw them as a modern opportunity to extend the expressive vocabulary of their art".[7] Roger's *tour de force* in this idiom, the Lloyd's Building in London was not competed until 1986, two years after the publication of Banham's 2nd edition.   There, in the building's environmental topography, we may trace a clear lineage from Larkin through Richards, with their shared form of a central, inhabited, 'servant' block surrounded by clusters of 'servant' towers, in which, once again, the circulation of people, in elevators or by staircase, is a service (Fig.4).

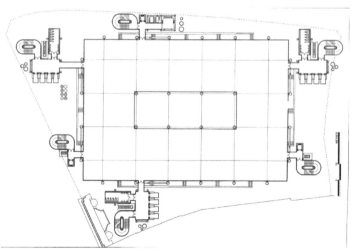

Fig. 4   Lloyd's Building, London.   Architect, Richard Rogers.   Floor Plan Galleries 1-6.   ©Rogers Stirk Harbour & Partners.

This building would surely have clinched Banham's argument for the primacy of *exposed power* as the ultimate and logical end point of environmental history to that point. The decorum of Wright's and Kahn's buildings has been superseded by a "new expressive vocabulary".

At this point, attention should be paid to Banham's alternative category of 'concealed' power.[8]   This is largely an analysis of certain strands in American architecture in the first half of the twentieth century. As mechanical services began to appear in the design and construction of the most ubiquitous American building type, the high-rise office building, so space had to be found for them.   We should note that the early skyscrapers of Chicago and New York, constructed at the turn of the century, were, in spite of their great height, structural sophistication and with circulation by elevator, environmentally primitive.[9]   They were conceived to be primarily daylit, before electric lighting became efficient and commonplace with the development and marketing of the fluorescent tube in 1938.[10]   Heating was by conventional hot water or steam systems and ventilation was a simple matter of opening a window.   So, the arrival of, first, mechanical ventilation, followed by air conditioning, demanded a response in order to integrate these into the fabric of buildings.   As Banham tells us this came in the form of the suspended ceiling.   In combination with the structural frame and, eventually, the curtain wall, a 'kit of parts' of immense utility evolved.   This allowed horizontal ceiling voids above which a plethora of ducts, cables and pipes could be concealed.   The examples Banham gives span the early and middle decades of the 20th century, with particular notice given to Howe and Lescaze's Philadelphia Savings Fund Society Building (1932) and Skidmore Owings and Merrill's Lever House (1951).   In the latter we have one of the great precedents for the fully air-conditioned, sealed and glazed envelope stereotype that has become, by virtue of its ubiquity, one of the most successful buildings types in the history of architecture.   The glass skin, first proposed by Mies van der Rohe in his environmentally speculative Berlin glass-skyscraper projects of 1919 and 1922, paradoxically, is not a source of illumination, but a weather excluding membrane.   All the environmental necessities of the building and its occupants, heat, light and air, now issue from the suspended ceiling.

In drawing the distinction between 'exposed' and 'concealed' power Banham was, I suggest, declaring his preference for one over the other, for 'exposed', with its 'new expressive vocabulary', over the decorum of 'concealed'.   This is evident when he wrote in *Well-tempered Environment*

> The achievement of invisibly serviced glass enclosures clearly satisfied one of the leading aesthetic ambitions of modern architecture, but in doing so it flouted one of its most basic moral imperatives, that of the honest expression of function ... [11]

Banham's history of mechanical services in buildings set us on the way. It was, however and understandably, imperfect.   We may now propose an alternative narrative and, from this, reconsider the crucial relation between mechanical systems and the fabric of the buildings that they serve.

An alternative history

A significant omission from Banham's history of environment was reference to the treatises that were published in the first part of the nineteenth century.   In Britain alone, we may list works by Tredgold (1824), Richardson (1837), Reid (1844) and Bernan (1845).[12] These and other texts are evidence of the extent to which such installations were in use at this time – theory, always and logically, follows in the wake of practice in these matters.   Buildings of all scales and many functions incorporated quite complex systems for warming and ventilation and, a crucial point, these were in many cases inconspicuously incorporated into their fabric.[13] These books also signalled the emergence of a new profession, that of the specialised consultant on the environmental services of buildings. A further and significant point of note is that the possibilities of these installations were quickly grasped by architects of the highest standing.

A good place to begin is the work of Sir John Soane. His status in the history of architecture has long been secured and his practical explorations of environmental possibilities were amongst the first to be studied in the new, post-Banham, wave of research in environmental history. One of the first contributions was by Robert Bruegmann.[14] This presented a survey of pioneering installations in buildings in Europe and the United States and made reference to Soane's systems at his house in Lincoln's Inn Fields. This building, the Bank of England, 1788 to 1831 and the Dulwich Picture Gallery, 1811-13, were the subjects of a detailed study by Todd Willmert in 1993.[15] Throughout his oeuvre, spanning four decades of practice, Soane incorporated innovative systems for warming and ventilation in buildings of many functions including, in addition to these the remarkable complex of Law Courts built in the 1820s at the Palace of Westminster. A key text in considering Soane's environmental ideas is Lecture VIII of the series he delivered between1810 and 1820 in his capacity as Professor of Architecture at the Royal Academy of Arts.[16] Here we find an eloquent statement of his perspective on the need to 'warm' buildings.

> The due and equably warming of rooms in cold climates, it must be admitted, is of great importance to the health and comfort of the inhabitants of every dwelling, from the cottage of the servant to the palace of the sovereign. So necessary is warmth to existence that we cannot be surprised at the various inventions that have been produced for the better and more economical warming of our houses.

Although there is no mention here of banks or picture galleries or law courts Soane applied this desire for 'due and (equable) warming of rooms' to all of his buildings and, as Willmert outlines,[17] pursued this end in collaborations with a number of specialist advisors and contractors. It is significant that Charles James Richardson, the author of *A Popular Treatise on the Warming and Ventilation of Buildings*,[18] was an architect who worked as an assistant in Soane's office from 1824 until 1837, the year of Soane's death. In that book we find the most detailed description of the final installation at Lincoln's Inn Fields, which used the Perkins system of heated water circulation.

> There are 1200 feet of pipe in the Soane Museum. It is divided into two circulations; one of which warms the picture-room, and the two rooms beneath. The other, which has the largest circulation annexed to it, first warms the office in which the expansion and filling pipes are placed; the pipe then traverses the whole length of the Museum, then passes through the breakfast-room under the long skylight, intended to counteract the cooling effect of the glass, it then passes through the floor into the lower room, forms a coil of pipe of 100 feet in the staircase, and returns to the furnace, passing in its course twice round the lower part of the Museum, a coil from the circulation is likewise placed under the floor of the dressing-room, which, by an opening in the floor and the side of the box, admits a current of warm air into the room above.

This description indicates the complexity and bulk of the early systems and raises the question of their impact on the architecture in which they were installed. As Willmert shows, the system at Lincoln's Inn Fields, all 1200 feet of pipe, was quite unobtrusively incorporated into the fabric. Perhaps more significantly, he suggests that Soane's experiments with spatial complexity in the planning of the office, museum, picture room, would have been impossible without central heating. This is, perhaps, a pre-echo of Banham's environmental analysis of Frank Lloyd Wright's Prairie Houses, of which he wrote,

Here, almost for the first time, was an architecture in which environmental technology ... was finally subsumed into the normal working methods of the architect and contributed to his freedom of design.[19]

At the Dulwich Picture Gallery, free from the complexities of working with an existing structure, Soane intended from the outset that the building would have an extensive heating system and provided for this in the construction by arranging a continuous duct beneath the floor of the galleries to house the pipes of the steam heating system to the design of Matthew Boulton and James Watt. This is clearly illustrated in the watercolour 'site record' made during the construction of the building (Fig. 5).[20]

Fig. 5 Dulwich Picture Gallery, London. Architect, Sir John Soane. Construction perspective showing floor duct for heating pipes. © Sir John Soane's Museum, London. Photo: Hugh Kelly.

By the middle years of the nineteenth century, buildings of all types were equipped with extensive systems for 'warming and ventilation'. In Britain, museums, law courts, gentlemen's clubs, libraries, theatres, schools and, significantly, the most important building project of the age, the Houses of Parliament all enjoyed these amenities. This was precisely the period in British architectural history when the principal concern was the question of style. A building should be either revived classical or gothic. As Summerson showed, most architects at this time were able, and willing, to work in either style.[21] They were also, with equal ease, able to incorporate the new environmental systems within their chosen stylistic approach.

The clearest example of this adaptability and expertise may be found in the work of Charles Barry, who, with Pugin, was appointed architect for the gothic reconstruction of the Houses of Parliament in 1836 and, the following year, received the commission for the Reform Club, in the manner of an Italian renaissance palazzo. The story of the design of the environmental systems at the Houses of Parliament is long and complex, with the figure (or spectre?) of Dr. David Boswell Reid featuring strongly in the drama. At the Reform Club things were more straightforward, perhaps significantly without Reid. Barry was instructed by the club's building committee, 'to confer with Mr Oldham in conjunction with Messrs. Manby and Price' on the design and installation of the building's system. The important point in the present discussion is that in both buildings Barry and his collaborators achieved a comprehensive synthesis of style and technology in which both form and detail worked together to meet the environmental ends.[22]

By the end of the 19th century we may catalogue not just these, but countless other buildings in which comprehensive environmental systems were accommodated within their physical and stylistic fabrics. To the work of Soane and Barry we may add, the Reading Room at the British Museum (1854-57) in which the librarian, Anthony Panizzi, worked with first, Robert and then Sydney Smirke in creating an almost hermetic environment at the heart of the museum. Alfred Waterhouse, in his practice in Manchester worked with the engineer George (G.N.) Haden on installations in the Assize Courts (1859), Strangeways Gaol (1861), The Town Hall (1868) and Owens College (1870). The triumph of this partnership was the Natural History Museum, South Kensington, completed in 1881.[23] In France, Henri Labrouste, at the Bibliotèque St. Geneviève (1838-50) and the Bibliotèque Nationale (1859-68), fused innovations in iron structures with equally advanced environmental systems.[24]

None of this was noted by Banham. He did, however, draw attention to a building that, at the turn of the century, achieved a remarkable synthesis of environmental services and building form, the Royal Victoria Hospital in Belfast, 1899-1906, by the Birmingham architects Henman and Cooper.[25] The building would now be called 'deep-plan' with its arrangement of seventeen, top-lit, mechanically-ventilated wards opening from a single corridor. The whole was serviced by a network of basement ducts through which air was propelled by a steam engine in a large engine room at the east end of the building (Fig. 6).

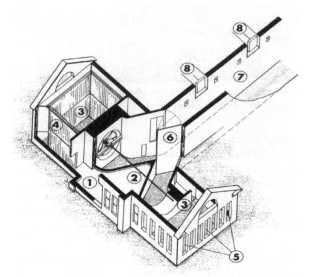

Fig. 6   Royal Victoria Hospital, Belfast. Architects, Henman and Cooper.   Axonometric drawing showing plant room.   After Reyner Banham.

The building provoked controversy, because of its reliance on mechanical ventilation, at a time when conventional practice was for natural cross-ventilation of wards.[26] But Banham was excited by the manner in which the adoption of mechanical ventilation had led to a transformation of the plan, from dispersed to compact. He was, however, dismayed to record that this considerable technical expertise had no impact on its appearance.

> ... in its detailing, what its designers doubtless regarded as its 'art architecture' it belongs dismally and irrevocably to a conception of 'Welfare' architecture fathered by the London School Board some forty years before, a style already thoroughly discounted and out of fashion amongst progressive architects in 1900.

To support his argument Banham invoked, Charles Rennie Mackintosh's, near contemporary, Glasgow School of Art, 1897-1910.[27] Here, for the first time, was building by an architect of significance in which he could illustrate advanced environmental services. He reported that the building was equipped with a comprehensive 'Plenum ventilation system' and observed that,

> The provision of such a system ... was a necessary concomitant of Mackintosh's use of huge north-facing windows ... and a humane provision where the life-class is concerned, for Glasgow is a chill city for nude models.

Here, Banham asserted, was a true synthesis of environmental technology and architectural form and language.

> ... new concepts of space, such as were pioneered by Mackintosh at the Glasgow School of Art, are crucial to their conception of modernity ... such spaces would usually be uninhabitable without massive contributions from the arts of mechanical environmental-management.

The environmental conception and technology of the Glasgow School of Art has been extensively explored, almost certainly prompted by Banham's discussion. In my own analysis,[28] I suggested that the key to the environment lies in the organisation of natural light, still at that date, the primary light source in buildings. In addition to the enormous studio windows of the north-facing Renfrew Street façade that so engaged Banham's attention, we find that light and space is carefully calibrated throughout all the spaces and function of the building. The celebrated library is brilliantly illuminated by south and west light through its tall bays and the concealed south side captures the light and warmth of the sun, which does shine in Glasgow, in the 'hen-run' passage and bay-windowed loggia that hover high above the city. The topography of the building reinforces this interpretation, with the great spine wall that runs east-west differentiating between the north and south environmental regions of the plan (Fig. 7).

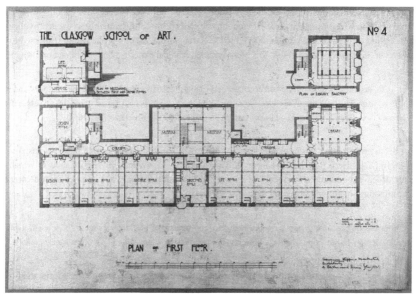

Fig. 7   Glasgow School of Art.   Architect, Charles Rennie Mackintosh.   First floor plan.© Glasgow School of Art

Banham drew attention to the network of ducts that are within or attached to this wall through which warmth and air were delivered throughout the building.   The full extent of the original system and the effectiveness with which it served the building has been fully explored by Ranald Lawrence in his recent analysis.[29]   There the technical competence of the building is revealed, both in the effectiveness of its mechanical installations and in their lucid integration into the fabric.

Where I depart from Banham's contention that this was evidence of Mackintosh's 'conception of modernity' is that, in the light of a more comprehensive history of services systems in the nineteenth century, this great building and the Royal Victoria Hospital for that matter, stands as a continuation of a lineage that runs, at least, from Soane.   In this sense the Glasgow School of Art is more cousin to the Dulwich Art Gallery than a 'pioneer of modern design'.

Space for services reconsidered

In an earlier exploration of this subject,[30] I referred to the alternative perspective on the relationship between technology and architecture that was proposed by Alan Colquhoun in his essay, 'Symbolic and Literal Aspects of Technology'.[31]   Colquhoun's argument is specifically concerned with questions of construction, but it may be shown to be to be equally applicable to environment and services.   Writing in 1962, seven years before the publication of Well-tempered Environment, Colquhoun observed that many buildings in the middle years of the 20th century.

... exploit heavy and traditional methods of construction. ... there is a tendency ... wherever the programme allows, to break away from the simple frame structure with panel infill to some form of structure that allows the building a greater plastic flexibility and gives its forms a greater density.

One of the examples that he used to illustrate his argument was Leslie Martin and Colin St. J Wilson's brick clad Harvey Court for Gonville and Caius College in Cambridge. This building is manifestly of its time, it could not be taken to be 'historicist' in any sense, but it is a far cry from being technologically 'literal'. In Colhoun's terminology, it has acquired 'symbolic' value.

Turning to environmental architecture, we can identify a parallel distinction in the architecture of the mid 20th century. This lies in the difference between buildings in which environmental provision has been wholly handed over to the mechanical services and those that continue to regard the form and fabric of a building to have a role in shaping its internal environment, albeit in most practical cases with the assistance of mechanical systems. The point may be illustrated by comparing two buildings, designed for a similar purpose at exactly the same point in the mid 20th century, but almost entirely different in their representation of both function and technology. These are Kahn's Yale Center for British Art at New Haven (Fig. 8) and Piano and Rogers' Centre Pompidou.

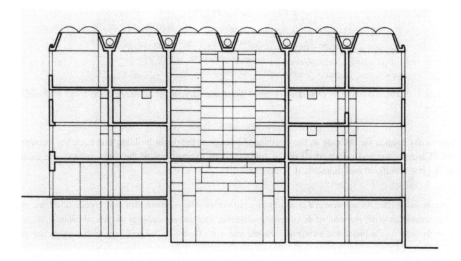

Fig. 8   Yale Center for British Art, New Haven, Conn. Architect, Louis Kahn.   Cross section. © Author.

Both were completed in 1977, were designed primarily for the display of art and use the technological 'kit of parts' of modernism – expressed structural frame, infill cladding and extensive mechanical services, including air-conditioning. But they could hardly be more different.[32]   I suggest that the difference between the two can be explained by their architects' position on the nature of the modern environment – symbolic or literal. For Kahn the environment of a building should derive from the preservation of natural light as its primary illumination. This idea most eloquently expressed in his drawing, 'Architecture Comes from the Making of a Room', with its caption, 'A room is not a room without natural light.' (Fig. 9)

Fig. 9   Louis I. Kahn, sketch.   'Architecture Comes from the Making of a Room', 1971. © Philadelphia Museum of Art.

This automatically locates the building in the continuous lineage of the daylit building that stretches throughput the history of architecture and informed all of the environmental experiments of the 19th century.   In contrast Piano and Rogers' standpoint was diametrically opposite.

> At the start of the '70s we were at a crossroads, we had to choose between two different concepts of culture; either institutional, esoteric, intimidating, or something unofficial, open and accessible to the general public.   We opted for the latter ... The building is a diagram.   People read it in a flash.   Its "viscera:" are on the outside, you see it all".[33]

At Yale, as at the slightly later Kimbell Art Museum at Fort Worth, 1966-72, Kahn's luminous, daylit galleries are served by mechanical systems that are discreetly integrated into the refined development of 'served' and 'servant' that he adopted in all his later buildings after the experiments of the Richards and Salk laboratories.   At Pompidou, the entire interior is artificially lit, day or night.   The one, Banham's 'concealed power', reflects historical continuity, the other, 'exposed power', endorses the new, in their respective conceptions of the 20th century environment.

Half a century after the construction of these buildings and the publication of *Well-tempered environment*, such strong distinctions are less strongly seen in most practice.   Indeed, the former exponents of 'exposed power' rarely feel the need to put their building's 'viscera' on display.   The majority of modern buildings have extensive service systems, but these are often accommodated with discretion and a lack of dogma. To conclude this survey, I turn to the work of Peter Zumthor, whose buildings seem to me to offer a case study of the best of this new practice. I have selected two buildings, Kunsthaus, Bregenz, 1989-97 and Kolumba Art Museum, Cologne, 1997-2007.[34]

Zumthor described Kunsthaus Bregenz as, 'a building that looks like a lamp'.[35] That is certainly appropriate for this glass cube on the shore of Lake Constance, but it conceals the originality with which the building provides an environment for the display of art. The gallery shows a succession of exhibitions of contemporary art in all conceivable media. This requires adaptability to meet the differing needs of these diverse displays, but the building must also provide controlled conditions to protect the works. The conventional solution is to install air-conditioning system and controlled artificial lighting, but Zumthor and his engineers sought an original alternative. The key is found in the cross section (Fig. 10).

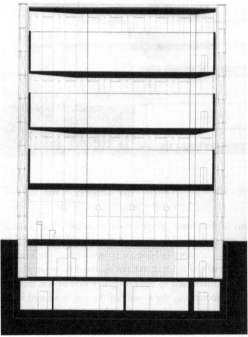

Fig. 10 Kunsthaus Bregenz. Architect, Peter Zumthor. Cross section.

Within the glass skin are three massive concrete walls. Supported by these, the floor slabs of the three gallery floors seemingly hover above the entrance foyer at ground level. Each is bounded by a perimeter wall of concrete that encloses, but does not support, and the space is capped by a taut glass suspended ceiling above which is an array of controllable artificial lighting. This provides almost infinite possibilities for illumination from natural to artificial. In the thermal system, in place of a conventional hvac system, temperature control is provided by the thermal mass of the exposed concrete of the floor slabs and three supporting walls. These contain coils of water pipes that circulate water drawn from a well deep beneath the building, cool in summer and warmed in winter.   A separate system of ventilation ducts supplies air at the junction between the floor and the walls and this is extracted through the ceiling void.   Structure and service, 'served' and 'servant', are redefined.

The Kolumba Art Museum stands at the opposite pole in museum culture.   It houses a permanent collection of European sacred art, with an emphasis on German medieval art.   This is contrasted with a collection of modern and contemporary works by many leading artists.   A unique element of the museum is the incorporation into its fabric of the remains of the medieval chapel of St. Kolumba that was damaged in the second world war and a small chapel, built in 1950 by Gottfried Böhm.   The form of the building is influenced by the complex condition of the site and, in this, has none of the Cartesian clarity of the Bregenz building (Fig. 11).

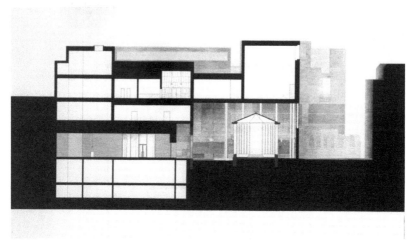

Fig. 11   Kolumba Museum, Cologne.   Architect, Peter Zumthor.   Cross section.

At ground level the remains of the chapel are presented as an exhibit in a remarkable space in which slender concrete columns rise from amongst the old stones and support a flat concrete slab high above.   The enclosing walls are of Danish brick with a clerestory of honeycomb openings.   The visitor traverses the space on a raised timber walkway.   Except for artificial lighting, the environment is 'untempered'.   There is no heating, so the temperature and ventilation are determined by the external climate as it is mediated through the openings in the wall.   This is acoustically transparent, so the sounds of the city are heard within.   The conventional gallery spaces are approached by a narrow staircase leading from the entrance lobby.   At the first floor a group of small, artificially lit galleries resemble, in their darkness, a 'basement' above the ground.   These display light sensitive works and a windowless 'Treasury' displays glistening sacred artefacts in spot-lit darkness.   On the top floor a sequence of day-lit galleries stands above the chapel ruins.   Three clerestory-lit 'tower' galleries at the perimeter define a central exhibition space that is side-lit by windows offering glimpses across the city.   Each tower has a different orientation and is entered through an artificially lit lobby.   The whole is air-conditioned by a system that is barely visible in this interior of polished concrete floors and ceilings and white walls.   Discrete air vents, similar to those at Bregenz, at the junction of floor and wall supply the conditioned air. The building has none of the topographical logic of Kahn's 'served' and 'servant', as this is realised in the Yale and Fort Worth buildings. In its place Zumthor adapts a strategy of *poché* in order to create zones within the building through which the services systems may be routed out of sight of the public spaces.   This is shown in the plans and sections on which, in Zumthor's drawings, these zones are rendered in solid black.   From plant rooms beneath the entrance block, vertical ducts give access to horizontal voids that deliver services to the galleries. Here the relation of 'served' and 'servant' has escaped the formal dogma of mid twentieth century theory and has returned to the easy assimilations of the nineteenth century pioneers of the art.

Conclusion

The Architecture of the Well-tempered Environment may truly be regarded as a *seminal* book. In it Reyner Banham brought the environmental function of architecture into the realm of architectural history. My aim in this paper has been to celebrate Banham's achievement and, almost half a century after the first edition, to offer a broad critique of its content and argument. Perhaps inevitably, pioneering work will have shortcomings. As I have suggested, one of Banham's most important omissions were the treatises on 'warming and ventilation' that appeared in great numbers from early in the century and both influenced and reported on the practice of numerous architects and their collaborations with the new profession of consultant engineers. Many of these men collaborated with leading architects, in Britain alone, Soane, Barry, Waterhouse, Mackintosh and many others, to transform the essential nature of buildings from the earliest years of the century. These events were paralleled in Europe and America. Again, Banham noted little of this.

Banham's sub-text was that history may influence practice. This is made clear in his classifications of type solutions for environmental strategies, such as the alternatives of 'concealed' or 'exposed' power in defining the relation of structure and services in new buildings. In reviewing practice since 1969, and the publication of Banham's 2nd edition in 1984, in which he promoted the 'exposed' power of the Centre Pompidou and Roger's Inmos factory, with their celebration of the 'viscera' of services systems, I suggest that, in the case study of buildings by Peter Zumthor, that leading contemporary practice has reached a more pragmatic understanding of the means of servicing complex buildings in which systems are once more unobtrusively present in the service of architecture.

References

[1] R. Banham, *The Architecture of the Well-tempered Environment*. London: The Architectural Press, 1969, 2nd edition, Chicago, Chicago University Press, 1984.

[2] Ibid., p. 11.

[3] In the substantially revised 2nd edition, Banham made no significant changes to his historical outline.

[4] Banham, (Note 1), 1st edition, p. 249, Kahn's statement was first published in *World Architecture*. London: Studio Books, 1964. The final sentence, in my italics, was omitted by Banham.

[5] P. Blundell Jones, *Modern Architecture through Case Studies*. Oxford: The Architectural Press, 2002, p. 236.

[6] F. L. Wright, *An Autobiography*. New York: Barnes and Noble, 1943, p. 150. Cited by Banham, (Note 1), p.86.

[7] Banham, (Note 1), 2nd edition, p. 299.

[8] Banham, (Note 1), 1st edition, Chapter 10, pp. 195-233.

[9] See C. W, Condit, *The Chicago School of Architecture: A History of Commercial and Public Building in the Chicago Area 1875-1925*. Chicago: Chicago University Press, 1964.

[10] See ibid, p.183.

[11] See Banham, (Note 1), 1st edition, p. 234.

[12] T. Tredgold, *On the Principles and Practice of the Warming and Ventilation of Buildings*. London: Josiah Taylor, 1824; C. J. Richardson, *A Popular Treatise on the Warming and Ventilation of Buildings: Showing*

the Advantages of the Heated Water Circulation. London: John Weale, Architectural Library, 1837; D. B. Reid, *Illustrations of the Theory and Practice of Ventilating*. London: Longman, 1844; W. Bernan, *On the History and Art of the Warming and Ventilating of Buildings*. London, 1845.

[13] The use of 'warming' in these titles seems preferable to the modern 'heating'. We seek warmth, not heat, in our buildings.

[14] R. Bruegmann, 'Central Heating and Forced Ventilation: Origins and Effects in Architectural Design', *Journal of the Society of Architectural Historians*, Vol. 37, No. 3, 1978, pp. 143-160.

[15] T. Willmert, 'Heating Methods and their impact on Soane's Work: Lincoln's Inn Fields and Dulwich Picture Gallery', *Journal of the Society of Architectural Historians*, Vol. 53, No. 1, 1993, pp. 26-58. This was followed by other studies of Soane as environmentalist. E. Ng, 'The Romantic Meaning of Light, Cambridge', PhD Dissertation, July 1991 (unpublished). N. Craddock, 'Sir John Soane and the Luminous Environment', Cambridge, MPhil Dissertation, 1995 (unpublished). See also D. Hawkes, 'Soane, Labrouste, Mackintosh: Pioneers of Environment', in *The Environmental Imagination*. London, Routledge, 2008, pp. 3-29, and D. Hawkes, 'Building in the climate of the nineteenth century city', in *Architecture and Climate*, Routledge, 2012, pp. 123-153.

[16] Sir John Soane, Lecture VIII, The Royal Academy Lectures. See D. Watkin, *Sir John Soane: Enlightenment Thought and the Royal Academy Lectures*. Cambridge: Cambridge University Press, 2000.

[17] Willmert, (Note 15).

[18] Richardson, (Note 12).

[19] Banham, (Note 1), 2nd edition, p. 111.

[20] The Boulton and Watt installation was unsatisfactory and leakages caused wet rot in the timber floor structure. See Willmert, (Note 15).

[21] J. Summerson, Architecture in Britain 1530-1830. Harmondsworth: Penguin Books, 1953, Chapter 29, 'Greek and Gothic: Architecture after Waterloo'.

[22] H. Schoenefeldt, 'The Temporary Houses of Parliament and David Boswell Reid's Architecture of Experimentation', *Architectural History*, Vol. 57, 2014, pp. 175-215. H. Schoenefeldt, 'The (Lost) First Chamber of the House of Commons', *AA Files*, No.72, 2016, pp. 161-173. H. Schoenefeldt, 'The Historic Ventilation of the House of Commons, 1840-52: revisiting David Boswell Reid's environmental legacy', *Journal of the Society of Antiquities*, Vol. 19, 2017, in press. J. Olley, 'The Reform Club', in D. Cruickshank (ed.), *Timeless Architecture*. London: The Architectural Press, 1985, pp. 24-46. D. Hawkes, 'Building in the climate of the nineteenth century city', in *Architecture and Climate*, (Note 19).

[23] J. Olley and C. Wilson, 'The Natural History Museum, London', in D. Cruickshank (ed.), *Timeless Architecture*, (Note 22), pp. 48-67. J. Cook and T. Hinchcliffe, 'Designing the well-tempered institution of 1873', *Architectural Research Quarterly (arq)*, Vol. 1, Winter 1995, pp. 70-78. and 'Delivering the well-tempered environment', *arq*, Vol. 2, Autumn, 1996, pp. 66-76.

[24] Hawkes, 'Soane, Labrouste, Mackintosh: Pioneers of Environment', (Note 15).

[25] Banham, (Note 1), pp. 75-84.

[26] RIBA Journal, Vol. XI, 3rd Series, 1902-04, pp. 89ff. Cited in Banham, (Note 1).

[27] Banham, (Note 1), pp. 84-86.

[28] Hawkes, 'Soane, Labrouste, Mackintosh: Pioneers of Environment', (Note 15), pp. 19-23.

[29] R. Lawrence, 'The internal environment of the Glasgow School of Art by Charles Rennie Mackintosh', *Construction History*, Vol. 29, No. 1, 2014, pp. 99-127.

[30] D. Hawkes, 'The Language Barrier', in *The Environmental Tradition: Studies on the architecture of environments*. London: E & FN Spon, 1996, pp. 88-97.

[31] A. Colquhoun, 'Literal and Symbolic Aspects of Technology' in *Architectural Design*, November, 1962, pp. 508-509. Reprinted in *Essays in Architectural Criticism*. Cambridge: MA, Oppositions Books, MIT Press, 1981, pp. 26-30.

[32] D. Hawkes, 'The technical imagination: thoughts on the relation of technique and design in architecture', *The Journal of Architecture*, Vol. 1, No. 4, Winter, 1996, pp. 345-366.

[33] R. Piano, quoted by M. Dini, *Renzo Piano: Projects and Buildings 1964-1983*. London: Electa/Architectural Press, 1984.

[34] For outline descriptions of these buildings see T. Durisch (ed.), *Peter Zumthor: Buildings and Projects*. Zurich: Verlag Scheidegger & Spiess AG, 2014.   Kunsthaus Bregenz is in Vol. 1, pp. 131-157, Kolumba, Cologne is in Vol. 2. pp. 145-173.   For Bregenz see also, D. Hawkes, 'The art museum: art, environment, imagination', *The Environmental Imagination*, (Note 15), pp. 157-183.

[35] P. Zumthor, *Introduction to Kunsthaus Bregenz, Archive Kunst Architektur*.   Werkdokumente: Ostfuldern-Ruit, Verlag Gerd Hatje, 1999.

History of Building Services

The hidden system: How district heating came to town

Jørgen Burchardt

National Museum of Science and Technology, Denmark

Introduction

District heating, where a building is kept warm by heat produced often a long distance away, has become a very common heating system. In many countries, half of the homes are heated this way. The first plants of this type were seen in the 1800s; in the early 1900s, several major systems were installed; but only in the 1950s did development begin to evolve significantly.

This article will discuss this development phase, as well as the specific installations used for district heating. Local installations in buildings will not be discussed, for the most part, as many installations are similar to central heating. The special facilities associated with the heating of the buildings are few.

Examples are taken from Danish history and based on documentation of the Danish district heating sector carried out at the National Museum of Science and Technology. In many ways, historical development is different from country to country, but the basic technical conditions have become international standards, so this knowledge is also of interest outside Denmark.

The first district heating

The first district heating plant in Denmark was installed in Copenhagen, when the Zoological Museum was built in 1863-69.[1] Its steam heating system was very advanced for the time (Fig. 1). It provided heat not only for the museum, but also for some other buildings in the central part of Copenhagen. This heating system worked well over time, even when the museum's premises were taken over by Copenhagen University. There was no thermostatic control of the radiators, so the fireman had to open and close the steam valves regularly. The author of this article, from his time studying there, can remember how the pipes in the rooms knocked and banged when they expanded or contracted.

Fig. 1 The steam radiators at the Zoological Museum from 1869 were in service for about 100 years. One of them is today at the National Museum of Science and Technology. The radiators could not be regulated, so the steam passed through the plant several times a day. Photo from 1960.

District heating was soon introduced in other countries. In the United States, in 1877, a system was installed in Lockport, N.Y., and the same designer established facilities in downtown New York, N.Y., in 1882-83.[2]

The next facilities in Denmark were established a few years later. The first was in 1900 at a sanatorium, where the heat of the institution's buildings was generated at a traditional boiler plant with coal fired in an independent economy building.

The next half century's expansion of district heating was not primarily established by a wish for the new energy supply, but as an economical and pragmatic use of surplus heat. After Hamburg, Germany experienced a major epidemic in 1892 due to the spread of contamination from waste, Frederiksberg, a municipality close to Copenhagen, decided to establish a combustion plant (which was built in 1903). The municipality was surrounded by the City of Copenhagen on all sides, and Frederiksberg's city council was worried about exposure to the city's waste. The waste incineration plant was designed, secondarily, to supply heat and electricity to the nearby hospital, to a bathing centre and to schools.

The downstream system similarly made use of waste heat — surplus heat from the big power stations built in the 1920s. This type first turned up in the smaller provincial towns of Brønderslev and Faaborg (Fig. 2), and between 1925 and 1929 it was established in Copenhagen, Esbjerg, Svendborg, Aarhus and Odense, and soon came to the other major cities in the country. Increasing electricity consumption required construction of new power stations and naturally provided an opportunity to spread district heating plants to more customers.

Fig. 2 The Faaborg Power Plant in 1925 had a diesel engine of 600 hp. It delivered heat to two schools and the manager's official residence. The power station was discontinued when electricity could be made cheaper on large power stations. However, a small power station was established in the city when the Faaborg district heating plant was built in 1995. Now, the generation of electricity has become almost a by-product of heat production. Photo: Faaborg Town History Archive.

In the 1930s, some systems that might be called district heating were installed. These block centres provided central heating to several of the homes in a settlement. If one strictly follows the definition of district heating in the official Dictionary of the Danish language — "heat delivered to multiple buildings from a heating plant" — it was district heating. If, on the other hand, the definition in Den Store Danske published by Gyldendal (the Danish counterpart to the British Encyclopaedia Britannica) — "distribution of heat through pipes to two or more properties with different owners" is used, these plants fell outside the definition. This combination of technical and legal criteria is the definition used by the district heating sector and partly in legislation (Fig. 3). In this article, however, I use the first definition, which is purely technological.

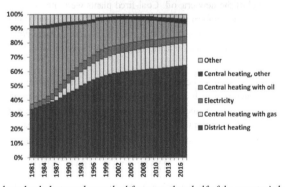

Fig. 3 District heating has slowly but surely reached far more than half of the country's households — by 2016, 64 percent. Around 85 percent of households receive piped energy when natural gas and electricity are counted. Source: Statistics Denmark.

The hidden system: How district heating came to town

The real breakthrough of district heating

While district heating was already a reality at the beginning of the twentieth century, the popular breakthroughs in the technology did not happen until later. After the establishment of plants to exploit surplus heat and the construction of block centres, interest in district heating waned, and from 1930 until the end of the 1940s only a few plants were created. One reason was, of course, that the war stopped societal development in many ways. The main reason, however, was that the easiest made plants had already been established.

We do not know the exact number of district heating plants that were in operation in Denmark during the first half of the century. At least a number of small district heating plants were shut down along with local power plants as the electricity sector centralized through the establishment of large power plants in the 1950s.

However, the number of new district heating plants exploded in the 16 years between 1950 and 1966. After the war, construction began slowly, with one new plant in 1947 and another in 1949. Then the number of new district heating plants rose to an average of five per year in the period from 1950 to 1958. Though that was a sharp rise, it was nothing compared to the explosion of district heating in the following years. In 1964, the biggest district heating year of all, 45 new plants came to be. In 1965, "only" half as many were established, and, in 1966, the number dropped to five new systems, and, in 1967, to only one. The big wave of development was over. In 16 years, more than 268 district heating plants had been launched.[3]

The reason for this unique period was that the post-war time was characterised by optimism everywhere that prosperity would return. The conditions did not normalise immediately after the end of the war. Everyone expected that product restrictions would be settled, but it took some time before reinforcing iron, radiators and oil could be purchased freely. The first district heating companies established just after the war, therefore, encountered major problems.

A popular movement

The new district heating plants were established with the boiler centre of primary importance. The plants were predominantly fired by the fuel of the new era: oil. Coal-fired plants were the exception, usually found in cities near brown coal fields. The spare heat from the power plants in the big cities was no longer the central source of heat; waste heat had become only supplemental. District heating, instead became the sole purpose of the plants, which often had no connection to a power station or municipal supply service.

With the use of oil, central heating could be for everyone. Growing car ownership had led to a residue from refineries, the so-called heavy fuel oil, which could not be burnt in the small furnaces of single-family houses. On the other hand, many households could agree on a large modern combustion plant with burners and preheaters that made burning of this fuel oil possible. It was no longer necessary to have a sweaty stoker shovel coal into the furnace. Automation meant the new oil burner only had to be inspected, and the oil was cheap and became still cheaper.

News of successful experiences with district heating in the first cities spread fast. Easy, cheap heat could be obtained by establishing a cooperative plant to serve owners of many houses. Enterprising engineers and blacksmiths travelled around the country and got busy designing installations and converting central heating systems in buildings. Homeowners met to discuss proposals, and often there was agreement that it should also be attempted at their area. In many cities, local associations of craftsmen and citizens took the initiative on establishing plants. A proposal was discussed, a committee was set up, and after some preparatory work an independent district heating association was established. Parish and town councils coordinated the public interest in some cities, but there were also examples of municipalities, for various reasons, responding in the negative to requests that they get involved with district heating.

The district heating movement was a strong popular uprising, entirely in the spirit of the cooperative movement.

Start-up of a district heating system

Homeowners and local craftsmen could not establish a project alone — experts had to join the effort. One engineering company, Bruun & Sørensen, was, for many decades Denmark's leading — and almost exclusive — district heating consultant. When, later, there was an increase in the creation of smaller and simplified plants, a wide range of competitors emerged. Salespeople often marketed aggressively. They gradually moved far from their hometowns, where they contacted local people they believed might be able initiate local projects.

A district heating plant could only be established when a sufficient number of contracts with homeowners who wanted to be connected were signed. The contracts were based on the size of the houses. While, today, one only needs to get a computer printout from the public register of buildings, back then it was necessary to send people to homes with a measuring tape to determine how many cubic meters had to be heated.

There was an exciting period during which individual homeowners considered the offer. Would there be enough who wanted to join the system? At first, enrolment in nearly every city went very slowly. After some time, the entries reached the desired number — often a sufficient number was only achieved years later, after repeated campaigns. But, in general more joined after the plant had become a reality. Membership would continue to rise for years, to an extent few had imagined.

Not everyone was in favour of district heating. People with new oil burners naturally refrained from joining. More serious was organised resistance, usually business interests that were put at risk by the new initiative. For example, in 1963, local fuel dealers in a provincial town issued a flyer to the town's households in which they drew attention to the benefits of coal. Similarly, in 1965, the large gasworks Strandvejs Gasværket in the metropolitan area advertised the benefits of gas.[4]

In some places, resistance was successful. In the provincial town of Rudkøbing, for example, trade unions and traders got the city council to temporarily stop plans for a local district heating plant in 1963. The plant would have allowed a single man to operate a district heating plant in an area which hitherto had been handled by 32 people employed by the city's fuel companies.

Apart from the relatively few cases where a municipality established a district heating plant, most were established by self-governing institutions. A private, consumer-owned company would be headed by a general meeting-elected board. This popular commitment was great, but at in one area it was not enough: the funding. Funds needed to be borrowed, otherwise the connection fee would be too high. A loan required a guarantor, and most district heating companies received a guarantee from the municipality. After the Ministry of Internal Affairs had assessed the pledge of the project plan, the loan would be issued by the public fund Kommunekredit.

The hidden system: How district heating came to town

However, some municipalities considered the projects risky, and dared not make the guarantee. In addition, lending was limited in 1965, when the state wanted to slow down the overheated economy.

The pipes are laid — and become leaky

In a typical district heating plant, there was a small and usually not very flashy building to house a few overgrown domestic boilers of 65 m or 150 m heating surface, depending on the needs to be fulfilled. Even if these calculations kept for quite a few months — connections soon exceeded the planned capacity.

The city also had to be dug up and the necessary heating pipes laid down. The method at the time was to cast a concrete channel in which steel pipes were laid. In 1964, national TV showed a feature on a brand new pre-insulated district heating pipe, which a copper smith in Løgstør had developed and patented. This plastic-wrapped tube later became a great success for the company Løgstør Rør (now Logstor). Unfortunately, this was not the type of pipe that had been laid in most places, so in the course of just a few years, damage began to occur. Steel pipes could tear, which, as demonstrated by water meters at district heating plants, resulted in increased water loss. In the District Heating Association's membership magazine, cigars were offered to those who could devise a method to find the breaks. One of the proposals submitted was to use heat-seeking cats, but it is unknown if this suggestion earned cigars. (Fig. 4)

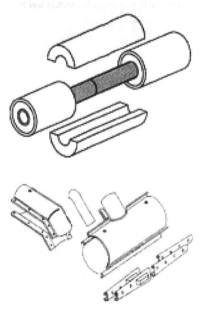

Fig. 4 Despite the fact that factories have developed a complete assembly set for district heating pipes, assembly has become a job for specialists. Illustration: Logstor.

Another problem was that pipes were often misplaced, a serious situation for many plants. One small district heating company had 30 to 40 pipe breaks in only one year. Several legal complaints were brought against the guilty engineers.[5] One of those accused was the pipe production department at the company E. Rasmussen. That was one of the reasons why the company's name was changed when it was incorporated into the former trading company I.C. Møller (now a part of ABB). In this way, what became one of the world's leading companies had shaken off its sins of the past.

In many places it was necessary to replace the pipes, which was an expense not all district heating companies could afford. Thus, some companies chose to shut down the works instead of renovating. But most cooperatives chose to relocate the pipes, and after some economically hard years, progress was made with continued improvements. (Fig. 5)

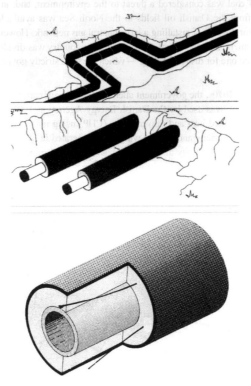

Fig. 5 A modern district heating pipe as supplied by the pipe plant. Around the inner steel pipe is insulation and there is a hard, protective layer. Inside the insulation are electrical wires used to locate possible damage.

Political management of the country's heating

On top of the technical problems with the pipes, new problems emerged. The price of oil rose dramatically during two energy crises, and, as a result, consumer heating prices also rose. This did not please consumers, who rarely had alternative heating options. And, if they did, the district heating plant had no interest in its customers using them. Several lawsuits led to consumers being forced to discontinue using their wood-burning stoves. In the

9

connection agreement with the district heating company, there was often a rule that it would supply all the heat customers used.

At the same time, the energy crises meant that the state and the public really began to interfere with the country's energy supply. It became official policy that the country should become independent of oil for heating. Across the country, oil-fired plants wholly or partially converted to coal in the early 1980s. That changed much, since heating with coal required more labour and a larger staff to care for the plants. Automatic firing stokers and computer-controlled coal-loading cranes were subsequently installed to reduce the cost of salaries.

However, the time of coal use was short. A few years later, political winds began to blow in the opposite direction. Now, the use of coal was considered a threat to the environment, and, in addition (and perhaps most importantly), natural gas from the Danish oil fields in the North Sea was available, and fixed district heating customers could help pay for the cost of installing a large natural gas network. However, natural gas could also be burned by individual consumers, and, to control development, the country was divided into separate areas — one for gas heating of houses and one for district heating — which the state strictly governed through legislation.

Since the energy crises of the 1970s, the government attempted, with both carrot and stick, to get the new policy implemented. The biggest stick was used by the Danish Energy Agency in 1991, when it wanted to convert to heat production based on combined heat and power plants (CHP) using natural gas and biofuels.[6] These new power plants would produce electricity and use the waste heat generated in the process for heating. There was a state reward for the production of electricity that was based on the number of produced KWh. (Fig. 6)

Fig. 6 Denmark's most widely used district heating system is found in Greater Copenhagen, the country's most densely populated area.

As mentioned above, exploitation of waste heat was not new. What was new was that even smaller communities could have the opportunity to establish district heating systems. If there were only a few hundred potential buyers in a fairly close settlement, then it would, at the time, pay to establish a decentralized CHP. Many new plants were set up as "greenfield" power plants in small towns. Denmark took the last steps needed to become one of the countries with the world's best-developed district heating. (Fig. 7)

Fig. 7 Avedøreværket is the main supplier of district heating to 500,000 homes in the western suburbs of Copenhagen. The fuels are today only biofuels. The last expansion, of block 2, was completed in 2002. Photo: VEKS.

The new architecture

The new wave of buildings benefited from an architectural innovation: the great accumulation tank (Fig. 8). All the new plants needed a place to store heat when no electricity was produced. It was only part of the day when the gas engines were engaged. An efficient operation would let the engines make electricity when there was "peak load" or at least a "high load" on the electricity service. The "low load" periods, when electricity companies did not pay much for the flow, would be avoided. The tanks were so large that the heat could be stored for use during the nights and weekends. When Monday morning came, and industry again needed electricity, the water in the tank could be heated again.

11

Fig. 8 Viborg Kraftvarmeværk, completed in 1996, is one of the 1990s' more architecturally beautiful facilities. It is built from a basic shape like two shells or hands that protect the machines. The shells integrate an accumulation tank for hot water. Photo: Energi Viborg.

The tanks, in their construction, are rather primitive. They are large insulated containers where the most technically sophisticated part is a so-called "vapor membrane" at the top of the tank, which prevents the air in the tank from circulating in the district heating system's pipelines. The tanks were installed in the hundreds across the country. They are so big that they far outweigh the adjacent buildings with machine houses and offices.

The expansion of facilities was very extensive in the 1990s. Where the buildings previously expanded gradually, in many cases large and complete plants were being built all at once. It enabled architects to design aesthetically beautiful and wholly owned plants. Where district heating plants were previously constructed anonymously and of the cheapest materials, the buildings were sometimes given an architectural expression — what first-generation electricity plants often had.

The hidden story

Strangely, nobody has systematised the historical knowledge of district heating in Denmark, the world's leading country in the field. Even the exact number of heating stations is unknown. A qualified estimate is that there are 1,600 stations, including everything from large buildings with waste incineration and/or central power generation, to small houses with a single, small gas engine, where the waste heat from electricity production is used for heating. In addition to the district heating plants themselves, many thousands of other construction sites should be included, such as pump and heat exchangers, valve wells, etc. With those buildings the district heating sector is not completely insignificant in the landscape image. One of the reasons for the lack of consideration of district heating may be that the system's main plant, the distribution plant, is hidden — buried well under the ground. It is estimated that there are more than 30,000 km of district heating pipes.[7] That number should actually be multiplied by two, because there are both supply lines distributing heat and return lines containing cooled water.

Danish museums with rich collections document the cultural history of warming when technology was simple. Low-tech tools such as the stove, coal bowl and peat are found in most museums. But it seems that the museums' interest in the history of heat production disappeared as technology became more complicated. (Fig. 9)

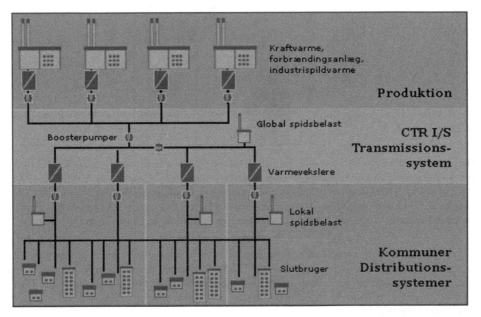

Fig. 9 The diagram shows the principle of the major utility company Centralkommunernes Transmissionsselskab I/S (CTR) in the metropolitan area with a number of large heating systems. To provide enough heat during the coldest periods, there are also a number of additional peak load systems.

The physical changes in the home

One of the major recent changes in home heating was the introduction of central heating. Instead of heating with heat sources in each room, warmth was now obtained from just one single "oven" in the building. Previously, you could only place heat sources where there were chimneys, which is why many rooms were unheated. With central heating, radiators could easily be placed in all rooms. Additionally, by locating these on external walls, better heat distribution could be achieved. (Fig. 10)

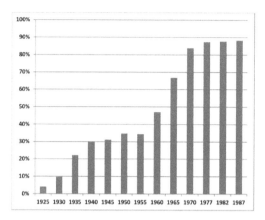

Fig. 10 Share of heating with radiators in Denmark. Until 1950 only apartments; later all kinds of homes. Source: Statistics Denmark.

The first central heating systems are lost in prehistory, but really began entering homes in the 1920s. However, it took a long time before a considerable portion homes were heated this way, and it wasn't until after 1960 that only half of Danish homes had central heating. This meant significant changes in dwelling construction, as stoves disappeared from rooms. In apartment houses, individual fuel burners disappeared, to be replaced by central heat sources in basements. With central heating, it was also easy to deliver hot water from a central hot water tank.

District heating offered the same benefits, although many of the technical installations disappeared: the central kettle and fuel storage room were removed. Similarly, a chimney was no longer necessary, which, at the same time, offered more flexibility in placement of interior partition walls. A pipe from the distribution line under the sidewalk brought 60 to 70-degree Celsius water into the house, while another carried 40-degree cooled water back for reheating. (Fig. 11)

Fig. 11 The cityscape with houses without chimneys shows that there is district heating. There could, theoretically, also have been electric heating, but that expensive heating method was not very widespread due to its cost and requirement to connect to district heating.

Special installations for district heating were few. Shut-off valves for flow and return of water, as well as thermometers, manometers, heat exchangers and multiple valves were most often located in a small unit with all valves and control panels. There should be a measurement to determine the amount of water used using simple energy meter. The latest ones also give digital readings, so the annual manual read is avoided. Larger installations, particularly, will also install a pressure gauge that stops the supply of water in case of a larger leak. Hot water is now easily produced via a heat exchanger, so a larger hot water tank is not required. New installations do not require more than a small cabinet in a utility room.

Personal relationship to heating before and now

Mrs. Andersen sits snug indoors while a winter storm is howling outside. From the radiators, heat flows into her apartment. The thermostats ensure that the temperature is constant — it is "summer" all year. She does not think of the heat, except when she receives the heat bill. She feels the same way as most other Danes, a majority of whose homes are currently heated by district heating. Mrs. Andersen is an older lady, and she remembers, from her youth, how to handle firewood. Then, during the late summer, peat, wood or coke would be stored for winter consumption. In the winter months, she had to fire up the ovens with newspaper and wood shavings, and when the fire burned, a damper had to be turned so that the fire would get the right amount of air. Regularly, the ash should be emptied and taken away.

To keep warm in Mrs. Andersen's youth, everybody had to master a great deal of knowledge. Today, no ordinary citizen needs to have any specific knowledge of home heating. Winter heat has become a "distant" heat that "is just there". That does not mean that necessary knowledge has disappeared. On the contrary, it has never been so extensive, but it exists primarily outside the home. At the specialized heating centres there is a great deal of knowledge about firing for daily operation. This is where the year's warming is being planned and the daily work is done. This extensive understanding is only a small part of the total knowledge needed, though. When constructing the plant, a host of counsellors and engineers are available to draw and calculate how to assemble the many components that come from subcontractors. The production of these components is further based on a high level of knowledge from the subcontractors. In addition, fuel suppliers contribute important information regarding obtaining and supplying required fuel, whether it is coal, gas or oil. Behind each machine, each process or component requires technological knowledge based on research from universities and other research institutions.

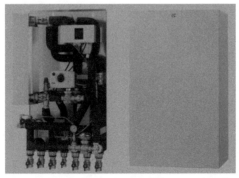

Fig. 12 Unit for a district heating installation in a small house. Illustration: Danfoss.

15

Conclusion

The combination of a political desire to control energy supply using less-polluting fuels, foreign policy concerns for suppliers and cheap prices for consumers has increased the use of district heating to 64 percent in Denmark.

The heat is produced in large plants of different types. Some heat comes from buildings intended exclusively to produce district heating. There are many different types depending on the size and type of fuel. Heat also comes as waste heat from the incineration of waste or the production of electricity. A distinctive type has been built since the 1990s to provide decentralized produced heat in parallel with the production of electricity. They are, in a way, a rebuilding of the small direct current power plants, which closed 60 years earlier. Their architectural expression is distinguished by their large hot water storage tanks.

Distribution of district heating inside buildings takes place in the same way as in central heating. There are major advantages for buildings that don't require chimneys, boiler rooms or fuel storage. Most of the special technical facilities are located in pipelines hidden under roads, and users shouldn't have to think much about their heat supply. The visible plant of district heating is usually far from housing, and the local installation can be stored in a closet. District heating has literally become a hidden system.

References

[1] Burchardt, Jørgen: "Sommer hele året – signalement af den danske fjernvarme", in: *Teknisk Museums Årbog 2003-2004,* 2005, p. 9, and Burchardt, Jørgen: *Signalement af den danske fjernvarme*, Danmarks Tekniske Museum 2005 (unpublished report with a registration of the Danish district heating sector), p. 22.
[2] Banham, Reyner: *The Architecture of the Well-Tempered Environment*, 2013, p. 46-47.
[3] Burchardt, Jørgen: *Signalement af den danske fjernvarme*, Danmarks Tekniske Museum 2005 (unpublished report with a registration of the Danish district heating sector), p. 34-47.
[4] Ibid., p. 30-31.
[5] Ibid., p. 32-33.
[6] Energistyrelsen: *Danmarks Enrgifortider. Hovedbegivenheder på energiområdet.* 2016, p. 31.
[7] Information from the Danish District Heating Association.

Building services in nineteenth-century Belgian cellular prison architecture

Jozefien Feyaerts

Ghent University, Belgium

Introduction

Between 1850 and WWI, the Belgian state built a network of cellular prisons to facilitate the regime of solitary confinement. The cellular (as opposed to communal) regime was the crown jewel of the young nation's modern penal system, that had emerged from changing views on the custodial sentence since the eighteenth century.[1]

The Belgian prison system has been studied mainly from a penological and legal-historical point of view.[2] Apart from a few unpublished master theses, little research has been conducted on its remarkable nineteenth-century purpose-built infrastructure.[3] In his study of the radial cellular prison typology Norman Johnston does pay attention to the Belgian case, yet with a mere focus on the radial layout of the prison plans.[4]

Nonetheless, the cellular regime had not only made its mark through the distinctive star-shaped floor plan of the cellular typology. The solitary system presented architects with the challenge of reconciling conflicting needs for separation and seclusion on the one hand, and health and hygiene on the other. High demands were made regarding environmental control of the prisoners' individual cells. As a result, nineteenth-century cellular prisons were an experimental ground for environmental technologies such as central heating and forced ventilation which, according to Bruegmann, were "an essential determinant in 19th-century architecture".[5]

This paper explores the heating, ventilation, lighting and sanitary systems applied in individual cells in Belgium's prison patrimony during the heydays of the cellular regime. These developments are contextualised within the historical development of environmental techniques, as well as within the discourse on health and hygiene in reformed penal design. Sources include contemporary publications, official prison construction programmes, circulars, measuring states and correspondence of the Ministry of Justice.

Hygienic concerns in reformed penal design

Early prison reform in England

Health and hygiene had already been a battlepoint in early prison reform. In the eighteenth century, outbreaks of epidemic typhus or 'gaol fever' were believed to be caused by putrid airflows.[6] Eighteenth-century prison reform not only crystallised in a changed view on the custodial sentence (which had to reform rather than punish the prisoners through classification and separation); it also prioritized a healthy environment to achieve this purpose. Early English prison reform's protagonist John Howard (1726-1790) had promoted security, salubrity and reformation as the "doctrines of reform".[7] These three "cardinal requirements of a reformed prison" brought about a change in penal design. [8] Reformed prisons necessitated a purpose-built infrastructure, reconciling the need for security (by means of enclosure), reformation through separation and seclusion (by means of compartmentalization) and salubrity through adequate water supply, drainage and ventilation (by means of exposure and fragmentation).[9] The material conditions of the prison had become crucial in achieving its penal goal.

The emergence of the regime of strict solitary confinement in the first half of the nineteenth century made prison architecture even more interlinked with its penal purpose. Prison reform had shifted its focus from preventing physical contagion, to preventing moral contagion. In order to avoid communication at all times, prisoners were now separated through the cellular architecture itself. With prisons becoming increasingly enclosed and cellularised, and hygienist requirements becoming more stringent as sanitary reform gained momentum, penal architecture needed yet again rethinking.[10] Earlier design principles based on the need for air and ventilation - basically turning prisons into "draughty and cold" "masses of small holes; large colanders jacked up on stilts"[11] - were no longer suitable.[12] The dilemmas that had already puzzled eighteenth-century reformed prison architects had only become more complex in the early nineteenth century. They boiled the conundrum down to the following question: "how could the circulation of air, water and waste be ensured in a place that is designed to impede the free movement of people?".[13]

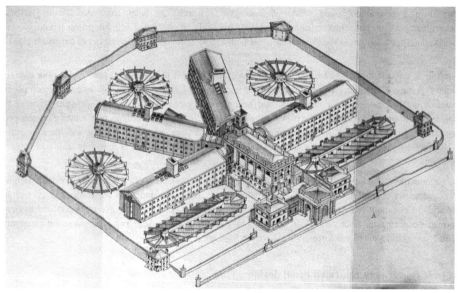

Fig. 1. Pentonville model prison (Description des plans de la prison modèle de Pentonville, s.l.: s.n., (ca. 1844), Pl. I.)

With technology rapidly evolving, architects experimented with new applications of heating, ventilation and sanitary services, which "found some of their earliest applications in the prisons of the first decades of the nineteenth century".[14] Pentonville prison (fig.1), constructed near London in 1840-42 as a model penitentiary,[15] indeed incorporated an innovative heating and ventilation system which was "one of the first systems to confront the problem of providing warm air to a large number of rooms from a single source".[16] Pentonville presented such a degree of sophistication and scale in mechanical servicing that Evans does not simply consider it the most advanced prison, but even one of the most advanced buildings of its time.[17] As such, it thoroughly influenced prison construction in Britain and continental Europe in the second half of the nineteenth century.[18]

Prison reform in nineteenth-century Belgium

Pentonville became the blueprint for Belgian prison building as well. In the wake of international prison reform, the young Belgian state rigorously implemented the new cellular regime in its (at that time communal) prison system. Belgium's first General Inspector of Prisons Edouard Ducpétiaux (1804-1868) was the separate system's main advocate. Via solitary confinement during night and day, and through labor, education and religion, he believed the regime to intimidate and reform detainees, while preventing moral contamination by avoiding communication between prisoners.[19]

The introduction of solitary confinement in Belgium required a radically new prison infrastructure. Throughout the second half of the nineteenth century until WWI, nearly thirty new purpose-built cellular penitentiaries gradually replaced Belgium's outdated prison infrastructure. In several publications Ducpétiaux provided prison architects with guidelines on penal design.[20] He presented a framework for architects to explore different possibilities of construction, technology and their imagination within the requirements of the cellular regime. Inspired by Anglo-Saxon experiments (in particular the Pentonville model prison), Ducpétiaux advocated a radial layout of cell wings converging in a central observatory. Keeping abreast with technological developments and penal design experiments abroad, he also provided guidance with regard to the adequate ventilation, heating, lighting and sanitary services.

Ducpétiaux's ideas on prison architecture have been determinative for the Belgian state's cellular prison construction policy until well after his mandate as General Inspector from 1830 to 1868.[21] His concept of the cellular typology was broadly continued by his successor Jean Stevens, who published several essays and guides on penal design as well.[22] It was only near the end of the century that the strict cellular regime was gradually mitigated,[23] which inevitably influenced its architectural design as well. The following overview presents the main tendencies in the application of environmental technologies during the heydays of the cellular regime.

Environmental building services in the nineteenth-century Belgian prison cell

Heating

In Belgium's early days of cellular construction, Pentonville was the pre-eminent example regarding any aspect of penal architecture. That also included its innovative combined heating/ventilation system, known as 'the Pentonville system' (Fig 2). The basement under each cell wing contained a furnace room, heating fresh air to transport it to each cell through ducts within the inner walls. A vent above the cell door introduced the warm air, while foul air was extracted through a grill near the floor on the opposite side of the cell. Via pipes in the outer cell walls leading to a large duct in the attic, the foul air was eventually evacuated to a chimney. The warm air heating functioned at the same time as a heat-driven forced ventilation system; a continuous air circulation was activated and guaranteed by heating the exhaust shaft in order to produce a strong draft. Introducing air into the top of the cell avoided unpleasant draughts and ensured the airflow – at this height, detainees could not block the vents. In order to prevent noise transmission and any form of communication, the air pipes were compartmentalized per cell.[24] Ducpétiaux specifically recommended the 'Pentonville system' in his memorandum in support of legislation on the cellular system in 1845.[25] It was applied in several projects around the middle of the nineteenth century; for example in the new cellular prison of Charleroi (1850),[26] the new cellular quarter of the Bruges prison (1851),[27] and the prison constructed in Verviers (1853).[28] Despite its innovative status, the system had its drawbacks which were increasingly subjected to critique. It lacked flexibility to adjust the temperature at nighttime - it took no less than 36 hours to lower the temperature in the cells. Heat was distributed in a very irregular way, depending on the orientation of the cells, their distance to the furnace room etc. Moreover, ventilation as well proved to be inadequate.[29]

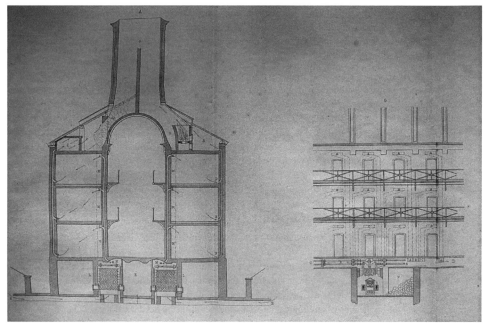

Fig. 2. The Pentonville warm air heating and ventilation system (S.n., Description des plans de la prison modèle de Pentonville, s.l.: s.n., (ca. 1844), Pl. IV)

To remedy these shortcomings, architects experimented with new combinations and arrangements. Henceforth, heating and ventilation were detached. Heating based on the circulation of hot water appeared to resolve most of the above mentioned issues.[30] A heater in the basement under each cell wing directed hot water to a special tank, placed in the exhaust chimney of the heating device. From there, the hot water was dispersed on each storey (Fig. 3-4). Two hot-water-filled pipes ran through the cells in the cell floor. Shielded by an iron plate, they provided a heat source in each cell. Through an opening in the iron plate, they uniformly released heat in the cells themselves and allowed a reduction of a few degrees when necessary. A valve on each floor could interrupt the circulation of hot water for a row of cells that were not occupied. [31] Hot water heating had been developed in the 1830s.[32] Around the middle of the nineteenth century, it was applied in prison construction abroad[33] and was introduced in Belgian penitentiaries as well. Architect Joseph-Jonas Dumont implemented the so-called 'thermosiphon' or low pressure hot water heating in the new prisons of Kortrijk (1853)[34] and Antwerp

(1853)[35]. A second cellular extension of the Bruges prison (ca. 1854), and Leuven central prison (1860) were also equipped with this system.[36] Instead of running the pipes through the cell floors, Stevens proposed in 1874 to place them ca. 50 cm above the floor, in an iron case over the width of the cell's outer wall, under the window (Fig. 5).[37]

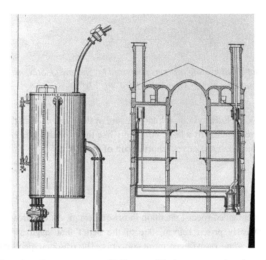

Fig. 3. 'Thermonsiphon' hot water heating system (J. Stevens, De la construction des prisons cellulaires en Belgique, Bruxelles: Muquardt, 1874, Pl. VIII)

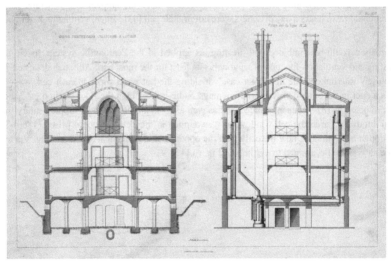

Fig. 4. Section of the Leuven central prison cell wings, illustrating the fixed toilet and water distribution system (l) and the thermosiphon heating system (r). Algemeen Rijksarchief, Ministerie van Justitie. Bestuur van de Gevangenissen en de Weldadigheidsinstellingen. Plannen van celgevangenissen II, 1822-1899, nr. 554. © Algemeen Rijksarchief

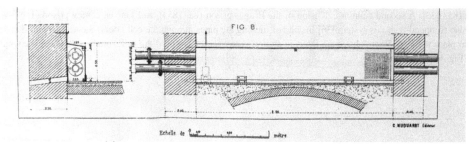

Fig. 5. Iron case to cover hot-filled heating pipes as proposed by Stevens (J. Stevens, De la construction des prisons cellulaires en Belgique, Bruxelles: Muquardt, 1874, Pl. VI)

Apart from the ordinary low pressure system, a high pressure system was used in the prison of Saint-Gilles.[38] This 'Perkins' system allowed heating of a large building - like the St-Gilles prison which housed 600 prisoners in five cell wings[39] – by means of a relatively short circuit of pipe.[40]

Ventilation

The ventilation of the cell demanded special attention in prison design. As we already mentioned had ventilation been a priority already in early prison reform, due to the belief that stagnant air caused disease.[41] The particularity of the cellular regime raised even more concerns. The prisoner spent about 22 hours per day – of which several laboring - in this 30 cubes space. The air was even more corrupted by the in-cell toilets. Therefore, a sufficient amount of fresh air was needed; preferably the air in the cell would be renewed every hour.[42] To prevent communication, natural ventilation by opening the cell window could was excluded. The tipping windows installed in most Belgian cellular prisons were to be used for supplementary ventilation, for example during the remaining two hours a day prisoners were not in their cell.[43] Hence, ventilation had to be forced.

Forced ventilation could be combined with heating, as applied in the Pentonville system. In the thermosiphon system, heating and ventilation functioned separately - at least for the most part. Although detached, both systems were still closely interlinked. The iron 'heat case' shielding the hot water pipes in each cell, was supplied with fresh air via a duct in the outer cell wall. The openings in the iron plate in the floor (or iron case above the floor as Stevens promoted in 1874) thus introduced heat as well as fresh air into the cell. Supplementary fresh air could be provided through a fan in the cell window, as was applied in the Leuven central prison (1860). Foul air was extracted through a 22-cm duct, near the ceiling on the opposite side of the heat and air supply. Via a large duct in the attic, the air was then evacuated to a chimney (Fig. 6).[44]

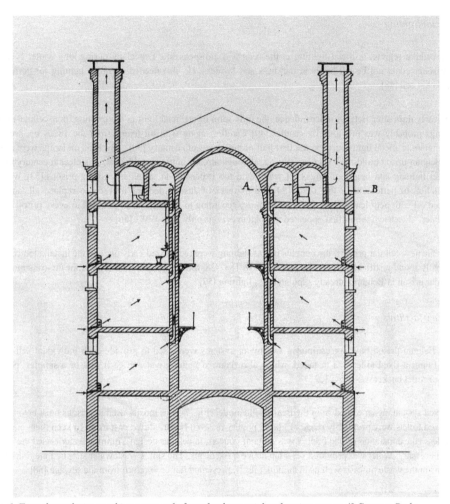

Fig. 6. Forced ventilation working separately from the thermosiphon heating system (J. Stevens, De la construction des prisons cellulaires en Belgique, Bruxelles: Muquardt, 1874, Pl. VII)

In his 1934 evaluation of the facilities in the Belgian prisons dating from the nineteenth century, Ernest Bertrand found these forced ventilation solutions inadequate.[45] In a time when separate confinement was no longer considered a panacea,[46] Bertrand advised to henceforth open the cell windows completely to suspend 'deceptive or annoying' forced ventilation through air vents altogether.[47]

Building services in nineteenth-century Belgian cellular prison architecture

Artificial lighting

In the cellular regime, artificial lighting in the cells was indispensable. Especially during long winter evenings, the prisoner could not be left hours in darkness and laziness. He also needed adequate lighting for performing labor in his cell.[48]

In the early days after Belgian independence, the only form of artificial light in the existing (non-cellular) prison buildings probably was provided by candles.[49] Candles, along with oil lamps from the 1820s on, were the predominant artificial light source in the first half of the nineteenth century.[50]   By 1850 oil lamps were used in most Belgian prison buildings.[51] Gas lighting, although already in use since the early nineteenth century mainly in street lighting and large buildings,[52] was found too expensive to install in existing prisons.[53] With the introduction of petroleum in the 1850s,[54] the minister of Justice decided in 1863 to replace all lamps on rapeseed oil with petroleum lamps.[55] Gas lighting, according to Bertrand, was installed in every prison "a few years later". Electric lighting first appeared in Belgian prisons only after WWI.[56]

As for the new cellular prisons, the benefits of gas lighting were recognized early on, and the installation cost was apparently found justifiable for new construction. In 1837-38, the earliest program drafted for the construction of a cellular prison in Belgium already stipulated gas lighting.[57]

Sanitary facilities

In the Belgian prison building campaign, two major systems were used to provide each individual cell with a toilet. Either a fixed toilet was installed, which also required running water in each cell, or a simpler 'portable toilet' or toilet bucket was provided.

The fixed system, again copied from the Pentonville model (Fig. 7), was mostly used in prisons built before 1863. The fixed toilets were preferably made of glazed pottery or, even better, glazed cast iron. To keep them clean and odourless (the emanation of bad odours was a major concern in cellular design), running water rinsed the system when necessary. Water was provided via a tap above a fixed sink. The sink's wastewater supplied the toilet flush. Siphons in the waste pipes as well as in the toilet itself, prevented fumes to return from the sewage.[58]

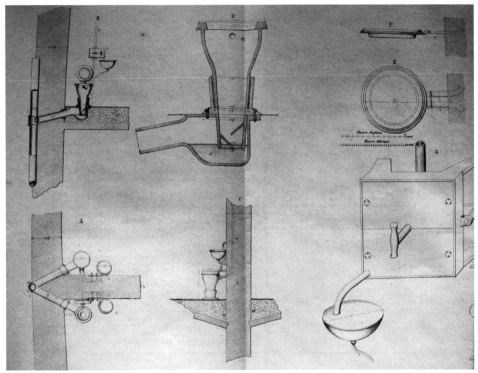

Fig. 7. Pentonville's fixed toilet system (S.n., Description des plans de la prison modèle de Pentonville, s.l.: s.n., (ca. 1844), Pl. VI)

Until 1863, Ducpétiaux had been a strong supporter of fixed toilets because of its ease of service. However, in order to function properly, the system necessitated water distribution in each cell via individual tanks of 25 to 30 litres, as well as seats and pipes made of solid and non-oxidizable materials that were drained to a septic well for each cell wing. These high demands could not always be met, and moreover they involved a considerable cost. Therefore, Ducpétiaux recommended in his étude de programme the use of 'portable toilets' which demanded an infinitely easier and cheaper installation. The toilet buckets, provided with a lid, were usually made of tin plate. They were placed in a ventilated niche in the wall towards the gallery, which were in some cases accessible via the gallery as well, by means of a double door. Emptied once or twice a day, toilet buckets did not require running water in the cells. Instead, prisoners were attributed a washbasin and water jug in pottery or stoneware. The jugs were filled with a daily supply of water from a tap installed per floor.[59]

In practice both systems were also combined, for instance in the prison of St-Gilles (1885). A ventilated niche contained a toilet bucket, while each cell was provided with running water and a fixed sink (Fig. 8).

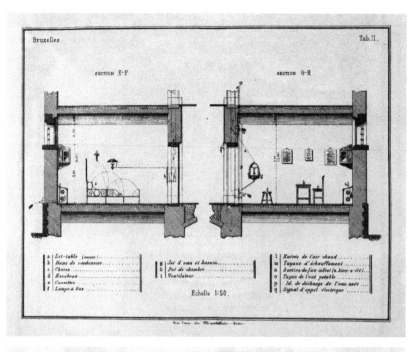

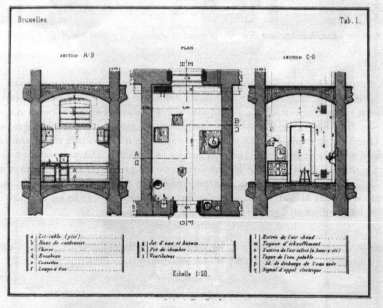

Fig. 8. Plans and sections of a cell in St-Gilles prison, with hot water heating, ventilation, gas lighting, a fixed sink with running water, and a toilet bucket in a ventilated niche in the inner cell wall (S.n., Actes du Congrès Pénitentiaire International de Rome 1885 (3 vols), Rome, 1888, Vol.3, Planches).

Conclusion

The implementation of the cellular regime in Belgium imposed high demands on its penal architecture. The new vision on the prison sentence had not only brought forward the need to provide for a single cell for every prisoner, it moreover had imposed an increased awareness on the importance of the prisoner's physical health for his moral recovery. The cellular prison typology was dependent on technologies of environmental control, that were rapidly developing in the nineteenth century and tested in several prison construction projects – abroad and in Belgium. Pentonville model prison's building services were copied in the first Belgian cellular prisons, following of Edouard Ducpétiaux' directives. Gradually, other systems like hot water heating or the portable toilet system were introduced in Belgian prison construction. It was only near the end of the century that the progressive loosening of the strictly cellular regime again rearranged the use of these building systems - a development to be further researched.

References

[1] E. Maes, *Van gevangenisstraf naar vrijheidsstraf: 200 jaar Belgisch gevangeniswezen*. Antwerpen: Maklu, 2009, pp. 119-148.

[2] See for instance: Jr. Delierneux and W. Crawford, 'Evolution of the Prison System in Belgium', *The Annals of the American Academy of Political and Social Science*, vol. 157, September, 1931, pp. 180-196; E. Maes, 'From Prison Sentence to Deprivation of Liberty. A Brief History of Two Centuries Regulation of the Belgian Prison Regime (1795-2006)', *European Journal of Crime, Criminal Law and Criminal Justice*, vol. 20, no. 1, 2012, pp. 81-97; B. Vanhulle, 'Dreaming about the prison: Édouard Ducpétiaux and Prison Reform in Belgium (1830-1848)', *Crime, Histoire & Sociétés/Crime, History & Societies*, vol. 14, no. 2, 2010, pp. 107-130.

[3] G. Vandersanden, 'De evolutie en de recente tendenzen in de Belgische gevangenisarchitectuur' (Master thesis, KU Leuven, 1980); B. Smets, 'L'architecture pénitentiaire en Belgique 1770-1900' (Master thesis, Université Catholique de Louvain, 1982); A. Autenne, 'La problématique de conservation du patrimoine penitentiaire belge: étude de la prison de Forest' (Master thesis, KU Leuven, 2006); M. Catrysse, 'De erfenis van Edouard Ducpétiaux: typologie van de gevangenis, 1830-1860' (Universiteit Gent, 2010).

[4] N. B. Johnston, 'The development of radial prisons: a case study in cultural diffusion' (Ph.D. thesis, University of Pennsylvania, 1958); N.B. Johnston, *The human cage: a brief history of prison architecture*, New York: Walker, 1973. N.B. Johnston, *Forms of constraint: a history of prison architecture*, Urbana: University of Illinois Press, 2000.

[5] R. Bruegmann, 'Central Heating and Forced Ventilation: Origins and Effects on Architectural Design', *Journal of the Society of Architectural Historians*, vol. 37, no. 3, 1978, p. 143.

[6] Y. Jewkes and H. Johnston, 'The Evolution of Prison Architecture' pp. 174-196 in Y. Jewkes, (ed.), *Handbook on Prisons, Portland: Willan*, 2007, p. 179.

[7] R. Evans, *The fabrication of Virtue: English Prison Architecture 1750-1840*, Cambridge: Cambridge University Press, 1982, p. 142.

[8] Ibid.

[9] Ibid., pp. 142-194.

[10] Jewkes and Johnston, 'Prison Architecture', (Note 6), pp. 182-183.

[11] Evans, *The fabrication of Virtue*, (Note 7), pp. 167, 162.

[12] Jewkes and Johnston, 'Prison Architecture', (Note 6), pp. 182-183.

[13] A. Corbin and K Van Dorsselaer, *Pestdamp En Bloesemgeur: Een Geschiedenis Van De Reuk*, Nijmegen: SUN, 1986, p. 144 (translation: J.F.).

[14] Johnston, *Forms of Constraint*, (Note 4), p. 47.

[15] Evans, *The fabrication of Virtue*, (Note 7), p. 346.

[16] C. D. Elliott, *Technics and architecture: the development of materials and systems for buildings*, Cambridge (Mass.): MIT press, 1994, p. 293.

[17] Evans, *The fabrication of Virtue*, (Note 7), pp. 363-367.

[18] L. Fairweather, 'The evolution of the prison' pp. 13-40 in G. Di Gennaro, (Ed.), *Prison Architecture. An international survey of representative closed institutions and analysis of current trends in prison design*, London: The Architectural Press, 1975, p. 22.

[19] Maes, *Van gevangenisstraf naar vrijheidsstraf*, (Note 1), pp. 141-149.

[20] E. Ducpétiaux, *Des progrès et de l'état actuel de la réforme pénitentiaire et des institutions préventives, aux États-Unis, en France, en Suisse, en Angleterre, et en Belgique* (3 vols), Bruxelles: Hauman, 1837-38;E. Ducpétiaux, *Mémoire à l'appui du projet de loi sur les prisons, présenté à la chambre des représentants de Belgique, dans la séance du 3 décembre 1844*, Bruxelles: Weissenbruch, 1845; E. Ducpétiaux, *Des conditions*

d'application du système de l'emprisonnement séparé ou cellulaire, Bruxelles: Hayez, 1858; E. Ducpétiaux, *Architecture des prisons cellulaires; étude d'un programme pour la construction des prisons cellulaires, accompagnée d'un plan*, s.l., 1863.

[21] Johnston, *Forms of Constraint*, (Note 4), pp. 104-106.

[22] J. Stevens, *Mémoire à l'appui d'un plan pour la construction d'une maison d'arrêt cellulaire*, Leuven: Vanlinthout, 1862; J. Stevens, *De la construction des prisons cellulaires en Belgique*, Bruxelles: Muquardt, 1874; J. Stevens, *Les prisons cellulaires en Belgique. Leur hygiène physique et morale*, Bruxelles: Ferdinand Larcier, 1891.

[23] Johnston, *Forms of Constraint*, (Note 4), p. 106.

[24] Elliott, *Technics and architecture*, (Note 16), pp. 293-294; Ducpétiaux, *Mémoire*, (Note 20), pp. 278-279; Ducpétiaux, *Architecture des prisons cellulaires*, (Note 20), pp. 18-19.

[25] Ducpétiaux, *Mémoire*, (Note 20), pp. 277-282.

[26] Algemeen Rijksarchief, *Ministerie van Justitie. Bestuur van de Gevangenissen en de Weldadigheidsinstellingen. Reeks I, 1790-1927*, nr. 288, folder *Plans, métré ...*, unnumbered document: measuring state, 28 June 1850.

[27] Algemeen Rijksarchief, *Ministerie van Justitie. Bestuur van de Gevangenissen en de Weldadigheidsinstellingen. Reeks I, 1790-1927*, nr. 282, folder *Paiements de l'entrepeneur ...*, unnumbered document: correspondence on heating system, 27 January 1849.

[28] Algemeen Rijksarchief, *Ministerie van Justitie. Bestuur van de Gevangenissen en de Weldadigheidsinstellingen. Reeks I, 1790-1927*, nr. 341, folder *Construction simultanée ...*, unnumbered document: measuring state, 17 april 185?

[29] The Builder, Vol. 5 (9 October 1847), p. 484; Ducpétiaux, Des conditions, (Note 20), p. 15; Ducpétiaux, *Architecture des prisons cellulaires*, (Note 20), p. 19; Algemeen Rijksarchief, *Ministerie van Justitie. Bestuur van de Gevangenissen en de Weldadigheidsinstellingen. Reeks I, 1790-1927*, nr. 291, folder *Adjudication ...*, unnumbered document: annexe to measuring state, 10 February 1853.

[30] Ducpétiaux, *Des conditions*, (Note 20), p. 15.

[31] Stevens, *De la construction*, (Note 22), pp. 17-18.

[32] Bruegmann, 'Central Heating and Forced Ventilation', (Note 5), p. 148.

[33] Ducpétiaux, *Architecture des prisons cellulaires*, (Note 20), p. 19.

[34] Algemeen Rijksarchief, *Ministerie van Justitie. Bestuur van de Gevangenissen en de Weldadigheidsinstellingen. Reeks I, 1790-1927*, nr. 291, folder Adjudication ..., unnumbered document: annexe to measuring state, 10 February 1853.

[35] Algemeen Rijksarchief, *Ministerie van Justitie. Bestuur van de Gevangenissen en de Weldadigheidsinstellingen. Reeks I, 1790-1927*, nr. 270, folder *Concours...*, unnumbered document: 'Mémoire explicatif', s.d.

[36] Ducpétiaux, *Des conditions*, (Note 20), p. 15.

[37] Stevens, *De la construction*, (Note 22), p. 16.

[38] S.n., *Actes du Congrès Pénitentiaire International de Rome 1885* (3 vols), Rome, 1888, Vol.3, p. 36.

[39] Ibid.

[40] Bruegmann, 'Central Heating and Forced Ventilation', (Note 5), p. 148.

[41] Bruegmann, 'Central Heating and Forced Ventilation', (Note 5), p. 149.

[42] Stevens, *Les prisons cellulaires*, (Note 22), pp. 15-16.

[43] Ducpétiaux, *Architecture des prisons cellulaires*, (Note 20), p. 21; Stevens, *Les prisons cellulaires*, (Note 22), pp. 17-18.

[44] Stevens, *De la construction*, (Note 22), pp. 16-20.

[45] E. Bertrand, *Leçons pénitentiaires*, Louvain: Imprimerie administrative, 1932-34, p. 305.

[46] Johnston, *Forms of Constraint*, (Note 4), p. 107.

[47] Bertrand, *Leçons pénitentiaires*, (Note 45), p. 305.

[48] Ducpétiaux, *Architecture des prisons cellulaires*, (Note 20), p. 22.

[49] Bertrand, *Leçons pénitentiaires*, (Note 45), p. 463.

[50] M. Stokroos, *Verwarmen en verlichten in de negentiende eeuw*, Zutphen: Walburg pers, 2001, p. 63.

[51] Algemeen Rijksarchief, *Ministerie van Justitie. Bestuur van de Gevangenissen en de Weldadigheidsinstellingen. Reeks I, 1790-1927*, nr. 257, folder *Systèmes d'éclairage ...* , unnumbered document: report on lighting, 1850.

[52] Stokroos, *Verwarmen en verlichten*, (Note 50), p. 72.

[53] Algemeen Rijksarchief, *Ministerie van Justitie. Bestuur van de Gevangenissen en de Weldadigheidsinstellingen. Reeks I, 1790-1927*, nr. 257, folder *Systèmes d'éclairage ...* , unnumbered document: report on lighting, 1850.

[54] Stokroos, *Verwarmen en verlichten*, (Note 50), p. 69.

[55] S.n., *Receuil des circulaires, instructions et autres actes émanés du Ministère de la justice ou relatifs a ce département: 1861-1863*, Bruxelles: Weissenbruch, 1864, p. 506.

[56] Bertrand, *Leçons pénitentiaires*, (Note 45), p. 463.

[57] Ducpétiaux, *De la réforme pénitentiaire*, (Note 20), Vol 2, pp. 255-267.

[58] Ducpétiaux, *Architecture des prisons cellulaires*, (Note 20), pp. 23-27; Stevens, *Les prisons cellulaires*, (Note 22), pp. 29-33.

[59] Ducpétiaux, *Architecture des prisons cellulaires*, (Note 20), pp. 23-27; Stevens, *Les prisons cellulaires*, (Note 22), pp. 29-33.

Roman building services and architectural manuals

John Gelder

School of Natural and Built Environments, University of South Australia, Australia

Introduction

Several Roman manuals dealing with aspects of construction survive, and all discuss building services to some extent. The earliest, and most famous, of these manuals is Vitruvius' *De architectura*, written 30-20 BCE. In terms of building services in particular, it is the fullest of the manuals.[1] Subsequent Roman manuals on construction include Faventinus, *De diversis fabricis architectonicae* (200-300 CE)[2] and Palladius, *Opus agriculturae* (ca. 450 CE).[3]

Though known to scholars during the medieval period, *De architectura* was 'rediscovered' in 1416 in the monastery library of St Gall,[4] and inspired several architectural manuals published during the Italian renaissance. These also discuss building services to a small extent, and include Leon Battista Alberti, *De re aedificatoria*, printed 1486,[5] Sebastiano Serlio, *Tutti l'opere d'architettura et prospetiva*, 1537-1575,[6] and Andrea Palladio, *I quattro libri*, 1570.[7]

This paper collects and compares material on a selection of building services – aqueducts, water pipes, hypocausts, sounding vessels in theatres, sundials and water clocks – across these architectural manuals from the Roman and Renaissance periods. Transmission between these manuals of ideas about building services is considered. Comparison is briefly made with the architectural record, to determine the extent to which these ideas were put into practice. Services not covered include water supply tunnels and siphons (Vit. 8.6), wells (Vit. 8.6.12-13), cisterns (Vit. 8.6.14-15), latrines and sewers (not in Vitruvius), hearths and artificial lighting (not in Vitruvius), the *analemma* – a chart used in the preparation of sundials (Vit. 9.7), and water-raising devices (Vit. 10.4-7).

Aqueducts

Though the invention of aqueducts is credited to the Romans, the oldest known (c. 690 BCE) served Nineveh and overall is 50 km long.[8] But before the Roman era, water supply tunnels were the norm. Greek examples include those at Athens, commissioned by Peisistratus (c. 535 BCE),[9] and at Samos, excavated by Eupalinos of Megaria (c. 530 BCE).[10]

Vitruvius (8.6) described the components (reservoir at source, regular cisterns, and a terminating reservoir with three compartments) and construction (e.g. to deal with pressure) of aqueducts. Gradients are key – too shallow and the channels will not self-clean, too steep and the water flow can be unmanageable. But achieving the necessary precision was difficult given the need to survey the topography and set out the falls using tools such as the *dioptra*

Roman building services and architectural manuals

(described by Heron of Alexandria in his book *Dioptra*, and dismissed by Vitruvius as inaccurate), water level and *chorobates* (known only from Vitruvius 8.5). Inevitably mistakes were made in practice.

Vitruvius (8.6.1) provided a minimum gradient for aqueducts, but the various manuscripts give two values, one being 1:200, the other 1:4800.[11] The former was not followed by any other author. The latter was followed by Pliny the Elder (*Natural History*, 31.31), who often followed Vitruvius on architectural matters.[12] Neither were followed in the quite steep gradients given by Faventinus (6), which were followed by Palladius (9.11). None of these values are unrealistic – gradients similar to them all can be found in built aqueducts (Table 1).[13]

Table 1: Gradients of Roman aqueducts

Approx. gradient	Roman manuals	Built Roman aqueducts
1:20000		
1:10000		Nimes (min, over a 10 km length) 1:14000
1:5000	Vitruvius & Pliny (min) 1:4800 [¼ inch in 100 feet]	Nimes (ave/min) 1:4000
1:2000		Nimes (ave) 1:3000/1:2941 General (min) 1:2900 General (min) 1:2640 Basse-Fontaine (min) 1:2500 Aqua Appia (ave) 1:2000 General (max) 1:1750
1:1000		Gier (min) about 1:1000 Vienne (ave) 1:860
1:500		Sabine Hills, Rome (ave) 1:700 General (min) 1:333
1:200	Vitruvius (min) 1:200 [½ foot in 100 feet]	
1:100		Gier (max) 1:151 General (max) 1:150
1:50	Faventinus & Palladius (min) 1:67 [1½ feet in 100 feet] Faventinus & Palladius (max) 1:40 [1½ feet in 60 feet]	General (max) 1:66 Yzeron, Lyon (ave) 1:60 Basse-Fontaine (max) 1:59
1:20		Rome (max) 1:33

Frontinus, as their administrator, devoted a book to the management of the Roman aqueducts: *De aquis urbis Romae* (80-100 CE).[14] These were the Appia (the first at Rome, built 312 BCE), Anio Vetus, Marcia, Tepula, Julia, Virgo, Alsietina, Claudia and Anio Novus. His work has been the subject of much study,[15] but provided no value for the gradient of aqueducts, since he was not concerned with their construction.

Alberti (10.7) gave a brief history of Roman aqueducts (from Frontinus), and described their component parts and explained their construction (from Vitruvius). Aqueducts were not mentioned at all in Palladio, and though Serlio mentioned them several times, he provided no technical information about them. Though at the time no aqueducts had been built since the Roman era, and all of the nine listed by Frontinus had fallen into disrepair, the Aqua Virgo was renovated in 1453 by Pope Nicolas V, and again in 1560-70, and still feeds the Trevi and other fountains.[16]

Water pipes

Terracotta water supply and drainage pipes are known from the Minoan city of Knossos, Crete (3200-1100 BCE).[17] They were also used in Greek cities such as Athens (6th century BCE).[18] Lead pipes were in use in Rome from at least 200 BCE.[19]

Vitruvius addressed water pipes, describing both terracotta tubes (tubuli) and lead pipes, arguing that the former are healthier and provide purer water (8.6.10). He described lead pipes in some detail (8.6.3). Table 2 presents an analysis of the pipe sizes given by Vitruvius. The first three columns provide Vitruvius' information, the rest are analysis. The approach to pipe sizes he describes works if the sheet thickness is the same for all pipe diameters. This affects strength – pipe walls should be thicker for bigger diameters – and so was not the case in practice in spite of weight considerations. Even so, at about 6.5 mm thick, Vitruvian lead sheet is very heavy lead by modern standards.[20] The weight of a single length of 5 digit[21] pipe corresponds to a modern 20 kg limit for safe manual handling at chest height.[22]

Table 2: Analysis of lead pipe sizes in Vitruvius

Pipe length	Sheet width	Weight	Lead weight/area		Sheet thickness		Weight	Diameter	Cross section area	Quinariae	Renard series (Q)
digit	digit	pound	pound/digit²	pound/foot²	digit	mm	kg	mm	mm²		R5
160	5	60	0.075	19.2	0.35	6.45	20.01	29.44	680.88	1	1.0
160	8	100	0.078	20	0.36	6.72	33.35	47.11	1743.06	2.56	2.5
160	10	120	0.075	19.2	0.35	6.45	40.02	58.89	2723.53	4	4.0
160	15	180	0.075	19.2	0.35	6.45	60.03	88.33	6127.95	9	10.0
160	20	240	0.075	19.2	0.35	6.45	80.04	117.77	10894.13	16	15.9
160	30	360	0.075	19.2	0.35	6.45	120.06	176.66	24511.79	36	39.8
160	40	480	0.075	19.2	0.35	6.45	160.08	235.55	43576.52	64	63.1
160	50	600	0.075	19.2	0.35	6.45	200.10	294.44	68088.31	100	100.0
160	80	960	0.075	19.2	0.35	6.45	320.16	471.10	174306.09	256	251.2
160	100	1200	0.075	19.2	0.35	6.45	400.20	588.87	272353.26	400	398.1

For the 8 digit sheet width it can be seen that Vitruvius made an error – the weight should be 96 pounds.[23] For simplicity, the calculations for diameter and cross section area ignore any sheet overlap needed to form the longitudinal joint.

The 5 digit pipe is the base pipe size, known to the Romans as the 'quinaria'. Other pipes can be described in terms of this size. The right hand column compares the quinariae to the Renard series of rationalised product dimensions – it can be seen that there is a close correspondence, though every number in the R5 sequence is not represented.[24] The conclusion is that Roman pipe sizes had been rationalised, to optimize choice and range. The Romans were ahead of their time.

Pliny the Elder (31.31) and Faventinus (7) based their text about pipe sizes on Vitruvius. In turn, Palladius (9.12) based his work on Faventinus, but made a number of errors.[25] See Table 3.

Table 3: Lead pipe sizes in Pliny, Faventinus and Palladius

	Pliny the Elder	Faventinus	Palladius
Designation	Weight (pound)		
5	60	-	-
8	100	100	100
10	120	-	-
20	-	240	240
30	-	360	450
40	-	480	600
50	-	600	680
80	-	960	840
100	-	1200	1200

Frontinus (1.23-63) provided an extensive set of pipe sizes, many more than those provided by Vitruvius, though he concedes that some were not used in practice. He acknowledged Vitruvius, but disagreed with his method of calculation and provided two others, the first – for smaller pipes – based on pipe diameter, and the second – for larger pipes – based on cross sectional area. As a result, the sizes provided are quite different, and much lighter. The first four columns in Table 4 give Frontinus' information, the others are analysis. Again, we see a close alignment with the Renard series. As we have seen, though authoritative, later authors did not follow him, preferring (or perhaps only being aware of) Vitruvius.

Table 4: Analysis of lead pipe sizes in Frontinus

Designation	Diameter	Circumference	Area	Diameter		Circumference	Area	Area	Weight	Quinariae	Renard series (Q)	
	digit	digit	Q	mm	mm	mm	digit^2	mm^2	kg		R5	R10
5	1.25	3.93	1.00	23.13		72.65	1.23	420.00	15.76	1.00	1.000	
6	1.50	4.72	1.78	27.75		87.18	1.77	604.81	18.91	1.44	1.586	
7	1.75	5.50	1.96	32.38		101.71	2.41	823.21	22.06	1.96		1.995
8	2.00	6.28	2.56	37.00		116.24	3.14	1075.21	25.21	2.56	2.512	
10	2.50	7.86	4.00	46.25		145.30	4.91	1680.02	31.52	4.00	3.981	
12	3.00	9.43	5.76	55.50		174.36	7.07	2419.23	37.82	5.76	6.310	
15	3.75	11.78	9.00	69.38		217.95	11.04	3780.04	47.27	9.00	10.000	
20	5.00	15.85	16.29	92.50	93.36	290.60	19.64	6720.08	63.03	16.00	15.855	
25	5.64	17.73	20.36		104.37	327.90	25.00	8556.25	71.12	20.37		19.953
30	6.18	19.42	24.43		114.34	359.20	30.00	10267.50	77.91	24.45	25.119	
35	6.67	20.98	28.51		123.50	387.98	35.00	11978.75	84.15	28.52		
40	7.14	22.42	32.58		132.03	414.77	40.00	13690.00	89.96	32.59		31.623
45	7.57	23.78	36.65		140.03	439.93	45.00	15401.25	95.42	36.67		
50	7.98	25.07	40.73		147.61	463.73	50.00	17112.50	100.58	40.74	39.811	
55	8.45	26.30	44.80		154.81	486.36	55.00	18823.75	105.49	44.82		

Designation	Diameter	Circumference	Area	Diameter		Circumference	Area	Area	Weight	Quinariae	Renard series (Q)	
	digit	digit	Q	mm	mm	mm	digit²	mm²	kg		R5	R10
60	8.74	27.46	48.87		161.70	507.99	60.00	20535.00	110.18	48.89		50.119
65	9.09	28.58	52.94		168.30	528.73	65.00	22246.25	114.68	52.97		
70	9.44	29.67	57.02		174.65	548.69	70.00	23957.50	119.01	57.04		
75	9.77	30.71	61.09		180.78	567.95	75.00	25668.75	123.19	61.12		
80	10.01	31.71	65.17		186.71	586.57	80.00	27380.00	127.23	65.19	63.096	
85	10.40	32.69	69.24		192.46	604.63	85.00	29091.25	131.14	69.26		
90	10.70	33.64	73.31		198.04	622.15	90.00	30802.50	134.95	73.34		
95	11.00	34.56	77.38		203.46	639.20	95.00	32513.75	138.64	77.41		
100	11.28	35.46	81.45		208.75	655.81	100.00	34225.00	142.25	81.49		79.433
120	12.35	38.83	97.75		228.67	718.40	120.00	41070.00	155.82	97.78	100.000	

All the manuals agreed that the Romans used standard sizes for lead water pipes, but they merely reported the fact – they were not the mechanism for standardization.[26] Again, this standardization is largely ahead of its time.[27]

Many Roman lead pipes have been found, but there appears to be no work correlating their dimensions with those in the manuals. Sizes vary for individual pipes, and of course from pipe to pipe. For example, we have pipes of diameter 95-125 mm, and 165-220 mm.[28]

Lead pipes and terracotta tubes for water were discussed in Alberti (10.7), who preferred terracotta tubes and described them in some detail, e.g. "the internal diameter of the pipe should be no less than four times the thickness of its wall".[29] Lead pipes were briefly mentioned in Palladio (1.6) but not in Serlio. Water pipes of various materials were widely used in the Renaissance, a famous example being the Villa d'Este (c.1560).[30]

Hypocausts

The hypocaust was an underfloor heating system used in Roman baths as far afield as the forts on Hadrian's Wall.[31] Hot air from a furnace was drawn into a series of subfloor spaces (under hot and warm baths – *caldaria* and *tepidaria*) in which the tile floor was supported on an array of small pillars. The system was extended to heat (hollow) walls and bathing spaces, and was also used in baths for large houses. Roman baths included a cold plunge pool, the *frigidarium*. Baths became a central part of Roman culture, and consumed vast amounts of wood and other renewables as fuel.[32]

The hypocaust is a Roman innovation. The earliest examples are the 2nd century BCE Republican Baths at Fregellae in Latium, and the Stabian Baths at Pompeii.[33] Given these dates, and contrary to Valerius Maximus (9.1.1),[34] Pliny the Elder (9.79) and others, the hypocaust was not invented by Sergius Orata (90-80 BCE), though he may have developed it for residential or other uses.[35]

Vitruvius described hypocausts in a section on baths (5.10), and Faventinus (16) and Palladius (1.39) both dealt with them. Plommer observes that "By the end of the series [of the 3 books], only the slope of the floor, the ball [used to check the slope] and the furnace-mouth survive from Vitruvius; and with Palladius the floor has become as heavy as it reasonably can on supports as slight as safety will require".[36] The three authors were mostly independent of each other, perhaps reflecting the evolution of the technology. For example, three separate boilers as described by Vitruvius were used at the Central Thermae at Herculaneum (beginning of 1st century CE). This was rationalised to one such vessel, of 4100 litres, serving the entire complex at the later military bathhouse at Exeter (c. 60 CE). Again, where Vitruvius had bronze vessels for boiling the water, Faventinus and Palladius had lead vessels with bronze base-plates, also found at Exeter.[37]

The technology was lost to the West with the fall of the Roman Empire, but was adapted from Byzantine examples for use in ritual bathing in the *hammams* of the Ottoman Empire (without the cold bath), and eventually made its way back to the West – to Ireland – in 1856, as the 'Turkish bath', and thence to the rest of the western world.[38] The hypocaust was therefore largely unknown in Renaissance Italy, and Alberti and Serlio did not write about it, though Alberti (8.10) and Serlio (3.88-92) did write about the layout of Roman baths. Palladio mentioned the hypocaust system, extended to include *canna* or *tromba* in the walls (1.27), but was more interested in adapting this approach for cooling.[39]

Sounding vessels in theatres

Ancient semicircular theatres relied on natural acoustics which could be enhanced in various ways, one such being acoustic resonance. Vitruvius recommended sounding vessels (echeia) (1.1.9 and 5.5), crediting Aristoxenus of Tarentum (fl. 335 BCE) for the theory behind them.[40] A series of inverted bronze vessels displaying different harmonics were distributed around the stone-built theatre seating, in chambers the distribution of which he described for small theatres (13 chambers) and large theatres (3 rows of 13 chambers).

Acknowledging that the system was not used in Rome, Vitruvius claimed that the idea was used in the provinces of Italy and many Greek cities, including Corinth, and that often terracotta vessels were used instead, to keep costs down. Though no bronze echeia have survived, terracotta vessels "apparently for this purpose" have been found.[41] Also, up to sixteen theatres with evidence of echeia have been identified, including the following:[42]

- Aizanoi, Turkey – 12 pairs of chambers.[43]

- Scythopolis, Syria – 7 pairs.[44]

- Nicopolis, Greece – 8 pairs.

- Gerasa, Jordan – 12 niches.

- Ierapetra, Crete – 13 niches.

- Gortyn, Crete – 13 niches.

- Lyttos, Crete – 3 x 13 niches.[45]

However, at best the vessels would have responded to just 7 notes and their harmonics. Pliny the Elder (11.112) argued that empty casks placed in the orchestra of a theatre will absorb the voice, and fixed (rather than loose) vases in several medieval churches seem to have been used in this way. Alternatively it is thought that they may have helped singers keep to the correct pitch. In other words, it is not clear whether they would have worked as Vitruvius claimed.[46]

Neither Faventinus nor Palladius wrote about theatres or their acoustics. Nor did Palladio (though he may have intended to). Serlio described several Roman theatres (e.g. the Theatre of Marcellus, 3.46),[47] but not their acoustics, but Alberti (8.7) had this to say:

> "... in suitable places such as these, at equal intervals, niches may be fashioned, where you may, should you wish, hang bronze vases upside down, so that the resonance of the voice improves as it reaches and strikes them. Here I do not intend to go into Vitruvius' theory, based on the divisions in music, from which he derives his method of arranging vases around the theatre to reflect principal, middle, and highest voices, as well as those in unison; an effect that is easy enough to describe, but only those who have experience know how to achieve. We should not ignore, however, the conviction also held by Aristotle,[48] that any empty vessel or well improves the resonance of the voice."[49]

Sundials

According to Herodotus, "knowledge of the sundial and the gnomon and the twelve divisions of the day came into Greece from Babylon".[50] From Greece, they came to Rome where they were common, too common according to some.[51] At least 35 have been found in Pompeii alone. The largest was built by Augustus in the Campus Martius, Rome. The gnomon was a 22 m obelisk from Heliopolis in Egypt.[52]

Vitruvius listed 13 types of sundial, and their purported inventors, all Hellenistic (9.8), but did not describe them further:

- Half-cylinder – Berossus the Chaldean (Babylonian, 3rd century BCE) – though relatively common in the Roman era, fewer than 100 such Roman sundials are extant;[53]

- Concave quadrant or hemisphere, and flat disc – Aristarchus of Samos;

- *Arachne* (spider) – Eudoxus or Apollonius;

- *Plinthium* or *lacunar* (plinth or coffer) – Scopinas of Syracuse;

- Quadrant for places studied – Parmenion;

- Quadrant for every latitude – Theodosius and Andrias;

- *Pelecinum* (double axe head) – Patrocles;

- Cone – Dionysodorus;

- Quiver – Apollonius;

- Conical spider, conical plinth, and 'the one facing north'.

- Portable versions of these – very rare – just 16 portable Roman bronze sundials survive.[54]

Faventinus (29) described two of these 'many and diverse' timekeepers in some detail: the *pelecinum* and the half-cylinder. He did not follow Vitruvius, which has no such detail, but used other sources. His descriptions deserve to be better known. He noted that sundials are imprecise devices, but that this did not matter since "almost everyone asks to know only what hour he is in".[55] This imprecision was nevertheless frustrating. For example, Seneca wrote "I can't tell you the exact hour, which is more easily agreed upon among philosophers than among sundials".[56]

Sundials were not described in Palladius, who instead offered a table of shadow lengths by the hour, for each month.[57] Nor were they discussed by Alberti, Serlio or Palladio. Renaissance authors on the sundial included Giovanni Padovani (1512-after 1570) and Giuseppe Biancani (1566-1624). Sundials were now in the realm of specialists.

Water clocks

Simple outflow water clocks were used to time speeches – an early example is from Egypt, dated about 1380 BCE.[58] For more sophisticated outflow water clocks, a shaped reservoir was needed so (in theory) the water discharged at a constant rate. A 3rd century CE papyrus from Oxyrhynchus in Egypt (*P. Oxy* 470) gave formulae for sizing and calibrating the reservoir of such a water clock.[59]

A detailed description of a large water clock was given in a treatise influential in the Arab world, attributed to Archimedes of Syracuse (died 212 BCE), perhaps with additions by Philo of Byzantium (c. 280-220 BCE), and surviving only in Arabic manuscripts.[60]

Vitruvius credited the development of the inflow type, with overflow to the reservoir and a constant supply of water (and so maintaining a constant head), to Ctesibius of Alexandria (285-222 BCE) in particular, and described his clock at length (9.8.2-7). The Romans divided each day (sunrise to sunset) into twelve equal hours, but as the length of the day varied from season to season, so did the length of the hour. While this variation was evident in the hyperbolic[61] shadow curves cast on a flat sundial, there was no such variation in a water clock – the water dripped at a constant rate all year round. Accordingly elaborate corrections were needed to convert the equal hours of the water clock to the unequal hours of the sundial, such as (in Ctesibius' clock) removable wedges or revolving columns with the hours and months marked. A monumental, and surviving example (though the mechanism is lost) is the Tower of the Winds in Athens (perhaps 2nd century BCE).

Vitruvius (9.8.8) also described an 'anaphoric' water clock (akin to an astrolabe), which indicated the signs of the zodiac as well as hours, days and months, using rotating discs. No water clocks were described in Faventinus or Palladius, or in Alberti, Serlio or Palladio. They were replaced by mechanical clocks from the late 13th century.

Summary and conclusion

Transmission between the manuals of Vitruvius, Faventinus and Palladius was inconsistent – for the six services described in the manuals, transmission occurred just three times (aqueduct gradients, water pipe sizes, hypocausts) and differently each time. On the other hand, the extent to which these technologies were put into practice in the Roman period was fairly consistent, with just two of the services being 'specialist' (sounding vessels, water clocks – Table 5). However, for none of the building services described here were the Roman manuals the route for implementation, though they advocated them in some cases (e.g. the use of *echeia* in Vitruvius). Aqueducts, lead pipes, hypocausts, sounding vessels, sundials and water clocks were all in use before Vitruvius, and the standards – if any – long established. In any case, the descriptions of these services in the manuals were generally incomplete, inaccurate or vague. The authors were out of their depth on these issues.

Table 5: Transmission and implementation of ideas about building services

Building service	Transmission between Roman manuals	Roman implementation	Transmission to Renaissance manuals	Renaissance implementation
Aqueducts	Gradients transmitted between Faventinus and Palladius, possibly also from Vitruvius to Pliny.	Rome had nine at the time of Frontinus – widespread across the Empire.	Alberti draws on Vitruvius and Pliny.	One Roman aqueduct repaired in the Renaissance, none built.
Water pipes	Pipe sizes transmitted between all three, but with errors, and to Pliny. Frontinus is not followed.	Widely used, in lead and terracotta.	No pipe sizes transmitted.	Terracotta pipes common.
Hypocausts	Transmitted between all three, but developed each time.	Widespread in public and private baths.	Not transmitted, bar a brief mention in Palladio.	No longer in use.
Sounding vessels in theatres	Described in Vitruvius but not transmitted.	Appear to have been used in some provincial theatres.	Alberti references Vitruvius.	Not in use – theatres of the Roman kind no longer built.
Sundials	Described in Vitruvius and Faventinus independently – not transmitted.	Common.	Not transmitted.	Still being studied and built, by specialists.
Water clocks	Described in Vitruvius but not transmitted.	In use but expensive.	Not transmitted.	Not in use – replaced by mechanical clocks.

Transmission to the manuals of Alberti, Serlio and Palladio was sparse – Alberti drew on Vitruvius for two of the services (aqueducts, sounding vessels) and Palladio, briefly, on one (hypocausts). One reason for the sparse transmission is that the extent to which these technologies were put into practice in the Renaissance was limited –

for example, one had been superseded (water clocks), and one had been lost (hypocausts) (Table 5). Three Roman building services transmitted – aqueducts, hypocausts, sounding vessels – were not implemented in the Renaissance. That is, the Renaissance manuals were not a route for implementation in this case.

Transmission of ideas about building services between Roman and Renaissance authors does not follow a consistent pattern. The Roman manuals reflected contemporary practice on building services – they were not theoretical. Though their architectural components (e.g. the Orders) were enthusiastically adopted in the Renaissance, they were generally anachronistic with respect to Renaissance building services practice.

References

[1] English-language editions include the following: Vitruvius (transl. M.H. Morgan), *The ten books on architecture*, Cambridge MA: Harvard University Press, 1914 (Dover reprint, 1960); Vitruvius (transl. F. Granger), *LCL 251 On architecture Books I-V*, Cambridge MA: Harvard University Press, 1931; Vitruvius (transl. F. Granger), *LCL 280 On architecture Books VI-X*, Cambridge MA: Harvard University Press, 1934; Vitruvius (transl. I.D. Rowland & T.N. Howe), *Ten books on architecture*, Cambridge: Cambridge University Press, 1999; Vitruvius (transl. T.G. Smith), *On architecture Books I-VI*, New York: The Monacelli Press, 2003; Vitruvius (transl. R. Schofield), *On architecture*, London: Penguin Books, 2009.

[2] Faventinus (transl. W.H. Plommer), *De diversis fabricis architectonicae*, in W.H. Plommer, *Vitruvius and later Roman building manuals*, Cambridge: Cambridge University Press, 1973 (UMI reprint 2001).

[3] Palladius (transl. J.H. Fitch), *The work of farming*, Totnes: Prospect Books, 2013.

[4] C.H. Krinsky, 'Seventy-eight Vitruvius manuscripts' *Journal of the Warburg and Courtauld Institutes*, vol.30, 1967 pp. 36-70.

[5] L.B. Alberti (transl. J. Rykwert, N. Leach & R. Tavernor), *On the art of building in ten books*, Cambridge MA: The MIT Press, 1988.

[6] S. Serlio (transl. V. Hart & P. Hicks), *On architecture, Volume One*, New Haven: Yale University Press, 1996.

[7] A. Palladio (transl. R. Tavernor & R. Schofield), *The four books on architecture*, Cambridge MA: The MIT Press, 1997.

[8] This length included the Jerwan aqueduct, a 22 m wide, 9 m high and over 280 m long limestone arcaded structure. J.H. Breasted & T.G. Allen, *Sennacherib's aqueduct at Jerwan*, Chicago: University of Chicago Press, 1935; S. Dalley, *The mystery of the Hanging Garden of Babylon: An elusive world wonder traced*, Oxford: Oxford University Press, 2015.

[9] T.P. Tassios, 'Water supply of ancient Greek cities', *Water Science & Technology: Water Supply*, vol 7/1, March 2007.

[10] Herodotus (transl. A. de Sélincourt), *The histories*, Harmondsworth: Penguin Books, 1972, 3.60, p. 228; K.D. White, *Greek and Roman technology*, London: Thames & Hudson, 1984, pp. 158-160. Now restored and open to the public.

[11] The manuscripts disagree. Granger used the oldest, Harley 2767, which has *semipede*, and Morgan used Valentin Rose's 1899 edition (Teubner 1912), which has *sicilico*. It might be that a manuscript editor modified Vitruvius to align with Pliny, on the basis that Pliny followed Vitruvius in this case.

[12] Pliny the Elder (transl. J. Bostock & H.T. Riley), *The Natural History*, London: Taylor and Francis, 1855. This compendium was written 77-79 CE.

[13] Various sources are used here: White, *Technology* (Note 10), p.165; J. Granier, *The Pont du Gard*, Monaco: Editions de Boumian, 1998, p.1; Vitruvius, *De architectura*, 1999 (Note 1), p.277; D.R. Blackman & A.T.

Hodge, *Frontinus' legacy: Essays on Frontinus'* de aquis urbis Romae, Ann Arbor: Michigan University Press, 2001, pp.52, 60; A. Hodge, *Roman aqueducts and water supply*, London: Duckworth, 2002, p.178.

[14] Frontinus (transl. C.E. Bennett), *LCL 174 Strategems; Aqueducts of Rome*, Cambridge MA: Harvard University Press, 1925.

[15] See for example: Blackman & Hodge, *Frontinus'* (Note 13). See also the journal *Schriftenreihe der Frontinus-Gesellschaft*.

[16] D. Karmon, 'Restoring the ancient water suppluy system in Renaissance Rome: The Popes, the civic administration, and the Aqua Vergine', *The waters of Rome*, vol.3, August 2005.

[17] A.N. Angelakis et al, 'Minoan and Etruscan hydro-technologies', *Water*, vol.5/3, 2013, pp. 972-987.

[18] HYDRIA Project, *The ancient Agora of Athens: Water works*, (online) 2009.

[19] A. Beall, 'Ancient Romans were drinking water from 'poisonous' lead pipes around 200 years earlier than thought', *Daily Mail*, 1 September 2017.

[20] The heaviest British standard lead sheet is Code 9 (i.e. 9 lb/ft^2). This is 4 mm thick, only available as sandcast, and manufactured by just a few specialist companies in the UK for heritage work.

[21] A Roman digit was 18.5 mm, and was 1/16th of a Roman foot.

[22] Health and Safety Executive, *Manual handling at work: A brief guide*, London: HSE, 2012 (Figure 1).

[23] This error was repeated in Pliny, Faventinus and Palladius, indicating that they used Vitruvius as a source and did not check the calculations themselves.

[24] The Renard series dates from the work of the military engineer, Charles Renard, in 1877-79, who rationalised the 425 evolved sizes of ropes in the French Army inventory to just 17. It is implemented in International Organization for Standardization, *ISO 3:1973 Preferred numbers – Series of preferred numbers*, ISO, Geneva, 1973.

[25] Discussed in: R.H. Rodgers, *An introduction to Palladius*, London: University of London Institute of Classical Studies, 1975, pp. 130-131.

[26] Given the use of preferred numbers, these sizes were probably devised, rather than evolved, perhaps by Frontinus' organization to manage its inventory. They were probably promulgated through the various contracts for pipe manufacture. Informal (i.e. not promulgated through standardisation organisations) technical standardisation was not unheard of in the ancient world. An imposed example is the Egyptian 'talatat' stone block, used under Akhenaten to speed the construction of Amarna, from c. 1346 BCE: L. Cailloce 'The lost city of Akhenaten' *CNRS News*, 4 November 2016. An evolved (through custom, trial-and-error etc.) example is the standard clay brick sizes of Babylonia: E. Robson, *Mesopotamian mathematics, 2100-1600 BC*, Oxford Editions of Cuneiform Texts 14, Oxford: Clarendon Press, 1999.

[27] Modern technical standardization begins formally, in the UK, with the establishment of the British Standards Institution in 1901. It had begun informally with the industrial revolution, from c. 1660. Good examples of informal standardization are standard railway gauges and screw threads, devised by individuals to tidy up an evolved mess of sizes in the marketplace. See, for example, D.P. Gross, 'The ties that bind: Railroad gauge standards and internal trade in the 19th Century U.S.' *Harvard Business School Working Paper*, No. 17-044, December 2016; J.K. Brown et al, *William Sellers and the United States standard screw threads*, The Franklin Institute & ASME, 2005.

[28] C. Bruun, 'Stallianus, a plumber from Pompeii (and other remarks on Pompeian lead pipes)', *Phoenix*, vol. 66/1-2, 2012, pp. 145-154.

[29] Alberti, *Art of building* (Note 5), p. 340.

[30] D.R. Coffin, *The Villa d'Este at Tivoli*, Princeton: Princeton University Press, 1960.

[31] Such as Chesters: English Heritage, *Guidebook: Chesters Roman fort and the Clayton Museum*, London: English Heritage, 2016.

[32] M. Mietz, 'The fuel economy of public bathhouses in the Roman Empire', unpublished MA thesis, University of Ghent, 2016.

[33] V. Tsiolis, 'The baths at Fregellae and the transition from *balaneion* to *balneum*', in S. Lacore & M Truenper (eds.) *Greek baths and bathing culture: New discoveries and approaches*, Leuven: Peeters, 2013, pp. 89-111; N. Diezemann, 'Antike Badefreuden', Freie Universität Berlin, Publikationen (online), 23 October 2016.

[34] Valerius Maximus (transl. D.R. Shackleton Bailey), *LCL 493 Memorable doings and sayings, Volume II: Books 6-9,* Cambridge MA: Harvard University Press, 2000.

[35] G.G. Fagan, 'Sergius Orata: Inventor of the hypocaust?', *Phoenix*, vol.50/1, 1996, pp. 56-66.

[36] Plommer, *Vitruvius* (Note 2), p. 16.

[37] White, *Technology* (Note 10), p. 45.

[38] M. Shifrin, *Victorian Turkish baths*, London: Historic England, 2015.

[39] Palladio, *Four books* (Note 7), p. 64.

[40] Aristoxenus (transl. H.S. Macran), *The harmonics of Aristoxenus*, Oxford: Oxford University Press, 1902.

[41] Vitruvius, *On architecture*, 1931 (Note 1), p. 277, Note 1.

[42] R. Godman, 'The enigma of Vitruvian resonating vases and the relevance of the concept for today', *The Journal of the Acoustical Society of America*, vol.122/5, 2007, pp. 3054 ff.

[43] Vitruvius, *On architecture*, 1999 (Note 1), pp. 245, 246.

[44] Illustrated in Vitruvius, *On architecture*, 2009 (Note 1), Fig. 12, p. 335.

[45] Like so much in Vitruvius, this is a Greek idea, and is found in locations where Greek influence was strong.

[46] Godman, 'Vitruvian resonating vases', 2007 (Note 42). Given the prohibitive cost of developing and creating bronze vases, Godman developed software to simulate their possible performance, and has used this in composition.

[47] As we have seen, none used *echeia*. In this description he stated: "We should uphold the doctrines of Vitruvius as an infallible guide and rule, provided that reason does not persuade us otherwise ...".

[48] Aristotle and other authors (*Problemata* 11.8) deal with the question: "Why is it that if a large jar or empty earthenware vessels are buried in the ground and lids placed on them, the buildings in which they are have more resonance ...?" Aristotle (transl. E.S. Forster) *The works of Aristotle: Volume VII: Problemata*, Oxford: Clarendon Press, 1927, p. 899b.

[49] Alberti, *Art of building* (Note 5), p.276.

[50] Herodotus, *The histories* (Note 10), 2.109, p.169.

[51] See quote from Plautus, *The Boeotian women*, in Humphrey et al, *Greek and Roman technology: A sourcebook*, London: Routledge, p. 517.

[52] T.W Potter, 'Astronomy in Etruria and Rome', in C. Walker (ed.) *Astronomy before the telescope*, London: British Museum Press, 1996, p. 94. Some of the bronze dial markings, inlaid in the travertine pavement, are to be found in Roman basements today.

[53] R. Schuster, '2,000-year-old sundial changes perception of ancient Rome', *Haaretz*, 8 November 2017.

[54] R.J.A. Talbert, *Roman portable sundials: The Empire in your hand*, Oxford: Oxford University Press, 2017.

[55] Faventinus, *De diversis fabricis* (Note 2), pp.80-85.

[56] Humphrey et al, *Technology* (Note 51), p.517.

[57] For example, in January, hour 4 had an adult shadow length of 12 feet. Palladius, *Farming* (Note 3), p. 85.

[58] D. Hill, *A history of engineering in classical and medieval times*, London: Croom Helm, 1984, p. 224.

[59] Humphrey et al, *Technology* (Note 51), pp. 529-520.

[60] Hill, *Engineering* (Note 58), pp. 229-232.

[61] Between the Arctic and Antarctic Circles. At the Circles the cast is parabolic, beyond them elliptical.

Ducts and Moldings: the Ambiguous Inventions of Franco Albini and Franca Helg

Silvia Groaz

Theory and History of Architecture Laboratory 3 (Lth3), École Polytechnique Fédérale de Lausanne (EPFL), Switzerland

Introduction

In the late 1950s architects began to take a stand over the need to integrate a range of technological systems into buildings, coming up with both practical and theoretical solutions. On the one hand, the attempt by architects like Le Corbusier and Louis I. Kahn to control services' intrusive nature through architectural design grew more and more radical, to the point of the assimilation of conduits into the purism of the primeval structure by those who, like Ludwig Mies van der Rohe and his followers, believed it was a problem that "should be solved in secret".[1] On the other, the adoption of stratagems for the integration of plant into the façade became an opportunity to regenerate the forms of modern architecture. The ever more decisive role played by services would induce Reyner Banham to devote an essay to the subject, reconstructing its evolution from the nineteenth century to the 1960s. In that essay a work by Franco Albini (1905-77) and Franca Helg (1920-89) was given a decisive place in the list of examples celebrating "exposed power", a stance that Banham considered the "fruit of a revolution in environmental management that is without precedent in the history of architecture".[2]

It was the La Rinascente store in Rome, built between 1957 and 1961, an Italian example of investigation of the role of services in the design of the façade and of appropriate forms for walls and moldings, that would be capable of integrating, hiding, or revealing them.[3] In the design of La Rinascente structure and services competed to find a new balance in which the ducts, once part of a design that turned them into a new kind of rib or molding, stood out to the point of overshadowing the lines of the structure. For Albini and Helg that work marked the beginning of a research program, conducted over a series of buildings, into the creative potential inherent in the intrusive presence of ducting. From La Rinascente in Rome to the SNAM office building at San Donato Milanese, Albini and Helg demonstrated the desire of Italian architectural culture to take the principles of the Modern Movement and Rationalist architecture in the direction of a recovery of historical figures, that would be in keeping with the most sophisticated technical and technological developments. All the "trapezoidal forms" and "bulging fairing" studied by Albini and Helg to wrap service ducts and integrate them into the architecture's design ended up turning into moldings, in some cases reproducing those of the past.

La Rinascente, the first project

Tradition and new technologies found a formal synthesis in the new La Rinascente department store in Rome, designed by Albini and Helg from 1957 onward. The Borletti family, owners of La Rinascente, commissioned a building on the corner of Piazza Fiume and via Salaria, in a district characterized by housing dating from the late nineteenth century and the powerful Aurelian Walls, two historical presences that would become significant for the project.

In a first solution, dated July 1957, Albini and Helg proposed a building of six blind stories, on the model of Marcel Breuer's De Bijenkorf department store in Rotterdam, and isolated on three sides.[4] In order to obtain sales floors as free as possible, with artificial lighting and ventilation, the structure took the form of a series of portals whose profile seemed almost to suggest a reinforced-concrete structure. (Fig. 1)

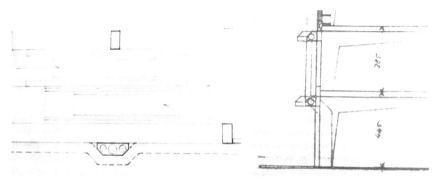

Figure 1. Albini-Helg, La Rinascente, Rome, 1957-61. Sketches of the air-conditioning system, 1st project, plan and section, July 1957 (Fondazione Franco Albini, Milan).

The air-conditioning system envisaged a plant on the basement levels and vertical and horizontal ducts along the perimeter, permitting a uniform distribution of air to all the floors. The ducts had a trapezoidal cross-section and produced articulations of the façades. The air-conditioning system would in fact guide the configuration of the structure and façades of La Rinascente in all the phases of design. In the first solution, however, simple ducts were set against the structure and the envelope, enclosed in geometric profiles so essential and pragmatic they appeared not to have been designed. Only in the case of the vertical ducts was there any sign of a desire to create a sort of sheath with chamfered sides, a design that would be expanded on and improved in the realization. (Fig. 1)

This first scheme entails the intuition of juxtaposing the service ducts, making them part of the design of the façade, as proposed in the plans of July 1957. This choice could be read in the background of the contemporary concept of New Brutalism as it had been defined by Banham in 1954 when he discussed the exposed plant of the school at Hunstanton.[5] From this very fist solution, Albini and Helg moved then toward a different way of absorbing plant into architecture, thanks to the change in the structural form.

In fact, in the project presented to the building commission in December 1957, the engineer Gino Covre maintained the structure of portals, to be made of steel owing to the particular characteristics of the ground and the rapidity of execution.[6] The profile of the portals' piers had rounded projections on which the horizontal ducts could be laid, letting them find a logical expression in the design of the façades. (Fig. 2) The vertical ducts ran instead in special cavities hidden inside the building's perimeter. In the complex play of relations between structure and services, it was the former that determined the overall lines of the composition, dominated by the broad and smooth horizontal bands, sloping like eaves, that sheltered the air-conditioning ducts and the valves of the firefighting system and divided the structure into horizontal layers. It is possible to recognize in this arrangement the nineteenth-century tradition of large iron constructions, conferring on the building what has been called "the plastic image of a selling factory",[7] accentuated by the presence of a garage on the top floor, accessible by mechanical elevators.

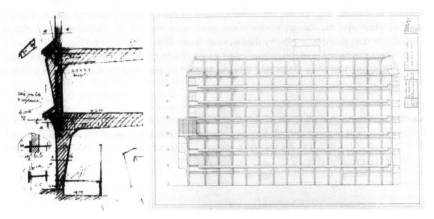

Figure 2. Albini-Helg, La Rinascente, Rome, 1957-61. Sketch of the structural proposal and elevation on via Salaria, 1st project, December 1957 (Fiori, Prizzon 1982, p. 23; Fondazione Franco Albini, Milan).

The air-conditioning and firefighting systems were designed to form an organic whole with the load-bearing structure and penetrate the floor slabs in a comb-shaped pattern. So forceful was the presence of the bands of sheathing that it was clear Covre had not designed a conventional framework but a portal tapering toward the bottom. The rationalist logic of leaving the structure visible, and the consequent expression of great static force suited to a department store, prevailed at this stage over the expression of the ducts on the façade. (Fig. 3)

Figure 3. Albini-Helg, La Rinascente, Rome, 1957-61. Model of the first proposal, 1957 (Fondazione Franco Albini, Milan; Fondazione La Triennale di Milano - Biblioteca del Progetto e Archivio Storico).

The dual-duct air-conditioning system

The client's desire to create an enclosed department store, impenetrable to the gaze, induced Albini and Helg to consult the engineer Balbino del Nunzio, professor of applied physics and electronics at Padua University, over modifying the air-conditioning system. The transformation of the La Rinascente store into an example of the integration of plant into the design of the form, was made possible by the adoption of the dual-duct air-conditioning system patented in 1950 by the Buensod-Stacey firm. This allowed Albini and Helg to locate the various ducts on the façade and leave the sales floors completely free. The design of La Rinascente's air-conditioning system was entrusted to the engineers Mario Sala and Carlo Biffi of the Uffici Tecnici Aster in Milan.

The dual-duct system has two channels of distribution, one for hot air and one for cold, allowing them to be delivered to each area as required through a mixing box for each room that can be adjusted independently with a thermostat. The air is distributed to the various areas by a system of delivery and recovery ducts, ensuring the exchange of air in each room. (Fig. 4)

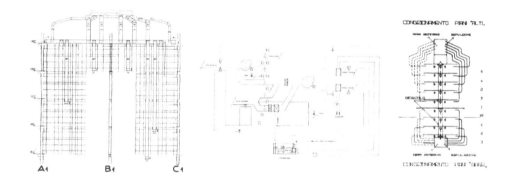

Figure 4. Albini-Helg, La Rinascente, Rome, 1957-61. Schemes of the dual-duct system (Sala, Biffi 1962, p.338, 341; L'architettura: cronache e storia, p.615).

This patented system offers a high degree of flexibility in managing climatic conditions in buildings subdivided into many rooms, as it facilitates a uniform control of the temperature to suit the most disparate uses. If at first sight the adoption of such a system might seem unjustified owing to the high cost of installation and the large number of ducts required,[8] its ability to handle variable loads makes it ideal for the automatic control of temperature in department stores thanks to the possibility of programing the air flow in different seasons and at different times of day, permitting considerable savings in running costs and energy use.[9]

In the case of La Rinascente, two treatment plants were installed, the main one on the sixth floor and the other on the third basement level. The delivery ducts on the top floor ran through the loft to the stories below, where they were connected to ducts running along the perimeter of the floor slab. This solution took up very little space on the various floors, despite the substantial amounts of air this sort of system moves around.[10]

Adoption of the dual-duct system became the precondition for a design that turned on the stylistic experiment of making the ducts an expressive part of the façade and on the envelope's relation of the with the structural system, "stressing chance as a positive factor", as Albini would put it, "by turning it into an occasion for invention".[11]

Variants of the second project

With the second project, dating from the summer of 1958, the structure was revised, substituting the portals with multiple frames arranged longitudinally with a series of central pillars.

The scheme of the air-conditioning system, with the presence of delivery and recovery ducts only on the long sides of the building, represented the starting point for the study of the position and arrangement of the plant in relation to the structure.

In the drawings dated July 1958, a mechanical principle was applied to the positioning of the delivery ducts next to the pillars of the structure, but asymmetrically with respect to the bay, as if to underline the independence of the rhythm of the ducts from that of the pillars. (Fig. 5) Although in the scheme the short sides have no ducts, other sequences of vertical articulations appear in the drawings of the façade and the plans. Their appearance should perhaps be seen in relation to the composition of the façade and the presence of the central pillar, combined to create a pattern of superimpositions and partitions of age-old origin.

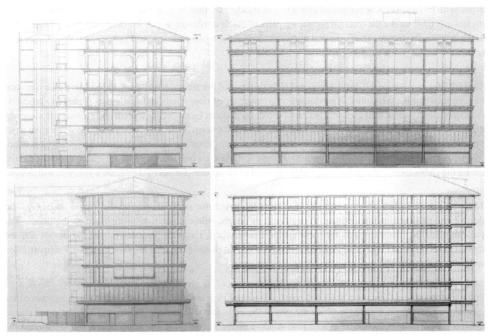

Figure 5. Albini-Helg, La Rinascente, Rome, 1957-61. Elevation studies, July 1958 (above) and November 1958 (below) (Fondazione Franco Albini, Milan).

Ducts and Moldings: the Ambiguous Inventions of Franco Albini and Franca Helg

The next step in the process of design confirms that Albini and Helg were trying to give the ducts an architectural character through combinations in which they were paired and set close together, apart from the bay on the side facing onto Via Salaria, where the ducts were placed farther apart, probably to mark an entrance. (Fig. 5) Through variants that envisaged a regular or irregular rhythm of the ducts, whose effects were studied through several copies made on drafting film, Albini and Helg examined the logic of the façade and the rhythm of the bay. What emerged during this investigation was an ambiguous and sometimes hesitant attitude, remote from the logical and pragmatic character suggested by the scheme of the ducts.

The structure produced a regulating system capable of becoming an "architectural frame"[12] for the arrangement of the services. And yet the necessity of a modular rhythm within each bay prompted Albini and Helg to have the ends of the joists, doubled in the vicinity of the pillars, protrude from the floor slab and thus be visible. This was at once a formal and a technical choice—the joists in fact supported the sheathing of the horizontal ducts.   It is possible to discern in the evolution of the design an incessant search for a logic of composition that would derive from the dimensioning and positioning of the ducts, so as to define a strong pattern and create a rhythm of projections right along the façade.

In the drawings dated November 1958, the ducts were reduced in thickness and multiplied to meet the needs of the dual-duct system. (Fig. 5) The increase in the number of ducts, and probably the role of the horizontal elements of distribution as well, meant that the structure was further revised, not just to solve the problem of the building's static equilibrium, but also to articulate and regulate the intrusive presence of the ducts, which now stretched along the whole perimeter and descended all the way from the sixth to the second floor. Thus the exposed metal structure was composed of a series of slender ribs flush with the envelope, creating a more relaxed rhythm this time, unlike the colossal protruding piers of the first solution, which it would have been hard to adapt to the ducts' tight rhythm. The horizontal ducts ran along the internal perimeter and guttering for the collection of rainwater was set on the external joists.

Through manipulation of the ducts Albini and Helg discovered the artistic potential of the building's services and became aware of the possibility of producing an architecture of ribs, reliefs and rhythmical patterns to articulate the façades with a close-knit cadence, like large moldings dictated by a need for pattern and measure, shadow and depth. The form of the duct was adopted as a pretext for the system of decoration in relief, freed from the strict functionality that had led to the motif's invention of that, right from the first designs with a trapezoidal section. Albini seems to have maintained a detached attitude toward the symbolic value of these elements, discovered during the elaboration of the project and boldly adapted to the formal choices of the façade's structure and design.

The multiplication of ducts went hand in hand with the search for an infill material that would encompass the ducting and introduce a strong pattern of lines with its panels, whose dimensions were based on the duct's. The cladding material first envisaged for these infills, marble slabs, confirms the evolution of the design and the rhythms toward an old-style composition. The slabs were supposed to be held in place by a metal support filled with insulating material.

In the juxtaposition of structure, shell and plant, Albini and Helg also found a solution for the expression of the main façade, on Piazza Fiume, in which the ribs at the ends framed the front, interrupted by a series of glazed openings, described by the studio as "the rose window of the façade".[13] The windows not only reasserted the symmetry that allowed transformation of the design into a proper façade, accentuating the "representativeness" of the building's use referred to by Ponti,[14] but at the same time drew attention to the presence of the central spine, which took on a symbolic quality. The central pillar in fact turned out to be the element capable of revealing the subordinate role of the envelope with respect to the structure and thus made known the interplay of the parts.

The final design

Once a regulating grid had been established, the formal research moved forward rediscovering, through graphic lines, the sense of the molding and the age-old play of multiple profiles. The pattern generated by the structural lines, the ducts and the joints between the slabs of cladding material responded to the desire to attain a new rhythm, even though the various solutions appeared at times rhetorical and unresolved.

Always reliant on divisions, multiplications and variations, the final solution freed the hermetically sealed envelope, or "container" as Helg called it, "from the typological constraint" of the department store with blind walls[15] (the design of the interiors was entrusted to the architects Carlo Pagani and Giancarlo Ortelli). At this point the design entered the world of infinite variations, in a game played with rhythms and surfaces that continued along the lines of the alternation of windows and infill panels first used in the INA office building in Parma (1950-54).

The dual-duct air-conditioning system was designed with ducts that, starting from the plant on the top floor, stopped at different heights on the floors they supplied. (Fig. 6) In this discovery of variation, at first sought in the continuity of these elements, paired and located asymmetrically with respect to the bay, the ducts grew more sparse as they descended, composing a "denser pattern of ducts at the top"[16] that seemed to evoke the chimney flues or buttresses which articulated the brick façades of medieval buildings.

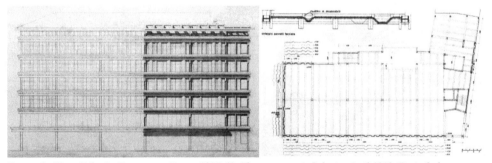

Figure 6. Albini-Helg, La Rinascente, Rome, 1957-61. Elevation on via Salaria, April 1959. Typical plan, December 1958 (Fondazione Franco Albini, Milan).

Both this reference and the decorative use of reliefs in the front onto Piazza Fiume show how Albini and Helg, in their handling of the ducts, were able to come up with a language similar to motifs of the past. Thus the wall in relief became a new order of architecture, one aimed at a multiplicity of effects, at symmetry in its offsets, at "variation in uniformity".[17]From the beginning of 1959 onward their research focused on the potential of this discovery, to which was soon added a variant within the vertical ducts, a triangular profile for "various services" that appeared in the version of May 1959 and would be confirmed in the finished building for the uprights of the firefighting system and the downspouts.

Ducts and Moldings: the Ambiguous Inventions of Franco Albini and Franca Helg

The final stage saw the decisive assertion of a structural principle: the bracket. Albini resorted to this system of overhangs and projecting beams, already tried out at Cervinia in the wooden structural work for his Pirovano hotel-refuge, built between 1948 and 1952, in order to insert coherently into the design of the façade what he himself described as a "strong framework, able to contain and formally settle the fortuitous aspects that would arise".[18] In fact the metal structure was conceived as a dovetailing of elements of reduced section, an operation that accentuated the assembly of the parts and would be viewed by critics as a latent classicism alluding to the triglyphs of Doric friezes[19] to the point of assuming the characteristics of a transposition of wooden structure into steel.[20] The bracket found its justification in the need to support the horizontal ducts, which ran around the perimeter inside a special sheath in the form of a trapezoidal metal box, protected by a bent aluminum rake that created the effect of a stringcourse.

In the final drawing of the horizontal sheath, dated November 1960, the overhanging section resembled a series of eaves, a figure Albini had also used for the new municipal offices behind Palazzo Tursi in Genoa (1950-63) and Villa Zambelli in Forlì (1956). The image to which Albini resorted is evocative of the roof, which at the top takes on immense size, supported by frames with horizontal panels and accentuated by the deliberate setting back of the envelope. This was not done for reasons of space but to make the mechanism of the bracket jut out and to close the structure with a theme that Helg dubbed the "cornice crowning the buildings all around".[21] (Fig. 7)

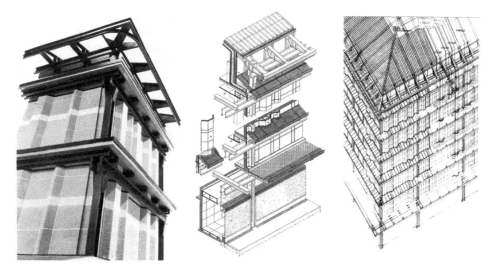

Figure 7. Albini-Helg La Rinascente, Rome, 1957-61. Model and axonometric drawings (A. Piva, V. Prina, Franco Albini 1905-1977, Milano: Electa, 1997, p.344; Baukunst und Werkform, vol.15, no.4, April 1962; L'architettura: cronache e storia 1962, p.615).

Owing to problems linked to the complexity of the relationship between the metal support, the insulation and finally the slab of stone attached with screws, the practice decided to abandon the marble cladding, "leaden and inert in the luminous dimension of Rome".[22] In the summer of 1959 work began on the prefabrication of panels made out of granite aggregates, cement and Rosso di Verona marble dust by the Fulget firm in Bergamo, specialized in granolithic industrial compounds. The panels for La Rinascente would later be marketed under the name "Silipol". The reddish tint was intended to blend in with the surrounding buildings and nearby Aurelian Walls. The process of fabrication of the panels allowed precise control over their composition and color, resulting in a technological concrete of artisanal character.

A lighter band, made with white granite dust, ran right across the panels, a decisive factor in asserting their continuity optically and underlining the continuous nature of the wall, which had not been entirely undermined despite the articulation of the ducts, leading Banham to declare that the envelope "constrains the servicing system within so rigid, yet timid, a classicising format that it goes almost unnoticed".[23] In this game where each element was judged for "the way it looks"[24] resides the quality and the enigma of this work, which, as Zevi suggested, went so far as to generate uncertainties about the actual structural role of that wall, almost competing with the metal structure by its plastic force, similar to that of a structural ribbed wall or series of buttresses, and choosing not to fully declare the contemporary technology it concealed. In the version actually constructed, the lines running across the façade became not just indications of a contrast, but also parameters of interpretation of the separation between the reddish infill panels and the grid of the burnished steel framework, in an orchestrated interplay of "materials used for the intrinsic values of their texture, their color and the way they are laid."[25]

Steel girders, eaves, ducts and brackets were by now part of the practice's structural and formal language, relying on materials devised and produced with industry and employing them in artisanal fashion, in order to "tackle the problems in the most modern way, expressing them in a deliberately traditional framework".[26] That recourse to tradition, which for Albini consisted, as he had declared in 1955, in a "collective awareness and collective recognition",[27] found concrete expression in the ambition, legible in the façade, to create "a building that belongs to the city", a "language that fits with people's experience".[28] In the desire for the work "to be 'popular'",[29] the architectural design opted for a domesticity that recalls the order and rhythms of the nineteenth-century Roman residential building, gradually altering and reinterpreting them to make them absolutely contemporary through the logic of the services and not of the structure.

It is no accident that this project was realized in the late 1950's and took the form of a personal reflection on the value of tradition in architecture founded on the principle of the "character of the environment",[30] as Albini put it, against the background of the debates animated by figures like Ernesto Nathan Rogers[31]— a theme that led an entire generation of architects, especially in Milan, to take sides, and to a fracture at the national level. However, for Albini this meant reasserting the artisanal character and conception of forms and materials and using them in a way that took new technology into account.

In the discontinuation between a proposition that seems exhaustive and resolved in classical terms and the revelatory windows and the ribs imposed by the plant, we can perceive the nature of a work in the making: it oscillates between a lofty and temple-like character and a vernacular and picturesque one and displays a certain degree of "ambivalence," as Tafuri suggested, precisely in the contrast between a sort of formal balance and a series of "unresolved fractures and fragments".[32]

The formal characteristics and ambiguous role of the moldings with respect to technology prompted the critics to interpret the various parts of the building as the union of several lines of research right from the time of its completion in September 1961. In Italy, where the debate over environmental preexistences was more heated, La Rinascente's façade was seen in relation to its context and dubbed "ribbed", "manneristic", "Gothic-style" and vernacular in places, to the point where those forms were interpreted as "pilaster-strips".[33] Helg herself called the cladding a "curtain wall", as if she saw those moldings as folds in a piece of fabric, or that wall of bygone taste were a variation on a contemporary theme. British critics, interested in the mechanistic world, would propose the "duct-wall" version[34] and not coincidentally view La Rinascente as an "aggressively mechanistic"[35] work free from any pretension of "historicism."[36]

Figure 8. Albini-Helg, La Rinascente, Rome, 1957-61. Photos of the building (Baukunst und Werkform, vol.15, no.4, April 1962; Fiori, Prizzon 1982, p.13).

Conclusion of the formal discoveries of La Rinascente in the SNAM offices

The formal research aimed at integration of services into the façade carried out for La Rinascente arrived at a refined stylistic coherence in the proposal for the SNAM offices at San Donato Milanese, built between 1969 and 1972 with the collaboration of Antonio Piva and Marco Albini. While in La Rinascente the formal aspirations generated by the plant still resulted in a degree of abstraction and uncertainty in the relationship between structure and envelope, in the SNAM offices the ducts' presence on the façade was the decisive theme of the project from the beginning. In fact, the predominant motif of the work became the continuous horizontal bands, modeled on the layout of the air-conditioning system. The line of research pursued by Albini and Helg, rather than aiming at a mechanistic expression of the ducts, insisted on exploiting the presence of those conduits to develop advanced and sophisticated profiles and shapes containing, like a skin, the "bulges" that had caught the studio's imagination.

The search for an ideal modeling of the SNAM offices has to be carefully evaluated through the corpus of working plans, which reflect the attempt to ensure a perfect execution by means of the instrument of drawing and copies on drafting film, allowing us to follow the birth and development of that motif. (Fig. 9) It is as if Albini and Helg had asked themselves what the formal character of that "bulge" ought to be, if it were going to be recognized as a genuine contemporary molding. That question, coinciding with the one of form and material, as well as of "recognizability" and "tradition", is what had preoccupied Albini since the project for La Rinascente.

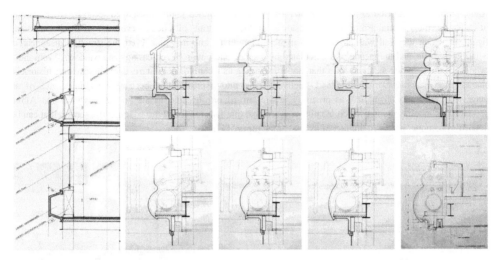

Figure 9. Albini-Helg-Piva, SNAM offices, San Donato Milanese, 1969-72. Detail studies for the services' "fairing", from February 1970 (right) to September 1971 (left, bottom) (Fondazione Franco Albini, Milan).

The first version of February 1970 envisaged the recourse to trapezoidal prefabricated panels, echoing the geometric motif and material of La Rinascente's envelope (the office was studying its application for the Madre di Dio complex in Genoa, 1972-79). It is precisely the choice of that shaped panel, proposed again in various projects, which makes it evident that the question of the ducts' appearance was everywhere influenced by a formal aspiration to turn it into a molding.

A detailed study of the sheath's profile commenced in October 1970. Once the number and arrangement of the ducts had been established, the study gave the modeling a connotation suited to the ideal profile they sought. Thus the desire to bring the sheath's profile closer to the shape and dimensions of the ducts led to an evolution of the envelope from prefabricated panel to curved and deep-drawn sheet metal, in order to make it as slender as it was strong, reflecting the fact that investigation of form was indissoluble from the search for a material that could be modeled at will. The horizontal profiles, modeled on the position of the internal ducts, end up giving the resulting figure a symbolic expressivity and a degree of coherence with the system it concealed. Still in search of the ideal profile, Albini and Helg also inverted the position of the ducts, not for technical reasons but as a formal expedient stemming from the desire to generate a profile with a more and more antique appearance, leading to a result that disengaged itself decidedly from the position of the ducts and resembled the shapes of the torus and fillet in classical moldings.

In the design phases this great freedom also produced profiles that helped to generate a range of aerodynamic forms. The fact that the sheath was repeatedly called "fairing", as if it were intended for use in aircraft, should not be overlooked if we want to grasp the ultimate sense of the figures generated by Albini and Helg, which redeem the geometry from its old-fashioned traits through the use of an authentically contemporary material.

The recourse to reinforced resin, apparently inspired by experiments with this material carried out at the time both in the automobile industry and on movie sets, is another crucial aspect of the SNAM offices that confirms how

Ducts and Moldings: the Ambiguous Inventions of Franco Albini and Franca Helg

Albini proudly saw himself as a craftsman and a designer who studied joints and shaped sections. The evolution of La Rinascente's formal principles now bestowed on them the traits of a design evocative of an all-embracing figure, in which the wall was molded into a sheath for ducts; one in which even the structure disappeared, withdrawn inside, and the façade was articulated by a single alternation of red casings and windows. From those cylindrical ducts sprang a curved form that, notwithstanding its technological nature, dared to take on a historicist character, to become Doric, Ionic and finally develop into a profile that became the quintessence of an outgrowing of Rationalism: it was precisely in the curved profiles and in the solemn rhythms that Albini perceived a formal aspiration which led him to assert that that fairing "found the courage of a section that can be defined as baroque, just from the fact of its containing pipes".[37] (Fig.10)

Figure 10. Albini-Helg-Piva, SNAM offices, San Donato Milanese, 1969-72. Photos of the building and construction site (L. Barbiano di Belgiojoso, D. Pandakovich, Marco Albini/Franca Helg/Antonio Piva, architettura e design, 1970-86, Milano: Arnoldo Mondadori Editore, 1986).

Acknowledgments

I would like to express my gratitude to the Fondazione Franco Albini, in particular Marco and Paola Albini, Elena Albricci and Stefano Setti for their assistance and support and for granting me access to the archival material that permitted a profound insight into Albini and Helg's design process.

References

[1] R. Banham, 'Stocktaking', *Architectural Review*, vol.127, no.756, Feb. 1960, (pp.93-100), p.100.

[2] R. Banham, *The Architecture of the Well-Tempered Environment*, London: The Architectural Press, 1969, p.264.

[3] See G. Marino, ''L'accidentalità tecnica': The Constraint as a Source of Architectural Composition. La Rinascente Department Store, Rome', *Building Environment and Interior Comfort in 20th-Century Architecture: Understanding Issues and Developing Conservation Strategies*, Lausanne: PPUR, 2016, pp.187-98; C. Conforti, R. Dulio, 'Un'architettura romana di Franco Albini e Franca Helg: La Rinascente di Piazza Fiume', *Rassegna di architettura e urbanistica*, nos.123-5, 2007, pp.169-78.

[4] Fondazione Franco Albini (henceforth FFA), handwritten note by Franco Albini, 1963.

[5] R. Banham, 'School at Hunstanton', *Architectural Review*, vol.116, no.693, Aug. 1954, pp.152-8.

[6] G. Covre, 'Il Nuovo Edificio in Acciaio de La Rinascente a Rome', *Acciaio*, no.1, Jan. 1963, pp.1-5.

[7] 'Rinascente: Rome. Machine Aesthetic', *Architectural Review*, vol.128, no.766, Dec. 1960, (pp.389-90), p.390.

[8] M. Sala, C. Biffi, 'Impianti di condizionamento d'aria e sistemi di regolazione automatica nel nuovo grande magazzino 'La Rinascente' di Roma', *Condizionamento dell'aria*, Nov. 1962, pp.337-51.

[9] C. Biffi, 'Modern Italian Commercial Buildings', *JIHVE*, Oct. 1963, pp.233-41.

[10] Sala, Biffi, 'Impianti di condizionamento', 1962, (Note 8).

[11] FFA, handwritten note by Albini, 1963, (Note 4).

[12] L. Fiori, M. Prizzon, 'Intervista con Franca Helg', *Albini-Helg: La Rinascente: disegni e progetto de La Rinascente di Roma*, Milan: Abitare Segesta, 1982, (pp.10-2), p.12.

[13] A. Rossari, 'La bestia domestica, produzione e tecnologia in Franco Albini', *Franco Albini 1930-1970*, ed. F. Helg, London: Academy Editions, 1981, pp.84-8, p.87.

[14] G. Ponti, 'La sede de La Rinascente in piazza Fiume a Rome', Domus, no.389, Apr. 1962, pp.1-20.

[15] P. Portoghesi, 'Rinascente in Piazza Fiume a Rome', *Architettura: Cronache e Storia*, vol.7, no.75, Jan. 1962, (pp.602-18), p.606.

[16] FFA, handwritten note by Albini, (Note 4).

[17] Fiori, Prizzon, *Albini-Helg*, (Note 12).

[18] FFA, handwritten note by Albini, (Note 4).

[19] Portoghesi, 'La Rinascente', (Note 15).

[20] V. Bacigalupi, 'La struttura di ferro nell'architettura', *L'ingegnere*, vol.37, no.3, Mar. 1964, pp.263-74.

[21] Fiori, Prizzon, *Albini-Helg*, (Note 12).

[22] Ibid.

[23] Banham, *The Architecture of the Well-Tempered Environment*, (Note 2) p.246.

[24] Fiori, Prizzon, *Albini-Helg*, (Note 12).

[25] FFA, handwritten note by Albini, (Note 4).

[26] Ibid.

[27] F. Albini, 'Un dibattito sulla tradizione in architettura', *Casabella-Continuità*, vol.29, no.205, Apr.-May 1955, p.46.

[28] FFA, handwritten note by Albini, (Note 4).

[29] Ibid.

[30] Ibid.

[31] E.N. Rogers, 'Le preesistenze ambientali e i temi pratici contemporanei', *Casabella-Continuità*, vol.29, no.204, Mar. 1955, pp.3-6; E.N. Rogers, 'Il problema del costruire nelle preesistenze ambientali', *Architettura: Cronache e Storia*, no.22, Aug. 1957, pp.255-6.

[32] M. Tafuri, 'La Rinascente di Franco Albini', *Superfici*, no.6, Sep. 1963, pp.60-3.

[33] Portoghesi, 'La Rinascente', (Note 15); Ponti, 'La sede de La Rinascente', (Note 14); Tafuri, 'La Rinascente', (Note 32); Bacigalupi, 'La struttura di ferro', (Note 20).

[34] 'Duct-wall', *Architectural Review*, vol.131, no.781, Mar. 1962, p.153.

[35] 'Rinascente: Rome', (Note 7) p.390.

[36] F. Atkinson, 'La Rinascente Store, Rome', *Architectural Review*, vol.132, no.788, Oct. 1962, pp.269-74.

[37] FFA, report on the SNAM offices project, 1972.

The Evolution of the Pompidou Centre's Air-Conditioning System.

Toward a new figure of architecture.

Boris Hamzeian

Theory and History of Architecture Laboratory 3 (Lth3), École Polytechnique Fédérale de Lausanne (EPFL), Switzerland

Introduction

The integration of technical services in architecture played a crucial role in the history of post-war construction. The Centre Pompidou, conceived and realized between 1971 and 1977 by the architecture studio Piano and Rogers and the engineering firm Ove Arup and Partners, is an excellent example in this regard.

Instead of reverting to traditional solutions such as service areas or suspended ceilings, Piano and Rogers chose to exhibit all the services of the building – from the air conditioning ducts to the movement system of people and goods – both in the interiors and exteriors. Exiled outside the envelope and placed within the "three dimensional walls" of the building, or rather clipped onto them, the Centre Beaubourg services were designed to serve the principle of "the maximum flexibility of use". During the design process the refinement of these elements and the surrender to the pioneering audiovisual screens intended to animate the Centre's main facades, created an unprecedented aesthetic value. Initially conceived as simple functional tools, the Centre Beaubourg services became symbolic and didactic devices designed to make the building a man-scale machine, both joyful and understandable.

This paper focuses on one of the main services of the Centre Beaubourg, the air conditioning system, and aims to retrace the genesis and evolution of this element thorough all the phases of the design process, from the first ideas animating the preparation of the competition's proposal to the prefabrication of the built solution.

The genesis of the Pompidou Centre's air-conditioning system

The configuration of the air-conditioning system of the Centre Beaubourg, today the Centre National d'Art et de Culture Georges Pompidou, must play a significant part in any reflection on the integration of plant into architecture since the Second World War. Its genesis, however, does not coincide with the solution presented to the international competition for the Centre Beaubourg by the Piano+Rogers and Ove Arup & Partners practices. It should be sought first of all in the reflections Richard Rogers and Renzo Piano devoted to such systems in the 1960s.

Crucial was the research Piano conducted into a total integration of plant within the envelope of the building, stemming from study of the solutions adopted by two of Piano's main influences, Marco Zanuso's designs of

The Evolution of the Pompidou Centre's Air-Conditioning System.
Toward a new figure of architecture.

factories and Franco Albini's La Rinascente department store. This research culminated in a series of design solutions, which included a scheme for the integration of the conduits for modular prefabricated housing (1969) and the transformation of the bars and ball joints of the Burrell Collection Gallery's roof into a sophisticated system for air distribution (1971). The research carried out by Rogers, however, proved decisive. Interested in the conception of flexible and uninterrupted spaces, he treated the plant as systems integrated into the envelope or as "clipped-on" equipment. Examples of this include the underfloor systems of the Sweet Heart Enterprise offices at Gosport (1969) and the energy equipment clipped onto the shell of the prototype Zip-Up House (1968-71), as well as the structural plans for the plant of the hospital unit for the Association of Rural Aid in Medicine (ARAM, 1970-71) designed in collaboration with Piano.

In the original conception of the Centre Beaubourg, traceable back to a series of sketches made by Rogers in the spring of 1971,[1] the principles destined to characterize the whole evolution of the project were already spelled out: a series of continuous free-plan platforms suspended above a large public square and supported at the sides by two steel structures called "three-dimensional load-bearing walls". Clipped onto the outside of these or plugged into them on the inside were the ventilation, plumbing and power systems, as well as a cutting-edge telecommunications system consisting of large audiovisual screens able to turn the building into a broadcaster of information.

For the air-conditioning system developed along with Tom Barker, service engineer at Ove Arup & Partners, the architects opted for a solution able "to maintain the flexibility and adaptability in space planning and usage which is considered essential in the philosophy of this building".[2] The solution proposed was a "recirculated fresh air system" based on a modular unit with an area equal to one of the twelve bays into which each floor (12.80 x 48.00 meters) was subdivided. Although the type of plant and its characteristics fitted perfectly into the project, its location immediately proved problematic since the guidelines of the competition called for these elements to be placed underground. This would have implied the vertical passage of the ducts through the ground floor (left free thanks to the elevation of the building on "pilotis"), compromising its complete visual and spatial permeability, regarded by Rogers and Piano as an indispensable principle.[3] It was precisely to preserve the empty space under the building that the team rejected the competition instructions and opted for a solution with plant rooms on the roof and a cascade distribution on the perimeter.

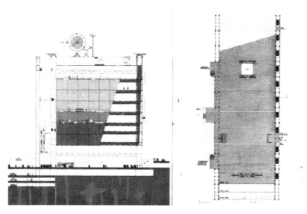

Figure 1. Piano+Rogers and Ove Arup & Partners, Centre National d'Art et de Culture Georges Pompidou, 1971-77. Section and plan of the competition proposal, June 1971 (RSHP Archives, London).

Figure 2. Piano+Rogers and Ove Arup & Partners, Centre National d'Art et de Culture Georges Pompidou, 1971-77. Competition model, June 1971 (Archives Nationales, Paris).

The final solution they submitted[4] consisted of a box-shaped plant room containing twelve independent "central station air-handling units" set on the building's roof. (Figs 1-2) The plant room was connected to a large horizontal duct inserted in the "three-dimensional wall" on Rue du Renard from which ran eleven pairs of vertical rectangular ducts (two per bay, one taking air in and the other discharging it). At the height of each floor slab the vertical systems intersected with two networks of horizontal ducts concealed behind the false ceiling and used for the distribution of conditioned air through "reheat boxes" and its recovery through vents.

At this stage the air-conditioning system already revealed specific architectural genealogies and intentions. For its overall configuration the model was the air-conditioning system of La Rinascente, a project on which Piano had worked in the two years he had been an intern in Albini's office, between 1960 and 1962.

Looking instead at the configuration of the plant room on the roof or of the ducts which could be glimpsed behind the audiovisual wall, the air-conditioning system reveals a more precise lineage, related to the projects and reflections of figures like Archigram, Cedric Price and Reyner Banham. It was due to their influence that the choice was made to locate the various components of the technical plant inside an isolated volume in a central position, as if to underline the unprecedented architectural nature assumed by a traditionally secondary and hidden element. In the plant room's configuration, the influence of Archigram is most apparent. It is a temporary "clipped-on" piece of equipment conceived as an expandable capsule on which, not coincidentally, Rogers bestowed the appearance of the Zip-Up House,[5] which had its roots in Archigram's research. The ducts' expressive shape belonged to the same world. Although it lacked the zoomorphic dynamism of Archigram's flexible pipes, the plant's insertion into the semitransparent structure of the "three-dimensional wall" probably derived from a similar solution adopted by Archigram in the Control and Choice Dwelling, a design exhibited with the housing prototypes of the Richard+Su Rogers office at the Fifth Paris Biennale (1967).[6]

Although these compositional stratagems already denoted an architectural sensitivity in the approach to the design of the air-conditioning system, this element was still treated with uncertainty and subject to a logic in which structure and shell prevailed. This was true not just for the interiors, where the systems were completely concealed behind false ceilings,[7] but also in the more ambiguous one of the front onto Rue du Renard.

The Evolution of the Pompidou Centre's Air-Conditioning System.
Toward a new figure of architecture.

Despite considerable inconsistencies between the competition plans,[8] there can be no doubt that the external structure of the "three-dimensional wall" and the audiovisual panels partially covered the plant, making it an element that could be glimpsed behind the façade. That the systems were not yet conceived as a predominant architectural element on Rue du Renard is further confirmed by the two models made by the architects between June and July 1971. (Fig. 3) In the first case this is shown by the decision to rework the model with a reflective film that hid the ducts inserted in the "three-dimensional wall" from view. In the second, produced following the announcement of the competition results, it is demonstrated by the total omission of the plant and the reduction of the "three-dimensional wall" to nothing but a translucent facade.[9]

Figure 3. Piano+Rogers and Ove Arup & Partners, Centre National d'Art et de Culture Georges Pompidou, 1971-77. Competition model (left) and the model realized after the winners' announcement (right), June-July 1971 (Archives Nationales, Paris)

The development of a decentralized air-conditioning system and the renunciation of the screens on Rue du Renard

During the first meetings between the team and the Délégation pour la Réalisation du Centre Beaubourg, the interdepartmental commission charged with overseeing the execution of the project, the air-conditioning system was mentioned only in passing. The disappearance of the plant in the second model and the reduction of the "three-dimensional wall" to a translucent surface distracted the Délégation's attention from the plant's configuration. The observations were limited to the acoustic problems caused by the plant's passage through the "three-dimensional wall" and the need to give the front onto Rue du Renard a "more intimate and enclosed" design, thereby revealing the desire to distinguish it from the one onto the square—a principle of asymmetry that would prove fundamental to the evolution of the design.[10] Crucial for the plant was the Délégation's proposal to reconfigure the top floor of the building with a series of museum galleries using natural light from above—a proposal that conflicted with the position of the plant room adopted in the competition.[11]

The uncertainties relating to the air-conditioning system were confirmed in the summer by the radical revision of the structure, which moved toward an alternation of continuous main floors with the same number of "structural decks" built out of immense Vierendeel trusses in which to insert "ancillary activities", including the services. This solution derived from Louis Kahn drew on a model Rogers and Piano had just applied in the ARAM project with its alternation of "activity zones" and "service zones".[12] Unlike this project, however, the proportions assumed by the "structural decks" of the Centre were so massive they would not be used solely to house the technical systems—"a series of services packages" conceived to ensure "maximum flexibility in the organisation of the building"—but also activities for the public and the staff.[13] (Fig. 4)

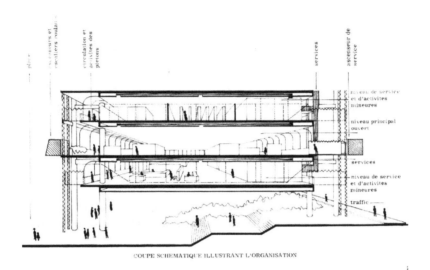

Figure 4. Piano+Rogers and Ove Arup & Partners, Centre National d'Art et de Culture Georges Pompidou, 1971-77. Schematic section, October 1971 (RSHP Archives, London)

Barker and his colleagues did not immediately set about studying this new decentralized configuration, called the "local system solution", in depth but continued to look at it alongside a variant known as the "centralised system solution", assessing the potentialities and disadvantages of both.[14] This was probably a reflection of the doubts that the engineers harbored over the "local system solution", an arrangement that on the one hand offered the advantage of complete integration into the Vierendeel structure and reduction in the time needed for its assembly and the number of ducts, but on the other would take up an enormous amount of space and require costly maintenance. Although the engineers' reservations were still to be found in the technical report produced by Barker and his colleague John Hampson in October,[15] the team adopted the "local system solution", including it in the *Avant-projet Sommaire*, the preliminary plan presented to the Délégation in November 1971.[16]

The new "recirculated fresh air system" consisted of a series of individually controllable "air-treatment units" located on each of the four "structural decks" and arranged on a rectangular band facing onto Rue du Renard and taking up about a third of the floor area. Each unit conditioned the bay in which it was located and the one immediately underneath it through a system of horizontal ducts once again concealed in the false ceilings. What had changed was the configuration of the ducts inserted in the "three-dimensional wall", now based on a module of two ducts used to take air in from openings set in the roof. The exhausted air was no longer channeled back to the upper floors but expelled directly from each "air-treatment unit" through rectangular grilles, called "*registres typiques*", set in the front onto Rue du Renard. (Fig. 5)

The Evolution of the Pompidou Centre's Air-Conditioning System.
Toward a new figure of architecture.

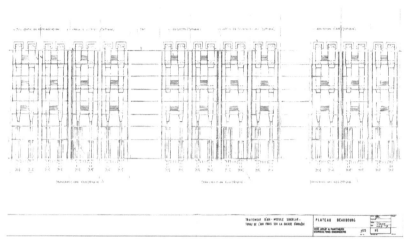

Figure 5. Piano+Rogers and Ove Arup & Partners, Centre National d'Art et de Culture Georges Pompidou, 1971-77. Service organization for the Rue du Renard elevation (conceived by Tom Barker and colleagues), October 1971 (Archives Nationales, Paris).

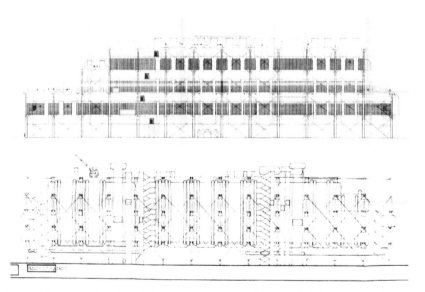

Figure 6. Piano+Rogers and Ove Arup & Partners, Centre National d'Art et de Culture Georges Pompidou, 1971-77. Rue du Renard elevation in the Avant-projet Sommaire. October 1971 (above) and March 1972 (below) (Archives Nationales, Paris)

It was precisely this technical detail that obliged the team to abandon the audiovisual screens on this front, although they were retained on the one facing onto the square. This choice resulted in an even greater asymmetry between the two main fronts of the Centre. With the elimination of the screens the front on Rue du Renard lost the last echo of a traditional façade, turning into a three-dimensional structure in which the plant acquired an unprecedented visual predominance that started reflecting compositional intentions.

A comparison of the engineers' technical dossier with the architects' slightly later one reveals many compositional variations with regard to the air-conditioning system. (Fig. 6 above) The pairs of vertical ducts were given a symmetrical reconfiguration and many of the technical elements designed by the engineers, such as the conduits for electric cables and *"registres typiques"*, were dispensed with entirely. On top of this came both the reshaping along Kahnesque lines of the air intakes on the roof. Its curved ends echoed the profile of certain towered elements used by Leonardo Savioli, and the plastic design of the "cooling towers", also on the roof.

Despite the abandonment of the audiovisual screens on Rue du Renard, the architects still displayed some uncertainty over the expressive value of the services set in the "three-dimensional wall". The concentration of the plant rooms on this side of the building, where their presence was marked by completely blank walls and the *"registres typiques"*, turned the façade onto Rue du Renard into a sort of rear whose aesthetic potential was still not clear.

The adoption of a "centralised system solution" and the exposure of the "air-treatment units"

After in-depth studies that included the development of an independent centralized air-conditioning system for the basement levels,[17] the Délégation rejected the Avant-projet Sommaire and the "local system solution" was dropped for good.[18] The air-conditioning system was criticized not just for its exorbitant cost but also for the excessive size of the plant rooms and the difficulty of deadening their noise for the activities to be located on the "structural decks".[19]

In an attempt to reduce project costs the architects opted for a single large plant room, a solution which Fred Dailey, a service engineer on Barker's team, helped to develop.[20] Given the impossibility of locating this element either on top of the building or in its basement, the architects chose to place the plant room on the lowest "structural deck" so that it would not interfere with the organization of activities at the Centre. To meet the same requirement of flexibility as the "local system solution" provided, the team used a "double duct system", a highly-efficient conditioning plant based on splitting the network of air distribution into two parallel ones carrying heated and chilled air to be mixed in the vicinity of individual rooms in order to create independent microclimates. The conditioning system's new configuration was characterized by the location of the intake and expulsion vents directly on the second floor, behind rectangular grilles, as well as by the splitting of the ducts in both the "three-dimensional wall" and the false ceilings.

These modifications turned out to have a value beyond mere functional efficiency, heightening the role of the plant as an architectural feature not to be masked by screens. It is just this aesthetic sensibility that explains Rogers's choice to abandon the Vierendeel solution which required the plant to be fitted into a narrow space concealed by a false ceiling.[21] The desire to give the plant more room led Rogers to imagine a beam that could leave the technical members visible and to go for an "open-truss" structure, something he and Piano had already tried out in offices and industrial establishments like the studio-workshop in the Genoese district of Erzelli or the Universal Oil Products plant at Tadworth, UK. The architectural sensibility that was emerging in the configuration of the new air-conditioning system already anticipated the character the element would take on in the second Avant-projet Sommaire, no longer a technological apparatus to be located at the back of a building but a genuine theme of façade.

From the conception of clipped-on "air-treatment units" to Laurie Abbott's "typical bay" scheme

The new air-conditioning system was employed for the first time in the revised Avant-projet Sommaire submitted to the Délégation in March 1972.[22] (Fig. 6 below) As a result of the renunciation of the "structural decks" in favor of a version with identical stories supported by Warren trusses, the team could no longer devote an entire floor to the air-treatment units. Out of this came the idea of reducing what had first been conceived as a large plant room on the building's second floor to an appliance to be hung underneath its slab, directly exposed to view. Configured in this way, the volumes housing the plant assumed the form of suspended equipment, resembling the modular units that Rogers had "clipped on" to the base of his Zip-Up House. With the display of treatment units on the outside of the building's envelope, the idea of making the ducts visible was now extended to all components of the air-conditioning system.

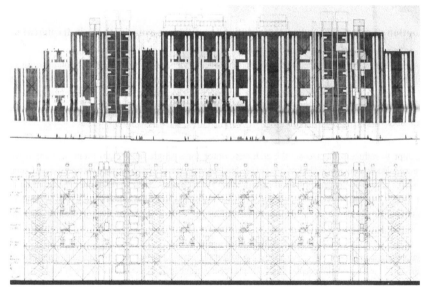

Figure 7. Piano+Rogers and Ove Arup & Partners, Centre National d'Art et de Culture Georges Pompidou, 1971-77. Rue du Renard elevation in the revised Avant-projet Sommaire and the Avant-projet Détaillé, May-December 1972 (Archives Nationales, Paris; Fondazione Renzo Piano, Genoa).

Although the architects could only count on still perfunctory technical information provided by the engineers, in the dossier of the revised Avant-projet Sommaire and in the one of the Avant-projet Détaillé[23] the idea emerged of making not just the ducts visible on Rue de Renard but also all the related technical devices, from the electrical substations to the transformers. (Fig. 7) The design of these elements gradually assumed such importance that

Rogers and Piano decided in the spring to set up the "Superstructure" team to oversee not just the structure but also the design of the "mechanical services". It is no surprise that the man put in charge of the team was Laurie Abbott, a former collaborator of the Richard+Su Rogers office summoned to Paris for his exceptional talents as a draftsman and his experience in vehicle design—characteristics that would prove crucial to the design of the front onto Rue du Renard. In May 1972 it was precisely his skill in the analysis and representation of complex mechanisms that allowed Abbott to devise a two-dimensional typological scheme, called a "typical bay", capable of integrating the still uncertain geometry of the ducts with all the new technical systems that were now housed in the "three-dimensional wall", from elevators and hoists to transformers.[24] (Fig. 8)

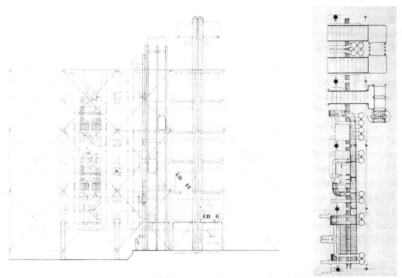

Figure 8. Piano+Rogers and Ove Arup & Partners, Centre National d'Art et de Culture Georges Pompidou, 1971-77. Elevation and plan of the "Typical Bay" scheme (designed by Laurie Abbott), summer 1972 (RSHP Archives, London; Fondazione Renzo Piano, Genoa)

The rate of progress in the summer of 1972 was so rapid that it caused difficulties for the engineers, who were slow to provide designs and detailed information on "overall plant sizes and positions" as well as on the individual components of the plant, from the "cooling towers" to "bulk items such as transformers and HV switchgears..."[25] Things slowed to such a point that Rogers was prompted to call a halt to work on the "mechanical services" owing to the lack of "detailed information".[26] The deep crisis over the air-conditioning system reflected the value now assumed by this element, which was first mentioned in the reports written by the architects in the summer of 1972. The plant now on show in every part of the building was no longer guided solely by the principle of "flexibility" but had to respond to "the architectural principle...of visual appeal" and to that of "symmetry"[27] in order to make "the technical elements of distribution of energy, conditioning and vertical movement...the architecture of the building".[28] It is no surprise that in a letter in which Rogers complained about the engineers' slowness the plant was presented as a fundamental element of the project on which all the other elements of the Centre depended, from the structure to the envelope: a dependence that had nothing to do with statics but alluded rather to a symbolic and visual predominance.[29]

The Evolution of the Pompidou Centre's Air-Conditioning System.
Toward a new figure of architecture.

The criticism of the Délégation and the humanization of the air-conditioning plant through the reinstatement of the audiovisual screens

The explicit formal value acquired by the plant prompted criticism from the Délégation and the other authorities involved in the Centre's construction, worried by the appearance the front onto Rue du Renard had now assumed. Evidence for this comes from the comments on the model presented to the interdepartmental council on May 30, 1972, relating to the industrial aesthetic of the front onto Rue du Renard ("large pipes that evoke an industrial building"[30]), and the anxieties of the Délégation, concerned about the hyper-technological appearance the Centre had taken on.[31] One of the observations made by the Délégation is crucial to the understanding of the air-conditioning system's evolution over the following months: the paradoxical visual predominance the air-conditioning systems assumed at the expense of the audiovisual screens, originally conceived as the principal element on Rue du Renard.[32]

The Délégation's comments were reflected in the proposal for reinstatement of the audiovisual screens contained in the Avant-projet Détaillé drawn up in the fall of 1972.[33] The restoration of this element did not imply, however, a return to the effect of partial visibility that had characterized the plant in the competition project. Notwithstanding the attempt to re-establish the lost balance between audiovisual surface and technical members, the air-conditioning system had by now acquired such significance that it could no longer be tucked away behind a semi-transparent façade. This was confirmed by the nature of the large vertical screens that Rogers and Piano were planning in collaboration with some of the leading exponents of the avant-garde Op Art movement—sem-itransparent panels designed to create "optical effects" by interacting with the technical members behind them, from elevators to ducts.[34] The unprecedented dynamism conferred on the front onto Rue du Renard was a reflection of the team's reaction to mounting criticism from the Délégation and public opinion: not a negation of the industrial aesthetic that was now a feature of every part of the Centre but an attempt to make it human and comprehensible by turning it into a work of art.

The evolution of the configuration of the "air-treatment units" on the roof

The aesthetic sensibility of the air-conditioning system found further confirmation in displacement of the "air-treatment units" on the building's roof, reconfigured, after a series of modifications, as a single opaque and level surface. There were several reasons for this change, including the functional problems connected with locating the air-treatment units just a few meters above the heads of passers-by,[35] but also the desire, still present, to retain the empty space under the building.

Appearing between July and October 1972 in a study model[36] and then in the dossier of the *Avant-projet Détaillé*, the new configuration of the "air-treatment units" was initially conceived as a simple box-shaped module set on each of the roof's thirteen bays. Over the course of 1973, Abbott abandoned the monolithic configuration of the "air-treatment units" and decided to free them of their casing, leaving all their components visible as formally recognizable elements. The compositional and figurative value imparted to the "air-treatment units" over their evolution is clearly discernable in the air intakes, which gradually took on the sculptural shape of industrial chimneys, turning, along with the "cooling towers", into truly monumental elements of the roof. Testimony to the aesthetic value of the "air-treatment units" is provided by the models made by Shunji Ishida, a member of the "Superstructure" team. (Fig. 9) These were produced not just to assess the three-dimensional configuration of the components of the air-conditioning system but also to study its spatial and figurative qualities.[37] This formal sensibility was finally confirmed in the *Projet Définitif* with the reconfiguration of the "air-treatment units" into six large bipartite modules, each spanning two bays, recognizable precisely by the symmetrical arrangement of the monumental air intakes.[38]

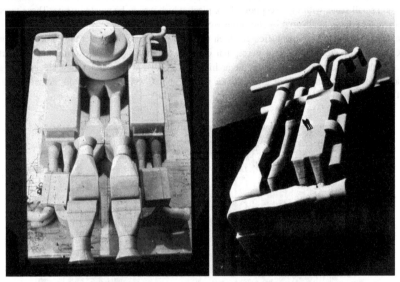

Figure 9. Piano+Rogers and Ove Arup & Partners, Centre National d'Art et de Culture Georges Pompidou, 1971-77. Study models of the air treatment units (realized by Shunji Ishida), 1973 (Fondazione Renzo Piano, Genoa; RSHP Archives, London)

From the fascination with Pop tones to the color code of the Beaubourg's plant

In the final solution presented in the *Projet Definitif* of fall 1973[39] the definitive elimination of the audiovisual screens on Rue du Renard led the architects to opt for another element capable of implementing that idea of comprehensibility and humanization of the technical members: color.

The question of color had already been tackled in the first *Avant-projet Sommaire* with tests based on the use of two Pop colors, yellow and red, amply utilized by Archigram but also by Rogers and Piano, from the structure of Wimbledon House (1966-68) to the roof of the prototype housing in Garonne (1970-71). Employed initially without a clear functional coding, these two shades remained predominant in the color tests carried out between 1972 and 1973. It was only in 1973 that Rogers and Piano, with the assistance of Alan Stanton, turned the Pop palette into a genuine educative and functional code capable of distinguishing the parts of the building and their functions, a solution whose models ranged from Le Corbusier's Unité d'habitation (1947-52) to Craig Elwood's Scientific Data Center at El Segundo (1966). In the new color code yellow and dark gray were used for the primary and secondary structure, green for the plumbing, red and blue for the ventilation ducts, orange for the electricity cables and sky blue for the compressed air supply.[40]

Until the end of 1973 all these experiments remained at the level of study tests reserved for the architects. In fact the Délégation had set up a committee to make the official choice of colors in December 1971. On it sat not just Victor Vasarely, Carlos Cruz Diez and Yaacov Agam, whose advice had already been sought on the façade's audiovisual system, but also Jean-Philippe Lenclos, a French colorist close to Pop Art, and Georges Patrix, a consulting engineer of industrial aesthetics known for the advice on color he had provided to major French industries. The committee opted at first for dichromatic palettes based on the use of color to distinguish elements on a large and small scale, with the exception of the plant, which was to be painted white. These tests would be followed by other variations favored by the committee, this time monochrome and based on, among others, the tones blue de France and khaki Tour Eiffel, in which the team's loss of control over the choice of color was now evident. Conscious of the material and perceptual dullness that these solutions would have imparted to the structure and other elements of the building, the architects succeeded in persuading the Délégation to go back to the functional coding that, apart from a few minor modifications, would be faithfully adhered to in the final version of the building. (Fig. 10)

Figure 10. Piano+Rogers and Ove Arup & Partners, Centre National d'Art et de Culture Georges Pompidou, 1971-77. Presentation model, 1974 (RSHP Archive, London)

The process of prefabrication and assembly of the plant

Once the call for tenders for the lots relating to the Centre's different services had been issued, Abbott and Barker set in motion a synergic operational process among the architects, engineers and suppliers based on the possibilities of making technical improvements and aesthetic and formal modifications to the suppliers' shop drawings.

This method was also used for the air-conditioning ducts, consisting of a galvanized-steel core, an intermediate insulating layer and an outer aluminum casing. For the elements' coloring—a complex question that involved technical components made of different materials and by different suppliers, the team resorted to a process of coloring in the factory based on coating with a pigment by electrostatic deposition and subsequent baking.[41] Once prefabrication had commenced, Abbott and Barker set about coordinating the complex procedure of installation. To organize all the people involved in the supply and assembly of the plant the "Superstructure" team produced thousands of coordination drawings, schematic sketches in felt-tip pen used to indicate the positioning, anchorages and connections of each element.[42]

Conclusions

With the completion of the building in January 1977 the evolution of the Centre Beaubourg's air-conditioning system came to an end. Viewed from Rue du Renard the construction presented the appearance of an unbroken wall of ducts and technical equipment. With the loss of the audiovisual screens, last trace of the traditional façade, the plant gained the upper hand, putting an end to the original balance between structure, envelope and technical members that Piano and Rogers had still sought in the competition project. The plant took predominance over the structure itself, reduced figuratively to slender milky white lines in support of a forest of piping that seemed to stand up by itself and at the same time hold the whole of the building together.

Before the Centre Beaubourg, all the leading architects of the first half of the century, from Le Corbusier to Kahn, had tackled the question of plant, seeking to contain and dominate it through the structure. No longer prepared to be overwhelmed by the structure, the plant erupted to the surface in Paris, turning the architectural object into a mechanical device. With its technical elements animated by an almost zoomorphic dynamism, the Centre Beaubourg took on the appearance of an enigmatic machine, looking almost as if it might get up and join the "walking cities", other mechanical creatures from the same universe.

References

[1] RSHP Archives, CO1/J0099, ARC89159, R. Rogers, 'Sketches for the Concours pour la réalisation du Centre Beaubourg', May 1971.

[2] Archives Nationales, 20100307, Art. 19, Piano+Rogers and Ove Arup & Partners Engineers, 'Plateau Beaubourg Centre, Paris', Jun. 1971, p.10.

[3] Ibid., p.4.

[4] Ibid., pp.10-2, 14, 16, 19.

[5] J. Young, Interview by Boris Hamzeian, 25 Jul. 2017.

[6]*Cinquième Biennale de Paris: Manifestation Biennale et Internationale des Jeunes Artistes, September 30 to November 5, 1967*, Paris: Musée d'Art Moderne de la Ville de Paris, 1967, p.75.

[7] Piano+Rogers and Ove Arup & Partners Engineers, 'Beaubourg', (Note 2) p.10.

[8] Ibid., pp.14-9.

[9] Archives Nationales, 20100307, Art. 19, 'Photographies maquettes'.

[10] RSHP Archives, CO1/ J0099, ARC84135, 'Notes on a meeting held at the Grand Palais on Monday 19 July 1971'.

[11] RSHP Archives, CO1/J0099, ARC73729, 'Centre Beaubourg-Programmation. 4 aout 1971'.

[12] RSHP Archives, CO1/J0002, ARC77586, Piano+Rogers, 'ARAM Module 1971'.

[13] RSHP Archives, CO1/J0099, ARC84135, M. Goldschmied, 'Notes on meeting on 18 August 1971'.

[14] RSHP Archives, CO1/J0099, ARC84135, Ove Arup & Partners, 'Notes on meeting held at 21 Ayebrook [sic] Street, London W.1, on 6th October, 1971'.

[15] RSHP Archives, CO1/J0099, ARC84160, Ove Arup & Partners, 'Centre Beaubourg Avant-projet Sommaire. Environmental Engineering', Oct. 1971.

[16] RSHP Archives, CO1/J0099, ARC31, Piano+Rogers, 'Centre Beaubourg, November 1971'.

[17] RSHP Archives, CO1/ J0099, ARC84135, J. Young, 'Service meeting on December 13, 1971'.

[18] Archives Nationales, 20100307, Art. 97, 'Déroulement des études du Centre Beaubourg, 16 Février 1971', pp.1-2.

[19] Ibid., pp.11-2.

The Evolution of the Pompidou Centre's Air-Conditioning System.
Toward a new figure of architecture.

[20] RSHP Archives, CO1/J0099, ARC84135, J. Young, 'Meeting with Fred Dailey on December 23, 1971'.

[21] RSHP Archives, C01/J0099, ARC84132, R. Rogers, 'Letter to Ted Happold' 24 Dec. 1971.

[22] Archives Nationales, 20100307, Art. 217, Piano+Rogers and Ove Arup & Partners, 'Centre Beaubourg', Mar. 1972.

[23] Archives Nationales, 20100307, Art. 266, Piano+Rogers and Ove Arup & Partners, 'Dessins pour la Consultation de la Commission Régionale des Opérations Immobilières et de l'Architecture (CROIA)', May 1972.

[24] RSHP Archives, C01/J0099, ARC71599, L. Abbott, 'Rue du Renard Typical Bay 29 05 1972'.

[25] Archives Nationales, 20100307, Art. 220, L. Abbott, 'Design coordination meeting Tuesday 20/06/1972'.

[26] RSHP Archives, C01/J0099, ARC8132, R. Rogers, 'Letter to Povl Ahm', Jun. 1972.

[27] Archives Nationales, 20100307, Art. 216, Ove Arup & Partners, 'Construction du Centre Beaubourg, Rapport de Base, Plomberie Sanitaire', 19 May 1972.

[28] Archives Nationales, 20100307, Art. 266, Piano+Rogers, 'Construction du Centre Beaubourg. Note descriptive', 28 Jun. 1972, p.4.

[29] Rogers, 'Ahm', (Note 29) p.2.

[30] Archives Nationales, Paris, 574 AP10, H. Domerg, 'Note pour Monsieur Le Président de la République', 08 July 1972.

[31] Archives Nationales, 20100307, Art. 214, Paris, R. Bordaz, 'Instructions données aux architectes du Centre Beaubourg par le Président de L'Etablissement Public', 4 Jul. 1972, p.6.

[32] Ibid., p.6.

[33] Archives Nationales, 20100307, Art. 219, Piano+Rogers, 'Documents provisoires pour la constitution du Rapport d'Avant-projet Détaillé, 27 10 1972', pp.18-20.

[34] Ibid., p.19.

[35] S. Ishida, Interview by Boris Hamzeian, 17 Jul. 2017.

[36] 'Photographies maquettes', (Note 9).

[37] Fondazione Renzo Piano, BE1-MOD 5538, 5539, S. Ishida, Photograph of the study model of the air-conditioning system on roof, 1973.

[38] Archives Nationales, 20100307, Art. 269, Piano+Rogers and Ove Arup & Partners, 'Dessins du Projet Définitif', fall 1973.

[39] Ibid.

[40] Fondazione Renzo Piano, BE1-MOD 5412, Piano+Rogers, Photograph of the structure schematic model, Oct. 1973.

[41] Archives Nationales, 20100307, Art. 129, R. Rogers, 'Letter to Robert Bordaz', 24 Jul. 1975.

[42] *"Apart from Laurie we were only five at that time, all Japanese. After the tender's results for the air conditioning lot, we had to produce the coordination drawings for the suppliers. We had to help them understand not only how to do the pieces but, most importantly, how to assemble them. This meant thousands and thousands of drawings... It was impossible to prepare proper technical drawings. Laurie started to make them using a black felt-tip pen. No preparatory drawing in pencil, no rules. He was an amazing draftsman, after all. We had to learn from him and soon we all began working like this"*. Ishida, Interview (Note 40).

The open-air school as an environmental Typology, 20th Century

Hala Roshdy Hegazy

Kent School of Architecture, University of Kent, UK

Introduction

This paper discusses the historic background of the Open-Air school as an environmental typology in the 20th century. The aim of the research, is to understand the design and the control regimes that were historically deployed to fulfill their thoughts and concerns at that era. The paper will evaluate the performance of the past environmental strategies and solutions taken in the 20th century to challenge the traditional and neoclassical styles dominated the school architecture.

Firstly, the paper focuses on the first open-air school erected in Germany in 1904 –named by *"Charlottenburg Wald-Schule"*. To illustrate the thinking behind and the aims sought to be achieved at that time. The construction of the school will be demonstrated with historic figures for more clarification. The section after identifies the open—air school constructions and their typologies. Some of the Results and records that were obtained are mentioned for the elucidatory of beneficial influences gained. Finally, influences of the Open-Air Schools on the Educational Policies that had been turned into basics in future schooling movement will be mentioned.

The methodology of this research paper was built on historic knowledge and statistical reports of different schools in Germany, England and several states in USA. Information concerning the German and English schools had been mostly depended on report published in 1908 by LCC – London City Council. In addition to some published theses and PhD paper that does not exceed 1920's. Much of the material related to open-air schools in USA build upon a wide range of content in a trusted digital archive. For example, journals named 'Educational Progress in 1909' or 'Open-Air Schools' published by Boston University and The University of Chicago Press. Furthermore, data regarding medical relief and control of tuberculosis were laid on Medical association reports and nurses' papers on tuberculosis and diseases at that time - municipal tuberculosis sanitarium among different countries.

Brief Background

Early 19th century, concerns regarding students' health began to challenge the traditional and neoclassical styles[1] that dominated school architecture, often independently, in scattered locations around the globe.[1] These schools came to be known as the "Open-Air School" movement, due to the emphasis of relying on air, light, outdoor learning and the easy circulation needed through school buildings. To enhance the students' physical health that were fundamentals of mental well-being. However, this specific type of schools looked rather less functional when compared to normal schools, in which students were kept in neat rows of desks within four walls, ceiling and floor.[2] Open-Air school was designed to note floor-to-ceiling windows and operable façades that emphasized large expanses of windows and connection to outdoors.[3] These features were considered as unusual boundaries of mainstream circles of architectural thoughts. Where the importance of rethinking about school building design was highlighted by scholars at that era.[2]

Open-air schools were introduced to school architecture in the beginning of 19th century and maintained through the 1930s to cure children with tuberculosis while meeting their educational needs. During this period, both adults and children were accomplished in sanatoriums for tuberculosis treatment. In which they were must be isolated to rest and to be exposed natural light and fresh air.[1] This isolation made it difficult for children to commit with schooling programs. Therefore, Open-air schools were the key solution of educating children at the same time as treating them with fresh air, sunlight, rest and nutritious food.[3] In other words, open-air school movement was a consequence outcome of a desire for better conservation of students' health, who were affected by tuberculosis, poor nourishment or any other health weakness conditions, and were incapable to profit their physical and mental work in regular indoor school life.[1] This movement signalizes one of the most important decisions that were undertaken in school architecture for many centuries.[4]

Since then, thoughts and new emphasizes had grown out with time on the value of health and facts discoveries bearing on nature to cure certain diseases were progressed. The dominant among these discoveries were the germs that caused tuberculosis and the correlation between its cure and out-door life.[5] In line with all the previous, Dr. Arthur T. Cabot, had expressed his opinion by *"in the future all schools will be open-air schools"*. As he kept in his consideration all results obtained from open-air schools that seemed to be eminently reasonable.[3]

Forces and Tendencies for Open-Air School to be erected

"an out-growth of the democratic movement in its ethical aspects"

Dr. Dewey of Columbia [1]

The open-air school movement ubiquitously was seen as paternalistic decision in which the education turned out to maintain student's mental and physical health. The main aim behind this movement was to combine the educational social process with the modernistic life features for individuals to successfully meet the emergencies and concerns.[6] As they believed that the highest degree of social efficiency is only achievable when all the powers and faculties of man are developed. The schools worldwide in that era had seen an increase in the percentage of physical wrecks among the students turning the education methods to be a serious indictment.[5] Diseases such as Myopia, hollow chests, and curvature of the spine were widely spread between schools. most educational systems were accused to be guilty of highly neglecting the physical welfare of the child.

"Tuberculosis, rickets, bronchitis, catarrh, and headaches, are aggravated, if not brought on, by impure air, ..." [1]

Dr. Stuart H. Rowe

In addition to the continuous increase of children affected near-sighted defections due to bad daylighting of classrooms. Day after day, the number of socially inactive individuals were increasing because of the physical impairment that was directly or indirectly traceable to the school. An alert thought was driven behind this situation which was – why to expand money every year on educating children who died before reaching the age of twenty (before being counted as socially efficient individuals).[7] From since, the globe aim was that the physical well-being of the child will be better looked after in the future than what has been in the past. Investigations began, the curative properties of fresh air and sunshine were beginning to be understood in order to find treatments of these diseases, chiefly those affecting the lungs.[3]

The idea of sanatoriums was initiated for the sake of curing tuberculosis in the subject of fresh-air treatment through the beneficial of out-door life. However, these sanatoriums were firstly admitted by parishes and local organizations to cure only men. Gradually, women and children were latterly given the same privilege after the announcement of "physical and mental well-being is the right of all" had been made. In order to prevent children from falling to far from their education, when being isolated in sanatoriums for treatment; open-air school movement begun.[1]

The First Open-Air School - Charlottenburg, Germany - 1904

In 1904, through medical inspections that had been done, the German empire took the first step in Open-air school movement.[4] Where Dr.H. Neufert, the city school director, and Dr. B.Bendix, Director School physician, both of Charlottenburg had decided that some provisions must be made for children who were unable to do their regular daily school work, because of the general physical weakness. Together they combined the features of sanitaria and school, then devised them in the first open-air school plan. This school was located in the forest near Charlottenburg, a suburb of the city of Berlin and therefore named *'Wald-Schule'*- Forest School.[1]

Thinking behind

Wald-Schule was initiated to achieve ***three main purposes***. The primary aim was to provide a place for children where their schooling could be carried on at the same time of regaining their health. This school hold back many children's education to be postponed as what definitely happened when sent to obtain their treatment in sanatoriums and been isolated. In addition of protection of students' physical health from a complete break-down and it's followed consequences if decided to stay in ordinary schools.[3]

The second aim was observably and experimentally aim to prove the correlation existed between individuals' mental and physical life. That the bodily weakness of children could increase their inabilities, or dullness in school activities routine. Data regards this hypothesis was insufficient to physician at that era, therefore this aim was to conclusively prove the theory.[8]

The German government had then realized the importance of class with physical and mental health to nations. Therefore, the third aim was to prevent schools from turning out to be socially inefficient for individuals whom suffered from physical and mental weaklings.[1]

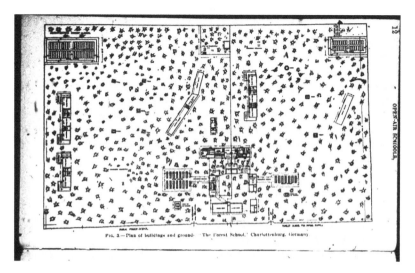

Fig. 1. Plan of the building and ground - Charlottenburg - Wald Schule. S. C. Kingsley and F. B. Dresslar, Open-Air Schools, 1917, p. 12.[3].

Construction

The school site was located three miles outside Charlottenburg in pine forest. The land acquired by school was about five acres where its boundaries was enclosed by a wire fence. At the time of initiation of the school, a building was already existed that was donated by national woman club. After then five additional buildings were erected. Each of them was one storey high with 81 ft. in length and 18 ft. in width. Each provided with adjustable sides and partitions that were made of weather-proof boards and wood materials.[8] These buildings were completely opened on the southern side, whereas closed other three facades. the closed sides were provided with heating plants that was only used in a very unpleasant cold weather conditions. To accommodate nearly 200 students in rainy weather. The students were compulsory had to rest in the afternoon, in order to be exposed for fresh air and desirable sunlight rays. This constant exposure to air and light destroyed the bacilli bacteria that causes tuberculosis. As in early 19th, the popularity of heliotherapy (sun exposure) had increased with growing the physicians' and doctors' knowledge about the relation between vitamin D and tuberculosis. As more theories and believes started to prove that the main source of vitamin D is the 'Ultraviolet Radiations'. Few years later, theories were taken further to prove that UV-radiations plays an important in inducing immunomodulation to be able to vanquish the bacteria causing tuberculosis.[16]

Students were required during school session to do light gymnastic exercises, in addition to proper methods of breathing were also taught. The classroom furniture was placed towards the opened windows in a way that children received fresh air at their backs and day light over their shoulders. the wall openings were tooled up with Venetian blinds to prevent out rain and too direct sunlight into the classrooms.[9]

The school also have two large sheds that were mainly used to serve dining rooms and protect from rainy weather or harsh sunlight. In addition to the scattered small mushroom shaped shelters, consist of only roof supported by

74

beams that covers table and benches. These were used for numerous day activities to encourage children to practice them in fresh air. School supervision were managed by nurses to maintain the level of hygiene in the school. Besides recording the weight and temperature of each student and gives care for their medical needs.[8]

Fig. 2 Charlottenburg large dining sheds. Lucy Wheelock Photo Collection 'Gemeinde-Waldschule Der Stadt Charlottenburg im Grunewald', 1900-1912.[17]

Fig. 3. Southern side of the Charlottenburg building in 1904. From Berliner Leben – Zeitschrift für Schönheit & Kunst Heft VIII, Jahrgang VII.[18]

The picture above showed the French windows on the southern side of Charlottenburg open-air school building, that which opens from floor to ceiling by swinging inward. These were provided for ideal ventilation of the room during and maximizing the desirable sunlight rays to penetrate. especially in stormy weather, these windows are sometimes needed to protect the sick students from a direct draft. In the treatment of tuberculosis, the window glass was substituted by window tent in case of economic advantage for less funded schools.[9] This type of construction will be demonstrated in detail in the next section of Open-air Constructions.

Results Obtained

The school physicians were tasked to carefully examine and select children whom their health cases needed to be sent to open-air school. Besides, their fully attention that must be given while students treatment. In which they cared mostly for heart, lung and overall development of the schools' children. By being regularly weighed and measured every specific period of time, for their conditions to be compared and noted upon their first entrance conditions.[10]

In order to maintain students' comfort in inclement weather, classes were held indoor the building with widely opened windows as possible as they could. Children were provided with heavy clothes and rugs that kept them stayed warm in undesirable weather conditions. Despite that, students were given more time for nature study and out-door gymnastic exercises, more frequently than in ordinary schools at that time. So as to, strengthen their muscles and bones when exposed to sunlight, as Vitamin D was being produced in their bodies. As well as, natural ventilating fresh-air prevent infectious bacterial to spread among students.[8]

The picture below shows how daylight penetrated to the indoor classroom through the large windows openings on the left-hand side of children. As well shows that almost all the students are upright seated, and their attention were given totally to the teacher.

Fig. 4 Daylight penetration through southern side of the classroom in Charlottenburg Waldschule in 1904. From Berliner Leben – Zeitschrift für Schönheit & Kunst Heft VIII.[19]

The table below noted improvement in students' health within the first three months session since the school was initiated. 25 children had been totally cured, whereas the largest percentage of 48 students' health was improved out of 107 children as total.

```
           Health record of the pupils after the first
                    three months' experiment.

    Name of disease.   "Aggravat-"  Un-   "  Im-  " Cured
                       "   ed.   "changed."proved."

    Anaemia                  1          9       11       13
     ( 34 children )
    - - - - - - - - - - - - - - - - - - - - - - - - - - - -
    Scrofulous diseases      —          8       22        8
     ( 38 children )
    - - - - - - - - - - - - - - - - - - - - - - - - - - - -
    Heart diseases           —          7        7        —
     ( 14 children )
    - - - - - - - - - - - - - - - - - - - - - - - - - - - -
    Pulmonary diseases       1          8        8        4
     ( 21 children )
    - - - - - - - - - - - - - - - - - - - - - - - - - - - -
    Total ( 107 children )"  2         32       48       25


    Ayres, "Open-Air Schools",p.76.
```

Fig.5. Health record of students for the first three months - Charlottenburg Wald-Schule. Lucile Winsted, 'The Open-Air School Movement', 1912, p. 27 [1].

Open-Air Schools – Constructions and Typologies

The pervious section had illustrated the construction features been used in Charlottenburg - Wald Schule. For more clarification this section will identify the open-air school typologies. In which the Charlottenburg - Wald Schule will be classified under the first type. The construction of open-air schools can be simply classified into two classes. The first category was often temporary in character and utilitarian structures following functional requirements of the treatment. Whereas, the second category named as "Fresh-air rooms". This type of schools was erected in individual rooms of the school building that can be altered when required to suit the new situation.[8]

First Open-air School type.

The first open-air school type that were temporary erected to be mainly devoted for a purpose, had ranged in buildings, relatively précised between the forest plants in Germany.[1] While in England this type school building was constructed on unoccupied country estates. Whereas, in Boston, New York and Chicago, they were erected on roofs of either schools or other different buildings.[10] This type of open-air school building is in a form of tents that built up of a combination of partly wood and other materials. Due to their small size, they can only accommodate from twenty-five up to thirty students as maximum. The description given below illustrates an example in New York buildings which were considered as typical features of the first type of open-air school construction.[13]

The building is a rectangular in shape covered with flat roof generally dimensioned 30 ft. long, 20 ft. wide and height of 12 ft. from floor to the highest point of the roof. Where the roof is built of tongued and grooved timber boards that laid on rafters (beams) and covered with rubberier roofing to proof rainfall water entering the

77

building. Timber columns of 4*4 inch supported the building roof at the corners and at the centers of the walls.[8] These columns are reinforced 4 feet distant on all the building sides by joints. Narrow timber floor boards laid on supporters and covered with battleship linoleum created the building floor. While board walls with 3 ft. high surround all the four sides of the room. Above this from the north and west side of the room, alternating panels of narrow timber boards and elongated windows hung from the ceiling. Above the wainscoting panels, from the south and west sides, there are openings that covered by canvas curtains on rollers, for undesirable wind and storm protection, thus carried out easily when not needed.[13] This building almost cost around $500 as a whole construction.

Fig. 6. Waldschule, Charlottenburg, Germany. Classroom and dining sheds, 1904. S. C. Kingsley and F. B. Dresslar, Open-Air Schools, 1917.[3]

Fig. 7. Franklin Park school, Boston, Class and roof building - side curtains lowered to manage light penetration. L. P. Ayre, Open-Air Schools, 1910.

Fig.8. Open-air school tent built on Chicago building roof - illustrate permanent construction. L. P. Ayre, Open-Air Schools, 1910.

Fig. 9. The Hartford Open-air school erected in an army tent. L. P. Ayre, Open-Air Schools, 1910, p. 129.

According to building and fire regulations in some cities, wooden construction is forbidden therefore, it was replaced by asbestos board -heat-resistant fibrous silicate material. It was also proven by experiments at time that this construction had successfully fulfilled the children's comfortability in Chicago schools. Even at very low temperature as long as they were protected from wind.[11] Even though, these buildings were cheap and simple, but they have not been seen essential in almost all cases. For example, in USA in different states as Chicago or Boston, the open-air school were initiated in tents and students were sheltered from inclement weather in near unoccupied dwellings houses.[13] Sometimes, also these unoccupied dwellings turn to be the main school building, where kitchen facilities in this case was been utilized to prepare food, and the top-roof rooms with large windows openings had been used as sleeping rooms for the duration of children's rest hours. To be exposed to sunlight and maximum fresh air ventilation while they were resting.[12] States like Hartford in USA took advantage from utilizing the unoccupied dwelling-houses for open-air school, in which they increased ample ground for provide the state with other estates needed.[9] Thus, many other places might be available for temporary use without necessity of purchasing it. Whereas, an alternative thought in constructive economy was found in New York, where they had utilized abandoned ferry-boats for open-air classes. This idea perhaps considered a better well-thought, as converting useless pieces of property to get benefit of useful new services within it. [1]

Second Open-air School type - "Fresh-air rooms"

'Fresh air rooms', were the second type of open air-schools. This type of open-air rooms varies in its construction from the first open-air school type, discussed before. However, these two types aim for the same concept of maximizing fresh air ventilation and day light penetration into the class. The Fresh air rooms were convenient remodelling of the schoolrooms to serve the features and get the advantage of previously classes.[8] This remodelling work was immediately started whenever a room was available within the public-school buildings. Sometimes these classrooms were available within school buildings that were abandoned by regular local classes. In which they were taken under remodelling processes to meet the new use with comparatively less expenses to original.[12] This idea was spread among many cities to re-utilize and amend old school building to Open-air schools.[8]

Southern exposure was the appropriate choice for the best lighted and best ventilated room, in order to fit this ordinary schoolroom with fresh-air room features. Then there were three methods of the remodelling operation to turn the four-sided room to three-sided by southern side demolished as can as possible. The first method, was to demolish the entire wall of southern side and then filling the openings with elongated windows from the floor to be hinged at top of wall. These windows were raised against the ceiling when needed with the use pulleys and cords provided from inside to be entirely opened for air and sunshine [12] Fig.10. The second alternative cheaper way was to remove the window stools down to the floor and then the openings were filled with window sashes that were also hinged from the top. Whereas, the third method was considered less expensive compared to the other two but was not as satisfactory as them. In which the window openings were left as they are and substituted by sliding full-length hinged sashes.[1]

Openings from floor to ceiling, created more endurable environment for tuberculate children by regular circulation of fresh air inside the classrooms. In addition of permitted them to look out door when obliged to gaze between four walls.[7]

Standards was followed in securing cross-ventilation within the schoolroom, which was considered as essential aspect for ideal fresh-air room. In case these standards were not achievable, and windows are found to be on one side of the room, then windows were opened at both upper and lower sashes. This arrangement allows the undesirable air inside the room to escape through the top opening, and fresh air given a way through to enter the room from below. Means of heating the school room must be provided, especially for low vitality sick students, who were in incessant need of care.[7]

Fig. 10. Fresh-air rooms - open-air school windows that were hinged at the top and can be totally opened when needed by cords and pulleys. L. P. Ayre, Open-Air Schools, 1910, p. 130.

Regarding to hygiene, the location of the open-air schools was preferred to be chosen away from dusty streets and roads, and in spot away from building baffles as possible to afford plenty of light and sunshine.[11] Also, Schools were always in abundant water supply. These two aspects prevent the danger of the infection spreading among students.[7]

When referring to internal design, after exterior alternations been made, the classrooms are then furnished with light movable chairs and desks. In order to follow the sun around the room all day. Proven by experiences, that the best to be seated was children's backs towards the open side of the room. When mechanical heating and ventilating systems are provided within the building, they were substituted from manual to automatic mechanism. [1] Whereas, if no heating plant was available in the school-room then an old-fashioned heating stove was installed. The experiences had many consensuses of opinion among that the classroom temperature should not be allowed to drop than 40-degree Fahrenheit (4 °C) even when the overall weather temperature drops below that.[8]

Both open-air school types that had been conducted previously, illustrated that compulsory changes needed to convert normal school-rooms into fresh-air rooms were relatively simple and inexpensive in either old or new buildings. After that time, open-air schools' construction had taken a way of development to accomplish classrooms with two or three opened sides to the outdoor.[3]

```
         Structures utilized for open-air schools
                  in the United States.(a)

Remodeled rooms  -  -  -  -  -  -  -  -  -  -  -  -  -  -  -  - 14
Special buildings  -  -  -  -  -  -  -  -  -  -  -  -  -  -  -   6
Roofs  -  -  -  -  -  -  -  -  -  -  -  -  -  -  -  -  -  -  -  - 6
Regular class rooms eith open windows  -  -  -  -  -  -   5
Boats  -  -  -  -  -  -  -  -  -  -  -  -  -  -  -  -  -  -  -  - 5
Tents-  -  -  -  -  -  -  -  -  -  -  -  -  -  -  -  -  -  -  -  - 2
Barn  -  -  -  -  -  -  -  -  -  -  -  -  -  -  -  -  -  -  -  -  1
```

Fig. 11. Structures utilized for open-air schools in USA. Lucile Winsted, 1912. [1]

Clothing

Fig. 12. Students provided with sitting-out bags to keep them comfortable even in coldest weather. L. P. Ayre, Open-Air Schools, 1910, p. 132.

The experiences had proved the proposition that children took advantage from open-air school treatment since they were well fed and kept warm. In frequently low temperature, if the schoolrooms were not provided with heaters, students were then provided with sufficient clothing and warm-fitting outer garments. These are supplied either directly by the school itself or indirectly by charitable agency.[7]

Records/Results obtains from Open-air Schools movement

In 1880's, hypothesis was made affirming that the air breathed contain a major cause of disease; which have threats on health with high probability of death.[20] This theory had been identified as "Miasma or Bad air theory",[21] it was speculated that both living bodies and dead organic material were the main emanating sources for these diseases such as typhus, scarlet fever and tuberculosis. Concerns was raised about this evidence and spreading of such diseases especially after many countries had experienced wave of tuberculosis immigrants.[15] The bacteria causing these diseases where proven to be tarnished by exposure to sun rays, therefore the health authorities tasked architects at that era to enterprise the maximum provision of sunlight penetration and fresh air movement while designing huge scaled public projects such as schools and hospitals. From then, open-air schools started to exist. The studies had showed that results obtained from open-air school were highly positive achieving the objectives behind erection of open-air schools.[11] Physically, tuberculous children committed with these schools for treatment, had noticeably gained weight, improved their overall health, lungs and hearts were greatly benefited and most of them became almost normed or totally cured. At Charlottenburg, Pupils showed immunity to colds and infectious diseases. As well, in United States medical reports indicates that children sight grew stronger and strengthen voice dedicate their improvement, as a result from their stay in open-air.[7] Mental and physical poise were maintained among both students and teachers throughout the whole day. The relief out-door environment offered in open-air schools, assisted children who had been for years with educational retardation[2] to be able to complete their studies and join the student in same age as them. In addition to development in persistence, intelligence and tenacity in their abilities in dealing with complex problems.

Reports from Germany showed a remarkable improvement in students' attention and alertness to school sessions as a result from their stay in Wald-Schule. While in England and Boston, reports had proved their mental endurance and interests in daily school routine work had increased. All previously mentioned relayed on regular treatment care, fresh air, healthy nutrition, wisely chosen lessons that fits students' abilities and regular exercising. These together created intimacy between teachers and children resulted in better natures and gentle manners. Incidentally, interacting with the out-door environment had developed the aesthetic side of the child's nature.[1]

The following figures shows examples of result among different open-air schools in different locations, in order to statistically prove the benefits gained by students' health committed with open-air schools:

For instance, the graph below shows the gain in percentage of hemoglobin for anemic class students within the open-air school up to nearly 85% since the beginning of the educational year. Whereas, showing a decrease by 6% with the normal indoor class in one of the public schools in New York city.[14]

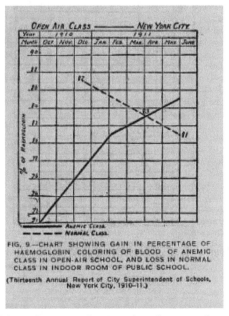

Fig. 13. percentage of hemoglobin with open-air class vs. indoor class room- Source: (S. WARREN, 1919) [14]

The next figure below shows a table of results in the Thackley open-air school maintained by the city of Bradford in England for nine weeks duration. The table clearly illustrated that there was a noticeable gain in weight among children. In addition to increase in chest measurements after nine weeks for both genders. The table also highlights that the student ages varies between 7 to 12 years as maximum, who were sent to these specific types of schools to attain treatment by fresh-air. All these results dedicate not only improvement, but the healthy growth of students within open-air schools.[8]

BOYS

Number	19
Ages	7 to 11 years
Average age	8.7 years
Average weight on admission	43.25 lbs.
Average weight nine weeks later	46.25 lbs.
Average increase . . .	3 lbs.
Average hæmoglobin percentage on admission .	78
Average hæmoglobin percentage nine weeks later .	88
Average increase in hæmoglobin percentage . .	10
Average chest measurement at full inspiration on admission	23.3 inches
Average chest measurement at full inspiration nine weeks later	24.3 inches
Average increase in chest measurement	1 inch

GIRLS

Number	21
Ages	7 to 12 years
Average age	8.5 years
Average weight on admission	44.5 lbs.
Average weight nine weeks later	50.2 lbs.
Average increase	5.7 lbs.
Average hæmoglobin percentage on admission . .	80
Average hæmoglobin percentage nine weeks later .	90
Average increase in hæmoglobin percentage . .	10
Average chest measurement at full inspiration on admission	23 inches
Average chest measurement at full inspiration nine weeks later	24 inches

Fig. 14. Thackley open-air school - table of results of nine weeks duration. L. P. Ayre, Open-Air Schools, 1910.

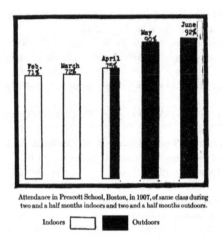

Fig. 15. Attendance bar chart for two and half months in the indoor and others in the outdoor - Prescott School -
Boston - in 1907 - United States. L. P. Ayre, Open-Air Schools, 1910.

The above chart indicated the percentage of attendance for students in Prescott School in Boston- United States,
when the class was taken indoor and outdoor. It shows that 92% of the student preferred the out-door teaching
and their attendance increased when regulated to have out-door sessions. While the percentage of student
attendance stayed the same when the classes were given indoor.[8]

However, the change in environment was not the limit to bring student to healthier but nutrition and continuous
medical check-ups were also included as affecting factors in the patient complete lifestyle of curation.

Conclusion

Undoubtedly, open-are school movement had wide-spread influences upon the educational policies made after
that era. Firstly, societies had learned how must the policies be expensive when it comes to vital problem such as
the education of the youth. The Architecture of openness to outside, was the remarkable print that open-air school
movement had left in the history of education. Forcing all school system policies that came after, to aim for health
to be contagious and not the diseases among students. Pure air, water and sunshine turned to be the rights pursued
for every child that had challenged to change the traditional thoughts and neoclassical styles dominated by school
architecture for years. As architecture aim to achieve the maximum equilibrium between healthy environment,
physical stimulation and thermal comfort/ neutrality either in outdoor or indoor.

In brief, open-air school movement combined ethical, physical, economic and social positive results in once. That
enhanced the careful consideration from all the thoughtful communities' individuals.

References

[1] H. L. Winsted, 'The Open-Air School Movement', University of Minnesota, MA Dissertation, 1912.

[2] L. Baker, *A History of School Design and Its Indoor Environmental Standards, 1900 to Today*. Washington, DC: National Clearinghouse for Educational Facilities, 2012.

[3] S. C. Kingsley and F. B. Dresslar, *Open-Air Schools*. Washington D.C.: Government Printing Press, 1917.

[4] E. Harwood, 'England's School - History, Architecture and Adaptation'. English Heritage, London. Hille, T., 2011.

[5] 'Eliminating the 'Great White Plague' Open Air Schools Advocated', 1915, Udspace.udel.edu. [last accessed 19 Dec. 2017].

[6] R. B. Westbrook, 'John Dewey (1859-1952)', *Prospects: The Quarterly Review of Comparative Education*, vol. 23, no. 1/2, 1999, pp. 277–291.

[7] J. B. Rollins, 'A Year In A Fresh Air School', Chicago: Little Chronicle, 1912.

[8] L. P. Ayre, *Open-Air Schools*. New York: Doubleday, Page & Co., 1910.

[9] J. E. Downey, 'Educational Progress in 1909', *School R.*, vol. 18, pp. 400-23.

[10] 'The Acland Report (1908)', Consultative Committee Report Upon the School Attendance of Children Below The Age Of Five. London: HM Stationery Office, 1908.

[11] A. Rasey, 'Open-Air Schools', *Journal of Education*, vol. 72, no. 10 (1796), 22 September 1910.

[12] T. B Sachs et al, 'Nurses' Papers on Tuberculosis. Chicago: Municipal Tuberculosis Sanatorium, 1914.

[13] R. G. Kirkby, 'The Design and Construction of Open Air Schools, *Journal of the Royal Sanitary Institute*, 1910.

[14] B. S. Warren, 'Open Air Schools for the Prevention and Cure of Tuberculosis Among Children', Public Health Bulletin, no. 58, Treasury Department, United States Public Health Service. Washington D.C.: Government Printing Office, 1912.

[15] K. Hill, 'The Decline Of Childhood Mortality - Department Of Population Dynamics School Of Hygiene And Public Health Johns Hopkins University', Department of Population Dynamics, School of Hygiene and Public Health, John Hopkins University, 1990.

[16] A. P. Ralph, R. M Lucas and M. Norval, 'Vitamin D and Solar Ultraviolet Radiation in the Risk and Treatment of Tuberculosis', *Lancet Infectious Disease*, vol. 13, no. 1, pp. 77–88.

[17] Wheelock College Library Archives, Lucy Wheelock Photo Collection, Box 9, Folder 2, 1A-79 'Gemeinde-Waldschule Der Stadt Charlottenburg im Grunewald', 1900-1912.

[18] Zentral- und Landesbibliothek Berlin, from *Berliner Leben – Zeitschrift für Schönheit & Kunst Heft VIII*, Jahrgang VII, 'Waldschule für kränkliche Kinder (translated: Forest school for sickly children)', 1904.

[19] Ibid., 'Waldschule für kränkliche Kinder (translated: Forest school for sickly children) in their classroom', 1904.

[20] N. Fogel, 'Tuberculosis: A Disease Without Boundaries', *Tuberculosis (Edinburgh, Scotland)*, vol. 367, no. 5, 2015, pp. 527-31.

[21] R. A. Robbins and S. A. Klotz, 'Profiles in Medical Courage: John Snow and the Courage of Conviction', *Southwest J Pulm Crit Care*, vol. 7, no. 2, 2013, pp. 87-99.

Case Study Analysis of the Baer House

Mariam Itani

Kent School of Architecture, University of Kent, UK

Introduction

The 20th century was the rise of renewable energy alternatives and passive architecture. It is the beginning of experimental thinking in solar buildings and technologies when innovative minds tried to use the sun instead of fossil fuels and oil as a means of heating buildings.

This paper will be discussing a specific type of solar technology, the drum wall or the water wall which was prominent at that time. It sheds light on the history of the drum wall which is when it was used in a simple residential building. This technology is basically a set of steel barrels filled with water and placed behind a transparent glazed façade. Thus, this "wall" will act as a thermal mass with a much higher thermal capacity than a regular wall. The first recorded solar building is the experimental MIT Solar House built in 1947. It was the first to use this approach as a space heating technique inside a residential building. In 1972, the Zome House, or also known as the Baer House is the next residential building that integrated this concept into the house's heating system. This innovative building at its time is the case study described in depth and analyzed in this paper and if it is possible to use the drum walls as an alternative for un-renewable sources of residential heating.

History of Drum Walls

Seventy years ago, in 1947, the Massachusetts Institute of Technology built what was probably the first water wall in the world in its second solar house. Solar II was one of six solar houses in an MIT research done by Hoyt Hottel and his students. Unfortunately, it was the first and only solar house built during the experimental researching by MIT. After World War II, Hoyt Hottel and his team continued to work on their research. This time they decided to develop a more economical heating system where they can collect, store and distribute solar heat in one single unit. They erected a wall of water containers which was behind a double - pane glass wall facing south. This was their solar - heating system that they called a 'water wall'. Dr. Albert G. Dietz, an MIT engineering professor explained how the water wall works.[1]

> "The sun hit the cans of water through a couple of sheets of glass. The water got warm, and then that energy was transmitted to the interior of the house. It was obviously a much simpler system than the usual" [2]

Image. 1. MIT Solar II showing its oblong form and the south wall where the 'water wall' is located (source: MIT, n.d.)

The building was of an oblong form with a long and narrow laboratory facing south as shown in Image. 1. It was divided into seven separate compartments each an experiment, slightly different from the other. The first cubicle had no water cans whereas 1- and 5- gallon water containers, painted black were stacked up just inside the glass façade of the other six cubicles. Four of them had insulating curtains covering the cans from the inside to avoid overheating and opened automatically whenever the temperature inside the house went under 22 °C. Similar to the sketch shown in Fig. 1. A, the wall was designed to have outer shades located right behind the south-facing edge-sealed double glass. These shades were kept open during the day and closed at night. Then came the water wall with 23 cm thickness was also covered by internal shades that operated automatically according to a thermostat inside the room. In the remaining two compartments, the wall had the same double glazed façade with the shades on its outer side, however, a fan blew room air past the water cans and back into the room. This approach was also controlled by a thermostat and was first used in the first MIT Solar house. This heating method contributed to 38 - 48% of the house's heating requirements. It lost a lot of heat which was mainly through the glass right behind the water cans. To reduce this heat loss the engineers installed aluminum curtains between the glass and the water cans. They weren't successful either since the heat loss was approximately 71 – 84% with the curtains. Several design faults led to the failure of the water wall in the MIT experimental house such as:

- Inadequate curtains between the water wall and the glass window

- Inadequate insulation at night – which wasn't then discovered until 1980

- Limited direct sun gain

- Separation of the water wall from the room by curtains

Due to this failure, the researchers did not pursue this experiment and went back to using active solar systems instead, in their designs. They didn't compare either the cost of such a simple heating system with the cost of a more complex one but they decided to get back to using expensive and unreliable solar systems.[3] In their case, the most prominent aspect that might have led to this failure was the dependency on active systems for operating a simple technique. Solar II had complex execution methods regarding the water wall so it constantly supplied with energy to operate as planned. The building was dependent on an outer source of power to function where it could've been almost completely passive. That was a dominant reason why the building wasn't completely successful and the complexity in its design created defaults which reduced its actual performance.

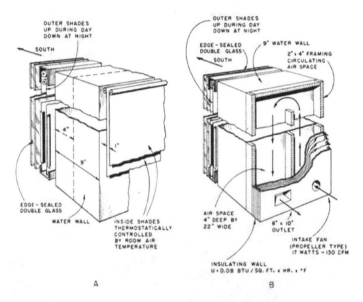

Fig. 1. Sketch of the solar water collectors in both the first four and the last two cubicles in the MIT research project (drawing: Perlin, 2013)

Drop City

Image. 2. A view of Drop City, the Zome house is the second from the left in the background (source: Richert C., 2012)

Case Study Analysis of the Baer House

In 1961, Gene Bernofsky, Jo Ann Bernofsky and Clark Richert, the founders of Drop City met as art students at the University of Kansas in Lawrence. The used to paint rocks and drop them from a window onto the street so they referred to this practice as 'Drop Art'. They had a desire to live rent free and create art without employment which led them in 1965 to buy a six acre (approximately 24,280 sq. meter) goat pasture right outside Trinidad, Colorado for $450. Their community was named after their gravity - driven art. Soon enough other artists, writers, and inventors joined them, and they started building a community where people could create and utilize creative work. The 'Droppers' had little to no building experience, but they were ingenious and original in their own ways. They used salvaged materials like lumber, bottle caps and chopped - out car tops. "We liked to collect the detritus around us and to make things..."[4] The community flourished and with a constant publicity in mainstream media, mainly through resident Peter Rabbit, led to a rise in the number of guests. By the time the community decided to stop its open - door policy, it was already too late. The founding members had already left and issues starting arising which led to its closure in 1973. The site was sold in 1978 and the group's work was held in exhibitions in New York City and in magazines.[5] Not until recently, Drop City became recognized as the first green economy of the 1960's and an inspiration for the new generation of scholars and DIY-ers (Do it yourself). Its architecture represented the 'bricolage' interpretation of Richard Buckminster Fuller's geodesic domes, a geometric structural system known as the Zome, and passive solar devices. It is a laboratory of experimental buildings and for cultural and environmental 'praxis'. Praxis, as Simon Sadler defined it, is used to describe Drop City as an exercise in practical reasoning, neither affecting a predetermined design nor indulging in abstract contemplation.[6]

Image. 3. School bus as the Baers' temporary home and in the foreground, the adobe bricks for the interior walls (source: Baer, 2012)

The Zome House

Steve Baer is considered a pioneer in solar housing and innovative technologies. He established his own company, Zomeworks, where all his inventions and creations are protected and reserved. His architecture was well known for its simplicity as well as its efficiency although he wasn't an architect. Baer was a man of low - income who lived with his wife Holly and his children on a school bus. Later, in 1972, Steve Baer moved to the Drop City and was one of the first arrivals there. He brought back the water wall and decided to build a house where he could live in with his wife and children. It was the first successful use of the water wall (drum wall) in an occupied and inhabited building. Although the house had a back - up heating system (wood fired stove), the drum walls worked efficiently. About one cord of wood (3.6 m3) was needed as back - up heating in the winter. After his house, Steve Baer went on using drum walls in other residential, commercial and religious projects. The Zome house is located in the U.S.A. in Albuquerque, New Mexico. It is still standing today on 1860 West Ella Drive, Corrales, with coordinates (35.23, -106.64).

Fig. 2. Location of the Zome House on the map through four images - Albuquerque, New Mexico (source: GoogleEarth, 2017)

Climate

The climate in Albuquerque is cold and semi - arid. It is in the northern tip of the Chihuahua Desert, near the edge of the plateau in Colorado. It is usually sunny and dry in Albuquerque, with 3,415 hours on average and 278 days of sunshine per year. On other days, periods of irregularly mid and high - level cloudiness block the sun, but extended cloudiness is rare. Albuquerque has four different seasons. Winter consists of chilly days and cold nights. The coldest month in the year, being December has a 2.4 °C average temperature although the minimum temperature is usually in January between -12 °C and -14 °C. Most nights in the coldest three months of the year, December, January, and February are usually below freezing. Spring is windy with a little unsettled rain sometimes, it is the driest part of the year. Many days of March and April are windy with the wind blowing at 32 to 48 km/h and this can cause blowing sand and dust. The summer heat is relatively bearable mostly because of the dry atmosphere. However, there are 2.7 days, mainly in June and July and rarely in August where the temperature reaches 38 °C and over. On average, 60 days reach a temperature of 32 °C and above. [7]

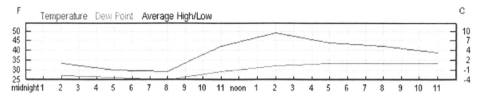

Fig. 3. Hourly temperatures (in red) in Albuquerque, NM in December 1973 (source: Wunderground, n.d.)

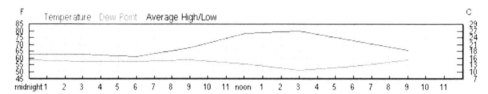

Fig. 4. Hourly temperatures (in red) in Albuquerque, NM in July 1973 (source: Wunderground, n.d.)

Date		Mean Temperature	Maximum Temperature	Minimum Temperature
December 1973	Actual	-4 °C	11 °C	-13 °C
	Average	0 °C	5 °C	-6 °C
August 1973	Actual	25 °C	32 °C	19 °C
	Average	23 °C	29 °C	16 °C
April 1973	Actual	13 °C	23 °C	3 °C
	Average	9 °C	15 °C	1 °C

Fig. 5. Actual and average temperatures in Albuquerque, NM in December, August and April 1973 (data from Wunderground, n.d.)

Anatomy

The house is made up of eleven single spatial units called Zomes. The organization of these Zomes in a clustered manner creates a U-shape with the longer side facing south. These units are connected by doors to let the air inside circulate from one to the other. The south - facing façade is glazed with single pane, R-10 insulated glass. In each of the Zomes, behind the windows is a 1.2 to 1.5 meter high stack of 56 - gallon steel barrels (245 liters),

90 barrels in total set on their sides in a steel angle iron rack. They are 95% filled with water so the house needs approximately 20,900 liters of water. The ends of the barrels facing the glass, and by default facing south are painted black for maximum sun exposure and absorption. The barrels of water used provided thermal mass and operated as a passive solar heating system. The water warms up from direct heat gain through the glass, then heat is distributed from the barrels by convection (the water inside in contact with the surface of the barrels and the latter warming up the air inside the house through convection). Baer had windows and a couple of glass doors along the perimeter of the house. These were mostly left open during the day so that the air warmed by the walls is moved through to the other compartments of the house. The house's walls are made of adobe brick and insulated aluminum sandwich panels for exterior cladding. The slab is 12.7 cm uncovered concrete with no basement. The slab and the adobe walls act as a thermal mass storing heat for later use in cold nights. Exterior aluminum shutters swing down and acting as mirrors, they direct adeditional sun radiation to the windows. Inside, curtains control the flow of warm air from the barrels to the room in case it gets too warm. The large shutters are insulated to prevent heat loss in winter, as well as unwanted heat gain in the summer. [8] Each Zome has a vent at the top which is hand - operated by a rope for ventilation. The roof also has 'Skylids'   which is a Zomework product and consists of a skylight with insulated louvres underneath. The louvres automatically open when the temperature between them and the skylight is higher than the interior temperature to allow the warm air into the house as well as to allow direct sunlight into the room and the adjacent Zome unit. [9]

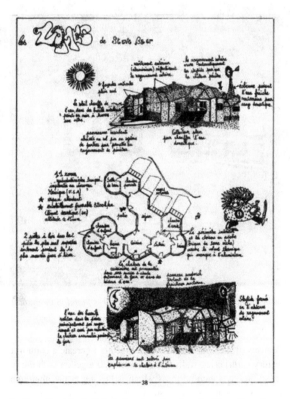

Image. 4. Page 38 from La Face Cachée du Soleil showing drawings by Steve Baer (source: Nicolas and Vaye, 1974)

Fig. 6. A transversal section through the building showing the drum wall, Skylids, aluminum shutters and the vents at the top of each Zome (source: Vollaard and Van Andel, 2012)

Analysis

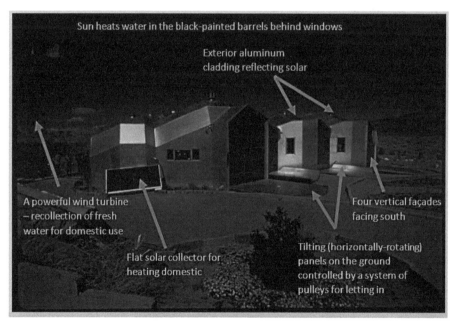

Fig. 7. A perspective view of the house showing the original features found in the building (source: Baer, 2009 edited by author)

Fig. 7 shows the main elements of the house which work together to create a comfortable environment inside in cold weathers. The adobe (dry earth) brick walls, the concrete slab together with the water containers, all shown in the section above (Fig. 6), act as a thermal mass which is lacking in the aluminium and create a large heat container and store the excess heat in hot weathers so that at night it could warm up the house. As the floor plan of the building (Fig. 9) shows, the form is a cluster of eleven exploded rhombic dodecahedra. According to Steve Baer, the rhombic dodecahedron is merging of the garnet crystal shape and the cell of a beehive. The zones are different lengths so they make different size rooms that meet at 120 ° angles instead of 90 ° angles which are more generous and spacious. The cladding of the Zome was formed of anodized 6 mm - thick aluminum skin with 7.6 cm - thick honeycomb core panels. The core was a paper honeycomb with urethane foam pressed in from both sides. The drum walls had enormous doors (shutters) made of the same aluminum skin 7.6 cm panels. Those were lowered in the morning and raised in the evening by winches with hand cranks. The drum walls were glazed with single - strength box - glass and lots of silicone sealant. [10]

> "We had Audrey and José raise and lower the four doors...We had a black, back insulated, single - glazed box parallel to the drum walls to judge when to open the doors. If the box was warm we opened them"

> "Single glazing (for the drum walls) seemed appropriate because the drums were never above 100 °F (37.8 °C) and the insulating doors were closed at night." [11]

This shows that the house required a significant amount of effort from the occupants to open and close the aluminium shutter and the roof vents. The floor plan also shows that the stove and the oven are surrounded by a mass of adobe blocks, so the heat released from the stove and oven will be accumulated and stored in the adobe walls. In the furthest rooms, the kids' bedrooms, there exist two wood heaters, one for each room, only for the worst ten days of winter. On the north - west side of the building where a hill stood, Baer drilled a well and installed a 4.26 meters high windmill and a 5,000 gallon (22,730 liters) tank as shown in (Fig. 10a). This mill was used for recollection of fresh water for domestic use and supplied water to three houses.

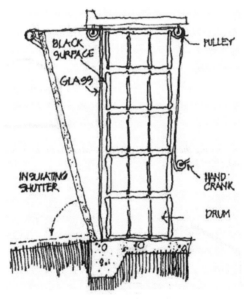

Fig. 8. A sketch by Steve Baer showing a section through the drum wall and the shutter's manual mechanism (source: Baer, 2009)

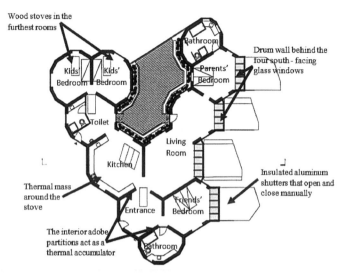

Fig. 9. The floor plan of the building showing its unique environmental feature (drawing: Baer, 2009 edited by author)

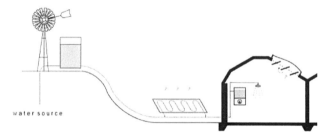

Fig. 10a. An analytical section showing the wind mill and its relation to the tank, solar collector and the house (source: Vollaard and Van Andel, 2012)

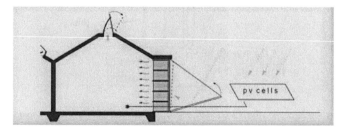

Fig. 10b. An analytical section showing the drum wall, the vents, the shutters and the PV cells (source: Vollaard and Van Andel, 2012)

The diagram (Fig. 11) showing the winter analysis of the drum wall's function describes graphically how the system works. Two diagrams are shown in Fig. 11, the first one shows the daytime functioning of the drum walls. At daytime, the shutters are left open, so the water in the barrels collects and store heat from solar radiation. The aluminium shutters act as mirrors so that they could reflect maximum sunlight exposure to the façade and thus, to the drum walls. Then, the warm barrels heat up the house's interior through conduction and convection. The lower diagram shows the function of the drum walls at night. At nighttime, the shutters are closed to ensure no heat is lost to the outside. The stored heat as thermal mass in the adobe walls, the concrete slab, and the water barrels warm up the air inside the house, keeping it at a comfortable temperature.

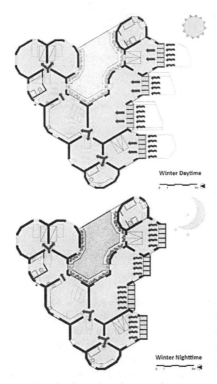

Fig. 11. The top and bottom figures show the thermal analysis on plan in winter at daytime and night-time respectively (drawing: Baer, 2009 edited by author)

The diagram (Figure 12) showing the summer analysis of the drum wall's function describes graphically how the system works. Two diagrams are shown in Fig. 12, the first one shows the daytime functioning of the drum walls. At daytime, to keep the house cool in hottest months, the insulated aluminium shutters are kept closed. This blocks sunlight from getting to the barrels and prevents the water from heating up. So the water barrels cool down the house's interior by absorbing excess heat inside. At night-time, the shutters are left open and the barrels are cooled through night cooling. The water releases the heat absorbed from inside the house, to the outside.

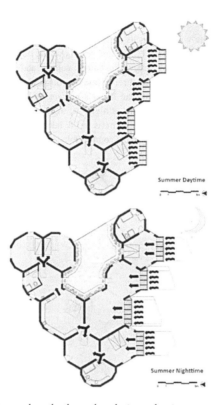

Fig. 12. The top and bottom figures show the thermal analysis on plan in summer at daytime and nighttime respectively (drawing: Baer, 2009 edited by author)

Fig. 13 below shows the sun path diagram in Albuquerque, New Mexico, and because the side of the Zome House in front of the drum walls is facing south so the solar path diagram in Fig. 13 should have the South pole facing upwards. So the diagram was compared with the hourly temperature ranges for July in Fig. 5 and similarly the hourly temperature records of the same figure in June and August. These three months were specifically chosen because, according to the climate in New Mexico, June, July, and August are the hottest months of the year. Then all temperatures ranging from 27 °C and above in each of the three months were taken into consideration and the times when these ranges existed are noted. On the solar path diagram, each month was marked (since the three months had temperatures ranging at 27 °C and above) according to the times noted respectively. Thus the sun path diagram in Fig. 13 below shows that in general, June has temperatures ranging from 27 °C and above between 12:00 and 19:00, July has temperature ranges between 13:30 and 15:00 and finally, August has those ranges in temperature between 14:00 and 17:30.

The solar path diagram emphasizes that June, July, and August are the three hottest months of the year. And it can be concluded that during these times, the three months have overlapping hours where all have a peak temperature of 27 °C or above. Thus, the hottest time of the day can be said to be between 14:00 and 15:00 o'clock, which is almost at midday.

At that time, the shutters would be closed and the roof vents could be opened for letting in ventilation, removal of stale air, and supply of fresh air if possible.

Regarding the building, the heating system worked efficiently in the Zome House. According to interviews with Steve Baer, the poorly - insulated house was "improbably warm". However, he also states how the house needed a lot of maintenance like the steel barrels that kept leaking slowly, or the wind turbine that had lasted for 25 years, or until 1996 but had to be fixed every once in a while and its oil had to be changed every few years. Baer said that eventually, in 1996, he discarded the wind mill and replaced it with a solar jack pump. It was obviously a better alternative to the wind mill, especially regarding the household's water usage: large in the summer and small in the winter. [12] And pictures below show how some features of the house changed. [13]

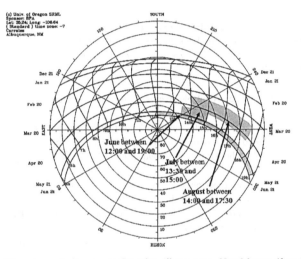

Fig. 13. An analysis of the solar path diagram in Corrales Albuquerque, New Mexico (drawing: University of Oregon, n.d. edited by author)

Another suggestion regarding the building is to manipulate the form a little.

In the summer, the building releases excess heat at nighttime through night cooling so the water inside the barrels becomes cool. At hot weathers, during one of the hottest three months, the building would need to benefit the most out of night cooling using every minute. However, the days of summer are longer while the nights are short. So if the four south - facing glass façades were slanted a few degrees into the inside so that the façade would be directed towards the night sky. This will help to cool at night become much more efficient. Thus, at daytime, the temperature difference between the house's interior and the exterior will increase, lowering the internal temperature by a few more degrees.

Conclusion

This article has provided an overview of the history of drum walls and time when they were first used experimentally, a thorough analysis of the Baer house which was the first time drum walls was used as a heating method in a residential building. The research shows how basic and simple Baer's design elements are taking into consideration he used relatively new technology for his time like the drum wall and the Skylids. The simplistic approach to the building was reflected from his modest background and it showed through the materials he used in the building (metal car tops and adobe bricks). Although the building was basic and less sophisticated than Solar II in MIT's experimental housings, the Baer House was properly functional and was inhabited by Steve Baer and his family up to this day. Baer had an advantage with more developed technology than MIT in 1947 especially with the insulated glass panels he used for the south façade however, the more straightforward and simplistic the design of the building is the better probability there will be for it to function properly and become successful.

References

[1] MIT Solardecathlon. (n.d.). SOLAR 7: History • Solar1. [online] Available at: http://web.mit.edu/solardecathlon/solar1.html [Accessed 2 Oct. 2017].

[2] Dr. Albert G. Dietz, quoted in, J. Perlin, *Let It Shine: The 6,000-Year Story of Solar Energy*. Novato: New World Library, 2013, p. 289.

[3] Ibid., pp. 289-291.

[4] 'Drop City – about', 2018, [online]. Available at: https://www.dropcitydoc.com/about [Accessed 18 Dec. 2017].

[5] J. Sternfeld, 'Ruins of Drop City, Trinidad, Colorado, August 1995', *The Baffler*, vol. 18, 2009, pp. 27-29.

[6] S. Sadler, 'Drop City Revisited', *Journal of Architectural Education*, vol. 59, no. 3, 2006, pp. 5-14.

[7] Wunderground.com. (n.d.). Weather History for Albuquerque, NM | Weather Underground. [online] Available at: https://www.wunderground.com/history/airport/KABQ/1971/12/23/DailyHistory.html?&reqdb.zip=&reqdb.magic=&reqdb.wmo= [Accessed 18 Dec. 2017].

[8] S. Baer, *Some Passive Solar Buildings with a Focus on Projects in New Mexico*. Albuquerque: Zomeworks Corporation, 2009, p. 7. [ebook]. Available at: http://www.zomeworks.com/wp-content/uploads/2012/04/Passive-Solar-Design-Slideshow.pdf [Accessed 19 Oct. 2017].

[9] K. Lee, *Encyclopaedia of energy-efficient building design: 391 practical case studies*. Boston, Massachusetts: Environmental Design and Research Center, 1977, p. 92.

[10] 'Steve Baer and Holly Baer: Dome Home Enthusiasts', Mother Earth News, 1973. [online] Available at: https://www.motherearthnews.com/nature-and-environment/steve-baer-holly-baer-dome-home-zmaz73jazraw [Accessed 14 Oct. 2017].

[11] S. Baer, 'I Think it is Finished Now', *Dash - The Eco-House*, no. 7, 2012, pp. 62-70.

[12] Ibid.

[13] J. Grossman, 'Drop City', 2012. [online] Drop City. Available at: https://www.dropcitydoc.com/about [Accessed 10 Dec. 2017].

Sanatoria for treatment of tuberculosis and the aftercare colonies (Early 20th century)

The Papworth Village settlement, Sanatorium Zonnestraal and the Paimio Sanatorium

Alisa Khan

Kent School of Architecture, University of Kent, UK

Introduction

Tuberculosis has been a growing public health concern during the 19th and 20th century. It was widespread all over urban Britain, as well as other parts of Europe and America. The quest for cure lead physicians to explore the therapeutic power of the sun, and the relation of fresh air in the prevention of disease. The medical and architectural profession, in concert, have created some notable examples of healthy architecture, over the years. Giving a brief account of the evolution, the paper discusses sanatoria architecture in detail, through analyzing the designs of three different sanatoria; the Papworth Village settlement, Sanatorium Zonnestraal and the Paimio Sanatorium. Focusing mainly on the patient wards and treatment areas it will explore how sanatoria, from the 20th century, were designed as environmental buildings for the treatment of tuberculosis. In addition, this paper also concentrates in distinguishing the role of indoor and outdoor therapy depending on the requirements and developments with time.

Background

Consumption, tuberculosis or phthisis has been a disease so common from the 18th to 20th century. It has correctly been named as "pulmonary tuberculosis" meaning tuberculosis attacking the lungs. The other two names were given to it owing to the fact that the disease consumed the individual, resulting in the loss of weight, as it progressed [1]. Consumption, as it was known was suspected to be caused in the aftermath of the industrial revolution. It is said that in the first decade of the 20th century it was responsible for the death of one in every eight and was the single greatest killer of men in the UK [2].

Causes of the disease

It was discovered by Dr. Robert Koch in 1882 that tuberculosis was caused by the presence of tubercle bacillus in any part of the body (commonly in the lungs) at the time when the body is incapable of properly defending itself. Tests showed that it was destroyed by bright sunshine and faces difficulty to grow outside a living body requiring heat and moisture. However, it could survive for a long time in dark corners of a dirty room. The most common causes of the disease were unhealthy conditions; unventilated, dark, overcrowded rooms, irregular habits, overwork and starvation. Dust particles in air irritate the mucus membrane of the air passages, and make them open to infection by the tubercle bacillus which is one reason why the number of consumptives in dusty towns was more, than in the countryside [1]. Then the expectoration of other consumptives by coughing and spitting lead to the introduction of bacillus into the air which resulted in the spread of the disease. Other ways were actual masses of sputum allowed to mix with dust and transferred by fingers or food to the mouth. Hence, the best ways to prevent the disease from spreading was to improve living conditions and returning to healthier ways of life [3].

The discovery of the tubercle bacteria gave scientists and medical professionals a direction to explore the cure of the disease. By 1877, Arthur Downes and T P Blunt, through their experiments had shown that sunlight light had a bactericidal effect [4]. Followed by their research, in 1897, a Danish physician Dr. Niels Finsen discovered the cure for Lupus Vulgaris (bacteria causing tuberculosis) in using concentrated ultraviolet radiation. By focusing ultra violet rays onto the faces of consumptive patients, he noticed that tuberculosis gradually disappeared [5]. It was now understood that the two major requirements for the cure were (1) surrounding the patient with the purest air obtainable and (2) maximum sunlight [3]. Keeping in mind the prerequisites of treatment, and knowing that dust in the air could infect people, sanatoria designers were encouraged to use the germicidal properties of sunlight to prevent cross infections and the spread of disease.

> ... every room occupied or visited by patients should be flooded by sunlight whenever possible, because, of all disinfectants, sunlight has been shown to be the most powerful. It is perhaps, together with pure air, the only certain non-liquid disinfectant for the tubercle bacillus [3].

The Movement

The sanatoria movement emerged in the mid-19th century, side by side with, 'Heliotherpeautic architecture' (Sun-responsive architecture that uses sunlight for the cure of diseases). In architectural terms, both are considered similar, but they are slightly different, in respect that sanatoria treatment does not deal with direct exposure of the patients to sunlight as in the case of Heliotherapy, where patients are tanned in the sun for the cure. Although both were oriented for sunlight, but it was used for different purposes. Open air sanatoria were designed in a way to maximize sunlight and fresh air inside, in order to hinder the growth of bacteria and prevent cross infections. Historic photographs show patients lying on balconies but covered in clothes or blankets and not having their bodies exposed to direct sunlight. So basically, sanatoria dealt with curing pulmonary tuberculosis, which was the main form, and heliotherapy, on the other hand, was for treating surgical tuberculosis, rickets and war wounds [6].

The sanatorium movement flourished from the late 19th to early 20th century. Sanatoria design which begin in the 1850s had two major considerations, the first being the 'Sitting and orientation of the buildings' and secondly 'Building layout and density'. For the orientation, keeping in mind the benefits of sunlight exposure, south, south-east, south-west was preferred. And the sanatoria buildings were usually sited at higher locations where the air was fresh [7].

In terms of Building Layout, it is seen that three arrangements evolved with time. The first one being the 'Resort Style'. Early sanatoria built before 1885 represented this style. They were actually modified private houses, mansions or hotels providing few specialized patient areas. Then came the 'Cottage Style'. It had a central administration block connected to a number of small patient cottages accommodating 2-6 patients in each cottage. This style had a spreading layout and there were different categories of patient areas. Physical isolation of patients was no more required when antiseptics were discovered in the early 1900s; as it was recognized that it could lessen the spread of diseases through infections. This is when the 'Pavilion Style' of sanatoria became popular. This design was more economical and efficient. It had one multi-storied building normally 3-4 stories high. The patient pavilions were connected to the administration through corridors or covered walkways [7].

Need for Aftercare colonies

Although tuberculosis was not entirely a disease of the poor but it was more prevalent amongst the working class. Instead of private sanatoria, that were for people who could afford a stay at the resort, the 'Volksheilstätten' (sanatoria for the workers in German), became part of a strategy to confront the spreading disease. Therefore, the Red cross, and some industrial and insurance companies began to build sanatoria for the recovery of their workers so that they could get back on duty [8].

The treatment in these early sanatoria wasn't much of a success. The patients did get well under therapy, but they suffered relapse sooner or later. This happened when the disease was not completely arrested and the patients returned to work unsuited to their physical strength, in the same unhygienic environment, that brought them back to the same condition. Hence, a need for after care of these patients now became a requirement.

In a book published in 1943, Lord Horder, considering why tuberculosis had not yet been bought under control, wrote, that the answer to this question is that "Varrier Jones is the only person who did see the problem of tuberculosis and did see it whole [9]."

Papworth Village Settlement, Cambridgeshire (1916-20)

Work in tuberculosis in the new colony system was started by Dr. Pendrill Varrier Jones, a Welsh physician. After finishing his medical training in 1910, he started his research in tuberculosis at Cambridge university. Varrier Jones did not believe that tuberculosis could be fully cured, he understood the need for an institution that could give permanent treatment to the consumptives. This lead to the establishment of the Cambridgeshire tuberculosis colony at Bourn in 1916, which was then later expanded to the Papworth Village settlement in 1918. The Papworth settlement served as a sanatorium for tuberculosis patients as well as an after care colony for their return to society [9].

The estate acquired for the colony was at Papworth to the west of Cambridgeshire. The area of the estate was about 350 acres. This site was chosen considering the requirement of a large area, and as the region was isolated it benefitted the establishment of a village settlement, away from the disturbance of the overcrowded and dusty towns. The main part of the establishment was on a slight rise, well elevated from the adjoining areas. On the east of the settlement was a woodland that provided shelter from the winds.

Compared to other sanatoria certain new principles for the treatment of tuberculosis were applied here at Papworth. These principles were set by Dr. Varrier Jones himself. The colony was exclusively established for the treatment of pulmonary tuberculosis. Patients in all stages of the disease; the early stage, the intermediate cases and the advanced cases, were treated here. The febrile cases were taken to the hospitals for treatment. The afebrile cases were described as sanatorium cases and were taken to the shelters. The shelters were mainly for those patients whose disease was arrested but they still were in need of medical supervision. After treatment under sanatorium shelters, when patients were better than before, they were then discharged to the village settlement. This included separate hostels for unmarried men and women, and cottages for those who were married so that they could live with their families [10].

Occupational therapy

Workshops and industries were also a part of the Village settlement. These workshops were run by the consumptives themselves. All separate departments were linked together under a business manager, himself an ex-patient, who had undergone treatment in the village settlement. Because, having suffered from the same disease could make him realize and understand the strength and capacity of the workers. People that were admitted here were mostly those who came from a working class. Hence, the consumptives working in the industries were paid depending on their medical condition relative to the amount of work they could do. Work at the Papworth industries was more gentle and easier as compared to the other business factories. Most of the work was done by the heavy machinery. So there was no stress on the workers, nor they had financial pressure [10].

The occupational therapy was one way of treating the tuberculosis patients. The patient could stay at the colony and work according to his strength in a social atmosphere where he could feel his importance. This is how the therapy had a psychological impact on the consumptives which facilitated in the healing process [10]. So, the advantage of this scheme of the Papworth settlement was that with the institutional section they had an industrial section, where the treatment may be prolonged but then the patients had a chance to get trained in a suitable occupation, and so that they could get employed to earn a livelihood.

The settlement had two or three separate hospitals for women and men. All of them were two to three stories high with large balconies adjoining the wards, where patient beds could be wheeled out. One of the building had a greenhouse which was converted into an open air ward. Patients treated here were in the advanced stages of the disease. Shelters were wooden cabins in the woods where patients could live individually for six months while working in the industries. There were large openings in the cabin walls to obtain maximum fresh air. All windows and doors had overhangs for shading, to prevent overheating in summers. Additionally, louvered chimneys on the roof provided fresh air circulation in the cabin, which was a prerequisite of sanatorium treatment.

In 1919, one of the buildings at the estate, St peter's house, was to be converted into a sanatorium for women and children. Dr. Varrier Jones had found out that patients under glass roofs respond well than those under normal roofs. So he proposed glass roofs for the open air wards in the new sanatorium, for light to enter. Behind the open fronted wards were dressing cubicles which provided space for patient beds to be wheeled in during harsh weathers [11][12]. (Figure 1)

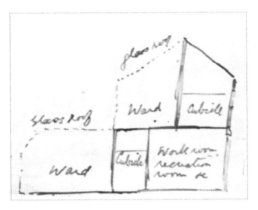

Fig. 1. Glass roofed open wards as designed by Varrier Jones, 1919 (drawing: National archives, Kew, MH 52/1)

The workrooms provided behind the cubicles on the ground floor, had a northern aspect and prevented the possible cross ventilation through the dressing cubicles and the work rooms which was not desirable. So an improvement in the plans were made in the same year and the work rooms were removed. Two bed cubicles opened fully in an open fronted pavilion or veranda with French windows, so that patient beds could be wheeled out for sun therapy. (Figure 2) A space of 2.5m was provided between two beds in the wards and the glass roofs were reduced providing an open air environment [12]. The balcony wards were preferable because of the fact that patients lying outdoors were more exposed to sunlight and fresh air, stimulating the cure, than those lying inside.

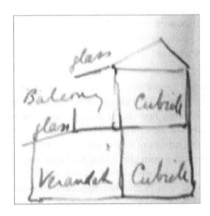

Fig. 2. Improvement in the design of patient wards, glass roofed wards converted to open balconies, 1919 (drawing: National archives, Kew, MH 52/1)

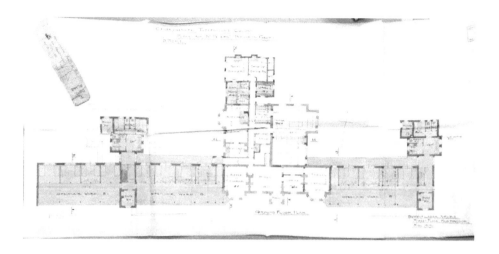

Fig. 3. Ground floor plan for St. Peter's House showing the open air wards , 1919 (drawing: National archives, Kew, MH 52/1)

Sanatorium Zonnestraal, Netherlands (1925-31)

By the early 1900s, there were a number of aftercare colonies in England, like Papworth, where consumptive patients were treated for a return to society. With adequate medical care (involving sunlight and fresh air), they took part in occupational therapy as well. In 1920, a Dutch architect, Jan Duiker along with medical director, Ben Sajet (as mentioned in his biography) went on a study trip to England to visit the aftercare colonies. There they paid a visit to the Papworth settlement. In their report in 1922, they concluded that the seriously sick belonged to hospitals whereas the sanatoria were to concentrate on the moderate cases. At this time, architects Jan Duiker and Bernard Bijvoet were commissioned for the design of a sanatorium in Netherlands, for which the Papworth settlement served as a model [13].

The Sanatorium Zonnestraal which means 'Ray of sunshine' in Dutch, was designed as a tuberculosis sanatorium for the workers of the Diamond Dust industry in Amsterdam suffering from tuberculosis. The name 'Zonnestraal' was given to it as a homage to the belief in the therapeutic power of the sun. Being a completely modernist building the sanatorium was an icon of the Dutch functionalist architectural movement, Nieuwe Bouwen'. Architects involved in this movement were to adopt modern technologies to create hygienic buildings. They focused on the need of a functional open plan with a flexible layout, a transparent and airy impression of buildings and a healthy environment with abundant fresh air and sunlight [14]. At Zonnestraal, they planned to expressed these ideas through open, well lit interiors, maximum glazing and open air recumbent areas for patients.

The sanatorium is situated in Hilversum, marking the boundary of Loosdrecht, some 35 km from Amsterdam. It is located on the latitude of <u>52° N</u> and <u>Longitude of 5° E</u>. It was designed during 1925-28. Due to a crisis in the Amsterdam Diamond industry, funds were extremely short at that time, which delayed the process, and hence the construction completed in 1931. The basic idea of the design was to capture plenty of sunlight and fresh air. An important aspect of the sanatorium was its transitory nature. As it was believed that tuberculosis would be exterminated within thirty to fifty years it was built as a temporary structure. The architect efficiently balanced the technical life span of the complex and the limited funds. A cheap construction method was employed, so reinforced concrete loadbearing frame was chosen, and prefabricated building components were introduced [15]. Remaining true to the ideas Duiker had gathered during his visit to the Papworth settlement, he gave a proposal for the spatial organization of the sanatorium in 1924. His proposal included an infirmary for 40 patients, pavilions for aftercare treatment, three to four workshops and aftercare dwellings [13].

Fig. 4. Zonnestraal Layout on the terrain (drawing: reproduced by Khan)

The complex is sited on the upper part of a gentle southward slope. (Figure 4) As Papworth, it too was located in an isolated area, a completely natural environment, in a heathland wooded with birch and pine trees; an ideal site for the establishment of a sanatorium. The main building of the complex is oriented slightly South-east, with two patient pavilions on either side. The Henri Ter Meulen Pavilion lies on the west of the main building in an open landscape and the Dresselhuys Pavilion to the east in the newly planted woodland. The configuration is an elaboration of the cottage style of sanatoria with a centrally placed administrative building but is more like the pavilion system with two patient pavilions. Each pavilion has two separate double-storied patient wings connected through a single-storied common room. The pavilions wings were placed at 45 degrees to each other with the intention to allow unhindered natural light and views for the patients inside the rooms [16].

Each patient wing is planned with the patient rooms on one side opening towards balconies to the sunward side and connected through a single corridor at the back. (Figure 5) At one end of the patient wards is a circular staircase that leads to the roof terraces. The floor slabs of the pavilion span 3m from girder to girder, providing 1.5m overhang on either side forming the corridor roof and an overhang to provide shade to the balconies at the time of excessive sun [13]. The patient rooms have large windows and doors towards the front so that the patient beds could be wheeled out on the balconies for therapy. The patients mostly laid outside on the terraces or balconies so that they could get fresh air as well as sunlight, which was necessary for the healing process. It seems that the extensive use of glass on the building's facades was not fulfilling the requirement of sun therapy which is why photographs of Zonnestraal show patients lying on balconies for exposure to sun.

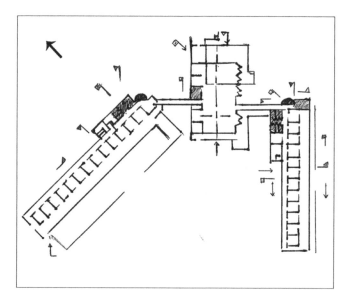

Fig. 5. Ground floor plan of Ter Meulen Pavilion, 1928 (drawing: reproduced by Khan)

The main principle that Duiker had borrowed from the Papworth settlement, was that of the occupational therapy. For this he designed five workshops for open air treatment. The five workshops were placed in a radial arrangement and were situated to the north-west of the main building. Similar to Papworth, patients who had undergone arrest under the sanatorium treatment, could work in these workshops where they were trained in different fields of work. Then there were cabins in the woodland that served as accommodation for patients who were in the last stage of their treatment. These cabins were built by the consumptives themselves. The cabins were timber framed, having large openable windows on all three sides for light and air [13].

Paimio Sanatorium, Finalnd (1929-33)

The Paimio sanatorium in Finland is greatly inspired by the Sanatorium Zonnestraal, which was visited by Alvar Aalto, soon after its completion in 1931. So, the Paimio has similar features to Zonnestraal, but the two differ in some ways as well [17].

The Paimio sanatorium which is located in the Village of Paimio in the south-west of Finland was designed in an architectural competition for sanatoria design. The competition held in 1928-29 was won by Alvar Aalto

[18]. The sanatorium lies on the latitude of <u>60° N</u>, and is sited among pine trees, fitting the sanatorium's functional requirement of isolation. Like Zonnestraal, it is placed on the highest part of the terrain on a north-south axis. The building has an asymmetrical plan, facing towards south-east, getting abundant of the morning sunlight, much required, and at the same time shielding it from the evening sun when it is in the west [17].[17]The sanatorium is located in a region having long summer days, with the sun setting around 10:30 PM and short winter days when the sun sets at 2:30 PM. The geographical orientation of the building plays a very important role in balancing the sunlight throughout the year. In winters the building is exposed to the sun throughout the day while in winters it only gets the morning and afternoon sun, preventing it from the evening sun when the building is already heated up.

The shape of the building is a result of a planning principle that naturally organizes different parts of the building according to their requirements. Hence, the placement and orientation of the different wings is determined in respect to their need for sunlight, ventilation and views. Spaces having a similar function and nature are arranged in the same wing, and then the different wings are linked to each other through a central building. Figure 12 is a master plan of the sanatorium showing different parts of the building. The A wing is the main patient wing, that has patient rooms and is facing south-east. B is the balcony wing having sun terraces on each floor facing due south. The C wing is the administrative block including the medical treatment rooms as well as the common spaces; dining hall, library and work rooms. D is for the services and staff accommodation and E houses the Boiler room and Heating plant. The blocks towards the west is the junior physicians housing.

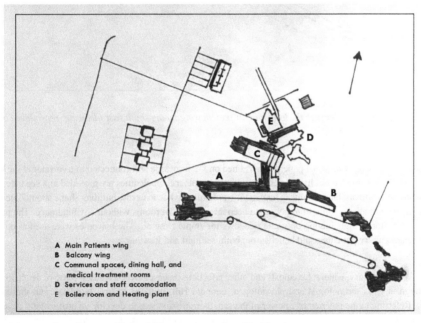

Fig. 6. Master plan of Paimio, Finland (drawing: reproduced by Khan)

Fig. 6 gives a picture of the effect of the morning sun when it is in the east. This shows that the main patient areas in the building are fully exposed to the sunward side, making maximum use of the sun in the morning and the afternoon when it is needed the most. Then in the evening when the sun is in the west, the building protects itself from overheating.

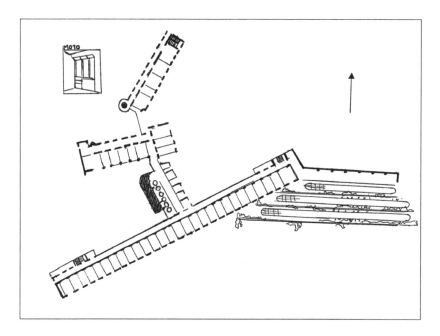

Fig.7. Ground floor plan showing the long narrow patient wing facing south east (drawing: reproduced by Khan)

The main patient wing consists of patient rooms lined on the front side and connected to a corridor at the back. (Figure 13) These wards do not have balconies with them, rather the balconies are provided in a separate wing towards the right and are facing south. The patient ward building has a narrow building shape about 7.5m deep [18]. In this way it allows sunlight to penetrate deep into the patient rooms without any hindrance. The patient ward is seven stories high, having openable windows for ample fresh air. The balconies were used as outdoor therapy spaces where patients could benefit from both, sunlight and fresh air.

In the mid-19th century, when tuberculosis and other infectious diseases were a leading cause of death, Francis Lamplough, a glass technologist and physiologist, Leonard Hill, initiated to turn buildings into therapeutic devices. Referring to the regenerative power of the sun, their mission was to develop an architectural glass that could let in the therapeutic ultraviolet rays into the buildings, as normal glass did not have the ability to transmit these rays. An English physicist, Sir William Crookes found out that the content of iron in normal soda lime glass was responsible for blocking ultraviolet light. Iron was not an ingredient of glass but it entered through impurities. Focusing on reducing the iron content with careful selection and handling of materials during the process, they were able to develop soda lime glass with a very low iron content, transmitting the therapeutic ultraviolet rays into the building. This specific type of glass was named 'vita' glass, bringing in health rays (as they were now known) through the windows. Chance Bros was England's first architectural glass manufacturing company to manufacture 'vita' glass [19].

Fig.8. Patients' room window drawings which show the floor curving up to the window sill (drawing: reproduced by Khan)

Taking advantage of this development in time, the Paimio sanatorium used 'vita' glass to enable the penetration of the UV rays in patient rooms, facilitating the therapy. Therefore, at Paimio, the patient rooms were the main therapy areas, in contrast to Zonnestraal where the balconies served the main purpose. A low curving window sill maximized the provision of natural light and venation blinds were provided for shading requirements [20]. (Figure 8).

While designing the sanatorium, Aalto's main aim was the physical and psychological well-being of the patients; resting in pleasant surroundings. He was concerned that a patient room should be different from an ordinary room. As an ordinary room is a room for a vertical person, who is well, whereas a patient room is for a horizontal person lying on the bed. Therefore, while designing for lighting, heating and other such features, this point should be kept in mind. As Aalto did, by positioning the ceiling radiator from where the rays could fall on the patient's feet rather than his head [20]. (Figure 9)

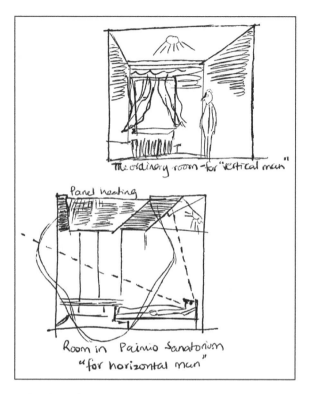

Fig. 9. Alvar Aalto. Sketches from 'The Humanising of Architecture' showing how patients inhabit a typical room at the Paimio Sanatorium (drawing: reproduced by Khan)

The Paimio sanatorium was well oriented according to the sun, planning the shape of the building in such a way, not to optimize the sunlight but balancing it throughout different seasons of the year. The spreaded layout of the building provided for better air circulation around the sanatorium and windows of the patient wings aided in cross ventilation.

Conclusion

It is seen that the main concern in the designs of all sanatoria has been the orientation of the buildings, mainly the patient wings. Orienting them either south, south-east or south-west, maximizes the sun exposure, which was a main requirement for sanatoria. Balancing the sunlight depending on the climatic variations of different geographical regions was also important. For example, in the case of the Paimio sanatorium which has a northern latitude at 60°, the asymmetrical plan of the building was erected to balance the large differences between the winter and the summer sun. In this way the building utilizes the sun throughout the short, cold and dark winters by extending the hours of the sun during the day. And at the same time the building protects itself from overheating in the summers, when the sun is at the west in the evening and the building is sufficiently heated up. Zonnestraal on the other hand, is located at 52°N where climates are not that harsh, so these aspects were not much thought of.

All the three sanatoria are sited in an isolated area, away from the overpopulated and dusty towns, benefiting from the natural environment around them. Placed among the woodlands having an abundance of trees that filtered the air in the surroundings and ventilated the rooms with as much fresh air as possible. As this too with sunlight, was another major requirement.

In all the three sanatoria; Papworth, Zonnestraal and Paimio the pavilion style of wards has been common. With wards facing south, connected to single corridor and balconies to maximize sunlight and fresh air which was recommended by Florence Nightingale (the pioneer of modern nursing) in the mid-1800s. The patient wards in these sanatoria were designed having a narrow building shape, so that maximum light could penetrate deep inside the rooms. The open air recumbent areas; sun terraces and balconies has been an important feature in all sanatoria.

The use of glass depended on the development according to the time period. The hospitals at Papworth settlement incorporated glass roofs and the Zonnestraal, depicting openness, has more glass than walls. The one used here was ordinary drawn glass and as discussed before, does not transmit ultraviolet rays from the sun. Here it makes us believe that this symbol of modern architecture was not serving medical ends at its fullest. The glazing had nothing to do with therapy but was for mere aesthetic reasons. Although the glass building looks more open and pleasing to the eye, but the indoors do not fulfill the requirement. It appears that the use of glass in Zonnestraal does not justify the modernist rhetoric of transparent and hygienic buildings. The architects may not have examined this deeply, as in the case of Paimio sanatorium. Paimio was not all glass architecture as Zonnestraal, considering the harsh weather conditions there in the winter months, more glass would create a cold and gloomy sanatorium. However, the tall windows of the patient rooms, having 'vita glass' provided plenty of sunlight for the treatment. And because of the use of 'vita glass', patients could be treated indoors, in their respective rooms, with less requirement of wheeling them out in the balconies as in the case of Zonnestraal and Papworth hospitals that had open air wards or patient wards opening up to the sun balconies, which Paimio did not have.

References

[1] F. R. Walters, *The open-air or sanatorium treatment of pulmonary tuberculosis.* London: Baillière, Tindall & Cox, 1909.

[2] L. Bryder, *Below the Magic Mountain: A Social History of Tuberculosis in Twentieth-century Britain.* London: Clarendon Press, 1988.

[3] A. Ransome, *The principles of open-air treatment of phthisis and of sanatorium construction.* London: Smith, Elder, 1903.

[4] A. Downes, and T P Blunt, 'Researches on the effect of light upon bacteria and other organisms', *Proc. R. Soc. London.*, vol. 26, 1877, pp. 488-500.

[5] R. Hobday, *The Healing Sun.* Findhorn Press. Forres, Scotland: Findhorn Press, 1999.

[6] R. A. Hobday, 'Sunlight therapy and Solar architecture', *Medical History*, vol. 41. no. 1, 1997, pp. 455-472.

[7] D. L. McBride, 'American Sanatoriums: Landscaping for Health, 1885-1945', *Landscape Journal*, 1998, pp. 26-41.

[8] E. Eylers, 'Planning the Nation: the sanatorium movement in Germany', *The Journal of Architecture*, vol. 19, no. 5, 2014, pp. 667-692.

[9] L. Bryder, 'Papworth Village Settlement - A unigue experiment in the treatment and care of the tuberculous?', *Medical History*, vol. 28, 1984, pp. 372-390.

[10] Anon., *Report on inspections of Village settlements*, Cambridgeshire : s.n., 1920.

[11] B. Kitchen, *Proposed new wings for St.Peters*, Cambridgeshire: s.n, 1919.

[12] B. Kitchen, *Wings at St.Peters*, Cambridgeshire : s.n., 1919.

[13] P. Meurs, *Sanatorium Zonnestraal : history and restoration of a modern monument*. Zonnestraal Estate: NAi Publishers, 2010,

[14] Anon., *NAi - Nederlands Architecture institute*, 2013. [Online] Available at: www.hetnieuweinstituut.nl/en/

[15] W. D. Jonge, *'Zonnestraal': Restoration of a transitory architecture*. Russia, s.n., 2003. [Online] Available at: http://www.wesseldejonge.nl/media/downloads/Zonnestraal_project%20ENG.pdf

[16] R. Vickery, 'Bijvoet and Duiker', *The MIT Press*, vol. 13/14, 1971, pp. 131-160.

[17] C. Volf, *Light, Architecture and Health*. Denmark: Aarhus School of Architecture, 2013.

[18] M. Ehrström, S. Jetsonen, T. Lindh, *Nomination of Paimio Hospital for Inclusion in the World Heritage List*. Helsinki: National Board of Antiquities, 2005.

[19] J. Sadar, 'The healthful ambience of Vitaglass', *Urban History*, vol. 3/4, 2008, pp. 269-80.

[20] M. Hipeli. & E. Laaksonen, *Paimio Sanatorium 1929-33*. s.l.:Helsinki: Rakennustieto, 2014.

The environmental role of transition spaces in Victorian architecture

Ranald Lawrence

Sheffield School of Architecture, University of Sheffield, UK

Introduction – transition spaces and thermal adaptation

Recent research in the field of thermal comfort has highlighted the importance of the inclusion of a range of dynamic environments inside buildings, offering more possibilities to provide thermal comfort to a greater range of occupants than static interior environments, as well as improving thermal comfort perception.[1] For example, research by Nikolopoulou and Steemers has shown how outdoor microclimates can enhance thermal comfort to a much greater extent that laboratory models suggest.[2]

Expanding on this idea, Pitts highlighted the role of thermal transition spaces in assisting adaptation to indoor microclimates, as well as their potential to reduce energy use by supporting the provision of a wider comfort range than in buildings conceived as only one environment.[3] Similarly, in 'Intermediate Environments', Potvin characterises adaptation as "difficult", "conscious" or "subliminal"[4], and argues that the most adept for promoting comfort is 'subliminal' adaptation, such that the individual is gradually exposed in steps to a change in environment.

It is possible to describe a hierarchy of microclimates, from outdoors to indoors. Transitional microclimates serve as intermediate spaces, which permit "a progressive adaptation to a new environment. Whereas environmental determinism creates uniformity, environmental diversity increases the morphological possibilities of architecture and urban form".[5]

Historic examples of transitional spaces

Some of the simplest historic examples of intermediate spaces come from the appropriation of glass to utilise solar gain. As Henrik Schoenefeldt has narrated, the history of 'glass architecture' is closely entwined to the development of horticulture in the 17th, 18th and 19th centuries, and the use of these environments for human purposes is a relatively late and radical experiment of the Victorian era.[6] In his history of arcades, Geist documented their specific historic importance as spaces of transition, either to provide direct access to shops and dwellings or to the interior of a block.[7]

Equally important to the evolution of transitional spaces was the relationship between the developing science of building physics and the study of disease. In *The Architecture of the Well-Tempered Environment*, Banham highlights the connection between research that physicians conducted into the causes of disease believed to be transmitted by air, and strategies for improved ventilation in the home. These included experts such as Dr.

Hayward, who designed his Octagon House in Liverpool (1867) as a testbed for maintaining a pure internal atmosphere in a domestic setting. All of the principle rooms of the Octagon House were arranged off intermediate lobbies accessed from the staircase by doors. This separation allowed the lobbies to function as a vertical supply duct of warm air – an active environmental buffer between the outdoor atmosphere and the family living spaces.[8]

At a larger scale, the environmental design and integration of technology in new public building types in the mid to late Victorian period demonstrated a profound level of understanding that was a combination of the new science of fluid dynamics (the efficient flow of air through buildings gained through decades of practical experimentation), and the intuitive application of this knowledge by architects who retained direct control of the physical dimensions of windows, room volumes, air inlets, and chimneys, that together constituted the chief variables determining the success or failure of building services. This paper examines three examples of such buildings: the new House of Commons, the Natural History Museum, and the Glasgow School of Art.

By contrast, the twentieth century saw a standardisation of environmental conditions as local climates and regional cultural responses were discarded in favour of new technologies and codified design guidance, for example regarding the sizing of air-conditioning systems. Much of the tacit and scientific knowledge gained in the previous century was lost; in particular the historic role of porches, lobbies and other transition spaces as thermal filters, assisting in the process of adaptation from outside to inside, or between spaces with different environmental requirements.

If we are to tackle the unsustainability of our current model of environmental control inside buildings[9] we need to understand how the question of provision of individual comfort was replaced by generic performance standards that assume that all internal environments should be broadly the same, regardless of location or purpose.

The House of Commons

David Boswell Reid was employed to develop heating and ventilating systems for the Palace of Westminster in 1840 following the destruction of the old Houses of Parliament in 1834.[10] Architect Charles Barry's design had envisaged conventional natural cross-ventilation through opening windows in combination with fireplaces for warmth, an arrangement that was deemed inadequate given the insalubrious atmosphere of London at the time. While the 'Great Stink' of 1858 was yet to occur, major cholera epidemics in 1831, 48-49 and 53-54 were widely attributed to airborne miasmas. Reid, who trained as a doctor, developed his first design over a period of six years, requiring intensive negotiations with Charles Barry regarding space for plenums and the treatment of air underneath the chamber itself.[11] Eventually the relationship between architect and doctor turned engineer broke down, and after two enquiries Reid's input was reduced to the design of the Chamber of the House of Commons alone.

Reid's design included two separate systems of inlets and extracts, one above the ceiling of the Chamber and one underneath the floor. The roof system was supplied from a roof inlet facing east to the Thames, or a secondary inlet above St. Stephen's Porch (depending on local air conditions). A fan located in the roof to the north of the Central Lobby drew the air across an array of steam pipes to the centre of the ceiling above the House of Commons, where it entered through vents in the ceiling adjusted by sliding valves. The floor system was supplied either through inlets in the Elizabeth Tower to the north or inlets from Cloister Court and the Commons' Inner Court to the south. From there the air was drawn through passages in the basement to heating and cooling chambers on the ground floor. Apparatus first tested and fine-tuned in the Temporary House of Commons was used to heat, cool, and adjust the humidity of the air, before mixing in an equalizing chamber.[12]

Treated air entered the Chamber through cast-iron plates in the floor, risers in the aisles, the back of the benches, and gaps in the central ceiling panels. Foul air was extracted from the ceiling either side of the central panels, as well as through the floor in front of the benches. During votes, valves were used to close the extracts in the ceiling and open extracts in the Commons' Lobby, the Ladies' and Stranger's Galleries and the Division Lobbies.

Following the opening of the chamber in 1852 it was found that the complexity of the system, with inlets and extracts at both ground and upper levels, made it difficult to balance the air pressure inside the House. The heat from the six gaslights of Barry's initial design also prevented air from the ceiling inlets from descending into the chamber, a problem compounded by the fact that the fan in the floor system had to be turned off because it resulted in too much noise.[13] Tests conducted in March and April 1852 showed temperatures ranging from 62F (17C) at ground level to 73F (23C) in the galleries (23C). This was considered to be too warm with 64F (18C) recorded as the 'most satisfactory temperature'.[14]

Reid's design was destroyed when the House of Commons was bombed during the Blitz, and the replacement post-war design by Giles Gilbert Scott included modern air-conditioning. However the layout of the reconstructed House is broadly similar, and it is possible to understand the architectural and environmental sequence of spaces from the original plans of the building. (Fig. 1)

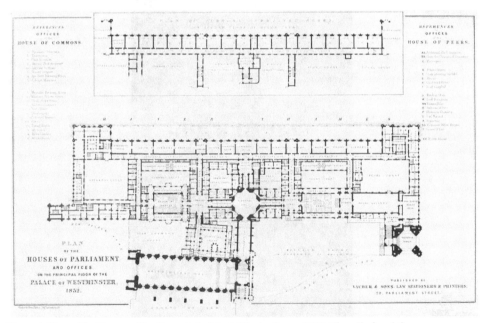

Figure 1. Plan of the Houses of Parliament. Architect, Charles Barry. 1852. Plan: Vacher & Sons.

The environmental role of transition spaces in Victorian architecture

The main entrance to the Commons' Lobby is from the Central Hall via the Commons' Corridor. From the Commons' Lobby, various offices belonging to parliamentary staff and committees are accessed via corridors to west and east, with the chamber itself accessed through an elaborate gothic screen and ante-chamber to the north. (Fig. 2)

Figure 2. Lobby of the House of Commons, Artist: Henry Barraud. 1872–1873.

Figure 3. The Chamber of the House of Commons. Report from the Select Committee on House of Commons-Rebuilding, Parliamentary Papers, 1943-44.

The original Commons' Lobby was a lofty glazed cathedral-like space serving as a waiting room for MPs to meet before and after debates. As Henry Barraud's painting of 1873 reveals, MPs would huddle together to discuss proceedings in their coats and top hats, which were not removed until inside the Chamber. (Fig. 3) When a vote or 'division' is called, members have eight minutes to assemble in either the Aye or No division lobbies, a pair of corridor-like ante-chambers either side of the main Chamber. The Aye lobby faces Star Chamber Court to the west, while the No lobby opens onto Commons' Court to the east. (Fig. 4)

Figure 4. The Aye Division Lobby. 1905.

The Aye lobby is entered from behind the Speaker's Chair at the north end of the main Chamber, whereas the No lobby is entered from the Common's lobby ante-chamber to the south. After eight minutes the doors are locked, and MPs names are counted as they exit at the opposite end of each lobby.

The Commons' and Divisions lobbies play a passive but nonetheless crucial environmental role, acting as air locks and thermal buffers to protect the fine-tuned conditions inside the House, designed in an age before insulation and air-tight sealing, permitting sensitive adjustments to be made to both temperature and airflow in response to feedback from the MPs and Speaker. These adjustments were essential given the chamber itself measured only 14 x 21m but could hold up to 800 people when fully occupied.

The rapid heat gains and losses experienced by parliamentarians filing in and leaving in short spaces of time must have presented more of a challenge than even the atmosphere of the city outside, and goes some way to explain the elaborate design of the system, as well as the time and effort that went into monitoring conditions inside the House (the chamber was fitted with eight thermometers, and temperatures were regularly recorded by the Sergeant-at-Arms and sent back to the superintendent so that adjustments could be made in the Equalizing chamber.[15]

Reid's concept of a continuous feedback loop that could respond to weather conditions, atmospheric pollution, as well as the continuously changing population and demands of the House was clearly ambitious given the technology available at the time. However, contemporary evidence suggests that parliamentarians were able to adapt to the changing internal conditions through adjustments to their dress, activity and location (for example, moving from a standing group discussion in the Commons' Lobby to a sedentary position in the Chamber itself, where coat and hat might be removed). The ritual of the 'division' also provided an opportunity for the build-up of hot air inside the Chamber to be purged, while parliamentarians might move into the fresher air in the division lobbies with views to the outside during breaks in proceedings.

While the design of the environmental systems of the House of Commons might therefore be summarised as a story of technological ambition ahead of its time[16], the lived experience of the spaces reveal the sophisticated ways in which the behaviour and activities of Victorian society were adapted and fine-tuned to the ever-changing environment indoors as well as outside.

The Natural History Museum

A combination of improved building technology and a greater sensitivity to personal hygiene drove the development of new methods of adequately ventilating the new, more complex types of public buildings that characterised the civic realm of the second half of the nineteenth century.

In Glasgow, the pioneer Wilson Weatherley Phipson installed a revolutionary fan and heating system at the University (designed by Sir George Gilbert Scott) between 1866 and 1870. Like Reid's design at the Houses of Parliament this was a fan driven system, but with localised boiler heating in dispersed chambers feeding groups of classrooms and lecture halls, and extraction assisted by the heat from the boiler flues running up the centre of the extract shafts. After his work at Glasgow Phipson's career took off, and he was responsible for installations at the Royal Albert Hall in 1871, the Natural History Museum in Kensington in 1881, and the Royal Infirmary in Liverpool in 1889.

The Natural History Museum was conceived to house the growing collection of specimens from the British Museum. Alfred Waterhouse was selected to design the new building after the death of Francis Fowke in 1865, and his idiosyncratic terracotta Romanesque design on the site of the 1862 International Exhibition building is a development of curator Richard Owen's 1859 diagram, 'Idea of a Museum of Natural History'. The collections were to be systematically catalogued as in an encyclopaedia. Either side of the main hall three storeys of galleries front the lawns to Cromwell Road. North of these galleries are twelve top-lit transverse specimen galleries. The Fossil collections are housed to the east and non-extinct specimens to the west of the main hall. (Fig. 5) A key concern was the protection of the specimens from excess heat or moisture - the target design temperature range was 54-60F (12-16C).[17]

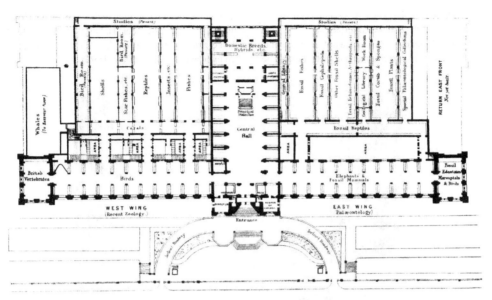

Figure 5. Plan of the Natural History Museum. Architect, Alfred Waterhouse. 1881.

The Great Hall is effectively the heart and lungs of the building. As the first space encountered on entry it provided a respite from adverse weather conditions as well as an opportunity for the Museum authorities to monitor and observe the circulation of visitors. It also protected the precious collections from the pollution of the street outside. The main hall is flanked by 58m towers to the south (serving as exhaust stacks), and 50m towers to the north, described by Waterhouse as "Smoke and Ventilation Towers", serving boilers in the basement. The heat from this central smoke shaft was also used to draw air up additional exhaust shafts surrounding it.[18]

The location of the air supply was carefully considered. Fresh air was drawn into six ducts from the Royal Horticultural Society gardens to the north. Prior to the construction of the Science Museum the gardens acted as a natural filter to the polluted air carried on the prevailing south-westerly wind. The ducts ran underneath the transverse galleries. Each duct was composed of a warm air channel, heated by arrays of steam pipes fed by the boilers, above a cold air channel, allowing the temperature to be locally mixed and controlled in each gallery. The air entered each gallery through grills located near the floor, and was extracted at ceiling level, making use of thermal buoyancy to guarantee continuous flow.

It is clear from correspondence with the client that Waterhouse had a good understanding of the spatial and logistical requirements necessary to integrate a complete heating and ventilation system into the design of the Museum, as demonstrated by his inclusion of the ventilation towers in the design prior to Phipson's appointment.[19] While the requirement for visitors comfort was apparently never explicitly elucidated[20] – the complex system was justified for purely functional purposes – we can see that was an important consideration in the design of the Museum, in parallel with the requirements of the collection.

The Great Hall was designed as a thermal buffer space between the outside and the collections held in the front and transverse galleries. (Fig. 6) Phipson proposed that the large volume of air in the Great Hall be actively heated to counter the heat loss through the main doors, tempering the thermal transition to the individual galleries, which were then conditioned further according to the requirements of the collections. Hot air was supplied to the hall through grates in the floor and from vents underneath the grand staircase. (Fig. 7) The location of the hall above the boilers also ensured that visitors would be warmed by heat radiating from the floor.

Figure 6. Central hall looking north. 1902. Trustees of the Natural History Museum.

Figure 7. Vents underneath the grand staircase. 1882. Trustees of the Natural History Museum.

This space is reminiscent of one of the grand Victorian train stations of the period, and would have been experienced in a similar way from a visitor's perspective, who would spend most of their time inside the building on their feet, in their outdoor clothes. The park benches lining the space reinforced the semi-outdoor quality of the main hall. From here visitors had the choice of moving at ground level into the south facing galleries, or rising up the grand staircase to the upper levels of the front galleries. The transverse galleries could only be accessed from the front galleries at ground level.

A visit to the Museum left much to chance: the path chosen dictating the exhibits that would be encountered. It would be impossible to see everything in one visit; instead the Musuem rewarded return visitors, who might choose a different route on each occasion, rather like weekend walks in the park. The nature of this experience meant that, rather like the Great Exhibition building, the Museum became a place to see and be seen as much – if not more than – an institution for education.

The maintenance of the collections at stable temperatures in all weather and seasons was a significant challenge given the unpredictability of the total number of visitors as well as numbers in individual galleries. Further local control was provided in the front galleries by opening windows or adjustable vents connected directly to the outside. In summer the skylit transverse galleries could warm rapidly in strong sunshine; however the visitor could be gradually acclimatised through their progression from the outside, to the main hall, to the front gallery, to the gallery in question. (Fig. 8) In winter, steam pipes and radiators provided further pockets of warm air for visitors to linger.

Figure 8. Diplodocus skeleton on display in one of the transverse galleries. 1905. Trustees of the Natural History Museum.

The Glasgow School of Art

Towards the end of the nineteenth century the use of sophisticated technology spread to more commonplace building types, for example schools. The medical profession had raised concerns about the health implications caused by overcrowding within school buildings as early as the 1860s.[21] The American surgeon John Billings' 1893 guide for architects, Ventilation and Heating, detailed various strategies for different building types, including schools and hospitals. He recommended careful analysis of existing practise and practical experiment as a means to perfect air quality.[22]

In America, the Sturtevant Company had offered combined fan and heating systems for installation in buildings from 1869.[23] In their standard design, a centrally located fan and boiler room in the basement would distribute tempered air through a series of radiating plenums to the external walls of the building, from where it would rise in a series of ducts to classrooms on each floor. The plan of the schools was kept as compact as possible to reduce the distance the air had to travel from the fan as well as minimising heat losses to the outside. Perhaps for the first time, orientation was demoted to a position of secondary importance.

Mackintosh worked with the Glasgow firm of James Cormack and Sons to install a Sturtevant system in the art school, with one fan supplying air to the first phase of the school (the eastern wing), completed in 1899, and a second fan added to double the power of the system with the completion of the western wing in 1910. However, similar to Waterhouse's design for the Natural History Museum, Mackintosh worked to completely integrate the technology with his own architectural and spatial aspirations. The linear form of the building had already been dictated to take advantage of the north orientation of the site to Renfrew Street for art studios, and so Mackintosh located the fan room underneath the central entrance, feeding into a single tapering plenum underneath the main corridor on the south side of the building.[24] (Fig. 9) The plenum fed ducts rising up the central spine wall of the building, the thermal hearth of the building. Hoppers that could be opened partially or fully then controlled the volume of conditioned air entering each space to north and south.[25] (Fig. 10)

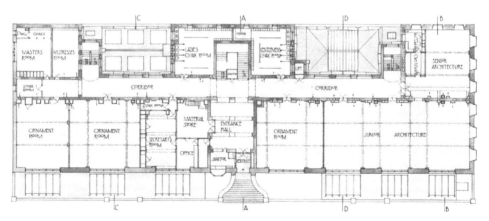

Figure 9. Plan of the Glasgow School of Art. Architect, Charles Rennie Mackintosh. 1910.

Figure 10. West corridor, showing ventilation hoppers on spine wall. Photographer, Thomas Annan. 1910. The Hunterian, University of Glasgow.

Visitors to the building follow a similar route, passing through a pair of double doors acting as an airlock into the entrance hall above the boiler room. From here a corridor leads east or west to north facing studios, and a central staircase gives access to the Museum and more studios at first floor level, and workshops in the basement.

When the system was tested in February/March 1910 temperatures in the studios and library ranged from 58-64F (14-18C). The life drawing studio measured 68-73F (20-23C), showing how the system could be adapted to provide different conditions as the use of different spaces dictated. Other spaces, including the corridors and loggia at the top of the building were allowed to be freer running, benefitting from solar gains from the horizontal sun in winter and with opening windows for additional ventilation in summer. The design of these spaces shows a sophisticated recognition of the pleasurable qualities of thermal sensation; particularly reflecting the importance of the sun in a cool and damp climate.

Conclusion

This paper has examined several examples of significant Victorian buildings and identified step changes in the role and design of transitional spaces, from the mid 19th to the early 20th century. The environmental role of key transitional spaces has been described in each case study in relation to the wider evolution of their design, and the developing discipline of building services.

In the twentieth century, HVAC technology has largely come to replace the key role transitional spaces played in Victorian buildings, which have often been dismissed as leaky, draughty and inefficient in use of space. Misplaced efforts have been made to retrofit modern air conditioning systems into these buildings at the same time as making the fabric more airtight. According to Colin Porteous, the development of modern air conditioning at the beginning of the twentieth century "signalled the loss of a science of ventilation that had prevailed for more than 60 years."[26]

The history of transition spaces demonstrated by these three case studies reveals a complex story. The use of transition spaces permitted the development of ever more sophisticated environmental systems to fine-tune and control conditions in critical environments – whether it be a debating chamber, a gallery of specimens or a life drawing studio – while at the same time ensuring the provision of experiential diversity through moderating environments connecting indoors with outdoors.

The first case study examined the design of a complex ventilation and heating system in the new House of Commons. Conflict between architect and engineer – probably partly caused by the radical complexity of the engineer's design – contributed to the partial failure of this system, which had attempted the complete thermal control of a relatively small space characterised by sudden fluctuations of heating load in the middle of the polluted atmosphere of Victorian London. Almost three decades later, the science of building services had advanced to the stage that Alfred Waterhouse could successfully integrate a complete system into the Natural History Museum in harmony with the site as well as the functional and experiential requirements of the building. Finally, at the turn of the century, Mackintosh's Glasgow School of Art shows the potential of the deployment of standardised equipment into a relatively small public building, but most importantly how this enabled the design of a diversity of environmental conditions that supported the ability of building occupants not only to adapt to their immediate environment but also to enjoy the building's relationship with climate and season.

However, Mackintosh's highly customised use of an off-the-shelf installation in the Glasgow School of Art proved to be an exception to the rule. Increasingly standardised equipment and a kit-of-parts approach to building services led to the conceptualisation of the environment as a machine, as Reid had predicted more than half a century before.

The invention of the air curtain has now made it possible to maintain all spaces, including entrance foyers, within ever-narrower comfort ranges. The ubiquitous use of raised floors and suspended ceilings to house services in modern public buildings and other places of work has reduced our connection to the outside world and increased the complexity and cost of construction, at the same time as building in obsolescence and reducing the useful lifespan of modern buildings. As the three case studies in this paper have demonstrated, perceived comfort temperatures have also risen dramatically over the past century. As we have become increasingly divorced from weather, time and season, we are seemingly less willing to adjust our clothing or activities to adapt to our environment.

However, in recent years, adaptive comfort theory has aided a rediscovery of the importance of transition spaces and transient environmental experiences, for example the impact of thermal history on thermal perception.[27]

Research suggests that it is possible to positively alter thermal perception through the judicious use of transition spaces, reversing the negative effects of air conditioning.[28]

The historic precedents explored in this paper demonstrate that environmental diversity not only offers improved opportunities for thermal comfort and adaptation compared with mechanically controlled interiors, but can also enhance our perceptions and experience of the architectural environment. Furthermore, the spatial cost of these spaces can be offset by the flexibility they offer for informal meetings, gatherings, and events, and the financial and energy savings to be made through a reduction in the scale and specification of HVAC equipment.

Environmental diversity is not an end in itself, but is about a connection to the climate of a place in order to avoid impoverishment of the built environment – a homogenous world where buildings look, and feel, the same regardless of where they are in the world. Use of space and comfort tolerance can be improved by a diversity of environmental conditions inside buildings achieved by the provision of transitional spaces that act as climate moderators, easing transition and offering possibilities for adaptation between different thermal conditions fine-tuned for different purposes, reflecting the local climate.

References

[1]   T. Parkinson, R. de Dear & C. Candido, in *Proceedings of 7th Windsor Conference: The changing context of comfort in an unpredictable world*, Windsor 2012, London: Network for Comfort and Energy Use in Buildings, 2012.

[2]   M. Nikolopoulou & K. Steemers, 'Thermal comfort and psychological adaptation as a guide for designing urban spaces', *Energy and Buildings*, vol. 35, no. 1, 2003, pp. 95–101.

[3]   A. Pitts, *Thermal comfort in transition spaces*, Buildings, vol. 3, no. 1, 2013, pp. 122–142.

[4]   A. Potvin, 'Intermediate environments', in K. Steemers & M.A. Steane (Eds.), *Environmental Diversity in Architecture*, Abingdon: Spon Press, 2004, pp. 121-142.

[5]   Ibid., p. 121.

[6]   H. Schoenefeldt, 'The Crystal Palace, environmentally considered', *arq: Architectural Research Quarterly*, vol. 12, no. 3-4, 2008, pp. 283-294.

[7]   J.F. Geist, *Arcades: The History of a Building Type*, Cambridge, Mass.: MIT Press, 1985.

[8]   R. Banham, *The Architecture of the Well-Tempered Environment*, Chicago: University of Chicago Press, 1969, pp.35-39.

[9]   See for example the performance gap between predicted and measured energy use.

[10] H. Schoenefeldt, 'The Historic Ventilation System of the House of Commons, 1840-52: revisiting David Boswell Reid's environmental legacy', *Antiquaries Journal*, vol. 98, in press, p. 3.

[11] The transformation of Barry's plans from openable windows to sealed building is retraced in detail in: H. Schoenefeldt, 'Architectural and Scientific Principles in the Design of the Palace of Westminster', in *Gothic Revival Worldwide: A.W.N. Pugin's Global Influence*, Leuven: University of Leuven Press, 2016, pp. 175-199.

[12] Ibid., pp. 21-25. A detailed examination of the process of fine tuning, taking into account Member perceptions of the indoor climate conditions, is provided in: H. Schoenefeldt, 'The Temporary Houses of Parliament and David Boswell Reid's architecture of experimentation', *Architectural History*, vol. 57, 2014, pp. 175-215.

[13] H. Schoenefeldt, 'The Historic Ventilation System of the House of Commons, 1840-52: revisiting David Boswell Reid's environmental legacy', *Antiquaries Journal*, vol. 98, in press, p. 28.

[14] House of Lords: 384, Ev 66, Q 675, Oral statement given by Goldsworthy Gurney, 8 May 1854.

[15] H. Schoenefeldt, 'The Historic Ventilation System of the House of Commons, 1840-52: revisiting David Boswell Reid's environmental legacy', *Antiquaries Journal*, vol. 98, in press, p. 26.

[16] Reid's description of the House of Commons as a 'piece of apparatus', and architecture's primary role as 'sustaining an artificial atmosphere', presages the architecture-as-machine metaphors of the early modern movement. See D. B. Reid, *Illustrations of the Theory and Practice of Ventilation*, London: Longman, Brown, Green, & Longmans, 1844, pp. 275, 70. See also R. Bruegmann, 'Central Heating and Forced Ventilation', *Journal of the Society of Architectural Historians*, vol. 37, no. 3, 1978, p. 160.

[17] Public Records Office: Works 17-18, p. 3.

[18] J. Cook and T. Hinchcliffe, 'Designing the Well-Tempered Institution of 1873', *arq: Architectural Research Quarterly*, vol. 1, no. 2, 1995, p. 74.

[19] Ibid., p. 74.

[20] Ibid., p. 71.

[21] One report by the Schools Enquiry Commission of 1868 estimated that only a quarter ofschools reached minimum acceptable environmental standards. See M.V.J. Seaborne & R. Lowe, *The English School: Its Architecture and Organization: 1870-1970*, London: Routledge & Kegan Paul, 1977, ii, p. 5.

[22] J.S. Billings, *Ventilation and Heating*, New York: The Engineering Record, 1893.

[23] B. M. Roberts and CIBSE Heritage Group, *Building Services Heritage*, CIBSE Heritage Group, 2003, p. 21.

[24] The fan room included the now familiar array of steam pipes, as well as horse hair screens for cleaning and humidifying the supply air.

[25] R. Lawrence, 'The internal environment of the Glasgow School of Art by Charles Rennie Mackintosh', *The Journal of Construction History*, vol. 29, 2014, pp. 112-113.

[26] C. Porteous, *The New Eco-Architecture: Alternatives from the Modern Movement*, London: Taylor & Francis, 2001, pp. 141–142.

[27] M. Nikolopoulou, & K. Steemers, 'Thermal comfort and psychological adaptation as a guide for designing urban spaces', *Energy and Buildings*, vol. 35, no. 1, 2003, pp. 95–101.

[28] G. Vargas, R. Lawrence & F. Stevenson, 'The role of lobbies: short-term thermal transitions', *Building Research & Information*, vol. 45, no. 7, 2017, pp. 759-782.

Owen Williams's Boots' "Wets" factory - a case study on the daylight factory typology

Samuel Leatt

Kent School of Architecture, University of Kent, UK

Introduction

The Boots' "Wets" factory (D10) is situated in Browtowe, Nottinghamshire, NG90 (Latitude: 52.9241 / 52°55'26"N Longitude: -1.1923 / 1°11'32"W). It is located on a large open site which was purchased by Boots in 1927 to provide a suitable premises for the company's pharmaceutical manufacturing operations. Designed by Sir Owen Williams (1890 – 1969), the factory building was constructed from 1930 to 1932. It received Grade 1 listed status in 1971.[1] Williams commented that it was built for "ten bob a square foot" (£5.55 per m²), making a total construction cost in 1932 of £18,500.00;[2] it is perceived to be his finest work.[3] Published literature on the building's environmental design features, such as its innovative use of glass and concrete in Britain to benefit its environmental performance is limited. Authors such as Alan Powers in his book, Britain, modern architectures in history (2007 1st Ed) and William J. R Curtis in Modern architecture (1996 3rd Ed), write about its clad glass 'curtain` wall façade as a design feature signifying the start of the modernist movement in Britain, rather than it being the factory's specific environmental engineering design intention. This paper will investigate the influences behind the D10's architectural typology and why Williams used a continuous glazed wall system separated by exposed concrete floors, and not the traditional method of masonry arches, piers and windows, which was heavily influenced by the work of Albert Kahn and the daylight factory typology.

Background

Williams started his career at the age of 16 as an apprentice at the Metropolitan Electric Tramway Company's Department of Building and Civil Engineering Works, whilst studying civil engineering at the Northern Polytechnic Institute. Following his graduation in 1911, Williams entered a world where reinforced construction was in its infancy. He worked for a British subsidiary of the Trussed Concrete Steel Company (Truscon), founded by Mortiz Kahn, from 1912 to 1916, laying the foundations for his expertise in reinforced concrete construction. His first project as an associated engineer for Truscon was the Gramophone Company Building in Middlesex (Fig.1), a factory constructed from concrete posts and beams, with brick infill up to sill height and large metal windows.[4] Its architectural form and specification was heavily influenced by the industrialist designs of Moritz's brother, Albert Kahn.

Albert Kahn was an architect based in Detroit Michigan, who worked alongside his brother Julius Kahn (a qualified engineer), who specialised in the design of industrial architecture from 1902 onwards. Julius was responsible for the development of the Kahn System®, where slabs were cast within wooden shuttering and hollow clay tile blocks were laid end to end in rows. The gaps between the blocks were separated by poured concrete, reinforced by the Kahn Bar and with a plain slab to finish.[5] This system empowered Albert Kahn to

129

design and build industrial buildings over multiple floors, using a reinforced concrete frame, enabling large window spans to be used which covered an internal grid of concrete columns, a typology defined as the daylight factory.

The Kahn system brought in new business and Albert accepted a commission from the Packard Motor Company in 1903, completing the famous Packard No. 10 in Detroit in 1905 (Fig.2). It has significant parallels with the Middlesex building, for example large double hung sash windows are used, framed by concrete to maximise light and air entry into the factory floors. At the time, this was a clear break from the previous mill framed industrial buildings and the design gained him further industrial commissions, most notably from Henry Ford, the factory being described by Banham in his book "A concrete Atlantis" (1989) as an "Innovative structure [that would] bridge the gap between the older tradition and the stunningly new type of factory". Albert, using the daylight factory typology, balanced the needs of the workers by considering their thermal comfort via heating systems, natural daylight design by large openable windows and incorporating health and safety features, primarily through its use of fire resistant materials (steel and concrete). He also kept his clients happy, by keeping the construction and maintenance costs low and offering flexibility in internal design and layout to facilitate advances being made in production techniques at the time.[6]

It is also important to note the works of Ernest Ransome during this period, as parallels can be drawn between the later Packard No. 10 designed by Albert Kahn and the second phase of the Pacific Coast Borax Company in Bayonne, New Jersey, completed in 1904 (Fig.3). Ransome had been both experimenting and constructing with reinforced concrete since 1870 and patented a twisted concrete reinforced rods system in 1884. The material's fire proof qualities also became evident in 1902, when a huge fire broke out in the first phase of the Company's Refinery, which he had also designed. Despite the scale and ferocity of the fire, Ransome noted that the structure had survived "with hardly any damage". His system the "monolithic unit construction" patented in 1902 differed from the Kahn System® by utilising a unit construction. This entailed manufacturing specific elements such as the columns, beams and girders off site, then the frame was erected and bonded via tie bars and grooves, and joined by floor slabs that were poured in situ and bonded in mortar. Ransome also secured another influential patent for the daylight factory typology, where the floor slab was exposed and extended further than the external walls, providing support for the wall piers and windows. This particular detail had not been incorporated in Kahn's early designs.[7]

Fig.1 Factory in Middlesex by Truscon 1912 (Picture: Fawcett, D., Thornburrow, K., Fellows, R., Yeomans, D., Cooper, P., Mark, B. and Hitchen, P. (2011). Conservation Management Plan for the Boots "Wets" Factory D10. 1st ed. Cambridge: Cambridge

Fig.2 Picture of the Packard No10 1905 (Picture: L. Kreager, J. (1998). Albert Kahn and the design of Angell Hall. LSA Magazine, (20-22), p4)

Fig.3 Picture of Pacific Coast Borax Company in Bayonne, New Jersey 1904 (Picture: L. Mortensen, J. (2015). Reclaiming the Daylight Factory: The Significance of Versatility in the Preservation of Early Twentieth Century Concrete Frame Industrial Buildings in Dayton, Ohio. Undergraduate. University of Washington, p23)

Legislation

The daylight factory was an evolution of the factory typology partially formed by legislation in the early nineteenth century. In 1802, the Health and Morals of Apprentices Act was introduced principally to improve the working hours and education of children within factory settings. However, it also covered the internal factory environment, requiring factories to be properly ventilated at all times and white washed twice a year to help combat mill fever and other health issues.[8]   Despite the Act's focus on children and factory inspectors finding it difficult to enforce, it recognised that the factory environment needed legislation to improve the health and working lives of employees.

The right for the public to have daylight within commercial and residential structures was also protected in law through the Prescription Act of 1832, giving people the right to have access to, and use of, light for 20 years, unless it was otherwise mentioned in a deed or an agreement.[9] This particular Act, which is still used in British planning legislation to this day, was a response to the poorly laid out urban planning slums seen in cities at the time, where daylight was not considered at all in the design process. The Factory and Workshop Act of 1878 obliged the rights of all workers to be protected whilst working in a commercial environment. It also required that the factory work space not be overcrowded to reduce injury, and ventilated in a manner to render "harmless, so far as is practicable, all the gases, vapours, dust or other impurities generated in the course of the manufacturing process".[10]

America copied the legislation and regulations set by Britain during the Industrial Revolution, but legislators there gave more powers to inspectors to enforce changes, such as the installation of mechanical ventilation where required. The Triangle Shirtwaist factory fire of 1911 lasted 18 minutes and killed 146 people, forcing the American government to compel the installation of sprinkler systems and larger fire escapes.[11] In New York, the Illuminating Engineering Society introduced the regulations for the amount of artificial illumination within a factory in 1915 (Fig.4) to combat the increase of accidents in poorly lit workspaces.[12] At this point, the daylight factory typology with its use of inflammable materials such as steel and concrete, its large openings to encourage natural daylight and ventilation, appeared to be a solution to compliance with the rules and regulations set by both British and American governments.

TABLE II
ILLUMINANCE REQUIREMENTS FOR FACTORIES, MILLS AND OTHER WORK PLACES (1915)

Class of Work	Minimum foot-candle intensity	Desirable foot-candle intensity
Storage, passageways, stairways, and the like	0.25	0.25 – 0.5
Rough manufacturing and other operations	1.25	1.25 – 2.5
Fine manufacturing and other operations	3.5	3.5 – 6.0
Special cases of fine work	-	10.0 - 15.0

Fig.4 Osterhaus, W. (1993). Office lighting: A Review of 80 yeards of Standards and Recommendations. 1st ed. [ebook] California: Windows & daylighting group Building Technologies Program Energy and Environment Division Lawrence Berkely Labratory, p2.

Chicago's daylighting design in commercial architecture during the late 1800s

Another influence in the development of the daylight factory typology was Chicago's commercial architecture in the nineteenth century. Its primary architectural design premise was shaped by maximising natural light for commercial buildings, so much so that the famous Chicago architect John Wellborn Root in his book "The Great Architectural Problem" stated that daylight design held more weight than foundation design or capacity. In 1850, the Chicago Gas Light and Coke Company controlled a monopoly over the gas supplies in the city making gas lamps expensive to run and therefore not the illumination of choice. By 1880, oil lamps were the primary source of artificial illumination, but they had a tendency to explode. During 1885, Edison lamps and dynamos were installed around City Hall, yet as this took two years to complete and cost 20 – 30% more to run than gas, many of the current suppliers in the city saw this as the technology's downfall. There were buildings, for example offices, that used two or three, 16 candle power lights in each space, but this did not, however, provide sufficient illumination for more detailed tasks. These factors contributed to Root's view that daylight was critical in tall office building design and as a result, he settled on the following window geometry as a solution; storey heights of 3.2m, sills of windows to be 700mm off the floor, lintels installed 150mm lower from the ceiling and windows to be no smaller than 1.83m in width. Yet without the use of reinforced concrete, these specifications were difficult to achieve under traditional masonry construction methods, and so the light court was used to promote natural daylighting in larger buildings.[13]

The use of light courts in Chicago became prominent after the American Civil War for a number of reasons: land values increasing, more demand for multistore office space/wholesale stores and higher rents for better daylit buildings. The large rectangular shapes of the new high-rise buildings were causing issues with daylight penetration, especially in the dark recesses of offices. One way of remedying this was either glazing the existing light wells, or creating new light courts in the construction phase. An example of an office building with a prominent light court by Root is the Rookery building in Chicago. Commissioned by him in 1886, the light court was supported on metal columns, connected via light weight steel trusses, enabling light to penetrate the office spaces internally. In addition, the internal walls were white enamelled brick to improve the space's reflectance.[14]

The influence of these architectural features used in Chicago's commercial buildings can be seen clearly in Kahn's daylight factory typology. The emphasis on window size and use of light courts to tackle economic challenges and to improve internal working conditions are evident throughout his commercial designs. Also, it is important to note that the daylight factor was identified by Alexander Pelham Trotter as far back as 1895, predating the daylight factories of Kahn and Ransome. Therefore, the knowledge regarding the need to calculate the daylight performance as a percentage existed, but there is no evidence to show that it was used in the design of the daylight factory.

The D10's daylight factory design

Moritz Kahn's book, *The Design & Construction of Industrial Buildings* (1917) is regarded as the book that Williams made reference to throughout the design process for the D10, a little over 10 years later.[2] In the preface Moritz states, "My experience of the construction of such buildings having been largely obtained in America, I have naturally found it convenient for my purpose to give a preponderance of illustrations of typical American factories: at the same time, some notable English examples are included". His primary reason for creating daylight factories was to reduce the amount of accidents due to poor lighting (Fig.5) and the physiological and psychological effects that gloomy surroundings have on the inhabiting workers, which he believed reduced the physical efficiency of human beings.[15] This train of thought was principally influenced by his brother Albert Kahn, whose primary drivers in the creation of beautiful commercial design were workers' needs, believing that the exterior should reflect the internal workings of a factory. He was disdainful of the over ornamentation of commercial buildings to flatter the ego of factory owners and stated that his designs were "90 percent business and 10 percent art".[6] This notion was shared by Williams who stated, 'The ideal structure is one in which the materials fit the conditions better than any other materials, and in which the form, both architectural and engineering, fits the material. It has been my endeavour as a guiding principle to use no material where another material would better serve'.[16] The parallels between Albert and Moritz Kahn's daylight factory design principles can be seen clearly in the D10's form, even though particular construction techniques may differ.

133

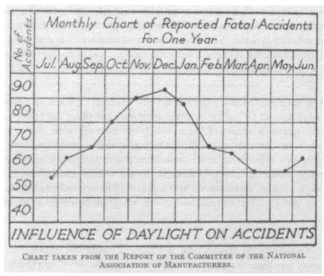

Fig. 5. Kahn, M. (1917). The Design and Construction of Industrial Buildings. 1st ed. London: Vacher & Sons Ltd.p20

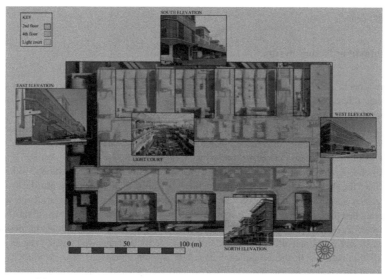

Fig. 6. Plan view of the D10 with elevations (drawing: Leatt)

The design of the D10 (Fig.6) was dictated by the need to move materials efficiently in order to improve the speed of the manufacturing process. The large atrium, whilst naturally lighting the four storeys below it, was engineered for the vertical and horizontal movement of materials via internal bridges connecting each level. The glazed four storey east and west elevations provided the backbone for the entry of goods via the two and four storey north elevation. These were then processed and manufactured and dispatched through the two and four storey south facing docks. Each elevation had a glazed ribbon daylight façade, separated by a concrete slab ready to be adapted for future extensions.[2]

Atrium

The roof construction of the D10 is formed of multi pitched concrete roofs with inset glass discs 206mm in diameter at 235mm centres and set in a 47.5mm reinforced concrete slab (Fig.7). This light court detail is prominent over the high-level packing hall atrium roof and other parts of the building, but it is not used over the third floor stores due to a possible fourth floor addition, pre-empted by Williams in the buildings design process.[2] The installation of glass in this way can be attributed to Hyatt Lights, the Luxfer Prism and Falconnier's blown glass bricks used in the early and latter part of the nineteenth century.

In 1845, Thaddeus Hyatt used glass cones and lenses in reinforced concrete frames for pavements, known as Hyatt Lights and these were seen as the preferred system for fire proof lighting in basements. The British inventor James Pennycuick filed a patent in the USA in 1882, which proposed glass with prismatic ridges which doubled the reflection and illumination of a single pane window.[17] Blown glass bricks were seen at the Stuttgart exhibition in 1897 with stout wire used in roof work as an early form of reinforcement. The wire was used within the cement mortar to bind it together by passing it under one brick and over the next. The bricks' double glazed form encouraged thermal mass and the permanent translucence of the glass provided privacy and reduced glare.[18] Each of these systems set out to improve daylighting through the manipulation of glass into a specific form to provide an environmental improvement internally.

The application of skylights to create light courts was also used by Albert Kahn to overcome the difficulties of naturally lighting a commercial factory, to aid the manufacturing process.[19] Kahn's well-known glass dome Conservatory for the Belle Isle Aquarium in Detroit (1904) was one of many projects to utilise glass and steel to maximise daylight design;[20] he also used glass in a similar manner in his daylight factories. The Highland Park Ford Plant number two, Detroit, completed in 1909 (Fig.8), used a sky lit central lightwell, a long expanse of glass to illuminate the long narrow building and translucent glass to reduce glare. In the George N. Pierce Company Plant, Buffalo, New York, (1906) Kahn used the saw tooth roof,[21] which allows for zenith sunlight to illuminate the building, providing good diffuse illumination and reducing the likely hood of glare or contrast to the light.[22]

By using roof glazing in the D10, Williams was focusing light into the packing hall or other dimly lit areas to improve daylight design and referencing Albert Kahn's use of glazed roofs in the daylight factory typology. The fact that they were cylinders set in concrete was a nod to the early innovators of glass and reinforced concrete and it also implies the desire of Williams to break away from Albert Kahn's specific construction techniques and use a technology of his own.

Fig. 7. Picture of glass-concrete roof. Fawcett, D., Thornburrow, K., Fellows, R., Yeomans, D., Cooper, P., Mark, B. and Hitchen, P. (2011). Conservation Management Plan for the Boots "Wets" Factory D10. 1st ed. Cambridge: Cambridge Architectural Research Ltd; p4-5

Fig. 8. Ford Highland Park Plant No2, Assembly Line Corridor, Detroit, Michigan: photo by Edward Burtynsky, 2008 (Edward Burtynsky Photographic Works)

Window façade

The D10 is enclosed by approximately 11,560m full height perimeter windows, separated by an exposed concrete floor slab. The original glazing was encased in ungalvanized Crittal medium universal steel glazing sections painted green, in 2340mm wide frames with frame heights ranging between 2705 to 3925mm adjusting to the different floor heights. The glazing panels were subdivided into three parts 775mm wide, with the central section having an openable side hung sash/vent and at the top of the frame a top hung sash/vent (Fig.9). The glazing was installed back to front to allow for installation from the inside and single glazed fixed with aluminium angle beads.[2] The windows' primary environmental design objective was to provide maximum natural daylight and ventilation (Fig.10).

The window design for the D10 follows Moritz Kahn's specification of being a fire proof steel sash, with sufficient ventilators. He preferred natural ventilation over a forced system (plenum) because of its feasibility and the increase of humidity associated with its use.[16] Albert Kahn also used natural ventilation via windows to good effect; indeed he was so confident in its performance that he used ventilated roof sashes as the main cooling strategy in the Ford Glass Plant (1927), where the furnaces reached nominal temperatures of 2500°C.[22] To reflect this, Williams encouraged natural ventilation via openable window sashes in the façade and slot ventilation in the roof (Fig. 9), and did not base his design on a ducted ventilation strategy.[2] The glass used in D10 on the façade was grouped together in three bands (Fig. 9), with clear glass in the centre and obscured above and below. Moritz Kahn stipulated this technique to be used whilst naturally daylighting a room via glazed windows, to diffuse the light, reduce glare and eye fatigue, and provide uniformity of light in deep spaces (Fig. 10). The middle pane was kept transparent to provide a view for the worker, which promoted well-being and happiness.[16] By installing the radiating heating pipes under the large windows of the façade (Fig. 9), Williams was improving thermal comfort via the steam heating system[2] to help combat the issues associated with large pane window design due to downdraft. This occurs when the warm internal air collides with the cold glass, cools and sinks, creating a convective current which causes discomfort due to the temperatures and air movement;[23] when the heating rails are placed under the glazing, the cold air is warmed (Fig. 10). This solution was suggested by Moritz Kahn, when he specified that there should be a well-designed heating system to combat heat loss via large windows during the winter. To regulate the thermal comfort for the confined worker at around 16°C, Kahn stipulated installing heating pipes at the base of the panes to take advantage of the incoming cold air and heat it.[16]

However, the glazed façade did suffer from environmental design issues. The original single glazing used suffered from condensation risks and large heat losses, resulting in the un- galvanised Crittal frame rusting and the damaged aluminium glazed beads being replaced with putty. The large pane windows, even with the obscured glazing, suffered from solar-overheating and glare problems. To help control this during the 1960s, projecting sun blinds were installed. These have since been replaced with double glazed neutral tinted windows, which were added in the 1990s.[2]

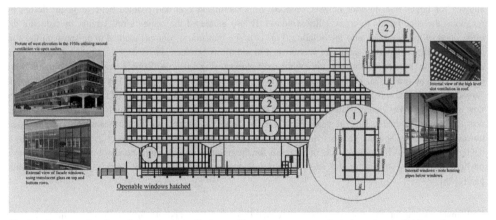

Fig 9.   Drawing detailing the original ventilation and heating strategy and window sizes on D10 south west elevation (drawing: Leatt).

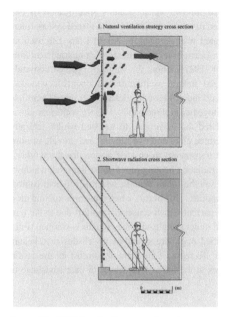

Fig. 10. Two cross section drawings of the D10 façade (drawing: Leatt)

Concrete slab & columns

Williams's use of specific reinforced concrete elements within the D10 benefited its daylight design. The factory's flat slab construction has an external thickness of 390mm and an internal thickness of 300mm. This allowed for larger floor-to-floor heights, reduced the construction cost and enabled better daylight design by removing the edge beams to create taller windows. It also increased the ceiling's reflectivity, by reducing the obstruction of light entering into the building (Fig. 10). The mushroom columns worked in unison with the slab and through their support, a cantilever was created to aid the weightless glazed façade, improving natural light and ventilation by not obstructing the ribbons of glazing (Fig. 10). Williams's mushroom columns were engineered to be spaced 7m x 9.563m apart, providing a column free area of 67m . They have been described as "broad inverted pyramids looking more like a thickening of the slab than a widening of the columns"[24] taking note of their larger top section designed to support the increased load from the slab. Primarily the column spacing was engineered to enable ease of adaptability for the factory's current and future manufacturing processes, however this larger spacing reduces the amount of physical obstructions for deeper penetration of natural daylight. Williams's choice of a white paint finish for the timber shuttered concrete also benefited the factory's daylight design, by increasing the internal light reflectance value from 0.25R (concrete) to 0.85R (white paint).[25]

Williams's vision for the use of reinforced concrete in the D10 and its further development to aid the manufacturing process to improve the daylight factory typology, was heavily influenced by the work he did in beginnings Truscon. The Kahns used a different system to Williams, the Hy-Rib (developed in 1909). This system's primary design function was to provide greater support for the heavier live loads placed on the upper storeys in hi-rise factories, which would need thicker floors and bigger columns to compensate without it. It

138

allowed for most of the load to be carried by intermediate beams and the hollow blocks for infill, in turn reducing the need for thicker columns.[26] However, the slab's thickness of around 750mm thick was reduced by over half in the D10, where Williams used a precast slab with rebar support, carried by his prominent concrete mushroom columns which were first used by Claude A P Turner, a railway engineer, in 1909.[27] The Kahn system usually laid out the column free area to create approximately 37m² of free space (50% less than Williams's system) for their multi storey factories.[2]. The columns were square, with long exposed reinforced concrete arches spanning from column to column and were used as an integral part of the façade.

For the floor heights, Moritz Kahn gave a rule of thumb for maximising daylight within a factory, stating that a theoretical factory of 18.3m in width should have a floor to ceiling height of 4.5m.[16] The D10 is approximately 200m long by 121m wide therefore, the equation $X = 121m \times 4.5m \div 18.3m$ calculates that the correct floor height to maximise daylight for the D10 should be 29.8m, but as the building is around 17m in height, this rule of thumb appears not to have been applied. Yet, Williams did follow Kahn's specification of using light coloured walls and white ceilings in the D10's design specification (Fig. 9), which exaggerated the importance of good natural lighting to improve the general health and the cheerfulness of workers.[16]

Concrete, as a key architectural element in the D10, has been used to great effect. Whilst designing the factory Williams was building upon the knowledge he learnt at Truscon and by using the mushroom column as a major structural element, he was embracing his early training as a railway engineer. The D10's dominant use of concrete as its primary material benefited its daylight factory design, by being flexible in its structural application, fire proof and providing the structural support of the factories iconic façade.

Conclusion

This paper has provided an overview of the daylight factory typology and how its specific principles were applied and built upon by Owen Williams's 'Wets' factory (D10). The fact that the building is still being used to manufacture pharmaceuticals nearly 100 years later (which was its original design purpose) is a testament to the selection of materials employed in its build and its flexible design. Yet, there have been issues with the ability to manage the factory's internal conditions via the glazed façade, which could have been better tackled if Williams had considered the building's orientation and the introduction of a shading strategy in the design phase. However, with modern day architecture's building management systems to illuminate, cool and heat a building and with the invention of double glazed window systems, Williams's design would have worked relatively well in its original form. Therefore, the D10's daylight design is an important reminder of the need to create commercial buildings that utilise their surroundings effectively to reduce energy consumption.

References

[1]   G. Stuff, *Building D10 at Boots Factory Site, Beeston Rylands, Nottinghamshire*, 2017. [online] Britishlistedbuildings.co.uk. Available at: https://www.britishlistedbuildings.co.uk/101247927-building-d10-at-boots-factory-site-broxtowe-borough-council-beeston-rylands-ward#.WgipG7p2scQ [Accessed 12 Nov. 2017].

[2]   D. Fawcett, K. Thornburrow, R. Fellows, D. Yeomans, P. Cooper, B. Mark and P. Hitchen, *Conservation Management Plan for the Boots "Wets" Factory D10. 1st ed.* Cambridge: Cambridge Architectural Research Ltd, 2011, pp. 1-5.

[3] S. Sanabria and K. Frampton, 'Studies in Tectonic Culture: The Poetics of Construction in Nineteenth and Twentieth Century Architecture', *Technology and Culture*, vol. 38, no. 4, 1997, p. 992.

[4] D. Yeomens and D. Cottam, *Owen Williams*. London: Thomas Telford Ltd., 2001.

[5] C. Meister, 'Albert Kahn's Partners in Industrial Architecture', *Journal of the Society of Architectural Historians*, vol. 72, no. 1, 2013, pp. 83-79.

[6] J. L. Kreager, Albert Kahn and the design of Angell Hall, *LSA Magazine*, (20-22), 1998, pp. 4-8.

[7] J. L. Mortensen, *Reclaiming the Daylight Factory: The Significance of Versatility in the Preservation of Early Twentieth Century Concrete Frame Industrial Buildings in Dayton, Ohio*. Thesis, University of Washington, 2015.

[8] A. Harrison and B. Hutchins, *A History of Factory Legislation*. Hoboken: Taylor and Francis, 2013.

[9] Legislation.gov.uk. (2017). Prescription Act 1832. [online] Available at: https://www.legislation.gov.uk/ukpga/Will4/2-3/71/section/3 [Accessed 27 Nov. 2017].

[10] A. Redgrave. *The Factory & Workshop Act. 1878*. 3rd ed. London: Shaw & Sons, 1878.

[11] Dol.gov. (2017). U.S. Department of Labor -- History -- 2. Factory Inspection Legislation. [online] Available at: https://www.dol.gov/dol/aboutdol/history/mono-regsafepart02.htm [Accessed 18 Nov. 2017].

[12] W. Osterhaus, *Office lighting: A Review of 80 years of Standards and Recommendations*. 1st ed., 1993. [ebook] California: Windows & daylighting group Building Technologies Program Energy and Environment Division Lawrence Berkely Labratory, pp.1-2. Available at: https://www.osti.gov/scitech/servlets/purl/10125246 [Accessed 12 Dec. 2017].

[13] T. Leslie, *Chicago Skyscrapers, 1871-1934*. 1st ed. Illinois: University of Illinois Press, 2013, p.36.

[14] M. Clausen, 'Frank Lloyd Wright, Vertical Space, and the Chicago School's Quest for Light', *Journal of the Society of Architectural Historians*, vol. 44, no. 1, 1985, pp. 66-74.

[15] M. Kahn, *The Design and Construction of Industrial Buildings*. 1st ed. London: Vacher & Sons Ltd, 1917, pp. 5, 19, 16, 23, 33.

[16] O. Williams, 'The Construction of the British Empire Exhibition', *Concrete and Constructional Engineering*, July 1924, pp. 421-432

[17] D. Neumann, '"The Century's Triumph in Lighting": The Luxfer Prism Companies and Their Contribution to Early Modern Architecture', *Journal of the Society of Architectural Historians*, vol. 54, no. 1, 1995 p. 24.

[18] 'Blown Glass Bricks for Building Purposes', *Scientific American*, vol. 76, no. 1, 1897, pp. 10-11.

[19] R. Fogelman, *Detroit's New Center*. Charleston, SC: Arcadia, 2004, p. 50.

[20] R. Matuz, *Albert Kahn: builder of Detroit*. 1st ed. Detroit: Great Lakes Books, 2002, p. 31.

[21] G. Hildebrand, 'Albert Kahn: The Second Industrial Revolution', *Perspecta*, vol. 15, 1975, pp. 32,34

[22] F. de Luis and M. Pérez-García, 'Parametric study of solar gains in saw-tooth roofs facing the equator', *Renewable Energy*, vol. 29, no. 8, 2004, p. 1223.

[23] L. Petermann, A. Menchaca and A. Love, 'Glazing design and thermal comfort: It's more than being cool', 2017. [online] Laboratory Design News. Available at: https://www.labdesignnews.com/article/2014/08/glazing-design-and-thermal-comfort-it's-more-being-cool [Accessed 17 Dec. 2017].

[24] D. Yeomans, *Construction since 1900: Materials*. London: Batsford, 1997, p. 124.

[25] R. Yarham, *Daylighting & Window Design - Lighting Guide LG10: 1999*. 1st ed. Dorchester: The Friary Press, 1999, p. 85.

[26] F. Sedlar, *Engineering Industrial Architecture. The Trussed Concrete Steel Company and Albert Kahn*, 2013, p. 20.

[27] A. kierdorf, 'Early Mushroom Slab Construction in Switzerland, Russia and the U.S.A. – A Study in Parallel Technological Development' in M. Dunkeld, J. Campbell, H. Louw, M. Tutton, W. Addis & R. Thorne (eds), *Proceedings of the Second International Congress on Construction History*, vol. 2, p. 1794.

Case Study: The Norris Cotton Federal Office Building

Kan Liang

Kent school of architecture, University of Kent, UK

Introduction

The Norris Cotton Federal Office Building, located in Manchester, New Hampshire, USA, was designed by Isaak and Isaak Architects Professional Association with a number of recommendations from NBS (National Bureau of Standards) and other architects. The building is located at an altitude of 104 m above sea level and is surrounded by some two-storey building and a high building located in the south. In 1972, the General Services Administration(GSA) assigned a contract to Nicholas Isaak hoping he could design a Federal office building. The design phase of this building began in 1973 and construction completed in 1976. This building is a 7-story government office building with about 11,000 m^2 total floor area. In 1970s, people were troubled by the oil crisis. Therefore, architects were aware that they need to develop a effective method to build a construction without high energy consumption. One of the measurements was applying some new energy-efficiency system. The figure 1 represents the climate data from 1977 to 1979 in Manchester, it showed that the range of temperature in this place was large so how to preserve heat was an important point in energy system design. The Norris Cotton Building as an experimental building played an important role in testing various energy-efficient systems. Moreover, The data of monitoring and analysis which majorly collected in the first three year after building accomplished would become an important reference for other similar building of 1970s. The immature energy-efficiency system as one of the special features in this building, which was combined with mini-computer, mechanism, solar and lighting system. Energy wastage could be decreased through operation of these system. And the performance of this building would be evaluated through energy consumption, user acceptance and cost analysis.

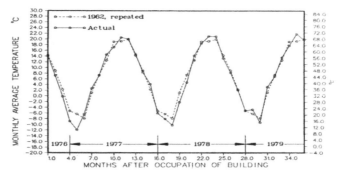

Figure 1. Average monthly outside air temperatures in Manchester [3]

Case Study: The Norris Cotton Federal Office Building

Background

The Norris Cotton Office Building was built in response to the oil crisis in the 1970s. In 1973, the OAPEC (Organization of Arab Petroleum Exporting Countries) declared oil export embargo because of dissatisfaction for the low oil price which became a serious bottleneck for the industrial society leading to higher demand of energy resources in an industrial economy.[1] As a result, some architects began to consider how to design a building with the low cost of energy. In 1976, a prototype energy-efficiency building was built in America, as an experimental programme to test the performance of different kinds of environmental technologies. During the period of the design phase, the NBS, as an organization established in 1901 while responsible for the design guidance of The Norris Cotton Office Building, was referred to a large number of specific recommendations which included the choice of mechanism system and design of the building from many architects with great experience, in order to gain the optimum methods. After the building completed in 1976, the NBS staff started to monitor the performance of The Norris Cotton Office Building during the period of the first three years [2]. The work of these staff involved not only analysis of energy consumption but also the research of effectiveness of various systems, the economic analysis of the building, operation situation of energy saving system and user acceptance for the building.

Due to the complexity of the mechanical system and the unconventional building details, the energy-efficiency design for performance was hard to be completely come true in 1970s (more detail will be showed in other section).[2] Therefore, selecting this building as a demonstration project for studying the effectiveness of energy-efficiency technologies and operation of a 1970s office building. While showing the firm commitment of the Federal Government to the energy conservation in the design, construction, and operation of Government buildings. If the performance of the energy-efficient system of the building was great, it might inspire architects and companies in the building industry to pursue energy conservation.

In general, a large types of useful information was offered by this building in the operation of heating, cooling and solar system, the analysis of the lighting system, economic analysis of the building, the degree of the user acceptance and some disadvantages. These content might improve development of energy-efficiency office building design after 1970s.

*NBS: (in the US) an organization, founded in 1901, whose function is to establish and maintain standards for units of measurements

Building elevation

A possibly small building surface of The Norris Cotton Office Building was achieved through making the shape of the building close to a cube. It could lower the building surface to volume ratio. The building was constructed of massive masonry and the thermal insulation covered with granite, the granite was mounted on the exterior wall outside with 30cm thick masonry blocks. Thus a thermal flywheel effect was established by this "inside-outside construction". It made the heat transfer coefficient (U value) of wall insulation reach $0.34W/m^2°C$.[3] One of the features of this building was that the window area just accounts for nearly 6 percentages of the entire building surface. Even the wall of the north building was designed without windows and the other walls of construction had the similar window area. Each window surrounded by overhangs and fins was equipped with double-glazed and adjustable louvers to adjust seasonal solar gain. The gap between two glazed was 3cm and includes some controllable louvers which could be adjusted depending on solar radiation and convection. It made the U value of windows arrive 3.3 W/㎡°C.[3] Meanwhile, the "open-plan" office without high ceiling walls between personal work area was implemented in this building. The experts thought that this unconventional office layout required less energy for lighting and operation while decreasing obviously cost of installation. Another reason was that this building might promote the development of the office building plan layout if it is successful.

Mini-computer data acquisition system

The Norris Cotton Building had two special systems which are the pneumatic system and the minicomputer system. The former acted as a part of control system while driving equipment. The latter could control building to select the model of the solar system, manage maintenance and monitor the performance of the critical devices. The performance of varies of energy production system could be combined to assign reasonable energy to the different part of building by the minicomputer system.

The minicomputer system was operated by a Johnson Controls JC-80/55 system. Its major task was monitoring and controlling the operation of equipment such as the selection of the solar system model and abnormality of the mechanical system, while acting as a data acquisition system(DAS).[3] Messages from computer, which could be used for analyzing operation of building and energy consumption condition, were obtained exactly by this smart system through sensors and loop remotes. Figure 2 showed the JC-80 system configuration. Each sensor of the instrumentation system linked to the computer by a loop remote which includes 50 point module cards. The building had total 19 loop remotes which had maximum link to 8 sensors. These loop remotes could convert the sensor analog signal to a digital value through the circuitry and the loop controller interrogates the loop remotes sequentially.[3]

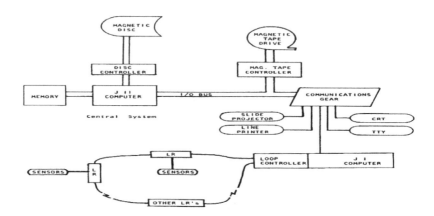

Figure 2. the JC-80 system configuration [6]

About every twenty seconds, the JC-80 central system scanned the system points. The amount of the sensor point values changed were collected in the central system 1/2-mega word magnetic disc storage which would convert the digital value from the loop controller to a digital number in engineering units through utilizing appropriate equations to the sensor type. Numerous software programs allowed the JC-80 to function as a DAS. One of the functions was the calculated point software that was applied for calculating point quantity and inputting to a specified equation. Some peripheral equipment was available such as a cathode ray tube terminal (CRT), line printer and teletypewriter (TTY) for the operator interface to the JC-80. Current values of system data points can be displayed and logged on the CRT, TTY or line printer, and the trend log would be operated to offer lists of system point values.[3] While DAS functions could be affected by the operators' interfaces. Points that were inputted to magnetic tape can be chosen and adjusted. In the 1970s, the computer control system had many limitations due to the immaturity of smart control technology. For example, the computer could only calculate the building energy requirement though inputted formula. It made the system limited as it could not timely adjust the energy assignment when some exceptional circumstances happened such as extreme climate and part of energy system failure. So this system needed to be monitored by some staff in order to change the computer calculated formula timely according to different situations. Nevertheless, It is difficult to deny that as an unconventional application in the 1970s building, the minicomputer system shows its potential of reducing energy consumption through monitoring operation of the energy system and distributing energy to a different part of the building.

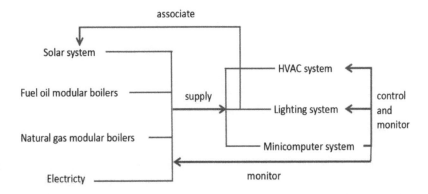

Figure 3. Connection of systems [3]

Mechanical system

The Norris Cotton Office Building's mechanical system or heating, ventilation and air conditioning (HVAC) system could be divided into two parts: the first three floors and the upper four floors. As an experimental building, the Norris Cotton Building still in a test stage in the mechanical system area, compared the effectiveness of two systems by decreasing complexity of energy supply net. In this building first three floors, a unitary water loop heat pump system includes 57 water-to-air pumps, was installed in building's ceiling and floor to serve these floors with a capacity of 350 kW for heating and 280 kW for cooling.[4] The thermal energy of the heat pumps was supplied by a closed water loop which acted as a heat sink for cooling. Meanwhile, the upper four floors were provided heating and cooling by some central systems. A hot water heating system was in charge of heating these floors. And the cooling system of the upper four floors operated through central chillers to offer chilled water which was driven by the pumps to a cooling coil or fan coil. The air without treating would be offered a mechanical device penthouse in order to promote ventilation and heating. However, even in winter, this building still generated excess energy because the evaluated heat needs of this building from the computer system were exaggerated high result in heating system which eventually generated a large amount of heat.[4] At that time, the conventional building usually removed the heated air through ventilation and air conditioning to outdoor, but the Norris Cotton Office Building used cool water to absorb excess heat for heating of perimeter units.

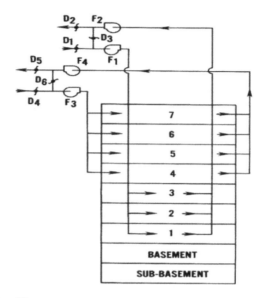

Figure 4. Ventilation system [1]

The Norris Cotton Office Building had two handing outside air systems which were the heat pump air system and the second air handling system. The former was used to supply ventilation to the first three floors by bringing outside air in. The air was transferred to the heat pumps which were installed on six floors before arriving the room of lower three floors to accomplish the heating and cooling. The latter was utilized for supplying ventilation air to the upper four floors. While a heat recovery system of this system could be used to preheat outside air by the energy generated from the exhaust air. The ventilating systems were operated with the outside air dampers, Dl and D4, closed to obtain nominal 100 percent recirculation while dampers D3 and D6 were open.[4] In addition to two other energy recovery measures were used in this building. One was to use condenser water from the chiller. The other was to operate a chiller to heat the water saved in the tanks for the hot water system.

Figure 4 showed the schematic of the energy conversion and supply equipment. It could be seen that this building consists of many energy conversion devices which can use electricity, gas, and oil to supply heated and cooled water for building water loops. The energy of the heat pump and hot water loops was provided by four 55 kW gas modular boilers and two 108 kW fuel oil modular boilers. The chilled water was provided by a 211 kW electric reciprocating chiller and an 88 kW hot water driven chiller. Meanwhile, a 150 kVA engine-generator which driven by natural gas was in charge of supplying electricity for the reciprocating chiller while the energy of heat recovery from the generator offers the absorption to the chiller.[3]

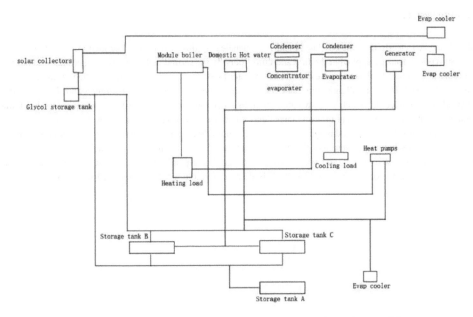

Figure 5. Schematic diagram of Norris Cotton Federal Office Building mechanical system [4]

Solar system

A 353 m solar liquid-type flat-plate collector inclined from 20 to 60 degrees was mounted on the roof. As a special feature in this building, the collector was settled at 60° from October to March and at 20° from April to September in order to gain possibly maximum solar energy.[4] Initially, a computer program was used to calculate the optimum degree of solar collectors and the staff of the Norris Cotton building had to change the angle of the collector for 8 times per year.[4] Then researchers found that the computer could not take the cost of operation of the account because it was just responsible for obtaining data and calculating which plan was the optimum option without considering the social elements. The adjustment of the solar panel could only be achieved by manpower because the system of automatically changing the panel's angle was not possible at that time. Later, researchers found that just adjusting the angle twice a year can acquire almost identical energy. Nevertheless, this measure confirmed one of the challenges of this system in the building was the cost of adjustment and complexity of tilting the arrays, however, the measure also could increase solar energy for space heating and the domestic hot water system. This solar system acted as a fluid collector and a heat exchanger between the collector loop and building solar storage loop in winter. In summer, the heat exchanger was ignored and the fluid collector works. The stored energy from the solar system could be saved in three 10 thousand gallon storage tanks, one of the tanks was used for chilled water storage tank in summer. Meanwhile, the energy provided by the solar system is supplied to the domestic hot water system. When the energy was not sufficient to support the operation of domestic hot water system, this system could gain thermal energy from natural gas storage. Due to the smoothing effects of masonry walls and thermal storage, the size of devices just needed to meet the size of the average load rather than the size of the peak load.

Lighting system

Table 1 showed clearly the types of lamps and lens installed on different floors. The identical luminaires with different types of lens are applied in the first and third floors. In the second and sixth floors, lighting system differ according to the number of windows and daylight. In order to avoid electricity wastage, the light used in the fifth floor is designed for only illuminating task areas. Three perimeter rows of lighting controlled by three independent photoelectric switch was switched on from outer rows to the inner rows if adequate daylight was available. Furthermore, 30 second time switches delay equipment was used in the lighting system. It could avoid too many switches in light when daylight levels change while reducing unnecessary energy consumption. One of the features of this lighting system was that the artificial lights could be turned off through the introductions of the minicomputer system if daylight was sufficient. As an "open-plan" lighting system, it provided practical illuminance data which could direct similar office building design on how to arrange the location of the lights to avoid similar problems.

Floor	Lamp Type	Lens Type
1	Fluorescent	Prismatic
2	Fluorescent (plus natural lighting and photocell control on perimeter)	Twin beam
3	Fluorescent	Polarized
4	High Pressure Sodium	Prismatic
5	Metal Halide and Fluorescent	Task-lit systems furniture
6	Fluorescent	Twin beam
7	Fluorescent	Prismatic

Table 1. Lighting Systems in the Norris Cotton Building [3]

Case Study: The Norris Cotton Federal Office Building

Performance

Energy consumption

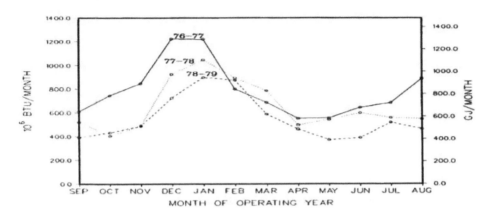

Figure 6. Total energy consumption of the Norris Cotton Building [3]

Year	Total energy used, MJ/m^2* (Btu/ft^2)*
September 76 – August 77	919 (80.6 x 10^3)
January 77 – December 77	813 (71.3 x 10^3)
September 77 – August 78	758 (66.5 x 10^3)
January 78 – December 78	730 (64.0 x 10^3)
April 78 – March 79	693 (60.8 x 10^3)
September 78 – August 79	641 (56.2 x 10^3)

* equivalent gross floor area = 10,900 m^2 (117,334 ft^2)

Table 2. Norris Cotton Federal Office Building annual energy consumption [3]

Total data of the Norris Cotton building energy consumption monitored by NBS in the first 3 years is showed in figure 6. It could be seen that the energy consumption of building decrease in different periods and the accurate data was given in table 2. A gratifying resulted from this table could be seen that for the third year the entire consumption reaches 178 kW·h/m² which was within 5 percent of the target of 176.6 kW·h/m².[3]

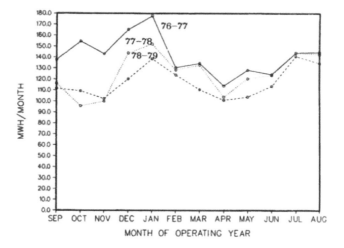

Figure 7. Electric energy consumption at this building [3]

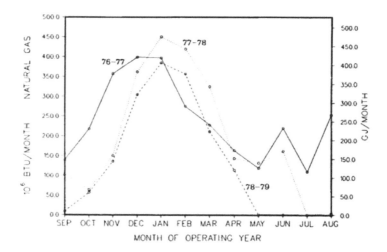

Figure 8.Natural gas consumption at this building [3]

From figure 7 and 8, it could be seen that electricity consumption decreases steadily from September to February but changes slightly in other months, and natural gas consumption reduced stably in first three years of operation. Nevertheless, the original goal of reducing at least 20 percent energy consumption was close to being fulfilled, the building was still not completely operating as expected. The design targets were not fully achieved in the performance of the building envelope and the operation of some mechanical devices. Actually, if some operating measures were not used in building then the there would be more energy saving.[5]

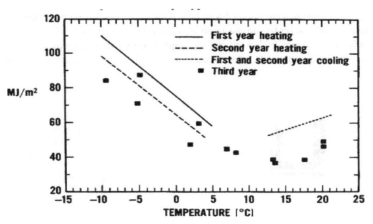

Figure 9. Gross Energy Consumption vs Outside Air Temperature [3]

The figure 9 showed that the relationship between gross energy consumption and outside air temperature in the first three years. It was clear that the energy consumption would increase from 5 to -10°C and from 12 to 21°C, and performance of energy consumption would become better due to the operation of the mechanical system that had been optimized after many corrections.

Problems

There were some typical problems in the first year after it's construction. For instance, high pump heating and cooling a space at the same time on the second floor and adjustments of mechanical systems. These problems were widespread in the new construction such as the operation of the solar systems, which hindered the building's cooling in the summer and reduced the air infiltration.[3] However, most of these problems were solved by monitoring. For example, during the winter 1976, the staff of the NBS found that the energy consumption was higher than the simulation from a computer while a number of occupants who worked near the outside walls felt unusually cold. Following the complaints made, the engineers investigated the heat and air leakage of this building. Investigations were carried out at night and on the inside because the temperature difference between inside and outside is big. The thermography device was utilized in this building to ensure whether some heat leaks happened in Norris Cotton building. At night, the outdoor temperature was about -7°C.[6] The staff sat up a temperature difference across walls and windows, which could differentiate between the two sides. Figure 10 showed the actual photo and the thermogram of the east wall on the first floor.[6] Depending on the difference between the two side dry-bulb temperatures and the insulation values of the window and wall, the concrete wall should be warmer than the window with several degrees. However, it was found from the figures that the wall temperature was close to the surface of the window temperature. A reason that may be explained why the inner and exterior walls were cold with undamaged insulation. The pressure within this building which was produced by a natural stack effect resulted in cool air to be drawn in the building through cracks, breathing holes and window frames, that may have been left open during construction, and researchers found that cold air flowed into the ceiling space. Therefore, people decided to survey the building using the findings from the wall temperature, thermograms, and qualitative examination that included simply feeling the walls and checking whether there were air leaks in the ceiling plenums. It was found that most of the exterior wall had the same problems and generally happened on the east and west walls. The problem was even found on the north wall that was designed without windows which could mean that the air possibly infiltrated the cavity space along with some different path than other three walls. Finally, according to the result of comparative survey from 1977, the air dampers were corrected to solve the problems of leakage and the construction's facade received extensive caulking. It is undeniable that the modification of the mechanical system plays an important role in reducing energy consumption.

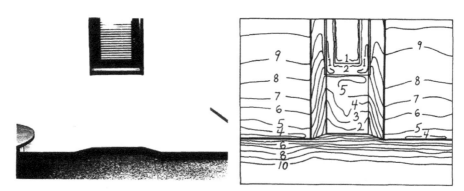

Figure 10. The thermogram of the east wall on the first floor [5]

User acceptance

The NBS workers collected occupants opinions of the Norris Cotton Building through two ways, one was selecting some agencies which worked at the building for interviews and the other was setting up two questionnaires which was handed out in different time intervals; firstly after the 6 months of occupancy and the other was utilized in 1977. Actually, the study plan focused on an examination of the relationships between the user's response data and physical data gained from sensors. However, the details of data were not available when the questionnaires were researched so the conclusions only could be obtained by investigating the subjective response data of the occupants.

The observations were made in August 1976, which involved employee reaction to their current environment and attitudes for the upcoming move in the Norris Cotton Building. Then in March 1977, the first questionnaire was distributed after the workers had experienced a winter in this building. Six months were sufficient for the occupants to realize the proper functioning of the mechanical systems of the building and ensuring whether the mechanical system operated correctly. A personal interview was conducted with the representatives explaining the objective of this questionnaire for the implementation of this survey. Each questionnaire was attached with a letter explaining about the project and anonymity was maintained. During the distribution of first questionnaire, a total of 292 questionnaires were handed out with each questionnaire containing 47 questions, out of which 75 percent were returned to the NBS. Likewise, the second questionnaire with similar questions was distributed in mid-November 1977.[1]

First Questionnaire (N=265)	Number	%	Second Questionnaire (N=213)	Number	%
Temperature	85	32	Temperature	105	49
Elevators	70	26	Elevators	39	18
Parking	48	18	Parking	37	17
Windows	47	18	Ventilation	31	14
Ventilation	45	17	Windows	26	12
Lack of cafeteria	35	13	Lighting	23	11
Heavy front doors	30	11	Lack of cafeteria	21	10
Lighting	29	11	Heavy front doors	16	7

First Questionnaire (N = 265)	Number	%	Second Questionnaire (N = 213)	Number	%
Location	55	21	Location	60	28
Appearance	38	14	Appearance	29	14
Newness	24	9	Newness	16	8
Cleanness	18	7	Lighting	15	7
Atmosphere	17	6	Atmosphere	13	6
Design	11	4	Cleanness	12	6

Likes   Dislikes

Table 3. Summary of occupants [5]

According to the table 3, it could be found that the occupants majorly favoured the location of the building, cleanness and lighting system. However, various dissatisfaction were also revealed from the response. The main problems pointed out were the following:

1. The temperature was considered to be too cold and too variable, which was mentioned before and had been solved.
2. The windows were too small and cannot provide adequate landscape.
3. The amount of ventilation was excessive during the summer and insufficient during the winter.
4. The lighting on the fourth floor distorted colours that led to annoying glare.

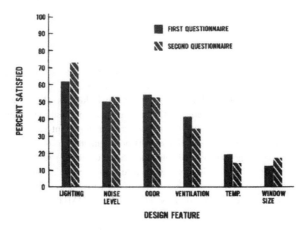

Figure 11. Satisfaction degree on different design features [5]

Figure 11 showed the people's satisfaction degree on different design features. It was found that the lighting was the most satisfactory design feature with an increase in satisfaction from 60 to 73 percent. To some extent, it could be guessed that the "open-plan" office have the positive effect on the performance of lighting. In contrast, the satisfaction of temperature and ventilation were low due to the air leakage problems which was later modified after the investigation. Another obvious problem was the size of the window. It was complained usually by occupants because more than 80 percent people thought that the windows were too small. Only no more than 20 percent of the respondents were satisfied with the size of the windows in two questionnaires. According to the detailed data, despite a slightly higher level of satisfaction for the window appeared on the second floor because it could provide a better view of outside, most of the users on this floor still thought the amount of the windows were insufficient.[7]

On the basis of the response of users, one critical question needed to be considered that is whether the comfort of the occupants is sacrificed to reach energy saving goal. Generally, the performance of the thermal comfort and the windows were less satisfied than other conventional office building but the lighting and noise environment better. The design features which occupants liked usually involved the way the building looks and dislikes are more happen in functions.[7] A similar result for the satisfaction of design features obtained in other studies. For instance, the lighting was the most satisfactory design features in their research.[7] Therefore, the dissatisfaction with design features should be treated objectively and not be excessively exaggerated.

In summary, the Norris Cotton Building did better in lighting and acoustics than other open-plan office buildings, but unfavorably in the size of windows and thermal environment. The users thought this building provided better suitability for their jobs but lower in comfort in comparison with the building they had worked before. Actually, it should be considered that the Norris Cotton Building was designed as an experimental building to test the energy conservation systems. Due to the experimental nature, this building was not expected to have a high-level satisfaction for its occupants. The objectives of the building evaluation research were to observe the energy efficiency of kinds of design alternatives and understand employee reaction for different environmental technologies. The architects and engineers could be assisted by the knowledge obtained from these research in designing environmental architecture with more comfortable environments for occupants.

Cost analysis

The purpose of the analysis was to test whether the additional construction cost caused by decreasing energy consumption can be adequately offset by the value of energy savings. Two buildings as examples which were used to compare with NCFOB were an Equivalent Conventional Building (ECB) and a Design Alternative Building (DAB). The first purpose of designing DAB was having a low cost with strict building standard. The construction and energy cost of these buildings were combined in a present value format to compare for the lifespan of 30 years. The construction costs of the ECB are estimated according to the 1969 GSA Design Handbook while its energy consumption cost was calculated by simulation.[5] And various of costs of DAB were simulated by computer. In general, a complete evaluation needed to take into account other costs such as costs of operation, maintenance and tax. Unfortunately, due to lack of these meaningful data, this analysis only based on the construction cost and annual energy costs of the NCFOB, ECB and DAB to evaluate.[5]

Table 4 shows the costs data for the NCFOB, ECB and DAB and table 5 simulated by computer represents present value costs and calculation of present value savings in 0 years, 15 years and 30 years. It is easy to find that resulting from strict design standard for DAB, it had an obvious advantage in performance for energy saving than NCFOB. It can be seen from table 5 that the construction cost of NCFOB was more than DAB $427,000, even more than ECB $327,000. Nevertheless, present value costs of ECB as a more meaningful reference would lower than NCFOB $141,000 in 30 years. And with the assumption made from figure 12, the discounted payback

153

period was considered to be about 12 years and later the NCFOB investment will lower than ECB. It was confirmed that the construction of the Norris Cotton Building not only could test various of energy conservation but also can reduce total investment compares with the conventional office building with a similar shape.

	NCFOB	ECB	DAB
construction costs	8,235,116	7,907,620	7,807,550
energy consumption10^6 Btu	7,250	12,250	6,961
cost of energy	91,003	141,375	76,964

Table 4. Costs of construction and energy for NCFOB, ECB and DAB [5]

BUILDING	LIFESPAN					
	0 Years		15 Years		30 Years	
	Cost	Saving	Cost	Saving	Cost	Saving
NCFOB	8235		8,916		9,088	
ECB	7908	(327)	8,962	46	9,229	141
DAB	7808	(427)	8,381	(535)	8,526	(562)

a/ Present value savings of the NCFOB over the ECB and DAB. Savings in parenthesis indicate negative savings, or more costly expenditures.

Table 5. Present value costs and calculation of present value saving ($1000) [5]

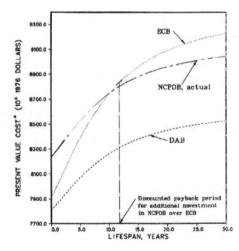

Figure 12. Present Value cost vs lifespan for NCFOB, ECB and DAB [5]

Refurbishment

Due to the Norris Cotton Building needed to develop to the next level in order to meet contemporary sustainability goals, a renovation construction contract for $13,388,000 was received by the Harvey Construction of Bedford in September 2004. Installing new windows and expanding the old ones were an essential task in this refurbishment. The goals of the renovation were conserving energy through the use of daylight, an energy efficient roof and expanding tenant space. Furthermore, in order to improve the energy efficiency of the building and reduce costs of the operation and maintenance, the previous mechanical systems were replaced with standardized systems. To some extent, these refurbishment measures alleviated the problem brought about by the too small size of windows.

Conclusion

In the first three years after the Norris Cotton Federal Office Building operated, NBS monitored the performance of various systems and collected a large amount of data that include users response and thermal leakage. According to these results, a number of conclusions can be obtained as follow:

1.It is possible to achieve the goals of energy consumption no more than 176.6 kW·h/m^2 per year in an office building designed for the northern climate. It is important for other places with similar climate because 176.6 kW·h/m^2 of energy consumption is less than normal office building consumption about 20 percents in the 1970s.

2.Most occupants were dissatisfied with the small windows in the building. The windows were also felt to be too small to provide a sufficient view, but this problem was modified in 2004 refurbishment. The size of building window as one of the serious problems affected occupants feeling. It makes other designers realize they should balance energy consumption and user feeling rather than just considering how to decrease building energy demand.

3.Designing an experimental building to compare the performance of kinds of energy efficient concepts is generally not compatible with a purpose of designing a building for energy saving because too many different environmental systems which are applied in this building will increase the entire mechanical system complexity and make it difficult to control. Actually, a successful and normal energy efficiency office building were more valuable in the 1970s, because the major function of this type of building was work rather than energy saving.

4.If some unusual construction situation appears in a similar building, it is important to pay attention to the thermal bridge and air leakage paths. The Norris Cotton Office building highlighted these potential problems and the corresponding solution were listed for future staff. It is helpful for architectures if they plan to design a more effective sustainable building.

5.Performance of thermal comfort was negative in the building. In addition, ventilation levels in this building were considerably high because engineers miscalculated ventilation required in different season. They overestimated the ventilation need in the building, but as an experimental building, some mistakes are unavoidable. The critical thing is to correct it in the later design.

6. The most positive design feature of the building from the user response was the lighting. As one of the factors which affects the performance is lighting, the"open-plan" office may be attempted in other office building design. According to the user acceptance data, this kind of the plane layout is likely to be accepted by the public and have a not bad effect.

7. According to the misjudgment on the angle change times of solar panels from the computer, it can be found that engineers not only should consider design parameters such as energy consumption and construction cost but also focus on maintenance cost, equipment replacement costs and so on. Applying computer system to monitor building to obtain a more adaptable operating way which was not possible in the 1970s. However, the success of the Norris Cotton Building points out the computer may be architect's right hand in the future.

8. The construction of the Norris Cotton Office Building was thought to be feasible because it was designed to replace a conventional office building. With the assumptions made from the computer simulation, the discounted payback period was around twelve years. In general, most of the purposes of design are accomplished.

References

[1] J. Elder & R. L. Tibbott, 'User acceptance of an energy-efficient office building: a study of the Norris Cotton Federal Office Building (No. DOE/PR/06010-T8)', *National Bureau of Standards, Washington, DC (USA)*. Center for Building Technology, 1981.

[2] W. B. May, 'Equivalent thermal parameters from measured data', *Batiment International, Building Research and Practice*, vol. 10, no. 6, 1982.

[3] J. E. Hill, W. B May Jr, T. E Richtmyer and C.M Hunt, 'Thermal performance of The Norris Cotton Federal Building in Manchester,New Hampshire', Proceedings of 'Thermal Performance Exterior Envelopes of Buildings Conference', Orlando, FL, Dec. 3-5, 1979. New York: American Society of Heating, Refrigeration and Air-Conditioning Engineers, 1981, pp. 781-797.

[4] W. B. May and L. G. Speilvogel, 'Analysis of computer-simulated thermal performance-the Norris Cotton Federal Office Building', *Ashrae journal-American society of heating refrigerating and air-conditioning engineers,* vol. 23, no. 7, 1981, pp. 43-50.

[5] J. E. Hill, W. B May Jr, T. E. Richtmyer, J. Elder, R. L. Tibbott, G. T Yonemura, C. M. Hunt, and P. T. Chen, 'Performance of the Norris Cotton Federal Office Building for the first 3 years of operation', NASA STI/Recon Technical Report N, 82, 1981.

[6] W. B. May, and L. G. Speilvogel, 'Analysis of Computer-Simulated Thermal Performance The Norris Cotton Federal Office Building', *Ashrae Journal-American Society of Heating Refrigerating and Air-Conditioning Engineers*, vol. 23, no. 7, 1981, pp.43-50.

[7] M. J. Brookes, 'Office landscape: Does it work?', *Applied Ergonomics*, vol. 3, no. 4, 1972, pp. 224-236.

[8] P. R. Boyce, 'Users' assessments of a landscaped office', *Journal of Architectural Research*, vol. 3, no. 3, 1974, pp. 44-62.

[9] B. Wolgers, 'Study of office environment — Attitudes to office landscapes and open-plan offices', *Build International,* vol. 6, no. 1, 1973, pp. 143-146.

The Drainage of the Fucine Lake in Antiquity and in the Nineteenth Century

Dermot O'Dwyer

Trinity College Dublin, Ireland

The draining of lake Fucino, (the Fucine lake, or lake Fucinus, of antiquity) has been achieved, or partially achieved, twice. First during the Roman era, when a scheme initially considered by Julius Caesar was implemented by Claudius and later repaired by the emperors Trajan and Hadrian, and more recently in the nineteenth century when the lake was finally drained successfully. The lake was the largest lake in central or southern Italy. It was elliptical in shape, 20 kilometres long and 11 kilometres wide and was completely enclosed by mountains so that the level of the lake fluctuated whenever the rates of precipitation and evaporation were dissimilar.

The original drainage works were described by Pliny the Elder, Suetonius, Tacitus and Cassius Dio. Their accounts generally agree and record that a total of thirty thousand workers were involved for a period of eleven years. The key element of this work was the construction of a tunnel 5.6 km long under Campi Palentine and Mount Salviano. This tunnel involved sinking about forty vertical shafts of up to a maximum depth of 122 metres. The tunnel carried a channel with an average inclination of 1½ in 1000. The scheme was well designed but poorly implemented. Subsequent repairs by Trajan and Hadrian allowed the partial drainage of the lake.

The successful nineteenth-century drainage works followed the line of the original Roman Tunnel and during these works an accurate picture of the original Roman construction was developed. These findings supported the accounts of the Roman historians and give valuable details of Roman tunnel and hydraulic construction practice.

The successful nineteenth-century drainage was undertaken by Prince Alexander Torlonia between 1854 and 1876. These works, which comprise the Torlonia tunnel and the water collection canals used to drain the lake, are described in this paper. The English Civil Engineers William Parker and Charles Hutton Gregory were involved in the project at an early stage but the detailed design was carried out by M. De Montricher assisted by M. Henri Bermont and M. Alexander Brisse.

Introduction

The Fucine lake, lake Fucino, was the third largest lake in Italy (Fig. 1). It was located in the Apennines 80 kilometres due east of Rome. Julius Caesar had been approached by the Marsi, the inhabitants of the shore of the lake, with a view to draining it but he was assassinated before a decision was made. However, Emperor Claudius undertook the drainage of the lake between 41 CE and 52 CE. This initial drainage was only partially successful. Claudius's works were not repaired or maintained by his immediate successors but there are records and evidence that the Emperors Trajan and Hadrian re-established the drainage.[1]

The Drainage of the Fucine Lake in Antiquity and in the Nineteenth Century

Figure 1. Panorama of the lake Fucino [2].

By the time the Roman Empire collapsed it is clear that the drainage works were defunct. There are accounts of attempts to repair the Roman system but it was not until the nineteenth century that serious progress was made in draining the lake. The first nineteenth-century attempt was by Afan de Rivera. This attempt resulted in the reopening of the original Roman system. However, the resulting flow through the Roman works seems to have resulted in the fresh, and more complete, failure of the tunnel in certain locations. However, in the middle of the nineteenth century Prince Torlonia undertook to drain the lake, a task he achieved. This was a mammoth and costly feat of engineering very deserving of attention in its own right, the cost in sterling was estimated to have been £1,800,000.[3] However, the focus of this paper is on the extensive information that was gathered on the earlier Roman constructions during the excavations of Prince Torlonia. Much of the detailed material presented in this paper has been taken from the account of the Torlonia drainage scheme written by Brisse and De Rotrou.[2]

Although the authors of this work stress that Prince Torlonia's primary incentive to drain Lake Fucino was civic, it is fair to observe that both the Prince and Claudius anticipated that the fertile land that would become available when the lake was drained would pay for the cost of the drainage works.

It is also appropriate to point out that although Claudius's drainage scheme was flawed, the almost 6 km long tunnel the Romans dug under Mount Salviano was the longest tunnel in the world until it was surpassed by the 12.8 kilometre long Mount Cenis Tunnel, which opened in 1871. Claudius's drainage works were probably the most ambitious engineering works of the Roman Empire. The scale of their achievement is only apparent when one reads the account of the difficulties overcome by the nineteenth-century engineers, and these engineers made extensive use of the Roman tunnels, shafts and galleries as part of their works.

Drainage works and tunnelling in the ancient world

Qanats, which comprise underground tunnels dug to bring water from a location where the water table is higher to an arid region, are still in use today.[4] They are believed to have been developed by the Persians and were well know in classical antiquity. The best known Greek tunnel was Eupalinos's tunnel under mount Kastro. Herodotus describes this tunnel in some detail and made a point of the fact that it had been dug from both ends,

> The Samians...dug a tunnel through a 900-foot-high mountain [Mount Kastro]; it is 4,080 feet long and 8 feet high and wide. Another channel, 30 feet deep and 3 feet wide, was dug along the entire length of the tunnel, into which

water is sent through pipes directly into the [walled] city of Samos from a huge spring. The builder in charge of designing and excavating this tunnel was a Megarian, Eupalinos son of Naustrophos. [5]

This work was constructed nearly six hundred years before Claudius's tunnel. This tunnel survives and numerous authors have described, often with photographs, the slight misalignment where the two tunnels meet.[4,5]

If a tunnel is not through a mountain that prevents a clear line of sight the horizontal alignment of a tunnel can be laid out on the surface. In such cases vertical shafts can be then be sunk from the surface and the tunnel dug from the base of each shaft. Figure 2 is a medieval illustration taken from Agricola's De Re Metalica showing the alignment of a tunnel.[6] However, where the tunnel is being dug through a mountain and where the tunnelling is to be commenced from opposite ends more sophisticated surveying procedures are necessary.

Figure 2. Alignment of a tunnel, from De Re Metalica [6].

The Eupalinos's tunnel was constructed in the sixth century BCE and as early as 396 BCE Roman engineers, perhaps using Etruscan technology, had dug an emissary to control flooding of Lake Albano.[8,9] Thus the surveying and tunnelling methods used to construct the Fucine tunnel were long established by the time of Claudius. Hero of Alexandria's work on surveying instruments, which was contemporaneous with the Fucine tunnel, describes the dioptra, which was akin to a theodolite and which could measure horizontal and vertical angles, as the appropriate instrument for setting out the alignment of a tunnel. [10,11] However, Vitruvius writing at approximately the same time proposes the chorobates as a better instrument for accurate levelling.[12]

However, the chorobates was a bulky instrument and many modern authors have questioned its potential accuracy. [11,13,14,15].

Tunnelling, particularly where watercourses are involved, would have required the builders to calculate levels accurately. Before the Roman emissary could have been planned a detailed levelling survey must have been undertaken so the levels of the lake bed, the river Liris, which the tunnel drained into, would need to have been known. Similarly, before the tunnelling, which commenced from the outflow, could have begun the level of the emissary's intake and the length of the tunnel would need to have been calculated and its inclination selected.

Works of Claudius 41 to 54 CE

Ancient sources

The earliest source of information on the draining of the Fucine lake is Pliny the Elder in his Histories, (Latin: Naturalis Historia) an encyclopaedic treatment of all knowledge.[16] Pliny the Elder, born Gaius Plinius Secundus, 23–79 CE, began his Natural History in 77 CE. Pliny refers to Claudius's works to drain the Fucine lake as follows,

> One of the most remarkable feats of Claudius, neglected by his successor [Nero], who hated him, is, in my opinion at least, the channel that he dug through a mountain to drain the Fucine Lake. This involved incalculable expense and the employment of an army of labourers over a period of many years, because where the inside of the mountain was earthy, the spoil had to be raised to the surface by hoists, and elsewhere bedrock had to be hewn away. These immense operations had to be carried out in darkness – operations imaginable only by those who saw them and which are beyond the power of words to describe. Book XXXVI.124

Most subsequent writers take this passage to imply that Pliny saw the workings. This view is consistent with the evidence of his curiosity. Pliny died, famously, during the eruption of Mount Vesuvius that destroyed Pompeii in 79 CE. The account offered by his nephew, Pliny the Younger, describes him taking a vessel across the Bay of Naples to observe the eruption more directly. He then went to the rescue of friends in Herculaneum but was caught in the eruption and died as a result of inhaling poisonous fumes.

Publius, or Gaius, Cornelius Tacitus c.56–c.120 CE, Senator and historian provides an account of the tunnel in his Annals [16]:

> ...About the same time [52 CE], the mountain between Lake Fucinus and the river Liris was bored through, and that this grand work might be seen by a multitude of visitors, preparations were made for a naval battle on the lake...When the sight was over, the outlet of the water was opened. The careless execution of the work was apparent, the tunnel not having been bored down so low as the bottom, or middle of the lake. Consequently after an interval the excavations were deepened and to attract a crowd once more, a show of gladiators was exhibited, with floating pontoons for an infantry engagement. A banquet too was prepared close to the outflow of the lake, and it was the means of greatly alarming the whole company, for the water, in the violence of its outburst, swept away the adjoining parts, shook the more remote, and spread terror with the tremendous crash. At the same time, Agrippina availed herself of the emperor's fright to charge Narcissus, who had been the agent of the work, with avarice and peculation. He too was not silent, but inveighed against the domineering temper of her sex, and her extravagant ambition. Book XII.56–57

A contemporary of Tacitus, Gaius Suetonius Tranquillus 69–c.122 CE provides an account of the tunnel and its opening in his work The Twelve Caesars, which is taken to have been written in 121 CE.[17]

> Claudius' public works, though not numerous were important. The included, in particular, an aqueduct begun by Gaius; the draining of the Fucine Lake and the building of the harbour at Ostia – though he knew that Augustus had turned down the Marsians' frequent requests for emptying the Lake....

> He [Claduius] undertook the Fucine drainage scheme as much for profit as for glory: a group of business men had offered to shoulder the expense if he awarded them the reclaimed land. The outlet took eleven years to dig, although 30,000 men were kept continuously at work; it was three miles long, and his engineers had to level part of a hill and tunnel though the remainder. Claudius.20

One must be careful when reading any translated work, particularly when the topic is of a technical nature because the translator is unlikely to be familiar with the technical concepts. As an example, consider the passage below, which is from a different translation of Seutonius.[18]

> After eleven years, partly by digging a canal, partly by tunnelling through the mountain, he finished the project with difficulty, even though 30,000 workers were employed continuously, without a break... Claudius.20

In this case the translator has technical expertise but appears to be working from a slightly different copy of Seutonius's work because there is no reference to the length of the tunnel. The translator's choice of the word "canal" in the translation is probably more accurate than the phrase "level part of a hill" from the first translation. However, a detailed review of the physical evidence unearthed by the Torlonia works might suggest the word "channel". Neither Seutonius nor Tacitus were construction experts and both were recounting events that had happened fifty years previously. Both authors give a more detail to the mock sea-battle (naumachia) than to the emissary, understandable perhaps, given the theatrical intervention by Claudius and the silver Triton that rose from the lake and blew a horn to announce the commencement of the fight. However, these accounts differ in the number of the combatants who took part.

The final substantial mention of Claudius's tunnel is by Cassius Dio, c.155–235 CE, who was a Roman statesman and historian of Greek origin.

> He gave many splendid banquets, usually in large halls, and at times invited no fewer than 600 guests. One banquet was held close to the debouchment of the Fucine Lake on the day it was emptied; but the water came rushing out in a deluge and almost drowned him...

> When the Fucine Lake caved in, Narcissus was severely blamed for it. For he had been in charge of the undertaking, and it was thought that after spending a good deal less than he had received he had then purposely contrived the collapse, in order that his wrong-doing might not be detected.

> He furthermore desired to make an outlet into the Liris for the Fucine Lake in the Marsian country, in order not only that the land around it might be tilled but also that the river might be made more navigable. But the money was expended in vain.

The Drainage of the Fucine Lake in Antiquity and in the Nineteenth Century

Existing Evidence

The key source is the account of the Prince Torlonia works because it details the Roman construction as uncovered in the course of the Torlonian excavations. The nineteenth century engineers made extensive use of both the original Roman vertical shafts and the inclined galleries and also followed the line of the original tunnel in the main and incorporated the original tunnel within their excavation where possible. This would have made their task much easier in many sections. Afan de Rivera had established that the Romans had succeeded in boring a tunnel under the Campi Palentine and Mount Salvino between the Liris and the lake. The Torlonia account records the Roman construction in detail and attempts to reconcile the tunnel, the lake outflow works and the Roman drainage canals with the existing original textual sources. They are very successful in this endeavour but one must always be cautious: there is natural tendency to interpret the evidence to support the ancient narrative. Thus, is it tempting and perhaps correct to see the evidence of the remodelling of tunnel entry as confirmation of Suetonius's and Tacitus's accounts. Similarly, the disparity between to overall planning of the drainage tunnel and the sometimes shoddy execution has been interpreted as evidence that Agrippina's accusation of Narcissus's misbehaviour was well founded.

The most interesting evidence reported is of the later drainage canals or ditches that Brisse and De Rotrou ascribe to Trajan and Hadrian. These remains suggest that the drainage system functioned to some extent in antiquity because there would have been no need to increase the extent of the drainage network into the lake bed unless the level of the lake had been dropped.

Construction of Tunnel

Figure 3 shows the cross-section of the Roman tunnel as revealed during the excavation. However, this ideal cross-section was not achieved in many sections of the Roman tunnel. The ideal section comprised a rectangle 1.8 metres wide by 2.1 metres tall topped with a semi-circular roof vault, giving a maximum height of 3 metres. The invert, vaulted roof and sides were of Roman concrete and the sides were lined with brick.

Overall, the tunnel was designed to have an average inclination of 0.15% or 1½ in 1000. However, there were sections of the tunnel that had a slope of 0.1% and sections where the tunnel slight slope was in the wrong direction.

The nineteenth-century works followed the original Roman tunnel and made use of the Romans' vertical shafts and inclined galleries. In some cases these needed some re-excavation and thus the nineteenth-century engineers unearthed the details of a timber-lined shaft some eighteen-hundred years after its original construction. This shaft was one of those in the Campi Palentine that had been sunk through soil. The shaft was 4.32 metres square and was subdivided into four 1.8 metre by 1.8 metre squares.

Figure 4 shows a longitudinal section of the tunnel under the Campi Palentine and Mount Salviano, taken from Brisse and De Rotrou.[2] This section shows both the original Roman emissary and the enlarged Prince Torlonia works. The vertical shafts shown are the original Roman shafts. These were used and where necessary reopened as part of the nineteenth-century works. The vertical scale is 1:1,000 while the horizontal scale is 1:20,000. Thus the vertical scale is twenty times the horizontal scale and as a result the inclined galleries shown on the section look more like vertical shafts. The section shows all the vertical shafts however, only a few of the most important galleries, or cuniculo, are shown. These include some of the galleries that penetrated beneath the summit of the mountain. The distance between shaft No. 22 and shaft No. 23, which are on opposite sides of Mount Salviano, was 889.72 metres.

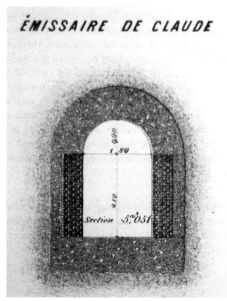

Figure 3. Section through the Claudian emissary [2].

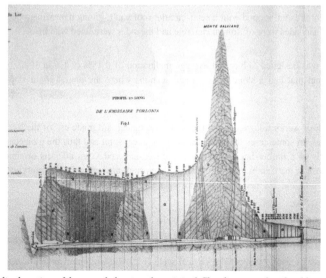

Figure 4. Longitudinal section of the tunnel showing the original Claudian tunnel with additional nineteenth century tunnelling works [2].

The Drainage of the Fucine Lake in Antiquity and in the Nineteenth Century

The galleries were often in the same vertical plane and in one case three galleries intersected a shaft at different heights. These galleries were important for ventilation and were used to remove excavated material in some locations. Brisse and De Rotrou surmise, from the presence of shunting points in some of the galleries, that excavated material was removed by hand cart.

Fucine relief showing two two-man vertical capstans

A number of Roman artefacts were found during the nineteenth-century workings. Perhaps the most significant artefact from the viewpoint of the tunnel was a relief that shows two vertical capstans.[12,19] Each capstan is worked by two men pushing on the ends of horizontal bars causing a drum, which may be formed by vertical bars in a manner similar to that shown by Jean-Pierre Adam. The vertical drum has two ropes wound around it in opposite directions in such a manner that, as one rope descends, being wound off the drum, the other is wound on and ascends. The presence of two such capstans in proximity, when taken in conjunction with the four cells of the vertical shafts has been interpreted as implying that two capstans worked each shaft with two buckets ascending and two buckets descending at any time. The workers also recovered a cylindro-conical bucket made of copper with hoops of soft iron. The bucked had a capacity of 40 litres. However, the bucket reported by Brisse and De Rotrou may be that preserved in the Torlonia collection, which has subsequently been dated to the medieval period.[19]

The relief of the capstan is illustrative only. It may have been worked by more than two people and it would not be sensible to assume that the lengths of the capstan bars and drum diameter are to scale. However, a very useful calculation can be performed without reference to the mechanical advantage of the hoist system. Regardless of the details of the mechanism work is being done. The power, or rate at which work is required to be done, can be calculated from the equation;

$$Power = \frac{Work}{Time} = \frac{Force \times Distance}{Time} = \frac{Mass \times g \times Distance}{Time}$$

A person working at approximately one fifth of a horsepower, which in practice might only be achieved for a short time, expends about 150 watts. This facilitates calculating an upper estimate of the total daily amount of work required. If the work is expended in lifting mass through a vertical height then one can easily estimate the mass a labourer could lift per day for a given height. For a height of 120 metres, which is close to the depth of the deepest shaft, this equates to approximately 11 tonnes in if the hoist is perfectly efficient.

$$\frac{150\,watts \times (60s \times 60min \times 24h)}{g \times 120m} = 11\,tonnes\,with\,100\%\,efficiency$$

This calculation is equally valid for earth moved in hand carts rolled up an inclined gallery or any other mechanical system. Naturally no one can work with one hundred percent efficiency twenty-four hours a day and all mechanisms have losses. In comparison with the Roman workforce of 30,000, the Prince Torlonia works used 2,000 workers.

The double rope detail makes considerable sense. With a deep shaft the weight of 100 metres of rope could be in excess of fifteen kilograms, which would significantly reduce the quantity of material that could be excavated with each lift. The double rope arrangement meant that the weights of the ascending and descending ropes cancel, and all the effort of the workers goes into lifting excavated material.

Figure 5 shows a diagram from Agricola's *De Re Metalica*, the earliest medieval treatise on mining (Fig. 5). The details of the timber shoring on the vertical shaft is broadly similar to that used by the Romans and the horizontal windlass, which lifts one rope while dropping a second, is similar in operation to the Roman capstan.

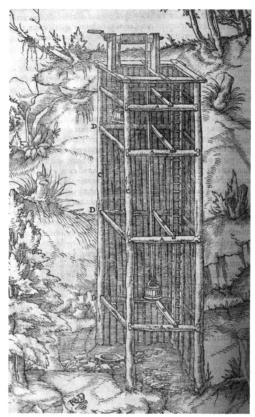

Figure 5. Windlass detail from De Re Metalica [6].

Works by Prince Torlonia

There are accounts of different attempts to re-establish the Roman emissary during the medieval and renaissance periods. Including one attempt by Domenico Fontana the architect and engineer to Pope Sixtus V who wrote an account of the movement of the Obelisk to the centre of St. Peter's square. Fontana's attempt was thwarted by the high level of the lake at the time. However, between 1824 and 1835 Afan de Rivera, working during a period when the level of the lake was low, was able to re-establish the Roman emissary and the tunnel was opened from end-to-end. Afan de Rivera's funding had been piecemeal and his work included temporary propping of sections of the Roman tunnel. Unfortunately, his work was not followed up directly and the subsequent rise in the level of the lake led to the inundation of the tunnel and the failure of the temporary works, leaving the tunnel in a condition as bad, or worse, than it had been prior to his intervention.

The Drainage of the Fucine Lake in Antiquity and in the Nineteenth Century

Eventually, a company was established to drain the lake. An early condition imposed by English capitalists involved in the project was that English engineers should be employed to draw up plans. As a result Charles Hutton Gregory and William Parker carried out some initial works and prepared a plan. The hydrological information required for such a project was absent and they had to extrapolate from very limited data. Prince Torlonia, who had originally purchased half of the shares in the company, realised that the manner in which the project was progressing meant that it was likely to fail and therefore he bought out the company and took sole control of the enterprise. He then engaged the French engineer Frantz Mayor de Montricher, who was the designer of the canal to convey water from the Durance to Marseilles, to take responsibility for the design of the new drainage works.

The new tunnel was designed to have a capacity of 50 cubic meters per second, whereas the original Roman design might have accommodated a flow of 16 cubic meters per second. In justice to the Roman scheme it is unlikely that the Romans intended the complete drainage of the lake and the evapo-transpiration regime in Roman times, when the surrounding hills were heavily forested, would have been different. The cross-section chosen for the new tunnel is shown in Figure 6.

This section is not only substantially larger but the plan was to increase the slope of the tunnel. Figure 7 shows both how the Roman emissary was incorporated along the new tunnel's length and the approximate condition of the Roman tunnel at different locations.

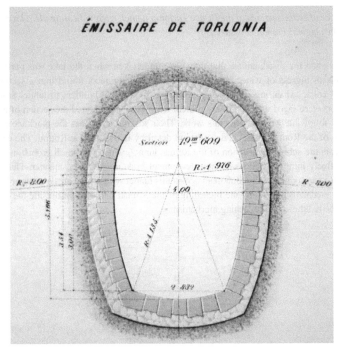

Figure 6. The cross-section of the nineteenth century tunnel [2].

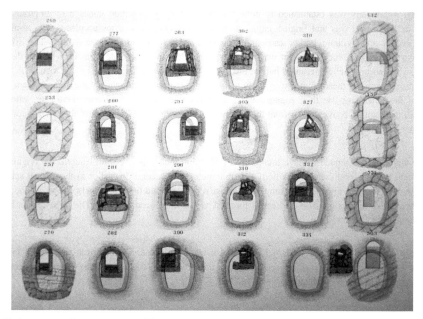

Figure 7. A sequence of cross-sections of the Prince Torlonia tunnel, each indicating the relative size, position and condition of the original Roman emissary [2].

The Torlonia works had the disadvantage that they were undertaken when the lake was particularly high. This added to the levels of ingress of water into the workings. The engineers found that a section of the original Roman works had collapsed during construction requiring the original builders to tunnel around the collapse. Torlonia's engineers were faced with a similar problem when they encountered the section of the Roman Tunnel that had collapsed following Afan de Rivera's work. Their scheme to bypass the blockage and break into the submerged section of the Roman tunnel is described in detail by Brisse and De Rotrou. The engineers could not allow the water from the submerged section of the Roman tunnel, which was in all probability still connected to the lake, to drain freely into the sections of their new tunnel in an uncontrolled manner. Thus they excavated a tunnel below the Roman tunnel, built a bulkhead across this tunnel with a pipe outflow controlled by a valve and organised a clever mechanism to allow the breaching of the Roman tunnel from outside the bulkhead. Figure 8 shows a detail of the bulkhead and breaching mechanism.

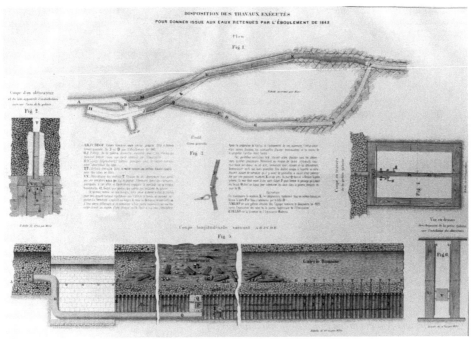

Figure 8. Showing the method adopted to bypass the collapse of the Roman emissary [2].

Once the submerged Roman tunnel had been breached the water was allowed to flow from the tunnel and the lake until the level of the lake had dropped. Tunnelling works were suspended during this drainage but once the level of the lake had been reduced the tunnelling restarted with a much lower rate of ingress of water. In addition to the tunnelling works the Torlonia project required the construction of an extensive network of drainage channels. The length of time taken for the actual excavation of the new tunnel was nine years eleven months.

Conclusion

The draining of the Fucine lake was a considerable enterprise for both the original Roman engineers, whose attempts were probably only partially successful, and for the nineteenth-century engineers of Prince Torlonia. Both sets of works deserve to be more widely known. The account Brisse and De Rotrou is particularly useful in that it gives valuable, accurate information about the original Roman emissary. Although the techniques used by the Romans had been demonstrated in earlier Greek works and in the Roman drainage of lake Albino, the scale of the Claudian tunnel emphasises the level of expertise and resources that could be mobilised by the Roman Empire.

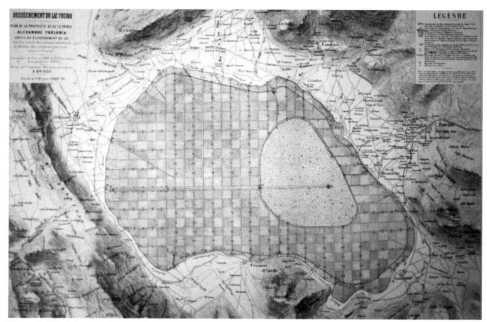

Figure 9. The lake post the initial Prince Torlonia drainage [2].

Satellite images of the lake today show that it was been drained completely. The drainage of Lake Fucino by Prince Torlonia reclaimed over 37,000 acres of land.

References:

[1] R. Shelton Kirby et al., *Engineering in History*. Dover Publications Inc., New York, 1990.

[2] A. Brisse and L. De Rotrou, *The Draining of Lake Fucino Accomplished by his Excellency Prince Alexander Torlonia: An Abridged Account Historical and Technical by Messrs Alesander Brisse, Engineer in Chief of the Draining and Leon De Rotrou, Late Chief Resident of the Administration, English Translation by V. De Jivoli, Jun.,* Propaganda Press, Rome, 1876.

[3] 'The Drainage of Lake Fucino, by A. Brisse and L. De Rotrou', *Minutes of Proceedings of the Institution of Civil Engineers; Abstracts of Papers in Foreign Transactions, etc.,* Vol. 51, 1878. pp 367-371.

[4] D. Parry, Engineering the Ancient World, Sutton Publishing, 2005.

[5] R.B. Strassler (Ed.), *The Landmark Herodotus the Histories: A New Translation by Andrea L. Purvis, Introduction by Rosalind Thomas,* Quercus, London, 2008.

[6] G. Agricolae, *De Re Metalica, 2nd* ed., Hieronymus Froben & Nicolaus Episcopius, Basil, 1561.

[7] J.P. Oleson (Ed.), *The Oxford Handbook of Engineering and Technology in the Classical World,* Oxford University Press, Oxford, 2008.

[8] E. Cresy, *An Encyclopaedia of Civil Engineering: Historical, Theoretical,* and *Practical (Volume 1): Facsimile of Volume 1 of 1861 edition.* Thomas Telford, London, 2010

[9] A. Burns, 'The Tunnel of Eupalinus and the Tunnel Problem of Hero of Alexandria', *Isis,* Vol. 62, No. 2, 1971, pp. 172-185

[10] Vitruvius, *The Ten Books on Architecture; Translated by Morris Hickey Morgan,* Dover Publications, Inc., New York, 1960 (Harvard University Press 1914).

[11] J.J. Coulton, 'The Dioptra of Heron of Alexandria', *Science and mathematics in ancient Greek culture,* C.J. Tuplin and T.E. Rihll (Eds.), Oxford University Press, Oxford, 2002, pp. 150-164.

[12] J.P. Adam, *Roman Building: Materials and Techniques, Translated by Anthony Mathews,* B.T. Batsford Ltd, London, 1994.

[13] M.J.T. Lewis, Surveying Instruments of Greece and Rome, Cambridge University Press, Cambridge, 2001.

[14] W.B. Parsons, *Engineers and Engineering in the Renaissance*, The M.I.T. Press, London, 1968.

[15] Pliny the Elder, *Natural History: A Selection, Pliny the Elder, Translated with an Introduction and notes by John F. Healy,* Penguin Classics, London, 2004.

[16] Tacitus, Annals, *Histories, Agricola, Germania, Translated by Alfred John Church and William Jackson Brodribb with an Introduction by Robin Lane Fox, Notes revised by Eleanor Cowan,* Everyman Library, London, 2009.

[17] G. Suetonius, *The Twelve Caesars: Translated by Robert Graves, Revised with an Introduction by Michael Grant,* Penguin Books, London, 1978.

[18] J.W. Humphrey, J.P. Oleson and A.N. Sherwood, *Greek and Roman Technology: A Sourcebook, Annotated translations of Greek and Latin texts and Documents,* Routledge, London, 1998.

[19] A. Campanelli, *Il Tesoro Del Lago: L'Archeologia Del Fucino E La Collezione Torlonia,* Carsa Edizioni, 2001.

Understanding Preservation and Comfort in the British Museum Reading Room

Surabhi Pandurangi

Kent School of Architecture, University of Kent, UK

Introduction

The British Museum underwent significant changes throughout the nineteenth century. The museum had housed two galleries dedicated to books. The King's library on the east and the Library of the printed books on the North. With the Public Library Act and the great acquisition in 1850, the trustees decided for the enlargement of the building to accommodate additional books and people.[1] This paper retracing the design development of the British Library Reading Room with a focus on environmental technologies. The context of the paper being nineteenth-century public libraries, the study concentrates on the design interventions which were carried out keeping preservation and comfort in mind. This involves examining new construction materials and methods which facilitated preservation, re-visiting the historical ventilation and heating system, comprehend the evolution of lighting and its implications on the people's perception of the space. In a larger framework, the study identifies the importance of collaboration between the Architect, the Librarian and the Engineer.

Background

The British Museum had displayed itself in a constant state of transformation from year to year in the nineteenth century.[2] It was designed and built as a hollow rectangular space with an indented parallelogram enclosed by galleries all around.[2] The original intention of the existing library block was '*reference only*' library and was said to be 'chiefly designed for the use of the learned and studious men' by the trustees.[3] However, after 1850 the state of the library had changed rapidly.

Antonio Panizzi became the keeper of the printed books in 1837.[3] He played a crucial role in bringing clarity to the concept of special functions associated with the national library. Kelly Thomas in his book describes that a combination of government grants and strict enforcement of the Law of Copyright Deposit led Panizzi to successfully increase the stock of the library by nearly three quarter million books.[4] This led the then Principal Librarian of the Museum to write a letter to the Secretary of the Treasury regarding the deficiency of space in the department of printed books, where space for storage was already found insufficient, and the Reading Room was small for the number of people.[5] The trustees agreed to the idea of expansion and thus began the process of preparation of conceptual plan to be presented at the House of Commons to get the required grant.

Conceptual evolution of the plan

The earliest proposal was made in 1849 by William Hosking, a professor of Architecture in University College London and a civil engineer.[6] He had proposed to convert a northern half of the King's library into the reading room and a new hexagonal sculptural gallery in the middle of the open courtyard of the museum.[6] The walls were proposed to be in thick masonry with niches to keep the sculptures.[7] The structure was to be topped with a domed rotunda. Similar proposals were made to build a new structure in the heart of the Museum only to be rejected by the trustees as they preferred to keep the quadrangle open and unbuilt.[8] This led them to look for buying additional land next to the museum and extend the building outwards.

Librarian's influence

Here, it is important to note that public library was a new typology of building for Architects during the nineteenth century. The evidence indicates that other proposed plans gave importance to the details of extrinsic qualities of the building without much attention to the arrangement of the bookshelves or the reader's tables in the extended reading room area implying possible lack of knowledge on detailed intrinsic requirements of the public library by the Architects. Panizzi at this point intervened and proposed to utilize the central courtyard area of the Museum to accommodate the proposed reading room.[9] He had made a conceptual sketch (fig. 1) of his idea of the reading room with a central point of supervision and reader's tables in a radial manner. Arundell Esdaile in his book *'The British Museum Library'* remarks that Panizzi must have been influenced by earlier domed reading rooms at Wolfenbuttel and the Radcliffe at Oxford. However, he argues that the plan proposed by Panizzi had emulated the advantages of all the other reading rooms and was far more practical.[10] It is important to observe that the conceptual plan was being proposed by the librarian with experience, who knew the functional requirements of library very well.

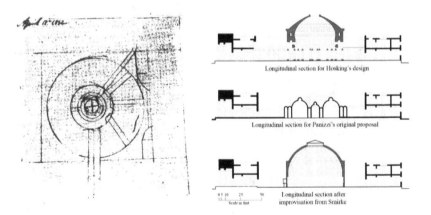

Fig. 1. Sketch showing the shape of the reading room, Panizzi, 1852(Photo: From D.Hawkes, Architecture and Climate, 2002)

Fig. 2. Comparative sections (drawing: Pandurangi)

The trustees accepted the idea and Sydney Smirke, the Architect was given a task of translating this sketch into architectural drawings.[9] Even though the trustees did not accept it the first time, after tweaking the floorplan and on the second submission in 1854, it was accepted by the treasury. Comparison of sections for all the three proposals was an interesting drawing for study. (fig. 2) It illustrates the difference between the Hosking's, Panizzi's and Smirke's reading room sections. Panizzi's clarity of furniture arrangement was far more superior compared to others, however, his structure looks way more grounded than others and lacked monumentality. William Hosking argued that in Smirke's proposal (the last cross-section in fig 2), due to the increased diameter of the reading room, the lack of light to the inner transceptal windows of both east and west gallery was identified. In the final drawing, this concern was addressed by Smirke.

Anatomical analysis of the plan

The final plan which was taken forward for execution was an improved version of Smirke's plan with lighting issues of the side galleries addressed by making the diameter of the building smaller to 140 feet (42.67m) (fig 3). Public access to the reading room was provided from Southside entrance of the Museum. This entrance passageway was flanked by cloakrooms, staircases and attendant's room. Conceptually the furniture arrangement inside the Reading Room was based on Panopticon principle as desired by Panizzi for the ease of supervision. The central space had supervisors table with 2 rows of concentric shaped catalog tables around. Beyond this were the radial-shaped reading tables.

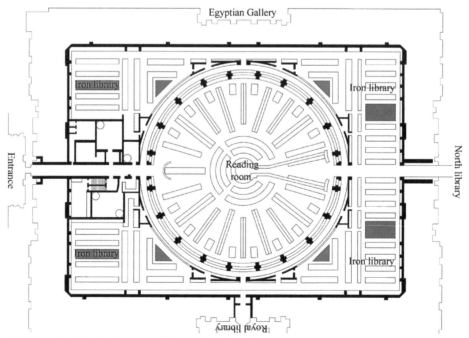

Fig. 3. Floor plan of the Reading room (drawing: Pandurangi).

173

The famous dome was built on twenty cast-iron frames economizing on the space,[11] as against thick masonry supports. In terms of influences, Esdaile points out that Smirke simply followed the tradition set by Wren in the Library of Trinity College, Cambridge[12] where the window(source of light), the bookshelf (perpendicular to the window) and the reader would come together in a triangle shape, the difference being Wren had a rectangular shaped floor plan.

The reading room was surrounded by the 'Iron library' with entire shelving erected in cast-iron. This lead to a reduction of fire risk and immense space saving by eliminating brick supports.[13] In the cross-section, the space between the Iron library and gallery was revised to allow ample light inside the gallery.

Design interventions accommodating preservation

Until the late twentieth century, Preservation was not introduced as a formal profession in the world of libraries.[14] However, the British Museum reading room had taken certain measures in its design and construction to accommodate preservation without really using the word 'preservation'. Edward Edwards gave an early narrative of the concept of preservation in the context of the economy of the libraries in his book '*The Memoirs of Libraries*' as follows:

> 'The building should be fireproof; walls, floors and roof should be exclusively formed of brick, stone iron and slate....'[15]

This implies that fire was believed to be one of the biggest fear in the library and measures taken to avoid the risk of fire was, not to allow it in the first place. This led them to look at materials which prevented the spread of fire. The dome was made up of sheets of fibrous material.[16] This was a nonconductor of heat & sound. In the wake of Joseph Paxton's crystal palace, iron was a popular material.[17] In the context of preservation, this was 'uninflammable' material. Hence this was extensively used as a main structural material for the dome, bookshelves and readers tables. The proposed bookshelves holding nearly a million books in the reading room and the iron library was built in cast-iron.[18] Esdaile appreciates the 'iron library' as the honored ancestor of every stack that was ever built later.[18] Apparently, the shelves were erected at a considerably small cost.[18] This news might have given a boost to various other libraries to urge them to use cast-iron shelving which was later improvised by using steel.

In the reading room area, we see a contradicting evidence of wooden flooring and wooden furniture in the form of tables being extensively used. Perhaps this was to create a feeling of warmth against the coldness of iron for the public. In one of the parliamentary proceedings, Mr.Wyld illustrates the example of British Museum library and points out that danger of combustion is due to the presence of wood.[19] However, he clearly states that books alone do not burn readily.[19] From the drawings, it is interesting to note that both vertically in section and horizontally in the plan, there seems to be a sense of clear compartmentalization being done to separate the space where wood is being used. In the section, the flooring has a solid slab on which wooden flooring has been laid out separating the basement area from the reading room area (fig 4). In the plan, the outermost circular cast-iron shelving acts as a separation between the reading room and Iron library(fig 4). Possibly this division was intentional so that the wood was still used to comfort people yet separating it from the space where books were kept. Between the multi-floor stacking of books, the intermediate floors were made up of the iron grill to allow for penetration of light indicating that they were aware of the necessity of good lighting for the shelving space. [20]

Design interventions accommodating comfort

By the nineteenth century, attempts were made to define comfort standards by Thomas Tredgold, Reid and John Billings. Reid had set the temperature standards by indicating 65 deg F as the most agreeable number with atmosphere moving in a very gentle stream.[21] Regarding system of thermal comfort, Tredgold had elaborated the local heating method using steam pipes specifically for large public spaces.[22] With this as the context, the study ahead looks at the various design interventions which were made to accommodate comfort. For the ease of study, the comfort parameters in the library have been divided into 1) Warming and Ventilation system and 2) Lighting.

1) Warming & ventilation system

Smirke had certain specific ideas about the warming and ventilation system. He believed warming the reading room by means of surfaces heated by hot water was the most appropriate system,[23] however, he was open to new ideas. It was decided to call upon a tender to decide on the Engineer who would take up the designing and execution of warming and ventilation system.[23]

The objective of the tender was to propose an arrangement of warming and ventilation system which was simple in its management, economical in terms of consumption of fuel, perfectly free from any risk of danger by fire and of the ill effects of impure air.[23] Smirke had even specified that the arrangement of warming of the reading room had to be kept distinct from the arrangements for the warming of the rest of the building. It was decided that the contract had to include the setting up of furnace, boilers, fitting of pipes, air gratings, building air shafts, channels, furnace room, smoke shafts etc implying that every work required to complete the execution of warming and the ventilating system had to be covered.[23] Trustees agreed that the Architect had to certify the successful execution of work and operation of the system before payments were made to the Engineers. Six different Engineers participated in the tender. George Haden, William Jeakes, Angier March Perkins, Turner, Sylvester and Price in April 1855.[23] Smirke had written that each party preparing tender was required to attach a detailed description of the proposal along with probable fuel consumption and a number of attendants required to maintain the apparatus.[23]

a) System specification by the Architect-Smirke had prepared a set of pre-requisites along with a conceptual drawing of warming and ventilation system to the Engineers (fig 4).

Tab. 1. Table showing highlights of the Architect's specification from a letter dated 17th March 1855 accessed at National Archives[23].

Parameter	Numerical Value	Remarks
Fresh air supply	10 cubic feet/min/person	To be designed for 500 people.
Velocity of air	Not more than 1 feet/sec	-
Indoor Temperature	60-70 deg F	Under all circumstances when artificial warmth was required.
Heated surface temperature	Not to exceed 212 deg F	-

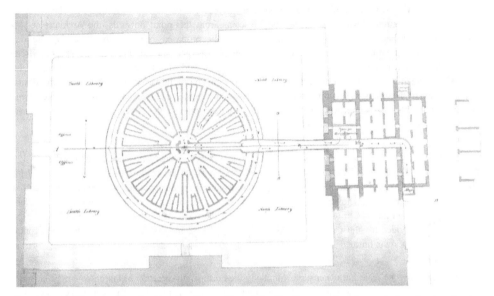

Fig. 4. British Museum: Circular Reading Room. Plan of Reading Room and center part of north wing showing heating ducts, S. Smirke (18th March 1855), (Photo: National Archives, (WORK 33/1137)

At this point, it can be noted that humidity was not considered in the specification, however, in 1857, in a report to General board of health on warming and ventilation in dwellings, humidity was considered an important aspect of comfort[24]. Subsequently, Billings in the context of health and comfort wrote that the relative saturation of air respired should be from 65-75%.[25] To compare the air change rates mentioned above, 3000 cubic feet/person/hour of fresh air for a mixed community of people was standardized by the end of the nineteenth century in an Annual meeting of Library Association held in Reading.[26]

Apart from above numerical, Smirke also clearly indicated that valves had to be provided at various junctions for local control. A hot water or steam pipe was to be provided to promote Summer ventilation over the heads of the windows or at the base of the lantern. Above written specification by the Architect shows that he had a meticulous idea of the system and the specifications were clearly driven by the performance of the system.

b)Architect's feedback on the tender drawings- Smirke wrote a letter to the trustees dated May 10th, 1855 after reviewing all the submitted plans for tender. He summarised that Sylvester's plan of introducing the warm air at the top of the dome would end up being expensive and ineffectual.[27] Perkin's and Turner's plans were considered inferior in terms of the position of the hot water pipes.[27] In principle, Jeakes plan was very similar to Haden's, however, it was found to be less economical in working.[27] In terms of cost, Haden's proposal was second highest after Turner's. However, Smirke reminded trustees about the seriousness of the public utility of the reading room. The building of such national importance could not afford to be affected by any error in the carrying of arrangements for warming and ventilation and therefore, he voiced his concerns about expenses not be taken as sole criteria of finalizing the tender contract.[27]

c)Description of the warming and ventilation system- George Haden from Trowbridge was chosen as the Engineer for the execution by the trustees of the Museum. From this point onwards, the Architect and the Engineer came together to work out the final tweaks for the proposed system before releasing the final construction drawings. Smirke did mention the reading room plan as 'peculiar' due to its circular shape.[28] This meant that the arrangement of pipes for warming system had to be worked out keeping this shape in mind. Both Smirke's and Haden's signature can be seen on the final drawing (fig 5), however, its unclear as to who drafted the final version of the proposal. It is observed that the executed system is a close combination of Smirke's initial proposal along with Haden's improved inputs. The following description of the system is partly by John Murray in a publication in 1867 and partly by the author.

The incoming supply of fresh air was from a 60 feet high shaft situated on the North side of the North gallery.[29] This was about 300 feet away, transferred via a tunnel to all parts of the reading room.[29] This tunnel had branches with valves to allow the air current either through the heating apparatus or through cold air flues depending on the season.[29] The heating apparatus, in this case, the boiler was kept below the North gallery. These had gauges and indexes to measure the temperature of the water in the boiler at all times.[30] Damper regulators were provided to adjust the draft of the boilers.[30] These indicate the awareness about the control regime of the system at the time.

From the boiler, a set of main hot water pipes run along the north-south direction in the basement air chamber. This chamber was 6'-0" high and was spread throughout below the reading room. This acted like a plenum to transmit the fresh air from the heating apparatus area to the reading room. Just before the air entered the reading room, it passed through a gauge blind for filtration. A little beyond this was a control valve for turning off the air completely from the source.

The fresh air passed around the surfaces of hot water pipes which were arranged in the radiating pattern in the air shaft and ascended up into space above at various heights depending on its function. Care was taken to see that occupants whether seated or standing, would get the supply of fresh air from different levels. Supply of fresh air in the Iron library was through iron floor gratings. The spacing of the grating was designed by the Architect.[30] in-line with the furniture layout indicating the book stacks. The floor gratings were provided in the center of the rows of book stacks and design of the gratings was as directed by the Architect. A similar arrangement of floor grating system was followed on the outer corridor of the reading room. Exclusive detailing in the furniture was done for the supply of fresh air for the seated readers in the main reading room.[31] Here the fresh air would pass over the hot water pipe, ascend as warm air and would come out at the top of the screen on the reader's table(fig 8 & 9) to make them feel comfortable during winter days. In the ladies' room, cloakroom and the copyrights room, the hot water pipes were encased in proper stands and support above the floor level instead of gratings along the floor.[32]

In summer, a large fan driven at high speed forced a constant current of cool air into the room through gratings. Possibly because in Summer, the fan would replace the thermal system used.

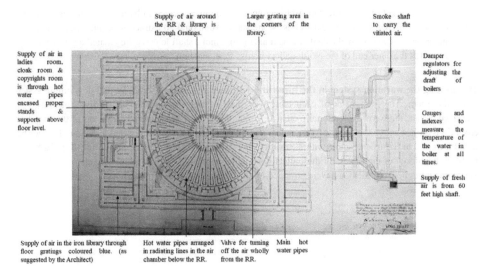

Supply of air around the RR & library is through Gratings.

Larger grating area in the corners of the library.

Smoke shaft to carry the vitiated air.

Supply of air in ladies room, cloak room & copyrights room is through hot water pipes encased proper stands & supports above floor level.

Damper regulators for adjusting the draft of boilers

Gauges and indexes to measure the temperature of the water in boiler at all times.

Supply of fresh air is from 60 feet high shaft.

Supply of air in the iron library through floor gratings coloured blue. (as suggested by the Architect)

Hot water pipes arranged in radiating lines in the air chamber below the RR.

Valve for turning off the air wholly from the RR.

Main hot water pipes

Fig. 5. British Museum: Circular Reading Room. Plan, section and details of boiler showing warming and ventilating arrangements, 22nd Dec 1855, Smirke and Haden (Photo: National Archives, WORK 33/1137)(Text added by author)

The dome was made up of two concentric air chambers (fig 9). The outer air chamber assisted in equalizing the temperature during extreme weather conditions and the inner layer was used to extract the stale air through an aperture which was provided on the soffit of the window.[33] All the windows and skylight were made up of double glazing to prevent the effects of condensation.[34] Coils of steam pipes between the double windows were used throughout the winter to equalize the temperature and to prevent the cold air from being driven downwards.[34]

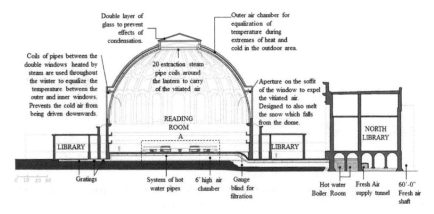

Double layer of glass to prevent effects of condensation.

Outer air chamber for equalization of temperature during extremes of heat and cold in the outdoor area.

Coils of pipes between the double windows heated by steam are used throughout the winter to equalize the temperature between the outer and inner windows. Prevents the cold air from being driven downwards.

20 extraction steam pipe coils around the lantern to carry of the vitiated air

Aperture on the soffit of the window to expel the vitiated air. Designed to also melt the snow which falls from the dome.

READING ROOM A

NORTH LIBRARY

LIBRARY

LIBRARY

Gratings

System of hot water pipes

6' high air chamber

Gauge blind for filtration

Hot water Boiler Room

Fresh Air supply tunnel

60'-0" Fresh air shaft

Fig 6-Cross section of the reading room showing warming and ventilation system (drawing: Pandurangi)

Due to the sheer height of the dome, the Architect and the Engineer seemed to be aware of the situations where enough pressure difference may not exist to assist the stack. Additional 20 extraction steam pipes were provided around the lantern to carry away the contaminated air(fig 6). Smoke shaft to carry the vitiated air was additionally provided towards the other end of the North gallery across fresh air shaft.

d)Integrating the warming system in the furniture- Furniture was used in the major part of warming system of the reading room. The framework of each table was made of iron, forming air distributing channels.[35] As mentioned earlier, these were intentionally created so that the air may be delivered at the top of the longitudinal screen division just above the heads of the readers (fig 8). A tubular foot rail connected to the air chamber below passed from end to end of each table with a current of hot water which acted as a foot warmer.[35] (fig 8). At the end of each pedestal of the tables, all the outlets were under control of the valve,[36] The catalog tables had air distributing tubes between them and were arranged in two concentric circles.

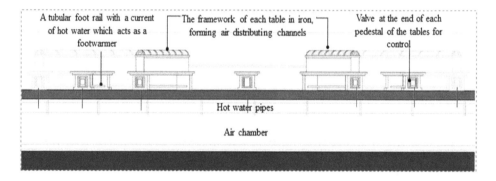

Figure 7-Detail at A showing the warming and ventilation system & the desks (drawing: Pandurangi)

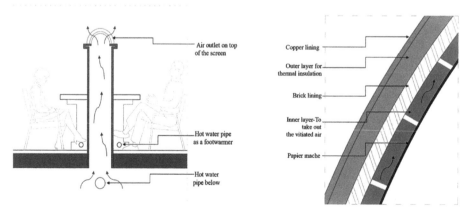

Fig 8- Section through desks showing hot water pipes. (drawing: Pandurangi)

Fig 9- Section through layers of the dome. (drawing: Pandurangi)

179

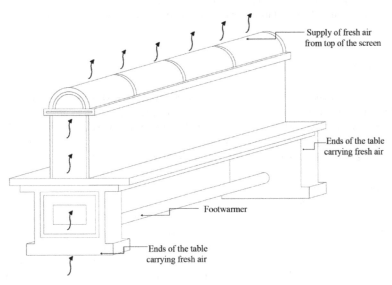

Supply of fresh air
from top of the screen

Ends of the table
carrying fresh air

Footwarmer

Ends of the table
carrying fresh air

Fig 10- Axonometric view of the furniture showing supply of fresh air. (drawing: Pandurangi)

The significance of above description of warming system incorporated into the furniture is that this was one of the experimental systems which integrated services at this scale. There is evidence which shows that the systems from Reading Room did influence libraries which were built later to have similar arrangements of warming system. Esdaile in his book 'The British Museum Library' mentions that, the plan and fittings here were admired by Labrouste and some of the features were even imitated in '*Salle de Travail*' of the Bibliotheque Nationale at Paris.[37] Dean Hawkes also draws a similar conclusion in terms of building adopting environmental technologies. He remarks that through the design of the desks, attention was given to the reader's thermal comfort and says, it must have surely influenced Bibliotheque Nationale.[38] We can consider another account from Panizzi's friend Prosper Merimee, a French writer, who described British Museum Reading Room as a building intended to serve as a type suggesting that this library had a set a standard for the public libraries to be built in future.

e) Historical records of the user experience- There is no available evidence which indicates the presence of thermometer kept in the reading room nor were there any systematic method of observing and recording temperature, humidity, air velocity data/user feedback. However, till the end of the nineteenth century, various newspapers published articles from which one can vaguely gather the kind of experience users had inside the reading room. On Jan 15th, 1875, an article was published in the '*Nottinghamshire Guardian*' in the context of the general unhealthiness of the British Museum Reading Room. It reported of two officials who died from the effects of 'cold and depression' inside the reading room and mentions complains about draughts going around relentlessly in the circular space.[39] Interestingly another evidence in summer of 1896 reported that the reading room was referred to as a 'refrigerator'[40] implying the feeling of cold possibly due to its sheer height. One of the user calls the reading room as 'the least warm place in London'. By 1893, a new article in January reported that the temperature inside was found comfortable and ventilation was good but the only sore point was lack of good lighting.[41] Given the fact that the above information was all from a newspaper source, it is hard to come to any solid conclusion in terms of the operation of warming and ventilation system nevertheless, the author elaborates on the study of lighting and its evolution in the reading room and how it affected the perception of the user.

2)Lighting evolution

Dean Hawkes writes in his book *'Architecture and Climate'* that when the reading room was opened, most people considered this as an 'unqualified success' specifically the readers who were used to sitting in the overcrowded and poor environment of older reading rooms. However, these impressions were soon contradicted by increased dissatisfaction with the ambiance of the room especially due to lack of artificial lighting.[42] John Murray also argued that reading room's greatest drawback was the absence of artificial lighting.

The main source of natural light for the reading room was 20 windows situated around the reading room and the skylight at the center. This meant that in winter, the reading room had to be closed by 4:00 pm and in summer by 6:00 pm. This being a public library, working class were expected to visit the reading room and hence the time restriction was found to be inconvenient. Smirke had originally proposed gas lighting from the outside of the lantern only to be rejected later by the trustees. Gas lighting was considered too dangerous for the books. In 1862 there was agitation for the introduction of gas lighting to allow evening opening. Due to the increased pollution levels in London when it became difficult to read during the daytime, the trustees decided to take some action to address this issue.[42]

In the beginning of 1879, the first experiment took place to use the electric lighting. This was considered as a failure.[43] In the same year, later second experiment for electric lighting was tested by Seimens and this was a success.[43] Four arc lamps hung from the bottom of the lantern each of 5000 candle-power was used.[44] Subsequently after many additional fixtures over the years(fig 11), finally in 1906, five arc lamps and 325 glow lamps were housed inside the reading room and the timing of the reading room was extended, keeping it open between 9 am to 7 pm throughout the year.[44]

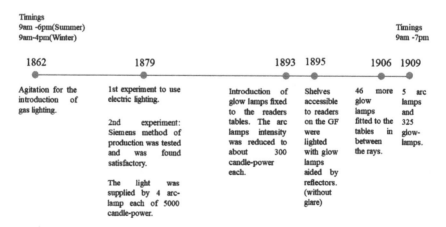

Fig. 11- Lighting evolution timeline (drawing: Pandurangi)

181

Here the context of lighting evolution signifies how development in the science of electric lighting improved the user experience overall, fostering comfort. Although the reading room originally was not designed to have electric lighting, due to the change in time and requirement, the building could contain additional services for the benefit of the public.

Conclusion

The study above gives a summary of the environmental aspects of the design of the public libraries in the nineteenth century in the context of preservation and comfort. From the beginning of the design process, the librarian was influential in converting his functional requirements into a concept sketch of the building which was later developed into a technical drawing by the Architect. Since fire was believed to be the only major hazard for the library, attempts to protect the books from fire were made through new construction materials and methods. Thermal comfort was also seen as significant design requirement, leading to a system that could provide an artificially controlled indoor climate under both summer and winter conditions and local controls. The fact that the architect Smirke provided detailed performance for the heating and ventilation system shows that environmental control was treated as an integral part of the design. The chosen Engineer collaborated with the Architect to develop the warming and ventilation system in detail. Elaborating on comfort, the introduction of artificial lighting played a substantial role in uplifting occupant's comfort levels. Lighting evolution in this building stands out as a good example of evolving technology and the building of national importance adapting to the change as and when needed to reflect the country's latest technological approach. Even with the mixed user satisfaction reports, the Reading Room in nineteenth-century has been highlighted for its latest construction methods and its environmental strategy. Although the development of the reading room was constantly driven by the public and trustees[45], the key observation here is the successful collaboration between the Librarian, the Architect, and the Engineer to produce a building which not only fulfilled the functional requirement but also reflected the experimental enthusiasm through executing variety of services like warming and ventilating systems and electric lighting systems at the time.

References

[1] A. Esdaile, *The British Museum Library*. London: George Allen & Unwin Brothers Limited, 1946, p. 117.

[2] W. Hosking, *Some observations upon the recent addition of a reading room to the British Museum*. London: Edward Stanford, 1858, p. C.

[3] T. Kelly, *History of Public Libraries in Great Britain 1845-1975 (2nd edition)*. British library cataloging in publication, 1977, p. 313.

[4] Ibid., p. 314.

[5] The return [557] to an order of the House of Commons, dated 22nd June 1852. Letter to the Treasury, July 25, 1851, p. 17.

[6] A. Esdaile, *The British Museum Library*. London: George Allen & Unwin Brothers Limited, 1946, p. 117.

[7] Letter from Panizzi to Hosking dated May 1st, 1857, in W. Hosking, Some observations upon the recent addition of a reading room to the British Museum. London: Edward Stanford,1858, p. 19.

[8] Ibid., p. 7.

[9] D. Hawkes, *Architecture and Climate: An Environmental History of British Architecture, 1600-2000*. London; Oxon: Routledge, 2012, p. 140.

[10] A. Esdaile, *The British Museum Library*. London: George Allen & Unwin Brothers Limited, 1946, p. 118.

[11] J. Murray, *British Museum, Reading room and New Library; With a Plan*. London: William Cloves and sons, 1909, p. 11.

[12] Esdaile, *The British Museum Library*, (Note 10), p. 118.

[13] Ibid., p. 119.

[14] Pearce-Moses, R, Society of Americal Archivists. 2005. [Online] Available at: www.archivists.org.[Accessed 16 October 2017].

[15] E. Edwards, *Memoirs of Library. 1st ed.* London: Trubner & Co, 1859.

[16] Anon., Huddersfield Chronicle (West Yorkshire, England) From British Library Newspapers, Friday, March 29, 1856, Issue 315, p. 3.

[17] Hawkes, (Note 9), p. 140.

[18] Esdaile, (Note 10), p. 119.

[19] Report from the select committee public libraries, house of Commons, 23rd July 1849.

[20] Hawkes, (Note 9), p. 142.

[21] D. B. Reid, *Illustrations of the theory and practice of ventilation. 1st ed. London:* s.n, 1844, p. 67.

[22] T. Tredgold, *Principles of warming and ventilating public buildings.* 2nd ed. London: Architectural Library, 1824, p. 163.

[23] National Archives, WORK 17/2/2, Sydney Smirke,17th March 1855.

[24] House of commons papers, Report of the commissioner appointed to enquire into warming and ventilation of dwellings, Vol 41, 1857, p-24.

[25] J. S. Billings, *Ventilation and heating.* 1st ed. New York: s.n, 1893, p. 112.

[26] H. Greenhough, *The Library.* London: s.n. 1890, pp. 421-433.

[27] National Archives, WORK 17/2/2, Sydney Smirke,10th May 1855.

[28] National Archives, WORK 17/2/2, Sydney Smirke.

[29] J. Murray, *British Museum, Reading room and New Library; With a Plan.* London: William Cloves and sons, 1909, p. 14.

[30] National Archives, WORK 17/2/2, Sydney Smirke,17th March 1855.

[31] Murray, (Note 29), p. 14.

[32] National Archives, WORK 17/2/2, Sydney Smirke,17th March 1855.

[33] Hawkes, (Note 9), p. 142.

[34] National Archives, WORK 17/2/2, Sydney Smirke.

[35] Murray, (Note 29), p. 14.

[36] National Archives, WORK 17/2/2, Sydney Smirke.

[37] Esdaile, (Note 10), p. 119.

[38] Hawkes, (Note 9), p. 143.

[39] Anon., Nottinghamshire Guardian (Nottingham, England), From British Library Newspapers 'There is much discussion going on relative to the general unhealthiness of the British Museum Reading room', Friday, January 15, 1875, Issue 1498, p. 6.

[40] Anon. Daily Mail (London, England) 'London in the heat', From Daily Mail Historical Archive, 1896-2004 Wednesday, July 8, 1896, Issue 57, p. 3.

[41] Anon. Liverpool Mercury (Liverpool, England) 'Our London Letter', From British Library Newspapers, Saturday, January 21, 1893, Issue 14056.

[42] Hawkes, (Note 9), p. 143.

[43] National Archives, WORK 17/3/4 (1-53)

[44] Murray, (Note 29), p. 15.

[45] Hawkes, (Note 9), p. 144.

"Symphony for Full Orchestra and Asbestos":

Tuning Albert Hall during WWII

Fiona Smyth

Trinity College Dublin, Ireland

Introduction

In May 1941, in the midst of the Blitz, I.G. Evans, Director of Britain's Building Research Station (BRS), received a letter from Basil Cameron, Chair of the London Symphony Orchestral Society and Associate Conductor of the Proms.[1]

London's Queen's Hall had been destroyed by an incendiary bomb just ten days prior to receipt of the letter. Orchestral music, and notably the Proms, was expected to relocate to the Royal Albert Hall where the acoustics were known to be problematic. Cameron's letter contained an impassioned plea to address the acoustics as a matter of urgency to "…ensure the continuance of orchestral music in London".[2] Significantly, the request was granted, although government work related to the acoustics of buildings at the BRS was in hiatus at the time, its Architectural Acoustics Committee suspended for the duration of the war.[3] Ensuing BRS involvement skirted a fine line between official and unofficial. In essence, while the BRS retained a definite advisory role, the official stance was that the acoustician Hope Bagenal was released from official duties to consult in a semi-private capacity:

> "All advice is to be given by the BRS: but BRS will not act as architect. At the same time owing to the useful experimental character of the work in acoustics, every help would be offered and Mr Bagenal's services loaned to the Philharmonic Committee".[4]

Regardless of any administrative intricacies, acoustic consultancy at the Albert Hall began the day the letter was received.[5] Relocation of the Proms and the associated letting conditions for the Albert Hall were confirmed by its Council two days after that.[6]

The process of acoustic adjustment at Albert Hall was interventional. Part optimisation and part experiment, mutability of the acoustic context was explored by the strategic use of reflecting surfaces to particular musical effect. Significantly, the process of acoustic adjustment continued throughout the Prom season using music as a gauge to assess and inform the material intervention.

Very little has been published on the wartime acoustic intervention at Royal Albert Hall. The little reference that exists is largely contained in books on music history, which make brief reference to the existence of the problem and the fact of its resolution and do not engage with the process of design and intervention.[7] With the exception of one contemporaneous report published in the RIBA Journal,[8] no meaningful examination has been made of the acoustic design process, its implementation, or its broader implications for subsequent work in auditorium acoustics in Britain.

This paper draws on primary source material in the form of archived documents, contemporaneous press coverage and the personal papers of the acoustician involved. It explores the wartime modification of acoustics at Royal Albert Hall and brings to light the work methods of the acousticians involved in aligning architectural intervention with musical intent. It presents the experimental work in the acoustics of Albert Hall as a prelude to the philosophies of design manifested in Britain's post-war concert halls, with particular reference to London's Royal Festival Hall.

"That dragon of an echo" and the acoustic design brief

There were multiple acoustic challenges in relocating the Proms from Queen's Hall to the Royal Albert Hall. At the quantifiable end of the spectrum were the issues of scale and form. The Albert Hall has a volume of approximately 3,000,000 cu ft, [9] whereas Queen's Hall had been much smaller with a volume of 422,000 cubic feet.[10] Queen's Hall had seated an audience of roughly 2,000, whereas the Albert Hall accommodated an audience of 7,000 with ease. Bagenal estimated that it would take an orchestra of 200 to generate sufficient loudness to 'fill' the Albert Hall, substantially more than the typical, moderate size of the orchestra for the Proms at Queen's Hall.[11]

Furthermore, Queen's Hall, reputed to have been designed in plan to replicate the bell of a trumpet, featured convex curvature to the stage area, with further convex profiling to the coving of the ceiling.[12] A pre-war acoustic survey of Queen's Hall, that was analysed with recourse to sound-path diagrams, demonstrates that where the plan was concave in form, (at the back of the auditorium), the effect was insufficient to cause echo.[13] By contrast, the dome, elliptical plan and large radius of the Albert Hall caused a pronounced echo. It was observed that in some parts of the hall, reflected sounds were often louder than direct sounds with sufficiently long delay to prompt sardonic comments about 'two concerts for the price of one' and 'a second concert in the roof a bar late'.

The echo had been an issue since the Albert Hall first opened its doors in 1872. Acoustics is never immune from subjectivity and nuance, but in the Albert Hall the echo famously varied by location. In some parts of the hall it was virtually inaudible, in others it was so pronounced as to obscure both speech and music. Hope Bagenal was later to describe the phenomenon as "...families of echoes - long and short, loud and soft"[14] around which "an entire acoustic mythology" had been propagated.[15]

In the years immediately following the opening of the hall, various techniques had been implemented to mitigate the effect of the echo. Wires and nets had been strung from the ceiling, the use of an electrophone had been trialled, and a large canvas velarium had been suspended beneath the dome. The only intervention still in place in 1941 was the velarium, although still the echo remained contentious. The effect of the velarium, noted Bagenal in an earlier study published in 1931 was "to make the hall just endurable". [16]

In 1941, Basil Cameron was associate conductor of the Proms. He had encountered Hope Bagenal some years previously in the acoustic work for Cowles Voysey's White Rock Music Pavilion in Hastings (1927). Aware of the acoustic problems in the Albert Hall, and knowing that a solution if possible might rest with Hope Bagenal,

Cameron nominated the acoustician as "the only St George I knew who could destroy this dragon of an echo…".[17]

The echo, despite its notoriety, was just one aspect of what was addressed. Much more nuanced challenges presented themselves in terms of the hall and its effect on musical tone. Cameron had particular requirements for the acoustic 'sense' that he wanted in the Albert Hall. Bagenal, as an acoustician, also had particular objectives, concerned to a large extent with shaping tone in terms of strength, brightness, and in solo as well as orchestral music. The nature of the brief as described by the acoustician is significant in this regard: "…the first object of the present treatment was strength of tone…".[18]

Within music, tone is a very nuanced, and hence difficult, concept to define. Different interpretations of the concept abound.[19] The term is much more defined in science, but in the acoustic work at the Albert Hall in 1941, tone was applied somewhat in the musical sense but with recourse to scientific description. If Royal Albert Hall was home to families of echo, Bagenal's work in acoustics can also be seen to have introduced tone in terms of 'families', considered in subcategories such as "bright tone", "singing tone" etc.[20] Varieties of tone were considered as phenomena structured by differing degrees of reinforcement across frequencies.

By necessity, both the aspirations behind the intervention, and the results of the progressive assessments, had to be communicable across disciplines. Physicists, musicians, engineers, architects, concert promoters and music critics all held a stake, and played a role in the process. The Albert Hall and the acoustic work therein, thus represented a substantial step forwards in defining a terminology for acoustics that was subsequently implemented in the design of the postwar concert halls in the 1950s. Arguably, it was most notably in the acoustic work for Royal Festival Hall where 'fullness of tone' was a specified design requirement, and where similar assessment procedures - test concerts and the alignment of objective analysis with subjective assessment - were employed to assess tone in terms of acoustics.

Interventions

In 1941, reverberation time was the only objective parameter for acoustic assessment. The other requirements, and their assessment, were subjective: mathematically undefined and conceptually difficult to articulate. The first evaluation placed the reverberation time as 3.8 s at 512 Hz, recognised as less than it might otherwise have been in a building of that scale, by virtue of the velarium, carpet and soft furnishings.[21] Even so, it was more than twice the measured reverberation time for the same frequency in Queen's Hall.[22]

Ultimately, the acoustic strategy that was designed both to combat the echo and to shape the intangible quality of tone was physically manifested in an installation that included a canopy and a screen. The canopy was to work inter-reflectively in tandem with an area of exposed parquet flooring. Curtains were introduced in strategic locations, and the velarium lowered in increments. Not only was the brief informed by musical requirements, and expressed in musical terminology, but the installation - its design, location, and angles of inclination - continued to be tempered and refined in response to issues highlighted by concerts and rehearsals as the season progressed.

It was not just tone that was addressed with recourse to music. As noted by Bagenal, 'the echo problem was dealt with experimentally'.[23] In the first instance, the velarium was brought down in increments in response to observations made at successive concerts. It was brought down by 30 ft for the first concert and a further 35 ft for the next. While this seems to have been relatively successful, it was subsequently observed that very loud or sharp (staccato) sounds manifested as problems, particularly with the trombone and the piano:

> "...they [the echoes] appeared to go through it [the velarium] and return with the full concentration of the dome above. The effect of this was that the hall was bad for Wagner, Tchaikovsky, Sibelius, but quite good, generally speaking, for Mozart and Beethoven".[24]

The echo was further addressed in terms of sound paths which were re-directed by the overhead canopy and lateral screen installation. The angles and positioning of this installation were adapted as and when issues with either echo or tone became apparent.

There were certain strictures which had to be observed in the design and construction of the installation. Wartime availability of materials was one. It is telling that the first sketch design was for an installation that was to be suspended on barrage balloon cables. And whilst plywood was ultimately the material of choice, a backup design had been produced, utilising asbestos sheets in the event that plywood would be unavailable in sufficient quantities. An equally significant stricture was the fact that the intervention was anticipated to be temporary. It was envisaged that a new permanent home would be found for the Proms. In the interim, the Albert Hall was intended to host the Proms for just one season, and it was to be a shortened season at that, extending to just six weeks between July 12th and August 23rd 1941.[25] Given this, and the multiplicity of other functions of the Albert Hall, the intervention had to be lightweight, portable, easy to assemble and demount. Given the constraints of time, it had to be designed and fully constructed within a matter of weeks.

Installation

Once permission to proceed had been secured, work advanced rapidly. The first design team meeting was held on May 23rd just two days after receipt of Cameron's letter. By this stage, representatives of both the National Physical Laboratory (NPL) and the BRS had provided suggestions regarding the canopy and screen, and initial sketch designs had been produced by the BRS.

The design at this stage was "to be hard and solid as feasible yet also light and portable". It also needed to be of sufficient scale to enclose a full orchestra and choir, and to make an impact in the vast interior of the Royal Albert Hall. A scheme of fluted precast units with an approximate height of 12 ft. was tentatively settled upon, the shape determined to provide the requisite stiffness in terms of its structure, and sufficient diffusion to avoid focusing effects in the auditorium. The same general type of units was to provide the basis of both canopy and screen. The suggested material at this juncture was hessian sprayed with cement, and the angles of inclination remained to be determined. [26]

While design and construction of the bespoke installation proceeded, a temporary form of screening was to be trialled at a series of concerts prior to the Proms. The temporary screen, was formed of studio flats, 20 ft in height.[27] These had been borrowed on a 6-week term from Denham film Studios in Buckinghamshire.[28] The borrowed arrangement, it was anticipated, would remain in place for the concerts for the concerts on May and June, to be replaced by the dedicated screen by opening night of the Proms. In the end, the dedicated arrangement was not fully in place until the end of July, and it continued to be adapted throughout the month of August.

The first concert was a Bach-Beethoven-Brahms programme performed by the London Symphony Orchestra, conducted by Basil Cameron. Fittingly, Myra Hess - who had played such an exceptional role in breaking the wartime cultural blackout with the instigation of the National Gallery concerts - was the soloist.[29] The Bach-Beethoven-Brahms programme was the concert at which the velarium was first lowered by 30 ft. In addition, heavy curtains were hung to increase absorption. The concert included Brahms *Piano Concerto in B Flat* (Hess), Bach's *Fugue in C Minor* (transcribed by Elgar), and Beethoven's *Second Symphony.* [30]

Newspaper reviews from music critics were largely positive, and made specific reference to the perceptible improvement in the acoustics. *The Sunday Times* referred to the intervention "resulting in great and much-needed improvement in the acoustics",[31] while the *Daily Telegraph* subtitled its article "Improved Acoustics", describing:

> "a great improvement in the acoustics, which in the past have caused much disappointment. The sonority of the Bach-Elgar Fantasia and Fugue in C Minor was rich but clean. Not a detail was lost in the delicate slow movement of Brahm's piano concerto in B Flat in which Myra Hess was the soloist".[32]

Another (unidentified) article was headed "Albert Hall has Beaten its Echo" and declared that the interval of the echo had been reduced from 4 to 2 seconds.[33] On a slightly more technical note, observations of the acoustician included that "the loudness of the direct sound was increased, echo slightly reduced, articulation improved".[34] However, the process of tuning the auditorium had only just begun and an afterword to the assessment he declared, "But we can do better".

The primary discerned inadequacy was a lack of "instrumental character" and a reduced "brightness" of tone. High frequency reflections, it was determined, needed to be reinforced. In preparation for the next scheduled concert on 31st May the introduction of a glossy surface was recommended to enhance the solo violin.[35] It was determined to clear a 10 ft x 30 ft strip of floor area in the stalls, just to the front of the stage platform, and to expose and polish the timbers. Brahm's Violin Concerto in D Major would be the essential test. Once again Basil Cameron would be the conductor.[36]

Bagenal referred to this as the Greek Orchestra Floor principle. The documented effect at the Albert Hall was that it was very good for increasing loudness in the solo voice and solo violin, and that it "improved the ensemble of tone" as heard from near seats.[37] A similar principle was later applied at Royal Festival Hall in the incorporation of a strip of exposed marble in front of the stage, analogously referred to as a reflective "lake".

Throughout the overall season, members of the design team attended the concerts, making note of discrepancies by location. Site meetings were held during rehearsals. It was observed at an early juncture that to accommodate Beethoven's *Ninth Symphony* - and a more complex staging with chorus plus soloists and orchestra - the initial design for the screening would need to be increased in height.[38] In view of this, it was also determined that plywood on a convex timber frame would be a more suitable material. The plywood was varnished to maximise the high reflections that Bagenal felt contributed to "brightness of tone".[39] The Proms season had already begun before the final screen and canopy were in place.

In its final iteration, the canopy weighed a ton and a quarter.[40] It was much heavier than anticipated. The original plan to use balloon cables and suspend it from winches in the gallery was, by necessity, re-addressed. The canopy was suspended from the dome on winches borrowed from the Strand Electric Co. with lateral stabilisation provided from the original winches in the gallery.[41] It was constructed of 1/4" plywood sheets to a convex profile and measured 40 ft in width and 27 ft in depth.

The first assessment of the new canopy in place was undertaken in late July at a rehearsal of Beethoven's *Fourth Symphony*. Assessment concentrated on definition, loudness, and the opportunity for players to hear themselves and one another. Improvements were noted in all of these aspects. Echo was observed to have been almost eradicated, perceptible only in slight lags from drums and timpani which fell outside the area of the overhead reflector.[42] The canopy was already as large as its weight would permit. However, the angle of inclination was steepened shortly thereafter in response to an imbalance of loudness in Mozart's *Concerto for Two Pianos* in *E Flat Major*.[43] The final readjustment of tilt and height took place towards the end of August.

Police Intervention

It was decided to reopen the Albert Hall on the 18th April 1941, after a period of closure subsequent to the outbreak of war.[44] Initial safety conditions for its reopening were agreed with an Assistant Commissioner of Police in late July 1941.[45] These were amended slightly in a letter of 31st July to take into account the risk of falling glass. It was recommended that the glass roof - which had already been damaged in shelling in 1940 - be treated with anti-splinter material.[46] Concern at the potential risks of falling glass however, had not been entirely assuaged. A subsequent (police) inspection took issue with the lowered velarium. It was deemed at risk of perforation in the event of shattered glass. On the 18th of August, Bagenal was notified by Keith Douglas of the London Philharmonic Society of a new safety requirement to raise the velarium to its full height. Douglas had commissioned and financed the acoustic work in the first instance. Although dubious as to the safety merits of the suggestion, and somewhat disparaging of the velarium: "that old gas-bag wouldn't stop the splinters at whatever position!", Douglas and the management of the Albert Hall duly complied.[47] The velarium was returned to its original position. "This has most successfully restored the echo!" declared Douglas in his letter to Bagenal. There were just four concerts left in that season's programme. Beethoven's *Ninth Symphony*, Prom 33 of that year and an acoustic concern from the outset - was scheduled for the next day. The auditorium, once again had to be re-tuned.

To compensate for the loss of low-level absorption, heavy curtains were hung from the gallery,[48] and to counter the echo the plywood canopy was raised and its angle of inclination increased once again. With the raised velarium, the balcony was re-opened accommodating a larger than usual audience.[49]

Beethoven's *Ninth* was generally deemed to be a success as was the new site for the Proms. Before the season had ended Henry Wood had made a request to hold the Proms at the Albert Hall again the following year, stating his pleasant surprise at how successful the venue had proved to be.[50] Financially that year's Proms were deemed a success. Furthermore, the screen and canopy installation found much favour. When the BBC resumed its association with the Proms the following year,[51] it was agreed first to rent them from Keith Douglas, and latterly to buy them outright.

Coda

Acquisition of the original installation did not go through as anticipated and the politics of negotiations in this regard have been discussed in other sources.[52] However, the upshot was that with the permission of Hope Bagenal and the BRS who had designed the intervention, it was proposed to build a replica, and to commission

Beck and Pollitzer as contractors to undertake supply and fit of a new screen and canopy.[53] (Messrs John Laing and Son were original contractors for the canopy.)[54] The cost was envisaged to be in the region of £1,150. It was end of September before wires, cables and hoists had all been procured and Keith Douglas's contribution had been returned to him.[55] History doesn't record what eventually happened the original installation, but the replica proved just as popular. As late as 1957, Sir Adrian Boult still insisted that it be reinstated every time he conducted.[56]

Conclusion: "Symphony for Full Orchestra and Asbestos…" [57]

If, as is reputedly the case, Queen's Hall was designed in homage to a musical instrument, in the acoustic intervention of 1941, the Albert Hall was understood as a musical instrument in its own right. This conceptualisation and the language used in support of it at the Albert Hall are both significant. Parallels with some of the practical aspects of the acoustic installation at the Albert Hall and Festival Hall are immediately evident. The reflective area to the front of the orchestra platform is one, the reflecting canopy designed to enhance loudness at source and direct sound towards the audience is another. In the general approach however, the conceptualisation of the building as an instrument, and the search for an interdisciplinary terminology predicated on shaping and enhancing music were also fundamental aspects in British postwar concert hall design.

In 1952, an article by the Times music critic written in response to one of Bagenal's papers summarised

> "Dr Martin's problem at the Festival Hall was not to make as good a shot as he could at a clearly defined goal but to extract from musician's a specification of what they wanted so that he might aim accurately at it".[58]

This is very much reminiscent of the entire design approach and attention to nuance that characterised the work at the Albert Hall. Substantial work into identifying and defining musical criteria in terms of design aspirations was undertaken in the years between the acoustic consultancies for Royal Albert Hall and for Royal Festival Hall. In an attempt to further understand and replicate that which constitutes 'good' in concert hall acoustics, post-war surveys put forward tonal quality as an attribute to be considered in ranking existing concert halls. This work fed directly into the design of the succeeding concert halls and was further explored the following decade in a 1963 BBC Study of *Tonal Quality in Concert Halls*.[59]

Tonal quality still has not been mathematically defined. It does not feature amongst the objective parameters for architectural acoustics in the international standards. It is not an objective measure of assessment. However, it is an important one, and it defined an approach to concert hall design in Britain in the mid-twentieth century that was relatively unique, and that warrants further analysis.

Commenting on the debate surrounding the acoustics of Royal Festival Hall, the aforementioned Times music critic concluded with the reflection that,

> "Buildings are in fact instruments of music and ideally we should choose the right auditorium for symphony, oratorio, or recital almost as if the composer presented it in the score thus - symphony for full orchestra and asbestos panels…".[60]

The Albert Hall however, while conceptualised as an instrument of music, proved to be less prescriptive than this. It was tunable.

Fig. 1 and Fig. 2: Canopy and Screen: Sir Henry Wood Conducting, Proms 1941, Journal of the RIBA August 1941.

References

[1]   National Archives, DSIR 4/654, Basil Cameron, improvement of Acoustics of Albert Hall, 'Letter of Basil Cameron to IG Evans, DBR', dated 20 May 1941.

[2]   National Archives, DSIR 4/654, Basil Cameron, improvement of Acoustics of Albert Hall, 'Letter of Basil Cameron to IG Evans, DBR', dated 20 May 1941.

[3]   F.M. Lea, *Science and Building*, London: HMSO; 1972.
DSIR, *Report of the BRB for the years 1940-1945*, London: HMSO, 1946.

[4]   National Archives, DSIR 4/654, Basil Cameron, improvement of Acoustics of Albert Hall, 'Minutes of Meeting/Memorandum of Interview', dated 23 May 1941.

[5]   National Archives, DSIR 4/654, Basil Cameron, improvement of Acoustics of Albert Hall, 'Memorandum of Interview: H. Bagenal and B. Cameron', dated 21 May 1941.

[6]   Royal Albert Hall Archives, 'Minutes for Mtg of Council 23rd May 1941' in RAH Minute Book no. 17, Council Minutes 1941.

[7]   J. Doctor and D. Wright, D (2007) *The Proms: A New History*, London: Thames and Hudson, 2007.
D. Cox, *The Henry Wood Proms*, London: BBC, 1980.
A. Jacobs, *Henry Wood Maker of the Proms*, London Methuen, 1994.

[8]   H. Bagenal, 'Concert Music in the Albert Hall' in *Journal of the RIBA*, August 1941, pp. 169-71.

[9]   According to Hope Bagenal's pencilled notes on his 1941 report (1941) in National Archives, DSIR 4/654, Basil Cameron, improvement of Acoustics of Albert Hall,

[10] Acoustic and architectural survey undertaken by Hope Bagenal in 1929. Bagenal Family archive at Leaside, uncatalogued.

[11] H Bagenal, *Practical Acoustics*, London: Methuen, 1944.

[12] R. Elkin, R., *Queen's Hall 1893-1941*, London: Rider & Co., 1944.

[13] Acoustic and architectural survey undertaken by Hope Bagenal in 1929. Bagenal Family archive at Leaside, uncatalogued.

[14] H. Bagenal, 'Concert Music in the Albert Hall' in *Journal of the RIBA*, August 1941. p. 169.

[15] National Archives, DSIR 4/654, Basil Cameron, improvement of Acoustics of Albert Hall, 'Introductory report'

[16] H. Bagenal and A. Wood, *Planning for Good Acoustics*, London: Methuen, 1931 (p. 65).

[17] See discussion succeeding lecture to the RIBA on concert hall acoustics, in H. Bagenal,'Concert Halls' in *RIBA Journal*, January, 1950, p. 93.

[18] H. Bagenal, 'Concert Music in the Albert Hall' in *Journal of the RIBA*, August 1941. p. 170.

[19] See V. Tzotzkova, *Theorizing Pianistic Experience: Tradition, Instrument, Performer* Ph.D. Dissertation (Columbia University 2012) for an exceptionally thorough and thoughtful engagement with this.

[20] H. Bagenal, 'Concert Halls' in *RIBA Journal*, January., 1950

[21] National Archives, DSIR 4/654, Basil Cameron, improvement of Acoustics of Albert Hall, 'H. Bagenal, Initial notes on conditions in the Albert Hall'.

[22] Acoustic and architectural survey undertaken by Hope Bagenal in 1929. Bagenal Family archive at Leaside, uncatalogued..

[23] Bagenal, 'Concert Music in the Albert Hall' in *Journal of the RIBA,* August 1941. p. 170.

[24] Bagenal, 'Concert Music in the Albert Hall' in *Journal of the RIBA,* August 1941. p. 170.

[25] Royal Albert Hall Archives, 'Minutes for Meeting of Council 23rd May 1941' in RAH Minute Book no. 17, Council Minutes 1941.

[26] National Archives, DSIR 4/654, Basil Cameron, improvement of Acoustics of Albert Hall, 'Minutes of Meeting/Memorandum of Interview', dated 23 May 1941.

[27] National Archives, DSIR 4/654, Basil Cameron, improvement of Acoustics of Albert Hall, 'Letter of Hope Bagenal to Keith Douglas' dated 1 June 1941.

[28] National Archives, DSIR 4/654, Basil Cameron, improvement of Acoustics of Albert Hall, 'Letter of Hope Bagenal to Keith Douglas' dated 1 June 1941.

[29] For more on this see *National Gallery Concerts,* London: The Trustees of London, 1944 . see also M. McKenna, *Myra Hess: A Portrait,* London: Ebenezer Bayliss and Son Ltd., 1976.

[30] 'LSO at Albert Hall', *Sunday Times,* (1 June 1941).

[31] 'LSO at Albert Hall', *Sunday Times,* (1 June 1941).

[32] 'LSO At Albert Hall: Improved Acoustics' *Daily Telegraph*, (2 June 1941).

[33] National Archives, DSIR 4/654, Basil Cameron, improvement of Acoustics of Albert Hall, clipping.

[34] National Archives, DSIR 4/654, Basil Cameron, improvement of Acoustics of Albert Hall, 'Letter of Hope Bagenal to Keith Douglas' dated 1 June 1941.

[35] National Archives, DSIR 4/654, Basil Cameron, improvement of Acoustics of Albert Hall, 'Letter of Hope Bagenal to Keith Douglas' dated 1 June 1941.

[36] 'Royal Albert Hall', *Times* (23 June 1941) p. 8.

[37] H. Bagenal, 'Concert Music in the Albert Hall' *in Journal of the RIBA,* August 1941. p. 171.

[38] National Archives, DSIR 4/654, Basil Cameron, improvement of Acoustics of Albert Hall, 'Letter of Hope Bagenal to Keith Douglas' dated 1 June 1941.

[39] National Archives, DSIR 4/654, Basil Cameron, improvement of Acoustics of Albert Hall, 'Letter of Hope Bagenal to Keith Douglas' dated 1 June 1941.

[40] (Arch Report no. 43)

[41] National Archives, DSIR 4/654, Basil Cameron, improvement of Acoustics of Albert Hall, 'Report of Hope Bagenal to Keith Douglas' dated 2 June 1941.

[42] National Archives, DSIR 4/654, Basil Cameron, improvement of Acoustics of Albert Hall, 'Meeting notes in Memorandum of Interview', dated 24 July 1941.

[43] National Archives, DSIR 4/654, Basil Cameron, improvement of Acoustics of Albert Hall, 'Letter of William Allen to Hope Bagenal' dated 24 July 1941. 12

[44] Minutes for Mtg of Council 23rd May 1941, RAH Minute Book no. 17, Council Minutes 1941.

[45] First Report of the committee Appointed by the Resolution of The Council dated 24th July. in Minutes of the RAH Council dated Aug 19th 1941.

[46] Letter of G Carmichael Asst Commissioner to Manager and Secretary RAH, dated 31st July 1941.

[47] National Archives, DSIR 4/654, Basil Cameron, improvement of Acoustics of Albert Hall, 'Letter of Keith Douglas to Hope Bagenal' dated 18 August1941.

[48] Royal Albert Hall Archives, 'Architect's Report no. 43'.

[49] 'The Choral Symphony' *Times* (21 Aug 21 1941) p. 6.

[50] (letter of HW to ASkew dated 1 Aug 1941)

[51] Doctor, J. and Wright, D (2007) *The Proms: A New History*, London: Thames and Hudson;
Cox, D. (1980) *The Henry Wood Proms*, London: BBC;
Jacobs, A. (1994) *Henry Wood Maker of the Proms*, London Methuen.

[52] Doctor, J. and Wright, D (2007) *The Proms: A New History*, London: Thames and Hudson;
Cox, D. (1980) *The Henry Wood Proms*, London: BBC;
Jacobs, A. (1994) *Henry Wood Maker of the Proms*, London Methuen.

[53] (Meeting of Council 15th July 1942)

[54] H. Bagenal, 'Concert Music in the ALbert Hall' in JRIBA

[55] (Royal Albert Hall Archives, 'Architect's Report no. 47', dated 30 Sept 1942.

[56] Royal Albert Hall Archives, 'Council Minutes Jan, 1957, RAH Minute Book No. 19.
A. Boult, *My Own Trumpet*, Western Printing Services Ltd: Bristol, 1973 p. 124.

[57] 'Taste And Acoustics', *Times*, (21 Nov. 1952) p. 9

[58] 'Taste And Acoustics', *Times*, (21 Nov. 1952) p. 9

[59] T. Somerville & C.L.S. Gilford, *Tonal Quality in Concert Halls*, BBC Research Department, Report No.B-079, 1963/52.

[60] 'Taste And Acoustics', *Times*, (21 Nov. 1952) p. 9

Case Study: The Temperate House at Kew—Controlling the climate under a glass sky

Qian Wang

Kent School of Architecture, University of Kent, UK

Introduction

In the royal botanic garden, Kew, the largest Victorian glasshouse in the world still exists — the Temperate House. It is one of the listed building of the world UNESCO heritage site. In 1859 the Temperate House was begun by the Architect, Decimus Burton, who was also involved in the Palm House designing process at Kew. After a gap of 30 years, work resumed on the Temperate House. Eventually, after the bankruptcy of one contractor, a rectangular building with glass-iron structures was finally finished in 1898 and opened in May 1899 as the world's largest plant house. At that time, along with the full completion of the building, the Temperate House became a topic of public discussion. However, due to a lack of technology, there remained many problems after it was put into use. This paper, taking the Temperate House as a case study, focuses on analysing the environmental controlling of the five zones of the building, relating to the functional requirement of each part. Moreover, this paper will explain how the Temperate House created various climate situations by the use of direct sunlight, ventilation and heating systems for plants from different countries. In addition, this paper will also outline the challenges faced in the building process and analyse how these problems affected the buildings performance after its opening.

Building expansion

In 1859, along with the opening of the Palm House, the number of the tourists visiting Kew garden increased from 64,000 in 1847 to 327,000 in 1851. Sir William Hooke, the director of the Kew garden, asked Decimus Burton to design another conservatory, similar to the Palm House. As a result, the Temperate House commenced barely ten years after the Palm House was opened.[1] Both the Palm House and the Temperate House are unique examples of British national heritage, with the Temperate House constructed twice as large as the Palm House. With the design of the Palm House the use of the wrought iron curved sliding sashes caused trouble with its operation and maintenance. As time went by, the wrought iron ribs started to rust and were falling away on the surface because of the rain and water surrounding the building. Burton was therefore asked to depart entirely from the use of curved cladding members and use instead the timber bars throughout the Temperate House. Also, as it was to house a unique combination of plants from different climates, the design of the Temperate House became much more complicated than the Palm House.[2] Considering the location, the building was sited on an east-west axis so that it could receive adequate daylight for the plants within.

The centre block was finished first in 1862, together with two octagons (Fig. 1). It was built 212ft 6 in length and 137 ft 6 in width.[3] The apex of the roof in the middle zone, which was known as the Winter Garden, was 60 feet from the ground. It combined growing facilities for the exotic species beloved of the Victorians with a

"Winter Garden" atmosphere being its aim. With regards to the two octagons, they firstly served as small lobbies before the two wings had been completed. What should be mentioned is that they had basements which originally housed the boilers. These two octagons with details shown on Burton's original drawing, used plain rectangular structural timber beams. In 1863, the two octagons and the centre block were opened to the public.

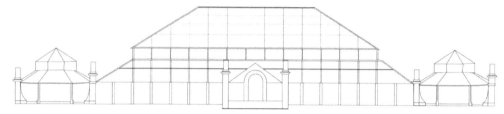

Fig.1.Facade of the Winter Garden and two octagons (Author's own work)

Although some work had been done on the foundations of the north and south wings, however, in 1894, the insufficient funds resulted in the construction of the North and South wings being delayed for 40 years until the Treasury approval was obtained.

At the very beginning, the government allocated £10,000 for the new conservatory. Due to the severe cost overruns, the project had to be stopped with only half of the whole garden being completed. However, after the financial failure, the construction of the two wings were built by different contractors. The South Wing was built 34 years later in 1897 by the designer who participated in the general pattern of the earlier blocks. He used a mixture of wrought iron and timber to build the main structure of the South Wing and added softwood timber to decorate the skin of the iron work. The North Wing was built by a third contractor who had also followed the general pattern of the main block construction. In this wing, the builder used mild steel and cast iron without the addition of any form of timber embellishment and was completed in 1898. These two later additions had the same structure, but differed in their detailing.[4] (Fig. 2)

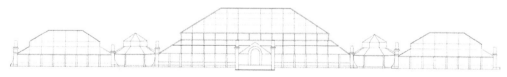

Fig.2.Facade of the whole Temperate House (Author's own work)

Aim and intention

In many respects, the most interesting and beautiful vegetation on the globe is found in climates warmer than that of Great Britain, but cooler than that of the tropics.[5] Fruits and flowers growing under those climates, which were quite peculiar to Britain at the time, were grapes, oranges, lemons, pomegranates, olives, and myrtle. The Temperate House was built with the aim to house these species. These plants were particularly popular amongst the upper classes, who wanted to find a way to protect these species and cultivate them within their own gardens. When the Temperate House was fully completed it housed a unique collection of 4,000 plants from around the world.[6] Following its completion, the Temperate House attracted huge numbers of visitors, including members of the Royal family. It functioned as a place of interest and provided a gallery for people to come and enjoy the various styles of plants that would have been impossible to view in Britain otherwise.

To create a suitable and sustainable environment for the non-native plants to survive the basic design of the Temperate House was of the utmost importance. The balance between the plant requirements and the structural and functional requirements of the building had to be found.

Functional Requirement

The Temperate House consisted of three different gardens, connected with two octagons. According to its horticultural character, the suitable location of the plants was the most important task for the design teams to solve. Therefore, to accommodate the plants from different climates, five different climatic zones were established. The North Wing, called the Himalayan House, was the coolest one among the three principal gardens, and was intended to be warm but not much warmer than the temperature out-of-doors. The South Wing, called the Mexican House, was the warmest section of the greenhouse, and was intended to create a semi-tropical climate.[7] The Winter Garden, the central garden, was intended to create in intermediate climate. The final two zones were located in the two octagons which connected the central garden to the two separate wings.[8]

Winter garden

Not only the biggest but also the most important part of the whole greenhouse was the great central garden: the Winter Garden. Neither the scale nor the plants inside could be compared with any other gardens in Kew. The plants in the Winter Garden were almost all from Australia and New Zealand. Due to the living conditions of these plants, the climate under the central zone was to be kept intermediate. That is to say, in the cold winter days, the temperature was often little over 40F. Thus, no fire-heating was needed for half the year, and numbers of the plants were grown in beds with the aim to reduce watering requirements and drainage problems. In addition, plants were grown on the side shelves in pots, maintaining a collection of numerous species. Plants thrived in the soft and still air so that people could find the Winter Garden always interesting to visit. On the other hand, when it came to the heat of summer, it was surprisingly much cooler than people imagined.

The Gum-Trees, Acacias, Tree-Ferns and Palms are the four typical plants found in the Winter Garden. The Gum-Tree which can heights of 480 feet high and has grey leaves, the edges of which turn towards the sun, unfortunately never lived very long in the Winter Garden. The season for the Acacias in the Winter Garden is from February to April, the flowers of which are various yellows and presented in tiny balls or cylindrical clusters. There are also two groups of Tree-Ferns at the north end of the Winer Garden worth visiting, each of which boasted exquisite crown of fronds surmounting a black, fibrous stem. The Palm, which has many diverse types, was also a favourite of the Winter Garden.

The beds, which were filled with plants from various warm areas in the world, were not only horticulturally attractive, but were also useful for the economic and scientific interest. Additionally, a Gallery ran along the upper floor around the entire garden, providing excellent viewing points for visitors.[9] As the plants within this house usually had tall slender stems, between 30 to 40 feet high,[10] surmounted by a crown of leaves, the Gallery was the best way in which they could be truly seen and appreciated.

Mexican House

The South Wing, the Mexican House, created a climate that was similar to the Mexican climate. In contrast to the Winter Garden, none of the plants were grown in pots.[2] Instead, the whole house was utilized for growing plants in plots of earth. In the central part of this house, the beds were divided into four rectangular areas, together with a seven feet wide border around the sides and the ends.[11] The unique role of this house was that it provided a temperature between the Winter Garden and the Palm House, a semi-tropical climate.

There were two typical kinds of plants living in the Mexican House, the Giant Cactus and some fruit trees with economic interests. For instance, the most striking plants in this house were the two groups of plants growing on rock work at the south end. Also, there were some fine examples of the remarkable cactus-like Euphorbias from South Africa.[12] All of these Cactus-like plants were very large in size, each of them nearly reaching about 9 feet high. As to an economic aspect, the most popular plants were mangoes. Further, the lemon, shaddock, guava, etc. also made a great economic influence for the Kew Garden. The tomato trees and the papaw trees also had remarkable edible fruits, and when the fruits were wrapped in their leaves, it was even more sweet for people to eat.

The Himalayan House

The North Wing, the Himalayan House, had the same structure as the South Wing, even the arrangement of the beds inside the house were the same. However, while the Mexican House kept warmer conditions than the Winter Garden, the Himalayan House was built for species requiring cooler conditions. Most plants in this house were from North Asia, especially from the Himalayas, China and Japan. Furthermore, some types of New Zealand and South American plants were placed within this zone as well. Although the climate in Britain was always too severe in the winter and too uncertain in spring, plants in the Himalayan House grew in the open air for eight to nine months of the year, with the intention of the house providing basic shelter for the plants. From 1847 to 1857, Sir Joseph Hooker made his first successful journey to the Himalayas, during which time he collected and brought back the seeds of these rare plants back to Kew.

During the growing process it was discovered that such plants could only survive in the open air, which resulted in the heating system being used only in the coldest winter days. As the blossoming time only for these plants only happened during the first five months of the year, they attracted large numbers of tourists during that period. Both the Rhododendrons and Camellias presented a colourful world in Spring, with colours ranging from blood-red, through to all the shades of rose and pink, to white. Moreover, a collection of climbers grew on the lower part of the roof as well.[13] In addition, two rock-pools afforded suitable conditions for moisture-loving plants too tender to survive successfully out-of-doors, but also imparted an agreeable diversity to the aspect of the house.[14]

Octagons

The two octagon zones were not intended for planting, instead they were built with an architectural aim, connecting and separating the three gardens.[15] Although the aim of both was the same, there were differences between the structures and plants housed inside. The North Octagon was built with plain rectangular structural timber beams within which were grown shrubs which were often clipped, such as Bay, Pittosporum and Myrtle etc.. On the other hand, the South Octagon was built with iron tracery-type arches instead of the rectangular timber in the building and was only used for the orange trees and its allies to live.

Environmental Strategies

The basic aim of the Temperate House was to create suitable growing conditions for the plants within. Thus, adequate light, suitable temperatures and the irrigation methods were the top three important factors in the growing process for the plants.

Corresponding to these conditions, as a horticultural building, the Temperate House needed to work out the design for daylighting, natural ventilation, heating systems and the drainage methods. A careful balance needed to be created for each house. For example, as the entire building was fully glazed, when the sunlight came through the glass the temperature increased, which could cause the death of some plants that required cooler conditions. Thus, direct sunlight could be harmful to various kinds of plants housed within the building. At the same time, to control the climate inside the house, both suitable ventilation and heating systems were needed to cool down and to heat up the house. As to the drainage methods, it needed to be made sufficient without causing waterlogging or causing undue humidity, because this could also damage plants than needed more arid conditions. On the contrary, if the plants were not sufficiently irrigated in warmer months, plants would also suffer. Consequently, keeping the balance of the temperature and climate was the key task in the design process of the Temperate House.

Daylighting

It cannot be denied that daylighting is an essential factor for plants to survive. Therefore, the primary task in the design of any glass house is to provide the maximum amount of daylight, especially during the winter when the daytime is short and the angle of the sun is low. However, in the 19th century the prevailing thought was that glass-houses should be built on a North-South axis. As a result, the Temperate House was built on this principle. While the daylight is necessary, getting too much heat from the solar gain in the hot summer can also be harmful to some kinds of plants. Thus, when building the Palm House, Mr Robert Hunt, F.R.S., suggested that the roof glass should be tinted green.[16] He thought "the green-tinted glass could intercept the heat rays, so the scorching effect of the sun in bright weather might be tempered". On the other hand, during the period when every ray of light is precious, this kind of colour glass may reduce the quantity of light in the winter or on overcast days. Nonetheless, the green-tinted glass was put into use in the construction of the Temperate House.[17][18]

Case Study: The Temperate House at Kew—Controlling the climate under a glass sky

This kind of green-tined glasses was firstly used in the Palm House, however after 40 years in 1887, the colourless glass was favoured once again. The use of green glass proved temporary which was partly due to changing environmental conditions and partly due to the failure to produce glass to the original specification. In the late nineteenth century, the atmospheric pollution had significantly reduced the light levels inside the house as well.[19] The changeable requirement for the plants and the unexpected air pollution had not been anticipated. Also, experience showed that in the large airy houses like the Palm House and the Temperate House, whatever the strength of the sunlight, it was powerless to injure the plants growing in there, even when using the ordinary glass. Instead, the effect was soon apparent in the improved vigour of the plants.[20]

Natural Ventilation

The reason why the ventilation in the Temperate House is important is not only to create a suitable environment for plants to live in, but also to provide a comfortable house for visitors to enjoy. According to the different climates under the five different zones of the Temperate House, some zones needed more ventilation to cool down the temperature, and some zones needed humid fresh air to comfort the plants inside as well. Ventilation, as its basic intention, is indispensable for a plant house to let the fresh air into the house. As has been mentioned before, in the North Wing and part of the Central Garden, many of the plants needed to grow in the open air for a long period of the year, so the windows needed to be kept open to ensure the fresh air flowed through the building.

The opening windows were laid both in the lower and upper structure of the house.[21] (Fig. 3) Also, there were sliding sashes on the top-roof of the building.[22] It was controlled by people at ground level, using the rope though a pulley to pull open the sliding sashes and to close them.   This enabled the rows of ventilator openings to be set easily and efficiently to achieve the plants requirements.

Depending on the different locations of the openings of the ventilation system, the temperature in the five zone could be controlled differently. In the warm zone, the glass could be fully closed and gain heat from the sunlight. On the contrary, if it needed the cooler conditions, once the windows were opened, the fresh cool air came though the upper level whilst allowing the hot air from inside the house to escape through the upper windows. This increased the air flow of and cooled down the overall temperature down by using the natural ventilation.

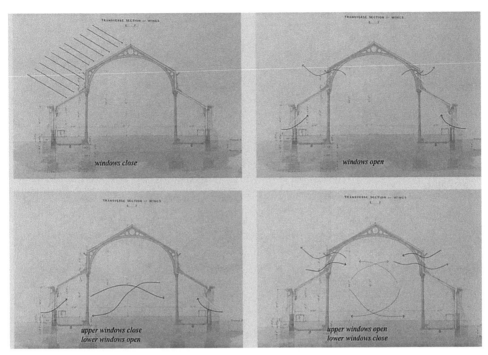

Fig.3. Temperate House, Kew Gardens. Architect, Decimus Burton. Plan showing section of wings to Temperate House, 1859

Heating pipe

Another important factor to maintain the temperature was the use of the heating pipes. These were used to achieve warmer conditions necessary during the winter period or on particularly cold days, especially in the South Wing and the Winter Garden.

Heating pipes were laid underground in the central garden in the centre and surrounding the house.[23] The two octagons have basements which originally housed the boilers.[24]

Once the water had been heated by the boilers, it flowed into the heating pipes throughout the building which then heated the air from outside. In the centre of the house, the heating pipes consisted of six pipes in length and four pipes in depth as a group (Fig. 4). Cool fresh air came through these groups and became warm when it came back to the house again. This heating system seemed to be the easiest way to warm the air at that time but not so sufficient in fact.

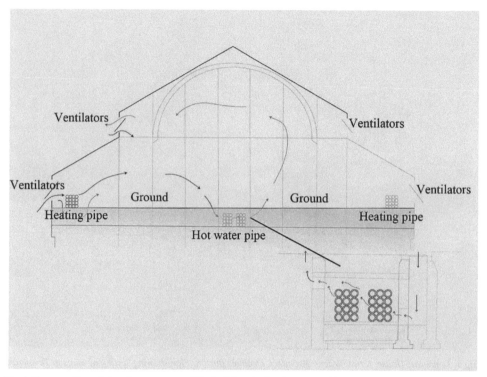

Fig.4. Cross-section of pipes in center part of the building (author's own work)

Drainage system

The problem of the drainage was as significant as the three factors discussed above. The depth of the beds was essential in the survival of rare and delicate plants, so as to avoid waterlogging on the one had or lack of water retention on the other. To secure the drainage so as not to damage to the plants, the arrangements of the drain-pipes were required to carry the surplus water efficiently out the house.[25]

Further, due to the wet climate of Britain rain that fell onto the roofs of the five buildings was collected and convened into six underground tanks. Originally, as the Centre Garden and two octagons were firstly built, only four tanks were set around the centre block in 1861 to 1862 which were used to collect the drainage from the building. When the water was needed for irrigation, pumps were used to elevate the water. When the two additional wings were constructed, two smaller tanks were added in 1898.[26]

Post-occupancy problems

Although the Temperate House was an advancement in horticultural building at that time, it was plagued by many problems once it was put to full use. Firstly, as the Temperate House was located on a north-south axis, during the winter the huge structure of the building allowed very little light into the house, so that the plants could not get enough sunlight to survive. Thus, many plants could not be grown in such dark environments. Secondly, as has already been mentioned, the octagons had the boiler underground, which caused the climate to be too hot and arid for the plants to thrive. Further, the chimneys laid in the octagons were built very low so that the waste fuel combustion would be deposited back on the glass roof, however this backfired by eventually turning the glass completely black.[27] Although there were not many plants in the octagons, this black caused by the chimneys obviously had an adverse effect on the plants within, due to the steady decrease of sunlight.

Moreover, the rain water supply also proved insufficient during the dry periods and many of the collection pipes underground became blocked due to this reason. However, in 1966 a new ring main was installed to link the six storage tanks together with cast iron pipes to keep a constant level of water in the system which led a more efficient and reliable water supply.[28]

Conclusion

This paper sought to explain the different character of the five zones inside the Temperate House and the technologies used to maintain the well-being of the plants it housed, despite the fact that these plants were from different climate from around the world. It also illustrates the important aspects required for a horticultural building of such a large size. The glass structure ensured adequate sunlight while the ventilation together with the heating system utilized the basic technology of that period. This research suggests that the whole system had achieved the original goal of its design — to provide a suitable environment for the exotic plant species in spite of using these basic technologies. At the time it was considered as a great success. However, after years of use, the Temperate House slowly revealed some problems which were not only a threat to the health of the plants but also endangered the building itself. The Temperate House not only functioned as a plant house, but also as a tourist attraction. Thus, the indoor comfort for both the plants and human were taken into consideration. To conclude, the problem for future designers to solve is to achieve the balance between the requirements of the plants and the buildings successfully which is the basic task when designing horticultural buildings.

Reference

[1] 'Damage from Bombs to the Royal Botanical Gardens at Kew', 1940, *Science*, 92 (2400), pp.597-598.

[2] J. Hix, *The glasshouse*, London: Phaidon, 2005.

[3] E. Salisbury, *The Royal Botanic Gardens*, Kew, 2017.

[4] National Archives, Work 32/338, Kew Gardens: Temperate House. Plan of centre portion of Temperate House showing proposed arrangement of earth beds and paths. Scale: 1 inch to 16 feet. By Decimus Burton, 1859.

[5] F. Hepper, *Bible plants at Kew*. London: H.M.S.O, 1981.

[6] Restoring the Temperate House at Kew Gardens, Available at: https://www.youtube.com/watch?v=q2KjCYjg-kc (Consulted on 13 Nov. 2017).

[7] H. Belloc, *On. Freeport*, N.Y.: Books for Libraries Press, 1967.

[8] National Archives, Work 32/338, Kew Gardens: Temperate House. Plan of Temperate House. Scale: 1 inch to 20 feet. By Decimus Burton, 1859.

[9] National Archives, Work 32/338, Kew Gardens: Temperate House. Quarter plan of upper roof of centre part of Temperate House. Scale: 1 inch to 4 feet. By Decimus Burton, 1859.

[10] A. Paterson, *The gardens at Kew*. London: Frances Lincoln, 2008.

[11] F. Hepper, *Kew, gardens for science and pleasure*. London: H.M.S.O, 1982.

[12] J.B. E Simmons, *Kew's architectural plant houses*. Kew: royal botanic gardens, 1982.

[13] D. C. Scoot, *The Palm House and Temperate House at the Royal Botanic Gardens, Kew.* London: Polytechnic of North London School of Librarianship and Information Studies, 1984.

[14] D. Oliver, *Guide to the royal botanic gardens and pleasure grounds, Kew.* London: British Library, Historical Print Editions, 2011.

[15] National Archives, Work 32/338, Kew Gardens: Temperate House. Ground plan of octagons. Scale: 1 inch to 4 feet. By Decimus Burton, 1859.

[16] The Horticultural Building, *Scientific American*, 65(3), pp.35-35, 1891

[17] National Archives, Work 32/338, Kew Gardens: Temperate House. Half roof plan of wings to Temperate House. Scale: 1 inch to 4 feet. By Decimus Burton, 1859.

[18] National Archives, Work 32/338, Kew Gardens: Temperate House. Roof plan of octagons. Scale: 1 inch to 4 feet. By Decimus Burton, 1859.

[19] H. Schoenefeldt, 'The use of scientific experimentation in developing the glazing for the Palm House at Kew', *Construction History,* 2011, Vol. 26, pp. 19-39

[20] F. Hepper, *Kew*, London: H.M.S.O, 1987

[21] National Archives, Work 32/338, Kew Gardens: Temperate House. Transverse section of centre part of Temperate House. Scale: 1 inch to 4 feet. By Decimus Burton, 1859.

[22] National Archives, Work 32/338, Kew Gardens: Temperate House. Transverse section of centre part of Temperate House. Scale: 1 inch to 4 feet. By Decimus Burton, 1859.

[23] National Archives, Work 32/340, Kew Gardens: Temperate House. showing the heating pipes. Also detail section of pipes. Scale: 1 inch to 8 feet; 1 inch to 2 feet. By Decimus Burton, 1860.

[24] National Archives, Work 32/338, Kew Gardens: Temperate House. Basement plan of octagons. Scale: 1 inch to 4 feet. By Decimus Burton, 1859.

[25] J. Guthrie, A. Allen, C. Jones, S. Hooker, W. Hooker, D. and Burton, 'Royal Botanical Gardens, Kew: Restoration of Temperate House', 1988, *Proceedings of the Institution of Civil Engineers*, 84(6), pp.1109-1143

[26] National Archives, Work 32/340, Kew Gardens: Temperate House. Roof plan of octagons. Scale: 1 inch to 4 feet. By Decimus Burton, 1859.

[27] "The Temperate House, Royal Botanic Gardens, Kew." *Illustrated London News*, 11 May 1867, p. 457. The Illustrated London News Historical Archive, 1842-2003, tinyurl.galegroup.com/tinyurl/5XPft3. Accessed 18 Nov. 2017.

[28] Report on the Progress and Condition of the Royal Gardens at Kew during the Year 1874, 1875, Nature, 12(307), pp.445-446

Ancient World

The beginnings of stone construction in archaic Greece

Alessandro Pierattini

School of Architecture, University of Notre Dame, US

Introduction

The Pindaric myth narrating the construction stages of the Temple of Apollo at Delphi, from the primitive laurel hut to the stone temple, is so embedded in humanistic culture and has generated such iconic visualisations throughout history that for generations art and architectural historians have addressed the origins of Greek stone construction mainly from a literary perspective. As emblematic as Pindar's passage, Vitruvius's description of how elements of Doric and Ionic stone architecture would have originated from wood construction has generated a conspicuous literature exploring the alleged ties between technique and the aesthetics of the orders. Yet stone construction appeared in Greece before the orders, and such a crucial innovation in Greek architecture has not duly been explored in the light of the physical evidence from the earliest Greek stone buildings. What triggered the development of Greek stone construction, and what can the first ashlar blocks of Greek architecture tell us about early construction technologies?

After the fall of the Mycenaean civilization, in the Early Iron Age (1100-700 B.C.) the use of stone in construction had mostly been confined to rubble socles supporting mud brick walls. It was between the eighth and the seventh centuries B.C. that squared stone blocks were first adopted in Greek architecture. In particular, two Greek areas lead the way in this connection: Ionia, in the east, and the Corinthia, in mainland Greece. As we will see, while early Ionian stone masonry was conceptually not too different from previous experiments in other eastern Mediterranean cultures, Corinthian stone masonry is to be regarded as the first true antecedent of later Greek ashlar construction. In this paper, I explore the origins of Corinthian stone construction and reflect on whether this was a genuinely local innovation or rather one inspired from abroad, as well as on why it manifested itself in this area around the mid-seventh century B.C. Moreover, I will re-examine features of the blocks that shed light on aspects of the Corinthian building process and on the early stages of crane technology, which represents a major Greek contribution to ancient construction.

Origins of Corinthian ashlar masonry

Ashlar masonry appeared in the Corinthia in two temples built during the first half of the seventh century B.C., which are those of Poseidon at Isthmia and of Apollo on Temple Hill, at Corinth. The remains of these two temples are so similar that they are regarded as two almost-twin products of the same local culture. While the evidence from Isthmia has been partly published,[1] that from Corinth is yet mostly unknown to the scholarly audience.[2] A brief description is in order. The blocks from the two temples (Fig.1) have a relatively modest size compared to those used in later archaic and classical architecture. Their thickness is 0.26 metres at Isthmia and about 0.22 metres at Corinth, while their width varies between 0.50 and 0.65 metres, and their average length is about 0.80 metres.[3] They were set in place without mortar or metal clamps, and their lateral and lower faces were slightly hollowed out in order to facilitate contact with their neighbors, which represents a first, rudimentary form of anathyrosis. They are made of oolitic limestone,[4] which is a characteristic component of the local geology. Abundance of this stone, which is compact enough to fit construction needs but relatively soft and easy to cut with iron tools, played a critical role in the early development of Corinthian stone architecture. Intensive exploitation of this resource would later become an important component of the local economy and would boost the creation of transportation routes on land and sea, as is testified by the presence of prominent monuments made of Corinthian oolitic limestone not only at Corinth but also at Delphi and Epidauros.

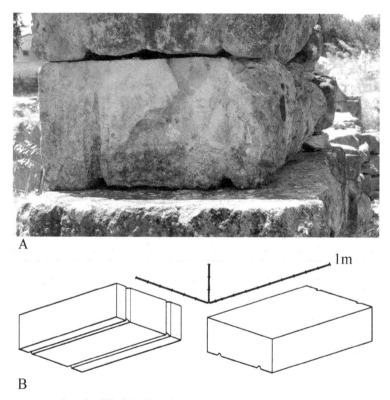

Figure 1. A: grooves on the side of block Ar 20 (Isthmia); B: typical groove disposition on the bottom of the block and going up one end. Drawing and photo: the author.

What makes early Corinthian blocks so interesting to us is that they were parallelepipeds as thick as the wall, therefore arranged as through stones in a single-wythe masonry, with courses of equal heights (isodomic). The idea of stone parallelepipeds squared on all sides might seem obvious in the light of later Greek architecture, but it was not so for Greek builders before the mid-seventh century B.C. The novelty of this concept becomes evident if we compare Corinthian ashlar masonry to the almost contemporary stone masonries of Ionia. Here, between the eighth and the early seventh centuries B.C., the Temple of Artemis at Ephesus and that of Hera at Samos were entirely built of stone. Differently from Corinthian masonry, in both Ionian temples the cella consists of double-skin walls, with blocks on the two faces of the wall and earth and rubble infill in between. While the blocks from Samos have a consistent height and thus their courses appear isodomic, both these and the ones from

Ephesus were only squared and smoothed on their exposed side, in addition to their top and lower surfaces, whereas their sides and back were left unworked. In the same period, even rougher walls were built on Crete and in the Cyclades with coarse stones not quarried but collected from the surface. In short, in Greece there seem to be no parallels or direct antecedents for early Corinthian ashlar masonry. This raises the question of its origins, whether local or inspired from abroad, as one might suppose considering the Egyptian primacy in stone working, or of the oriental influence that characterizes this period of Greek history. In this connection, E. Gebhard has compared the peculiarities of Corinthian stone work with ashlar masonry in other cultures of the Eastern Mediterranean.[5] Ashlar masonry with rectangular exposed faces was used in this broad area ever since the Bronze Age. In particular, its beginnings can be traced in Egypt as early as the 27th century B.C., and during the second and early first millennia B.C. stone block masonry appeared on Crete, in northern Syria, on Cyprus, in Phoenicia and in Palestine. Egyptian wall blocks were usually squared on their exposed face and on their horizontal surfaces, as they were mostly used as facing in thick walls with a core of roughly worked stones.[6] (Fig. 2) Isodomic masonry with regular joints did exist since the beginning, as shown by the funerary complex of Djoser (mid-27th century B.C.), but it is relatively rare, and the frequent change in course height and the presence of oblique or stepped joints demonstrate that the builders aimed at saving material rather than at obtaining regular wall patterns. Moreover, ever since the Old Kingdom (beginning from around 2600 B.C.), Egyptian blocks were tied to each other by means of wooden or metal clamps, which were not used in Corinthian masonry and would appear in Greek construction only later in the Archaic period.

Figure 2. Stone masonry types in Egyptian construction. Drawing and photo: the author, after Arnold 1991, p.148, fig. 4.72.

On Crete, stone block masonry appeared in monumental architecture in the Early Palace period (beginning from around 2000 B.C.). A distinctive feature of Cretan walls[7] is the presence of orthostates, which do not seem to have been used in Corinthian masonry. Analogously to Egyptian blocks, Cretan orthostates were used as facing in thick double-skin walls with earth and rubble infill, and only their exposed surfaces were squared and dressed. Usually, the superstructure of the wall consisted of a wooden framework with rubble and mortar infill. In some cases, however, the whole wall was made of blocks, but these, too, were only squared and finished on one exposed face. Even though in some cases a block was almost as thick as the wall, the back was left unworked and covered with plaster.[8] (Fig. 3) Patterns were relatively regular, with horizontal beddings and vertical joints. However, although courses of about the same height are occasionally observed, apparently Cretan builders were not interested in obtaining an isodomic pattern, and block heights vary a great deal in some cases. Between the mid-second and the early first millennia B.C., walls consisting of thick orthostates supporting wooden structures with rubble infill similar to the Cretan ones were also built in northern Syria and on Cyprus, where coursed ashlar masonry was apparently not used.

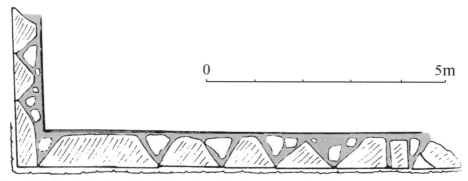

Figure 3. Palace of Kato Zakro (Crete), plan of a wall on the western side of the Central Court. Drawing and photo: the author, after Shaw 2009, p. 270, fig. 122.

It is in Palestine in the Early Iron Age that we find the closest parallels for Corinthian ashlar masonry. Examples from Samaria and Megiddo show blocks of a standard size and sometimes squared on all six faces like those from the Corinthia. Another similarity with the Corinthian blocks is that Palestinian ones are used without clamps or other metal elements. On the other hand, these blocks are usually arranged in characteristic patterns of alternating sets of headers and stretchers, all standing on edge, and they were combined with wooden structures. Moreover, as we will see in short, Corinthian blocks have characteristic grooves that served specific purposes in construction. These are not observed on Palestinian blocks, which points to differences in the building process. In brief, it seems from the above that no previous experiments with ashlar masonry in the Eastern Mediterranean qualifies as a direct antecedent for Corinthian masonry, and the idea of a single-wythe wall with blocks squared on all sides appears rather as a local innovation, potentially inspired from mud brick construction. A local origin is also supported by the Corinthian manufacture of stone sarcophagi, dating back as early as the second half of the tenth century B.C.,[9] which demonstrates that the Corinthians had long been able to quarry, carve, and transport sizeable parallelepipeds of the local stones by the time they started using similar, smaller blocks as building components.

We now turn to a second aspect of the question, which is why such a radical innovation appeared in the mid-seventh century Corinthia. In the eighth century B.C., isolated blocks were already adopted for particular purposes[10] in Corinthian buildings made of rubble or mud brick. The decision to construct whole buildings with standard-size, fully squared blocks was a radical and ambitious one with profound implications on technology, specialization of craftsmanship, and the local economy. We have already introduced two key factors that made this possible in the Corinthia, namely the availability of suitable stone and the presence of a local stone working tradition. Interestingly, the same is true for Ionia, a region rich in stones and where the use of blocks in construction had an antecedent in the ninth century B.C. fortifications at Old Smyrna.[11] Yet a peculiarity of the Corinthian phenomenon has led scholars to believe that it was a technical reason that triggered the transition to stone construction in this area. Interestingly, in the two mid-seventh century B.C. Corinthian temples stone walls appeared since the very beginning in combination with the first terracotta roof tiles of Greek history, which suggested a close relationship between the two phenomena. Indeed, beginning from this period tiled roofs replaced thatched ones in Greek architecture, and the concurrent adoption of stone masonry instead of mud brick has been seen as dictated by the greater weight of tiles as opposed to thatch. This view has since been generalized and appears in most handbooks of Greek architecture. As rational as this explanation appears, however, at a closer look it proves unfounded. To begin with, early stone temples in Eastern Greece (Ionia and the Cyclades) and Crete had no tiles but flat clay roofs, or in some cases thatched ones. On the other hand, while tiled roofs spread quickly in Greece from the mid-seventh century on, in most regions mud brick remained the usual material for cella walls for over half a century thereafter. Some Late Geometric temples, such as that of Artemis Aontia at Ano Mazaraki (ca. 700 B.C.), had their original thatched roof replaced by a tiled one during the sixth century B.C., but there was apparently no need to replace their mud brick walls with stone. Moreover, in Etruria, where tiled roofs spread at the same time as in Greece and were used even more frequently, stone masonry never replaced mud brick. It is plain enough, in brief, that the seemingly compelling cause-effect rationale of this explanation has no historical foundations, and the following technical reflections confirm that we should discard it altogether. While there is no question that terracotta weighs much more than thatch, volume being the same, we must note that a substantial layer of thatch is needed in order to seal the roof effectively, while tiles are relatively thin (usually 0.02-0.04 metres). Estimates based on findings of tiles from archaic Greek and Etruscan contexts show that the load of a tiled roof varies from 60 kg/m2 (Etruscan roofs at Aquarossa[12]) to about 94 kg/m2 (mid-seventh century tiles from Isthmia and Corinth[13]), whereas the overall load of a thatched coat is between 25 and 50 kg/m2, depending on thickness and on the kind of thatch employed. However, while tiled roofs have a shallow pitch, thatched ones are remarkably steep, usually from about 45 to 60° or more. This means that, roof plan being the same, the slopes of a thatched roof are substantially longer than those of a tiled one, and with a 60° pitch their total surface is almost twice as large. (Fig. 4) As a consequence, a thatch coat and the wood beams that support it are not necessarily much lighter, if at all they are, than a corresponding tiled roof.

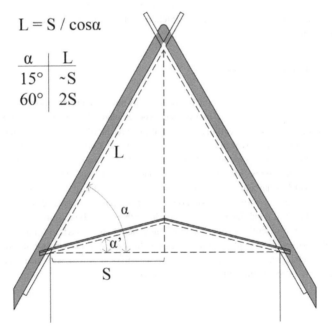

Figure 4. High pitch thatched roof and low pitch tiled roof: relationship between the pitch and the length of the slopes. Drawing: the author.

One more point deserving attention is that, while limestone is a much stronger material than mud brick, nonetheless, the latter has a compressive strength up to more than 30 kg/cm2,[14] so that a wall 0.50 metres thick, which is usual in early archaic Greek architecture, would be able to support loads immensely larger than the heaviest possible tiled roof.[15] As a matter of fact, mud brick walls were used in tall, multi-story buildings in ancient Rome and, later, especially in the Middle East, so the idea that this material could not support a single tiled roof is simply implausible. Rather than technical, the reason that prompted Corinthian builders to adopt stone walls seems more probably related to its longer durability, which is a particularly desirable feature in a monument. After all, as we have seen, in previous centuries the stone had almost only been used for sarcophagi, which were meant to guard the remains of distinguished warriors indefinitely. Interestingly, in general, shift in focus from the funerary sphere to cults was a distinctive feature of early archaic Greek culture. Indeed, while in pre-urban Greek societies burial had represented the only tangible form of status display, in eighth century B.C. Greek poleis ritual offering to the gods became the main way for citizens of all social levels to display their wealth and establish their status. This fact and the remarkable wealth achieved by some Greek cities in this period have a direct bearing on our topic, for the temple embodied a community's ultimate gift to the gods and thus its construction became the foremost target of public outlay. In particular, building became a priority in the political agenda of Cypselus, the aristocrat who overthrew the oligarchic regime of the Bacchiads and established a tyranny at Corinth right before the middle of the seventh century. The unlawful origin of his power prompted him to display strong leadership by undertaking ambitious, unprecedented public projects, and the continuity of his reign, which lasted for over thirty years, allowed him to bring them to completion. All things considered, the appearance of Greek stone monumental architecture hic et nunc, in the mid-seventh century Corinthia, seems consistent with the extraordinary conditions at play in this area during this crucial period of Greek history: abundance of local stone and the ability to square it into blocks, accumulation of wealth and a cultural and social value system that conveyed it towards temple construction, and a strong leadership that saw in this process a major tool for propaganda.

Early Corinthian building technology

Having explored the origins of Corinthian stone masonry, let us now examine the most characteristic trait of the Corinthian blocks, which is the presence of two parallel grooves along the bottom and continuing vertically up one end. As we will see, these peculiar cuttings are critical to understanding how the wall blocks were lifted and assembled. According to the first excavators of the early temples at Corinth and Isthmia, S. Weinberg and O. Broneer, respectively, the grooves served to hold ropes used in lifting each block and lowering it into place with a crane and then to extract the ropes, after the block was placed in contact with its neighbor (Fig. 5). This idea entails that the crane, which is among the major Greek inventions in building technology, was already adopted in stone construction since the very beginning. However, the earliest positive evidence for the use of this machine dates to about one century and a half later, at the end of the sixth century B.C. Moreover, it has been questioned whether the grooves were sufficiently deep to accommodate ropes strong enough to lift a block and allow them to be extracted after the block was set in place.[16] Addressing these questions is a matter of some importance to the history of ancient construction. I will begin with the practical aspects and will then examine the historical plausibility of the use of a crane in the mid-seventh century B.C.

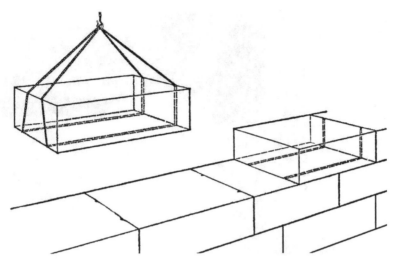

Figure 5. Grooves and ropes interpreted as devices for lifting with cranes. Drawing: the author, after Robinson 1976, p. 226, fig. 7.

In a recent article, F. Hemans has briefly reported that most of the blocks from Isthmia have grooves deep enough to accommodate modern sisal ropes sufficiently strong to support the heaviest blocks.[17] For a more accurate assessment, I have re-examined the blocks from the two early temples at Isthmia and Corinth with the support of the American School of Classical Studies at Athens and of the University of Chicago Excavations at Isthmia. In particular, I have measured their grooves and examined the data in relation to the weight of the largest blocks and to the strength of the ropes arguably employed by the Corinthian builders. The grooves have a triangular or trapezoidal shape in cross-section, and their width is usually about twice as large as their depth. At Corinth, the minimum depth that I have recorded is 0.01 metres (occurring only in one case, block n. 165). (Fig. 6a) The remaining blocks have groove depths between 0.012 and 0.037 metres, with maximum frequency between 0.018 and 0.023 metres. Because the blocks from Isthmia were used to reconstruct a portion of the cella wall, their grooves are often inaccessible. However, 45 of the 162 preserved blocks[18] are in such positions that allow measurement of their grooves. The minimum depth value is 0.011 metres (block IA 1382, Fig. 6b), while in most cases depth ranges from 0.02 to 0.03 metres, with a maximum of 0.035 metres (IA 1587). As the minimum value is 0.01 metres, we now need to assess whether ancient ropes of a compatible thickness could lift the heaviest blocks, which are the cornice blocks from Isthmia, weighing up to 360 kg. (Fig. 7) Among the plant species mentioned by ancient authors in relation to rope fabrication,[19] flax (*linum usitatissimum*), broom (*spartium junceum*), and bulrush (*scirpus holoschoenus*) were endemic to Greece. Flax was probably used for this purpose ever since the Late Bronze Age, as suggested by Linear B sources stating that the city of Pylos was well known for the cultivation of flax and the fabrication of ropes.[20] We may conclude that ropes of flax and probably other fibres of comparable strength would have been available in the seventh-century B.C. Corinthia. This seems natural if we consider Corinth's advanced ship building industry in this period,[21] for strong ropes are an essential in nautical technology. A traditional flax rope 0.008 metres in diameter, which could easily be accommodated by the grooves, has a breaking load of about 500 kg, which is more than necessary to our purpose. We must thus conclude that, technically, the idea that the grooves served for lifting is plausible. But would it have been possible to extract the ropes after setting a block in place, given the high friction coefficient of oolitic limestone and the relatively low flexibility of traditional ropes?

Figure 6. Samples of minimum groove depth. A: Block no. 165 (Corinth). B: Block Ar 70 (Isthmia); the block is upside down, so the groove faces upwards. Photos: the author.

Figure 7. Isthmia, cornice blocks from the early temple. Photo: the author.

To answer this question, I have carried out experimental tests on replica blocks of the same dimensions and material as the original ones. (Fig. 8a-c) Grooves have been cut on the replicas using the original tooling process, which can be reconstructed on the basis of the tool marks observed in the grooves: a first, rough processing by adze or axe and then, in some cases, further finishing by chisel. In this experiment, I have used traditional broom and flax ropes (Fig. 8b) with diameters of 0.008, 0.010, and 0.012 metres, which have been slipped out of grooves with depths of 0.010, 0.012, and 0.015 metres, respectively. While the critical point was the 90° angle at which the grooves turn up on the end set against the adjoining block, on the whole, the operation proved to be relatively effortless and produced no damage on the stone surfaces.

Figure 8. A: replica block with a groove 0.012 m deep accommodating a 0.010 m thick rope. B: broom (top) and flax (bottom) ropes 0.008 m thick. C: rope extraction test. Photos: the author.

We now turn to the historical aspect of the question. In a seminal essay, Jim Coulton argued that the use of the crane was not common practice in the Greek world until the late sixth century B.C.[22] It was in this period that metal devices used to suspend blocks from ropes became usual tools in Greek construction, as is shown by the widespread presence of tong and lewis holes on contemporary archaic blocks. At the same time, a reduction in the maximum size of blocks employed in Greek monumental architecture has been interpreted as a clue that some radical change occurred in lifting technology – presumably a shift from the inclined plane to early crane prototypes, whose loading capacity was presumably limited at the beginning. The blocks from the two early Corinthian temples antedate this period by about a century and a half. This fact suggests caution in accepting that they were lifted with a crane rather than on a ramp of earth, as we must assume was usual during most of the Archaic period. However, if we look back to how the Corinthians handled their stone sarcophagi since the second half of the tenth century B.C., the idea that some prototype of the crane might have been used in construction in the seventh century B.C. does not seem too implausible. Corinthian sarcophagi are monoliths weighing up to over 2.5 tons that were lowered into pits that were too narrow to allow for the use of a ramp. More likely, these massive blocks were moved vertically by means of some kind of apparatus. Was this a crane? The formidable performances that earned cranes a prominent place in later Greek and Roman technical literature[23] (Fig. 9) were due not so much to their frame as to the sophisticated mechanisms that were associated with it in order to gear down the load – the multiple-pulley hoist – and to multiply the effect of manpower – the winch or capstan, and the windlass.[24] Evidence for the latter devices is found since around 600 B.C. at the Diolkos – the paved trackway created across the Isthmus of Corinth under Periander (625-585) –, where rope marks and holes have been interpreted as traces from haulage of heavy cargo with capstans.[25] The earliest evidence for hoists, instead, is in the pseudo-Aristotelian Mechanics 18 (ca. 270 B.C.), although these devices might already have been part of the crane in the late sixth century B.C. In brief, we cannot assume that advantageous mechanisms were used in the ancient world before 600 B.C. However, a simple, mechanically non-advantageous device consisting of ropes passing over a wooden framework used to change the direction of pull[26] would have been an obvious system throughout the Eastern Mediterranean since the Bronze Age. This is shown by representations of sail vessels from Egyptian reliefs and wall paintings and from Greek vases (Fig. 10), which suggest that all sail maneuvers employed systems of ropes and frameworks redirecting pull, just as in modern boats. It was probably a mechanism based on the same concept, which we may consider as a forerunner or a component of the crane, that the Corinthians employed to move their monolithic sarcophagi and, later, to lift the first ashlar blocks of Greek architecture, in the mid-seventh century.

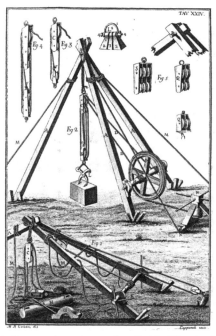

Figure 9. Cranes with hoists, windlasses and capstans as described by Vitruvius, illustrated by Berardo Galiani (L'architettura di Marco Vitruvio Pollione, Naples, 1758, pl. XXIV).

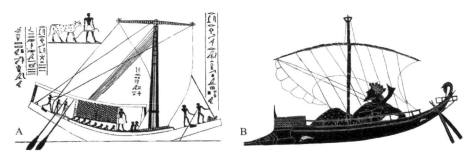

Figure 10. A: sailing craft in an Egyptian painting from the tomb of Kaem'onkh at Giza (2400-2300—B.C.). B: Dionysos's boat from the cup by Exekias (540–530 B.C.). Drawings: the author.

One last aspect of the Corinthian blocks deserves attention in connection with the building process. My examination of the evidence has revealed cuttings that have been overlooked in previous scholarship. These occur on most blocks, at the bottom of a contact end, which is where a lever hole is usually found on blocks from the later Archaic period onwards. The lever served to maneuver each block into place tightly up against its neighbor – a complex operation that required absolute precision. While the cuttings on the early Corinthian blocks are roughly made and do not always appear on the same side,[27] they most likely served a similar scope and thus represent the first evidence for the use of levers in Greek construction.

Conclusions

The masonry of the two mid-seventh century temples of the Corinthia, which represents the first true ashlar construction of Greek history, seems to have been a local innovation and was made possible by the availability of suitable local stone and by a well-established stone working tradition. The adoption of stone walls was not due to the need to support a tiled roof, as previously thought. Rather than a cause-effect relationship, the fact that these two momentous innovations appeared in combination in early Corinthian architecture suggests that they were both prompted by the builders' ambition to lend their monuments a centuries-long durability. On the other hand, financially, stone construction required considerable resources that became available only when thriving Greek communities organized themselves and chose to invest a substantial part of their wealth in the construction of monumental architecture. Finally, what triggered this process in the Corinthia was the political agenda of a tyrant who saw in architecture a powerful tool to legitimize his leadership. The blocks from the early temples at Corinth and Isthmia also cast light on the beginnings of Greek stone construction technologies. Analysis of their distinctive grooves, study of ancient ropes and experimental tests confirm that the blocks were plausibly lifted by means of machines as early as the mid-seventh century B.C. Regarding the nature of this apparatus, it was probably a framework serving solely to redirect pull. Only later, during the sixth century B.C., would such a framework be combined with the winch and the hoist, which would turn it into the advantageous lifting machine that responds to the definition of a crane. Finally, cuttings observed on most blocks show that levers were already employed to maneuver blocks into place since the very beginning of Greek ashlar construction.

reference

[1] O. Broneer, *Isthmia I: The Temple of Poseidon*, Princeton: The American School of Classical Studies at Athens, 1971. pp. 3-56. This monograph includes references to previous articles on the temple.

[2] For partial descriptions of the blocks, see references in R. F. Rhodes, 'The Woodwork of the Seventh Century Temple on Temple Hill in Corinth," in A. von Kienlin, (Ed.), *Holztragwerke der Antike: Internationale Konferenz, 30. März–1. April 2007 in München, Byzas*, vol.11, 2011, pp. 109–124.

[3] Width and length figures refer to the blocks from Isthmia, some of which preserve their original dimensions, whereas the blocks from Corinth do not.

[4] C. L. Hayward, 'Geology of Corinth: The Study of a Basic Resource', in Williams and Bookidis, 2003 (Note 2) pp. 16–17.

[5] E. R. Gebhard, 'The Archaic Temple at Isthmia: Techniques of Construction', in M. Bietak, (Ed.), *Archaische griechische Tempel und Altägypten*, Vienna: Verlag der Österreichischen Akademie der Wissenschaften, 2001. pp. 47–50.

[6] D. Arnold, *Building in Egypt: Pharaonic Stone Masonry*, Oxford: University Press, 1991. pp. 148-178.

[7] J. W. Shaw, *Minoan Architecture: Materials and Techniques,* Padova: Aldo Ausilio, 2009. pp. 54-73.

[8] Shaw, 2009 (Note 8) p. 270, fig. 122.

[9] G. Sanders, S. A. James, I. Tzonou-Herbst, J. Herbst, 'The Panayia Field Excavations at Corinth: The Neolithic to Hellenistic Phases', *Hesperia*, vol.83, 2014. p. 36.

[10] Gebhard, 2001 (Note 6) pp. 51-53.

[11]   R. V. Nicholls, *Old Smyrna: The Iron Age Fortifications and Associated Remains on the City Perimeter,* The Annual of the British School at Athens, vol. 53/54, 1958/1959, pp. 68-71, 96-100.

[12]   O. Wikander, *The Roof-Tiles: Typology and Technical Features,* in *Acquarossa VI.2,* Stockholm: Åström, 1993. pp. 128-30.

[13]   P. Sapirstein, 'The Emergence of Ceramic Roof Tiles in Archaic Greek Architecture' (Ph.D. thesis, Cornell University, 2008), p. 352, n. 886.

[14]   G. Gaeta, E. Lo Giudice, 'Mattoni crudi e mattoni in terracotta: confronto delle proprietà meccaniche e limiti strutturali', in M. L. Germanà, R. Panvini, (eds), *La terra cruda nelle costruzioni: dalle testimonianze archeologiche all'architettura sostenibile,* Palermo: Nuova Ipsa Editore, 2008. pp. 227-34.

[15]   35 Kg/cm2 x 5000 cm2 = 175,000 kg.

[16]   R. F. Rhodes, 'Rope Channels and Stone Quarrying in the Early Corinthia', *American Journal of Archaeology,* vol.91, 1987, pp. 545–51. Further objections regard blocks with peculiar groove dispositions. A more extensive discussion of the grooves and their function will appear in A. Pierattini, 'Interpreting Rope Channels. Lifting, Setting, and the Birth of Greek Monumental Architecture', in preparation.

[17]   F. Hemans, 'The Archaic Temple of Poseidon: Problems of Design and Invention', in E. R. Gebhard, T. E. Gregory (eds), *Bridge of the Untiring Sea* (Hesperia suppl. 48), 2015, p. 47.

[18]   These include those published in Broneer 1971 (Note 1) and some unpublished ones.

[19]   On ancient sources, see L. Casson, *Ships and Seamanship in the Ancient World,* Princeton: Johns Hopkins University Press, 1971, p. 231.

[20]   R. Williams, 'Nestor's War Effort', *Classical Quarterly,* vol.36.1, 1986, pp. 280–3.

[21]   Thucydides (I, 13) recounts that the Corinthians modernized shipbuilding and invented the trireme, and that the Corinthian shipwright Ameinocles built four ships for the Samians around 704 B.C.

[22]   J. J. Coulton, 'Lifting in Early Greek Architecture', *Journal of Hellenic Studies.* vol.94, 1974, pp. 7, 16.

[23]   Hero, *Mechanica,* 3.2; Vitruvius, 10.2.8–10.

[24]   The main difference is that the winch and the capstan have a vertical axis, whereas the windlass has a horizontal axis.

[25]   G. Raepsaet, 'Le diolkos de l'Isthme à Corinthe: son tracé, son fonctionnement, avec une annexe, Considérations techniques et mécaniques', *Bulletin de Correspondance Hellenique,* vol.117, 1993, p. 255.

[26]   Sanders et al., 2014 (Note 9) pp. 39-40.

[27]   On some blocks it appears on the grooved side, on others on the opposite end.

Middle Ages

The Vault over the Crossing Tower in Lincoln Cathedral in the Context of European Gothic Architecture

José Calvo-López[1], Enrique Rabasa-Díaz[2], Ana López-Mozo[2], and Miguel Ángel Alonso-Rodríguez[2]

1. Universidad Politécnica de Cartagena, Spain; 2. Universidad Politécnica de Madrid, Spain

Introduction

In addition to quadripartite or tierceron vaults, Late Gothic builders in many European countries used other particular layouts. Among many others, groups of tierceron vaults and asymmetric vaults are particularly puzzling. They pose some interesting questions: did these types arise independently in different locations, or are they a result of knowledge transfer between distant lands? Did the masters who adopted a solution which originated in a different country hear about it somehow, or did they have a deeper technical knowledge of these solutions? We should take into account that the horizontal projection of a vault, or at least its basic diagram, can be deduced from simple visual inspection; however, it is not easy to grasp the spatial layout of the ribs and the height of the bosses of these members without direct involvement in its construction.

The group of four tierceron vaults in the crossing tower in Lincoln Cathedral (c. 1306) furnishes an outstanding case study of these issues. Looking at the plan, it seems a simple juxtaposition of four ordinary tierceron vaults. However, there is no central pier between the four vaults, as would be usual in hall vaults, for example. Instead, a main keystone is placed at the top of the vault, much above the springers. As a result, the keystones of the individual tierceron vaults are relegated to the role of secondary bosses. The vault at Lincoln crossing is one of the oldest examples of this type,[1] which spread later through Poland, Germany, France, Spain and Portugal. The general layout of the vault can be easily appreciated from the floor of the crossing. However, the precise shape of the diagonal and transverse ribs cannot be determined from mere visual inspection alone; thus, it is not easy to tell whether the similarity between Lincoln and the Continental vaults extends to their spatial layout.

All this has led us to survey both the Lincoln crossing vault and a significant number of vaults of this type in the Continent, using automated photogrammetry to measure both their plan layouts and their spatial configurations with precision. In this paper, we shall explain in detail the results of our Lincoln survey, also including a general, schematic view of its Continental counterparts, in order to analyse the influence of English vaulting systems in Europe and the mechanisms of knowledge transfer.

The vault over the Lincoln crossing tower

The crossing of Lincoln Cathedral was built in the 13th century; however, around 1306, Richard of Stow added a new story, building a new vault formed by an array of four tierceron vaults. If we leave aside for the moment its spatial layout, the plan involves four individual cells, each one with the layout of an ordinary tierceron vault including, as usual, peripheral arches, diagonal ribs, tiercerons and liernes (Fig. 1). The latter are extended all the way to the peripheral arches, crossing the whole vault, as usual in English ridge ribs. However, they are not real ridge ribs, since the association of four tierceron vaults brings about noticeable changes in the spatial organisation of the vault.[2]

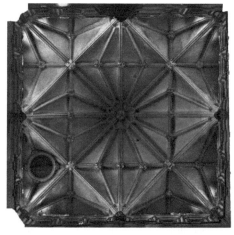

Figure 1. Vault over the crossing tower of Lincoln Cathedral. Ortophotograph prepared by automated photogrammetry.

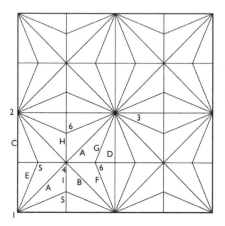

Figure 2. Vault over the crossing tower of Lincoln Cathedral. Schematic plan. Ribs are marked with letters; keystones and bosses are marked with numbers, as explained in the text.

José Calvo-López. Enrique Rabasa-Díaz, Ana López-Mozo, and Miguel Ángel Alonso-Rodríguez

Before tackling this issue, we should take into account that the mere association of different tierceron vaults brings about important changes in the role of each of these constituent elements. First, there are two different kinds of diagonal ribs (Fig. 2). For each individual cell or unit, a diagonal rib (A) is placed along the diagonal of the whole ensemble, while the other one (B) is just the diagonal of an individual unit, going from the midpoint of one side of the area to the midpoint of the next side. The sides of each cell or lesser square are treated in different ways. Those placed at the periphery of the ensemble (C) are not materialised as actual ribs; the severies of the vault simply intersect the crossing tower vaults in the shape of pointed arches. However, these intersections take the shape of two pointed arches on each side of the ensemble, one for each cell. Each of these pointed arches springs from a corner of the ensemble and an intermediate pier placed at the midpoint of a side of the area; thus, there are eight springers in total (1, 2). By contrast, the sides of the cells that are placed at the axes of the ensemble (D) go all the way from one side of the vault to the opposite one, meeting with each other at the main keystone (3) placed at the centre of the vault. There are also three different kinds of tiercerons: for each cell, two pairs of tiercerons (E) are placed along the peripheral walls, starting from springers and reaching secondary keystones (5) while the other two pairs are placed along the ribs over the axes of the ensemble. The latter can be further classified into tiercerons starting from the springers placed at the midpoints of area sides (F) and reaching secondary keystones (6), and tiercerons of a different kind (G) which start from secondary keystones (6) and rise to the main keystone (3). Finally, liernes can be divided into those that start at the perimeter (H) and the ones that meet at the axial ribs (I). All of them are placed at lines that divide the plan into one-quarter and three-quarters of the side of the area.

As for keystones, an ordinary tierceron vault involves just a main keystone and four secondary keystones or bosses. In the Lincoln model, there is a main keystone, placed at the centre of the vault (3), where the edges of the individual units meet. The main keystones of the cells are relegated to the role of second-order keystones (4), while the secondary keystones of the units are in turn demoted to third-order keystones. In theory, there are two different kinds of third-level keystones, those next to the corners of the area (5) and those next to the main keystone (6); however, this distinction is not essential, as we shall see. Also, the keystones of the peripheral arches of the individual units are now placed either in the walls of the crossing tower (7) and thus not materialised, or in the axial ribs; the latter are executed as an additional kind of boss (8). All in all, five different kinds of keystones.

All this can be appreciated with the naked eye. However, the possible solutions for the spatial layout of a vault with this plan are quite different, as we shall see when dealing with Continental vaults. Also, it is not easy to determine the precise shape of diagonal and transverse ribs or tiercerons from the floor, in particular in Lincoln, where the height of the crossing tower does not help to see the vault from a distance. Thus, in order to analyse thoroughly the geometry of the Lincoln vault, a precise survey is essential; we will deal with it in the next section.

Surveying the vaults at Lincoln crossing and other locations

We have surveyed the vault at the Lincoln crossing using automated photogrammetry, processing a number of photographs in a specialised program, namely Agisoft PhotoScan Professional. In particular, we have used 115 photographs, taken with a Nikon D810 camera, with a resolution of 7360 by 4912 pixels, using a 70-200 mm lens, set at 125 mm. In order to achieve maximum sharpness, camera and lens were set at ISO 64 and f/11, and a medium-weight tripod was used. Speeds were measured by the camera, ranging between 2,5 s and 5 s.

The Vault over the Crossing Tower in Lincoln Cathedral in the Context of European Gothic Architecture

After taking the photographs, they were processed in the office using Photoscan. First, this program scans the images looking for corresponding groups of points in the images; then it uses these groups of points to perform internal orientation, computing the relative positions of the lens in each photo and constructing a sparse point cloud. Second, Photoscan matches correlative points in the oriented photographs to increase the density of the point cloud. As a third step, a polygonal mesh is interpolated from the points in the dense point cloud. Then, the program projects the photographs onto the polygonal mesh to build a textured 3D model of the vault, which can be exported to standard formats, such as VRML or 3D PDF, or used to prepare orthophotographs representing plans, elevations, or axonometrics. Photogrammetry is based on conic or central projection, as perspective, and thus it cannot measure absolute distances by itself. In other words, no self-standing photogrammetric process can scale models or furnish a reference for verticals. To overcome this limitation, we have taken the coordinates of three easily identifiable points, such as the intersections of the three-quarter ribs with the peripheral walls, using a Leica DistoS910, which includes a laser distance meter, a compass, and an inclinometer. This instrument is quite convenient as a supporting device in photogrammetric surveys, since it can be mounted on a photographic tripod using a special head, thus reducing the additional weight and volume carried when working out of the office. The specially-designed head guarantees that the instrument keeps its centre fixed while rotating around horizontal and vertical axes. Also, points taken with the DistoS910 can be imaged by a low-resolution video camera included in the instrument. The combination of a distance meter, an inclinometer, and a compass provides spherical coordinates; the internal software of the instrument converts them to rectangular ones, with a precision of +- 1 mm. These coordinates may be imported into PhotoScan, either in the field or the office; using this additional information the program can refine the internal orientation of the photographs, also allowing users to add scales and vertical references to three-dimensional models.

The geometry of the vaults at the Lincoln crossing

The model of the Lincoln vault, imported in Rhinoceros 3D, a powerful CAD program, has allowed us to determine several important features of the vault. In this case, the ribs placed at the axes of the ensemble (D) are simple pointed arches, made up of two circular arcs (Fig. 3); tiercerons (E, F, G) follow the shape of a circular arc, as usual; ribs placed at three-quarters of the side of the ensemble (H, I) are nearly horizontal; diagonals of the lesser squares (B) are pointed arches; and finally, the main diagonals (A) are traced as a particular kind of oval.

This last detail may be striking, but it gives a clue to the whole design procedure of the vault. We should take into account that the shape of the diagonal is conditioned by five points: its start and end at the springers (1); its intersection with the ribs placed at three quarters of the side of the vault (H), which are horizontal, at second-level keystones (4); and the main keystone (3). The choice of simple shapes for the ribs over the axes (D) and the three-quarters ribs (H), in contrast with the diagonals (A), does not seem to be casual; it hints that the shape of the diagonals is a result of the constraints placed by the simpler members.

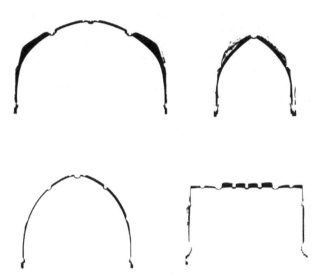

*Figure 3. rib profiles, taken from the point cloud gathered by automated photogrammetry. From left to right and
top to bottom, diagonal rib(A), unit diagonal(B), axial rib(D), three-quarter rib(I,H).*

Thus, we can put forward a hypothesis for the tracing procedure for the vault in the Lincoln crossing, starting from an axiom: simpler members were traced first and the shape of complex members was conditioned by constraints set by the preceding members. Probably, the ribs over the axes of the ensemble were traced first, as ordinary pointed arches, using standard procedures.[3] Next, the three-quarter ribs were traced as horizontal members. Their level is determined by the height of their intersection with the axial ribs. Probably, some trial and error were needed at this stage, since the intersections of these three-quarter ribs with the peripheral walls are placed a few feet above the apices of the lancet windows in the wall. Then, the diagonals were set out so that their directrices pass through the springers of the vault (1), the intersections with the three-quarter ribs (4), and the main keystone (3). The lower tiercerons (both E and F) are traced taking into account the level of the springers and their intersections with the three-quarter ribs, while the upper ones (G) pass through these intersections and the main keystone. Of course, two ends do not determine a circular arch; a third condition is needed. In this case, the tangent at the start (1 or 2) of the lower tierceron (E or F) is approximately vertical, as usual, while the tangent of the upper tierceron (G) at its junction with the main keystone (3) is horizontal, also following standard practice. Finally, the other diagonals of the individual cells (B), going from one perimeter wall to the other (2) without crossing the main keystone, can be traced using the same method as in the lower tierceron; that is, keeping its tangent at the springer (2) vertical. However, these later operations involving approximate tangencies were quite probably carried out by trial and error; even in the 16th century, the drawing for a tierceron vault in the manuscript of Hernán Ruiz shows some hits and misses for the centres of the tiercerons, as has been known for some time.[4]

It is not likely that such complex geometry was produced without the help of some drawing or tracing. In a quadripartite vault on a square or rectangular plan, for example, diagonal ribs will cross automatically at the main keystone as a result of the symmetry of the piece, without the need for any special method of formal control. By contrast, in an ordinary tierceron vault, nothing guarantees that tiercerons and liernes will meet in space unless their curvatures are well controlled. Full-scale tracings of Gothic architectural members are not unusal in England or the Continent[5]. However, most of these tracings depict gables, flying buttresses and the like; vaults are very scarce. A remarkable exception is a huge tracing of a net vault in Szydłowiec, in Poland[6], but it seems to have been executed as a demonstration for the patron rather than as a working drawing for the construction of the vault. Other examples of full-scale tracings for rib vaults can be found at the other end of the continent, in Tui and Montederramo, both in Northwestern Spain, but they date from the 18th century.[7]

The lack of surviving tracings for Mediaeval vaults can be explained by a well-known passage from a lost manuscript by Rodrigo Gil de Hontañón, a prominent Spanish 16th-century master mason, which was reproduced in a later manuscript by Simón García.[8] Hontañón explains how to construct a complex ribbed vault, stating that

> ... you should prepare another scaffolding at 5 (in the accompanying figure). This second scaffolding should be entirely covered with strong planks so that you can draw and trace all the ribs on it, as seen in the plan. Once you have done that and all keystones are marked in the plan on the planks, you should hang plumb bobs from the vaults (to the tracing) for the keystones placed along the diagonals[9]

Thus according to Hontañón, tracings for vaults were prepared on a scaffolding, rather than in floors or walls; this explains that few of them have survived. They were used not only to determine the curvature of the ribs and the height of keystones in the design stage; they were reused during the execution phase in order to control the correct placement of the keystones using plumb bobs in order to ascertain that they were placed exactly over their theoretical projection, as depicted in the tracing. Such practices were quite sensible. If the masons were to prepare the tracing of a vault on a cathedral floor, oscillations of the plumb line and difficulties in communication between masons on the scaffolding and their mates down on the floor would make the method unreliable or even useless for the control of voussoir placement. All this explains why vault tracings have been preserved in Tui and Montederramo: they were executed for the construction of low-rise members. By contrast, the Hontañón method makes sense in the case of Lincoln, given the great height of the crossing vault. Quite probably, a full-size tracing for the vault was prepared on planks laid out on a scaffolding and lost.

Arrays of tierceron vaults in Continental Europe

Similar arrays of four tierceron vaults can be found in the churches of Orneta and Branievo, now in Poland, dating from the mid-14th century, both executed in brick. Later examples can be found in Spain, for example in the chapel of Our Lady of the Old Cathedral in Seville,[10] built in 1485 by German masters[11] (Fig. 4). There are also arrays of four stars in the church of Saint Mary of the Pomegranate in Niebla, west of Seville, dating from 1515[12], in the crossing of the Royal Hospital in Santiago de Compostela (Fig. 5), executed around 1527[13], the church of Saint Mary of the Harbour in Santoña, begun around 1530 and probably finished in 1562[14], and the retrochoir of Salamanca cathedral, built in 1598 by Juan del Ribero Rada. Possibly the latter used a basic scheme by Juan Gil de Hontañón, the father of Rodrigo Gil.[15]

Figure 4. Vault over the chapel of Our Lady of the Old Cathedral in Seville.

Figure 5. Vault over the crossing of the Royal Hospital in Santiago de Compostela.

In addition to arrays of four stars, there are extensions of the Lincoln type, for example in Santoña: next to the four-cell example we have mentioned and dating from the same period, there is a six-cell vault (Fig. 6). The crossing of the Hieronymite monastery in Belém, near Lisbon, much larger than all preceding examples, is also solved using an array of three by two units (Fig. 7). It was built between 1516 and 1522 by Juan del Castillo, a mason born in Liérganes, near Santoña, who had worked in Seville before arriving in in Lisbon, which may explain some common traits with the Old Cathedral example, although the overall result is quite different.[16] The vaults in the church of Saint-Eustache in Paris (Fig. 8), built around 1532, and Lidzbark Warminski, in

Poland, dating from around 1497, also feature two by three units. However, as we will see, in these latter examples the number of vaults in the longitudinal direction is not really relevant.[17]

Figure 6. Vault over the crossing of the church of Our Lady of Harbour in Santoña.

Figure 7. Vault over the crossing of the church of the Hieronymite monastery in Belém.

Figure 8. Vault over the cathedral of the church of Saint-Eustache in Paris.

As noted, in most of these examples the plan follows the Lincoln scheme closely. There is simply a juxtaposition of tierceron vaults, except in Seville and Belém, where ribs do not reach exactly the corners of the cells, a typical Late Gothic fancy detail. However, spatial layouts are quite different. First, intermediate supports along the perimeter are used only in Lincoln, Santiago and Bélem. The rest of the examples solve the problem with the corner springers; in other words, peripheral arches that span each of the sides of the area. Paris and Lidzbark Warminski stand at a middle ground: arches span the shorter sides of the plan, including two cells; by contrast, there are supports in all unit corners along the longer sides; the result resembles a barrel vault with lunettes.

However, even in Santiago, the shape of the transverse and diagonal ribs differs from the Lincoln model: the member that seems to govern the layout of the vault is the semicircular diagonal rib. In Orneta, Seville and Niebla diagonal ribs are also semicircular. However, the effect is quite different, since there is a single peripheral arch in each side of the area, in contrast with two arches per side in Santiago. Thus, the final result in Seville or Niebla resembles a sail vault, that is, a spherical vault cut by four vertical planes in the sides of the area. The general shape of the Salamanca vault is similar, although in this case, diagonal ribs are oval, in an attempt to limit the height of a vault placed over a large, rectangular area.

There are still other solutions. In Belém, the transversal arches that separate each pair of units from the next one are semicircular. By contrast, the axis of the central unit, placed over the the symmetry axis of the vault, is a three-centre oval. Gómez Martínez remarked on the formal similarities between the Santoña vaults and the Bélem ones.[18] However, their spatial layout is quite different. Leaving aside the four-unit vault, which is quite different to the six-cell Bélem ensemble, in the six-star vault in Santoña there are no intermediate supports in the perimeter. As a result, transverse arches do not start from the springers' plane but rather from an intermediate point in the peripheral arch; quite reasonably, they are surbased to avoid excessive height. Given the six-star layout, the diagonals of the area are not materialised by ribs; the nearest thing to a diagonal rib are the diagonals of groups of four vaults, starting in a corner of the ensemble and ending in an intermediate point in the opposite side of the area. These "fake diagonals" are semicircular and seem to be the governing members in the Santoña six-cell vault.

Despite geographical and chronological differences, the examples in Paris and Lidzbark Warminski are remarkably similar. Both designs are based on two units in the transversal direction, since there is a single arch spanning the width of the area. By contrast, the use of one arch per unit in the longitudinal direction allows the vault to grow indefinitely, at least in theory; in practice, there are two by three units both in Paris and Lidzbark. Transversal arches are oval, while the rib placed over the longitudinal axis of the vault is horizontal. This layout leads to the general shape of a barrel vault; however, tiercerons and liernes allow raising the surface of the vault to form the equivalent of a series of lunettes. While the spatial strategy is the same in Paris and Lidzbark, the formal treatment is quite different. As remarked by Norval White, in this church the ornament is classical, implying that the general spatial design is Gothic; however, the use of classical decoration signals the beginning of the end of this essentially Late Mediaeval constructive type.

Conclusion

Lincoln Cathedral is well known for its innovative vaulting systems, such as its early tierceron vaults, which later crossed the English Channel to the crossing of Amiens cathedral, and its "crazy" vaults, which furnished a model for many Late Gothic vaults in Poland, Germany, France and Spain.[19] The importance of the vaults at the crossing tower must also be stressed: they are laid out in the plan as an array of four tierceron vaults, but they feature a complex spatial layout; this vault, and maybe other English examples, fostered a rich family of star-vault arrays, spreading along most of Continental Europe, from Eastern Prussia to Western Iberia.

However, different geometrical solutions were used in most Continental pieces. The key to the spatial solution of each vault is the member that directs the layout. In Lincoln, this role is played by the axial ribs, which control the horizontal three-quarters ribs, which in turn determine the unusual shape of the oval diagonal ribs. The solutions in Belém, Paris and Lidzbark, are similar, although in these cases the controlling member is not placed exactly at the axis of the vault, but rather at a transversal arch. It should be stressed that in none of these vaults are the results identical with Lincoln; none of them uses an array of four vaults or independent arches on the perimeter. By contrast, in Orneta, Seville and Niebla, featuring two-by-two arrays, the directing members are the semicircular diagonal ribs. Variants of these solutions can be found in Salamanca, where the directing member is still the diagonal, although it is traced as an oval in order to avoid excessive height, and Santoña, where the controlling "diagonal" does not cross the full area of the vault, but rather a group of four cells, out of a total of six units.

All this suggests different levels or routes of knowledge transfer: the builders of many significant examples in Western and Central Europe may have heard about the English scheme, but had no detailed knowledge of the particular solution used in this cathedral, or else they wished to explore alternative paths. In other words, the use of the English model in the Continental examples was anything but mechanical or unimaginative.

José Calvo-López. Enrique Rabasa-Díaz, Ana López-Mozo, and Miguel Ángel Alonso-Rodríguez

Acknowledgements

This paper is part of the research project "Construction of Late Gothic Spanish Vaults in the European Context. Innovation and Knowledge Transfer" (BIA2013-46896-P), financed by the Ministry of Economy and Competitiveness of Spain.

Reference

[1] J. T. Frazik, 'Zagadnienie sklepień o przęsłach trójpodporowych w architekturze średniowiecznej', *Folia Historiae Artium*, vol. 4, 1967, pp. 5–91, mentions a similar vault in Westminster Abbey, built in the mid-13th century and destroyed in 1941.

[2] About the architectural history of the crossing, see G. Webb, *Architecture in Britain. The Middle Ages* London: Penguin Books, 1956, and P. Kidson, 'Architectural History', in Owen, Dorothy (Ed.), *A History of Lincoln Minster* Cambridge: Cambridge University Press, 1994, pp. 14-46.

[3] About these procedures, see R. Branner, 'Villard de Honnecourt, Archimedes, and Chartres', *Journal of the Society of Architectural Historians,* 1960, vol. 19, n° 3, pp. 91-96; L. R. Shelby, 'Setting out the keystones of Pointed Arches: A note on medieval "Baugeometrie" ', *Technology and Culture,* vol. 10, 1969, n° 4, p. 537-548; R. Bechmann, *Villard de Honnecourt. La penseé technique au XIIIe siécle et sa communication*, Paris: Picard, 1991.

[4] H. Ruiz el Joven, 'Libro de Arquitectura', Biblioteca de la Escuela de Arquitectura de la Universidad Politécnica de Madrid, 1550 c., f. 46v; facsimile ed., 2005. Madrid: Universidad Politécnica de Madrid, 2005. See also E. Rabasa Díaz, 'Técnicas góticas y renacentistas en el trazado y la talla de las bóvedas de crucería españolas del siglo XVI', in Casas Gómez, Antonio de las, et al., (Ed.) *Primer Congreso Nacional de Historia de la Construcción, Madrid 1996*, 1996: Instituto Juan de Herrera, Madrid, p. 423-434.

[5] See J. Harvey, 'The Tracing Floor in York Minster', *Annual Report of the Friends of York Minster,* 1968, n° 40, pp. 1-8; A. Holton, 'The Working Space of the Medieval Master Mason: the Tracing Houses of York Minster and Wells Cathedral', in Dunkeld, Malcolm, et al., (Ed.), *Second International Congress on Construction History, Cambridge 2006*, 2006: Construction History Society, Cambridge, pp. 1579-1597; C. F. Barnes, Jr., 'The gothic architectural engravings in the cathedral of Soissons', *Speculum,* vol. 47, n° 1, 1972, p. 60-64; F. Claval, 'Les épures de la cathedrale de Clermont-Ferrand', *Bulletin Archéologique du Comité des travaux historiques et scientifiques,* n.s., n° 20-21, 1988, pp. 184-224, to quote only a few relevant studies.

[6] M. Brykowska, 'Quadratur des spätgotischen Gewölbes im Chorraum der Pfarrkirche zu Szydowiec/Polen', *Architectura*, vol. 2, n° 22, 1992, p. 101 - 108.

[7] M. Taín Guzmán, 'The drawings on stone in Galicia: Types, uses and meanings', in Huerta Fernández, Santiago, (Ed.), *First International Congress on Construction History, Madrid 2003*, 2003: Instituto Juan de Herrera, Madrid, p. 1887-1898, in particular p. 1892; M. Taín-Guzmán; M. Á. Alonso-Rodríguez; J. Calvo-López; P. Natividad-Vivó, 'Stonecutters' literature and construction practice in Early Modern Gothic: the tracings for a rib vault at the Cathedral of Tui in Galicia', *Construction History, n°* 27, p. 1-21, 2012.

[8] S. García, 'Compendio de arquitectura y simetría de los templos, conforme a la medida del cuerpo humano', Biblioteca Nacional de España, MS 8884, 1681. Facsimile edition, Valladolid: Colegio de Arquitectos, 1991.

[9] "... se ará otro segundo andamio como 5. Y este tan quajado de fuertes tablones, que en ellos se pueda traçar, delinear, y montear, toda la cruceria ni mas, ni menos de lo que se ve en la planta. Esto echo y señaladas todas las claues en su lugar sobre los tablones dejar caer perpendiculos, de la buelta a ellas, esto es para las que

están en los cruzeros o diagonales". Transcription by Cristina Rodicio Rodríguez, taken from the 1991 facsimile edition.

[10] The name refers to a fresco of the Virgin Mary, painted in a wall of the old mosque, which was used a cathedral. The fresco itself has been preserved in the eponymous chapel of the extant 15th-century cathedral.

[11] J. Gómez Martínez, *El gótico español de la Edad Moderna. Bóvedas de Crucería*, Valladolid: Universidad de Valladolid, 1998, p. 86; see also M. Á. Aramburu-Zabala Higuera, 'La iglesia de Santa María de Puerto en Santoña', *Monte Buciero,* 2000, n° 5, p. 7-28, in particular p. 16.

[12] E. Infante Limón, 'La cabecera tardogótica de la parroquial de Santa María de Niebla (Huelva): una obra promovida por el arzobispo fray Diego de Deza', in Alonso Ruiz, Begoña ; Rodríguez Estévez, Juan Clemente (Ed.), *1514. Arquitectos tardogóticos en la encrucijada,* Sevilla: Universidad de Sevilla, 2016, p. 237-248.

[13] J. Villaamil y Castro, 'Reseña histórica de la erección del Gran Hospital Real de Santiago, fundado por los Reyes Católicos', *Galicia Histórica,* vol. 2, n° 8, 1903, p. 475; J. Gómez Martínez, *Gótico español* (note 11), p. 72-73; A. A. Rosende Valdés, *El Grande y Real Hospital de Santiago de Compostela*, Madrid: Electa, 1999, p. 37-39.

[14] M. Á. Aramburu-Zabala Higuera, 'La iglesia de Santa María de Puerto en Santoña', *Monte Buciero,* n° 5, p. 7-28, 2000, in particular p. 15.

[15] Gómez Martínez, *Gótico español* (note 11), p. 88.

[16] Gómez Martínez, *Gótico español,* (note 11), p. 87; see also Aramburu-Zabala, 'La iglesia de Santoña' (note 14), p. 16; S. Genin, 'Voûtes à Nervures Manuélines' (Ph. D. thesis, KU Leuven, 2014), p. 42.

[17] J. T. Frazik, 'Zagadnienie ...' (note 1).

[18] Gómez Martínez, *Gótico español* (note 11), p. 87.

[19] P. Frankl, 'The "Crazy" Vaults of Lincoln Cathedral', *The Art Bulletin,* vol. 35, n° 2, 1953, p. 95-107; A. López-Mozo; R. Senent-Domínguez, 'Late Gothic Asymmetrical Diamond Vaults in Spain', *Nexus Network Journal,* vol. 19, n° 2, 2017, p. 323-343.

King's College Chapel Vault; Movement, Restraint and Foundation Loading

Michael D. Wood

Fellow of Gonville and Caius College, Cambridge University, UK

Abstract

It is now known that the vault of King's Chapel has suffered small distortions in geometry in the five centuries since it was built. The distortions are small, in the region of ten to fifteen centimetres in a span of ten metres.

The article investigates the loading which must be supported by the ground beneath each buttress, by considering the gravitational forces acting on various parts of the structure and the reactions required for stability. It is then shown how the vault movements may be qualitatively correlated with the loading.

George Gilbert Scott inserted transverse iron ties in the wooden roof structure in 1860. Their importance is demonstrated, showing that they limit undesirable loading on the structure.

Figure 1. King's College Chapel. Exterior from South.

King's College Chapel Vault; Movement, Restraint and Foundation Loading

Introduction

King's College Chapel is widely regarded as one of the finest examples of English Perpendicular Gothic architecture. (Fig.1). The original design was laid out by Henry VI in the document of 1448 known as his "Will". It was always intended that the Chapel should have a stone vault and strong buttresses featured in the original design. Construction was intermittent during the upheavals of the "Wars of the Roses" but by 1485, at the conclusion of the war, the eastern six and a half bays had been completed and roofed [1]. There was no further progress until 1506 when Henry VII finally authorised completion, appointing John Wastell as master mason [2]. The main structure was completed in 1512. Wastell was then commissioned to build the celebrated Fan Vault (Fig.2) which was finished in 1515 [3].

Figure 2. King's College Chapel. The Fan Vault.

The Chapel structure will have been monitored since completion for signs of movement and cracking. In the 1860 George Gilbert Scott was retained to give advice [4]. He detected certain cracking in the vault which he attributed partly to "spreading" of the wooden roof structure. He noted that when the roof was originally built it required no horizontal thrust from the stonework, the collar beams within the structure providing the necessary horizontal restraint internally (See Fig.3a). Gilbert Scott argued that over the centuries the collar beam pegs might have loosened, leaving the rafters as a simple triangulated structure requiring large horizontal restraining forces from the buttresses to provide stability. In turn, these forces would contribute to an "outward lean" of the buttresses [5]. He therefore recommended that iron ties should be inserted to prevent the roof "wedging action" which he deduced was partly responsible for the cracking. The ties were installed in 1863.

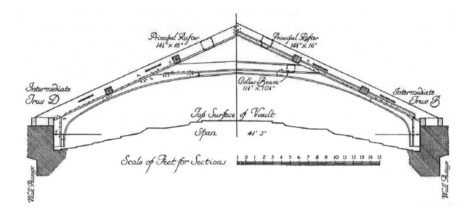

Figure 3a. Roof Truss.

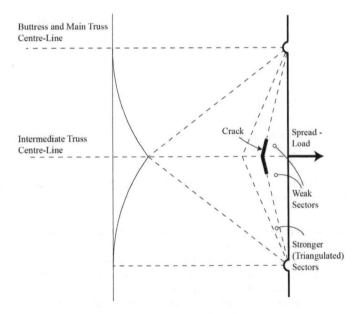

Figure 3b.   Schematic Spread-Loading on Vault from Intermediate Truss (Plan View).

King's College Chapel Vault; Movement, Restraint and Foundation Loading

This article explores the loading exerted on the buttresses in order to understand the directions of possible buttress movement, which in turn, would result in distortion of the vault geometry. Attention is then given to the loads exerted by the "spreading" of the wooden roof structure which was counteracted by the iron roof-tie restraint installed by George Gilbert Scott.

Our knowledge of the geometry of the vault has been greatly extended by recent "laser-scan" investigations. Ochsendorf and De Jong reported the results of such an investigation and considered whether the gravity loads which were revealed, were consistent with the clear, "global stability" of the buttresses [5]. In this context, global stability concerns the possibility that each buttress might topple over by rotation about ground level at its outside extremity. As expected, global stability in this sense was found to be assured by the weight distribution compensating for the over-turning effect of the vault thrust on the buttress.

This article extends the analysis to consider the restraint required to be supplied by the foundations beneath each buttress, and hence to improve understanding of the observed distortions of the vault.

Buttress Movements

Fundamentals

Fig.4 shows the conventional terms used to describe the vault geometry.

It is convenient to regard each buttress above ground level as a solid, capable of movement in each of three ways in a single vertical plane:

(i)   Horizontally, by sliding

(ii)   Vertically, by sinking

(iii)   Rotationally, by differential vertical movements along its length about a horizontal axis through the mid-point at ground level.

It is intuitively the case (and supported by natural laws) that any movement (or rotation) must be the result of a net force (or net moment) in the corresponding direction.

Each buttress is carried on a foundation which consists of "rough stonework" carried down to a depth of 12 ft 6 in and then resting on gravel (Note 2). The present article concentrates on the above-ground buttress and the loads which it must support.   It is assumed that each buttress must in turn be supported by its underlying foundation which with the gravel beneath, will respond to the loads applied by permitting small movements. No attempt is made to explain details of these movements below ground level.   It is merely asserted that they must have occurred (to explain the distortions in the vault structure) and that they will always be in the directions implied by the loading on the above-ground buttress.

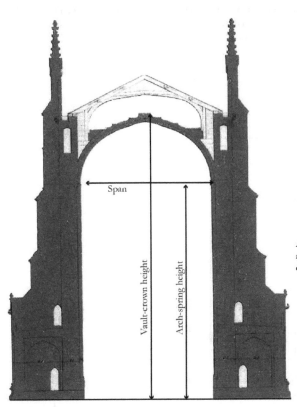

All vault-crown heights and
arch-spring heights measured from
common horizontal datum level.

Figure 4. Vault Terminology.

Movement of Buttress Corner

The upper corner of each buttress, where it supports the vault, is of particular interest (point H on Fig.5). If it sinks, and the buttress on the other side of the chapel east-west centre-line sinks symmetrically, then the vertical movement will be directly transmitted to the vault, which will also sink. Should the two buttresses sink by different amounts, the vault crown would be expected to sink by the mean of the two amounts.

This same buttress corner may also move horizontally as the buttress slides or, additionally, if the buttress rotates. These two separate movements might combine to increase the vault span. Providing the north-south pair of buttresses move symmetrically, then the increased span will result in a drop in the height of the crown of the vault on the chapel centre-line. Fig.5 shows a cross-section through the vault and buttress adapted from Ochsendorf and De Jong's work [5]. It is marked with a point "I" which would be the instantaneous centre for any movement of the half vault-span caused by horizontal movement of the top of the buttress. It appears that any such horizontal movement would inevitably cause the vault crown to drop by a slightly larger amount (proportional to the distances from I), providing the north and south buttresses move by similar (small) distances. It is clear that it may not be possible to allocate any partial increase in vault span either to sliding or to rotation. However, this division is of little importance since it is the sum of the two which is relevant to any drop by the vault crown. The total movement of each corner has been detected by the laser scan and is referred to as "sinking", vertically, and "sliding", horizontally, which increases the span.

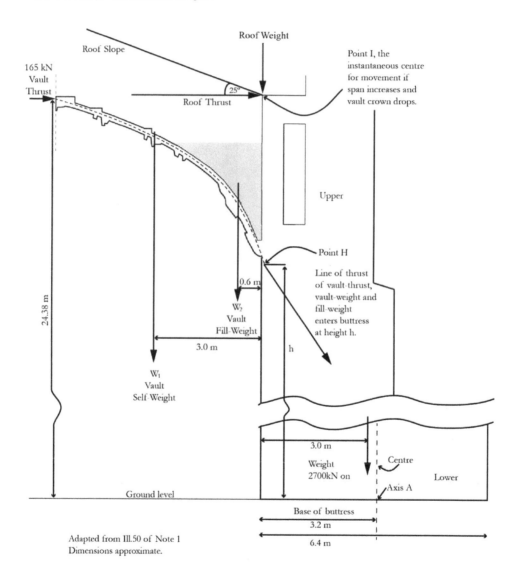

Figure 5. Vault/Buttress Loading.

The Laser Scan Results

These comments relate to some of the findings reported in J Ochsendorf and M DeJong, *King's College Chapel 1515-2015* [5]. In particular:

i.   The vault crown-height decreases progressively from east to west, the west end being some 10 cm lower than the east end. The east end vault crown height is taken as datum. It is not therefore possible to detect sinking of the east end since no early records of its height are known to the accuracy of the laser scan.

ii. The upright buttress walls show small rotations from the vertical which increase progressively from east to west. The rotation direction would increase the vault span in each case.

     Additionally, Dr DeJong has provided some extra information during private correspondence which was not described the paper cited.

iii. The spring heights for the vault at each buttress decrease from a true horizontal by some 19 cm from east to west on the north side and by some 8 cm on the south side.

iv. The total span of each section of the vault opposite each buttress increases by some 12 cm from east to west but there is no correlation between the increased span and the height of the vault crown above each springing level (as explained in Ochsendorf and De Jong [5]).

v.   Certain discontinuities were found in the height of the main ridge towards the west end of the chapel. It was suggested that buttress settlement might have occurred during the construction of the final building phase of the west end, and that the masons compensated for the sinking by introducing these corrections to maintain a perfectly level vault-crown in successive bays.

     It is interesting that the measured distortions of the vault are all of the order of 10-15 cm, which is equal   to the average thickness of the vault stonework. The vault remains stable even though it has suffered movements equal to its own thickness.

Analysis

Vault Loads

Fig.5 has been adapted from Ochsendorf and De Jong [5] (Illustration 53) to show the loads imposed on a half span of a typical length of vault supported by a single buttress. The horizontal thrust of 165 kN corresponds to that given by several independent estimates and is deemed to be a reliable value. The weight of the buttress, 2,700 kN, corresponds to the known volume of that element of the structure and is also accepted as reliable. Values for the vault weight W1 and conoid filling weight W2, are estimated afresh in this article and are shown to correspond to the requirements imposed by "Line of Thrust" considerations.

Vault Weight Estimates

The plan view of the part of the vault carried by one buttress would be a rectangle 7 metres wide (east-west) by 6 metres (north-south). The vault curves downward from the arch centre towards the outside walls so that, for the purposes of a weight estimation, the 6 metre dimension should be increased, (by examining the cross-sections shown in Ochsendorf and De Jong [5]) by some 10% to 6.6 metres. The average thickness of the vault has been taken as 17.8 cm (making allowance for the ornamental ribs, the solid thickness being 12.5 cm). The stone density is taken as 2310 kg/m^3 giving a weight estimate of 7.0 x 6.6 x 0.178 x 2,310 x 9.8 or   186 kN.

The two quarter conoids on each side of a typical buttress are approximately equivalent to a half cone of base radius 2.0 m and height 3.0 m. Hence the estimate for the weight of the fill is

$$\frac{1}{2} \times \pi \times (2.0)^2 \times 3.0 \times 1/3 \times 2310 \times 9.8 \quad \text{or 142 kN}$$

it being assumed that the rubble fill has the same density as stone.

These weight estimates may be checked for consistency with the requirements for the height of the "Line of Thrust" as it exits the vault and enters the supporting buttress. The predicted location must be within the stonework. If not, the stonework may be subjected to bending rather than simple compression, which would lead to instability and possible collapse.

Consider the moments exerted by the vault thrust, the vault self-weight and fill-weight about the point where the line of thrust enters the buttress. On Fig.5 this is designated to be at a height   h metres above ground level. The buttress side is deemed to be vertically below the outer edge of the conoid fill, as shown schematically in the Figure.

The moments must sum to zero since, by definition, there is no moment along the line of thrust. Thus 165 x (24.38-h) the vault-thrust moment, must be balanced by 186 x 3.0, the vault-weight moment, plus 142 x 0.6, the fill-weight moment. This leads to the value h=20.48 metres, which has been indicated on Fig.6. The weight estimates lead to the conclusion that the line of thrust enters the buttress slightly above the junction of the outside of each inter-bay rib with the side of the buttress. This corresponds with the location suggested by Heyman [7]. He shows that the line of thrust deduced from appropriate hanging chains super-imposed on an inverted concave conoid requires the line of thrust to pass into the solid fill of the vaulting conoids slightly above the rib-buttress junction.

The vault-weight and fill-weight estimates therefore lead to a predicted position for the line of thrust at entry to the buttress which is in accord with expectation. The weight estimates are therefore accepted as realistic and suitable for use in further analysis.

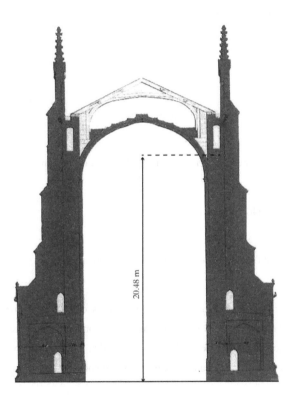

Figure 6.   Height of Thrust Line at Entry to Buttress.

Foundation Loading

It is possible to determine the total moment which must be provided by the foundation reaction to counterbalance the moments imposed on each buttress. Components of the total are established separately and are computed about a horizontal axis which passes through the buttress centre line at ground level, which is mid-way along the 6.4 m buttress length, as shown in Fig.5.

(i)   Vault thrust moment:

      165 kN at a height of 24.38 m   4023 kNm (clockwise)

(ii)   Vault self-weight moment

      186 kN at (3.0 + 3.2)m   1153 kNm (anticlockwise)

(iii)   Fill-weight moment.

      142 kN at (0.6 + 3.2)m   540 kNm (anticlockwise)

(iv)   Moment from displaced buttress self-weight (displaced by 0.2m from ground centre-line)

      2,700 kN at 0.2 m   540 kNm (anticlockwise)

(v)   Roof-weight moment (A small amount compared with other quantities)

A simple estimate using suitable dimensions for the rafters, collar beams, purlins and roof covering of lead suggests a roof-weight load for each buttress of some 50 kN. Some of this load would be carried to ground by the wall plates and nave walls so that less than the total would be carried by the buttress. Thus the most that would be carried as a moment by the buttress would be:-

      50 kN at 3.2 m 160 kNm (anticlockwise)

The sum total of these moments is a net clockwise value of 1790 kNm which might be reduced by a maximum of some 9% if the small effect of roof weight is included. This analysis shows that the moment exerted on the buttress which must be resisted by ground reaction, would have been predominantly outwards from the time of the completion of the vault in 1515. It would therefore be expected that the vertical walls at the buttress inner sides should incline outwards as a consequence of the deduced   loading.

Roof Spreading

George Gilbert Scott examined the vault in the mid-nineteenth century and observed cracks in the vault structure. He deduced that these faults might be partly due to "spreading" of the wooden roof structure. Fig.3 shows the wooden roof design. It was intended for a higher vault crown than that actually built by Wastell. There is only a high collar beam rather than a tie beam to prevent spreading. Gilbert Scott considered that the wooden pegs which locked the component parts of each roof truss together, might have deteriorated. If that happened, then each roof truss would require a restraining force from the stonework to prevent it "spreading". When the roof truss was new, it would have had its collar beam pegged to the rafters and there would have been no tendency for the truss to spread, nor any requirement for a restraint force from the stonework. If the pegs loosened, then a force would be required. It is possible to estimate the magnitude of the force under the extreme assumption that the pegs are entirely ineffective and the rafters are left to support the roof weight as a simple triangulated structure. In this worst case, the roof weight per buttress, estimated at 50 kN, would need to be supported by the thrust in the rafters set at an angle of 25° to the horizontal. The thrust would thus need to be 50 kN ÷ sin 25° which would have a horizontal component (50/sin 25) cos 25 or 107 kN. This horizontal force acting at a height of 24.38 metres would therefore exert a moment of 107 x 24.38 or 2609 kNm (outwards). It appears that Gilbert Scott was correct in deducing that the moment produced by roof spreading was important. The present analysis shows that roof spread might potentially add 2609 kNm to the outward moment of 1790 kNm attributed to the earlier stonework loads. Gilbert Scott had iron ties installed across the wood roof trusses to restrain any roof spreading in 1860. These ties would have reduced, or eliminated, the loads on the stonework due to the wedging action of the roof structure.

It is noted that the "Main Trusses" are aligned with the buttress themselves so that any wedging action load would be transferred directly to the top of a buttress. By contrast, the "Intermediate Trusses" are located between the buttresses. Any load caused by spreading of each Intermediate Truss would be transmitted to a weak section of the nave wall as shown schematically in Fig 3b. There are clear signs of incipient cracking between the pairs of the east/west sections of the vault conoids and adjacent sectors. These cracks run in an east/west direction at right angles to the direction of the intermediate trusses. Attempts have been made to bridge the cracks with iron clamps. It is these cracks to which Gilbert Scott presumably drew attention in 1860. Thus it seems that although Gilbert Scott ties were "desirable" in the Main Trusses, they may be seen to be "essential" in the Intermediate Trusses. Without these ties, any further deterioration of the intermediate truss pinning would have resulted in growing cracks in the vault. This analysis shows that the Gilbert Scott ties, in place for 150 years, have probably had a highly beneficial effect in reducing vault cracking. Fig.7 shows the ties resting on the top of the vault stonework.

There would be no danger of the buttress toppling over its outer lower corner even with the worst roof spreading moment. Global stability is assured by the buttress weight of 2700 kN acting at a distance of 3.4 m from the outer corner, which dominates other moments. This confirms the finding of Ochsendorf and De Jong [5] that global stability is guaranteed even including an estimate for the roof spread moment.

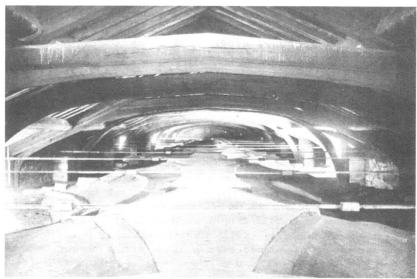

Figure 7. Iron Roof Ties.

Foundation Reaction Under the Buttress

It is not possible or necessary to determine the precise pressure reactions at every point under each above-ground buttress. These reactions will depend on possible fragmentation of the foundation structure and on the response to increases in penetration of the gravel subsoil by the very bottom of each buttress. Further, the local response under any particular buttress is likely to be time dependent as the buttress sinks or rotates. In spite of this uncertainty over the fine detail of the response pressures, it is necessary for the ground reaction to provide, at all times, the reaction which will balance the applied loading. It is therefore possible to speculate on the form of the pressure distribution which would satisfy this requirement. A possible schematic arrangement is shown in Fig.8.

First, the foundation below ground level, must provide a shear force F to balance the horizontal component of the vault thrust and, if relevant, by an addition for the roof-spreading effect. This force will be 165 kN for vault thrust only or a total of 272 kN if the worst case value for roof-spreading is considered. The shear force will be supplied by the "rough stonework" beneath ground level and will be reacted by soil pressure on the vertical faces of the below ground foundation together with the horizontal shear force exerted by the gravel layer on which the foundation rests.

The below-ground foundation must also provide vertical pressure loading on the bottom of the above-ground buttress to balance the applied vertical loads, that is the weights of the appropriate sections of vault, conoid filling and self-weight of the buttress as indicated in Fig.5. These weights will exert moments on the buttress foundation and the pressure distribution must match and balance these applied moments as well as the applied loads.

Fig.8 shows the schematically possible distribution of pressure immediately below ground-level. Equilibrium requires a balance of shear forces, vertical loads and moments exerted about the axis designated A in the Figure.

It is clear that the pressure distribution shown in the Figure is only one of a whole family of different possible curves any one of which could satisfy the equilibrium requirements. Each buttress will have its own curve which will satisfy local foundation and ground properties and which may even vary with time. On the other hand, it seems likely that the actual distributions will have a general appearance similar to the one shown.

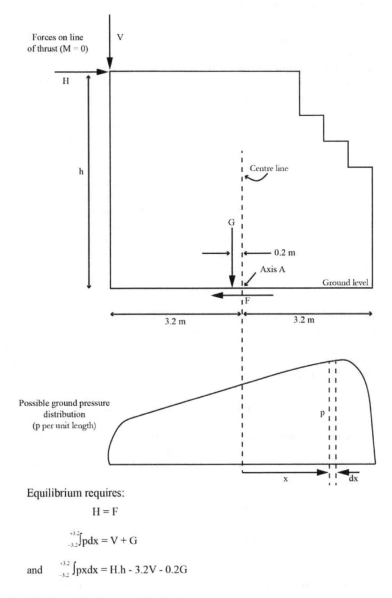

Equilibrium requires:

$$H = F$$

$$\int_{-3.2}^{+3.2} p\,dx = V + G$$

and $$\int_{-3.2}^{+3.2} px\,dx = H.h - 3.2V - 0.2G$$

Figure 8.   Possible Foundation Pressure Distribution.

Comparison with Observations

The calculated moment exerted on each buttress foundation would have been <u>outwards</u> from the time that the vault was completed. The roof-spread loading might have increased this moment but in the same direction until restrained by the Gilbert Scott ties. This accords with the observation of the outward "lean" of the buttresses.

Attempts were made to calculate the sinking of the vault crown due to span increase at each transverse arch (ie between pairs of buttresses on a north/south line). It is necessary to make the calculation on the basis of assumed hinge-line locations for the distortion mechanism. The simplest model is indicated on Fig 5 with the half vault moving about the point I as instantaneous centre. The increase in semi-span is assumed to move the 'tas de charge' outwards, and the resulting drop in the vault crown follows from consideration of the rotation of the part-vault about the Instantaneous Centre, I. This mechanism would require the development of Sabouret cracks between the conoid filling and the top of each buttress. Close examination of the location in the chapel itself, disclosed no sign of any such cracking. However, the source material for Note 1 suggested that a hinge-line (without cracking) might have formed at the junction of the flat top of the conoid fill with the vault arch because a slight "kink" in the vault profile was detected at that point. It is possible to repeat the calculation for the drop in the vault crown for given span increase according to a second mechanism which assumes that two hinge lines occur, one close to the crown and the second at the observed kink point. This kink point would move with the buttress as the span increased. Movement of the part-vault between kink point and crown would be about a new instantaneous centre immediately above the kink and on the same level as I. The results for the second mechanism show larger values for the predicted height reduction at mid span than for the first mechanism, typical values being 5.8 cm for the second mechanism compared with 3.4 cm for the first (for bays towards the west end of the chapel). These values are smaller than the total reduction in local vault height of some 10 cm detected by the laser scan in the same area.

Comparison of the possible drop in the vault crown caused by the increased spans with that due to simple sinking of the buttresses, shows that the two effects are of comparable magnitude. In both cases the effects are in the range up to 10 cm with the greatest values at the west end of the Chapel. Ochsendorf and De Jong noted that this increase towards the west end may be associated with the presence of the river which is only a distance away equal to the length of the chapel itself [5].

It has also been observed that the sum of the measured sinking of the springing of the vault spans, together with the expected drop of the vault crown caused by increase of each span, <u>exceeds</u> the actually observed drop in the vault crown. In some cases, towards the west end of the chapel line the excess may be as much as 12 cm. This effect is attributed to a "correction" which appears to have been built-in to the vault by the stonemasons during construction. The vault crown shows discontinuities in height between bays 3 and 4 of 6 cm and of 4 cm between bays 7 and 8 and 4 cm between bays 11 and 12. In each case the discontinuity reduces any loss of vault height from the starting level at the east end. It is deduced that the western buttresses must have sunk during the building period of 1508 to the latter stages of the vault construction (completed by 1515). The stonemasons would have easily built in a running correction to successive vault bays as construction proceeded and it was required that the vault crown should be strictly horizontal along its length. The evidence is far from precise, but no other explanation would easily account for the actual observations.

The explanation would also show why there is no correlation between the increases in span and the corresponding changes in height between springing levels and the vault crown. The running corrections made by the stonemasons would have changed the height differences in a way which was unrelated to subsequent changes in span.

Conclusions

a)   This investigation confirms that the loading of the foundation beneath each buttress is in accord with the observed movements of the vault. It is not possible to determine the fine detail of the resulting ground pressures, but a general pattern which satisfies the required equilibrium conditions has been presented.

b)   The mass distribution of vault and buttresses shown implies that there has been a net outward moment exerted on the buttresses, and hence on the foundation beneath, since the time the vault was completed in 1515. This moment has produced a small increase in the vault span which, in turn, has produced a small drop in the vault crown. This drop combines with that due to direct sinking of the buttresses in order to explain the reduction in the height of the vault crown at the west end compared with that at the east end. (It is not possible to determine the magnitude of any sinking at the east end).

c)   The drop in the vault-crown at each buttress position is less than the sum of the sinking of the corresponding springing points together with that due to an increase in vault span. It is concluded that some sinking of the western buttresses must have occurred in the 1508 – 1512/14 period after the buttresses were first built, but before the vault was completed in 1515. The stone masons would have compensated for the sinking of the buttresses by "stepping up" some of the vault crowns in order to maintain a truly horizontal level. This hypothesis accords with the discontinuities in vault-crown levels observed by the laser scan, and was originally proposed by those documenting the scan results.

The hypothesis would also explain why there is no correlation between the increase in span and the height from springing to vault-crown. The initial "corrections" by the stone masons would have been present before any subsequent height changes due to the increased span.

d)   The Gilbert Scott roof ties, inserted in 1860, have played a key role in preventing undesirable loading on the stone structure. Firstly, the ties limit the possible spreading load which might be exerted on the buttresses which in turn would add to the outward tilting of each buttress. Secondly, the ties fitted to the intermediate roof trusses reduce the spreading load to a weak part of the vault and nave wall, where cracking may be seen. It is recommended that tension in the roof ties should be checked as part of the regular maintenance programme.

Acknowledgements

The author wishes to acknowledge with gratitude, permission from King's College to publish the results of his investigation, and to include Figures drawn from college publications. He also wishes to pay tribute to Dr. DeJong's pioneer work on the Laser Scanning of the Chapel, and to thank Prof J. Heyman and Prof R. Blumenfeld for stimulating discussions during the preparation of this article. Lastly, he wishes to thank Jane Howson and Belen Tejada-Romero for creating elegant text and computer diagrams.

References

[1] F. Woodman, *The Architectural History of King`s College Chapel and its Place in the Development of Late Gothic Architecture in England and France*. London; Boston: Routledge and Kegan Paul, 1986, p. 221.

[2] Ibid., p. 157.

[3] Ibid., p. 197.

[4] J. Ochsendorf and M. DeJong, 'The Structure and Construction of the Chapel, in J. M. Massing, N. Zeeman (eds.) *King's College Chapel 1515-2015*. London: Harvey Miller, 2014, 74.

[5] Ibid., pp. 63-77.

[6] Ibid., plate 42.

[7] J. Heyman, *The Stone Skeleton*. Cambridge: Cambridge University Press, 1995, p. 82.

Medieval counter rebated doors. A door from the Diocese of Lund compared with the English examples

Karl-Magnus Melin

Department of Conservation, University of Gothenburg, Sweden

This paper is about medieval counter rebated doors in general and particularly about a door in the collections of Lund University Historical Museum. Counter rebated doors have been seen as an English phenomena but the actual door in question is from St Olofs church in Skanör, built in the diocese of Lund in medieval Denmark. In England there are a number of extant counter rebated doors, made in the 11th and 12th century, but the door from Skanör is the first example to be found and described outside of England.[1] In order to understand this unique door's eventual connection to the English examples investigations were done both from a Scandinavian and an English viewpoint. The features of the Skanör door were compared with the features of the English doors. The door was investigated from a carpentry/craft research perspective where the tool marks, the material and the manufacturing techniques were interpreted. The features and ironwork were also analysed through style orientated, historic eyes. The church and the door´s original location were investigated in the search for clues. These investigations led to the hypothesis that the door was most probably younger than the English examples. The hypothesis was tested with a dendrochronological analysis of the ledges that not only dated the door but also gave further information about the provenance of the timber and timber trade connected to the hanseatic league. Yet one of the main questions remains unanswered, why is there a counter rebated door in Skanör 874 km and 200 years away from the closest known example in England?

Introduction

An ordinary counter rebated door has boards where the small sides are jointed with rebates, also called half-lap joints. But instead of a continuous rebate the joints step back and forth as the rebates change direction. Or as conservator Hugh Harrison describes it, *"Board A projects over Board B, and below the joggle, the situation is reversed with Board B projecting over Board A ".*[2]

Medieval counter rebated doors. A door from the Diocese of Lund compared with the English examples

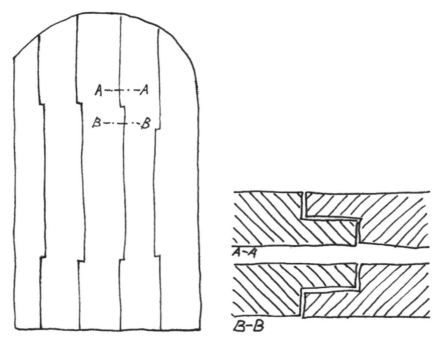

Figure 1. Diagrammatic representation of the counter rebated door from Stillingfleet. Drawn by author after Karlsson 1988: 403.

The art historian Lennart Karlsson made an extensive inventory of decorative ironwork on medieval doors in contemporary Sweden including the diocese of Lund, that was a part of Denmark until 1658. In his two volume book he presents over five hundred medieval doors with the focus on the ironwork. He also mentions the carpentry of the door leaves. He is aware of the English counter rebated doors and concludes that not one single example is known from Scandinavia[3]. The art historian Jane Geddes presents hundreds of English churches with doors that have decorative ironwork and the counter rebated doors receive special attention, but as in the work of Karlsson the carpentry is not the main focus[4]. Both Geddes and Karlsson make many references about doors from other countries in Europe but not one single mention is made concerning counter rebated doors outside of England. In later years a number of English doors have been dendrochronologically investigated. The results, that include two counter rebated doors, are put forward in a paper by Martin Bridge and Daniel Miles[5]. Conservator Hugh Harrison discusses the wood work behind the counter rebated doors, in particular the door from Bristol cathedral, in a manner close to what I call craft research. He is aware of the risk of jumping to the wrong conclusions if craft from a different time is judged by modern norms of good / bad craft methods or craftsmanship. For example he writes *"A real insight into the original craftsman's work methods can be seen where board edges with indentations were made good by shaping projections in the adjacent boards. With our traditions of straight edges, this is a delightful reminder that it was not always so."*[6] As a craftsman that has worked with medieval craft for many years he has a close empirical understanding of woodworking techniques which makes it easier for him to see and understand subtle details from the work process that is hard to grasp without craft experience. David Yeomans has written about medieval doors from a structural engineer's viewpoint and counter rebated doors are mentioned in his papers among other types of doors.[7]

Figure 2. The map show the distribution of the known churches with counter rebated doors. The three circles with dark background show the location of "false" counter rebated doors.

In order to put the counter rebated door from Skanör into context this paper starts with an introduction in which the English counter rebated doors are briefly presented. Then the church from Skanör is presented followed by a more thorough description of the door and the trans-disciplinary investigations undertaken to interpret it. Especially the dendrochronological results are discussed in context with medieval timber trade in connection with the hanseatic league. A door from the church in Hörup, that has some features that reminds one of counter rebated doors, is also presented since it also is unique among existing doors in Scandinavia. Then follows a discussion about English counter rebated doors and the door from Skanör, their similarities and differences, and the techniques used to make them. The paper finishes with a conclusion, remaining questions and forthcoming research.

Counter rebated doors in England

Geddes lists 13 churches with counter rebated door boards in England.[8] All of these doors are supposed to have been manufactured during the 12th century so the use of counter rebating is a dateable feature. Other features that indicate an early date are: rounded ledges with or without roves clasping the ledges, see fig. 9, and boards joined with counter groove and free tongue. Two of these doors have since then been dendrochronologically dated, St Peters church in Old Woking to 1106-1138 and St Marys church Kempley to 1114-1144[9]. Additionally Harrison noticed a hitherto unknown medieval counter rebated door at Bristol cathedral in the year 2000.[10]

251

Medieval counter rebated doors. A door from the Diocese of Lund compared with the English examples

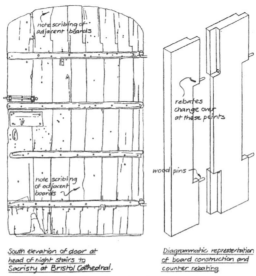

Figure 3. Drawings of the counter rebated and scribed door from Bristol church. Drawings by Peter Fergusson, in Hughes 2007.

These counter rebated doors show variation and two of the doors presented by Geddes I would like to question, are they counter rebated or do they just have some similar features?

The doors from Castle Hedingham are a more complicated variation since they have stepped counter rebates, a feature which is interpreted as highly innovative by Sharpe.[11] Without having had the opportunity to investigate the doors from Castle Hedingham I still want to suggest that it is possible that the stepped counter rebates are an adjustment to maximise the usable width of curved boards. If I am correct, the variation is done for practical reasons. Harrison points out that the Bristol door has counter rebates that are scribed to fit exactly with irregularities in the adjacent board.[12] Whether or not this manner of scribing has been used on other doors has not been investigated. The door from Skanör does not have any scribed irregularities. The door from Edstaston only has "counter rebates" on one side of the door leaf according to Geddes.[13]

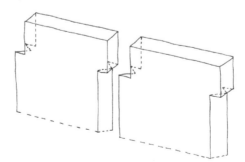

Figure 4. A diagrammatic representation of the construction, of the door from Little Hormed, with shouldering boards joined with butt joint and V edged joints, Drawn by the author after Yeoman Hughes 2014.

Finally the doors from Elmsett and Little Hormead actually have boards with V-edged joints and although they at first glance appear to be counter rebated doors, they are not.

St Olofs church in Skanör and the south door of the nave

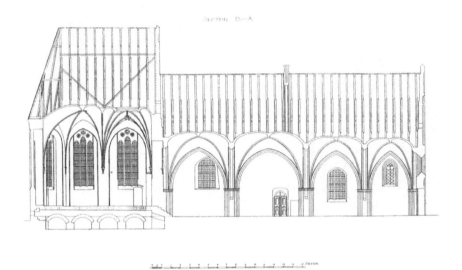

Figure 5. the chancel is to the left in this sectional drawing. The portal in the middle of the south wall of the nave is where the counter rebated door hung until the end of the 19th century. Drawing by architect Theodor wåhlin 1905.

As one of the clues to understand the Skanör door it is necessary to give a short description of the medieval church and the town it came from. In medieval times Skanör was one of northern Europe's most important international trade centres, especially for the herring trade. On a yearly basis the Scania market was held and it has been estimated that it had 30-40000 visitors. This can be compared to a common Danish town in the same period that had a couple of thousand inhabitants. In total Skanör had six churches. Trade cities as Rostock, Weimar, Bremen and Amsterdam had assigned areas. Merchants also came from England, Normandy and Scotland. In other words the town was multicultural and craftsmen as well as tradesmen came from all over Europe.[14]

The oldest parts of the extant church were built in the 13th century, but there might have been a predecessor from the 12th century. With this in mind it is possible that the door was recycled and could be older than the extant church. Until the late 19th century, the door was hung in a portal between the nave and a tower that is supposed to have been built in the 14th century. Whether or not the portal is of the same age as the tower or older is unclear. The tower is thought to be younger than the extant chancel that is supposed to has been built after 1425. The roof trusses of the chancel have been analysed dendrochronologically and have an estimated felling age of 1435 but other features such as heraldic weapons suggest a slightly older date to before 1428.[15] The size of the chancel indicates that there also were plans to rebuild the nave. But the trade policy of the hanseatic league and the

253

decline of herring finally led to a collapse for the Scania market which in turn took away the basis for grand rebuilding plans.[16]

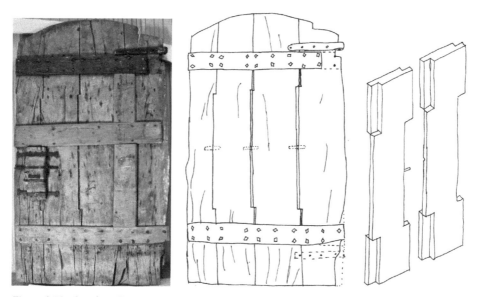

Figure 6. The door from Skannör. In the diagrammatic drawings the lock and secondary boards have been left out. Three dowels are drawn, but there might be more. Photo and drawings by the author.

Since the 19th century this door has been in the collections of Lund University Historical Museum[17]. The door leaf is 274 cm high, 159 cm wide and the oak boards are 3 cm thick. The leaf consists of four counter rebated oak boards that have been whip sawn out of fast grown oak. Although not proven it seems that the boards are sawn from the same tree. On the backside the door has two original oak ledges that are fastened with two rows of rivets and diamond shaped roves. These oak ledges are made from good quality forest grown oak. The wooden fibres of the boards, are curved and the two left hand boards have fibres that are convex to the left and the two right hand boards have fibres that are convex to the right. This arrangement in combination with the use of boards that have not been well seasoned and have only two ledges has resulted in curving and shrinkage. The bent fibres, the shrinkage and tension in the wood have created a gap between the two middle boards whereas a third ledge could have prevented this[18]. The gap probably occurred early on, and wool was used to caulk it. One original oak dowel can be seen on the backside. Probably others are obscured by the oak ledges and the secondary pine boards. The door has one intact original iron hinge and one that is fragmented.

On the front secondary panel boards cover most of the leaf. Some parts of the panel have been removed and show that the original boards are covered with graffiti in the form of house marks.[19]

The forensic investigation of the door

Figure 7. The front of the door has not been fully documented yet. But the door leaf is full of house marks. The right photo shows the fleur de lis end of the upper hinge, patly hidden by the panel from the 18th century. Photos by the author.

The door gives clues that point in different directions. Counter rebating, and roves in some circumstances, are from an English view typical features for the 11th and 12th century. From a regional Scanian view boards whip sawed from poor quality oak point to the 15th century, take or give one century. On the other hand, the high quality oak in the ledges could point to the 12th century.

Therefore pictures of the iron hinges were sent to diocese antiquarian Gunnar Nordanskog who did a PhD project about the underlying meanings and purpose of the medieval decorative ironwork on church doors[20]. He pointed out that the door was unusually big if it was supposed to be from the 12th century. Further he could tell that the iron hinges were crude and the distinct fleur the lis shapes of the end of the hinges could be at the earliest from the 14th century, but is more likely to be from the 15th century[21].

The portal, where the door leaf was hung originally, has a slightly pointed arch. This is a clue that tells us that the portal is probably not original, but the door leaf could still be reused and be older than the portal.

The clues so far in the investigation pointed to the 15th century, when viewed from a regional craft research standpoint. But there were clues pointing to other directions and since the regional standpoint might be misleading when used on a medieval church in an international marketplace, we had to continue our investigations.

Medieval counter rebated doors. A door from the Diocese of Lund compared with the English examples

The dendrochronological analysis and medieval timber trade

When dendrochronologist Hans Linderson, Lund University, and the author examined the door we concluded that the best option was to make an analysis of the ledges that were made of slow grown forest oak. We also thought that the ledges probably were from another source than the boards. Generally oak used for buildings in the diocese of Lund in the 11th and 12th century is slow grown forest oak, and then from the 14th century and onwards it tends to be fast grown oak of lesser quality. The analysis was carried out with an USB microscope[22] on the end grain of the oak ledges. The use of a conventional microscope, for measuring year rings, give an accuracy of 1/100 mm. This can be compared with the use of photographs, for measuring year rings, that give an accuracy of 7/100 mm. Linderson estimates that the photographs taken with the USB microscope gives similar accuracy as measuring on ordinary photographs.[23] The analysis resulted in that the source of the timber was northern Poland. It could also be concluded that the oak ledges came from different trees. The upper ledge gave the best result and it was interpreted that the timber started to grow between 1050-1090 and that it was felled between 1348-1398.[24]

Less than four kilometres away from the Skanör church, at the area used by the Lübeck tradesmen during the Scania market, an archaeological investigation was conducted in 2014-15. Among the finds there were ten herring barrels, buried for secondary use as water containers. Eight of these had the provenance of northern Poland and the upper ledge had very good correlation to one of the barrels which might be interpreted as they came from the same tree.[25] If this is correct it is possible to tighten the timespan, of the felling of the tree the ledge came from, to 1363-1378. In previous research, about the origin, assortments and transport of Baltic timber during the middle ages, dendrochronologist Tomasz Wazny has shown that the majority of polish timber were exported from Danzig that then was a centre for timber trade. The export from Danzig had its peak in the period 1350-1600 and mainly oak was exported to Holland, England and France. On the timber trade route all the cargo ships had to pass the sound between Denmark and Scania, were Skanör is situated. Danzig had close trading contacts with Lübeck and took an important role in the Hanseatic League. Export of logs and beams seems to have been rare. Polish timber was mainly exported as small size semi manufactures of which more than a dozen types are known by name. Wainscots, thick high quality boards made from oak logs radially cleft into pith-free boards, and barrel staves were of primary importance in the timber trade. A description of staves, from the beginning of the 15th century, says they were boards at least 5 feet long and 5-9 inches wide. A later description gives smaller measurements but adds to the description the thickness as 3 fingers.[26] The ledges of the Skanör door and the barrels staves can be put in context with Wazny´s research. With the timber trade route in mind the provenance of the ledges and stave barrels makes sense. The ledges dimensions indicate they can have been made either of wainscots or stave barrels. It might be of importance that the barrels were found on the area assigned to the tradesmen from Lübeck as Lübeck and Danzig had close contact. Maybe future archaeological investigation and / or historic manuscripts can give more information. But one conclusion is that the barrels most probably were manufactured at the Scania market. Wazny writes that the exported Polish oak was of high quality that easily could be cleaved in contrast to the knotty or crooked oaks that were common in many parts of Western Europe.[27] On the Skanör door the boards are made from knotty crooked oak that could not be cleaved but had to be whip sawn. The quality of the boards indicates it is of local origin. It can also be mentioned that wainscots were used for doors in medieval England. For example imported wainscots were used for doors 1366 in More End and a contract from 1369 specifies that the doors shall be made of imported oak boards.[28]

Thoughts about how the counter rebates may have been done

Cecil Hewett writes the following about the construction of counter rebated doors: "*they not only illustrate the highest point of complexity in this field, but also indicate the approaching end of such work, which must have entitled very high costs.*"[29] My hypothesis is that it is not very difficult to make a counter rebate and if the same tools are used it does not take significantly more time than making a common rebate. After studying the Skanör door I believe the main tools used to make the rebates were mallet and chisel[30]. A rebating plane was not used at all.[31] Other tools that probably were used are: awl, soot line, hand axe, auger and a square. A future full scale reconstruction, of counter rebated and common rebated boards, with medieval methods and replicated tools will help to confirm or deny my hypothesis.

A seemingly counter rebated door in Hörup´s church

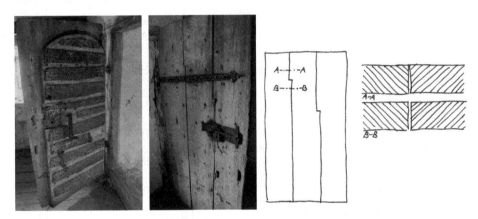

Figure 8. The door from Hörup seen from both sides and diagrammatic representations of the door's construction with shouldering boards and butt joints. Photos by the author.

Photographic evidence indicated that an old door in the tower of Hörup´s church is counter rebated. But after examination it was clear that this door has been made with butt jointed boards that have no rebates. The door is made of pine and has two iron hinges, one on the inside and one on the outside. On the outside of the door there are horizontal panels that are partly hidden by iron plates. The boards are whipsawed. Between the iron plates there are some graffiti markings. It is worthy of mention that there are two inscriptions that might indicate the years 1366 and 1445. One of these numbers could signify the year when the door was constructed[32]. Even without considering the graffiti marks the door leaf would be given a probable date in the period 1350-1600. The door can be seen as an example of a quite modest door that has features that can be mistaken for counter rebates. In a way this door is more peculiar than the door from Skanör. If no similar doors are found my best hypothesis would be that this door has no link to the counter rebated doors from England or the door from Skanör. It might instead be an invention by a carpenter who just solved a specific problem in a somewhat unconventional way.

Medieval counter rebated doors. A door from the Diocese of Lund compared with the English examples

English doors compared to Scandinavian doors

Scandinavian doors made before the 16th century are often made in a carpentry- and not in a joinery manner. This could lead to a presumption that the same craftsmen could do everything from choosing a tree, felling it, making boards and finally the door leaf. There is no known written account about medieval door making from Scandinavia. But in England there are preserved accounts concerning new doors for the hall of Wethersfield Manor in Essex in 1428-29.[33] The accounts tells us that John Walforde felled the timber, John Herd transported it and finally John Langford made the doors. The source does not say whether or not John Langford had assistant carpenters or if there was a smith to make the ironwork, but at least three people were involved in felling, transporting and making the doors. In the case of the door from Skanör it is most probable that many persons were involved, not at least because the boards and the ledges are made of wood from different sources.

Churches with counter rebated doors or similar	dendro date estimated felling	Style G=Geddes, B&H= Bettey & Harrison	roves	ledges	height, width cm
St Peters church Old Woking	1106-1138	G 1100-1125	no	no	311 x 149
St Marys church Kempley	1114-1144	G 1100-1120	?	?	236 x 98
Bristol cathedral	inconclusive	B&H c1140	no	yes	ca 267 x 155
St Anne and St Laurence church Elmstead	-	G late11th-early 12th century	no	yes	190 x104
All saints church Sutton	-	G 1100-1150	?	?	249 x 113
Mashbury church (original boards?)	-	G 1100-1150	?	?	141 x 67
St Helens church Stillingfleet (clinched roves)	-	G c1150-60	yes	yes	280 x 170
Castle Hedingham St Nicholas church 1 door + 2 fragmentary	-	G 1175-1185	?	?	269 x 124
Peterborough cathedral, double doors	-	G 1177-93	?	?	?
Worfield church double doors	-	G late 12th century		yes	262 x 93
St Marys church Edstaston	-	G c1200	no	yes	256 x 169
Ely cathedral double doors	-	G 1198-1215	?	?	?
St Peter church Elmsett not counter rebated but V edged	-	G 1175-1200	no	yes	243 x 116
St Marys church Little Hormead not counter rebated but V edged	-	G 1125-1150	?	?	216 x 104
Skanör church diocese of Lund (diamond shaped roves)	1348-1398	15th century	yes	yes	274, 159
Hörup church diocese of Lund butt joined boards with shoulder	-	after 1350	no	no	164 x 93

Table 1.   Known counter rebated doors and three doors with similar features.

Bridge and Miles write that the English doors generally are made of the finest imported oak and in this respect have more in common with furniture than structural carpentry.[34] The medieval doors from the Diocese of Lund, including the door from Skanör, and the Swedish doors examined by the author seem to have more in common with structural carpentry than furniture. Or rather there's a similar roughness in the structural work and the doors until approximately the 16th century when the doors get closer to furniture. The quality of the oak used for the doors generally corresponds to the contemporary oak used for the roof trusses. In the 12-13th century very fine straight forest oak cleaved into boards is used and in the 15th century poor quality sawn oak is more common. The timber used seems to be mostly local, a hypothesis future dendrochronological analysis might confirm or deny. In the diocese of Lund two extant examples of probable 12th century doors are made of pine[35] and therefore made of imported wood since pine did not grow in this region in the medieval times. The ledges on the door from Skanör are also made of imported oak.

In England sawn boards were used for the 11th century door called Pyx from Westminster Abbey and later on the 12th century doors from Staplehurst church and Chepstow Castle[36]. In Scandinavia the oldest documented use of whip sawn planks are dated to 1315.[37] The use of sawn boards on Scandinavian doors are quite common from the 15th century and onwards.

Figure 9. Left: The 11th century, common rebated, door from Hadstock church have rounded ledges with claw like roves that clasps the ledge. The surface is smoothly hewed.   Right: The roves or washers on the Skanör door are smaller and diamond shaped. The ledges have a rectangular crossection. On the upper rounded part of the door complementary roves can be seen that secure the boards from warping. A housemark can also be seen. The surface is whip sawed. Photos by the author.

The use of roves on doors are previous only documented twice in Scandinavia, on one from Hafslo in Norway and on another from Ekeby in Sweden[38]. Although roves have a long history of use in boat and wagon building in Scandinavia they have not been common on doors. The early medieval roves on English doors are generally long and claw like and clasp the ledges, later roves are reduced to flat washers.[39] It is only the door from Stillingfleet that is documented to have both counter rebated boards and clasping roves. The roves on the Skanör door are not claw like but rather flat and diamond shaped. They in fact points to a late medieval date from an English typological viewpoint.

Most of the unaltered English doors, including the door from Skanör, have ledges but the doors from Old Woking and Hörup do not. It is only on the doors from Elmstead and Little Hormead that the ledges are wedged in recesses on the boards. In the case of Elmstead this can be seen as superfluous since the counter rebating has similar effect as the wedged ledges but for the door from Little Hormead it is more understandable.

The door from Skanör was made with sawn boards and there was no use of a plane to make the boards smooth. On the counter rebated English doors there were more concern with the finished surface.

Medieval counter rebated doors. A door from the Diocese of Lund compared with the English examples

Conclusions and remaining questions

The door from Skanör with counter rebated boards is unique in a Scandinavian context. The fact that Skanör was not an ordinary town but an important trade centre might be an important clue to why the door has unique features. The only other known doors of this construction are from England, but the door from Skanör is around 200 years younger. The difference in time makes it hard to see a connection with no known intermediate examples. This leaves the question, of why a counter rebated door appears in a medieval church in the Danish diocese of Lund, still mostly unanswered. However it is a good example of the need to be critical when constructional details, dateable in one region are used for dating details in another context.

So why is there a counter rebated door in Skanör church, 874 km away from the closest extant English door? The door from Hörup could have been an experimental construction made only once. The Skanör door on the other hand seems to be a completed construction which make it improbable that it was a one-hit wonder with no connection to any original model. Possible explanations could be: The Skanör door was made as a replica of an older door in the church that was made by English carpenters. It was done by a travelling carpenter who had seen similar doors in England. Or counter rebated doors were not only common in 11th and 12 century England. Maybe there are other extant counter rebated or "false" counter rebated doors from various times around Europe waiting to be found?

Answers and questions that emerged by chance was due to a nearby archaeological investigation, that among other results found oak barrels that were dendrochronologically analysed to be contemporary with the door´s ledges. The provenance of the barrels and the door ledges were northern Poland. This can be seen in the context of medieval timber trade in the Baltic region where Danzig was an important trade centre for Polish oak. The trade routes to England, Holland and France had to pass through the Sound where Skanör and the Scanian market. The oak was exported as smaller semi manufactures as Wainscots and barrel staves which give us the information that the Barrels were manufactured in Skanör. The ledges of the door can have been manufactured of either wainscots or barrel staves. But is it a coincidence that the barrels were found on the Lübeck tradesmen´s area? Lübeck and Danzig had good trading contacts so one possible explanation could be that the Lübeck tradesmen among other things sold polish oak on the Scanian market.

Acknowledgement and forthcoming research

Research in this article was initiated through the project *Historic carpentry art in the diocese of Lund*. In this project, among other things, an inventory is made of the dioceses extant medieval church doors from a carpenters viewpoint[40]. A number of these medieval doors are examined by craft research methodology[41] and some undergoes dendrochronological analysis. The Skanör door has lots of graffiti marks on the front of the door leaf that wait to be documented and interpreted. Further understanding of counter rebating and door making can be gained from a full scale reconstruction. This door has been 3D modelled and can be viewed, among other doors and roof trusses on Sketchfab; https://sketchfab.com/models/c1f35074d11748be82210788cab70d6b. The author's research also is part of a doctoral project called *Sacral carpentry art* at the University of Gothenburg. This paper could not have been done without help from: antiquarian Petter Jansson and diocese antiquarian Heikki Ranta, colleagues in *Historic carpentry art in the Diocese of Lund*. Hans Linderson who did the dendrochronological analysis. Diocese antiquarian Gunnar Nordanskog who analysed the ironwork. Antiquarian Anders Ohlsson who made the door accessible at Lund University Historical Museum. Richard O. Byrne for critical reading and for checking the spelling and grammar. My supervisors, professor Gunnar Almevik and associate professor Peter Carelli for critical reading. David Yeomans and Martin Bridge who supplied me with relevant papers. Peter

Ferguson Dip. Arch. (UCL) RIBA Hugh Harrison Conservation for permission to use the drawings of the door from Bristol cathedral and for comments on the paper.

references

[1] C. A. Hewett, *English Historic Carpentry*. Sussex, England: Phillimore & Co., 1980, p. 72; J. Geddes, *Medieval Decorative Ironwork in England*. London: Society of Antiquaries, 1999, pp. 29 and 315; L. Karlsson, *Medieval Ironwork in Sweden volume I & II*. Stockholm: Almqvist and Wiksell, 1988, 402f.

[2] Description in, H. Harrison, `Church Woodwork´, *Regional Furniture*, vol. 21, 2007, p. 54.

[3] Karlsson, *Medieval Ironwork*, (Note 1), p. 402.

[4] Geddes, *Decorative Ironwork*, (Note 1).

[5] M. Bridge and D. Miles, `Dendrochronologically Dated Doors in Great Britain', *Regional Furniture,* vol. 26, 2012, pp. 73-103.

[6] Harrison, 'Church Woodwork', (Note 2), p. 54.

[7] D. Yeomans, H. Harrison and A. Smith, `Repairing a Medieval Door´, *Advanced Materials Research*, vol. 778, 2013, pp. 739-746; D. Yeomans and H. Harrison, `The construction and structure of medieval gates´, in J. W. P. Campbell et al (eds), *Proceedings of the First Conference of the Construction History Society*, Cambridge 2014, Cambridge: Construction History Society, 2014, pp. 475-482; D. Yeomans, `Ancient Carpentry of doors and gates´, *Construction History Society Magazine,* no. 93. 2015.

[8] Geddes, *Decorative Ironwork*, (Note 1), p. 30.

[9] Bridge and Miles, 'Dendrochronologically Dated Doors', (Note 5).

[10] J. H. Bettey and H. Harrison, `A twelfth-century Door in Bristol Cathedral', *Transactions of the Bristol and Gloucestershire Archaeological Society*, vol. 122, 2004, p. 169.

[11] G. R. Sharpe, Historic English Churches. London: I.B Tauris & Co Ltd, 2011, p. 122.

[12] Bettey and Harrison, 'A twelfth-century Door', (Note 10), p. 169.

[13] Geddes, *Decorative Ironwork*, (Note 1), p. 322.

[14] L. Ersgård, *Skanör-Falsterbo. Medeltidsstaden 53. RAÄ*, 1984, p. 8; L. Ersgård, `Sillmarknaderna I Öresund under unionstiden´, in P. Grinder-Hansen (ed.), *Unionsdrottningen, Margareta Ioch Kalmarunionen.* Stockholm, 1997, 117ff; P. Carelli, *Det medeltida Skåne. En arkeologisk guidebok*. Stockholm: Historiska Media, 2010, 163ff.

[15] T. Bartholin, `Dendrokronologiske undersøgelser af Ystadområdets kirker', in H. Andersson and M. Anglert (eds) *By huvudgård och kyrka*: studier i Ystadsområdets medeltid,. Lund Studies in Medieval Archaeology 5. Stockholm Bartholin: Almqvist & Wiksell, 1989b, pp. 211–219; L. Dufberg, Skanörs kyrka St Olof. 1994, pp. 3-11.

[16] Carelli, Det medeltida Skåne, (Note 15), p. 165.

[17] Inventory number, LUHM 21065 B.

[18] A secondary ledge of pine was mounted, probably in the 18th century.

[19] House marks look very similar to mason's marks but were used by, for example, farmers as owner marks on tools and as signatures.

[20] G. Nordanskog, *Föreställd Hedendom. Tidigmedeltida skandinaviska kyrkportar i forskning och historia*. Lund: Nordic Academic Press, 2006.

[21] Nordanskog´s interpretation was done from a Scandinavian viewpoint.

[22] In essence, USB microscopes are a webcam with a high-powered macro lens and generally do not use transmitted light, but rely on incident light from in-built LEDs lights situated next to the lens. The light reflected from the sample then enters the camera lens.

[23] Orally Linderson 2018, see also Nordanskog 2006:167ff.

[24] H. Linderson, *Dendrokronologisk analys av den gamla kyrkodörren i Skanör kyrka, LUHM 21065B fotoanalys.* 2017. If the analysis of the ledges had resulted in a 12th century date, we would have taken samples of the boards to date them with Carbon-14 in order to be sure that the ledges were not reused and older than the rest of the door.

[25] Ibid.; A. Knarrström and S. Lindberg, Falsterbo 2:40-44 och 2:1 m.fl. Tomter, tunnor och en smidesverkstad på lübeckarnas fit på Skånemarknaden. Arkeologerna Rapport 2017, p. 130.

[26] T. Wazny, `Historical timber trade and its implications on dendrochronological dating', *Lundqua Report*, 1992, pp. 331-333; T. Ważny, 'The origin, assortments and transport of Baltic timber', in C. Van de Velde, H. Beeckman, J. Van Acker, F. Verhaeghe (eds), *Constructing Wooden Images: Proceedings of a Symposium on the Organization of Labour and Working Practices of Late Gothic Altarpieces in the Low Countries. Brussels, Belgium, 25-26 October 2002.* Brussels: VUB Press, 2005, pp. 115-126.

[27] Wazny, 'Baltic timber', (Note 26), p. 119.

[28] L.F. Salzman, *Building in England down to 1500. A documentary history.* Oxford: Clarendon Press, 1997, p. 246.

[29] Hewett, *English Historic Carpentry,* (Note 1), p. 72.

[30] The medieval Scandinavian doors with uninterrupted rebates seems to have been made without the use of a plane, at least the examples documented by the author.

[31] If a rebate plane was used on the English counter rebated doors is not known but at least in the case of the Bristol door it seems most unlikely.

[32] Another possibility is that the numbers are just graffiti with no connection to the making of the door.

[33] J. Harvey, Mediaeval craftsmen. London, 1975, p. 50.

[34] Bridge and Miles, 'Dendrochronologically Dated Doors', (Note 5).

[35] The doors are from the churches in Barsebäck and Häglinge. Both of these doors are under investigation by the author and will be reported later.

[36] Harrison, `Church Woodwork', (Note 1); Bridge and Miles, 'Dendrochronologically Dated Doors', (Note 5).

[37] T. Finderup and H. Rensbro, `Træværket fra Stege Borg´. KUML, 2005.

[38] Karlsson, *Medieval Ironwork*, (Note 1), p. 86.

[39] J. Geddes, 'The construction of Medieval doors', in S. McGrail (ed.), *Woodworking Techniques before A.D. 1500*. British Archaeological Reports, Intl. Series S129. Oxford: BAR, 1982, 313ff.

[40] A medieval door from Ronneby church is discussed, in K-M. Melin, `Timmermanskonst i Sankt Laurentius kyrka´, *Blekingeboken. 2016 (94)*, s. [6]-19.

[41] For more information about the methods used, see K-M. Melin & O. Andersson, *Behuggningsteknik i Södra Råda och Hammarö kyrkor. 1300-tals yxor i litteratur och magasin. Södra Råda gamla kyrka. Förundersökning X.* (Knadriks Kulturbygg rapport 2008:18), Kristianstad, 2008; G. Almevik, K-M. Melin, 'Traditional craft skills as a source to historical knowledge. Reconstruction in the ashes of the medieval wooden church Södra Råda', *Mirator* 2015:16. The Finnish Society for Medieval Studies, Helsingfors, 2015; K-M. Melin, `Techniques of cleaving wood with an axe and mallet- Deconstructing present craft knowledge, in order to reconstruct historic´, in J. W. P. Campbell et al (eds), *Proceedings of the Fourth Conference of the Construction History Society*, Cambridge 2017, Cambridge: Construction History Society, 2017, pp. 89-100.

Trace Methods of the Romanesque Churches of Val D'aran (11th-13th Centuries) Orientations

Mónica López Piquer and Josep Lluis i Ginovart

School of Architecture UIC Barcelona, Universitat Internacional de Catalunya, Spain

Abstract

Val d'Aran is a region of Spain located on the north slope of the central Pyrenees, the Catalan Pyrenees, and is limited on the north by France. Val d'Aran preserves twenty-nine Romanesque churches, whose date of construction range from from the 11th to the 13th century. The first studies and topography surveys of Val d'Aran churches were done by the construction historians Viollet-le-Duc (1814-1879), Lluís Domènech i Montaner (1850-1923) and Josep Puig i Cadafalch (1867-1956), in their expeditions in 1833, 1905 and 1907, respectively, but they did not take into account the orientation of these Romanesque churches.

A topological study of the data and information obtained from the mass data capture, with a Terrestrial Laser Scanner (TLS), of the Romanesque churches of Val d'Aran has been done. Topology, from the Greek words τόπος 'location', and λόγος 'study', is the mathematical frame that is dedicated to the 'study of the location' and its properties, from the geometrical point of view. Through the topological and visual analysis of these religious buildings, several hypotheses have been raised, the one studied in this paper is whether clerics and lay people had some knowledge of orientation and astronomy. This achieved by analysis of the methods used to align the Romanesque buildings from the 11th to 13th centuries, and its relations between the methods and sources used, such us: Vitruvius (c. 80-20 BC) in his treatise *De architectura* (c. 30-15 BC), the orientation techniques used by the Roman *gromatics* or surveyors in the 1st and 2nd centuries, as for example Hyginus Gromaticus (c. 98-117), in his *De limitibus constituendi*, the texts written by Gisemundus at the monastery of Santa María de Ripoll, *Ars gromatica siue geometría Gisemundi* (c. 880), near the Val d'Aran and, finally, the hypothetical use of the compass, which is mentioned in documents dating as far back as the 12th century.

Liturgy and orientation of sacred buildings

A collection of Romanesque churches situated in the region of Val d'Aran in northern Spain, built between the 11th and the 13th century, is presented in this paper. Several authors, such as José Antonio Iñiguez Herrero[1], Santiago Sebastian[2], Nicolas Reveyron[3], Francesca Mambelli[4], Constant J. Mews and Eduardo Carrero[5], claim Romanesque buildings were designed under the influence of the main liturgies from that period: *Gemma animae* (c.1120) by Honorius of Autun (1080-c.1153); *Mitralis de Officio* (1190) by Sicard, bishop of Cremona (1185-1215); *Rationale divinorum officiorum,* (c.1150) by Jean Beleth (fl. 1135-82); and, lastly, *Prochiron, vulgo rationale divinorum officiorum* by Guillaume Durand (1230-96)[6]. In this regard, special significance was attached to the orientation of these sacred buildings.

Isidorus of Seville (c. 5561-636), in his *Originum sive etymologiarum libri viginti* (c.630), chapter IV: *De aedificiis sacris*, wrote that large buildings —*templa*— should be built facing the equinoctial east (*Etymo*. L XV. iii, iv)[7]. Rabanus Maurus (c. 776-856) said the same thing in his *De Universo libri viginti duo* (c.844): *orientem expectabant æquinoctialem* (*Uni*. L XIV. XXI)[8]

Trace Methods of the Romanesque Churches of Val D'aran (11th-13th Centuries)
Orientations

This tradition prevailed in Romanesque liturgies such us: Honorius of Autun, *ecclesiae ad orientem vertuntur ubi sol oritur (Gem. Ani. I, 129, De situ ecclesiae)*; Sicard, bishop of Cremona, *Ad orientem, id est, ortum solis aequinoctialem (Mitra. I, 2, De fundatione ecclesiae)* and Guillaume Durand, *Yerus ortum solis aequinoctialem, ad denotandum quod ecclesia quae in terris militât (Prochi. I, 8, pp.5)*, amongst others.

The orientation of churches and the position of the altar and throne evolved from the fact that apses used to face west[9]. After few changes, the altar was located the rear end, where the officiant faced the *Sancta Sanctorum*, towards the east, and the chair in front of the apse was moved forward towards the epistle side of the church, on the right-hand side of the altar. This last arrangement is concurrent with the chronology of the Aranese Romanesque[10].

The Romanesque churches in Aran were built within this liturgical context. Josep Puig i Cadafalch (1867-1956) connects them to the tradition of Lombard architecture[11]. The churches in Aran differ greatly from the churches in the rest of the Iberian Peninsula, which followed the Mozarabic rite and later adopted the European liturgy[12][13].

Some churches thus preserved the Canonical orientation (apse facing east), inherited from the Roman tradition[14], while other churches display festival orientation. They are aligned with the sunrise or sunset position on the feast day of the patron saint to whom the church was dedicated[15]. The knowledge available at that time to determine the Canonical orientation from east to west through geometrical tracing processes, however, is more difficult to ascertain.

Feast days of saints were those of martyrs included in the Julian calendar. They commemorated each martyr every year on the day of his or her death. In the *Gemma animae* liturgy (c.1120) by Honorius of Autun, only the most important saints appear. Feast days were celebrated the day before (*Gemma Animae*, LIV.VI), so the orientation could also be determined by the sunset. The *Martirologium Hieronymianum* is a liturgical calendar, a medieval list of martyrs, compiled in the 6th century in different parts of the Christian world of the time.

However, the approach to the knowledge of the orientation of these medieval churches can be established from different direct sources[16]. From an epistemological point of view, when ascertaining the knowledge available to determine the orientation of these churches, we can establish links between: a) the methods $[M_1, M_2]$ stated by Vitruvius in his treatise *De architectura*[17], written in the 1st century and later referenced by Moritz Benedikt Cantor (1829-1920)[18], b) the orientation techniques used by the Roman gromatici (land surveyors) in the 1st and 2nd centuries, methods $[M_3, M_4, M_5, M_6]$, c) the texts written by Gisemundus at the monastery of Santa María de Ripoll (c. 880)[19], near the Val d'Aran $[M_7, M_8]$, and, lastly, d) the hypothetical use of the compass $[M_9]$, which is mentioned in documents dating back to the 12th century[20].

Methods

All seven topographic surveys (2014-15) used terrestrial laser scanning technology [TLS] for data acquisition, which enabled a non-invasive, contact-free measurement. The geometric and radiometric surface information obtained[21] is very accurate[22]. All measurements were made using a Leica ScanStation P20, and Leica Cyclone software was used to process the information in order to obtain a point cloud. Next, a 3D mesh of the object was generated with the software 3DReshaper. The estimated geometric error of the set of points resulting from this process is [0.02-0.01 m] (Fig. 1).

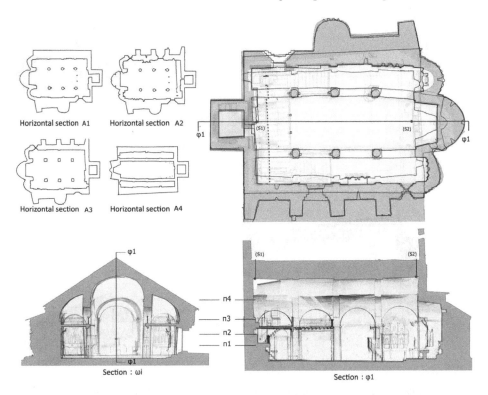

Figure 1. methodology for the topological determination of Romanesque architecture.

By using massive data acquisition techniques by means of terrestrial laser scanning (TLS), a three-dimensional rendering of these buildings was made. A distinction is made between *templi* (*Gem. Ani.* L. 1, Cap. CXXVII) (*Mitra.* L.1, Cap. V) and *capellis* (*Gem. Ani.* L. 1, Cap. CXXVIII) (*Mitra.* L.1, Cap. V) in Romanesque buildings from the 11th to the 13th century. We determine a plane [τ] in order to achieve a unified methodological criterion for orientation. This plane is the longitudinal section [τ], as defined by the highest point of the chancel's opening —point [s_2] of the *Sancta Sanctorum*— and the corresponding point [s_1] on the wall opposite to the *Sancta Sanctorum*, dropping perpendicular lines to the floor plan (Fig. 2). Section [τ] determines an imaginary axis, which shows the orientation of the building on the floor plan—see *De pavimento* (*Gem. Ani.* L. 1, Cap. CXXXIV). Having defined the longitudinal axis of the church, the latitude [ϕ] and longitude [λ] of the church are said to be the latitude and longitude of the central point [O] of this longitudinal axis.

Figure 2. 3D Representation of Terrestrial Laser Scan data of Santa Maria de Arties (XIII).

The technique used to determine the building's topography has an error of [0.25°] at the azimuth [A]. The calculation of the declination based on the azimuth and horizon altitude has an error of [0.50°]. The cumulative error in the calculation process of the astronomical declination [δ] is close to [1°], so the accuracy of the orientation determination is close to [± 1 day].

Determination of the Sunrise on the horizon

The methods used by archaeoastronomy are based on determining the church's location —latitude [ϕ] and longitude [λ]—, as well as its orientation —degrees from the geographic north—, the real geographic azimuth [A], the horizon altitude [h] in the direction of the church and the astronomical declination corresponding to that orientation [δ].

Thus, the orientation of the sacred building is obvious, placing a gnomon, or *pertiga*, oriented towards the sunrise on the feast day of the patron saint, either in its horizon or its sunset. For this reason, it is necessary to determine the height of the visible horizon [h] in the direction of the building, at the point where the sun rises or rises over the mountainous profile of the Val d'Aran. This procedure was carried out by locating the point [O].

Once the horizon altitude [h] was determined for each location, we provided latitude and longitude [ϕ, λ], the topographic height from the sea [a] through the program *heywhatsthat* (Calculator: http://heywhatsthat.com. Last query 17-11-2017). The visible horizon is perfectly verifiable using Google Earth and its astronomical

266

applications. The astronomical declination [δ], corresponding to that orientation, can be calculated using the Calculator of the Astronomical Applications Department of the U.S. Naval Observatory, (http://aa.usno.navy.mil/data/docs/AltAz.php) and Spencer's formula (1971)[23].

In order to find a match with the day of the patron saint, it must be borne in mind that the present liturgical calendar is based on the Roman calendar authorized by the *Mysterii paschalis celebrationem* (1969) of Paul VI (1897-1978)[24]. This calendar is different from those used during the reference epoch —11th to 13th centuries—, usually the *Martirologio Hieronymianum* (s.VI)[25]. The Gregorian calendar was introduced in 1582 by the papal bull *Inter gravissimas*, issued by Pope Gregory XIII (1502-85), in order to stop the drift of the Julian calendar with respect to the equinoxes —*aequus nocte*, when the plane of Earth's equator passes through the centre of the Sun— and solstices. In order to determine a date in the ecclesiastical calendar, the mismatch between the Julian calendar (used during the period under study, 11th-13th centuries) and the Gregorian calendar must be taken into account. This mismatch is of [5-7] days in the 11th and 13th centuries (https://carta-natal.es/calendario_gregoriano.php), and for the year 1150 the mismatch is 7 days.

After surveying the Romanesque churches [11th-13th century] by means of terrestrial laser scanning [TLS], using archaeoastronomy techniques, we established an error of one day. Spencer's formula (1971) has a small relative error, but it creates uncertainty because it relies on an experimental result. When a solstice is nearing, a decimal second means one day. The cumulative error of both the instrumental method and the data collection process, with respect to the tropical year, can be [±2 days]. Thus, when determining the position of the sun by means of its gravitational pull, the problem lies in establishing the instrumental error and the one produced by the refractive effect of the star, which we can determine at 3°-5°. The cumulative error for both the instrumental method and for the data acquisition process is [1.92%] (deviation from the solar year 1150). Therefore, we estimate that the difference between the astronomic declination [δ], and the day of the sun's rising given by Spencer's formula, is almost one week.

Layout of the canonical orientation

Another possibility is that these buildings were built using an instrumental system. Vitruvius, in *De architectura* (*De archi. LI.VI.6*), puts forward two methods for constructing a wind rose[26]. Based on historiographic sources, the following methods can be established:

Method [M₁]: The first method uses a gnomon, translated as *sciothiras* by Miguel de Urrea (1582) and as *sciatheras* by José Ortiz y Sanz (1787) in their respective editions of Vitruvius' treatise. A circumference is drawn with its centre at the gnomon and a radius equal to the length of the shadow projected by the gnomon in the morning. Point [S₁] is marked. In the afternoon, when the shadow of the gnomon intersects the circumference, point [S₂] is marked. The bisecting line [S₁, S₂] to the centre of the circumference is the north-south line, the Roman *cardus* (Fig. 3.a).

Method [M₂]: In *De architectura* (*De archi. LI.VI.12*), Vitruvius determines points [S₁, S₂ and S₃] on the basis of the shadows cast by the gnomon. Point [S₁] is determined by the longest shadow; point [S₃] is determined by the shortest shadow —corresponding to noon— and point [S₂] is any intermediate point. Three right triangles are built with the length of each shadow as a leg and the gnomon as the other leg. By rotating the shortest shadow length towards the other two shadow lengths, points 1 and 2 are found. Points [S₁, S₂] define a straight line, and points (1-2) define another straight line; the intersection between these two straight lines provides point 3. Line [S₃-3] is the *decumanus* (the East-West line) (Fig. 3.b).

Trace Methods of the Romanesque Churches of Val D'aran (11th-13th Centuries)
Orientations

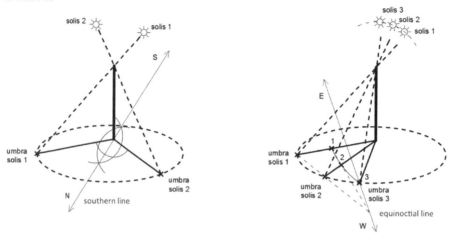

Figure 3. Marco Vitruvius Polión (c.80- c.20 aC).   a) De architectura (LI.VI.6).   b) De architectura (LI.VI.12).

Method [M₃]: Hyginus Gromaticus, in his *De limitibus constituendi* (*Die Schri.* 166-208), uses the rising sun to determine the direction of the *cardus* (the north-south line) and the *decumanus* (the east-west line). This can be done if the equinoxes are known. Gromaticus says: *aut forte cierunt errorem et neglexerunt, ei contenti tamen regioni ortum et occasum demetiri.* (*Die Schri.* 182-183).   This method is also used by Sextus Julius Frontinus (c. 30-104) in his *De limitibus constituendis: Postesta hoc ignorantes non nulli secuti; ut quídam agri magnitudinem, qui qua longior erat, facerunt decumanum* (*Die Schri.* 29).

Method [M₄]: Hyginus Gromaticus, in his *De limitibus constituendi* (*Die Schri.* 188), uses the shadow cast at the sixth hour (i.e., at midday) as the basis to determine the meridian line: *Optimum est ergo umbram hora sexta deprehendere et ab ea limites inchoare, ut sint semper meridiano ordinati.* Having aligned the groma with the midday Sun, the *cardus* is determined when the shadow cast by an object is the shortest.

Method [M₅]: This method presented in *De limitibus constituendi* (*Die Schri.* 188-189) by Hyginus Gromaticus is similar to Vitruvius' method [M₁]. A circle is drawn in a flat place on the ground. When the shadow cast by the *sciotherum* enters the circle after the sunrise, that point of the circumference [S₁] is marked. When the shadow intersects the circumference again, point [S₂] is marked. The central point of segment [S₁- S₂] is determined and a perpendicular line is drawn to the central of the circle: that is the meridian line (N-S) or *cardus*.

Method [M₆]: This method presented in *De limitibus constituendi* (*Die Schri.* 189-181) by Hyginus Gromaticus is similar to Vitruvius' method [M₂]. It uses three shadows cast by a gnomon, which defines three points [S₁, S₂, S₃] on the circumference. Point [S₃] is determined by the shortest shadow, and point [S₁] is determined by the longest shadow.   By rotating the shortest shadow length towards the other two shadow lengths, points [1] and [2] are found. Points [S₁, S₂] define a straight line, and points [1-2] define another straight line; the intersection between these two straight lines provides point [3]. Line [S₃-3] determines the groma's alignment.

Method [M₇]: Gisemundus (c. 880), in his *Ars gromatica siue geometría Gisemundi*[27], uses the shadowcaster method and the movement of a shadow around a reference circumference. This method is similar to method (M₁) by Vitrubio and method [M₅] by Hyginus Gromaticus. After sunrise, there is a long shadow [S₁], then a shorter shadow S₂ intersecting the circle line, and after that an even shorter shadow [S₃] which gets inside the circle.

Later, the cast shadow intersects the circle line again in [S$_4$] and gets out to reach [S$_5$]. The two points of intersection on the circle [S$_2$, S$_4$] form the equinoctial line (Fig. 4.a).

Method [M$_8$]: Gisemundus (c. 880), in his *Ars gromatica siue geometria Gisemundi*, provides a method based on two neighbouring shadows which determine points S$_1$ (longer shadow) and [S$_2$] (shorter shadow). The longer shadow [S$_1$] is made equal to the length of the shorter shadow [S$_2$], thus obtaining point [1']. The line [S$_2$-1] is drawn, and the alignment is solved with the groma. This alignment is not clearly explained. This seems to be an evolution of methods [M$_2$] and [M$_6$]. The first two points [S$_1$, S$_2$] render the equinoctial line (Fig. 4.b).

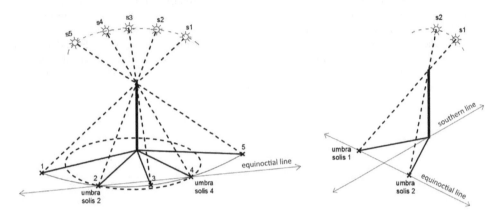

Figure 4. Ars gromatica Gisemundus (c880) a) Method [M7]. b) Method [M8].

Method [M$_9$]: A further possibility is using a compass. There is evidence that European seafarers in the 12th century used a lodestone —called *Leidarstein* by Nordic seamen— as a mariner's compass. Alexander Neckam (1157-1217) mentions a similar instrument. Guiot de Provins (c. 1150-c. 1208) calls it a *pierre laide et brunette*[28]. It has been hypothesized that a magnetic needle could have been used in some churches located in Central Europe, in countries such as Denmark[29], Germany and Austria[30]. In the field of architecture, the first source referring to this instrument is Lorenz Lechler (c. 1460- c. 1538). In his book *Unterweisung für seinen Sohn Moritz* (1516), he explains to his son how to orientate the church choir using a compass[31]. This is also mentioned in a letter which Raphael Sanzio (1483-1520) wrote to Pope Leo X in (1519), in a section entitled *della forma e misura propria della bussola della calamita*[32].

After analysing the geometric methods, we find that the simplest methods are: [M$_1$] by Vitruvius (c.80- c.20 BC), (M$_5$) described by Hyginus Gromaticus (s. I-III), and [M$_7$] by Gisemundus (c.880), all of which can find both the meridian line and the equinoctial line. Methods [M$_2$, M$_6$] by Vitruvius and Hyginus Gromaticus, which draw the equinoctial line, show the highest geometrical complexity. The method by Gisemundus [M$_8$] cannot be interpreted accurately and it might be flawed. As for method [M$_9$], there is no certainty that compasses were being used at that time, since the first direct sources date from the Renaissance period.

The gromatic methods [M$_3$, M$_4$], based on the direct observation of the sun, are relatively inaccurate when establishing the altitude of the sun and the orientation of the church. They have an approximate error of [1°][33].

The most accurate instrument used at that time was the groma, but it is not mentioned in the *Originum sive etymologiarum libri viginti* (c.630) by Isidorus of Seville. Therefore, the continued existence of this instrument by the year 1000 is uncertain. Thus, in all likelihood, the methods mentioned in the treatise *Etymologiarum* (XIX.18, *De instrumentis aedificiorum*) by Isidorus of Seville, and in *De Universo* (XXI.11) by Rabanus Maurus, were the methods used in the period under study. The error of methods (M_1, $M_2 M_5$, M_6, M_7, M_8) is within the range of [3°-5°]. To the possible deviation of the orientation, we must add a degree in the imprecision of the determination of the azimuth (A), the total relative error of which is [1.64%].

Results, discussion and conclusions

A distinction is made between *templi* (*Gem. Ani.* L. 1, Cap. CXXVII) (*Mitra.* L.1, Cap. V) and *capellis* (*Gem. Ani.* L. 1, Cap. CXXVIII) (*Mitra.* L.1, Cap. V). *Capellis* were ancient itinerant churches, consisting of a tent made of goat skin. It is also the designation given to the priests wearing Saint Martin's cloak in those tents. Nowadays, these constructions are called hermitages[34]. From the whole ensemble of First Romanesque churches in the Val d'Aran, 36.36% of them have a basilica floor plan with three naves, whereas the remaining [63.64%] have a single nave. In the Second Romanesque, [30.77%] have a basilica floor plan and the other [69.23%] have a single nave. (Table 1) shows the results of our research.

Town	Church name	Longitud (λ) decimal	°	'	Latitud (φ) decimal	°	'	Topogra. height (m)	Azimut (A)	Horizon height (h')	Solar time	Day-month 2016/17	Declin. (δ)	Day-month 1150	Patron saint 1150
Tredòs	Santa Maria de Cap d'Aran	0,92°	0	55	42,70°	42	42,17	1.319	111,05°	12,89°	7:50	4-Mar	-9,78°	25-Feb	16-feb Maria
Tredòs	Sant Estèue de Tredòs	0,91°	0	55	42,70°	42	42,04	1.328	105,87°	12,40°	7:32	13-Mar	-3,22°	6-Mar	13-feb Stephanus
Unha	Santa Eulària d'Unha	0,90°	0	52	42,71°	42	42,57	1.290	94,45°	13,81°	6:59	5-Apr	2,82°	29-Mar	13-feb Eulalia
Bagergue	Sant Feliu de Bagergue	0,92°	0	55	42,72°	42	43,09	1.411	101,96°	22,80°	7:44	7-Apr	3,62°	31-Mar	1-abr Felix
Salardú	Sant Andrèu de Salardú	0,90°	0	54	42,71°	42	42,45	1.266	96,56°	9,82°	6:56	25-Mar	-1,61°	18-Mar	10-feb Andreas
Arties	Santa Maria d'Arties	0,87°	0	52	42,70°	42	41,88	1.144	93,03°	14,07°	6:55	8-Apr	4,02°	1-Apr	1-abr Maria
Casarilh	Sant Martin de Casarilh	0,83°	0	50	42,70°	42	41,98	1.040	71,44°	10,95°	5:42	25-May	19,49°	18-May	21-may Martinus
Escunhau	Sant Pèir d'Escunhau	0,83°	0	50	42,70°	42	41,80	1.053	53,70°	14,06°	-	-	-	-	- Petrus
Betren	Sant Estèue de Betren	0,81°	0	49	42,70°	42	41,86	1.008	107,93°	14,63°	7:49	13-Mar	-6,38°	6-Mar	13-feb Stephanus
Vielha	Sant Miquèu de Vielha	0,80°	0	48	42,70°	42	42,08	976	120,05°	12,82°	8:18	17-Feb	-14,90°	10-Feb	8-may Michael
Vielha	Santa Maria de Mijaran	0,80°	0	48	41,71°	42	42,63	949	101,81°	26,02°	7:52	14-Apr	6,38°	7-Apr	8-abr Maria
Gausac	Sant Martin de Tours	0,79°	0	48	42,71°	42	42,45	997	106,36°	11,16°	7:30	10-Mar	-7,53°	3-Mar	25-ene Martinus
Casau	Sant Andrèu de Casau	0,79°	0	47	42,71°	42	42,39	1.109	87,89°	11,96°	6:33	14-Apr	6,38°	7-Apr	10-feb Andreas
Vilac	Sant Fèlix de Vilac	0,80°	0	48	42,72°	42	43,30	1.019	128,74°	21,11°	9:06	21-Feb	-13,62°	14-Feb	14-feb Felix
Betlan	Sant Pèir de Betlan	0,79°	0	47	42,73°	42	43,70	1.031	98,70°	13,50°	7:11	27-Mar	-0,81°	20-Mar	24-mar Petrus
Montcorbau	Sant Estèue de Montcorbau	0,79°	0	47	42,73°	42	43,87	1.192	110,33°	9,73°	7:40	28-Feb	-12,27°	21-Feb	13-feb Stephanus
Aubèrt	Sant Martin d'Aubèrt	0,78°	0	47	42,73°	42	43,85	927	125,48°	7,64°	8:19	22-Jan	-21,27°	15-Jan	26-ene Martinus
Arròs	Sant Joan d'Arròs e Vila	0,77°	0	46	42,76°	42	45,53	1.210	43,19°	14,04°	-	-	-	-	- Johanes
Vilamòs	Santa Maria de Vilamòs	0,73°	0	44	42,75°	42	44,86	1.250	107,74°	1,76°	7:10	17-Feb	-14,90°	10-Feb	8-may Maria
Vilamòs	Sant Miquèu de Vilamòs	0,74°	0	44	42,75°	42	44,76	1.279	88,57°	9,34°	6:28	8-Apr	4,02°	1-Apr	8-may Michael
Begòs	Sant Ròc de Begòs	0,74°	0	44	42,74°	42	44,42	974	109,50°	2,52°	7:18	15-Feb	-15,52°	8-Feb	saint of XIV century
Jos	Sant Fabian d'Arres de Jos	0,71°	0	43	42,75°	42	45,30	1.222	162,01°	8,22°	-	-	-	-	- Fabianus
Bossòst	Era Mair de Diu dera Purifacion	0,69°	0	42	42,79°	42	47,15	714	120,57°	22,25°	8:41	7-Mar	-8,67°	28-Feb	15-feb Maria
Les	Sant Blai de Les	0,72°	0	43	42,81°	42	48,90	660	126,02°	29,54°	9:13	15-Mar	-5,60°	8-Mar	18-jul Blastus

Table 1. Result of the research.

Most of the twenty-four churches analysed, are oriented between the 8th of February and the 7th of April, which represents [79.17%] of the total number of churches. The majority of the azimuths of the churches are concentrated mainly among in the third octant [90°-135°] (Graph 1). Therefore, we can say that [75.00%] of the churches are oriented towards the east-south, as are most Romanesque churches in southern Europe.

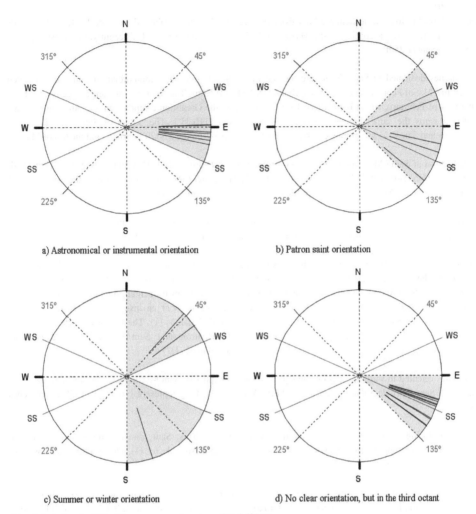

Graph 1. Azimuths (A) of Romanesque churches of Val d'Aran.

If we consider any of the geometric methods [M_1, $M_2 M_5$, M_6, M_7, M_8], and the gromatic methods [M_3, M_4], the relative error would also be within this range. We conclude that the churches that face the equinox (Feast of the Annunciation, March 25th) are from the First Romanesque: Santa Eulària d'Unha and Sant Miquèu de Vilamòs, and from the Second Romanesque: Santa Maria d'Arties and Sant Andrèu de Casau.

Other churches with canonical orientation to the equinox, calculated by astronomical methods, with an error of one week [18th March – 1st April], can be: Sant Fèlix de Bagergue, Santa Eulària d'Unha, Sant Andrèu de Salardú, Santa Maria d'Arties, Sant Pèir de Betlan, Sant Andrèu de Casau and Sant Miquèu de Vilamòs.

Three churches face a point that falls outside the band of possible sun rising points, because their astronomic declination [δ] is greater than [± 23.50°]. These are: Sant Pèir d'Escunhau, Sant Joan d'Arròs e Vila and Sant

Trace Methods of the Romanesque Churches of Val D'aran (11th-13th Centuries)
Orientations

Fabian d'Arres the Jos. All of them are First Romanesque churches. Sant Fabian d'Arres de Jos tends to face its patron saint's feast day, according to the *Martirologio Hieronymianum* (in the 13th century, this feast day took place on December 25th).

The churches dedicated to Sant Estèue are located in Tredòs, Betren and Montcorbau, and they are oriented between the 21st of February and the 6th of March [IX Kal - II Non]. The feast day of Sant Estèue is celebrated on the Ides of February, which is February 13th, according to the Gregorian calendar, but the three churches are oriented towards the same direction, between [105,87°] and [110,33°]. The Saints of San *Saturninus*, San *Sebastianus* and San *Valerius*, among others, were celebrated between the 21st of February and the 6th of March.

The dedication of Santa Maria is celebrated on different dates: February 2nd, 16th and 25th, March 13th, April 1st, 5th, 8th, 16th, 24th and 27th and May 10th and 13th. Therefore, they could coincide with the orientation of the churches of: Santa Maria Mijaran, April 7th, and Santa Maria Vilamòs, February 10th.

According to their orientation, the Romanesque churches in the region of Val d'Aran can be classified in four groups, specifying if they are from the (1) First Romanesque or from the (2) Second Romanesque:

a) We can find three different groups of churches that have a canonical orientation, as prescribed by medieval liturgy, depending on the method used to orientate the building (Graph 1a). Astronomical orientation: Sant Fèlix de Bagergue (1), Sant Andrèu de Salardú (2) and Sant Pèir de Betlan (1). Instrumental orientation: Sant Andrèu de Casau (2) and, finally, churches that could either have an astronomical or an instrumental orientation: Santa Eulària d'Unha (1), Santa Maria d'Arties (2) and Sant Miquèu de Vilamòs (1). They represent [29.17%] of the churches considered. Some of these possibly coincide with their patron saint: Sant Fèlix de Bagergue (1), Santa Maria d'Arties (2), Sant Pèir de Betlan (1) and Sant Miquèu de Vilamòs (1).

b) Churches oriented towards the day of their patron saint (Graph 1b): Sant Martín de Casarilh (2), Santa Maria Mijaran (1), Sant Fèlix de Vilac (2) and Santa Maria Vilamòs (1). They represent [16.67%] of all the churches considered.

c) Churches facing oriented towards the summer (Graph 1c), such as: Sant Joan d'Arròs (1) and Sant Pèir d'Escunhau (1), or facing the towards winter, such as Sant Fabian d'Arres de Jos (1). They represent [12.50%] of all the churches considered.

d) Churches for which we still have not been able to determine a clear orientation. They are possibly oriented towards the east-south, i.e. in the third octant (Graph 1d): Santa Maria de Cap d'Aran de Tredòs (1), Sant Estèue de Tredòs (1), Sant Estèue de Betren (2), Sant Miquèu de Vielha (2), Sant Martín de Tours de Gausac (2), Sant Estèue de Montcorbau (1), Sant Martín d'Aubèrt (2), Sant Roc de Begòs (1) and San Blai de Les (1). They represent [41.67%] of all the churches considered.

References

[1] Íñiguez, J. A. (1986). La simbología del templo cristiano en el comienzo del periodo gótico (Honorio de Autún y Sicardo de Cremona). *Biblia y hermenéutica: VII Simposio Internacional de Teología de la Universidad de Navarra*. José María Casciaro (ed). Servicio de Publicaciones de la Universidad de Navarra, pp. 667-681.

[2] Sebastián S. (1994). *Mensaje Simbólico del Arte Medieval. Arquitectura, Liturgia e Iconografía*. Madrid: Ediciones Encuentro, pp. 352-355.

[3] Reveyron, N. (2003). Architecture, liturgie et organisation de l'espace ecclésial. Essai sur la notion d'espace dans l'architecture religieuse du Moyen Âge. *Les cahiers de Saint-Michel de Cuxa*, n° 34, pp. 161-175.

[4] Mambelli, F. (2004). "Il problema dell'immagine nei commentari allegorici sulla liturgia: Dalla Gemma Animae di Onorio d'Autun (1120 ca.) al Rationale divinorum officiorum di Durando di Mende (1286-1292)". *Studi Medievali*. Jun 2004, Vol.45 I.: 1, pp. 121-158.

[5] Mews, Constant J. (2009). Liturgists and Dance in the Twelfth Century: The Witness of John Beleth and Sicard of Cremona. *Church History*. Volume 78, Issue 3 September 2009, pp. 512-548

[6] Durand, G. (1775). *Prochiron vulgo rationale divinorum officiorum. Auctore Gulielmo Durando*. Matriti: Ex typographia Blasii Roman.

[7] Isidorus of Seville. (1919). *Isidori Hispalensis episcopi. Etymologiarum sive Originvm libri XX. Recognovit brevique adnotatione critica instruxit W. M. Lindsay*. Tomus II. Oxonii: e Typographeo Clarendoniano.

[8] Rabanus Maurus. *De Universo Libri Viginti Duo*. Documenta Catholica Omnia. De Scriptoribus Ecclesiae Relatis. Migne JP. Patrologia Latina, MPL111, Col. 0009 - 0614B, 1864.

[9] McCluskey, S.C. (2004). "Astronomy, Time, and Churches in the Early Middle Ages", in M.-T. Zenner, Villard's legacy: *Studies in Medieval Technology, Science and Art in Memory of Jean Gimpel*. Ashgate, Aldeshot: 197-210.

[10] Vogel, C. (1962). Sol aequinoctialis. Problèmes et technique de l'orientation dans le culte chrétien. *Revue des Sciences Religieuses*, n° 36, pp. 175-211.

[11] Puig i Cadafalch, J. (1906). *Influences lombardes en Catalogne*. Congrès Archéologique de la France, Carcassonne-Perpignan, pp. 684-703.
Puig i Cadaflach, J. (1908). Les iglesies romàniques ab cobertes de fusta de les Valls De Bohí y d'Aran. *Anuari de l'Institut d'Estudis Catalans*. MCMVII, pp. 119-136.
Puig i Cadafalch, J., (et al). (1918). *L'Arquitectura Romànica a Catalunya*. Vol III. Barcelona: Institut d'Estudis Catalans.

[12] Martínez Tejera A. M., (2002) Cenobios leoneses altomedievales ante la europeización: San Pedro y San Pablo de Montes, Santiago y San Martín de Peñalba y San Miguel de Escalada. *Hispania Sacra*. Vol. 54. No 109, pp. 87-108.

[13] González-García, A.C. and Belmonte, J.A. (2015). The Orientation of Pre-Romanesque Churches in the Iberian Peninsula. *Nexus Network Journal,* Volume 17, Issue 2, pp 353-377.

[14] Delcor, M. (1987). Les églises romanes et l'origine de leur orientation. *Les Cahiers de Saint-Michel de Cuxa* 18, pp. 39-53.

[15] Benson, H. (1956). Church Orientations and Patronal Festivals. *The Antiquaries Journal* 36, pp. 205-213.

[16] Incerti, M. (2103) Astronomical Knowledge in the Sacred Architecture of the Middle Ages in Italy. Nexus Network Journal, n°15, pp. 503-526

[17] Vitruvius, M. (1899). *Vitruvii. De architectura Libri Decem*. Iterum edidit Valentinus Rose. Lipsiae: In aedibus B. G. Teubneri.

Vitruvius, M. (1878). *Los diez libros de archîtectura de M. Vitruvio Polión, traducidos del latín, y comentados por Don Joseph Ortíz i Sanz presbítro.* Madrid: Imprenta Real

[18] Cantor, M. (1880). *Vorlesungen über Geschichte der Mathematik, von Moritz Cantor Erster Band.* Von den ältesten Zeiten bis zum Jahre 1200 n. Chr. Leipzig: Druk und Verlag von B.G. Teuberner, pp. 454-456.

[19] Millàs Vallicrosa, J. Mª. (1931). *Assaig d'història de les idees físiques i matemàtiques a la Catalunya medieval.* Vol I. Barcelona: Institució Patxot.

[20] Nissen, Heinrich (1906). *Orientation. Studien zur Geschichte der Religion.* Berlin: Weidmannsche Buchhandlung.

[21] Pesci, A., Bonali, E., Galli, C., & Boschi, E. (2012). Laser scanning and digital imaging for the investigation of an ancient building: Palazzo d'Accursio study case (Bologna, Italy). *Journal of Cultural Heritage,* 13(2), 215–220.

[22] Guarnieri, A., Vettore, A. and Remondino, F. (2004). Photogrammetry and ground-based laser scanning: assessment of metric accuracy of the 3D model of Pozzoveggiani Church. In *Working Week, The Olympic Spirit in Surveying.* Athens.

[23] Spencer, J.W. Fourier Series Representation of the Position of the Sun. *Search,* n° 2, (1971), pp. 162-172.

[24] Pablo VI. *Calendarium Romanum ex decreto Sacrosanti Decumenici Concilii Vaticani II instauratum aictoritate Pauli PP. VI promulgatum.* Typis Polyglottis Vaticanis, Vaticano, 1969, pp. 23-32.

[25] Smedt, C; Backer I (et alt). *Praemissum est Martyrologium Hieronymianum endentibus Iohanne Baptista de Rossi et Ludovico Ouchesme. Sanctorum novembris collecta digesta illustrata.* Tomi II pars prior, Apud socios Bollandianos, Bruxellis, 1894, pp. 1-156.

[26] Cantor, M. (1875). Die römischen Agrimensoren und ihre Stellung in der Geschichte der Feldmesskunst. Eine historisch-*mathematische Untersuchung von Dr. Moritz Cantor.* Leipzig: Druk un verlag von B.G. Teubner.

[27] Andreu Expósito, R. (2012). *Edició critica, traducció i estudi de l'Ars gromatica siue geometria Gisemundi.* Tesi Doctoral codirigida pels doctors: Dra. Cándida Ferrero i Dr. Oriol Olesti. Departament de Ciències de l'Antiguitat i de l'Edai Mitjana. Universitat Autònoma de Barcelona.

[28] La Roncière, C. (1897). *Un inventaire de bord en 1294 et les origines de la navigation hauturière. Bibliothèque de l'école des Chartes.* Vol. 58 N. 1 pp. 394-409.

[29] Abrahamsen, N. Evidence for church orientation by magnetic compass in twelfthcentury Denmark. *Archaeometry* 34 (1992), pp. 293-303.

[30] Arneitz, P; Draxler, A; Rauch, R; Leonhardt, R. Orientation of churches by magnetic compasses? *Geophysical Journal International.* Vol. 198, Iss. 1, (2014), pp.1-7.

[31] Frankl, P. *The Gothic: Literary Sources and Interpretations through Eight Centuries,* Princeton University Press, Princeton, New Jersey, 1960, pp. 916.

[32] Visconti, P. E. *Lettera di Raffaello d'Urbino a papa Leone X. Raffaello Sanzio.* Tipografia delle scienze, Roma, 1840, pp. 15-35.

[33] Orfila M. (et alt.) (2017). Urbanizar en época romana: ritualidad y practicidad. Propuesta de un procedimiento homologado de ejecución. *SPAL* n° 26, pp. 113-134

[34] Monge España, Esther. (2013). Capèles romaniques d'origina romanica ena Val d'Aran. *Era Batalha de Murèth, 1213. Era Queremònia, 1313. Era grana patzeria, 1513. Tres hites importantes entara Val d'Aran. Jornades d'estudi.* Val d'Aran, 18-20 October 2013. Salardú, pp. 111- 118.

Transformation of the interior of Gökhem, a Swedish romanesque church - results of an investigation of the attic

Mattias Hallgren[1] and Robin Gullbrandsson[2]

1. Traditional carpenter/crafts researcher; 2. Västergötlands museum, Phil. mag. in archaeology, Heritage Officer[2]

Figure 1. Gökhem romanesque church, dated 1140.

Introduction and background

During 2017, the authors made a damage inventory and archaeological cleaning prior to a forthcoming restoration of the attic of Gökhem church from the 12th century.[1] This revealed several interesting traces from the transformations of the church interior throughout the ages: from the open romanesque nave-roof which was part of the sacred church room, to a secluded attic behind a flat wooden ceiling that later was remodeled into limestone vaults.

Covered in dirt and bird nests, several traces have never been seen before. Due to the lack of written detailed technical references, the church itself become the reference when we interpreted its construction. The article both adds to, and partly revises, previous knowledge. [2]

Transformation of the interior of Gökhem, a Swedish romanesque church - results of an investigation of the attic

The interest for Gökhem church is based on its unique roof trusses over the nave, dated to 1140/1141. Already during the early 20th century the Swedish romanesque churches were well known for their many well-preserved original wooden roof constructions from the 12th and 13th centuries.[3] Several investigations and drawings were made by restoration architects all over the country up until the 1940s. When the science of dendrochronology started to form in the early 1980s, a new interest in the medieval churches started to grow. At the same time a restoration architect, Peter Sjömar, started to examine the churches from a craftsman's perspective. [4]

In spite of the early origins, systematic surveys of the Swedish medieval roof constructions only started in the 2010s. In recent years, several dioceses have carried out or are about to do, identification projects aimed at the medieval wooden constructions. During 2011-2015 the authors have done projects in Skara dioceses about belfries and roof constructions.

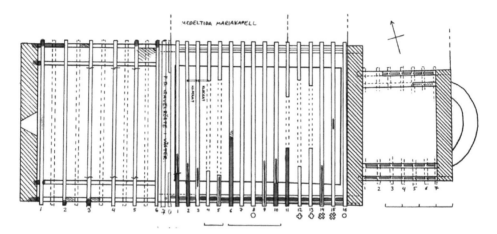

Figure 2. Gökhem church, plan of the attic. Dark marking shows damages in tie beams and wall plates.

Purpose and questions

The paper's main goal is to show the large potential of knowledge a church attic has in both its preserved constructions and all the dust and loose material, mainly considered as "trash", that has accumulated over the years. The authors aim in Gökhem was to develop a suitable method for archaeological cleaning while doing a building archaeological examination.

Figure 3. Archaeological cleaning and building archaeological examination.

In this article the authors want to present conclusions that can be drawn from finds made during the cleaning and from traces in the masonry and roofing. These are new clues to the building's chronology, changes in the church room and traces of the renovation stages of the roofing. In the cleaning process, the authors were given the opportunity to get to know the object with "open minds". Going through an attic systematically, basically every inch of the roof trusses and every square foot of the walls and heads of the vaults, gives a holistic view.

Based on the Gökhem church as an example, we will discuss the following issues in the article. What values are there in a cluttered church attic? What can the "trash" tell about the use of the church, building chronology, crafts and techniques? What do single finds tell about the social context? What clues about the building hide beneath the cultural layers? The authors claim that conscious cleaning produces new knowledge. [5]

Geographic and historic context

The church of Gökhem is located in the Swedish province of Västergötland, which coincides with the country's oldest diocese, Skara, instituted in the early 11th century.

Much suggests that Västergötland was the first province to be christianised in the emerging medieval Swedish kingdom. Together with the province of Östergötland, east of Lake Vättern, Västergötland came to be the core of the medieval kingdom.

Transformation of the interior of Gökhem, a Swedish romanesque church - results of an investigation of the attic

Already in the 12th century, Västergötland had developed a dense structure of church buildings, often founded by local noble families. This was certainly the case with Gökhem. Easily-worked sand- and limestone enabled the construction of expensive buildings, which initially demanded foreign stone builders' skills.[6]

164 churches in today's Diocese of Skara have medieval origins, originally there were around 400. The mentioned survey has identified wholly or partly well-preserved medieval roof constructions and traces of such in the attics of almost 70 churches. 28 roofs can be regarded as having well-preserved roof trusses with tie beams, dating from the 12th century and the first half of the 13th century. Ten are only partly preserved and 18 remain as reused parts in later constructions.[7]

Together with preserved roof constructions in other medieval provinces in mid-Sweden, this is possibly one of the largest concentrations of its kind in northern Europe. Hewing techniques like "sprätthuggning" (fish-bone pattern) and hewing with broad-axe occur side by side, the former is generally considered to be synonymous with the Nordic Middle Ages.[8]

The majority of the churches with preserved medieval roof trusses are concentrated to the area around Kinnekulle and Falbygden with their Cambro-Silurian hills, as well as the neighbouring area southwest of the latter, formerly known for vast oak forests. Large scale modernization and demolitions during the 18th and 19th centuries have largely affected the grade of preservation, thus leaving large areas of the diocese with hardly any traces of the medieval wooden constructions.[9]

Figure 4. Decorated roof trusses at Gökhem over the nave, once visible from the floor during the 12th century. Every truss has a unique decoration, some of them are asymmetric.

278

The Gökhem church is located in the Cambro-Silurian area of Falbygden. The romanesque church is constructed of crude limestone and sandstone from the immediate area. The church consists of a nave, extended by a bay to the west, an apse chancel in the east, north of the chancel a sacristy with pulpit roof and north of the centre of the nave, a former Mary chapel, now a porch. It is unclear when in the Middle Ages, the chapel, the western extension and the sacristy were built. In the late 15th century, the church room was vaulted and painted. In the 18th century, the church received its current window openings. In the 19th century, the outer roof shingles were replaced with roof tiles. A major restoration was carried out in 1913. The work resulted in, among other things, a new roofing of tiles and a chimney from the stove in the chancel (opening a hole at the top of the gable, in the attic, between the chancel and the nave). In the western extension an older cross vault was replaced.[10]

The roofing in the original part of the nave

The nave roofing consists of 16 pine roof trusses with six crossed struts attached with nails, and with dowels in the tie beam. The trusses are spaced about a cubit's length apart and rest on oak wall plates. The roof was originally visible from the church nave floor, similar to that in most contemporary parish churches.[11] Particular to Gökhem is that the eastern half of the roof has decoratively designed joints between the struts. Nothing similar is preserved elsewhere in the Nordic region. The beauty of the embellishments is related to the church's direction to the east, escalating towards the holiest.[12]

The dendrochronological samples and the analyzes of the roofing over the older part of the nave show, due to the occurrence of wane, that the timber was cut down in the winter of 1140/41.[13] The perfectly fitting joints between the tie beam, rafters and struts show that the twisting of the dried wood has clearly been taken into account. Thus, the cutting of the joint has not been done in fresh wood, which indicates that the actual assembling of the roof construction may have been completed at least one or more years after the felling. The visible parts of the meeting between the tie beam and the wall plate show that the tie beams are more or less wedged into the recesses of the wall plate, in most cases one side of the tie beam has been hewn to fit for this purpose. The wall plate is not locked to the masonry which is otherwise common in early medieval roofs.

Traces of the original appearance and changes of the roof

A closer study of the walls above the nave's vaults has given new information after the cleaning. The walls carry at least two layers of a slightly yellowish lime plaster, but not all the way up to the tie beams. The first layer should be the original from the middle of the 12th century, the second layer is likely to be linked with the later insertion of a flat wooden ceiling (see below).

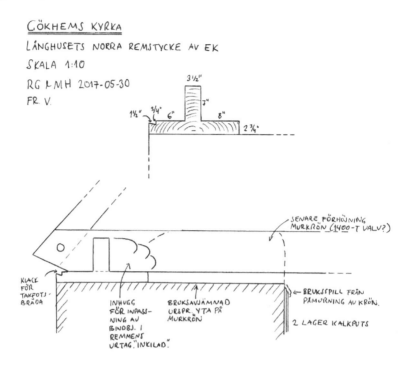

GÖKHEMS KYRKA

LÅNGHUSETS NORRA REMSTYCKE AV EK

SKALA 1:10

RG & MH 2017-05-30

FR. V.

Figure 5. Wall plate meeting tie beam (the later masonry extension indicated with a broken line). The wall plate is without attachment to the masonry, lying "loose", held by friction.

At one place on the north side (at truss No. 4) you can see that someone drew his fingers in the still wet plaster. It is now also apparent that the present height of the northern and southern walls is not the original. After cleaning, we could see that the wall plates of oak are shaped like up-side-down T:s with an outside shelf for the footboard. The wall plates are placed on a horizontal surface that has been very carefully smoothed with mortar. That is the original top of the masonry. The tie beams are wedged into the recesses in the tall and thin vertical part of the plate. The tie beams have therefore originally not been in contact with the masonry. Only later, the masonry has been raised between and on top of the tie beams and, especially in the north, completely embedded them all the way up to the roofboards. Earlier this was thought to be an original masonry.[14] The added masonry is quite sloppily done without smoothing the mortar between the stones. The lime plaster has poured out at some places on the inside of the wall and trickled down on the broken top edge of the plastered wall and created rills. (fig 12) According to the observations, the roof initially rested directly on the wall top by its own weight. There was no attachment to the masonry. So, when was the height of the walls increased with up to half a meter, and why? Why did the craftsmen want a firm foundation of the roofs in the walls (despite the risk of rotting)? The question is discussed further in the following.

It is a fact that the roof was initially open to the ridge. Not only do the decorative struts speak for this. In line with one of the two original (now plugged) window openings on the south side, two of the tie beams have been given a planed profile along the lower edge to the west, which must have appeared in relief in the light from the window.

Figure 6. North wall with masonry extension, built tight in between the tie beams. Here partly disassembled due to earlier restoration of the outer roof.

Figure 7. Profile on tie beams near the original windows. Parts of the roof have probably been painted. Foto Daniel Eriksson.

Similar profiles have been shown on the tie beams in the churches of Od and Våmb and on a loose beam in the church of Fivlered. [15] In the northwestern corner of the nave, two small liturgic bells were hanging from recesses on the upper side of the tie beams belonging to the trusses 2, 3 and 4. Here you can see both the abrasion

281

in the recesses and the marks in the sides of the beams where the lower edge of the bell has been scraping when ringing. There is no evidence that the gable of the chancel has been plastered, but much of the original mortar joints remain, in one spot there are even fingerprints.

Remodeling with a flat wooden ceiling

A remnant of full-width pine board from the former ceiling was found between the eastern roof truss and the gable of the chancel. The sides are straight edged and there are two nail holes in line, with impressions of large-headed handforged nails. Two such medieval nails were found in close proximity and correspond well to the holes and imprints. The width of the board is 6" and the thickness 3/4". Like small shadings, the imprints of these ceiling boards without tongue and groove can be seen on the underside of the tie beams. The width of the boards has been varying between 6" to 10" and the boards were nailed in every second tie beam. The boards were nailed end to end with two nails in each. They were probably of the same length, which created a contiguous joint. This ceiling should have been put up in the 13th or 14th century and traces of such ceilings have been observed in several medieval churches in Sweden. [16] Whether the roof has been painted can not be commented today, and the theories differ as to why ceilings were generally put up in the churches. [17]

Figure 8. Piece of the former ceiling with its original nails.

Vaulting during the second half of the 15th century

During the second half of the 15th century, the nave was provided with limestone vaults. According to a now lost inscription, vaults and walls were painted by master Amund, a famous painter in 1487.[18]

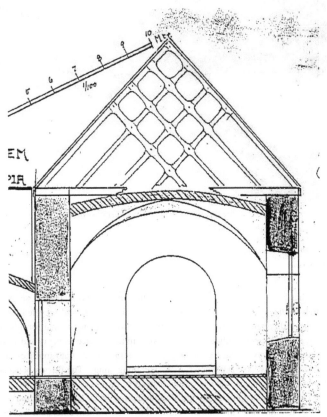

Figure 9. Section of the nave with cut tie beams for the vault. Antikvarisk-topografiska arkivet.

The vaulting was started by tearing down the ceiling. After that, five tie beams were cut where the top of the two vaults would be. In the adjoining roof trusses, the tie beams were cut out slightly underneath before the vault was built. The authors' interpretation is that it was then that the masonry tops in the north and south were extended. Because the existing roofing with wall plates rested on the masonry without locking attachment, only friction, we can assume that the 15th-century craftsmen were afraid that the pressure from the vaults would push the walls outward. Small limestone slabs have been wedged under and alongside the tie beams. The height of the masonry was increased by half a meter, in some places up close to the primary outer roof. The top of the extended masonry has been smoothed with mortar. When cleaning the broken parts of the extended masonry, residues of organic matter appeared in between the stones and under thick layers of mortar. These are probably traces from the demolition of a worn out roofing, that could possibly be linked to a contemporary renovation of the roof. The extended masonry as described here, has been found in other contemporary churches around the country and often been considered as original. A new look at these could strengthen the authors' theory.

Figure 10. Loose mortar from the masonry extension dropped down on the broken plaster. This is one of the evidences that shows that the height of the walls has been altered.

The western extension

The western extension has been paid surprisingly little attention in previous studies, despite the fact that it must have been built in high-medieval times. Wall plates with "sprätthuggning" and recycled parts indicate a dating before the middle of the 14th century. [19]   The roof trusses have in their original form been of a gothic type. They have double wall plates, recesses indicate that they were initially twice as many and were placed at 1-cubit intervals (24"). In the gable trusses (1 and 6), the original tie beam remains with mortices on the upper side for two vertical posts. Several beams have been hewn with "sprätthuggning". The trusses between the first and last ones probably had sole and ashlar pieces/collar beams instead of tie beams/posts, in other words a pronounced gothic roofing adapted for vaults. Dendrochronological sampling has so far not been carried out here, but it would be of great value in order to understand the church's chronology. The western extension was probably built with a vault (groin or barrel), before vaulting the rest of the nave (by 1487).

What was the function of the western extension?

A comparison can be made with the neighbouring church of Marka, where the barrel-vaulted ground floor of a romanesque tower served as a baptistery. [20]   We know that the nave, at some time in the middle of the Middle Ages (before 1487), was provided with a (later?) groin-vaulted Mary chapel in the north. The roof has not been inspected nor tested for dendrochronology. Separate side chapels are known only from a few medieval churches in Västergötland. [21]

In what remains of the original western gable of the nave, we can see the lower part of what may have been a nook for passage into the nave attic. It is located next to where the gable meets the north wall. Probably, this has been the only access to the attic after the vaulting, but it may have existed from the beginning. Interestingly, this is where the two bells were placed before the vaulting.

The roof of the chancel

The apse chancel's relationship to the nave remains to be studied. Continued cleaning and investigation of the chancel's attic will certainly generate new observations that facilitate interpretation. What we know is that the chancel had trusses of gothic type that were totally different from the nave's, that is, the trusses were adapted to vaults where the tie beams and beams were replaced with sole and ashlar pieces and collar beams. This type of roof truss has double wall plates. It is these, on the surface very weathered remnants of wall plates of oak and one remaining sole piece, that have conflicting dates, on the one hand 1113-1117[22] and on the other hand 1239. [23] The latter date seems more plausible considering the truss type; we do not yet have any datings of Gothic trusses from the 12th century in Sweden. The truss type indicates that there was a vault when the roof was (re)built. Is this the existing groin vault, or was there an older barrel vault of wood or stone?

Traces of older roofings

A large amount of oak shingles has been found on top of the masonry and vaults. The shingles have been pre-drilled, so as not to break at nailing. This has nevertheless occurred and the discarded shingles have apparently been thrown into the church attic. Some shingles have nails in their visible lower part, probably made deliberately as an exclusive decoration in the Middle Ages when iron was something expensive. Only one shingle has been found with a remaining B-shaped nail, which is usually considered a medieval type of nail. Otherwise, the shingles most likely originate from shingle roofs from the 17th and 18th centuries. Three oak boards with trapezoidal shape are interpreted as primary roof boards. They have nail holes after at least two generations of shingle coverings. The shingle coverings have been long lasting, at least 100 years.

When investigating the vaults and above all the masonry, a large amount of iron nails of different ages and appearances was discovered. To some degree we observed a stratification that gives a rough chronology (nails of medieval types were generally at the bottom, near the masonry and head of arches), comparisons can also be made with nails that still are in their original contexts in this church and elsewhere.

Figure 11a and b. B-shaped nails like this, indicate medieval shingles.

Transformation of the interior of Gökhem, a Swedish romanesque church - results of an investigation of the attic

Around seventy nails with characteristic B-shaped, thin heads were found on the masonry and vaults. The majority was found beneath dust and trash on top of the masonry and head of arches, together with decomposed wood. The type is known from late medieval depictions and occurs in other medieval constructions. However, it does not appear after the Middle Ages. [24] The interpretation is that these long, B-shaped nails have been used to attach primary roof boards and shingles and that they are found in a demolition layer that should be connected with the renovation of the church in the 18th century and the laying of new roofing.

Other categories of finds

The examination generated a large amount of finds of organic material in the form of textiles, leather and rope as well as withies. Lots of material has probably ended up in the attic due to birds and rodents. In terms of time, parts of it are rather late, that is, from the 20th century. However, single fragments seem to have a greater age and would need a closer study by a textile historian.

Hundreds of skeletal parts were found in the attic above the original part of the nave, especially a bit down in the large bird nest by the eastern end of the gable, which may have accumulated for a long time. The majority of the bones are human and many parts are noticeably weathered. The interpretation is that the bones have lain visible above ground at the cemetery and been collected by birds. Even at the beginning of the 19th century, the graves were dug shallow and it is possible that cattle got in and rooted among the graves.[25]

Archaeo-botanics and -genetics

A lot of plant material could be found in the cultural layers, such as straw, flower stems and some seed ears, also manure and horsehair. In general, the attic has a large archaeo-botanic and -genetic potential, especially in spandrels, cracks and other spaces that have not been disturbed. Preserved dry plant material of great age is very rare. During the cleaning, archaeo-botanist Jens Heimdal and archaeo-geneticist Matti Leino from the Nordic Museum visited us. The southern spandrel (with the romanesque window nook) between the two medieval nave-vaults was considered interesting for a future archaeological survey in connection with restoration. Its likely untouched layer may have accumulated for more than 500 years.

Conclusions

The authors' archaeological cleaning and investigation of the attic in the Gökhem church generated new knowledge about the changes and uses of the building. The transformation from visible roof trusses, through ceilings to vaults has left clear traces of the processes in the attic. Additionally it has given a lot of information about roofing history. Accumulated cultural layers on the vaults and walls provide a great future research potential to understanding how society and surrounding areas have changed. Conscious archaeological cleaning is a way to increased knowledge, therefore such spaces should be handled carefully.

Figure 12. Archaeo-botany has great potential to find valuable reference material on the attic. Matti Leino, The Nordic Museum, examining the "trash" in the southern spandrel, by a former Romanesque window.

References

[1] R. Gullbrandsson and M. Hallgren, *Gökhems kyrka. Antikvarisk städning och undersökning av vind och taklag. Byggnadsvårdsrapport 2017:19.* Skara: Västergötlands museum, 2017, pp. 5 f.

[2] K. Linscott, *Tidigmedeltida taklag i Skara stift. Rapport 2013-01-04.* Skara: Skara stift, 2013, pp. 3–23; K. Linscott, *Interpretations of old wood. Figuring mid-twelfth century church architecture in west Sweden.* Gothenburg: University of Gothenburg, 2017; R. Gullbrandsson, *Medeltida taklag i Skara stifts kyrkor.* Skara: Skara stiftshistoriska sällskap, 2015, pp. 86–94.

[3] O. Janse, 'Om forna takkonstruktioner i några Östgötakyrkor', *Svenska fornminnesföreningens tidskrift 11.* Stockholm, 1902, pp. 313–320; S. Curman, 'Två romanska träkonstruktioner', *Från stenålder till rokoko. Studier tillägnade Otto Rydbeck den 25 augusti 1937.* Lund: University of Lund, 1937, pp. 194 f.

[4] P. Sjömar, *Byggnadsteknik och timmermanskonst. En studie med exempel från några medeltida knuttimrade kyrkor och allmogehus.* Gothenburg: Chalmers, 1988.

[5] R. Gullbrandsson and M. Hallgren, *Gökhems kyrka. Antikvarisk städning och undersökning av vind och taklag. Byggnadsvårdsrapport 2017:19.* Skara: Västergötlands museum, 2017, p. 34.

[6] M. Dahlberg, *Skaratraktens kyrkor under äldre medeltid.* Skara: Västergötlands museum, 1998, pp. 209 ff.

[7] R. Gullbrandsson, *Medeltida taklag i Skara stifts kyrkor*, Skara: Skara stiftshistoriska sällskap, 2015.

[8] O. Storsletten, *Takene taler. Norske takstoler 1100–1350. Klassifisering og oprinnelse.* Oslo: University of Oslo, 2002, p. 8; P. Sjömar, *Byggnadsteknik och timmermanskonst. En studie med exempel från några medeltida knuttimrade kyrkor och allmogehus.* Gothenburg: Chalmers, 1988, pp. 263–268; G. Almevik and K-M. Melin, 'Att bygga en kyrka i trä', *Bebyggelsehistorisk tidskrift nr 74/2017.* Uppsala: University of Uppsala, 2017, pp. 48–64.

[9] R. Gullbrandsson, *Medeltida taklag i Skara stifts kyrkor*, Skara: Skara stiftshistoriska sällskap, 2015.

[10] R. Gullbrandsson, *Medeltida taklag i Skara stifts kyrkor*, Skara: Skara stiftshistoriska sällskap, 2015.

[11] P. Sjömar, 'Romanska takkonstruktioner – ett värdefullt och outforskat källmaterial', *Från romanik till nygotik. Studier i kyrklig konst och arkitektur tillägnade Evald Gustafsson.* Stockholm: Kungliga

Vitterhetsakademien, 1992, pp. 56–66; P. Sjömar, 'Romanskt och gotiskt – takkonstruktioner i svenska medeltidskyrkor', *Hikuin 22. Kirkearkæologi i Norden*. Højbjerg, 1995, pp. 207–212; R. Gullbrandsson, 'Medieval Roof Trusses in Churches of Northern Småland', *Lund Archaeological Review 2013*. Lund: University of Lund, 2014, p. 91; K. Linscott, *Interpretations of old wood. Figuring mid-twelfth century church architecture in west Sweden*. Gothenburg: University of Gothenburg, 2017, pp. 177 f.

[12] K. Linscott, *Interpretations of old wood. Figuring mid-twelfth century church architecture in west Sweden*. Gothenburg: University of Gothenburg, 2017, pp. 170–176.

[13] R. Gullbrandsson, *Medeltida taklag i Skara stifts kyrkor*, Skara: Skara stiftshistoriska sällskap, 2015; P. Sjömar, 'Romanskt och gotiskt – takkonstruktioner i svenska medeltidskyrkor', *Hikuin 22. Kirkearkæologi i Norden*, Højbjerg, 1995, p. 79.

[14] R. Gullbrandsson, *Medeltida taklag i Skara stifts kyrkor*, Skara: Skara stiftshistoriska sällskap, 2015.

[15] R. Gullbrandsson, *Medeltida taklag i Skara stifts kyrkor*, Skara: Skara stiftshistoriska sällskap, 2015, p. 22.

[16] R. Gullbrandsson, 'Dendrokronologisk undersökning av två kyrkor i Linköpings stift – Kumla och Norra Solberga', *Fornvännen 2016/3*, Stockholm: Kungliga Vitterhetsakademien, 2016.

[17] Sjömar, 'Romanskt och gotiskt – takkonstruktioner i svenska medeltidskyrkor', *Hikuin 22. Kirkearkæologi i Norden*, Højbjerg, 1995, pp. 227 f.; K. Linscott, *Interpretations of old wood. Figuring mid-twelfth century church architecture in west Sweden*. Gothenburg: University of Gothenburg, 2017, pp. 177 f.

[18] Hernfjäll, V. *Medeltida kyrkmålningar i gamla Skara stift*. Skara: Västergötlands museum, 1993, pp. 175 fff.

[19] K-M. Melin & O. Andersson, *Behuggningsteknik i Södra Råda och Hammarö kyrkor. 1300- tals yxor i litteratur och magasin. Knadriks Kulturbygg rapport 2008:18*, Kristianstad: Knadriks Kulturbygg, 2008.

[20] R. Gullbrandsson, *Medeltida taklag i Skara stifts kyrkor*, Skara: Skara stiftshistoriska sällskap, 2015, pp. 184–189; R. Gullbrandsson and M. Hallgren, *Marka kyrka. Antikvarisk städning och undersökning av vind och taklag. Byggnadsvårdsrapport 2017:15*. Skara: Västergötlands museum, 2017, p. 7.

[21] *Västergötland – landskapets kyrkor. Sockenkyrkorna – kulturarv och bebyggelsehistoria*. Stockholm: Riksantikvarieämbetet, 2002, s 61.

[22] H. Linderson, *Dendrokronologisk rapport Gökhems kyrka*. Lund: University of Lund, 2012, pp. 1 f.

[23] A. Seim et al, 'Diverse construction types and local timber sources characterize early medieval church roofs in southwestern Sweden', *Dendrochronologia 35*, Association for Tree-Ring-Research, 2015, pp. 45.

[24] C. How, *Historic French Nails & Fixings*, Victoria: Furniture History Society of Australasia, 2017, M. Helje, *Medeltida byggnadsspik. En undersökning av spikmaterialet från Södra Råda gamla kyrka*. Mariestad: Hantverkslaboratoriet, University of Gothenburg, 2015.

[25] *Ett levande kulturarv – Kyrkogårdar i Växjö stift*. Växjö: Växjö stift, 2009.

Earth Mortared Masonry Construction – Its Symbolism and Functionality – An Irish and United Kingdom Perspective

Shirley Markley

Department of Environmental Science, Institute of Technology Sligo, NW Ireland

Summary Introduction

Pioneering research in Ireland and Britain has identified the extensive and selected use of earth mortar in masonry construction across social classes from the early medieval to the post medieval periods [1]. The durability and structural stability of earth mortared masonry construction is borne out in the survival of earth mortared masonry buildings both in standing structures and in the archaeological settlement record. This paper looks at the prevalence and choice of earth mortar in upstanding ecclesiastical stone buildings with a view to presenting the potential imbued symbolic, sacred function which promoted its use. Historically, earth embodied sacred, curative, protective and spiritual properties. The paper proposes that the use of earth mortar in stone church construction across time periods may have provided a tangible associative link to a founding saint. It is hoped that future researchers may add evidence substantiating this theory.

Ireland – Earth Mortared Masonry Construction

The case has already been made documenting the heretofore unacknowledged but widespread presence of earth mortared masonry construction throughout the later medieval settlement record in Ireland in the previous fourth volume of these proceedings [2]. By the mid to late twentieth century, earth mortared masonry construction became acknowledged and synonymous with post medieval (eighteenth to twentieth century) vernacular building construction, principally farm houses and outbuildings associated with the poorer agricultural classes [3-8]. However, regional field survey of later medieval upstanding buildings in north-west Ireland (Counties Sligo, Leitrim and Roscommon), in association with extensive national documentary research has provided evidence for this forgotten tradition of building extending much further back into later medieval (1100-1600AD) and early medieval (400-1100AD) Ireland. In County Sligo, 28% of later medieval buildings surveyed were revealed to be of earth mortared masonry construction. Comparative percentages comprised 17% in County Leitrim and 20% in County Roscommon. National documentary research re-examining both above ground standing structures and below ground archaeological excavation records identified the presence of earth mortared masonry construction in almost every other county in Ireland ranging in date from the early medieval to post medieval periods.

In Ireland, the non-survival of an above ground later medieval domestic building stock has resulted in an inadvertent skewing of analysed data based upon regional field survey. Castles, tower houses, hall houses and churches predominate in the virtual absence of standing later medieval domestic dwellings. Interestingly, stone and earth mortared ecclesiastical buildings ranked as the largest building category identified representing 85% of all upstanding buildings recorded through regional field survey. These ecclesiastical buildings were classified as later medieval parish churches forming 79% of the record, building (non-denominated function at an ecclesiastical site), comprising 8% of the record and religious houses constituting 13% of the upstanding ecclesiastical record. Meanwhile re-interpretation of building records, based upon examination of both above ground and below ground excavation records nationally, identified stone and earth mortared buildings across a wide range of building categories comprising domestic (28%), agricultural (25%), ecclesiastical (21%), defensive (19%), industrial (5%) and public (2%). The reinterpretation of archaeological excavation records has been instrumental in uncovering the extensive use of earth mortared masonry construction in the later medieval Irish settlement record.

Britain – Earth Mortared Masonry Construction

Preliminary research investigating the potential presence of earth mortared stone buildings for the later medieval period was also undertaken on the UK in tandem with national Irish research. Secondary documentary sources were examined across England, Scotland and Wales which identified the widespread presence of stone and earth mortared construction from the early medieval to post medieval periods. This was an important finding establishing a precedent for stone and earth mortared construction in Western Europe from the early medieval period. Indeed, research has shown that stone and earth mortared construction dating to the wider medieval period (400-1600AD) has been identified from Denmark to the Channel Islands, France and Italy.

ENGLAND

L. F. Salzman's publication expounding the building construction process in England in the later medieval period from examination of primary documentary sources established the use of earth mortar in stone built construction dating from the mid 14th to the sixteenth century. At Clarendon in 1363AD building accounts refer to "digging and carriage of 2 cartloads of white earth for making mortar" [9]. In 1367AD, an account of repairs to the lodge at Beaumont (Beaumond) in the Forest of Rutland described "digging earth for *mortarherthe* for the said lodge" (Ibid, 152). At Oxford in 1453AD "a cartload of red earth for making mortar" is described in building ledgers [10] and at Collyweston, Stamford, Northamptonshire building accounts described costs "for siftying of *mortar erth* owt of the old wallis" dating to 1504AD [11]. Unfortunately, no such evidence for the documented use of earth mortar from building construction accounts has been found to date for Ireland.

Salzman citing William of Malmesbury who quoted Bede referred to Benedict Biscop, who had built monasteries at Monkwearmouth and Jarrow, County Durham *c.*670AD, "being the first person who introduced into England builders of stone edifices and makers of glass windows" [12]. Excavation by Rosemary Cramp identified extensive evidence of stone and earth (clay) mortared wall construction across numerous buildings including churches, cloisters and ancillary buildings at both sites dated between the seventh and ninth centuries. Cramp was confident of the unequivocal use of clay bonded wall construction and further compared them to Irish stone buildings suggesting her acknowledged use of this construction technique in similar dated buildings in Ireland [13].

Elsewhere in England a cluster of early medieval examples denoting the use of earth mortared masonry construction are evident in Cornwall comprising St. Piran's Oratory and Church [14-15], Oratory of St. Gwythian [16], Oratory and Well of St. Maddern [17] and Oratory of Porth Kernou [18], all dated to between the fifth and sixth centuries. The Anglo-Saxon Church of St Paul-In-The-Bail, Lincoln [19] was similarly constructed and dated from the seventh century with later extensions and additions occurring until the early twelfth century. Meanwhile, excavations at Norton Priory in Cheshire, originally founded by William fitz Nigel *circa* 1134AD, revealed the guest quarters and the north aisle of the church were constructed of stone and earth mortared wall construction dating to the early thirteenth and fifteenth century respectively [20]. Similarly, excavations at St. Giles Graveyard, Winchelsea, East Sussex revealed the surviving remains of the former stone and earth mortared graveyard boundary wall dating to the late thirteenth century [21].

SCOTLAND

In Scotland, early medieval ecclesiastical earth mortared masonry constructed sites include a church and stone building at Hoddom in Annandale, Dumfries and Galloway [22] dated to between 450-700AD; the chapel and enclosure wall on Ardwall Isle, Kirkcudbright [23-24] dated to the early eighth century; the enclosure to chapel Finnian, Luce Bay, Wigtownshire [25-26] dated to the sixth century and the fifth to early eighth century excavated church underlying Whithorn Priory church in Wigtownshire [27-28]. Three miles south of Whithorn, at The Rhinns, Galloway, Luce Bay, St Ninian's cave excavations revealed stone and earth mortared church wall construction dating to the sixth or seventh century interpreted as the likely hermitage site associated with Whithorn [29]. Archaeological excavations at Hoddom and Whithorn record the earliest use of stone and earth mortared wall construction in ecclesiastical sites in the fifth century in Scotland. A number of stone and earth mortared built late medieval ecclesiastical buildings were identified in Dumfries and Galloway in south-west Scotland. Excavations uncovered two stone built and earth mortared churches at Brydekirk, Annan, one dated to the pre twelfth century and the other to between the twelfth and sixteenth century [30]. A stone and earth mortared chapel was identified through excavation to be 13th century in construction and occupied until the sixteenth century at Kirkmirran, Dalbeattie [31]. Similarly archaeological excavations revealed that Barhobble Church, Airylick, Mochrum dated to the early twelfth century [32]; St. Ninian's chapel and enclosure wall on the Isle of Whithorn dated to the twelfth century [33]; the north cloister and infirmary range at Whithorn Priory dated to the twelfth century [34] and the later medieval Priory Gatehouse in Whithorn dated to *circa* 1500AD [35] were all constructed of stone and earth mortar wall construction.

The use of stone and earth mortared wall construction at Whithorn Priory gatehouse is significant. Oram relates the high social status of the prior and priory in the construction and siting of its buildings:

> At every monastery where grants of free regality were made, the superior social status of the head of the community was underscored by the construction of a monumental gatehouse. Dominating the market-place, its heraldic display would have been a constant reminder of the priory's status and, by means of the Royal Arms, the source of that influence. [36]

The use of stone and earth mortar with lime mortar repointing in its construction emphasises the selective use by the prior and affluent priory in constructing this symbolic structure when it is assumed the priory finances could well have provided for a different construction method i.e. lime mortared construction.

WALES

Cursory appraisal of excavation records in Wales revealed stone and earth mortar wall construction at two later medieval ecclesiastical sites. At Greyfriars Franciscan friary in Carmarthen, excavations over an eight year period revealed substantial evidence of earth mortared masonry construction. The thirteenth century Greyfriars church choir as well as foundations of the western building range (Room 1323) of the north cloister dating to between the fourteenth and fifteenth century were of earth mortared masonry construction. The thirteenth century Chapter

House foundation walls and the surviving portions of the north-east Chapter House wall were likewise of stone and earth mortared wall construction. In addition, buildings to the north and north-east of the Chapter House were of stone and earth mortared construction and dated to between the fourteenth and fifteenth century [37].

The stone church of Capel Maelog, Llandrindod Wells, Powys constructed in two phases, the first commencing in the late twelfth century and the second phase in the thirteenth century, were both constructed of stone and earth mortar wall construction [38].

The Symbolic Function of Earth Mortar in Masonry Construction in Ireland and Britain

The cult of relics, with its development at the outset of Christianity in Ireland, spawned a fundamental desire by ecclesiastics to obtain the relics of saints, either corporeal or associative relics [39]. The former comprised the physical human remains of the saint while the latter comprised any object that had come into contact with the saint (hand bells, croziers, shoes, cloaks, manuscripts, books shrines, belts and *brandea* comprising pieces of cloth that had come into contact with the saint [40].

Documentary Evidence

Documentary sources communicate that earth or clay was extracted from the graves of saints both nationally and internationally and used for medicinal, curative and restorative purposes and it had protection properties also. Where access was reduced to saint's graves, pieces of cloth were touched to the earth where the saint lay as well as to oil from lamps burning at the saint's shrine. The healing properties of soil came from the belief in the early and later medieval period that earth constituted an associative relic. Pilgrims believed that earth taken from the saints graves had been sanctified because of its proximity to the saint's body [41].

Large scale pilgrimage was known deriving from the east and from as far west as Spain, France and Britain to Kala' at Simian in Syria where Simeon the Stylite (c.390-459) sat upon a pillar for thirty years. Simeon was credited with numerous miracles during his lifetime. Anything that came in contact with him was utilised for this purpose, his unused food and the earth from the site partially mixed with water [42]. As early as the fourth and fifth centuries, pilgrims ventured from Britain and possibly Ireland to Rome [43]. Pilgrims sought dust (earth) taken from the grave of St Martin of Tours, France in the fourth century, which when mixed with water or wine, had miraculous and curative properties [44]. By 1000AD pilgrimage had gained momentum to Western Europe [45]. It was common practice for pilgrims to generally leave a gift or token at the grave of the saint. Equally pilgrims took with them secondary relics such as a cloth, dust (earth), oil or water which had come into contact with the saint's remains in the hopes that the saint's blessing would be imparted and retained upon the pilgrim and his family [46]. In the eleventh century Ua Cinn Fhaelad, King of the Deisi in south-east Ireland is one such notable pilgrim who, according to the *Annals of Inisfallen*, visited Jerusalem in 1080AD [47].

Hagiographical sources further demonstrate the importance and use of earth in the ecclesiastical record. Significantly, in the *Life of Colman mac Luacháin*, a seventh century Irish abbot, founder and patron saint of Lann (Lynn, Co. Westmeath), recounted how he and his companions sought out soil from St. Peter's tomb and from graves of other apostles and saints in Rome which was brought back to Ireland and spread in Irish graveyards:

"... collected the soil of Peter's tomb and of the tomb of every other apostle and of every saint in Rome ... Thence Colman went to Lann Mic Luacháin with the load of seven men of the soil of Rome and of the tombs of the apostles ... and [it] was thereupon scattered in every direction in the cemetery of Lann, so that each one who has been buried there since has been buried in Roman soil". [48-49]

The *Annals of the Four Masters* recorded Clonmacnoise, County Offaly as the earliest place of pilgrimage in Ireland where a pilgrim died in 606AD. In the *Annals of Clonmacnoise* pilgrims at the site were recorded in 617, 754 and 832AD. The *Annals of Tigermach* noted another date of 722AD for pilgrimage at Clonmacnoise while *The Annals of the Four Masters* note its continuity in 834, 1100 and 1118AD [50]. In Scotland, the *Miracula Nynie Episcopi*, a poem dated to the last quarter of the eighth century recounts the numerous miracles wrought by St. Ninian. In one instance, a woman was cured of blindness by pressing her forehead against the earth in the hollowed out cave associated with St. Ninian [51].

Hagiographical sources document the miraculous properties of the clay from the saint's grave at Clonmacnoise, Co. Offaly. Macalister's first and second *Latin lives of St. Ciarán* relate an original episode of how Colum Cille was given clay from Ciaran's grave when he visited Clonmacnoise and how some of this clay later saved him from a whirlpool at sea [52]. Manning estimates this legend dated to the early eighth century [53]. Harbison citing Caesar Otway recounted the hollowed out place of St. Ciarán's grave within the church being dug by pilgrims to extract the sanctified earth:

"Here it was that the people, to be deposited, have rooted diligently for any particle of clay that could be found, in order to carry home what holy earth, steep it in water, and drink it, and happy is the votary who ... to pick up what has the semblance of soil .. as means of grace or a sovereign remedy". [54-55]

At St Kevin's church, Glendalough, County Wicklow, the Priests House was much visited given it was purported to be the burial place of a thirteenth century priest. The eastern portion of the house, closed off by a wall, marks the burial place of the relics of the saint. The wall contains a slit window opening providing a narrow view of the interior. Harbison citing William Wilde noted that the wall was likely put in place to reduce loss of relics from the burial place of the saint. Visitors could look inside and indirectly use a piece of cloth to touch the sanctified earth through the slit window opening [56]. Reverend Power described the extraction and use of sacred soil at the twelfth century St. Declan's grave, Ardmore, County Waterford:

"Generations of reverent clients have scooped out and carried away the sanctified earth from his narrow bed so that the latter has come to be a mere rectangular, and by no means shallow, pit in the floor of the ancient building". [57]

At the tomb shrine of St. Chad in St. Mary's, Lichfield, Staffordshire, England, access to the saint's remains was, according to Bede, through:

"A hole in the wall, through which those that go thither for devotion usually put in their hand and take out some of the dust (earth), which they put into water and give to sick cattle or men to drink, upon which they are presently eased of their infirmity, and restored to health". [58]

In 1938, Skillen recounted that there was a tradition of earth being transported from Ireland for the foundation of Lindores Abbey, Newburgh, Fifeshire in the twelfth century. Skillen citing F. J. Hogan's *History of the Irish in Australia* denoted that "a cartload of Irish earth was brought over to that country for the same purpose" [59]. He also referred to earth from St. Maccarthin's grave at Clogher being used for the prevention of diseases at Downpatrick and Clogher, County Down [60]. Harbison cited James Gandon who in 1846 makes a reference to the use of holy water in the mixing of mortar to sanctify the construction of stone built reliquaries to house saint's relics from the eighth century onwards:

> "The Ordo Romanus compiled in the ninth century directed that mortar for such receptacles to be made with holy water. A great number of these cryptical buildings exist, such as at Cashel, Portaferry, Saul, Killaloe, St. Doulagh's near Dublin and other places". [61]

The Material Symbolism of Earth Mortar used in Masonry Construction

Bishop Durandus [62], Petrie [63] and Ó Carragáin [64] describe the profoundly symbolic nature of the architectural tools used in church construction which portray an emotive and spiritual resonance. Viewing this material symbolism from a slightly different perspective, it may be inferred that, stone represented a material of the wider landscape, its use an aspiration, beyond the wherewithal of the masses for building construction in the early medieval period. Stone formed the building blocks in church construction. It symbolised the embodiment of a higher power with God at its centre and therein the people's desire to move closer to that power. Earth, likewise a common material of the landscape, had an indelible link to the people and the land they lived on, worked upon and used in their house constructions. Its very essence in the core of church construction symbolised the people who it was built to serve. The stone church with its core fabric of stone and earth symbolised the union of God the Creator (providing strength, protection and shelter by the stone church) and the people (the earthly dwellers). The intentional simplicity of construction and the materials employed in these early churches is in direct contrast to the acknowledged, exemplary and superior artistry evidenced in early medieval Irish church metalwork and illuminated manuscripts. The innate craft skills and building expertise utilised in both early and later medieval Ireland contrasts with the use of these simple materials, earth and stone, in ecclesiastical constructions which it is postulated were borne out of choice rather than need or lack of skills.

The symbolic and spiritual importance attached to the soil taken from saints graves may have promoted the use of sacred earth in the construction of early medieval and later medieval stone built churches. To date, no documentary sources have been found to validate this theory. The sheer number, however, of instances documenting the importance of soil taken from saints graves and spread in graveyards for the consecration of graveyards, earth digested for curative properties or pilgrims retaining it as a token for protection and security, supports the conceivable theory that sacred earth was most likely used in the consecration and construction of the most important structure on ecclesiastical sites i.e. the stone church. The continuity of earth mortar in the construction of later medieval masonry churches may have promulgated this sacred link with an earlier founding saint. It is argued that this may also have occurred at church sites where continuity of use and new church construction occurred between the early and later medieval periods.

The importance of *spolia,* the practice of reusing building materials is significant in the context of the continuity of earth mortared masonry churches in the later medieval period. It is suggested that sanctified earth may have been taken from the site of, or from the earliest church building, and was reused in later buildings on the site. Ó Carragáin proffers support to this theory when he wrote:

"The act of rebuilding in the same manner possibly using some of the same materials was a way of paying homage to the founding saint and affirming the authority of their successors. It effectively enshrined the hallowed form of the original church and made it immutable". [65]

While the spreading of earth in cemeteries transported from continental saints graves is documented in hagiographical sources, similarly it may be argued, that earth taken from continental saints graves, transported to Ireland and partly used in the construction of stone churches sanctified the whole space i.e. church and graveyard in both the early and later medieval periods. This may have formed an essential ritual used by Irish clerics in the consecration of sites replacing tomb shrines when relics were not possible to attain on the continent. This may have allowed less important sites to compete with those of larger importance such as Armagh. It is further postulated that the importance of pilgrimage in the later medieval period, highlighted by chroniclers, combined with the established and continuing use of earth mortar in stone built churches, supports the theory that it may have facilitated church sites to maintain their prominent saintly associations.

Conclusions

This paper has emphasised the widespread, yet largely unrecognised, number of ecclesiastical buildings from the early and later medieval periods across Ireland and Britain that demonstrate the use of earth mortar in their stone construction. It remains unclear whether or not earth mortar utilised in their construction had a symbolic sacred importance. This paper shows, however, that documentary sources provide ample evidence of the immutable importance of sacred soil at ecclesiastical sites, its acquisition and transport from continental saints graves to Irish grave sites and vice versa, the symbolic ritual incorporated into the materials and manner of construction of church buildings to its much sought after use for curative properties. In this regard the use of earth mortar may have had a particularly important symbolic function and overlooked role to play in the construction of ecclesiastical buildings.

References

[1] S. Markley, 'Filling the Void – Earth Mortared Masonry Buildings, Unearthing Ireland's Medieval Settlement Record' pp.121-132 in J. W. P. Campbell, N. Baker, M. Driver, M. Heaton, Y. Pan, T. Rosoman and D. Yeomans (Eds), *Building Histories The Proceedings of the Fourth Conference of the Construction History Society.* Cambridge: University Press, 2017.

[2] *ibid.*

[3] C. Ua Danachair, 'Some Primitive Structures Used as Dwellings', *Journal of the Royal Society of Antiquaries of Ireland*, vol.75, no4, 1945, pp.204-12.

[4] C. Ó Danachair, 'The Traditional Houses of County Limerick', *Journal of the North Munster Archaeological Society*, vol.5, 1946-9, pp.18-32.

[5] C. Ó Danachair, 'Materials and Methods in Irish Traditional Building', *Journal of the Royal Society of Antiquaries of Ireland,* vol.87, no.1, 1957, pp.61-74.

[6] C. Ó Danachair, 'Traditional Forms of the Dwelling House', *Journal of the Royal Society of Antiquaries of Ireland,* vol.102, no.1, 1972, pp.77-96.

[7] M. Sheehy, 'Architecture in Offaly', *Journal of the County Kildare Archaeological Society*, vol.14, 1964-6, pp.1-19.

[8] F. H. A. Aalen, 'The Evolution of the Traditional House in Western Ireland', *Journal of the Royal Society of Antiquaries of Ireland,* vol.96, no.1, 1966, pp.47-58.

[9] L. F. Salzman, *Building in England Down to 1540: A Documentary History*. London: Routledge, 1952. p.152.

[10] *ibid*.

[11] *ibid*.

[12] Salzman (Note 9) p.1.

[13] R. Cramp, R. 'Excavations at the Saxon Monastic Sites of Wearmouth and Jarrow, Co. Durham, an Interim Report', *Medieval Archaeology*, vol.13, 1969, pp.58.

[14] Rev. Hasham, Rev. W. 'Ancient Oratories of Cornwall', *Journal of the Royal Archaeological Institute*, vol.2, 1845, pp.225-39.

[15] A. C. Fryer, 'St. Piran's Church, Cornwall', *Journal of the British Archaeological Association*, vol.48, 1892, pp.81-2.

[16] Hasham, (Note 14) pp.231-4.

[17] *ibid.*

[18] *ibid.*

[19] B. Gilmour, 'The Anglo-Saxon Church at St Paul-In-The-Bail, Lincoln', *Medieval Archaeology*, vol.23, 1979, pp.214-218.

[20] J. P. Greene, *Norton Priory The Archaeology of a Medieval Religious House,* Cambridge: University Press, 1989.

[21] D. Martin and B. Martin, 'The Defences' pp.41-66 in D. Martin and D. Rudling (Eds), *Excavations in Winchelsea Sussex 1974-2000*. Monograph 3, Norfolk: Heritage Marketing and Publications Ltd, 2004.

[22] C. Lowe, 'New Light on the Anglian 'Minster' at Hoddam. Recent Excavations at Hallguards Quarry, Hoddom, Annandale & Eskdale District, Dumfries & Galloway Region', *Transactions and Journal of Proceedings Dumfriesshire and Galloway Natural History and Antiquarian Society*, Third Series, vol.66, 1991, pp.11-35.

[23] C. Thomas, 'Ardwall Isle: The Excavation of an Early Christian site of Irish Type', *Transactions and Journal of Proceedings Dumfriesshire and Galloway Natural History and Antiquarian Society*, Third Series, vol.43, 1966, pp.84-117.

[24] C. Thomas, 'An Early Christian Cemetery and Chapel on Ardwall Isle, Kirkcudbright', *Medieval Archaeology*, vol.10, 1967, pp.127-188.

[25] C. A. Ralegh Radford, 'The Excavations at Chapel Finnian, Mochrum', *Transactions and Journal of Proceedings Dumfriesshire and Galloway Natural History and Antiquarian Society*, Third Series, vol.28, 1949-50, pp.28-40.

[26] C. A. Ralegh Radford, 'The Churches of Dumfriesshire and Galloway', *Transactions and Journal of Proceedings Dumfriesshire and Galloway Natural History and Antiquarian Society*, Third Series, vol.40, 1961-2, pp.102-17.

[27] C. A. Ralegh Radford, 'Excavations at Whithorn, First Season, 1949', *Transactions and Journal of Proceedings Dumfriesshire and Galloway Natural History and Antiquarian Society*, Third Series, vol.27, 1948-9, pp.85-162.

[28] C. A. Ralegh Radford, 'Excavations at Whithorn (Final Report)', *Transactions and Journal of Proceedings Dumfriesshire and Galloway Natural History and Antiquarian Society*, Third Series, vol.34, 1955-6, pp.131-94.

[29] *ibid*, p.165, 169-70.

[30] C. Crowe, 'Excavation at Brydekirk, Annan, 1982-1984', *Transactions and Journal of Proceedings Dumfriesshire and Galloway Natural History and Antiquarian Society*, Third Series, vol.59, 1984, pp.33-40.

[31] C. Crowe, 'An Excavation at Kirkmirran, Dalbeattie, 1985', *Transactions and Journal of Proceedings Dumfriesshire and Galloway Natural History and Antiquarian Society*, Third Series, vol.61, 1986, pp.55-62.

[32] W. F. Cormack, 'Barhobble, Mochrum – Excavation of a Forgotten Church Site in Galloway', *Transactions and Journal of Proceedings Dumfriesshire and Galloway Natural History and Antiquarian Society*, Third Series, vol.70, 1995, pp.5-107.

[33] Ralegh Radford, (Note 26), (Note 27), (Note 25).

[34] C. Tabraham, 'Excavations at Whithorn Priory, Wigtown District 1972 and 1975', *Transactions and Journal of Proceedings Dumfriesshire and Galloway Natural History and Antiquarian Society*, Third Series, vol.54, 1979, pp.29-38.

[35] C. E. Lowe, '53 George Street, Whithorn: The Late Medieval Priory Gatehouse, together with a note on a series of possible Ritual Marian Marks', *Transactions and Journal of Proceedings Dumfriesshire and Galloway Natural History and Antiquarian Society*, Third Series, vol.78, 2004, pp.93-110.

[36] *ibid*, p.105.

[37] T. James, 'Excavations at Carmarthen Greyfriars, 1983-1990', *Medieval Archaeology*, vol.41, 1997, pp.100-194.

[38] W. J. Britnell, 'Capel Maelog, Llandrindod Wells, Powys: Excavations 1984-7', *Medieval Archaeology*, vol.34, 1990, pp.27-96.

[39] R. Ó Floinn, *Irish Shrines & Reliquaries of the Middle Ages*, Dublin: Town House and Country House, 1994.

[40] *ibid*, pp.5, 33.

[41] http://pilgrimagemedievalireland.com/tag/dirt-saints-graves (Consulted May 19th, 2016).

[42] P. Harbison, *Pilgrimage in Ireland. The Monuments and the People*. London: Barrie and Jenkins, 1991. pp.13-4.

[43] *ibid*, p.15.

[44] *ibid*, p.17.

[45] *ibid*, p.20.

[46] *ibid*, p.26.

[47] *ibid*, p.29.

[48] *ibid*, p.31.

[49] T. Ó Carrigáin, *Churches in Early Medieval Ireland. Architecture, Ritual and Memory*. London: Yale University Press, 2010. p.190.

[50] Harbison, (Note 42) p.51.

[51] W. MacQueen, 'Miracula Nynie Episcopi', *Transactions and Journal of Proceedings Dumfriesshire and Galloway Natural History and Antiquarian Society*, Third Series, vol.38, 1959-60, p.47.

[52] C. Manning, 'Some Early Masonry Churches and The Round Tower at Clonmacnoise' p.71 in H. King (Ed.), *Clonmacnoise Studies 2: Seminar Papers 1998*, Dublin: *Dúchas*-The Heritage Service, 2003.

[53] *ibid*.

[54] Harbison, (Note 42) p.115.

[55] A. MacDonald, 'The 'Cathedral, Temple Kelly and Temple Ciarán: Notes from the Annals' p.131 in H. King (Ed.), *Clonmacnoise Studies 2: Seminar Papers 1998*, Dublin: *Dúchas*-The Heritage Service, 2003.

[56] Harbison, (Note 42) p119-20.

[57] Rev. P. Power, 'Excursion Guides – I. Jerpoint & *c*, II Ardmore', *The Waterford and South-East of Ireland Archaeological Society Journal*, vol.4, 1898, p.160-3.

[58] D. M. Waterman, 'An Early Christian Mortuary House at Saul, Co. Down: With Notes on Similar Monuments in Ulster', *Ulster Journal of Archaeology*, vol.23, 1960, pp.86.

[59] J. Skillen, 'Irish Earth', *Ulster Journal of Archaeology*, Third Series, vol.1. 1938, p.141.

[60] *ibid*.

[61] Harbison, (Note 42) pp.73-4.

[62] T. J. Westropp, 'Notes on the Antiquities around Kilfernora and Lehinch, Co. Clare Part II', *Journal of the North Munster Archaeological Society*, vol.1, no.2, 1909, pp.92, 94.

[63] G. Petrie, *The Ecclesiastical Architecture of Ireland Anterior to the Anglo-Norman Invasion. An Essay on the Origin and Use of The Round Tower in Ireland*, Shannon, Ireland: Irish University Press, 1979. p.191.

[64] T. Ó Carrigáin, 'Habitual Masonry Styles and the Local Organisation of Church Building in Early Medieval Ireland', *Proceedings of the Royal Irish Academy. Section C: Archaeology, Celtic Studies, History, Linguistics, Literature*, vol.105C, no.3, 2005, pp.101-2.

[65] Ó Carrigáin, (Note 58) pp.156-7, 165.

Seventeenth and Eighteenth Centuries

Lee Prosser

The Roofs of Inigo Jones Revisited

Lee Prosser

Historic Royal Palaces, London, UK

Dendrochronological analysis at Hampton Court Palace has dated two hitherto overlooked roofs to the mid-1630s, placing them firmly within the tenure of Inigo Jones as Surveyor of the King's Works. These lie above the ante-chapel to the Chapel Royal, and the historic Tennis Court. Both roofs comprise king-post trusses, but display remarkable differences in carpentry and jointing while also retaining residual vernacular techniques of construction. These discoveries have prompted a re-evaluation of Jones's other surviving roofs at the Queen's House Greenwich and the Queen's Chapel at St James's Palace. Previous study was forced to rely largely on the interpretation of antiquarian drawings and extrapolation, but the new discoveries provide us with a greater sample and allows close examination of Jones's carpentry. This paper will present and describe these roofs in detail for the first time, comparing differences and similarities. It will show that, as previously suggested, Jones may have used specific printed prototypes, but that later, a degree of experimentation was employed to perfect and refine his trussed roof form.

Inigo Jones became Surveyor of the King's Works, and thus overseer of all royal building projects in 1615 after spending the previous five years as surveyor to the ill-fated Henry, Prince of Wales and his brother Charles, the future king. Though Jones re-orientated the architectural direction of royal building by introducing classical styles, the period coincides with a general decline in the quality of the official documentary record, so that while his principal achievements can be traced through surviving drawings or by reputation, much of the detail, and his more minor works are not recorded in enough detail to be useful to the building specialist. This represents a major gap in our understanding. Furthermore few of the more substantial royal commissions Jones is known to have executed have survived, and where they have, their roofs are lost or fragmentary, thus hindering a better understanding of the architect. Jones's roof of the Banqueting House at Whitehall was replaced in its entirety by Sir John Soane in 1830, while the Queen's House at Greenwich was renewed in the nineteenth century. Only by virtue that the tie-beams held up the coffered ceiling below, was any part of it spared. The most important survivor until now has thus been the roof of the Queen's Chapel at St James's Palace, long inaccessible to scholars. Until the present day, it had been imagined that the canon of surviving work by Inigo Jones was largely definitive, despite what Summerson described as a "swarm of misattributions".[1] The juxtaposition of firm date and structural form in a royal context, however suggest that two further commissions can now be added to the list.

Hampton Court Palace is managed by Historic Royal Palaces, a charitable trust established by Royal Charter in the late 1980s. It has become an acknowledged leader in the quality of research before major repair or conservation works. Key to refining an understanding of the palace, where almost six acres of roofscape survive, has been the science of tree-ring dating, which has begun to re-write the conventional history of this complex building as cyclical repairs are undertaken. Broadly speaking, the roofs can be divided into two major groups; those traditional oak structures of the Tudor period, and the later oak and softwood reconstructions by Wren, principally around the new lodgings built for King William III and Queen Mary II between 1689 and 1700. Some eighteenth and nineteenth century work can be identified, but it is not extensive. Very little work of the interim period has hitherto been identified, and Simon Thurley, in his magisterial work on the palace asserted that "Inigo Jones did not make a single alteration at Hampton Court".[2] This was an understandable conclusion to reach, given the paucity of the documentary record and difficulty of access for close forensic study. The roof over the ante-chapel was damaged by incendiary bombs during an enemy attack in 1940. Though repaired, the structure was consequently assumed to be the work of Wren, whose carpentry was then under-appreciated. The Tennis Court poses difficulty of access during long hours of play, so that no specialist had ventured into the roof-space in living memory.

In 2005 structural movement was detected in the mezzanine of the royal pew or ante-chapel within the Chapel Royal. Even though repairs did not directly affect the roof structure, a tree-ring survey, which took place to the affected lower timberwork, was extended throughout the building in order to gain a more complete understanding of the structure. Five years later, a proposal to re-tile the Tennis Court prompted a similar programme of research. This was encouraged and ultimately permitted by English Heritage (now Historic England) following a rigorous brief and specification.

The results have served to confound the historical narrative, but also to reopen the study of Jones's roof structures, which were last reviewed, in what might then have been considered a definitive study, by David Yeomans over thirty years ago, and reiterated in its wider context several years later.[3] The analysis revealed that the ante-chapel roof was constructed of timber felled in 1634-5, and the Tennis Court in 1635-6.[4] This prompted a re-examination of the Queen's House at Greenwich, which, under the management of Royal Museums Greenwich embarked on a major representation in 2016. The opportunity to examine normally inaccessible areas of the building was seized, and funding was secured to conduct tree-ring analysis on the floor joisting. The roof was also sampled to confirm that the residual roof structure was indeed Jones's, and produced a felling date of 1634, but furthermore matched the source of the timber used with that of the ante-chapel at Hampton Court in the Thames Valley.[5] More recently, representations have been made to the surveyors of the Royal Household, and permission granted to gain access to the roof of the Queen's Chapel at St James's Palace for more in-depth analysis. Tree-ring dating will take place there in due course.

Figure 1. Aerial view of Hampton Court Palace showing respective locations of the Jones roofs (Historic Royal Palaces).

Hampton Court Palace

The building of Hampton Court in its current form was initiated by Cardinal Thomas Wolsey on the site of an earlier manor house. His building accounts begin in 1514 and thereafter the palace grew rapidly, particularly after its confiscation by King Henry VIII. For the second half of the sixteenth century, few additions of note were made, and by the reign of James I in the early seventeenth century, Hampton Court no longer attracted attention as a primary royal residence, but instead began to assume the role of an ancestral palace, preserved for its curiosity value. Most notably however, it continued to be an important venue for ambassadorial or state receptions and for hunting.[6] Examination of the expenditure throughout the period reflects careful maintenance of the palace, but nothing more.[7]

Figure 2. The ante-chapel roof. Photo: author.

The ante-chapel

The Chapel Royal lies at the heart of the palace as part of the original ceremonial sequence which included the Great Hall and State Apartments. The western end of the chapel, though physically contiguous, is separated by an upper balcony or mezzanine known as the royal pew, or formerly the holyday closet, from where the Tudor monarchs would take mass in enclosed chambers with large glazed windows overlooking the main chapel. Decoratively, the chapel as it exists today is a result of modifications under Wren for Queen Anne in the early 1700s, though the basic structural outline was retained, and the closet converted to a royal balcony. Only the fictive timber vaulted roof of 1537 survived a general stripping out and destruction of its Tudor splendour by Parliamentarian soldiers in 1644. At roof level the two components are separate, with the trusses of the ante-chapel aligned east-west, at right angles to those of the chapel proper. (Fig. 1) The main chapel roof above the Tudor vaulting was replaced in its entirety around 1845, but at its western end, a single truss of 1635 survives to span the gap and provide support for the lateral ante-chapel trusses.

Figure 3. Shouldering at the foot of the king-post. Photo: author.

The ante-chapel roof spans some 41 feet (12.5 m) and is constructed of five trusses, three of which are supported by the wall-plate truss noted above by tenons and iron straps. (Fig. 2) They support a shallow-pitched, leaded roof. Each has a king-post and raking struts. They are linked by three in-line butted purlins in each pitch. The king-posts are shouldered or 'joggled' at the top and bottom, but where the raking strut is jointed at the base of the principal, the carpentry is sophisticated; the post is partly cut into and comprises two shoulders for maximum compressive restraint. (Fig. 3) The butted purlins are also morticed with a double tenon with diminished haunches in the seventeenth century manner. (Fig. 4) These once supported common rafters morticed into the upper and lower faces of the central purlin with similar early mortices, sailing over its companions in two flights. These are strutted on either side from the base of the king-posts. There is evidence that originally a robust ridge-purlin carried the common rafters at the apex, but this has been replaced.

The lateral surviving truss within the body of the chapel is of similar interest, having stepped joggles at the head instead of the foot of the king-post, but the two are clearly from the same hand and employ similar techniques and scantling. (Fig. 11)

Figure 4. Double-tenon to the purlin. Photo: author.

Tennis Court

The Tennis Court occupies the north-eastern corner of the main palace complex, but is only physically connected to the main building by a narrow corridor which terminates the main northern axis of Tennis Court Lane. (Fig. 5) It is enclosed by high walls, with continuous glazing extending between the brickwork and roof on its long sides. This is punctuated by supporting posts which are part of the original structure. Charles I enjoyed tennis, and an account of 1625-6 records 'ripping and taking downe the bourded walles round the Tennis court', clearly reflecting the replacement of a flimsy structure with brick.[8] At that time it remained an open or uncovered court, which was only enclosed in the 1630s by the addition of the raised frame and existing roof.

Figure 5. The Tennis Court. Photo: author.

Compared to the ante-chapel, the Tennis Court is an altogether more monumental structure – extremely tall with an angular pitch of 45 degrees to reflect the fact that it is tiled and not leaded, and furthermore sits on a lower structure of principal posts at the bay divisions, which are braced inwardly to the tie-beams with short curved braces, now acting as a matrix to form a deep inner coving to the boarded ceiling below. (Fig. 6) The wall-plates are scarfed at every second bay, suggesting that the building was raised in the manner of a traditional timber-framed building in pairs of bays, rather than simply hoisting the trusses into place once the underlying masonry had been raised to full height.

Seven trusses of king-post form survive, though we can be certain that originally eleven were present, as the earliest surviving depictions show the roof with gabled ends.[9] The existing outer hip trusses are now of queen-post form in slender Baltic softwood. The king-posts are 14 feet tall (4.5 m), with a truss span of 42 feet (12.8 m), but they are shouldered at top and bottom, and cut into by the strutting, as we see with the ante-chapel roof, though the shoulder is simple in form. Laterally, the roof is supported by three in-line butted purlins in each pitch, though the lowest purlin is positioned just above the wall-plate, presumably to throw the common rafters far beyond the wall plate and provide shelter to the formerly unglazed interior space with deep eaves. The joints are fairly orthodox. The common rafters are morticed into the central purlin only, extending over the outer faces of its upper and lower companions as in the ante-chapel. The lower posts were sampled during the archaeological survey and proved to be primary with the building. They are chamfered and have decorative lambs-tongue stops. This embellishment does not extend to the upper structure. Many of the purlins and common rafters have been replaced with nineteenth century Baltic softwood, but in a similar pattern.

Figure 6.   Tennis Court roof. Photo: author.

Queen's House Greenwich

The roof of the Queen's House at Greenwich now repays further analysis, as previous commentators clearly had no lengthy access to it, and the definitive study of the building by Chettle makes no mention of the roof at all.[10] The roof, or more properly that above the central hall is now fragmentary, comprising only three tie-beams, with a later trussed roof of softwood above, and much early twentieth century steel introduced to provide yet more bolstering, making access very constricted.   (Fig. 7) The tie-beams were tree-ring dated in 2017, corroborating Colvin's understanding of the completion of the building in 1636.[11] James I had intended to create a 'house of delight' for Queen Anne of Denmark, but work was halted on her death in 1619, and only completed in the 1630s for Queen Henrietta Maria under the direction of King Charles I.

Figure 7. Greenwich roof tie-beam, showing the splayed and tabled scarf. Photo: author, with permission.

The original roof only ever had three tie-beams, but these survive with many of the common joists which provide support for the decorative hollow coffering, which is the principal architectural feature of the hall below. However, sufficient other residual elements are also present to enable a fairly confident reconstruction of its original form. It can be presumed that the roof was hipped as at present, as there is little structural evidence for further trusses or gable ends, which would have been conspicuous above the balustraded parapet.[12] The three tie-beams are of 55 feet (17 m) in length, each scarfed in two parts with a long splayed and tabled joint of some nine feet (2.7 m) in total length. The scarf was secured by the central king-post and also by outer iron rings, which must have been forged before construction, and tightened by hammering wedges into the soffit, but are also notched flush into the upper face of the timber to prevent movement. The central tie-beam scarf runs counter to its outer companions.[13] On the west side of the south tie-beam, a stump of the original principal rafter survives within the wall socket, allowing the original pitch of the roof to be established as broadly in line with the existing roof, thus confirming a shallow and challenging pitch from the very beginning. Each of the tie-beams has a central through-mortice for the lost king-post, pegged above and below the scarf by three pegs arranged in a triangle, so six in total, for maximum strength at this point of weakness. The king-post mortice was perhaps further secured with an iron strap, though no trace now survives. Further out, shallow mortices supported struts, though it is not certain whether these would have been upright, as in the Tennis Court, or inclined.

The form of this roof presents challenges – the immense span and forces bearing on the extremely shallow pitch, together with its hipped ends, suggest that a common purlin roof was more likely to have been employed.

Figure 8. St James's roof. Photo: author, with permission.

St James's Palace

St James's Palace is now a fragment of a once large Tudor complex, which nevertheless still contains many interesting buildings concealed by a security perimeter. From 1604 the building was used as the residence of Henry, Prince of Wales on his arrival from Scotland, and passed to his younger brother, the future Charles I on his death. Colvin suggested that Jones was responsible for other, now lost buildings on the site, such as the prince's buttery, constructed between 1617-19, which was classical in character.[14]

The Queen's Chapel was a hasty project, initiated by the proposed marriage of Prince Charles to the Spanish Infanta, which was under negotiation in 1623. Accounts suggest that the work proceeded quickly at first, but may have been halted when the marriage plans were abandoned.[15] Within two years, however, Charles by now king, had married the French princess Henrietta Maria, and a visitor reported that the chapel was nearing completion.[16]

Figure 9. Dovetail joint on external face of the principal rafter. Photo: author, with permission.

The chapel retains eight trusses, spanning 33 feet (10.2 m), but inexplicably these are irregularly-spaced, differing by up to 27 inches (0.7 m) between each other. Though simple in concept, this roof retains many idiosyncratic features which are not found elsewhere. (Fig. 8) The king-posts are shouldered, but at the expense of the post, which is notched into as we see at Hampton Court, but furthermore the shoulders are not of sufficient width to accommodate the raking struts, which are partly jointed over the straight edge of the post.   No outer strutting is present, suggesting that the span of the roof was not considered sufficient to require them.   Few trusses have any iron strapping, and where it is present, it is secured with modern forms of fixing such as threaded bolts and nuts, in contrast to the earlier system of forelock bolts with twisted wedges which would be expected. Further research might establish whether this is indeed secondary. The most curious feature of the trusses however is the original purlin form, where four members were locked into place on the outer faces of the principal rafters with double-dovetail joints. (Fig. 9) One purlin sat almost at the junction of the principals with the tie-beam near the outer edges.   Two of these joints in each pitch are now redundant and accessible for inspection, but the others remain utilised by modern steel.

While these roofs provide empirical evidence, several others were recorded before their destruction and were surveyed by Yeomans. Among these is the only other surviving truss attributed to Jones at Stoke Bruern in Northamptonshire, which has not formed part of this study, but also extant drawings for St Paul's, Covent Garden, burnt in 1795 and the Banqueting House at Whitehall, which, as noted above was destroyed in 1830. In it he discussed the inherent problems of interpreting details of structural carpentry and of distinguishing the subtleties of phasing, given the dubious reliability of the drawings. Though three drawings for the Banqueting House roof exist and are discussed extensively, Yeomans lamented the fact that Soane made no record drawing of this roof.   However, Soane did much better than this, and produced at least two scale models of the original roof in timber which he had commissioned in advance of his repairs.   They compare favourably to both a detailed drawing by John Webb now in the Chatsworth archive and an engraving published by Peter Nicholson in 1826. These allow the discussion to progress further.[17] (Fig. 10) They represent, for example the scarfed tie-beam which was clearly depicted by Nicholson, but in more convincing detail and reveals it to have been, like Greenwich of splayed and tabled type. Similarly, the shoulders at the base of the king-post are not fully developed, confirming that the diagonal metal tensioning was created by rods and not straps. We also see three large butted purlins in each pitch. Similarly, a thickening of the raking struts, curiously indicated on the earlier drawing is represented, though still difficult to interpret. We might presume that these technical details are accurate, particularly if the model was made by a carpenter, who would have had an eye to the nuances of Jones's carpentry, and did not attempt to correct them to a more conventional form.

Figure 10. Sir John Soane: model of the Inigo Jones king-post and queen-post trusses. Sir John Soane's Museum, M1215.

Discussion

The surviving trusses and the model reflect as many differences as similarities. (Fig. 11) Technical analysis of the carpentry is particularly revealing. Jones clearly understood the basic form of the truss and details such as the requirement for shouldering at the top and bottom of his king-posts for restraint, but there are many differences which suggest that the feature was not fully resolved and subject to experimentation, particularly in the 1630s. The earliest survival, at St James's Palace is the most primitive in this respect, where the shoulder was created by notching the king-post, thus weakening its strength, but furthermore then engaged with a wide strut which was forced to extend beyond an insufficient shoulder, fixed on each side only with a single peg. In this respect, the detail of this truss most closely resembles an example drawn by Daniello Barbaro in his interpretation of Vitruvius, and illustrated by Yeomans.[18] (Fig. 12). The detail of the Egyptian Hall in Palladio's second book also shows a notched king-post in the same manner.[19] These features became less pronounced by the time the Tennis Court was constructed, with a shoulder sufficiently wide to carry the strut in its entirety. A further detail at St James's is the curious lockable purlin mortice which was not repeated again. The use of such a shallow, unfixed method was clearly risky, but this feature notably accords again with Barbaro's drawing, where the purlins seem to extend over the outer face of the truss, seemingly only notched in for support.

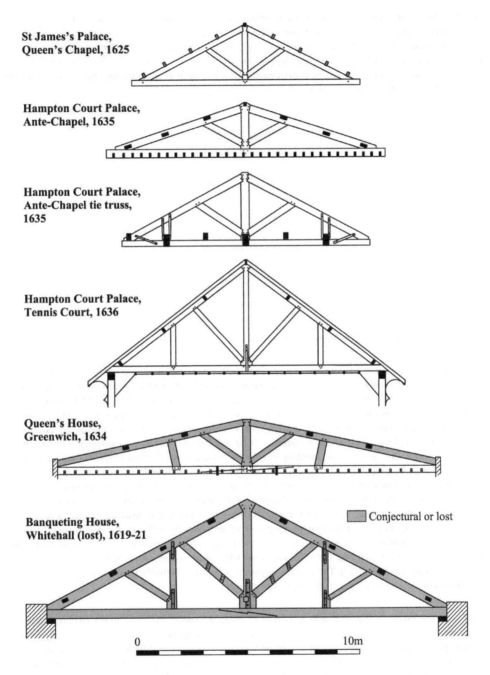

St James's Palace,
Queen's Chapel, 1625

Hampton Court Palace,
Ante-Chapel, 1635

Hampton Court Palace,
Ante-Chapel tie truss,
1635

Hampton Court Palace,
Tennis Court, 1636

Queen's House,
Greenwich, 1634

Banqueting House,
Whitehall (lost), 1619-21

Conjectural or lost

0   10m

Figure 11. Comparative truss drawing.

On all the trusses, the vernacular legacy remains, offering a salutary lesson not to consider the truss in isolation. Traditional carpentry methods are present, and reflect those to be found on any conventional roof of the period, such as the typical seventeenth century treatment of rafters, joists and jointing. Similarly the tennis court roof retains decorative embellishments and the wall-plates are scarfed at every second bay. They need not have been, as adequate lengths of timber would have been easy to procure, but it is clear that this enabled the roof to be raised bay by bay in the manner of a barn.

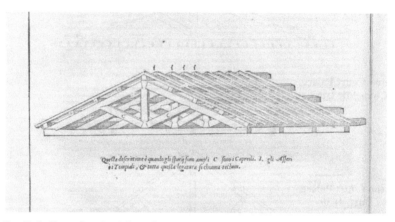

Figure 12. Detail of a Truss, from Danielo Barbaro.

Ultimately the evidence allows us to revisit the question whether these trusses were an outright copy of something else, a response to the nature and requirements of the building, or whether they represent a slow, experimental progression, presumably by the carpenters towards a competent truss form which could be adopted with confidence. Jones would have relied on his carpenters to interpret some technical aspects of the framing, and the records in this respect are worth touching on. The specific documentary record as a whole is very poor for all Jones's work. Completion of the Queen's Chapel at St James's Palace is largely circumstantial, and only thanks to an eyewitness do we know that the building was almost finished by 1625, when Henrietta Maria arrived and required a Roman Catholic chapel for worship. At Greenwich, the relevant building accounts give no detail and only through the existence of warrants for payments, can a date be pinned down.[20] The records are similarly poor at Hampton Court. A single clue to the alterations of the ante-chapel occur some ten years earlier than the roof with preparations to create a place for Catholic worship for the queen. The closet was refitted in 1631-2, and a new organ installed in 1636-8 following the completion of the works. At the Tennis Court an account of 1636-7 records that James Carver had turned "two pyramids", and payments were made to James Bayes of 63 shillings for "woorkeing and setting upp the firste Pyramides and taking them downe againe from the top of Teniscourte with other carpentrywoorke".[21] The isolated payments would not normally be considered as marking the construction of the whole roof, but in context, we can see that they do.

Some evidence exists for the carpenters employed to frame the roofs. The royal works employed teams of carpenters working under a master, with clerks of works overseeing large projects. Many can be identified through payments made, though locating them on specific sites is more difficult. In overall charge at the beginning of the period was William Portington, master-carpenter since 1579, who died in 1629, well within the period when the Banqueting House, the Queen's Chapel at St James's and several other suspected commissions were undertaken. Perhaps more relevant to the new discoveries is of Portington's successor Ralph Brice, who became Master Carpenter in 1629 and served until 1640, and so the later commissions were not only supervised under his authority, but we can assume that he had worked his way through the ranks of the royal works under Portington and so was presumably familiar with the earlier commissions too.[22] Nicholas Haughton, another carpenter served as clerk of works at Hampton Court in 1635-6 after the death of Edward Basil, going there immediately after the completion of Greenwich. He was thus present and overseeing these projects in precisely the right time-frame.

We can be sure that the form of the king-post roof was not wholly unfamiliar to the carpenters in the royal works, nor to Jones himself, even without speculating on the degree to which he was familiar with them in Italy. Not a few metres from both newly discovered roofs at Hampton Court is precisely that: a king-post roof above the Great Watching Chamber, built exactly a century earlier by William Clement under the surveyorship of James Nedeham, Henry VIII's most talented builder, master-carpenter and engineer.[23] This roof was designed for precisely the same purpose; to span a large room with a flat, under-drawn ceiling and to have a shallow, lead-covered roof profile. It retains a thick king-post, shouldered at the head, with inclined struts and butted, jointed side-purlins for lateral strength. This of course is not a truss and relied on timber of huge scantling for brute strength. But it proves that royal carpenters were working in the traditions of the earlier king-post form. On balance, the new discoveries at Hampton Court sit within a tradition where the truss is an interloper within a fairly standard roof form. The St James's roof however reflects several structural differences which places its form more in line with the printed sources, suggesting that Jones and his carpenters replicated the form of Barbaro's drawing, with which it accords in many ways. Later, the truss was recombined with tried and tested traditional techniques. Ultimately the precise relationship between carpenters and the architect may never be resolved fully, but the theoretical and practical dynamic remains an important consideration. The evidence in the earliest roofs however, suggests copying, but later a more pragmatic approach to the structural needs and a degree of experimentation. As Colvin noted, Jones himself was unlikely to have been a bystander in this process, and that "all the evidence at our disposal suggests that every substantial work emanating from the works during his surveyorship, received the impress of his mind."[24]

Acknowledgements

The author would like to thank the surveyors of the Royal Household, and to Glen Smith at Royal Museums Greenwich for facilitating access to the Queen's House during the works and to Clive Dawson of Hockley and Dawson for discussions on the nature of the earlier Jones roof at Greenwich. Tansy Collins kindly drew the comparative trusses.

References

[1] J. Summerson, *Inigo Jones*. New Haven and London: Yale University Press, 1966, p. 1.
[2] S. Thurley, *Hampton Court: a Social and Architectural History*. New Haven and London: Yale University Press, 2003, p. 114.
[3] D. Yeomans, 'Inigo Jones's Roof Structures', *Architectural History*, vol. 29, 1986, pp. 85-101. D. Yeomans, *The Trussed Roof: its History and Development*. Aldershot: Scholar Press, 1992.
[4] D. Miles, The Tree-Ring dating of the Chapel Royal, Hampton Court Palace, Middlesex. Oxford Dendrochronology Report, 2007/37. D. Miles, The Tree-Ring Dating of the Real Tennis Court, Hampton Court Palace. Oxford Dendrochronology Laboratory Report, 2010/52.

[5] M.C. Bridge and D.H. Miles, *The Dendrochronological Dating of the Roof of the Great Hall and First Floor Timbers at the Queen's House, Greenwich*. Oxford Dendrochronology Laboratory Report, 2017/23.

[6] Thurley, *Hampton Court*, (Note 2), p.115.

[7] H. Colvin (ed), *The History of the King's Works. Vol IV, 1485-1660 (Part II)*, London, 1982, p. 144.

[8] National Archives, E351/3259.

[9] Only one surviving image shows the building gabled, all later images, including one from the 1670s depict a hipped roof.

[10] G. Chettle, The Queen's House Greenwich. Survey of London, 14th monograph, London 1937.

[11] Bridge and Miles, Dendrochronological Dating.

[12] The rest of the building is roofed by a series of short spans of little structural sophistication, essentially creating a series of very shallow, almost flat leads. Those roofs on the east side were set alight during the Second World War, and though the principal timbers survive, they are badly charred. Pine boards over the King's Presence Chamber, inserted to prevent dust from building up on the rear of the paintings were also sampled, and found to be Swedish pine, of 1630s date.

[13] Yeomans erroneously ascribed two tie-beams. Yeomans, *Roofs of Inigo Jones*, p.97.

[14] Colvin, *History of the King's Works*, vol 6 (II), p.246.

[15] National Archives E351/3260.

[16] Historical Manuscripts Commission, Rutland I, p.473.

[17] Sir John Soane's Museum, models M1215, 1216, 1217, 1221. Peter Nicholson, *Practical Carpentry, Joinery and Cabinet Making*. London 1826, plate 20.

[18] Daniello Barbaro, *I Dieci Libri dell' Arhcitettura di M. Vitruvio*, Venice 1552, p.168. Illustrated in Yeomans, Roofs, p. 89.

[19] I Quattro Libri Dell'architettura Di Andrea Palladio. Venice 1570, II, 42; James Campbell has also discussed the influence of this and similar sources on Sir Christopher Wren. J. Campbell, 'Sir Christopher Wren, the Royal Society, and the Development of Structural Carpentry 1660-1710'. Unpublished thesis, University of Cambridge, 1999, p. 108.

[20] National Library of Wales, Wynnstay MSS nos, 175, 176, 179, 181, 183, cited in Colvin.

[21] National Archives E351/3270.

[22] National Archives E351/3263.

[23] Colvin, History of the King's Works, VI, p. 129.

[24] H. Colvin History of the King's Works, vol III, 1485-1660 (Part 1). London 1975, p.138.

Theatre Construction in Eighteenth-Century France: The Opera of the Palais-Royal in Paris and its Impact on Theatre Construction

Aikaterina Maria Chalvatzi

Institute of Conservation and Building Archaeology, Federal Institute of Technology in Zurich (ETHZ), Switzerland

Introduction

Theatrical renaissance in France started in the seventeenth century and was a successor to the Italian theatre revival of the sixteenth century. In Italy theatre construction was already underway, supported by the development of the opera and by technical progress in machinery and stage design. Strongly influenced by the trend, France followed the Italian example and at the end of the seventeenth century the first 'Salles de spectacle' emerged. Among those early objects were the Hôtel de Bourgogne (1588) and the Salle des Machines in the Palais des Tuileries (1662) [1]. Although admiration was rising, existing theatre spaces were small and uncomfortable [2] and the demand for specialized construction consequently increased [3].

Nevertheless, the need for appropriate buildings was unfulfilled, creating discourse around designs for new theatre projects. The majority of early theatre buildings were private and often attached to residences or palaces. The intensification of the discourse [4] in the eighteenth century directed theatre construction towards modernization of both architectural form and structural techniques.

Several theatres were erected in Paris in the eighteenth century, as a response to the increasing demand. Each project reflects the theoretical background and represents diverse solutions, for instance the theatres 'de la Gaité' (1764) [5], 'de l'Ambigu-Comique' (1769) [6], 'de l'Odéon' (1782) [7].

This research attempts to reconstruct the context, in which the Theatre of the Palais-Royal was built. On the one hand it is positioned rather late in the career of the architect Victor Louis (1731-1800), who had already designed and constructed a major theatre in Bordeaux. The direct comparison of the two theatre projects, these examples in Bordeaux and in Paris, reveal both the intention of the architect and the evolution in construction techniques.

This article focuses on the example of the Opera in the Palais-Royal in Paris and on the work of the architect Victor Louis on theatre construction. The example in Paris is representative of the evolution of theatre structures in France and is a reflection of the factors that influenced and determined to some extent theatre design in the nineteenth century.

Theatre Construction in Eighteenth-Century France: The Opera of the Palais-Royal in Paris and its Impact on Theatre Construction

Paris Opera until 1781

Until 1672, the Opera in Paris was accommodated in the Théâtre de Vaugirard [8]. In 1673, opera performances were transferred to the premises of Palais-Cardinal, today called Palais-Royal, at the time property of Cardinal Richelieu (1585-1642). In the right aisle of the Palace, designed in 1635 by Jacques Le Mercier (1585-1654), there was already a small theatre with a capacity of 500 people, used by the theatre company of the Marais [9].

Being a renowned culture enthusiast, the cardinal renovated the theatre space of the palace in 1641 to accommodate theatre representations in presence of the King [10]. In 1674, the theatre was refurbished by the director of the Musical Academy Jean-Baptiste Lully (1632-1687) [11], in order to respond to the requirements of the opera. In 1749, the owner of the palace Louis Duc d'Orléans (1703-1752) transferred his theatrical privilege to the municipality of Paris [12].

Opera at the Palais-Royal built by Moreau

On the 6th of April 1763, the Opera of the Palais-Royal was destroyed by fire. Given the scale of the destruction, the palace required complete renovation, which was time-consuming. Due to the pressure for a new opera, the City of Paris commissioned the chef architect of the city, Pierre-Louis Moreau Desproux (1727-1793) [13] to construct a new opera. This was inaugurated in 1770 [14], in the same location as its predecessor and was considerably larger. Moreau rejected the modern forms proposed for the design of the opera and based his design on the opera at Lyon designed by the architect Jacques-Germain Soufflot (1713-1780) [15]. The theatre had an elliptical auditorium, four rows of loggias and fire-proof staircases. Due to the absence of vertical supports at the front of the loggias, the impression was that of a continuous balcony. Furthermore, the opera was furnished with a foyer placed on the first floor behind the auditorium [16].

The structure and the machines of this theatre are documented in contemporary publications such as in the Supplement of the Encyclopédie (1772) [17], in Krafft (1820) [18] as well as in the Parallèle of Dumont (1774) [19]. The structure of the roof consisted of wood following Italian examples (fig. 1). The trusses formed a purlin roof with tie beams set on the masonry walls. The roof structure extended on three levels, the first two formed with queen posts and the last with a king post. The queen posts were connected to the tie beams with metal straps and the principal rafters were double on the first level. Wooden struts connected the straining beams with the queen posts and the principal rafters. Over the auditorium, the roof spanned 19 m. The machines for the scenery, or 'flies' were positioned in the basement and connected with ropes to the roof [20].

The opera occupied this theatre until 1781, when it was again destroyed by fire.

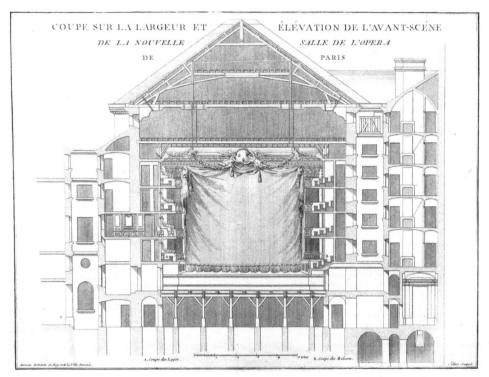

Figure 1. Section of the Opera of Moreau at the Palais Royal(1770),Dumont,Parallèle,1774(Note 19).

A temporary Opera

The reconstruction of the Opera of the Palais-Royal was an imperative demand of its owner, the Duc de Chartres (Louis-Philippe I Duc d'Orléans, 1725-1785), who requested that the city of Paris take over the expense. The city was reluctant to accept the Duke's claim, however Paris needed a theatre without further delay [21]. Indecisiveness and legal complexity led to the construction of a temporary Opera in order to cover the immediate need. This theatre was constructed next to the Porte Saint-Martin by Samson Nicholas Lenoir (1733-1810) and was slightly smaller than Moreau's Opera. It was inaugurated in October 1781 after three months of rapid construction [22]. The theatre had an elliptical auditorium and four rows of loggias. The wooden structure of the roof was as its predecessor a purlin roof with queen posts and a king post [23] (fig. 2).

Although the theatre was constructed as a temporary space, it presented acoustic qualities and refined machinery for the scenery. In parallel, the construction of a new permanent theatre located in the Palais-Royal advanced [24].

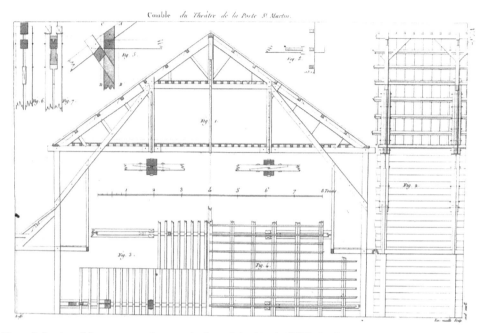

Figure 2. Section of the temporary Opera at the Porte Saint-Martin(1781), Kraft,Traité,(Note 18), Pl,57.

Theatre construction by Victor Louis

Already before the fire of 1781, the Duc de Chartres (Louis-Philippe II Duc d'Orléans, 1747-1793) was planning to refurbish the Palais-Royal. In 1780, the project was probably already assigned to Victor Louis, the architect of the Grand Theatre at Bordeaux [25]. The Duke became acquainted with Victor Louis during his visit to the construction site of the theatre and acknowledged his talent. In 1781, Victor Louis was in charge of the design and construction of the left wing started in June of the same year [26].

Victor Louis, the architect of the theatre

Victor Louis (1731-1800) was born in Paris and studied at the Académie Royale d'Architecture [27]. In 1755, he obtained the Grand Prix de Rome, which granted him three years of research in the Italian capital. Following his return to Paris in 1760, Victor Louis was assigned the restoration of the church Notre-Dame de Bon Secours, in the Faubourg Saint-Antoine [28]. Several further projects for decoration and restoration of churches, including the cathedral of Chartres, allowed him to establish a name as an architect. In 1765, he was acquainted to the King of Poland, Stanislaus II (1732-1798), obtaining later the title of the first architect of the King of Poland [29].

In 1767, Victor Louis took over the restoration of the private palace of the Maréchal de Richelieu (1696-1788), who became his protector [30]. He became Richelieu's personal architect and worked on refurbishing his private property. It is because of the suggestion of Richelieu to King Louis XV, that Victor Louis was assigned the construction of the Grand Theatre at Bordeaux in 1773 [31], a project that was to define his career.

The Grand Theatre at Bordeaux

The city of Bordeaux desperately needed a theatre, as the existing one had been destroyed by fire and the temporary hall did not meet contemporary expectations [32]. Attempts to raise money, find a suitable site and obtain the approval of the King delayed construction. Although a project by a local architect, Nicolas-François Lhote (1743-1808), already existed [33], the intervention of the Maréchal de Richelieu was crucial for the selection of Victor Louis. Consequently, he arrived at Bordeaux in April 1773, to assume construction of the theatre he had already started to design, following the advice of Richelieu [34].

In 1774, financial hindrance caused by a change of minister delayed construction, but the intervention of Turgot in 1775 resulted in support to proceed further [35] and the theatre was inaugurated in April 1780 [36].

The Grand Theatre at Bordeaux is a majestic structure that established Victor Louis as a renowned architect. Every aspect of the theatre's construction reflects cutting-edge techniques of its time. The construction of the walls is in masonry of high quality, using techniques of precise stereotomic cutting of the stone. The portal of the main façade is made of flat arcs, *'plates-bandes'* in stone with iron reinforcement [37]. The auditorium has a circular hall, four rows of loggias and eight staircases made in stone. On the roof, the architect designed water tanks filled with pumped water from the Garonne River [38].

The roof is a wooden structure spanning 23 m, constructed as a mansard-purlin system (fig. 3). Each truss consists of two sets of double rafters and three collar beams, the higher aligned with the walls, one before the mansard angle and one above it at the height of the next purlin. Diagonal posts connect the lower beam with the purlin at the mansard angle and a king post reaches the level of the middle beam. The roof was conceived without separation between stage and auditorium and repeats the circular shape of the latter with a complex structure of double rafters and a central tension post (fig. 4).

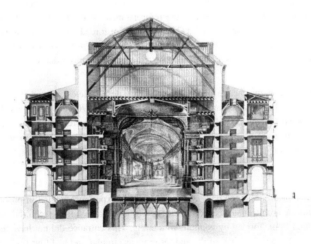

Figure 3. Section of the Grand Theatre at Bordeaux, V. Louis, Salle De Spectacle De Bordeaux. Paris: L'auteur, Chez Espritt,1782, Pl.18.

Theatre Construction in Eighteenth-Century France: The Opera of the Palais-Royal in Paris and its Impact on Theatre Construction

Figure 4. Aspect of the wooden roof of the Grand Theatre at Bordeaux, Holzer 2017.

Construction of the Opera of the Palais-Royal

The construction of the theatre in Bordeaux, a major structure, already attracted visitors even before its completion [39]. As the site work was drawing to its end, Victor Louis went back to Paris to receive a new assignment by the Duc de Chartres, concerning the refurbishment of the Palais-Royal. The plans were already prepared in 1781, but the destruction of the old Opera due to fire forced Victor Louis to revise his original plan. The new proposal was signed in 1784 [40] and the theatre was placed at the corner of St Honoré and Richelieu, thus not in the location of its predecessor [41]. However, financial difficulties delayed construction [42].

In 1786, the construction of the theatre then called 'Théâtre des Variétés' started [43], and Victor Louis was actively involved on site. The theatre was inaugurated on 15th May 1790 but was not used for the opera, despite the demands of the Duc d'Orléans and of the architect himself [44]. The architect wrote a letter in 1789 to defend his structure, claiming that the theatre was larger than its predecessor and the Opera at the Porte Saint-Martin [45]. The remarks concerned the space for the machines and the number of spectators, rather than the actual structure.

For the design of this theatre, Victor Louis had applied all his experience gained in previous projects. The site was very narrow, but the architect succeeded nonetheless to incorporate all the required functions. The entrance hall was on the ground floor, formed by columns in a circle. This entrance did not have the impressive stairs of Bordeaux due to lack of space. The hall of the auditorium was circular and had four rows of loggias. The ceiling was a dome resting on pendentives and half-domes (*culs-de-four*). The arcs supporting the ceiling where not identical, two were double and ornamented [46].

In the Theatre 'des Variétés' (fig. 5), the interesting fact is the transition accomplished in the structure. The major remark concerning the structure is that the roof is no longer made of wood, but of wrought iron and hollow bricks. According to Kaufmann [47], the walls supporting the roof structure were impressively thin (rather reinforced masonry). The iron frames distributed their load on a larger surface on the walls with the help of vertical posts embedded in the masonry. Supporting buttresses punctuated the weaker parts of the masonry assisted by the vaults in iron and hollow bricks, which covered the surrounding corridors. The vaults resting on the exterior walls, gradually transferred the load to the ground.

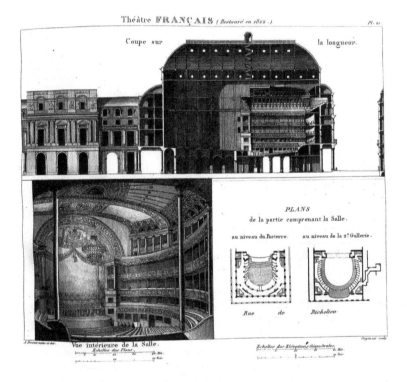

Figure 5. The Theatre of Victor Louis at the Palais-Royal, Kaufmann, Architectonographie, (Note 47), Pl. 21.

The roof frames (fig. 6) consisted of two three-piece arcs held together by several vertical struts. The interior arc was more curved than the exterior. The outer parts of the arcs resting on the walls were covered with smaller arc-formed iron ties to strengthen the supports. The iron struts closer to the walls were elongated in order to connect the arcs with the horizontal collar tie rods. There were two collar ties, one aligned with the walls and one almost two meters lower, both connected with the vertical posts, which were embedded in the walls with reinforced iron braces. They were also composed of three pieces mounted with bolt and nail like connections. A long diagonal tie at each side was connected to the exterior arc with iron struts, the higher collar tie and the vertical posts in the walls, providing stability and stiffness. A vertical hanging tie connected the highest point of the arcs with the two collar ties, forming staple-like joints.

Theatre Construction in Eighteenth-Century France: The Opera of the Palais-Royal in Paris and its Impact on Theatre Construction

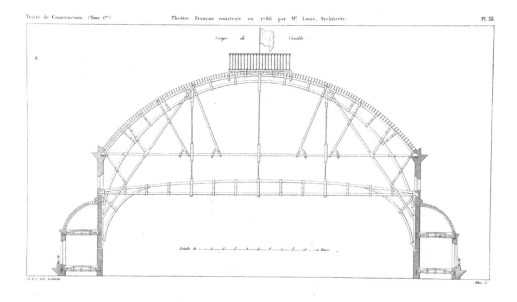

Figure 6. Theatre of Victor Louis at the Palais-Rpyal. Section of a frame of the roof with the hollow bricks. C. G. Eck, Traité de construction en poteries et fer, à l'usage des bâtimens civils, industriels et militairs, suiyi d'un recueil de machines appropiées à l'art de bâtir…, Paris: J.-C. Blosse (Carilian-Goeury), 1836, Pl. 31.

The structure of the roof supported both the dome shaped ceiling and the intermediate floor over the scene with all the machinery, which was directly resting on the collar beams. All connections were designed to take into account the dilatation of iron, in order to prevent deformation and rupture.

The roof trusses were connected in the longitudinal direction with iron struts forming frames, which were filled with hollow bricks and covered with plaster and 'ardoise' stone. The hollow bricks were forming vaults and they were covering the iron struts. The result was a highly fire-proof roof structure, which consisted of iron and masonry vaults.

In the centre of the roof there was a lantern, accessible by an iron staircase. The total span of the roof was about 21·90 meters.

Transition to Iron

According to Fontaine, the wish of the Duc d'Orléans for the theatre, was to construct an object "majestic and extraordinary" [48], with the intention of bringing the opera back to his palace. A crucial question in the construction of the theatre concerns the influence of the Duke in the choice of materials. Victor Louis was definitely a talented architect, who was willing and capable of applying high-quality techniques and innovations in his structures.

As owner of the theatre, the Duke stands behind Victor Louis and the choice of iron/hollow bricks had to be approved by him. His acquaintance with the architect Alexandre-Théodore Brongniart (1739-1813) [49] and further research on the latter's work [50], might suggest a probable influence of the Duke on the choice of this particular roof structure. Nevertheless, in this stage of research, it is unsubstantial to question the decision concerning the application of iron. For the theatre at Bordeaux, the architect followed closely the construction process [51]. Given the importance of the theatre in the Palais-Royal, Victor Louis must have been involved in every aspect of the realisation and construction of his project.

Simultaneously with the theatre, another roof construction of smaller scale was erected in iron, the Salle Carrée in the Louvre [52]. The identification of similar structures is attested by contemporary literature and archival research.

Although mentioned and admired in several contemporary publications, the impact of the iron roof was not rapid. After the erection of the Theatre of Victor Louis, several theatres followed his example, including the Cirque-Olympique (1827), the Théâtre de l'Ambigu-Comique (1828) and the Théâtre Ventadour (1829) [53]. However, these examples were erected almost four decades after the theatre in the Palais-Royal. At the same time, several prestigious theatres were constructed with traditional wooden roofs, such as the Théâtre de l'Odéon (1808, 1819). Although the fear of fire was well known, and the theatres had to be reconstructed regularly, the fire-proof structure applied by Victor Louis did not find immediate imitators.

Current status of the Theatre of Victor Louis

The Theatre of the Palais-Royal has been damaged and altered since its creation in 1790. Furthermore, the French Revolution resulted in its poor maintenance. Already in 1822, a project for its restoration was effected. Since then, the theatre has been dedicated to the Comédie-Française [54]. Nevertheless, the iron roof skeleton survived the fire of 1900 which completely devastated the theatre. The fire-proof structure of Victor Louis survived the flames, but had to be demolished, to allow a reconstruction. A photograph after the fire published in Prudent-Guadet [55] shows the situation of the roof before the demolition.

The theatre was reconstructed by the architect Julien Guadet (1834-1908), who acknowledged the accomplishment of Victor Louis in the theatre of the Palais-Royal. Together with Henri Prudent, the architects published a book [56] dedicated to Victor Louis, with precious contemporary research concerning its state before the destruction.

Conclusion and remarks

This Theatre by Victor Louis was inaugurated at the break of the French Revolution. The architect did not produce a detailed publication to present his project, as he did for the Grand Theatre in Bordeaux. The actual structure is not conserved, leaving a gap in its documentation. Original plans and contemporary descriptions of the construction, illustrate how the structure was built. Archival research will be complemented with building research, in order to locate possible remnants and determine the contemporary situation of the structure. It is nevertheless certain that the Theatre of Victor Louis in Paris had a large brick vault reinforced by an iron structure. The architect was familiar with the use of iron since the flat arcs (*'plates-bandes'*) of the Theatre in Bordeaux.

A further major question concerns the reasons behind the choice to apply an iron and brick roof system to this project. The theatre had a large span and the roof demanded technical expertise. Victor Louis had already successfully constructed a theatre with a wooden roof. He must have had a strong reason to innovate, instead of repeating a familiar solution. There are several hypotheses explaining the reasons that possibly obliged the architect to apply iron, including the danger of fire particularly in theatres, the demands of his client, the quest for technical innovation.

Furthermore, the theatre was erected in Paris, where wrought iron application emerged. Iron was produced in better quality than before. This fact was due to the introduction of new techniques. It is essential to identify which techniques and systems were applied at the time in different structures and the technical and theoretical level that allowed their erection.

References

[1] J. Lorcey, La Comédie Française, Paris: Fernand Nathan, 1980, p. 10-16.

[2] D. Rabreau, Apollon Dans La Ville: Le Théâtre Et L'urbanisme En France Au XVIIIe Siècle, Paris: Editions Du Patrimoine, Centre Des Monuments Nationaux, 2008, p. 13.

[3] The demand for specialized theatre construction is expressed in the Permission of the King for the construction of the theatre of Bordeaux, Ordonnance of the 4th of September 1773, Archives Municipales Bordeaux Métropole, Folder DD 36 A.

[4] C. de Chaumont and Monginot, *Exposition des principes qu'on doit suivre dans l'ordonnance des theatres modernes. Par M.*** Comte des guerres, & Sre de M. de D. de C.,* Paris: Charles Antoine Jombert, 1769.

[5] N. Wild, Dictionnaire Des Théâtres Parisiens Au XIXe Siècle: Les Théâtres Et La Musique. Vol. 4, Paris: Aux Amateurs De Livres, 1989, p. 167.

[6] Wild, Dictionnaire, (Note 5), p. 32.

[7] J. C. Daufresne, Théâtre De L'Odéon: Architecture, Décors, Musée. Sprimont (Belgique): Mardaga, 2004, p. 13.

[8] Plans des principales salles de théâtres de Paris. Théâtre des Italiens, Paris: Jonas-Lavater, Book not dated, signature in the Bibliothèque Nationale de France : FRBNF38767752.

[9] S. Serre, L'Opéra de Paris (1749-1790): politique culturelle au temps des Lumières, Sciences De La Musique, Paris: CNRS éditions, 2011, pp. 171-172.

[10] E. Dupezard, Le Palais-Royal de Paris. Architecture et décoration de Louis XV à nos jours, Paris: Eggimann, 1913, pp. 3-7.

[11] Serre, Opéra, (Note 9), pp. 174-175.

[12] Dupezard, Palais-Royal, (Note 10), p. 10.

[13] Dupezard, Palais-Royal, (Note 10), p. 10.

[14] Dupezard, *Palais-Royal,* (Note 10), p. 13.

[15] Musée Carnavalet, *Le Palais Royal: Musée Carnavalet, 9 Mai - 4 Septembre 1988.* Paris: Edition Paris-Musées, 1988, p. 128.

[16] P. Patte, Essai Sur L'architecture Théatrale, ou, de l'Ordonnance la plus avantageuse à une Salle de Spectacles, relativement aux principes de l'Optique & de l'Acoustique: Avec un Examen des principaux

Théâtres de l'Europe, & une Analyse des écrits les plus importans sur cette matiere, Paris: Chez Moutard, 1782, pp. 107-112.

[17] Recueil de Planches sur les Sciences, les Arts Libéraux et les Arts Méchaniques avec leur explication, Vol.10, Paris: Briasson, 1772.

[18] J. C. Krafft, Traité Sur L'art De La Charpente, Plans, Coupes Et élévations De Diverses Productions: Exécutées Tant En France Que Dans Les Pays étrangers, 1st edition. Paris: Chez L'auteur, 1805, Plate N. 56.

[19] G. M. Dumont, Parallèle De Plans Des plus Belles Salles De Spectacles D'Italie Et De France: Avec Des Détails De *Machines Théatrales*, Paris, 1774.

[20] Recueil, Briasson, (Note 17), pl. XXI-XXII.

[21] Serre, *Opéra,* (Note 9), pp. 202-205.

[22] Serre, *Opéra,* (Note 9), pp. 212-214.

[23] Krafft, *Traité* (Note 18), Plate N 57.

[24] Dupezard, *Palais-Royal,* (Note 10), p. 14.

[25] C. Taillard, *Victor Louis (1731-1800): Le triomphe du goût français à l'époque néo-classique*, Paris: PUPS, 2008, pp. 252-253.

[26] H. Prudent and P. Guadet, *Les Salles de Spectacle de Victor Louis*, Paris : Librairie de la Construction Moderne, 1903, pp. 32-33.

[27] C. Marionneau, *Victor Louis: Architecte Du Théâtre De Bordeaux : Sa Vie, Ses Travaux Et Sa Correspondance : 1731-1800*, Bordeaux, 1881, pp. 1-9.

[28] Marionneau, *Louis*, (Note 27), pp. 11-44.

[29] Louis has the title of the 'first Architect of the King of Poland' on the first payment receipt for the Theatre of Bordeaux dated the 27. November 1773, Archives Municipales Bordeaux Métropole, Folder DD 36 A.

[30] Marionneau, *Louis*, (Note 27), p. 89.

[31] Taillard, *Louis* (Note 25), p. 164-165.

[32] Marionneau, *Louis*, (Note 27), p. 104.

[33] Taillard, *Louis,* (Note 25), p. 167-168.

[34] Marionneau, *Louis*, (Note 27), p. 132.

[35]   Letter by Turgot on the 15 March 1775, Archives Municipales Bordeaux Métropole, Folder DD 36 A.

[36] Marionneau, *Louis*, (Note 27), p. 420.

[37] L.E.H. Gaullieur-L'Hardy, *Porte-feuille ichnographique de V. Louis*, Paris, Bordeaux: Carillan-Goery, chez les principaux libraires, 1828, Plate IV. The term 'plates-bandes' is explained thoroughly in: J. B. Rondelet, *Traité Théorique Et Pratique De L'art De Bâtir*. Tome troisième, livre sixième, seventh edition Paris: Firmin Didot Frères, 1834, p. 306-309.

[38] J. P. Avisseau, V. Monthiers andM. Laruë-Charlus, *Le Grand Théâtre De Bordeaux*. Bordeaux: William Blake and Co, 1991, p. 29.

[39] Marionneau, *Louis*, (Note 27), p. 277.

[40] Marionneau, *Louis*, (Note 27), p. 493.

[41] The plan is published with a date in: C. Percier, and P. F. L. Fontaine, *Résidences de souverains. Parallèle entre plusieurs résidences de souverains de France, d'Allemagne, de Suède, de Russie, d'Espagne et d'Italie*. Paris: chez les auteurs, au Louvre, 1833, Plate 37.

[42] Taillard, *Louis,* (Note 25), p. 267.

[43] Marionneau, *Louis*, (Note 27), p. 508-509.

[44] Marionneau, *Louis*, (Note 27), p. 509.

[45] Letter of Victor Louis on 9 May 1790 in: Recueil: Journal académique 1789, Réponse à un écrit qui a pour titre Mémoire justificatif des sujets de l'opéra, Paris: Chez Gattey, 1789.

[46] Prudent-Guadet, *Louis* (Note 26), pp. 43-44.

[47] J. A. Kaufmann, *Architectonographie des Théâtres ou parallèle historique et critique de ces édifices, considérés sous le rapport de l'architecture et de la décoration*, seconde série, Paris: Mathias, 1840, pp. 122-126.

[48] C. Percier and P. F. L. Fontaine, *Résidences de souverains. Parallèle entre plusieurs résidences de souverains de France, d'Allemagne, de Suède, de Russie, d'Espagne et d'Italie*, Paris : chez les auteurs, au Louvre, 1833, pp. 307-308.

[49] B. Lemoine, 'Alexandre-Théodore Brongniart', *Paris. Tête d'affiche*, no.3, March April May 1986, p. 77.

[50] Brongniart is the architect of the Bourse (1807-1825), which is covered with a similar structure of iron and hollow bricks. J. B. Rondelet, *Traité Théorique Et Pratique De L'art De Bâtir*. 6th Edition, Paris: Chez l'Auteur, 1831, Pl. CLVI.

[51] Victor Louis' involvement in the construction of the theatre in Bordeaux is preserved in the Archives Bordeaux Metropole (DD 36 A-J).

[52] J. B. Rondelet, *Traité Théorique Et Pratique De L'art De Bâtir*. Tome quatrième, deuxième partie, Paris: Chez l'Auteur, 1816, Pl. CLXXXI and G. Fonkenell, 'The Roof Frame of the Salon Carré' pp. 515-524 in R. Carvais, (Ed.), *Nuts & Bolts of Construction History: Culture, Technology and Society,* Vol. 3, Paris: Picard, 2012.

[53] Kaufmann, *Architectonographie,* (Note 47), Pl. XX, XXXI.

[54] Dupezard, *Palais-Royal,* (Note 10), p. 16.

[55] Prudent-Guadet, *Louis,* (Note 26), Pl. 13-14.

[56] Prudent-Guadet, *Louis,* (Note 26).

The Dry Dock at Ramsgate: Smeaton or Rennie?

A developmental history

Mark Samuel

Independent Heritage Consultant, UK

Introduction

The developmental history of the Dry Dock at Ramsgate has never been examined although the published reports of the famous Civil Engineer John Smeaton[1] and the unpublished notebooks of John Rennie still exist.[2] The Dry Dock represents one of Smeaton's last works in a long career; his most famous task, the Eddystone Lighthouse.   No attempt has previously been made to relate the surviving designs to what exists today. An important paper on the "No. 3 Dry Dock" at Chatham made no mention of Rennie's near-contemporary commitments at Ramsgate.[3]   This paper therefore amalgamates archaeological technique and source criticism to clarify how Rennie used his experience at Ramsgate as a technological forcing ground.

The paper is developed from a report originally commissioned by Thanet District Council in 2014. This was intended to provide background information for an application for EU Community funding. The *Yacht Valley Project* was an act of international cooperation between the coastal regions of France (Nord-Pas de Calais), England (SW, SE, and E), Belgium (Flanders) and the Netherlands. It was partially funded by the EU-based INTERREG IV A2 programme for seas. The funding was to allow the histories of individual North Sea harbours to be researched; the aim - to improve these old harbours as amenities for tourism and leisure use.

Methodology of the Report

Apart from Smeaton's publication and Rennie's notebooks, the main source of historical information were the photographs, engravings, maps and other views held in the Local History collection of Ramsgate Library. Some key images only exist as copies made before arsonists destroyed the original library in 2005.

Great reliance was placed on photographic survey; the bare minimum of survey was carried out, and that to address specific research questions. The survey presented here is schematic, for no modern survey of the Dry Dock apparently exists.

Geology and history of the pre-Dry Dock setting

Thanet is a small stub of a great promontory that ran into the nascent North Sea 7000 years ago.[4] The Ramsgate haven originated as a flooded valley, created by subsequent sea levels rises. It is now no more than an indent in the south edge of an exposed syncline of chalk. The topography of this syncline ridge was created in the last ice

The Dry Dock at Ramsgate: Smeaton or Rennie?

A developmental history

advance, where permafrost allowed both running water and solifluction. As a result of these processes, a valley formed that was then partially filled in by head deposits and (more recently) anthropogenic hill-wash.

The 'contour-determined' coastline was rapidly modified by sea currents and wave-cut platform formation.[5] In Roman times, projecting headlands probably flanked a natural harbour. By medieval times, the haven had become no more than a "gate" (depression) in a curving cliff face which presented no natural shelter.

The lost natural harbour was certainly used by the Romans, but we only know this from chance discoveries in the nineteenth century. A brick-built sewer and "the timbers of an ancient pier" seen at a depth of 7 metres in the 1850s[6] illustrate significant urban development yet to be found.

Ramsgate probably existed well before the first survivals of documentation in the thirteenth century when it became a member of the Cinque Port of Sandwich. There is no evidence to see continuity between this fishing hamlet and the Roman settlement. The depth of the Roman pier illustrates a significant sea-level rise in the intervening period. This is in accordance with one model of sea-level change, which posits first-century CE sea level as 3-4 metres below the present level.[7]

A timber pier was first mentioned in Henry VIII's reign. This pre-existing pier influenced the position of the Dry Dock. It probably survives in a 'fossilised' state within the vastly greater works of the eighteenth and nineteenth centuries.

By its nature, the timber pier needed constant repair and modification. A Board was therefore decreed to supervise the harbour. The "Glorious Revolution" (1688) marks the turn in Ramsgate's fortunes.[8] The town underwent accelerated growth as a result of expanded trade with Russia and the "East Country" (The Baltic States'). The benefits of the "Late Wars" was also mentioned by a topographer in the 1730s.[9] Lewis mentioned that the timber pier was:

> "...considerably enlarged...For the maintenance of this Pier, Orders and Decrees of the Cinque Ports, by which the Inhabitants are impowered to choose Wardens, to look after the Repairs of the faid Pier, and to collect fuch Droits or Rates, as by the faid Decrees and antient immemorial Custom are payable for Shipping and Goods brought into this Pier".[10]

The pier provided little protection and a severe storm of 1748 lead to the creation of a Board of Trustees at Ramsgate. Their purpose was to provide a safe harbour for ships at risk in storms.[11]

Fig. 1. "A Plan for peirs (sic) to make an Harbour at Ramsgate in the County of Kent", c. 1750; Ramsgate Local Studies Collection, photo Mark Samuel, (by kind permission of Kent County Council –Libraries Registration & Archives)

The design of the harbour seems to have caused considerable interest, and various designs were submitted (Fig. 1). The construction of a stone East Pier commenced soon after the necessary Act of Parliament in 1749.[12] One of the trustees, William Ackenden, projected a stone east pier and wooden west pier, and this was "...carried on with great spirit for three or four years".[13] Commencement of the stone east pier is shown in a lost oil painting of 1751.[14]

The committee, alarmed at the cost, demanded that the harbour be contracted in size; rendering it useless (as the sailors did not hesitate to point out!). The disagreements were only eventually resolved by a petition to Parliament. It was not until June 1761 that the offending west wall was removed and the original design re-instated. A vast amount of money was wasted and the new harbour started silting up at an alarming rate.[15]

The Dry Dock at Ramsgate: Smeaton or Rennie?

A developmental history

Fig.2 The Ramsgate Dry Dock, Ramsgate Harbour, 2014 (Photograph Mark Samuel).

The dispute between the harbour committee and sea captains reflects a long-established problem of this harbour. It served as a refuge for shipping on the Goodwin Sands, but the degree of trade that it brought never compensated for the expense of maintaining it. Repair work of storm-damaged ships was however a frequent requirement. A dry dock was required to allow the hulls of ships to be repaired. Stone-built Dry Docks of this type were still a novelty; the technical problems far from solved.

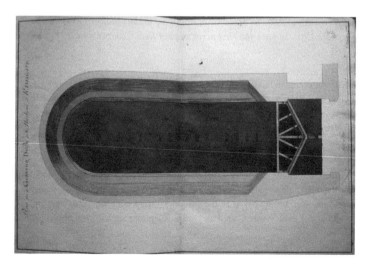

Fig. 3 "Plan for a Graving Dock at the Harbour in Ramsgate", 1783. Photo Mark Samuel. J. Smeaton vol. V Fos 138-195 l.s. [XVI], 142, modern. ref. JS/5/139, (reproduced by kind permission of the Royal Society)

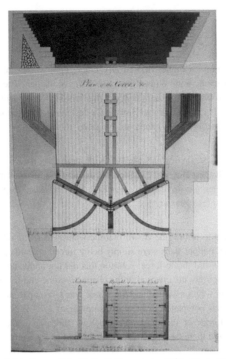

Fig. 4 "Section...Plan...and upright of one of the Gates", Ramsgate, 1783. Photo Mark Samuel, J. Smeaton vol. V Fos 138-195 l.s. [XVI], 144, modern. ref. JS/5/140, (reproduced by kind permission of the Royal Society)

John Smeaton's stately hand provides the tangled tale of the Dry Dock's construction.[16] He came to Ramsgate with the main body of his achievement behind him. This "J.S. Bach of Engineering" was scrupulously patient and fair-minded with his clients and would-be rivals. He had cause to be! His association commenced in 1774, initially in a consultative capacity.

The "sullage" (silting) of the new harbour exercised the trustees more than any other concern. His ideas were admired and imitated by one Thomas Preston, previously in charge of dredging. This man directed the building of a "Cross Wall" across the harbour. This enclosed a separate bason (sic.) to the north. Water trapped at high tide could be released through sluices, to wash the silt away. On completion of the wall, the first trials went ahead in August 1779. Smeaton's ideas were vindicated. An extension of the east pier also dealt with the rare but devastating "nor-easters". The trustees, scenting the profit from ship repairs after storms, hit upon the idea of a "graving" (dry) dock. Smeaton continues:

> "1784, 26th July. From Mr Barker's Report upon this visitation it appears, that a new Dock being determined upon by the Trustees, to be built according to Mr Smeaton's Plan, it was immediately begun, and Mr Barker [the master mason] laid the first stone, 31st July; and the workmen were directed to proceed with all possible expedition. *Here it may be proper to observe that had Mr Smeaton's Plan been in reality complied with, it would probably have taken the whole of this season to have completed and laid down the timber floor, before a single stone could have been

laid; but it was thought proper to begin with the Walls according to Mr Smeaton's lines, exclusive of the Floor" [original italics].[17]

The 1783 design (Figs. 3, 4) shows a timber-floored Dry Dock, upon which the stone walls of the Dry Dock rested. Smeaton was justifiably exonerating himself from what was to happen. The Trustees understood that if the floor was completed before the walls were commenced, this would delay opening by a year. The Chair (Mr Barker) and the master mason Mr Cull over-ruled Smeaton's design for this reason.[18] Their alternative design made sense to them, being of stone throughout and thus avoiding "the worm".

"1785. Ramsgate, 5th August. On this visit, Mr. BARKER reports that the Dock was in great forwardneff, for the Walls were built up twelve feet high, and 3,065 feet of pavement had been laid at the bottom. That the Gates were made, and ready for hanging, and that the whole feemed to be an exceeding good piece of workmanship; and that it was likely to be ready for ufe by February next..."[19]

On the 5th of August Barker had to inform the Board that the water was rising up though the joints between the paving stones so fast, that the individual slabs were simply being forced upwards.[20] The master mason Mr Cull came up with an ingenious but flawed 'brute-force' solution that did not understand the role the water pressure of the springs was playing. He proposed an 'inverted arch' of massive one-and-a-half ton (1.524 tonne) blocks of Portland stone.[21] The Board however assented and the whole was taken apart and the necessary blocks ordered from Portland. The new floor was completed in the early summer of 1787.[22] This would in theory be bound even harder together by the forces of the water from below. Smeaton made a record of this design,[23] presumably as a precaution should there be an enquiry. This had led to the confusion about the authorship of the second stone- floored dry dock.

It was not until the 3rd -7th of August 1787 that the master mason made a trial of the dock. Mr Cull had to inform the board that:

"...by the time it was high water, the greateft part of the pavement was disjointed, and hove up; and what was yet more aftonishing, near 100 feet in length of the North Wall was hove up alfo"

Barker summoned Smeaton and Mr Aubert (soon to be Barker's successor). A further test was carried out, and water was seen to pour between the stones as the tide rose. Smeaton calculated the pressures involved and quickly got to the root of the problem. The solid Dry Dock floor was acting like the hull of a ship, the trapped water forcing it up through its own buoyancy. In its turn, it was pushing out the north wall of the Dry Dock. Smeaton suggested a return to his own design. He diplomatically blamed the site conditions rather than Cull and Barker.[24]

Alexander Aubert was appointed Chair on the death of Barker in November. Smeaton was permanently appointed as engineer in 1788, and remained in post until his death in 1792. His faithful assistant Mr Gwyn was appointed 'resident surveyor' because Smeaton had many other responsibilities.[25]

In 1788, the trustees decided that resources should be prioritised on the other parts of the harbour; the Dock reconstruction only occurring during pauses in the other work.[26] By the summer of 1791 (the year before his death), Smeaton was able to proudly announce:

"As an addition to this second edition of my report, I have the pleafure of informing the public, that on the Seventeenth July 1791, at a high spring tide, the New Dry Dock, built in the Bason, for repairing ships, was tried in the prefence of the Chairman, for the first time since it was found neceffary to build it with a timber floor, which is of a new and peculiar construction, on account of the springs rising from the chalk, so powerfully under it, that the stone floor which with it had been twice tried formerly [i.e. tested twice], was forced up. The experiment answered in the completeft manner; the Dock remaining perfectly dry till low water, when the fluices of the Bason were opened for scouring the harbour; so that this very desirable object, that has been so much despaired of, is now fully obtained, and must prove of great utility to the public".[27]

We understand why Smeaton's timber floor avoided self-destructing. On the other hand, the reasons for its water-tightness were not divulged – a trade secret clearly!

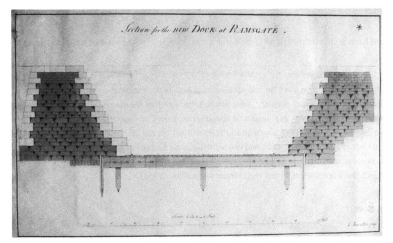

Fig. 5 "Section for the new Dock at Ramsgate", 1788. Photo Mark Samuel, J. Smeaton vol. V Fos 138-195 l.s. [XVI], 138v, modern. ref. JS/5/135, (reproduced by kind permission of the Royal Society)

An engraving of 1795 (not shown) seems to be the only view of Smeaton's completed dock.[28] High tide was depicted but no dock gates were shown. This absence can be explained by the empty dock, when the gates would be concealed in their reveals. An old "storehouse" was shown north of the dock on the harbour edge. It also appeared on a plan of the harbour in Smeaton's 1791 edition of his *Report* (not shown)[29]; the only record in plan of the realised Dry Dock. The appearance of this building illustrates a sixteenth century date, but it was soon to be removed (see below).

By 1813 the Dry Dock and Cross Wall had become the concern of a new generation of engineers. At about this time, John Rennie was employed by the Navy Board as a general adviser in new building schemes[30]. Although extremely busy at Chatham and Sheerness, he was the obvious choice to help out at Ramsgate. In February 1815, he set down the following in his unpublished (and unedited) *Reports*. [31]

"...The Dry Dock in the Basin is in a bad state, the floor near the entry neck is loose and a great deal of water gets into it....The Wings of the Gates are cracked in various places and must be taken down...these repairs will therefore become expensive and when so much is to be done, I would beg leave to submit for your consideration whether it would not render the Harbour more generally useful if this Dry Dock were to be lengthened 20 feet which might easily be done by substituting a floating gate in place of common gates" (author's italics). [32]

Rennie eventually went for a more radical solution (see below), because the Dry Dock was part of a much larger project. He laconically mentioned it as "enlarged" in February 1816. The rest of the harbour, as he makes clear, was also in a bad way:

"...The cill of the new entry neck [through the Cross Wall] is [in]sufficiently deep. One great benefit is therefore lost to many vessels which enter this harbour and this is particularly felt when they are damaged and might be repaired in the Basin or Dry Dock which has now been enlarged if they could get to them [author's italics]...The Dry Dock though enlarged wants capstanes, pumps etc. The expense of these respective works will amount to about £ 7000".[33]

The work must have gone on through 1815 and was a *fait accompli* by the time of Rennie's next report. In July of 1816, he:

"...went to Ramsgate on the 12th and spent several days in the examination of the Works. I found the Dry Dock completed in a satisfactory manner... there will be little to employ the masons unless the Basin Wall and Sluices are put in hand. These Sluices and Basin will altogether be a work of considerable expense but as they are only to be done progressively the annual expenditure I hope will not out run the funds of the Harbour...The next Sluices that should be done after the last mentioned two are those at the east end of the Cross Wall by the head of the Dry Dock. One of these sluices has at present a 10 feet opening and the other a 6 feet opening. I would advise the two new sluices to have openings of 12 feet each similar to the other...."[34]

In November, Rennie:

"... took a view on the proceedings of the works at Ramsgate Harbour on the Nineteenth instant where I found what I had long foreseen. Namely that owing to the great exertions which were made last year and the early part of the present to complete the enlargement of the Dry Dock and New Entry neck [of the Cross Wall] that it would be difficult to keep the Masons at work during the present winter".

He therefore efficiently discharged "some of the inferior workmen" and masons shortly before Christmas.[35] The ninth volume shows work in full swing on the sluices, where *Bramley-tall stone* and *Craigleith stone* were used due to their exceptional resistance for the Cross Wall facings and sluices respectively.[36] In August 1817, an order was sent to the quarry master near Edinburgh for Craigleith stone. This set out the specification for the cut stone in great detail.[37] At this point, all reference to the Dry Dock ends. Rennie returned his attention to the massive No.3 Dry Dock at Chatham which was not completed until a year after his death in 1821[38]. Unsurprisingly, this bristled with innovations.

Because no description or drawings of the Ramsgate dock are currently located, we are reliant on examination of the extant fabric to understand the changes made (see below).

The fortunes of the Ramsgate Dry Dock were chequered from that date, but it operated in its intended role until 1893. An 1822 map of Ramsgate shows the reconstructed Dry Dock with its distinctive curved gates (see

334

below).[39] A view of the harbour (not shown)[40] shows the enlarged Dry Dock in the company of the Clock House and Obelisk. These structures (1817 and 1823) survive to this day.

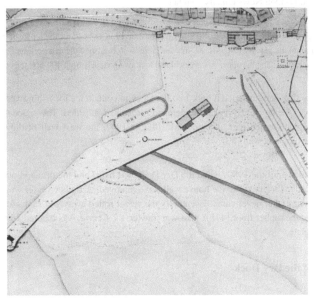

Fig. 6 "Map of Ramsgate. 10 inches = one mile, Lieut A. Hill RE. Levelled by Lieut W. Wynne RE ", detail of the Dry Dock, 1872, photograph Mark Samuel, (copied by kind permission of Michael Dance, Ramsgate).

The Rennie Dry Dock was included in an excellent map of the town surveyed by Royal Engineers in 1872. The data was used in the first 'official' Ordnance Survey of Ramsgate. It is not clear why this more detailed and coloured original was commissioned. Perhaps it was a proving exercise for urban survey?

Fig 7. "The Old Dry Dock Ramsgate", c.1870, (Postcard original lost. Copy reproduced by kind permission of Ralph Hoult, Ramsgate)

The Dry Dock at Ramsgate: Smeaton or Rennie?

A developmental history

Incapable of housing anything larger than a barque (a workhorse vessel), the dock was no longer "fit for purpose". The lack of draft in the Inner Basin made the Dry Dock inaccessible to modern seagoing vessels. An article in the Illustrated London News tells its own tale:

> "...Another great work at Ramsgate is the Slipway, constructed in 1838-9, for the repair of damaged vessels. It was built according to the patent of Messrs. Morton, of Leith, who furnished the ironwork and machinery. It is 480 feet long and 60 feet wide; and the apparatus is calculated to draw up vessels from 400-500 tons burthen".[41]

In 1893 the Thanet Ice Company inserted a hulk into the Dock to contain ice for fishing vessels. Most of the Dry Dock was covered by an ice house. By 1923, the demand for ice had subsided. The "...ice wells were [therefore] covered with concrete and formed part of a car park".[42] In 1947, the west wall of the car park ticket office rested on the ice house blocking wall.[43]

This sorry state continued until the 1980s when the Dry Dock was listed and the decision was taken to return it to view. All later accretions other than the ice house wall were removed. A timber vessel was hoisted into the Dry Dock to await a restoration that never came. Eventually the vessel rotted away and sank. Attempts to remove the wreck further damaged the timber floor.[44] A post-war trawler, the Cervia, was moored within the entry neck for restoration; now complete.

The archaeology of the Dry Dock

336

Fig 8. The Dry Dock, Ramsgate. Surviving pivot block of Dry Dock gate, 2014. Photo: Mark Samuel.

Archaeological attention was mostly paid to the Dry Dock entry neck and surrounding area. As far as Rennie's Dry Dock was concerned, the 1872 survey proved impressively accurate (when checks were made). For the purpose of easier description, round *imperial* measures originally employed (where confidently identified) are given before metric equivalents. Marked asymmetry of the entry neck passage was apparent; the facing of the north side was an untidy mass of cement repairs that sloped noticeably with no sign of concavity.

A concavity in the south side is *c. 6.05* metres long (approximately twenty feet) and at least 4 metres high. Two vertical slots (Fig. 10) ran the full height of the concave reveal. An irregular pattern of sockets was also cut into the reveal (Fig. 8) near an inverted round pivot socket (now infilled with cement). Heavy masonry oversails the socket.   The bottom of the reveal is submerged.

On the north side, radiating blocks can be seen in the pavement over; clearly the remains of a similar arrangement.   It was concluded that the passage was originally narrower, the thickness of masonry removed in ?1893 was *c. 50* centimetres.

The author's uncorrected photographs of the Royal Society Archive drawings (Figs. 3-5) were compared and analysed in a CAD environment to create composite reconstruction plans (Figs. 9 & 10).

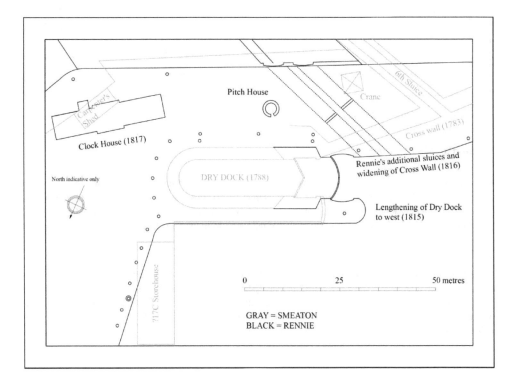

A developmental history

Fig 9. *Topographical relationship of the 1788 and 1815 Dry Docks (1872)*

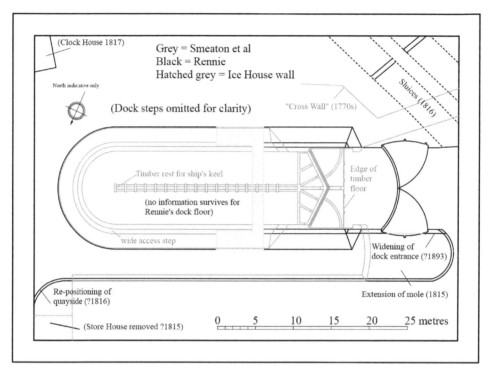

Fig 10. *Evolution of the Dry Dock (1788-2014).*

Smeaton's 1788 Dry Dock

The original Dry Dock was built with a narrow opening 31 feet wide (9.45 metres); a dimension that also set the width of the floor. The basin was 19 feet deep (5.79 metres) and 91.5 feet (27.88 metres) long, with straight sides 66 feet (20.11 metres) long. The east end of the dry dock was a precise semi-circle with stepped sides 10 feet (3.048 metres) in batter. There were 14 "steps" down; the fourth from the Dry Dock floor being 2 feet wide (0.61 metres) to allow workers to walk on it.

The gate consisted of two flat leaves which swung when open into reveals 19 feet long (5.78 metres). When closed, they met at an angle. The bases rested on heavily-braced timber beams in the floor. Grooves allowed the gates to run on wheels. Smeaton's method of dealing with the groundwater is unknown. Perhaps he devised a system for using water pressure to discharge the groundwater outside the Dry Dock. The 1783 plan (Fig. 3) hints at this, for the west end of the timber floor appears to be open to the sea (Fig. 10).

338

Rennie's reconstruction

We know from Rennie's reports (see above) that he rebuilt an existing pair of sluices adjacent to the Dock gate. Blocks, possibly of Craigleath stone, are skilfully run across one to the other, so that the sluice and Dry Dock entry neck appear to be contemporary.

The un-submerged parts of the dry dock appeared homogenous in detail and material. The steps were cut from a permeable yellow limestone; now suffering badly. The overall width of the floor was greater (approximately 10.57 metres) than its precursor (9.45 m). The anecdotal mention of recent damage to a timber floor (see above) illustrates that Rennie imitated Smeaton's floor. The present basin is 15.82 metres wide at pavement level, i.e. slightly greater than Smeaton's basin (15.60 metres wide).

Scans of the 1791 and 1822 maps were compared in a CAD environment; this allowed the two to be topographically related. This provided a surprise for rather than simply extending the dry dock to the east, Rennie had entered on a more radical solution.

He massively "thickened" the Cross Wall on both sides (its eighteenth-century precursor presumably survives deeply encased within the later work). An entirely new dock entry neck was built within the land thus reclaimed (Fig. 9). He also took the opportunity to remove the east wall of the Inner Basin, rebuilding it on an obtuse angle. This did away with the old "Storehouse". A "Carpenters' Shed" was also swept away to clear the site of the Clock House, and the south pier wall was rebuilt on a single alignment through which a pair of new sluices exited.

The position and action of Rennie's lost gates could be reconstructed in some detail (Fig. 10). Each formed a segment of a single arc, struck from a centre lying on the long axis of the Dry Dock. The significance of the vertical slots and the multiple sockets (Fig. 8) is unknown. Could there be some connection with Rennie's proposed "floating gates"?

Conclusions

No less than three attempts, the last successful, were required to build Smeaton's Dry Dock. Rennie's comprehensive rebuilding in 1815 extended the dock c.10.36 metres (an overall measurement) to the west. This is what we see today.

Smeaton cannot be held to blame for the failure of the first two attempts. He was pressurised by other work and was content to let less able men take a lead – with predictable results. His original design, when finally executed, worked well for twenty years. How he dealt with the groundwater problems was however a secret that died with him. The drawings in the Royal Society Archive were demonstrated to be different "states" of an evolutionary process.

Rennie's notebooks make little mention of the Dry Dock, for he was constantly exercised about the Cross Wall and other large concerns. We can now see that he took a hammer to what he found leaving not a single part of Smeaton's work. He set about altering Smeaton's Dry Dock (Fig. 9) by lengthening it westwards; the extant entry neck being built independently of the pre-existing entry neck. His original written proposal was therefore much less radical than his final solution. When the new entry neck was complete, the old entry neck and dry dock were removed.   This may have been a more practical course, for it allowed the new dock to be commenced while the old dock still functioned. The lengthened dry dock followed its predecessor in overall design, but was entirely new, with straight sides 10.95 metres longer. Smeaton clearly wrote "51 Feet" on his 1788 section (Fig. 5) and the extant dock is only 23 centimetres wider. It follows that the fall of the sides was sharper in the rebuilt dock, given its wider floor.

Rennie's rebuilt sluices with their joggled arches appear contemporary with the Dry Dock, but the notebooks record that these sluices were built in the following year. The implication is that Rennie built the east side of the adjacent sluice "in advance" as the first act in thickening the Cross Wall. The riverside end of the entry neck at Rennie's No. 3 Dock at Chatham was sealed by a floating chest called a caisson. Filled with water, it could rest on the bed of the river, but once pumped free of water, could be floated and re-positioned[45]. The peculiar slots and sockets in the concave reveals of the gate at Ramsgate hint at some such arrangement; this was short-lived, if it ever existed.   As far as we know, no pumping device was used at Ramsgate.

The Public Record Office and National Maritime Museum hold the records of the work at Chatham.[46] It is therefore possible that information relevant to Ramsgate remains to be found.

The construction of "Morton's Patent Slipways" (1838-9) marked the start of a 35-year decline in the Dry Dock's fortunes, although the Dock was still in full use as late as the 1870s. In 1893, his Dry Dock was put out of commission for good, being adapted to form an ice house for fishing. It had presented no problems during its eighty-year existence.

One can only hope that a new and happier era in the Dry Dock's history might yet hove into view. The Ramsgate dock was overlooked by past researchers, but can now rightfully take its place in the context of Rennie's career and the development of his ideas; brought to perfection at the Chatham Dry Dock.

Acknowledgments

The author would like to thank Reinier Steensma (waterfronts.nl) and Nick Dermott (Thanet District Council) for permission to re-use research originally carried out for the Yacht Valley Project, and for resourcing the first report[47], of which this is a substantial re-working. The Cervia Volunteer Crew allowed the Tug as a means of inspecting the Dry Dock; providing much useful information about its recent vicissitudes. The staff of the Royal Society Library allowed reproductions to be made by the author and Katherine Marshall waived reproduction charges and provided full archive references. Heather McNally of the Kent County Council Archive Service likewise waived reproduction charges of images made by the author. Carole Morgan at the Archive of the Institute of Civil Engineers provided facilities and advice. Michael Child and Ralph Hoult are to be thanked for allowing reproduction of images in their possession.

References

[1] J. Smeaton, *An Historical Report on Ramsgate Harb*our: written by *order, and delivered to the Trustees By John Smeaton. Civil Engineer FRS and Engineer to Ramsgate Harbour,* 2nd edn., London, 1791

[2] Institution of Civil Engineers Archive, REN/RB/01&09, *The Rennie Reports* 1790-1821, vols 8 and 9, (Vol. 8 mis-numbered '1')

[3] P. MacDougall, 'Granite and Lime: the building of Chatham Dockyard's first stone Dry Dock', *Cantiana* , vol. 107, 1989 (published 1990), pp 173-191.

[4] G. Moody, *The Isle of Thanet from Prehistory to the Norman Conquest*, Stroud, Tempus, 2008, fig.10.
5Ibid., chapter 2.

[6] Ibid., p.152.

[7] G. Milne, *The Port of Roman London*, London, Batsford, 1985, p. 92.

[8] W.H. Ireland, *Kent's Topographer. A New and Complete History of the Isle of Thanet*, London, Geo. Virtue, 1828-29 (2 vols) (Michael's Bookshop, Ramsgate, reprint ?2000, new pagination, p.105).

[9] J. Lewis, *The History and Antiquities, as well Ecclesiastical as Civil, of the Isle of Tenet*, in Kent,   London, sold by J. Osborn, 1736, 2nd edn., p.175.

[10] Ibid., p.176.

[11] C. Busson, *The Book of Ramsgate*, Buckingham, Barracuda Books, 1985, p. 21.

[12] Ibid.

[13] Ireland, *Thanet* 1828, p.106.

[14] Busson, *Ramsgate*, 1985, p.26 (original photograph held by Kent County Libraries – destroyed 2005?).

[15] Ibid., p.21.

[16] J. Smeaton, *An Historical Report on Ramsgate Harbour: written by order, and delivered to the Trustees By John Smeaton. Civil Engineer FRS and Engineer to Ramsgate Harbour*, 2nd edn., London, 1791, pp 60-70.

[17] Ibid., p.55.

[18] Smeaton, Report, 1791, p.55

[19] Ibid., p. 56.

[20] Ibid., p.59

[21] Ibid.

[22] Ibid.

[23] Royal Society Archive: 'Engineering Designs'. J. Smeaton FRS, vol. V, Fos 138-195 l.s. (XVI), 139v, (modern ref. JS/5/137), "Section of the Dock - The present Pavement – width at top 50 feet – [floor =] 31 feet"   [1787?]

[24] Smeaton, *An Historical Report*, pp 61-3.

[25] Ibid., p. 68

[26] Smeaton, *Report*, 1791, p.69.

[27] Smeaton, *Report,* 1791, p.86

[28] Ramsgate Local Studies Centre, "*Ramsgate*. Plate 77. Engraved by Storer from an original sketch by Mr Orme. [sic] Published April 1795 by J. Walker, No. 18 Rosaman's Street, London" April 1795.

[29] Smeaton, *Report*, 1791, "Plan of Ramsgate   Harbour".

[30] MacDougall, 'Granite and Lime...', p.176.

[31] Institution of Civil Engineers Archive, REN/RB/01&09, *The Rennie Reports* 1790-1821, vols 8 and 9, (Vol. 8 mis-numbered '1')

[32] Ibid., vol. 8; p. 120, (16 February   1815).

[33] Ibid., p. 317 (18 February 1816).

[34] Ibid., p. 401 (25 July   1816)

[35] Ibid., p. 423 (28 Nov 1816)

[36] Ibid., vol. 9, pp 143-4 (28 July 1817), .

[37] Ibid., p. 146 (1 August 1817)

[38] MacDougall, 'Granite and Lime...', p.181-2.

[39] R. Collard & G. Hurst, *Ramsgate, the Town and Royal Harbour* 1822, published by R. Collard, Broadstairs 1823, *c.* 1:33,000, (repr. Kent County Council, Supplies Department, West Malling)

[40] Ramsgate Local Studies Collection "*Ramsgate from Nelson Crescent*. Drawn from Nature and on Stone by G. Stowe. Published by G. Wooll, Hastings", c.1825., .

[41] *Illustrated London News* (22 June 1850), p. 441.

[42] Busson, *Ramsgate,* 1985, p.25

[43] Ramsgate Local Studies Collection , *Ramsgate Harbour,* Aerofilms, 1947.

[44] Michael Houckham (pers. comm.).

[45] MacDougall, 'Granite and Lime...', p.176.

[46] Public Record Office ADM 140/33-4; National Maritime Museum CHA/B/30.

[47] M.W. Samuel, *The "Ice House" Dry Dock, Ramsgate*: Historical and Archaeological Survey (NGR TR 383 647), 2014, for the Yacht Valley Project and Thanet District Council

Nineteenth Century

The First Wire-Nail machines & their origins

Chris How

Retired engineer, Australia

Abstract

This paper examines the manual processes that led to the first patents for wire nail-making machines. It introduces a recent discovery, backed by provenance and analysis, dating the first proper wire nail machine to 1816, some 30 years earlier than previously accepted. It shows how the assemblages, hence much of the technology that we enjoy today, are pre-eminently French, and dispels some of the myths that have accumulated in the accepted literature concerning wire nails.

The paper is based on research into the original patent dossiers from 1808 to 1825 held in Paris. As part of this analysis, errors relating to the so-called wire nail-making machine of James White of 1810 are identified. The paper shows how early reporting had distorted the inventor's own claims.

Introduction

The paper continues a series on nail history aimed at better understanding changes in nail morphology for use in dating buildings and artefacts. It follows an article published in the magazine of the Construction History Society in 2016, and some of this information is repeated in order to give context [1]. The paper traces the development of the manual processes that appear, first in 1761 in a work dealing with the manufacture of needles and pins, and then in further detail in the *Grande Encyclopédie*. Wire nails made by hand were briefly described in *L'Art de Menuiserie* in 1769 [2], and the relevant passages from both works have been translated into English. [3] For brevity, repetition of the translations is kept to a minimum within the article. Some technical developments relating to the first French wire nail-making machines, which have escaped previous analysis in English, are presented and explained here.

As it has proved difficult to obtain any samples of these early wire pin nails, it is hoped that this article will alert CHS members and conference delegates to look out for these small, unusual and easily ignored items.

The First Descriptions

The first mention of nails being made from wire occurs in *L'Art de l'Epinglier* (1761), which deals with needle and pin manufacture [4]. This is the least known of the French works on nails yet, in several ways, it sheds light on why the French persevered with wire nails when neighbouring countries apparently had no tradition in their use. Three eminent contributors took turns in the text to explain various aspects of technology, metallurgy, workshop practice, tools and the different usages relating to this apparently mundane subject. They were the famous scientist and metallurgical expert René Antoine Réaumur; the Minister for the Marine, botanist and agronomist Duhamel du Monceau; and lastly the renowned engineer and technical educator Jean-Rodolphe Perronet FRS, famous for his innovative Neuilly bridge design.

> Pin-nails are, in effect, short thick pins. The pin-makers make them from wire of iron and of brass. Their heads are made by being folding down at the extremities of the wires by use of a hammer. In size they run from one and a half inches (or even larger) down to one ligne [2.5mm]. [5]

The first reference to their being made in Paris was also made by Réaumur and this helps explain why the colloquial description, *'pointes de Paris'* (Paris points), was used in lieu of the more correct term, *'clous d'épingles'* (pin nails):

> As part of their normal work the pin makers of Paris also make a pin nail for the use of cabinet makers, joiners, and for the makers of fine linen coffers, etc.... These little nails are made of iron and brass.... Sculptors, makers of fine boxes, and sheath makers, use a better formed head pin-nail which is round.

In some places a fuller explanation was given than in the works that followed. Contrary to what Diderot was to write in the *Grande Encyclopédie*, the best-quality brass wire was deemed to be from Hamburg and was noted to be of a light-coloured brass. This was closely followed by three Swedish brands, which entered France through Rouen, and the text advises that the brass wire from Switzerland should be ignored. A comment by Perronet, the engineer, clarifies the reference made by Diderot that the best (or stiffest) wire came from Aachen (Aix-la-Chapelle) by a rider: *'in time of war the needle makers are often forced to use wire coming from Germany'*.

It is a surprise to learn that the needle and pin makers were aware of the strain-hardening effect caused by the wire drawing process. (Fig.1) Réaumur comments;

> In the better workshops, they always select thicker wire than is needed so as to provide a margin for re-drawing the wire through several holes of the draw plate, in order thus to get a stiffening effect.

Duhamel du Monceau, in his contribution, repeats this and refers to passing the bobbin through several holes of the draw plate to obtain extra stiffness in the wire.

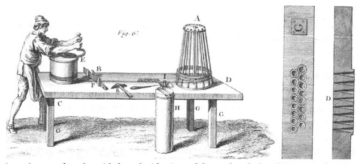

Fig. 1 Re-drawing wire on a beach , with face & side view of draw plate holes, Réaumur, plate I.

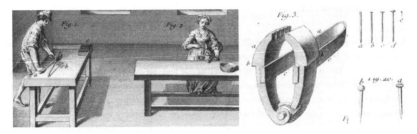

Fig. 2 Paris pin-nail workshop with cutting & heading benches. Gripper(mordant), and the different varieties of pin-nails. After Réaumur, plates V &VII.

The workshop scene shows shears on the cutting bench, with one arm fixed down to allow bundles of wire to be cut to length using only one hand, and next to it is the heading bench. (Fig. 2, left) A young woman is show forming flat heads to the pin-nails using just a flat-faced hammer. The gripper shown in the treatise has protruding lugs that allow it to sit in a quick release vice, and clearly shows the spring with which automatic opening and speed was achieved between heading operations. (Fig. 2, second image) The grooves in the gripper in which the pieces of wire were held to be headed are described as being dented towards their tops. Conical points were ground onto both ends of the cut wires before they were cut in half, to then be deposited as headless points in the felt tray shown on the second bench.

Plates V and VII include two sets of pin-nail illustrations. Accompanying the part of the text prepared by Réaumur are shown five variations of pin-nail. (Fig. 2, top right)

The production range of pin-nails comprises the first four items of the nail types shown. (Fig. 2, top right, labelled a, b, c & d on the original plate) These were:

(a)   Headless

(b)   Minimal head, made with a light strike of the hammer, and convenient for boot-makers

(c)   Flat heads – similar to modern tacks – whose heads were spread by a strong blow, as used in box making, and by
        sculptors and joiners

(d)   Rounded heads. These had to be formed by an initial hammer strike, followed by one using a punch with a
        semi-spherical bottom cavity. This formed a hollow domed head, likened to a skull cap. The best of the heads
        formed this way were favoured by certain sorts of high-quality coffer makers, some sculptors and the makers of
        sheaths for tools or weapons.

(e)   The last tiny nail shown was also used in the making of small sheaths.

The text adds:

> One can whiten, like as for needles, the iron nails and the brass ones, and one can brighten to a yellow the brass
> ones.

347

The process is described in the text:

> Some of the shanks are sold without heads, but most are supplied with a head, but not a rolled wire head as is the case for needles, but by a blow of the hammer instead and for which a special tool is required, called a gripper (mordant), fig 3. This is a little vice with two projecting side lugs 'bb' having a big spring 'cc'. On the thickened part of the teeth 'aa' it has some indented small grips at the upper end to catch the shank from slipping back when it is struck from above by the hammer in forming the head. One puts the gripper in a large vice, fig. 2, the ears sit onto the vice jaws, in loosening the screw the large vice also opens he gripper, it holds an offcut in one of the notches. With his right hand the operator sets a shank length which exceeds the jaw surface by a slight amount. He closes the big vice and takes with his right hand the hammer set on the table, and strikes a slight blow to the top of the shank projecting above the gripper, sufficient to form a small head 'b', fig. 4, which suits the cobblers. If the nails are for box-makers, or for joiners or sculptors, etc. he gives again a little blow, then a strong one; then he forms thus a flat head and a wider one than used by most cobblers. Whilst the left hand undoes the screw & loosens the vice, the right hand has taken an offcut & makes the headed nail drop loose, & substitutes in its place a fresh off-cut which he holds in his right hand. On the space he tightens the vice with his left hand & takes with the right the hammer which lies on the table, then he strikes the head and replaces the hammer on the table to take with the right hand a new off-cut.... But with respect to the nails he must make a head to each shank, which takes time.

The second image of two nails is in the section of the text that refers specifically to the making of wire screens, and these two types of nail were used to secure the ends of the wires woven into a frame [6]. (Fig. 2 bottom right) These screens were used in certain public buildings, such as libraries, and were often of brass wire. More prosaic screens were those used in mangers and for cleaning seed or cereals, when iron wire and iron pin-nails were used.

The Parisian master craftsman Roubo, in his magnum opus *L'Art de Menuisier*, uses only the term 'pin-nails' (*clous d'épingles*); and he endorses their suitability for high-quality joinery and furniture. They could be of iron, in which case they were tinned to avoid staining the timber, or they could be of brass:

> The joiners also use another type of nail, called pin-nails. These nails are made with brass wire in different lengths according to their thicknesses; their head is round or flat and is made cold. One finds these nails in all sorts of lengths, that is to say, from a quarter inch to two inches; they are very suitable for lining works. This sort of nail is sold in packets of 100; but those joiners who use them a lot buy them by the pound whereby there is greater profit [7].

In the later revision of the *Grande Encyclopédie* by Panckoucke, the *Encyclopédie Methodique* of 1786, the term 'pin-nails' was used also for a type of wrought pin [8]. (Fig. 3) His illustrations show a square pin with a pointed end, as well as the round wire version.

Fig. 3 clous d'épingles and square pin, after Panckoucke.

The Technical Train

Among those things mentioned in *L'Art de l'Epinglier* are the procedures that still govern wire nail production to this day:

- 'Dressing', or straightening wire fed off the supplied coils (Fig. 4)

- Cutting the wire and forming the pointed end

- Grasping the wire and then gripping it so that there is no movement during the head-forming process The various ways of forming serviceable heads

- The methods of releasing the jaws and freeing the finished nail.

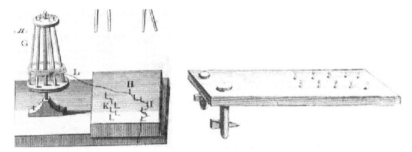

Fig. 4 Spool-feed and dressoir, after Réaumur(left); and dressoir, by Diderot(right).

Dressing

The process of dressing the wire is described in detail and illustrated by both Réaumur and Diderot. In the *Grande Encyclopédie* the feeder for the spools of wire is shown mounted on a post, whereas Réaumur shows it mounted at bench level. (Figs 4 & 5) The 'slalom' or staggering of the metal pins through which the wire is to pass is explained best in *L'Art de l'Epinglier* in the description by Réaumur:

> In passing through the first, second and third pin on the dresser it takes up a contrary curve to that with which it started. If it were to leave the dresser at this stage then one would find that it had taken up a curve in the opposite sense, or perhaps a little less, since the disposition of these parts to the original curve is not quite overcome in one instant. One overcomes this curve in leading it through between the fourth or fifth pass, and then finally through the last one, at which point the wire should be quite straight if the pins have been well set up. It is never easy to pre-determine this exact disposition since the wires are of different sizes and their spool radii changes also.

The *Grande Encyclopédie* describes the cutting and grinding process:

> The cutting bench (*banc à couper*) comprises a strong bench and a (fixed) large set of snips with one long handle and one short. The bench has edges to contain the bits of wire, with a measure for the length to be cut. Above all elsewhere there are edge borders, except for one side gap which serves to draw in the wire for the points. The tool is fixed in such a way as to cause the least fatigue to the person doing the cutting. [9]

Cutting the wire and forming the pointed end

A similar process is described in both *L'Art de l'Epinglier,* as seen in Figure 4 above, and the *Grande Encyclopédie*, which points to the pin-nails being ground on a steel grinding wheel. (Fig. 5)

Fig. 5 Grinding points and dressing the wire(left) and 'tabernacle'(right), after Réaumur,p1.II.

In the centre can be seen a wooden frame holding a glass plate set at an incline, which serves to stop the sparks, which continuously escape off the grinding wheel, from hitting the eyes of whoever is doing the grinding. The grindstone & equipment are shown in figs 11 & 12 and only the front of the bench which serves as a base is seen... in fig 5. [10]

Grinding wheel. The wheel connects to the grindstone by means of a cord which passes inside the throat crossing on its circumference, from there into a small pulley wheel on the axis of the grindstone. The grindstone is made of tempered steel, about three to five inches diameter and its circumference is coated with lime. This mill and its fittings are supported by small bearings of copper or of iron, located onto two small mounts or dollies by a half-circular base. This is fixed securely on a frame composed of two trestles and some planks which attach it. On this frame is a box which is termed a 'tabernacle'. [11]

Heading

Two types of heading devices are introduced by *L'Art de l'Epinglier* that may have only slight relevance to the production of pin-nails, except in respect of the very small ones noted above, but which re-emerge later in French patents. These are pedal controlled and allow a heavy weight to plummet a short distance to form pin or small nail heads. (Fig. 6)

Fig. 6 Headers of fixed weight, left, and variable concentric weights, right, after Réaumur, plates VII & V. Pin-nail hammer and punches, after Diderot.

A simple flat-faced hammer was used to produce the flat heads. For the domed heads, a punch or a small trussel (*poinçon à étamper*) was used after first initiating the set of the head by hammer. The type used for the pin-nailers differed to that which the French used in forging nails and had a rear-facing angle to the face. This presumably relates to the need to give a substantial square blow to the head when cold forging flat heads. (Fig. 6, third image) The punches included one to form a shallow-rise dome and a square heavy punch with a full-hemispherical bottom cavity. Forming the heads took time, as both these latter types had to be punched with the appropriate hand-die [12].

The French Nail-making Patents (Brevets d' invention)

The Revolution affected the normal patterns of life in France until Napoleon re-established order and identity in 1804. Within two years there was a flowering of innovative ideas that have continued ever since. However, in 1790 both Britain and the infant USA had developed pragmatic solutions to nail-making by machine, resulting in patents on both sides of the Atlantic.

The patent dossiers show that between 1806 and 1825 seven wire-nail making patents were issued, some of which have amendments to the original designs under a subsequent patent number. However, with two of them it is first necessary to weed out the factoidal information that has accrued since, often abased by incorrect reporting in early times.

Japy Brothers, Colmar, award of 1806 (1BA344)

The dossier for the ingenious Japy Brothers' patent of 1806 for a screw-making lathe included a disingenuous claim that it could also produce pin-nails. Each screw was given a machined conical point and so, although the claim might be true, each pin-nail would have had to be hand machined and take longer to make than by manual means. The patent examiner noted in the dossier that the applicant, Louis Japy, was well aware of how the process depended on the wire being of particularly high quality, which would have added to the already inflated costs for pin-nails made this way [13].

James White, Paris, award of 1810 (1BA611)

An American, James White, made one application on 7 September 1810, followed by a subsequent application and separate drawing on 27 November of the same year [14]. The initial application included a single pencil drawing showing eight devices, which he described in his application as:

> Descriptive Memoir; for several machines intended to facilitate the accepted methods more rapidly to form the shanks and to forge nail heads.

The first five drawings show a variety of cutting, cold-heading, threading and planishing devices. But it is the next group that has been the most misreported. (Fig. 7) In this group, a device is shown with a handle that reverses the slant of the cutting blade in order to cut tapering slivers of iron. This suggests that it was restricted to thin plate and hence could only produce small nails. (Fig. 7, left) There is a strong possibility that the nails were required for provision boxes for the *Grande Armee*.

The First Wire-Nail machines & their origins

The following two images show a magazine carousel that had radiating expanding grooves. (Fig. 7) A nail plate can be seen in both of the first two images, the second showing outlines of cut iron slivers. Two cut slivers (shaded grey) are shown on the magazine plate. James White described these as being loaded into position by children (*des petits*). The heading and pointing of the sliver ends were described as being done in one action and a following drawing shows the magazine loaded in a vertical plane on the heading device.

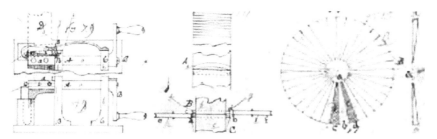

Fig. 7 Side and plan view of iron-ribbon cutter, first image; nail plate centre image, top; and cut-nail disc magazine, third image. Brevet dossier 1BA 611

This group of drawings includes a waffle-plate clutch to be fitted on the same axle, and with it is a selector gear to rotate the magazine one slot at a time. A trip-operated die-hammer would form the heads and the trip would advance the selector one notch at each descent of the hammer, such that heading took place at top dead centre. A foot treadle fitted to a sturdy wooden-framed holding device was used to hold the magazine securely for each blow of the hammer.

These devices are conventionally quoted as being for the heading and pointing of pin-nails (as in wire nails), but it is clear from the drawings that they were cut nails – cutting being the nail-making method most favoured by the Americans.

In November of 1810 the descriptive memoire for the second application by White reads:

> of a method of cutting rolled iron to serve as nails in a method which Monsieur James White wishes to join with his application of tenth of September last for the which he has requested a patent.

This application, which is mostly legible, reveals a conventional sliding journal assembly in two main parts, oscillated by an eccentric working through a slotted hole. The off-cut sliver is shown held by a special cavity of appropriate depth, which was transported laterally to be headed. It was an ingenious solution, nevertheless it trailed behind those of his contemporary countrymen such as Perkins and Dyer. One of the drawbacks to the device would have been wear in the driving parts.

The reporting of James White's application was covered by several publications in precis form, and these publications mostly adopt the standard wording of the *Bulletin*, each in two separate but successive entries;

> he receive a patent for 15 years for a machine intended to make pin-nails and wrought nails. [15, 16, 17]

This entry is immediately followed by:

> in accord with his request for a certificate of improvement to his patent of 4 March 1811.

The précised form starts the slide to further incorrect reporting, which might be attributed either to James White himself or to his patent agents, since the second cut-nail machine functioned on different principles to the earlier devices, which might best be described as manual aids to production. This description of these aids, *'to facilitate the accepted methods more rapidly'*, is exactly what James himself wrote in his application descriptive memoire. The pragmatism of conjoining the two very different approaches must have been compelling.

However, a third departure from the proper description was then made by the *Chronological Dictionary of Discoveries* in September 1824, in which the reporter is carried away by a jumble of facts and what could be termed hyperbole:

> This machine, for which the inventor has obtained a patent for 15 years, and sometime after, an award of improvement, produces around 100 nails per minute. The small nails, called pin-nails, are made cold, and large ones made when hot. These nails show a perfection which is impossible to tell from forged nails: their points are so fine that a simple thumb pressure suffices to hold them in the wood. Children's hands suffice to feed the machine and it is only necessary to feed the iron ribbon from which the nails are cut. The head of these nails is made by a successive blow following separation of the shank from the rolled band of which the breadth is pre-calculated according to the nail size. The advantage of this invention lies in the constant mobility of action of the two pieces comprising the cutters; the first of these stops once having operated, as the second piece advances with the cut-off shank to uncover the end part destined to become the head, which is formed with a second blow. Should we receive more details of this machine they will be published in our annual dictionary. [18]

To what extent the term 'pin-nails' was used for a forged item still remains conjecture. The stated output can only relate to instantaneous, and not sustainable, production. Likewise, shearing always leaves its signature on a cut nail and this claim can be discounted. It seems that the description is based on the second submission, and the substance of the passage was repeated in a major work of 1912, and has become accepted knowledge ever since [19].

François Daguet, patent number 713, 16 July 1816 (1BA632)

This invention deserves to be acknowledged as the first true wire-nail making machine. It is remarkable in that it anticipated steps in production that were to last as long as iron wire nails were in existence:

- It established a square grip to the neck
- It used teeth indentations to reinforce the grip during heading
- It established facet points in lieu of conical ones
- The dressing marks show that the wire was straightened by the same methods as were to continue for the next 90 years (essentially little different to the pin-nail workshop dressoir described by Diderot).

In other ways, too, the invention is a breakthrough in converting wheel drive, fly wheels, gearing and lever activation. It is remarkable that the inventor has been essentially bypassed in the history of technology, and that the introduction of these features has gone unnoticed in the field of nail-making.

Verification of these aspects came from a conservator of musical instruments in Melbourne. While restoring a French horn musical instrument case he found that the maker, Courtois Neveu Aisne, had resided at Rue des Vieux Augustins in Paris between 1816 and 1825. The case used early wire nails for fixing hinges and corner plates. All of the nails had been clenched, but several had broken-off heads. The close dates, Paris address, and the early style of instrument confirm that the wire nails came from the Daguet machine [20]. A headless sample was supplied to the author for cleaning and analysis: (Fig. 8)

Fig. 8 Instrument case, c.1818. Photo: Jerome Deakin. Pin-nail magnified x 10. Author.

Daguet described the machine as executing the process in five principle movements:

1. Loading-in the wire

2. Cutting the wire to length and pointing the end

3. Gripping the nail shanks

4. Striking the head

5. Releasing the finished nail from the jaws.

He then describes each of these functions of the machine in some detail.

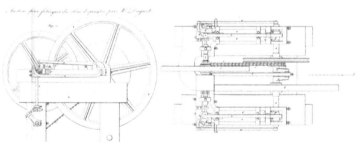

Fig. 9 The Daguet machine of 1816. Plate 18, patent 713, 'Descriptions des machines—dans les brevets d' invention Vol. 9. Issues 614—814, 1824'

The Daguet design made clever use of advancing cogs, slides and transfer arms to achieve the fabrication process, and it first introduced the concept of facetted points to wire pin-nails [21].

Maillot of Lyon, patent, 1821 (1BA1597)

This was a light device mounted on a wooden bench and driven by a simple toothed wheel. The feed wire ran through a fixed anvil and was severed and headed by a striker. It may have been hand or whim driven and have worked well for light gauge wire, but it is doubtful that it could cut iron wire of greater than 2mm diameter. [22]

Laroche & Monier of Marseille patents, 1821/23 (1BA1615)

The machine sat on a wooden bench with cut-outs for gear wheels. It was of the order of 18 inches (450mm) wide, 3 feet 2 inches (950mm) long, and the header mast rose a total of 3 feet (900 mm) above the bench. From this we can assume that it was capable of making medium-gauge pin-nails, say, typically 1¼ inches (40mm) long.

The dossier shows two stages of development, with a change to a plummet heading device reminiscent of Réaumur's images. The device worked through a chain drive connection and meshed gear wheels, and the points of the pin-nails were turned to give a conical point [23].

Chevenier & Company of Lyon patent, 1823 (1BA1700)

This machine was larger and more robust than the Maillot or Laroche machines, but it essentially comprised an aide to manual production, with wire cutters worked by a handle, and it included a foot pedal to activate the heading tool [24].

Bruyset of Lyon patent, 1825 (1BA451)

This comprised a complete-product wire nail-making machine which had the advantage of being self-loading from off a spool. It included a set of pins for dressing the wire straight. After pointing and cutting to length, a holding box was shifted laterally to lie plumb with the header. This may have been the first machine to incorporate automatic dressing of wire [25].

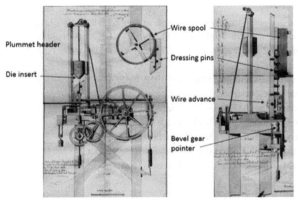

Fig. 10 The Bruyset machine of 1825, notations by author. Brevet dossier 1BA 451

Conclusion

In the progression towards mechanical production, the ergonomics of manual production of pin-nails were followed in an irregular series, but the various elements remained much the same. With the widespread locations of different inventors, a melange of manually assisted machines was inevitable as adaptions were made to suit local conditions. There was a reluctance to abandon the concept of conical points to pin nails, which in retrospect is difficult to understand. All the devices shown would have had the ability to produce pin-nails suitable for softwood boxes and for lathing, for which there was a large demand, and they can therefore be considered commercial successes.

References

[] C. How. 'An Historical Look at English Roofing Nails', *Magazine of the Construction History Society*, vol. 1 (Aug) 2016, Cambridge.

[2] J. Roubo, *L'Art de Menuisier* (réimpression de l'édition de 1769–75, 4 vols), ed. Léonce Laget, Paris: L'Academie Royale des Sciences, 1976 (1769). P.259, pl. 98.

[3] C. How, *Historic French Nails & Fixings,* Warrnambool: Furniture History Society of Australasia, 2017. pp.39-48.

[4] R. E. Réaumur, *L'Art de l'Epinglier,* Paris: Saillant et Nyon, 1761. Pp.53, 72, pls V & VII.

[5] Réaumur, *L'Art de l'Epinglier.*

[6] Réaumur, *L'Art de l'Epinglier.*

[7] J. Roubo, *L'Art de Menuisier.*

[8] C.-H. Panckoucke, *Encyclopédie Méthodique,* Liège: Plomteux, 1782. Pl. VIII.

[9] D. Diderot, *L'Encyclopédie: Ou, Dictionnaire Raisonné des Sciences, des Arts et des Métiers par une Société de Gens de Lettres,* Paris: Briasson et al., 1769. Vol. 3, p.137, pl. I.

[10] D. Diderot, *L'Encyclopédie.*

[11] D. Diderot, *L'Encyclopédie.*

[12] D. Diderot, *L'Encyclopédie.*

[13] http://bases-brevets19e.inpi.fr/ File 1BA344 (accessed November 2017).

[14] http://bases-brevets19e.inpi.fr/ File 1BA611 (accessed November 2017).

[15] *Bulletin des Lois de l'Empire Français,* 4ieme Serie, Paris: Imprimerie Imperiale, 1811. Vol. 4, July, pp.342–78.

[16] *Journal des Mines,* 2nd semestre, Paris: Bossanges et Masson, 1811. Vol. 13, p.449.

[17] *Annules Forestiers,* Paris: Arthus-Bertrand, 1811, vols XXXIII–XLIV. P.343.

[18] *Dictionnaire Chronologiques et Raisonees des Déscouvertes* 1789–1820, Paris: Louis Colas. Vol. 16, pp.270–71.

[19] C. Frémont, *Le Clou,* Paris: Philippe Renouard, 1912. P.35.

[20] J. Deakin. Personal correspondence, June 2017

[21] http://bases-brevets19e.inpi.fr/ File 1BA632 (accessed November 2017).

[22] http://bases-brevets19e.inpi.fr/ File 1BA1597 (accessed November 2017).

[23] http://bases-brevets19e.inpi.fr/ File 1BA1615 (accessed November 2017).

[24] http://bases-brevets19e.inpi.fr/ File 1BA1700 (accessed November 2017).

[25] http://bases-brevets19e.inpi.fr/ File 1BA451 (accessed November 2017).

Cells and *Epines-Contreforts* for a New Kind of Vaulted Roofing:

The Church of Saint-Jean-de-Montmartre in Paris

Beatrice Lampariello

Theory and History of Architecture Laboratory 3 (Lth3), École Polytechnique Fédérale de Lausanne (EPFL), Switzerland

Introduction

In the second half of the nineteenth century cisterns and tanks began to be constructed in the form of shells covered by depressed vaults, using a mixed system of metal and concrete to ensure a fire-resistant and waterproof structure that was quick and cheap to build. This led at the end of the century to a spread in the use of slender vaulted roofing made out of concrete reinforced in various ways for industrial buildings, public buildings and monuments. Many structures were built, patents applied for, studies and research carried out, sometimes with the aid of tests of tensile strength, with the aim of clarifying theoretical aspects, the composition of the material, the configuration of the structures and the modes of their construction. Mathias Koenen, Paul Christophe and Emil Mörsch played a crucial role in the development of the early methods of calculation. While Joseph Monier, François and Edmond Coignet, Jean Bordenave, Thaddeus Hyatt, Ernest Leslie Ransome, Alexander Matrai, Aimé Bonna, Josef Melan, Franz Habrich, Gustav Adolf Wayss, the brothers René, Henri and Marcel Demay and François Hennebique were just some of the engineers, entrepreneurs and inventors who were involved in perfecting vaulted roofing made of concrete reinforced in various ways.

It was in this context that the French engineer Paul Cottancin (1865-1928) proposed a system of construction with metal, concrete and bricks, known as *ciment armé* from the late 1880s, when the first small-scale works were realized and a patent filed for the configuration of the metal reinforcements,[1] until the beginning of the twentieth century with the construction of the roofing of important buildings and the invention of a method that aimed to reduce the amount of centring.[2] *Ciment armé* differed from contemporary proposals in a variety of ways, all of them designed to produce structures capable of integrating other functions and ranging from the composition of the material to the configuration of the structures themselves. The metal reinforcements were made out of wire interlaced to form a regular mesh without a break, to be combined with fragments of any shape and size, bars and tubes.[3] The concrete was reduced to the role of a stiffening and protective material, with a composition that would allow it to engulf the mesh perfectly: a fat mortar, with no gravel and a high proportion of cement. Not coincidentally one of the ways in which Cottancin chose to describe his *ciment armé* was as a *construction métallique petrifiée* ("petrified metal construction").[4] Metal reinforcements and concrete were combined with perforated bricks to obtain a construction that on the one hand harked back to the tradition of masonry and on the other generated structures with functional cavities. Cottancin's studies led him to propose a construction method that no longer relied on casting the concrete on site, but on the assembly of pieces connected by bars fitted with screws so that they could be tensioned and installed by means of tie beams anchored in the wall or fixed to a temporary wooden structure.[5]

Cells and Epines-Contreforts for a New Kind of Vaulted Roofing:
The Church of Saint-Jean-de-Montmartre in Paris

The most important applications of *ciment armé* in the construction of vaulted roofing were developed at the end of the century together with the architect Anatole de Baudot (1834-1915). Cottancin contacted him at the beginning of the 1890s and they worked together on several buildings, the most outstanding of which was the church of Saint-Jean-de-Montmartre in Paris.

Cottancin vs Hennebique

The story of the church began in the first half of the 1890s, when the archbishopric of Paris staged a competition for the construction of a church on an irregular and sloping plot in Rue des Abbesses, recently acquired by the parish priest of the church of Saint-Pierre de Montmartre, Father Sobaux.[6] This was the first occasion for a confrontation between two of the main protagonists in the process of development of the mixed metal and concrete system, against the backdrop of a rivalry that was destined to grow ever fiercer: Cottancin and Hennebique. In fact the design that won the competition was the one by the architect Edouard Bérard (1843-1912) for a church with a nave and two aisles and a reinforced-concrete structure. Two proposals for the project are known to us:[7] in a submission signed by Bérard, the roofing took the form of a single pointed vault with a regular arrangement of beams and pillars that covered smooth vaults. In the basement, the vaults were turned into horizontal structures to be used instead of the traditional slabs and with functional cavities for the passage of conduits. (Fig. 1)

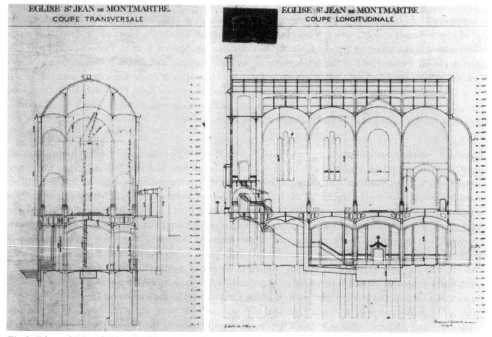

Fig 1. Edouard Bérard, Church of Saint-Jean-de-Montmartre, Paris. Sections (Simonnet 2005, p.132)

In another submission dated 1896 and signed by Hennebique, a trussed roof with a different arrangement of beams, pillars and tie beams was used to cover ribbed vaults. In this case illumination was provided by windows set in the sides of the church or by skylights in the roofing, chosen to avoid revealing the reduced thickness of the reinforced-concrete walls – the skylight could also assume a spherical shape and was located above the altar. (Fig. 2)

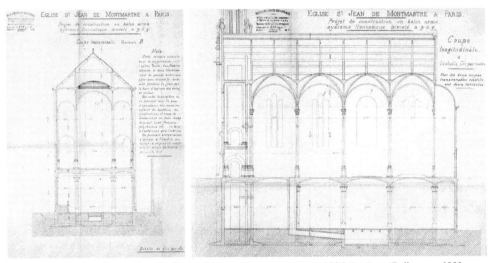

Fig 2. Francois Hennebique, Church of Saint-Jean-de-Montmartre, Paris, 1896. Sections (Delhumeau 1992, pp.20-1)

De Baudot and Cottancin's design envisaged a building with a similar layout of a nave and two aisles, with widths of 11.50 and 4.25 metres respectively. (Fig. 3) The roofing did not consist of a diversified superimposition of vaults and roofs, as in the solutions proposed by Bérard and Hennebique, but a single closure. The nave was in fact covered by three vaults of octagonal shape, with a central oculus protected by a cupola, and a rectangular cloved vault. The galleries were closed instead by similar cloved vaults and a flat roof. All the vaults were made up of cells and ribs, in keeping with a concept that Cottancin had started to develop between 1889 and 1890 with the objective of covering ever larger spans without increasing the thickness of the roofing. The vaulting cells consisted of two slender structures set one on top of the other and separated by a cavity to increase the strength of the roofing and create an insulation gap. The ribs, referred to variously in 1890 *as épines, contreforts and contreforts-épines,*[8] would instead be described *as épines-contreforts rationnelles* ("rational stiffening spines") from 1896 onward[9] to stress the fact that their new configuration with a T-profile and rounded edges, proposed in a patent, was efficient from the structural viewpoint and made construction easier and quicker. These ribs constituted the crucial detail of Cottancin's system for several reasons: structural, they ensured the static equilibrium of roofing on a large scale; they provided aid during construction, as they also functioned as supports for the centring of the vaulting cells; and decorative ones. In fact the ribs were interlaced in geometric patterns similar to those of Gothic ceilings. In its effort to represent the French tradition of construction that Eugène Emmanuel Viollet-le-Duc had identified with the Gothic during the nineteenth century, de Baudot and Cottancin's project succeeded in expressing the style that architects were trying so hard to find. But the distinctive nature of construction in *ciment armé* bestowed an unprecedented character on this style, that of a monolith hidden in the structure of buildings of traditional appearance. And *monolithe* was indeed the word de Baudot used to describe the church, once its construction was complete.[10]

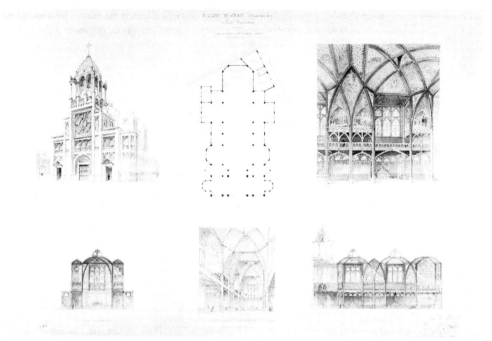

Fig 3. Anatole de Baudot, Paul Cottancin, Church of Saint-Jean-de-Montmartre, Paris,1894-1904. Project drawings (Dumont, Ramat 1996; p.47)

The choice of de Baudot and Cottancin's design over that of Bérard and Hennebique was probably due to the economies provided by the construction system they proposed. Thanks to its particular composition, in fact, *ciment armé* permitted more slender structures, using a smaller quantity of concrete and no gravel. The reinforcing bars, while greater in number, had the smaller cross-section of wire.

> "*Ciment armé* should not be confused with *béton armé* [reinforced concrete]", explained de Baudot. "These two methods are based on the same scientific data, that is to say on the surprising fact that iron is better preserved in mortars made from sand or pebbles and a greater or lesser amount of cement. What differentiates them are the proportions of the mix and the method of reinforcement with metal bars. In addition, pebbles and sand are used for *béton armé*, while only sand is used for *ciment armé*; as a result, the thickness of the components is very different; for *béton* this is variable; for *ciment* it is, as it were, fixed and greatly reduced in comparison, thanks to the much superior strength of the metal reinforcements and the mix adopted in the latter case".[11]

Construction

The construction of the church to de Baudot and Cottancin's design began in 1897 with the crypt, but was already put on hold in 1899, only to recommence with regularity in 1901 and be concluded in 1904.[12] The long lead times were the result of difficulties in funding, errors in the bureaucratic procedure and doubts over the slender structure developed by Cottancin.[13] It was in fact solely owing to the experience he had gained in projects and on construction sites since the 1880s that Cottancin was able to determine the thicknesses, dimensions and details of the structures. It was a form of empirical know-how not so distant from the kind that had been used to build Gothic cathedrals during the Middle Ages. Cottancin did no structural calculation, and would never do so for any of his other projects. Partly as a result of the collapse of a cantilever roof built with the Matrai system for the Paris Universal Exhibition of 1900, however, it became necessary to regulate and control construction with the recently adopted mixed metal and concrete systems. And so, in order to check the stability of the church's structure, the Conseil Général des Bâtiments Civils and the Conseil Général des Travaux d'Architecture de la Ville required inspections of the building site to be carried out, with an analysis conducted by three architects, Émile Trélat, Eugène Train and Émile Vaudremer. De Baudot and Cottancin requested instead an intervention by the general inspector of the Ponts et Chaussées, Cyrille Boutillier. "From above the nearby houses, from the dominant crest of the church, the wind, the storm, hurricane, the cyclone will come. What is going to happen?" asked the report on the church.[14] Thus, at the end of the inspection, the church, owing to its "extreme precariousness" and "worrying appearance", would be subjected to load tests to check its stability. The lack of any structural calculation and the reliance on experience alone for the stability of buildings would lead to the failure of Cottancin's system in 1906. The French government circular of 20 October signed by the Minister of Public Works, Louis Barthou, on the use of reinforced concrete[15] made it a requirement that the calculations of strength which Cottancin had never been able to provide be carried out for any work.

> "If the rapporteur had seen Cottancin's ciment armé being made ... he would have understood what degree of confidence an architect can reach after many years of experience and results", explained de Baudot. "He would have understood that, independently of a method of calculation supposedly as reliable as the one applied to iron, one could, just as the architects of our great cathedrals did, ... proceed to a certain extent by empiricism and claim absolute safety".[16]

In confirmation of the difficulties encountered during the construction of the church, Cottancin would be dismissed and his place taken by Gustave Degaine (1866-1928), an employee of and later a partner in Cottancin's construction firm, he was to found one of his own in 1899. In the same manner and around the same time, following the failure of the pillars in the crypt of Oran Cathedral built out of *ciment armé*, the Perret brothers would be called on to replace Cottancin.

Every structural detail and all the different stages in the construction of the church vaults in Paris were designed to meet the objective of leaving visible, on the inside, the lower surface of the *épines-contreforts* in continuity with the pillars and of emphasizing, on the outside, their upper surface. (Fig. 4) The decision to leave the *épines* visible, along with the need to build two cells separated by a space to be filled with *béton de mâchefer pilonné* ("pounded clinker concrete")[17] entailed a series of special construction based solutions. Prefabrication, a process for which Cottancin had taken out a number of patents during the 1890s,[18] was combined with complex operations of an artisan character carried out on site for the interlacing of the metal mesh, the casting of the concrete and the laying of the bricks.

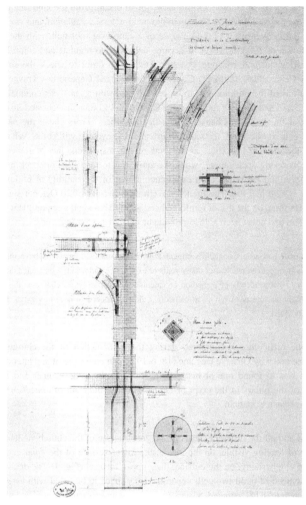

Fig 4. Anatole de Baudot, Paul Cottancin, Church of Saint-Jean-de-Montmartre, Paris,1894-1904. Structural details (Dumont, Ramat 1996; p.48)

The *épines* were made on the ground and their configuration varied in relation to their position. (Fig. 5) The ones at the base of the vaults consisted of a concrete slab reinforced with pieces of wire and, along its edges, long and narrow bricks – the space between the bricks was filled with clinker.[19] The connection between these *épines* and the pillars, built of reinforced brick masonry, was made with pieces of wire. The *épines* along the cells consisted instead of two concrete ribs with a rectangular cross-section, each 7 centimetres thick and separated by a gap of 22 centimetres, reinforced with bars bound together with pieces of wire interlaced in an orthogonal mesh. From the *épines* of the base and the ones on the vaults, long pieces of wire branched off that were knotted in turn around other bars added on the upper surface of the *épines* themselves and left protruding. The peculiar composition of the *épines* was established in the earliest publications devoted to this system of construction used for the church, in which the ribs were sometimes described as made of *briques armées* ("reinforced bricks") and at others as built of *ciment armé*.[20]

The cells, which were 7 centimetres thick, were not homogeneous structures because their metal mesh was reinforced by flat bars, arranged diagonally, these were added to the *épines* to provide an invisible stiffening and bracing of the ribs. *Barres auxiliaires* was the definition Cottancin had used for these reinforcements in a patent he filed in 1890 relating to the configuration of the metal mesh.[21] In confirmation of their role as an additional reinforcement, other pieces of wire similar to the ones sticking out of the *épines* were knotted around these *barres auxiliaires*.

The construction of the vaults was organized around the *épines*, which therefore represented at once the essential element of stiffening and stability of the vault and the structure of the centring for the realization of the cells.

Fig 5. Anatole de Baudot, Paul Cottancin, Church of Saint-Jean-de-Montmartre, Paris,1894-1904. The construction of the vaults (Dumont 1992, p.36)

The *épines* at the base of the vaults were installed first, and then the ones along the cells, mounted on site with the aid of a temporary wooden structure. The fundamental role of the metal mesh in Cottancin's system is confirmed by the fact that the pieces of wire used to reinforce the concrete also served as the connections for the temporary structure, instead of the more common hemp ropes, tarred or covered with copper.[22] Wooden boards were set between the *épines*, and then the *barres auxiliaires* and the metal mesh, for the construction of the lower cells. The pieces of wire resting on the boards were connected to the ones knotted around the *barres auxiliaires* and the ones that stuck out from the *épines* in order to create the most homogeneous and extensive metal lattice possible and then embedded in the concrete.

For the construction of the upper cells, the pieces of wire protruding from the *épines* and *barres auxiliaires* were made to pass through a series of superimposed bricks.[23] (Fig. 6)

Fig 6. Anatole de Baudot, Paul Cottancin, Church of Saint-Jean-de-Montmartre, Paris, 1894-1904. The construction of the vaults (Berger, Guillerme 1902, p.847; H. Chaine 1905, no. 6, p.47)

From the section drawings, it appears that other bars were laid on top of the bricks and the protruding reinforcements knotted around them.[24] Incisions were made on the upper surface of the lower cells, along the springers, where the slope was greater. They took the form of more or less parallel strips to facilitate the installation of the "clinker concrete", which performed the dual role of an insulation layer and support for the construction of the upper cell. The various operations required for the construction of the cells on top of this layer were carried out at different times, depending on the position of the cells themselves in the roofing. The aim was to obtain an upper surface that would not be smooth and continuous, but have the *épines* in relief. The largest cells were realized first, until the upper surface of the two ribs that made up each *épine* had been covered. Only then did the builders move on to the cells above the small sectors comprised between these two ribs, in such a way as to make the geometric patterns that run along the lower surface evident on the roofing too.[25] On these sectors, therefore, an additional layer of "clinker" was added to bring them up to the same level as the upper surface of the adjoining cells, then the usual mesh, and finally the concrete was poured. The entire lower surface of the roofing was given a coating of plaster with decorations of a small size, painted by F. Aubert. (Fig. 7)

Fig 7. Anatole de Baudot, Paul Cottancin, Church of Saint-Jean-de-Montmartre, Paris,1894-1904. The upper and the lower surface of the vaults (E. Chaine 1905, no. 29, p.340; Boileau 1905,no.51, plate 72)

At the end of the construction process, the need for further checks on the actual stability of the structure after the analysis carried out while the work was in progress entailed the execution of new load tests with a 60-centimetre-thick layer of sand spread over an area of 12 x 12 metres, with a weight of 700 kilos per square metre. The results, measured after three weeks, showed a flexure of 2 millimetres.[26]

Conclusions

With the church of Saint-Jean-de-Montmartre, the traditional freestone vault of Gothic derivation became a combination of ribs and slender cells that gave nothing away with regard to its weight, its static function or even the transmission of thrusts and forces. Thanks to *ciment armé*, that vault had now attained an ideal dematerialization, taking on a different consistency from that of traditional figures while retaining their appearance and even their mystical intensity. Thus, while *ciment armé* replicated the traditional forms, it was the material itself that undermined the original value of those figures, turning them into simulacra.

As soon as the work was complete, the extreme thinness of the vaults and every other structural element of the church, viewed as a monument whose sheer mass was intended to ensure its persistence in time, became the subject of a fierce debate that was followed closely in magazines of architecture and the bulletins of the Union Syndicale des Architectes Français. "The Folly of the Century", a "shed" or "too slight a building" with no "flesh" on it were some of the criticisms levelled against the church.[27]

> "If rational construction in reinforced concrete were to be adopted, I fear that we must say goodbye to monumental architecture, that is to say architecture that suggests to the mind it is going to last forever", a reader wrote to the magazine *La construction moderne* for example. "... The church of Saint-Jean de Montmartre reminds me much more of a piece of furniture than of a monument, and for that reason gives me the impression of a temporary shed rather than a building constructed to last for centuries".[28]

Le Corbusier would also criticize the church, which he considered so "hideous" that it had prevented him from perceiving the potentialities of Cottancin's invention.[29]

The use of *ciment armé* for the construction of vaults did not just challenge the configuration of traditional roofing but was destined to result in a "complete overturning" of all certainty. Even the terms commonly used to describe masonry vaults and their various parts no longer seemed correct.

> "Can we call vaults upper caps so thin that, far from thrusting against the thin walls, ... they are instead absolutely one of a piece with them as if the whole thing were just an object made of cast-iron or porcelain?" asked Henri Chaine in an article on the church.[30]

The mixed metal and concrete system had now disrupted every aspect of the traditional figures, to the point where at the beginning of the twentieth century, engineers and architects had already started to propose other definitions capable of reflecting the new consistency of the vaults: "dome shell", for example, was the description used for the roofing of a chapel built at Annapolis in 1905.[31]

Reference

[1] P. Cottancin, *Notice sur la parfaite construction moderne,* Paris: n.d.; P. Cottancin, *Procédé de fabrication d'ossatures métalliques sans attaches et à réseau continu*, FR Patent, no.196773, 18 Mar. 1889.

[2] G. Lavergne, 'Les travaux en ciment avec ossature métallique', *Le génie civil,* vol.XXVI, no.648, 10 Nov. 1894, pp.23-6; G. Lavergne, 'Constructions en ciment armé', *Le génie civil,* vol.XXX, no.857, 12 Nov. 1898, pp.22-4; G. Lavergne, *Etude des divers systèmes de constructions en ciment armé,* Liège: Librairie Polytechnique Ch. Béranger, 1901; C. Berger, V. Guillerme, *La construction en ciment armé: Applications générales, théories et systèmes divers,* Paris: Dunod, 1902, pp.801-54; E. Procida, 'Paul Cottancin, ingénieur, inventeur et constructeur' pp.597-607 in R. Carvais, A. Guillerme, V. Nègre, J. Sakarovitch (Eds), *Edifice et artifice. Histoires constructives: Recueil de textes issus du Premier Congrès Francophone d'Histoire de la Construction,* Paris: Picard, 2010.

[3] P. Cottancin, *Travaux en matières plastiques avec ossature composée,* FR Patent, no.210293, 18 Dec. 1890.

[4] P. Cottancin, 'Expériences du plus haut intérêt pour le Ciment Armé', in Cottancin, *Notice sur la parfaite construction moderne,* (Note 1) (pp.28-32), p.31.

[5] P. Cottancin, *Construction armée sans cintrage,* FR Patent, no.305778, 7 Nov. 1900.

[6] F. Boudon, 'Recherche sur la pensée et l'œuvre d'Anatole de Baudot, 1834-1915', *Architecture, mouvement, continuité,* no.28, Mar. 1973, (pp.2-67), pp.42-8; M.-J. Dumont, 'La pietra filosofale: Anatole de Baudot e i razionalisti francesi', *Rassegna,* vol.XIV, no.49, Mar. 1992, pp.36-43; M.-J. Dumont, 'Fortuna di un precursore', *Rassegna,* vol.XVIII, no.68, 1996, pp.6-13; M.-J. Dumont, M. Ramat (Eds), 'Chiesa di Saint-Jean-Baptiste de Montmartre, Parigi, 1894-1904', *Rassegna,* vol.XVIII, no.68, 1996, pp.46-9.

[7] G. Delhumeau, 'Hennebique e la costruzione in calcestruzzo armato intorno al 1900', *Rassegna,* vol.XIV, no.49, Mar. 1992, pp.15-25; C. Simonnet, *Le béton, histoire d'un matériau: Economie, technique, architecture,* Paris: Parenthèses, 2005.

[8] Cottancin, *Travaux en matières plastiques avec ossature composée,* (Note 3).

[9] P. Cottancin, *Fabrication de l'épine-contrefort rationnelle,* FR Patent, no.260250, 7 Oct. 1896.

[10] A. de Baudot, 'L'église Saint-Jean-de-Montmartre', *La construction moderne*, no.32, 6 May 1905, p.375. See too H. Hartung, 'Ein Architektursystem des Eisenbetons?', *Deutsche Bauzeitung Mitteilungen über Zement, Beton-und Eisenbetonbau*, no.2, 23 Jan. 1907, pp.5-7.

[11] Anatole de Baudot, *L'Architecture. Le passé, le présent*, Paris: Librairie Renouard, 1916, p.163.

[12] E.C. [E. Chaine], 'L'église Saint-Jean-de-Montmartre', *La construction moderne*, no.29, 15 Apr. 1905, pp.340-43; E.C. [E. Chaine], 'L'église Saint-Jean-de-Montmartre', *La construction moderne*, no.30, 22 Apr. 1905, pp.351-54; E.C. [E. Chaine], 'L'église Saint-Jean-de-Montmartre', *La construction moderne*, no.31, 29 Apr. 1905, pp.363-67. See too E. Leduc, 'Eglise Saint-Jean de Montmartre', *L'Union des Architectes et des Artistes Industriels*, 1 Apr. 1904, pp.53-4.

[13] P. Planat, 'La future Eglise de Montmartre', *La construction moderne*, no.43, 26 Oct. 1901, pp.37-9; P. Planat, 'La future Eglise de Montmartre', *La construction moderne*, no.47, 23 Nov. 1901, pp.85-7. See too H. Degeorge, 'Architectes, Attention!', *L'architecture*, no.45, 9 Nov. 1907, pp.370-72.

[14] Archives Nationales, Paris, VM 31-37, supplément 17, Conseil d'Architecture, 'Rapport Eglise Saint Jean de Montmartre', 15 Aug. 1900.

[15] L. Barthou, Ministre des Travaux publics, des Postes et des Télégraphes, *Circulaire du 20 octobre 1906, concernant les instructions relatives à l'emploi du béton armé*, 20 Oct. 1906.

[16] Archives Nationales, Paris, A. de Baudot, 'Eglise Saint-Jean de Montmartre', 20 Oct. 1899 (Boudon, 'Recherche sur la pensée et l'œuvre d'Anatole de Baudot', Note 6, p.43).

[17] E.C., 'L'église Saint-Jean-de-Montmartre', *La construction moderne*, no.29, (Note 12) p.343.

[18] P. Cottancin, *Constructions démontables en matière plastique avec ossature*, FR Patent, no.242238, 20 Oct. 1894; and Cottancin, *Construction armée sans cintrage* (Note 5).

[19] See the drawing entitled *Détails de la Construction* (Dumont, Ramat, Eds, 'Chiesa di Saint-Jean-Baptiste de Montmartre, Parigi, 1894-1904', Note 6, p.48).

[20] Berger, Guillerme, *La construction en ciment armé: Applications générales, théories et systèmes divers*, (Note 2) p.846; E.C., 'L'église Saint-Jean-de-Montmartre', *La construction moderne*, no.29, (Note 12).

[21] Cottancin, *Travaux en matières plastiques avec ossature composée* (Note 3).

[22] 'Note sur les échafaudages en usage dans le Bâtiment', *L'Union des Architectes et des Artistes Industriels*, 1 Feb. 1905.

[23] See the photograph of the building site published in H. Chaine, 'L'église Saint-Jean-de- Montmartre', *L'Union des Architectes et des Artistes Industriels*, no.6, 1 Jul. 1905, (pp.44-7), p.46.

[24] See the drawing entitled *Détails de la Construction* (Dumont, Ramat, Eds, 'Chiesa di Saint-Jean-Baptiste de Montmartre, Parigi, 1894-1904', Note 6, p.48) and the one published in 1905 (E.C., 'L'église Saint-Jean-de-Montmartre', *La construction moderne*, no.29, Note 12, p.342).

[25] See the drawing entitled *Détails de la Construction* (Dumont, Ramat, Eds, 'Chiesa di Saint-Jean-Baptiste de Montmartre, Parigi, 1894-1904', Note 6, p.48). The photograph of the roofing taken at the end of the construction process confirms the presence of ribs in relief (E.C., 'L'église Saint-Jean-de-Montmartre', *La construction moderne*, no.29, Note 12, p.340). The section drawing published in 1905 showing the roofing with a smooth upper surface does not correspond to what was actually built (E.C., 'L'église Saint-Jean-de-Montmartre', *La construction moderne*, no.29, Note 12, p.342).

[26] E.C., 'L'église Saint-Jean-de-Montmartre', *La construction moderne*, no.29, (Note 12) p.352.

[27] E. Dupuis, 'L'architecture et le ciment armé', *L'architecture*, vol.XVIII, no.37, 16 Sep. 1905, (pp.351-52), p.351; E. Dupuis, 'La raison, la logique, le beau, l'art', *L'architecture*, vol.XVIII, no.33, 19 Aug. 1905, pp.315-16; L.-Ch. Boileau, 'Le nouveau matériau', *L'architecture*, vol.XVIII, no.48, 2 Dec. 1905, pp.442-43; L.-Ch. Boileau, 'Le ciment armé et l'art de l'architecture', *L'architecture*, vol.XVIII, no.49, 9 Dec. 1905, pp.454-57; L.-Ch. Boileau, 'Le ciment armé et l'art de l'architecture', *L'architecture*, vol.XVIII,

no.51, 23 Dec. 1905, (pp.471-73), p.471; L.-Ch. Boileau, 'Causerie', *L'architecture,* vol.XIX, no.34, 25 Aug. 1906, pp.303-06, plates 56-66; L.-Ch. Boileau, 'Causerie', *L'architecture,* vol.XIX, no.37, 15 Sep. 1906, pp.325-28; L.-Ch. Boileau, 'Causerie', *L'architecture,* vol.XIX, no.39, 29 Sep. 1906, pp.347-50; Ch. F. Marsh, *Reinforced concrete,* New York: D. Van Nostrand Company, 1904, p.429; A.R. Galbraith, *The Cottancin System of Armoured Construction,* Ipswich: Cowell, 1904, p.26.

[28] L. Harvey, 'M. de Baudot et le ciment armé', *La construction moderne,* no.231, 10 Mar. 1906, (pp.271-72), p.272.

[29] Le Corbusier, 'Introduction à la première édition', in Le Corbusier, Pierre Jeanneret, *Œuvre complète 1910-1929,* Paris: Les éditions d'architecture, 1964, (pp.7-10), p.10.

[30] H. Chaine, 'L'Eglise de St-Jean-de-Montmartre', *L'Union des Architectes et des Artistes Industriels,* no.4, 1 May 1905, pp.28-9.

[31] 'Reinforced concrete, chapel building, U.S. Naval Academy, Annapolis MD', *Engineering News,* vol.LIV, no.2, 13 Jul. 1905, pp.25-31.

Scaffolds for the iron-and-glass roof of Gallery Vittorio Emanuele II: challenges, design and evolution

Iva Stoyanova

Independent Researcher

Introduction

Gallery 'Vittorio Emanuele II' (1867-77) is acknowledged as the zenith of nineteenth-century glazed shopping arcades.[1] It belongs to the Monumental Phase of their typological development. The Gallery was dedicated to the first king of unified Italy and exemplified a new concept for grand, national architecture. It brought international recognition to the city of Milan and Italy at the time of its construction.[2] It is usually referred to in relevant twentieth-century literature as an emblematic example of iron-and-glass architecture.[3] While most nineteenth-century glazed arcades have been destroyed, the Gallery in Milan has survived, and recently celebrated 150 years of existence since its official inauguration on 15 September 1867.

The Gallery consists of two streets that cross perpendicularly, with an octagonal space at their intersection. The four wings of the cruciform plan are covered with glazed vaults, and the intersection is surmounted by a monumental dome with a cupola. (Fig. 1) The vaults have larger spans (15 metres) than those of earlier glazed arcades,[4] and the dome is internationally renowned for its large, harmonious proportions and monumental spatial effect. Because of these large dimensions, the roofs were built with a primary metal structure, which supported the glazing.[5] The primary structure originally consisted of arches and purlins for the vaults, and arches and rings for the dome. They were made from rolled wrought-iron angle sections and flat plates, riveted together. The roof ironwork was produced by the French company of Henry Joret, whose factories were located in Montataire, and transported to the construction site in Milan. These prefabricated elements were installed on-site between January and May 1867.[6]

Figure 1. Three-dimensional model of the iron roofs. The components of the primary ironwork can be observed.
Image: © Iva Stoyanova & Tihomir Stoyanov

Scaffolds for the iron-and-glass roof of Gallery Vittorio Emanuele II: challenges, design and evolution

After the Gallery had been finished and opened to the public, it became a large public facility that required maintenance. In the first half of the twentieth century there were two large-scale campaigns for conservation and repainting of the roof ironwork, in 1907 and 1928.[7] A key condition for the projects was to leave the Gallery open for public access during the execution of the work, which lasted respectively for three and six months.

Although the Gallery has been the object of extensive studies, less attention has been paid to the scaffolds for the construction, and especially to those for the maintenance of the roofs. What scaffolds were used to lift and install the heavy prefabricated pieces of the iron vaults and dome? Who designed them and what challenges needed to be addressed? What were the scaffolds for the maintenance campaigns like? Did their design resemble the scaffolds that were employed for the installation of the roofs? The answers to these questions will add to an understanding of the construction history of the Gallery and of scaffolds more generally. This understanding could also be relevant for the future design of scaffolds for the roofs.

Scaffolds for the construction work: heavy loads at great heights

The scaffolds for the installation of the roof needed to fulfil several requirements at once: to supply a work platform at the necessary height, to provide a means to lift the prefabricated pieces to it and to support the first pieces to be installed in the right positions. Among the first pieces to be installed were 38 arches for the vaults (1174.50 kg each), 16 meridian-wise arched segments (2602.30 kg each), eight parallel-like rings (the uppermost 313.88 kg and the lowest 1247.68 kg) and the crown ring (4605.97 kg)[8] for the dome. The adoption of putlog scaffolds was possible because the masonry walls that supported the roofs had already been built.

Figure 2. A sketch of the service scaffold that was used for the installation of the iron-and-glass roofs of the Gallery. Image: © Iva Stoyanova. Cantù, Album dell'Esposizione industrial italiana, (note 14) p.89

All the scaffolds for the construction of the Gallery were designed by the local master builder Giorgio Pellini.[9] He was well known for being the building contractor for the Gallery and for Piazza del Duomo, of which the project for the Gallery was a part.[10] He also worked on the design of the scaffolds for the construction of the vestibule of Central Station in Milan (1861-64). Pellini was awarded a bronze medal at the Italian Industrial Exposition in 1871 for the improvements he introduced in building machines and scaffolds.[11] One of the featured scaffolds was a rolling pier scaffold that was employed to install the ironwork in the Gallery's roofs.[12] (Fig. 2) A very similar scaffold designed by Pellini was described by engineer Luigi Mazzocchi in his technical treatise on timber construction.[13]This description reveals that one of the improvements was the possibility to extend and retract the uppermost section through a mechanism of iron rolls that were installed vertically.

Apart from this service scaffold, larger and much more elaborate structures were also employed, which are shown in historical photographs of the construction site taken by Francesco Heyland and Hyppolite Deroche. According to nineteenth-century technical literature and archival documentation, the scaffolds for the roofs were combined into two large systems, one for each type of roof being installed, vaults or dome.

System with rolling scaffolds for the vaults

The scaffolding system for the vaults involved a movable timber framework that rolled on rails supported on ledges along the side walls. It is illustrated and described in a chapter about temporary timber structures in the above-mentioned treatise by Luigi Mazzocchi.[14] (Fig. 3) Three main components of the scaffold system can be distinguished in the drawings: console supports, a two-level rolling framework and a rope pulley. The supports were to be sustained on putlogs in the lower end and by the floors of the adjacent buildings in the upper end. However, a historical photograph[15] clearly shows that instead of this, the consoles were supported by the wooden standards of scaffolds along the walls. In the design described by Mazzocchi, the supports were installed in pairs. The axial distance between the supports in one pair was 1.5 metres and 3 metres between two consecutive pairs. All pairs were braced lengthwise by timber beams that were framed along the length of the vault. These supported iron rails along which the framework rolled.

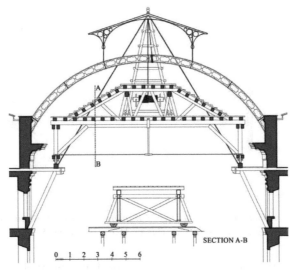

Figure 3. A drawing of the rolling framework that was designed for the installation of the iron vaults. Image: © Iva Stoyanova. Mazzocchi, Trattato, (note 14) plate 46

The two levels of the framework were constructed as a system of crosswise and lengthwise timber frames that were further strengthened by diagonal wind-bracing and tie-rods. The framework spanned 12 metres and was 3.5 metres deep. Its second level was accessible from two symmetrically disposed flights of stairs. The lower level supported a triangular structure with a pulley at the top. The summit of the structure was secured with ropes that tied it to the framework supports.

The framework structure rolled on four cast-iron wheels along the rails until it reached the designated position for installation. Presumably, this position was marked for each iron arch by the already-constructed pilasters that protruded from the supporting walls into the same plane where the arch was to be installed. The trajectory of the ropes in the scaffold drawing suggests that the weight of the rolling scaffold was used as a counterweight for lifting the iron arches. Although the drawings depict the iron frame of the lantern above the arch, the lantern was not installed together with the arch, but rather after the arches were in place, as historical photographs confirm.[16]

System with revolving scaffolds for the dome

According to historical photographs of the design drawings,[17] the dome scaffolds consisted of a tower-like scaffold (approximately 40 metres high) and a round elevated platform (approximately 35.9 metres in diameter). (Fig.4 left and centre) The historical photographs of the construction site reveal that there was also a revolving scaffold. (Fig.4 right) The revolving scaffold was comprised of four inclined standards, ledgers and diagonal braces. Rectangular platforms at three different levels were accessible through stairs inside the volume of the scaffold. This scaffold rolled on four pairs of rollers along rails made of wooden planks that circled around the main platform.

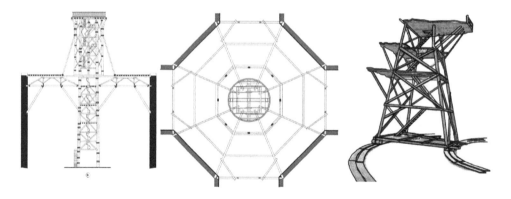

Figure 4. Crosswise section of the dome scaffolds. (left) Plan of the dome scaffolds. (centre) A sketch of the revolving scaffold. (right) Images: © Iva Stoyanova. C.P.A.o.M.,C.P.o.M (note 15)

The tower-like scaffold was a fixed pier resting on the ground. It consisted of an inner full-height core (approximately 40 metres high) and an outer shorter part (approximately 18 metres high) starting at the platform and extending upwards. In plan, the two parts appeared as a smaller square (side of approximately 5.5 metres) contained within a larger square (side of approximately 6.5 metres) rotated by 45°. The standards of the outer part were tied to those of the core with diagonal braces, forming one spatial structure. A round platform (approximately 11.5 metres in diameter) was constructed on top of the tower scaffold where the top ring of the dome was to be placed. This round platform was sustained by eight assemblies of inclined poles that transferred the load from the round platform to the lower and larger one.

The load-bearing components of the main platform were eight queen-post frames that were arrayed radially in accordance with the angles of the octagon. One end of the frame was supported on putlogs in the masonry walls and the other end, by the tower core. These frames were braced by transverse components, some of which were diagonal while others formed, in plan, a series of concentric octagons. This primary structure supported a subfloor of beams. Planks were used for the floor decking as can be seen in most historical photographs of the construction site. The construction workers could reach every level of the scaffold by a system of stairs built inside the tower. The timber elements of the framework were tied with metal fasteners, as shown in the drawings.

Guiding the iron dome and installing the crown ring

Comparing the scaffold and the iron dome in layout reveals how the disposition of some scaffold elements closely aligned with the position of installed iron components. For example, the location of the eight frames of the large platform and the eight assemblies of inclined poles were built in accordance with the radial disposition of the 16 dome arches. Furthermore, the scaffold tower and the round platform corresponded in position to the location of the top iron ring. This suggests that the scaffold elements functioned also as guides during the installation work.

The fact that the crown ring of the dome is the only iron component depicted in the drawings suggests that it was the first element of the dome to be installed. The literature consulted does not explain how the crown ring was lifted to the large platform, or to the top one and placed on the latter. It is unlikely that the ring departed from the rest of the prefabricated ironwork and was assembled on-site. Indeed, such a solution would have been easier because all the components of the crown ring would have been separately lifted to the top platform and then riveted to one another there. However, such a hypothesis is improbable because the crown ring is described in a technical report about the ironwork as being a single piece.[18] This report is especially valuable because it describes the pieces of the roof structure along with the rivets needed for their installation or assembly on-site. Rivets for the crown ring were not reported because none were needed. Hence, the crown ring was not assembled on-site.

Given the large weight of the crown ring, it was likely that it was raised in two steps at least: first to the large platform and then to the small platform on the top. One suggestion is that this happened after the whole scaffold had been built. In this case, the ring would have been raised to the large platform sideways, manoeuvring in the open space of one of the four wings. For these operations, either triangular frameworks such as those used for the installation of the vaults or special types of service scaffolds similar to the one with the extending uppermost section were used.

Another suggestion is that the ring was raised while the scaffold was being constructed so that the tower could be built inside the ring and used as a giant pole against which the ring would be pulled up later. In this case, the ring would have been raised to the large platform sideways right after it had been built with only half of the tower ready. Thus, the ring could be placed in the centre and the rest of the tower could be constructed inside the ring. Once the whole tower was erected with the ring surrounding it, the ring could have been pulled up to its place by means of pulleys. It would have been temporarily supported on a number of points while the small platform was constructed quickly under it. If so, the assemblies of inclined poles supporting the small platform would have been installed after the ring had been lifted and put into position.

Scaffolds for the iron-and-glass roof of Gallery Vittorio Emanuele II: challenges, design and evolution

An analysis of the drawings shows that another major challenge for the design of the dome scaffolds was the suitable division of load transfer between tower and platforms, between the ground and the surrounding buildings. Live loads created by the revolving service scaffold or the lifting of the heavy pieces can be assumed as most consequential. The challenge of load distribution could explain why the tower was designed as a two-part instead of a single structure. If the tower had been built as a one-part scaffold it would transfer the loads principally to the ground. Since the outer part was supported by the platform, loads were transferred also to the surrounding buildings. Thus, thanks to the two parts, all loads could be divided more equally between the ground and the surrounding buildings. Furthermore, the two-part configuration of the tower allowed it to be constructed with greater precision. It was easier to build an 18-metre high tower more precisely than a 40-metre high one.

Scaffolds for maintenance work: public safety and statics

The requirement that the Gallery remain open during the execution of maintenance campaigns created a two-fold challenge for the design of the scaffolds. First, the scaffolds needed to be designed so as to minimize obstructions for pedestrians inside the Gallery. Second, measures needed to be taken against the risk of objects falling from the scaffolds. Therefore, the design of scaffolds also became a matter of public safety.

Rolling and suspended scaffolds in 1907

These challenges for the scaffold design were particularly compelling during the 1907 campaign because it was the first large-scale one since the construction of the roofs. Hence, various problems with the scaffolds had to be addressed for the first time, which meant that their design had an experimental character. The design and execution of the scaffolds was handled by the Municipal Technical Office, which was in charge of the Gallery's maintenance, and a local painting company, headed by engineers Edoardo Piatti and Emilio Clerici.[19] The surviving correspondence reveals that initially there were intentions to support the scaffolds on the roof ironwork and the cornices of the Gallery.[20] However, these plans were abandoned due to concerns for public safety.[21] According to the contract, pier scaffolds were to be used for work on the vaults, and suspended scaffolds for work on the dome. More specific information about their design is contained in a technical report that was prepared by the contractors, Piatti & Clerici Company, for the 'Associazione degli Industriali d'Italia per prevenire gli infortuni del lavoro avente sede in Milano' [Association of Industrialists in Italy for preventing accidents at work in Milan] in order to prove that the scaffolds would be safe for passers-by as well as for the workmen.[22]

The pier scaffolds for maintenance of the vaults rolled and depended on the simultaneous movement of three mobile supports. They used diagonal strings for wind-bracing as well as ropes for manoeuvring. The most complicated manoeuvres involved turning the scaffold between the perpendicular wings in the Octagon.[23] It is recorded that deformations of one of the standards hampered the simultaneous movement of the three mobile supports and of the wind-bracing strings.[24]

The suspended scaffolds for maintaining the dome are better documented, by some sketches in the report. (Fig. 5) From these it can be observed that their design was very simple and relied on the suspension of wooden decks from the load-bearing ironwork of the dome. For this purpose, parallel-wise composite I-profiles with minimum dimensions of the section 100 mm x 120 mm were to be installed. Safety meshes were put under the scaffolds to catch falling objects and workmen. All workmen needed to be secured with safety belts that would fasten them to the iron arches of the dome.

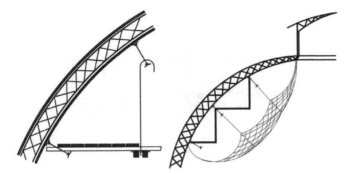

Figure 5. Scaffolding decks and safety meshes suspended from the iron dome. The additionally installed plate beams can be observed. Associazione degli Industriali d'Italia, 1927. Images: © Iva Stoyanova. C.o.A.,C.F. (note 19)

Flying scaffolds in 1928

The contract[25] for supplying scaffolds necessary for the 1928 campaign was between the Municipality of Milan and the local company Pasqualin e Vienna, which also executed the maintenance work themselves. A specialized chapter of the contract specifies details of the design and components of the scaffolds, and these are illustrated in project drawings proposed by the company. Scaffolds for both the vaults and dome were of an overhead type.

The vault scaffold was designed as a tiered structure with the dimensions of a single vault span (5.00 metres x 15.00 metres). (Fig. 6) It was comprised of five glulam frames (90 mm x 140 mm) with timber tie-beams that were connected with bolts and metal straps. The frames were braced together with diagonal bracing and with lengthwise sections that shaped the tiers. The whole structure rolled on ten pairs of wheels along special rails that were installed on the cornices. Hence, the rolling scaffold in this form was possible because of the load-bearing capacity of the walls supporting the roof. Preliminary calculations showed that with the scaffolds, the cornices were stressed to their admissible limits.[26] For this reason, a proposal was made to reinforce them by embedding iron between the walls and the consoles.[27] (Fig. 7)

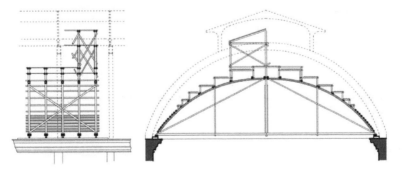

Figure 6. Rolling scaffolds under the vaults. Pasqualin & Vienna Company, 1928. Image: © Iva Stoyanova. e.C.A.o.M., folder 94 (note 20)

Scaffolds for the iron-and-glass roof of Gallery Vittorio Emanuele II: challenges, design and evolution

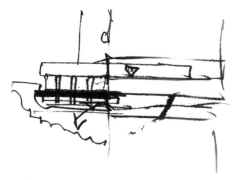

Figure 7. Sketch of the cornices without name and date. It can be suggested that this illustrates necessary reinforcement, involving embedded metal sections. Processed photo: © Iva Stoyanova. e.C.A.o.M., folder 94 (note 20)

The dome scaffolds were comprised of two sets of seven ladders. (Fig. 8) One set was designed for maintenance work on 1/8 of the ironwork. In the meantime, the other set was being installed. The ladders were suspended from the parallel-wise rings of the dome.[28] The decks for the workmen were sustained at one end by the ironwork and at the other, by the ladders. Materials are not specified other than the necessary metal fasteners. It can be suggested that the same materials – glulam and timber, which were used to build the vault scaffolds – were also employed for the dome scaffolds.

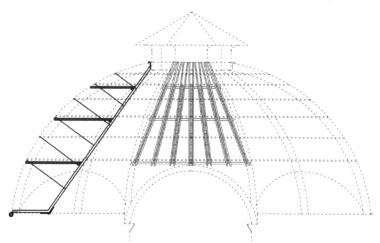

Figure 8. 1/8 scaffolds under the domes. Pasqualin & Vienna Company, 1928. Image: © Iva Stoyanova. e.C.A.o.M., folder 94 (note 20)

Conclusions

The main scaffolds that were used to erect the iron roof were designed as two systems of complementary scaffolding facilities, one for the vaults and another for the dome. Both systems share features, in that they combined fixed supports (the consoles with rails for the vaults and the tower with the platform for the dome) with a movable structure (the rolling platform for the vaults and the revolving scaffold for the dome). It is very likely that both systems counted on the proper weight of the main scaffolds to serve as counterweights when lifting the iron pieces.

The dome scaffolds stand out for their complexity and compelling dimensions. The accord in the disposition between the scaffolds members and the iron ones strongly suggests that the scaffold was also designed so that its components could serve as guide marks during installation. Therefore, its construction required the utmost precision and careful division of the loads between the elements of the system. Thus, the design of the main scaffolds, especially those of the dome, stand out for their thoughtfulness, functionality and adaptability, and the same can be said of the service scaffolds. Their design provides a better understanding of the contribution of master builder Giorgio Pellini to the construction history of the Gallery and its roof.

The maintenance scaffolds were mostly designed as overhead ones so that their supports would not interfere with pedestrians passing underneath. The overhead design was scarcely considered for the vault scaffolds in 1907, and rolling pier scaffolds were used instead, although their operation proved to be very problematic. The design of the overhead scaffolds evolved from the simple hanging decks in 1907 to the elaborate rolling and hanging systems used in 1928.

The 1928 overhead structures constituted a significant temporary intervention into the statics of the roof ironwork and its supporting walls. The design was experimental to a large extent because it relied on the load-bearing capacity of the existing structures, which most likely were not built to support such large temporary loads. The fact that the same type of rolling scaffold was employed in 1867 and in 1928 for the vaults, suggests that the type of scaffold used for initial construction was also suitable for its maintenance. Therefore, the scaffolds for the construction of the roofs prove to be another viable starting point for the design of future scaffolds for the maintenance of the roofs.

Acknowledgements

Special thanks to Prof. Sara Wermiel for editing the paper.

References

[1] J. F .Geist, Arcades: *A history of a building type*, Cambridge, MA: MIT Press 1985. p .371.
[2] ibid., 75.
[3] N. A. Pevsner, *History of Building Types*, Princeton, JC: Princeton University Press, 1976. 265. H.-R. Hitchcock, *Architecture: Nineteenth and Twentieth Centuries*. Harmondsworth: Penguin books, 1985. P.75, 120,146. M. Mackeit, *The History and Conservation of Shopping Arcades*. London, Ney York: Mansell,1986. pp.40–43.
[4] I. Stoyanova, I. Wouters & I. Bertels, 'Glazed wrought-iron arcades: building technologies and spatial effects', *International Journal of the Construction History Society*, vol.30, no.2, 2015, pp.45-66.
[5] I. Stoyanova, 'The roof of the Gallery Vittorio Emanuele in Milan: reconstructing the original building technology' pp.277-294 in J. W. P. Campbell, B. Nicholas, M. Driver, M. Heaton, P. Yiting, M. Tutton, C. Wall & D. Yeomans, (Eds), Further studies in the History of Construction. *The proceedings of the Third Annual Conference of the Construction History Society*, Cambridge: Queens' College, 2016.

[6] G. Chizzolini & F. Poggi, 'Piazza del Duomo e Galleria Vittorio Emanuele' in *Milano tecnica dal 1859 al 1884*. Milano: Ulrico Hoepli, 1885, 195–220.

[7] I. Stoyanova, 'The iron-glass roof of the milan gallery Vittorio Emanuele II: knowing the past for understanding the present and preserving for the future' pp.75-86 in C.A. Brebbia & S. Hernández, (Eds), *Structural Studies, Repairs and Maintenance of Heritage Architecture XIV*. Southampton, Boston: WIT Press, 2015.

[8] Civic Historical Archive of Milan and Trivulziana Library, Collection Piano Regolatore, folder 1382, file 2, 'Perizia della copertura in ferri e vetri della Galleria Vitorrio Emanuele II', 23 November 1868. pp. 1,3.

[9] I. Cantù, *Album dell'Esposizione industriale italiana*, Milano: Tipografia editrice di Enrico Politti, 1871, pp.63.

[10] ibid., p.90.

[11] ibid., pp.271, 90-91.

[12] ibid., p.89. fig.12.p.90.

[13] L. Mazzocchi, *Trattato sulle costruzioni in legno*, Milano: Antonio Vallardi, 1871. p.389.

[14] L. Mazzocchi, *Trattato sulle costruzioni in legno*, Milano: Antonio Vallardi, 1879. pp.82-86.

[15] Civic Photographic Archive of Milan, Collection of Photographs of Milan, FM Albo G 107/30, 'Galleria Vittorio Emanuele. Cupola. Cantiere' by Deroche & Heyland.

[16] C.P.A.o.M., C.P.o.M., FM Albo G 107/27, 'Galleria Vittorio Emanuele. Copertura in ferro' by Deroche & Heyland. (note 15)

[17] C.P.A.o.M., C.P.o.M., Albo G 107.29 'Galleria Vittorio Emanuele. Disegno' and Albo G 107.29b 'Galleria ittorio Emanuele. Disegno'. (note 15)

[18] C.H.A.o.M. and T. L., C.P.R., folder 1382, file 2, 'Perizia della copertura in ferri e vetri della Galleria Vitorrio Emanuele II', 23 November 1868. (note 8)

[19] Citadell of Archives of Milan, Collection Finances, folder 253, file 4, Contract entitled 'Contratto per la verniciatura delle parti in ferro della tettoia della GVE in Milano', 27 May 1907.

[20] ex-Civic Archive of Milan, folder 94, letter from Piatti & Clerici Company to the Municipal Technical Office of Milan, 21 March 1907.

[21] ibid.

[22] C.o.A., C.F., folder 253, file 4, Technical report by 'Associazione degli Industriali d'Italia per prevenire gli infortuni del lavoro avente sede in Milano', 17 June 1907. (note 19)

[23] C.o.A., C.F., folder 253, file 4, letter from Piatti & Clerici Company to the Municipal Technical Office of Milan, 8 June 1907. (note 19)

[24] C.o.A., C.F., folder 253, file 4, letter from Piatti & Clerici Company to the Municipal Technical Office of Milan, 14 June 1907. (note 19)

[25] e.C.A.o.M., folder 94, Contract entitled 'Contratto di appalto per la fornitura di armature e ponteggi in legname occorrenti per la verniciatura della Galleria Vittorio Emanuele II', 21 December 1926. (note 20)

[26] e.C.A.o.M., folder 94, Letter from Pasqualin & Vienna Company to the Municipal Technical Office, 31 January 1927. (note 20)

[27] e.C.A.o.M., folder 94, Letter from Pasqualin & Vienna Company to the Municipal Technical Office, 8 February 1927. (note 20)

[28] e.C.A.o.M., folder 94, Letter from Pasqualin & Vienna Company to the Municipal Technical Office, 1 June 1926. (note 20)

The Rise and Fall of Fox Henderson 1840-1856

Robert Thorne

Independent Scholar

Gone are the days when it was acceptable to refer to the Crystal Palace as being solely the work of Sir Joseph Paxton. The erection of the exhibition building in Hyde Park and its subsequent removal to Sydenham in south London made the names Fox Henderson household names. Although those names later faded from people's minds they have been resurrected in most recent accounts of the Crystal Palace. [1] The Paxton side of the story is beguiling and will always merit retelling, but his reliance on Fox Henderson as engineering contractors is integral to that story; indeed without it the story is half told and unconvincing.

However, the renewed acknowledgement of the role of Fox Henderson at the Crystal Palace has yet to translate into a general interest in the firm and its fortunes. The company is mentioned in many discussions of engineering and building projects of the 1840s, enough for it to be obvious that it did not spring from nowhere at the time of the Great Exhibition, and in addition the Crystal Palace was accompanied and followed by a trail of other projects. Somewhere in the biographies of numerous mid-Victorian engineers lies mention that they served time with the company, many of them making a notable contribution to its success. Yet like many such firms, its fame was short-lived, for it ceased trading in October 1856 and was wound up a year later. Many of those associated with it, notably its co-founder Sir Charles Fox, went on to successful careers elsewhere: other individuals fade from view, perhaps ruined by the firm's collapse after such a meteoric passage.

There are two interconnected sides to the Fox Henderson story. The first, of interest to engineering historians, is the development of the firm's structural expertise, which can be studied through contemporary descriptions and drawings of the roofs, bridges and other structures which they produced, often augmented by what was said about these at lectures and meetings. The Hyde Park Crystal Palace was in the limelight from the day work began, generating unprecedented interest in the process of its conception, but there were also many other projects which attracted professional attention. The second aspect of the story concerns the management of the firm, more a matter of business history but equally important to understanding its success and failure. There is a constant sub-theme in the history of industrialisation, never as glamorous as the evolution of machines and products, which looks at how firms were run – recruitment, research, investment, innovation, planning and coordination. Pioneering companies such as Boulton and Watt at the Soho Foundry in Birmingham are highlighted for their management techniques, but how far their example was followed is less clear. [2] Firms in every sector had to find the right balance between technical know-how, production and marketing, plus how to manage the whole operation. They did so at a time when there was no recognised body of management thought. It was always foolish to allow any one aspect of an enterprise to get the upper hand, which is perhaps what happened to Fox Henderson. But for a newly-established company, intent on gaining a reputation for innovation and lacking guidance on professional management, the risks and temptations were only too obvious.

Where the business history of an industrial enterprise has been written it is usually because there is a surviving archive of reports, accounts and business correspondence. In the case of Fox Henderson there is no such body of material, the records presumably having been destroyed after the firm was wound up. Therefore, a review of how the business was run has to be pieced together tangentially from sources outside the firm. Fortunately, however, in addition to such sources there is one particular surviving record, written as much from inside as outside, which is potentially as illuminating as any bundle of letters or financial ledger. Before launching into the history of the firm it may assist to outline the use and limitations of this source.

In 1868, twelve years after the collapse of Fox Henderson, the engineer F. R. Conder (1815- 89) published a memoir *Personal Recollections of English Engineers*. Because he was describing recent people and events many of his references were opaque or anonymous and he chose to write under the pseudonym 'A Civil Engineer'. It is known from the memoir and other sources that he served an apprenticeship with Charles Fox 1834-37, returned to work with Fox in 1843, and was directly involved with Fox Henderson from 1845 until perhaps 1851. He later set up a partnership to build railways abroad, and after the failure of one of those projects he developed a new expertise in water supply and sewage purification. The tantalisingly guarded references in his memoir would be infuriating were it not that a copy has survived in the Institution of Civil Engineers Library annotated by a member of the Fox Family, either Sir Charles Fox's son Sir Douglas Fox (1840- 1921) or his grandson Francis Douglas Fox (1868 –?). With the aid of these annotations it is possible to get closer to the ups and downs of decision-making in the firm and thus to understand why it failed so soon after its triumph at the Crystal Palace. [3]

Fig. 1 Charles Fox (1810-74). From Francis Fox, 'River, Road and Rail' London: John Murray, 1904

The Establishment of the Firm

The genesis of Fox Henderson began in 1834 when John Henderson (1811-58) joined John Joseph Bramah, engineer and machinist and nephew of Joseph Bramah of hydraulic press fame. [4] The Bramah foundry was in Ecclestone Place Pimlico. Five years later, in 1839, Charles Fox (1810-74) joined the firm, having resigned as Resident Engineer on the London Birmingham Railway, in the construction of which his engineering talent had already come to the fore (Fig.1). [5] With the arrival of Fox the decision was made to move the enterprise to Smethwick in the West Midlands, where it was established as Bramah Fox and Co. at London Works in 1840. It is said that Fox himself designed the works and supervised its construction. [6] Bramah left the firm in 1842 (he died four years later) and it then received the name by which it is best known, Fox Henderson and Co.

Industrial history is peppered with the names of double-headed partnerships, which always raises the question of how responsibilities were divided. The usual assumption is that one person contributed the technical or scientific expertise and the other the business acumen. Boulton and Watt is cited as a classic early example of that kind of partnership or, from the 1830s, the alliance at Nasmyth and Gaskell of James Nasmyth's expertise in precision-engineered machinery with Holbrook Gaskell's commercial and marketing energies.[7] In the case of Fox Henderson the division has been characterised as between Fox the designer and Henderson the works manager, but for a firm operating in a sphere where design was so inextricably linked to a knowledge of materials and the production process, that dichotomy may be too simplistic. Undoubtedly Fox brought to the partnership a reputation, while still in his twenties, of being a very bright engineer who, while working on the London and Birmingham Railway, had designed an innovative bowstring bridge over the Regent's Canal and the wrought iron trussed roof of the Euston terminus: in addition he had patented a type of railway points.[8] He was also later characterised by an engineer who had worked with him on the London and Birmingham as a man of "imagination and malevolence", which may possibly have infected how the firm was run.[9] John Henderson on the other hand is a slightly more shadowy figure, brought to life in F. R. Conder's memoirs as a "self educated Scotchman, shrewd, keen, not unkindly, but of an essentially combative disposition". For Conder, Henderson's inadequacies stemmed from his being "only a magnified or glorified workman", an unsystematic manager whose inability to spot priorities was concealed behind his ceaseless, bustling energy; someone who generally got things done but under whom "contracts are made only to be broken". Conder's caustic portrait needs to be balanced by what is known of Henderson's commitment to local churches and schools and the distinguished list of those who came to the support of his widow and child after his death in 1858. He obviously was regarded as more than just a behind-the-scenes supervisor of no particular distinction.[10]

Fox Henderson was set up in Smethwick at a time when a diversified iron industry was already well developed, in the west Midlands and elsewhere, supplying a whole range of infrastructure, transport and engineering projects. Accounts of visits to the works mention anchors, railway wheels, steam boilers, cannon and shells.[11] What distinguished the firm was the ability it could offer, not just to fabricate iron products but to design them as well. In the 1840s this came to the fore in two spheres, railway structures and the supply of roofs for naval dockyards.

The first major boom in the authorisation of new railways 1833-37 took time to result in actual construction, with the result that the firm was able to benefit from that boom in its early years. It was even better placed for the 'mania' in construction of 1845-49 when railway investment accounted for 55% of fixed capital formation.[12] Station roofs became one of its specialities: amongst the first it supplied were those at Cowlairs Station, Glasgow (32ft- 10m span, 1841-42) and Norwich Thorpe (two spans of 50ft- 15.6m, 1844).[13] The collapse during construction of the roof at Bricklayers Arms station in London (three spans of 52ft 6ins-16.2m, 1844) had the indirect result of revealing how much work of that kind it had secured. Two men were killed, apparently because the ridge beams and skylights were not properly supported during construction. Giving evidence at the subsequent coroner's inquest Fox claimed, "I speak from experience, as we have erected 28 acres of such roofs lately", and he went on to have similar roof trusses tested in front of fellow experts.[14] Fox Henderson emerged from that collapse apparently with its reputation unscathed and went on to build further roofs for stations and railway workshops. Their roofs of the 1840s culminated in 1849-50 with a project for the Lancashire and Yorkshire Railway at Tythebarn Station Liverpool, carried out with the engineer John Hawkshaw: a series of triangulated trusses of 128-136ft (40-42.5m) span entirely of wrought iron – riveted T-sections for the main rafters, purlins and struts, plus rounded iron tie rods (Fig.2).[15] A textbook on railway construction of 1850 aimed mainly at the foreign and colonial markets took its examples of roof construction all from Fox Henderson examples (Fig.3).[16]

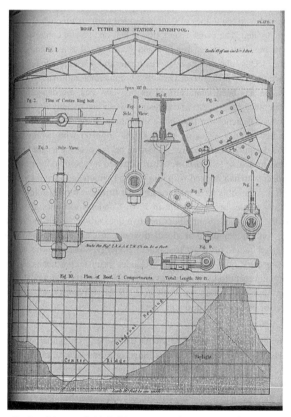

Fig. 2 Roof of Tythebarn Station, Liverpool, 1848-50. From Civil Engineer and Architect's Journal, Vol. 16, February 1853.

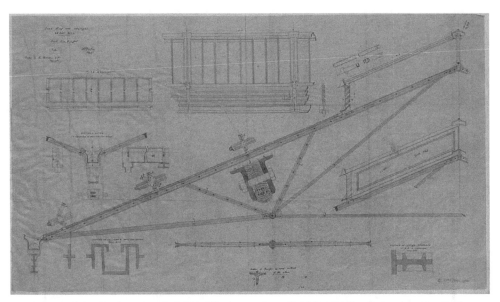

Fig. 3 A typical Fox Henderson roof, of 48 ft. (15m.) span, drawn by F. Brodie. The National Archives RAIL 1057/3507.

As with the roofs which the firm supplied, its iron railway bridges ranged from relatively modest examples that any foundry might have produced to innovative structures in which its design input is evident, often traceable to Fox's work for the London and Birmingham Railway. In the modest category were cast iron girder bridges produced for the Cubitt-engineered Great Northern Railway.[117] Two bridges which attracted far more attention were fabricated for Joseph Locke's London & Blackwall Extension railway in east London, 1848-9. Both were bowstring arch designs, of 120ft (37.5m) and 130ft (40.6m) span, distinguished by the use of box girder ribs with overhanging top section tied by flat tie bars.[18] A bowstring bridge incorporating even greater spans was produced for the railway crossing the River Shannon at Athlone in Ireland engineered by George Hemans, 1850.[19]

What Fox Henderson were not to know when the London Works was opened was that a major segment of their work would come from the Admiralty as a result of the decision of its Works Department in 1842 that dockyard roofs for shipbuilding should be constructed in iron rather than timber. Iron would reduce the risk of fire and promised to be less expensive and easier to maintain, but it had the disadvantage that the Works Department lacked expertise in designing iron structures. As James Sutherland showed in his pioneering article of 1989 this opened the way for design and build projects by engineering contractors, led by Fox Henderson.[20] The firm contracted to build two roofs at Pembroke Dockyard (Nos. 8 and 9, 1844-45), "taking the responsibility of stability upon themselves".[21] The frame design of these roofs, as well as their No. 7 roof at Pembroke and Roof No. 6 (1845) at Woolwich Dockyard, was modelled on their timber predecessors but with the struts and ties sized for iron. The slightly later roof over Slip No. 4 at Woolwich (1847-8) broke new ground in having a rigid frame of uniform height, avoiding the constricting eaves of the earlier designs: the tall central space, with wrought iron trussed roof similar to their station roofs, was braced by two side aisles with cast iron arches (Fig.4).[22] In their early years Fox Henderson also supplied a light trussed roof for a boiler house at Woolwich (1844).[23]

Boiler Makers Shop & Store. Late Woolwich Slip Roof Nº 4.

Fig. 4 Slip No.4 from Woolwich Royal Naval Dockyard in process of re-erection at Chatham Dockyard, 1876. The National Archives, ADM 195/7.

The Roots of the Firm's Success

The achievements of the firm in its first ten years help clarify what is meant in saying that it was a design-build enterprise. Neither Fox nor Henderson (nor Bramah before he retired) set out in writing how they wanted the firm to develop and there was no theoretical model for them to follow. Yet it is obvious that they had a vision of how design, research, manufacturing and marketing could be combined to exploit the engineering needs of the mid-nineteenth century industrial economy. Their strategy, if it can be so called, was based on their expertise in iron at a time when wrought iron was beginning to supersede cast iron for many types of structure. Whatever they designed or made and however they chose to publicise their work, almost everything was related to that expertise. And as with any firm, they depended on who they could recruit to work for them and how the whole operation was managed.

The London Works at Smethwick was both the head office and factory. It was arranged around a square with a boiler house (incorporating two 75 hp steam engines) and 70 forges. In the frantic production of components for the Crystal Palace it is said to have had about 30 pattern makers and 120 moulders.[24] The capacity for forging and moulding indicates an ability to produce wrought and cast iron elements, probably using pig iron and wrought iron brought in from elsewhere. Charles Fox was closely interested in the working of wrought iron but it seems that he out-sourced its rolling to other firms: in the line-up of companies which made parts for the Crystal Palace, Fox Henderson kept the lighter castings in-house but went to other firms for larger castings and wrought iron components.[25] That demands of that project, which called for the orchestration of manufacturers and suppliers from across the west Midlands, was no doubt repeated on other projects. But one thing which was definitely kept in-house was the trial erection and testing of beams, girders, and other components.

Also on the London Works site, a visitor in 1850 was told, there was a collection of "30, 012 drawings and tracings, catalogued with precision".[26] This clearly implies a scale of activity, plus an investment in collective knowledge, of an exceptional kind. At a time when most engineering firms had fewer than ten employees, Fox Henderson reached a significantly larger scale. And because of its size, and the projects it was attracting, it had the capacity to support research and nurture engineering talent. Thanks to the publicity which the Crystal Palace gained it is possible to identify 18 individuals who worked on the project in its two versions – engineers, draughtsmen, estimators and resident engineers. They included engineers such as Edward A. Cowper and Charles Heard Wild who made their reputation while at the firm as well as others – Rowland M. Ordish, John W. Grover and William Dempsey – who rose to distinction later on. At least 14 other people are recorded as having spent time at the London Works on other projects. Amongst them was, for a short time in 1845, the future philosopher Herbert Spencer and in 1848–c.1852 (Sir) William Siemens, who was given facilities at the works to develop his proposed regenerative steam engine and regenerative evaporation apparatus.[27] At a time when academic engineering was still in its infancy the firm provided a powerhouse of ideas, allied to the practical experience of direct involvement in the fabrication of structures.

When, as in the case of dockyard roofs, structures were directly attributed at the time to Fox Henderson, their contribution was beyond dispute. On projects where there was also a consulting engineer involved, the division of responsibility is often less clear-cut, for instance when they were answerable to John Hawkshaw, engineer for the Tythebarn Station in Liverpool or John Locke, designer of the Blackwall Extension Railway. Well before the 1840s there were instances of an engineer designing a structure such as a bridge or in iron-framed mill but entrusting the detail to the ironfounder. Fox Henderson took the role of the ironwork contractor much further, riding on the back of Fox's knowledge of wrought iron in the years when it was rising in favour. The all wrought iron roof trusses which became one of the firm's hallmarks were the offspring of his trainshed roof at Euston, and the bowstring bridges can also be related to his designs for the London and Birmingham Railway. Others helped develop these ideas particularly Edward Cowper, " his chief engineering manager", who was involved in the design and calculations for the Blackwall Extension bridges and most probably devised the framing of the roof over Woolwich Slip No. 4 with its tapered openwork struts, and another Fox Henderson hallmark.[28] At a time when structural design in wrought iron, based on calculation and testing, was rising to the fore it is easy to understand why even experienced consulting engineers were ready to rely on the knowledge of such a well-versed contractor.

What is more, Fox Henderson were not shy about broadcasting their abilities. Once the Hyde Park Crystal Palace was under way it required no effort to get publicity, but before then they were unusually zealous in grabbing every opportunity to display their abilities. For instance when the arched trusses for the two bridges on the Blackwall Extension Railway were ready they sent out descriptions of the design and invited engineers to witness the proof testing of one of the smaller (120 ft- 37.5m span) trusses at Smethwick (Figs.5-6). Amongst those who attended were Captains Simmons and Wynn of the Railway Inspectorate, Charles Vignoles, William Fairbairn and Prof E. S. Cowper of King's College London, father of Edward A. Cowper who worked on the design and helped measure the deflections. The truss was successfully proof tested to 240 tons, twice the maximum expected load. To squeeze the most out of this event they then issued a booklet about the design. Few other firms were so assiduous in courting the attention of potential customers.[29]

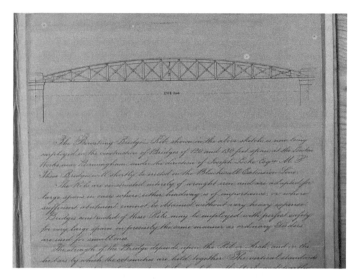

Fig. 5 Bowstring Bridge, Blackwall Extension Railway. Drawing and description circulated by Fox Henderson, 24th. August 1848. Tower Hamlets Local History Library.

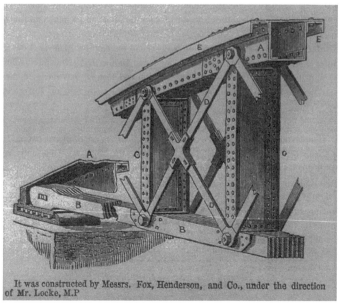

It was constructed by Messrs. Fox, Henderson, and Co., under the direction of Mr. Locke, M.P

Fig. 6 Detail of one of the Blackwall Extension Railway bridges. From the Illustrated London News, 6th. January 1849.

Management Skills

However innovative and good at marketing a firm might be, ultimately it was organisational skills that were crucial to prolonged success. This was particularly true for firms such as Fox Henderson which aspired to combine design with supply and construction. If F. R. Conder is to be believed John Henderson, whatever his other qualities, was not the most efficient of works managers. No doubt as one of the founding partners he contributed to the reputation which Fox Henderson had achieved by 1850, but it is reasonable to surmise that the smooth operation of the London Works at that time could also be traced to others. This is what makes Conder's memoirs particularly interesting. He devotes a whole chapter, 'Our Own Correspondent', to the description of another manager, someone whose calm ability was in stark contrast to Henderson's temperament.[30] As usual he doesn't name the particular individual, but thanks to the annotated copy of the memoirs, we know that it was Charles-Samuel Stokes. It was Stokes, described as "one of the partners", who showed a local journalist around the works in November 1850 and the following year his name appears, along with Fox, Henderson and others, as parties in an agreement with the French Government for the building of the Western of France Railway (Versailles to Rennes).[31] But for all that Conder admired Stokes as someone for whom "work contrived to do itself" he also detected in him a flawed personality, like "a costly and highly-finished instrument in which there was some lurking imperfection."[32] For Stokes, we are told, was of High Anglican, not to say Catholic sympathies, which meant for Conder that the conscientious simplicity of his life was vulnerable to over-indulgence. He moved to Paris, probably in 1851 or 1852, still acting for the firm but then, having set up in business for himself, he met his downfall in 1856 as a result of a foolish speculation.

Conder's delight in censuring Stokes's religious beliefs can easily be a distraction from the fact that he was obviously a very capable manager who understood what was needed to control the flow of projects through the works. The fact that he was employed at Smethwick in the years when the firm developed its reputation, and had left for Paris at the time when its first managerial weaknesses began to appear, may say something about the entrepreneurial strengths that Fox Henderson could command.

The Two Crystal Palaces

Speaking at a dinner in Derby to celebrate the completion of the Crystal Palace, Fox described his role on the project as being to "mature and realise" Paxton's idea of a building of iron and glass.[33] In that remark he pinpointed an aspect of the project which was potentially more significant than the scale, transparency and materials of the building that had recently opened. From the moment that an exhibition on an international scale was decided upon, it was obvious that the structure to house it would have to be exceptionally large and, as one commentator suggested, "should be altogether subordinate to the uses of the building and should be of the kind that would express them".[34] Thus it was anticipated that the chosen design might break architectural conventions in its form and materials. What was less foreseen, even as the Building Committee for the exhibition reviewed the design submissions and struggled to resolve its own design, was the critical question of whether the usual methods of building procurement could deliver what was required. Because of their experience in combining design, fabrication and assembly, Fox Henderson were ideally placed to supply an exhibition building, not just of novel form but through a novel type of delivery.

The story of how Fox Henderson became involved has often been told.[35] In short, Paxton entered the running for the design of the exhibition building at the last moment, having realised how unworkable the Building Committee's design was. The loophole which allowed his proposal to be considered was that those tendering on the specification for the Building Committee project could also submit an alternative costed design based on the same brief. Paxton, having gathered initial support, approached Fox Henderson who agreed to take the contractual risk using this two-pronged approach. They developed the design, based on the scheme drawings which had been produced, four by Paxton and one by the railway engineer W. H. Barlow, and were able to meet the tender deadline of 10th July 1850. Four days before that deadline an engraving of Paxton's proposal appeared in the *Illustrated London News*, to the acclamation of those who were looking for a viable alternative to the much-despised Building Committee design. Having as required tendered on both proposals, Fox Henderson were given verbal agreement on their price for the Paxton design on July 15th and so took possession of the site two weeks later and embarked on the hectic preparation of construction drawings. Work started on site in September 1850, ahead of the final contract being signed in October. Growing public support for the Paxton-Fox Henderson scheme, plus its attractive cost, made the Building Committee's decision almost a foregone conclusion, but many on the committee will have known the firm's reputation for railway and dockyard structures and their "deserved character for punctuality in their work".[36]

In his speech at Derby, Fox elaborated on the significance of the firm's role: "If any other course had been taken, or if, as is usual in the construction of large buildings, the drawings had been prepared by an architect, and the works executed by contractors instead of, as in the present case, these separate functions being combined by my making the drawings and superintending the execution of the works, a building of such dimensions could not have been completed within a period considered by experienced people altogether inadequate for the purpose".[37] A celebratory dinner was not the time or place to go into greater detail about how the firm fulfilled its role – how the design and structural analysis were undertaken, how the thousands of components were fabricated, and how the transport and assembly were organised. This was indeed a logistical exercise of an unprecedented kind, carried out in the face of an absurdly short deadline.

Fox was not shy about portraying himself as the key person responsible for turning Paxton's initial concept into reality, working 18 hours a day at his drawing board to produce "every important drawing of the Building as it now stands with my own hand".[38] However crucial his role may have been, other engineers at the London Works deserved some of the credit, including Edward A. Cowper, Rowland M. Ordish and Bernhard Schmidt (Table 1). C. H. Wild was officially part of the team monitoring the project on behalf of the Building Committee but didn't shrink from helping with the structural calculations and methods for testing components.[39] Indisputably the concept of a largely iron, timber and glass building based on a modular grid was Paxton's, as were many details of the design such as the ridge and furrow roofing and the glazing system which derived from his experience in building his conservatories at Chatsworth. This project was the climax of his vision of the use of industrialised construction, which was now to be put at the service, not of plants but of the exhibition-going public. But if the original idea was his, Fox Henderson took on the challenge of translating it into a buildable project for a specific site. The structural analysis which they undertook was demanding enough were it simply, as Paxton envisaged, a modular structure based on a 24ft (7.5m) grid with a regular ridge and furrow roof from end to end. That could have generated a wholly repetitive system based on a column-girder frame made up of uniform components. In practice the design was made more complicated because of many factors – the slightly sloping site, the building's stepped section, the introduction of the arched transept and the need for additional diagonal bracing. What is striking about the finished drawings that were published in 1852 is the huge variety of components – different beams and trusses, ten different column types, varied connections and a large diversity of façade treatments.[40] To plan, analyse and draw for such complexity, always with production and assembly in mind, make this a prefabrication project like no other.

NAME	HYDE PARK	SYDENHAM	ROLE
John H. Abbot	✓	-	Draughtsman
W.G. Brouger	✓	?	Surveyor
Charles Clark	✓	-	?
John Cochrane	✓	✓	Resident Engineer
Edward A. Cowper	✓	-	Chief Engineer
J. Dalrymple	✓	-	Site Supervision
William Dempsey	✓	✓	Assistant
Joseph Fisher	✓	✓	?
Charles Fowler Jnr.	✓	-	Site Supervision
John W.Grover	-	✓	Assistant
C. A. Hanson	✓	-	Estimator
Rowland M. Ordish	✓	✓	Draughtsman
Joseph Phillips	✓	✓	Outdoor Superintendent
Bernhard Schmidt	✓	✓	Draughtsman
F.W. Shields	?	✓	Engineer
George Spencer	✓	-	Draughtsman
Charles Heard Wild	✓	✓	Inspecting Engineer/Engineer
Joseph W. Wilson	✓	-	Mechanical Engineer

Table 1. The Crystal Palace Team. Compiled from obituaries in the Minutes of the Proceedings of the Institution of Civil Engineers, the Biographical Dictionary of Civil Engineers Vols 1 and 2, and local newspapers

Visitors to the works at Smethwick were in awe, not just at the number of drawings being produced but also the amount of activity in the foundry: 80 – 90,000 separate castings were produced for the building.[41] But this was a project which Fox Henderson could not handle on their own. The contribution of Chance Brothers in the supply of sheet glass is the most well-known aspect of what became a collaborative exercise of west Midlands industries, embracing amongst others Cochrane and Co. and Robert Jobson for other castings and Fothergill and Co. for wrought iron components, as well as firms from further afield such as the Aberdare Iron Co. Many of these were paid separately from the main contract.[42]

But what attracted even more attention was the co-ordination of the flow of components to the Hyde Park site, their testing, assembly and erection (Fig.7). Paxton's previous experience in producing timber and glass roofs was developed further for the project with the help of Cowper's sash-bar drilling machine and Fox's design of a travelling stage for the glazing of the roof. The derrick crane devised by John Henderson's brother David was brought into play.[43] And Wild's testing machine, using a version of Bramah's hydraulic press, was set up to test every cast iron beam as it arrived on site (Fig.8). Yet such fascinating machinery was only effective, in what was still a deeply labour-intensive project, because of the careful programming of construction. Many aspects of what was achieved, such as the erection sequence for the transept roofs, relied simply on muscle power. It was in that aspect of the works on site as much as any other that the virtues of the direct link between design and construction, as preached by Fox, shone through.

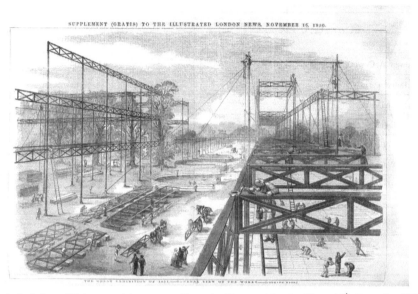

Fig. 7 Hyde Park Crystal Palace, work in progress. From the Illustrated London News, 16th. November 1850.

Fig. 8 Hyde Park Crystal Palace, proof-testing of girders with an adapted version of Bramah's hydraulic press. From the Illustrated Exhibitor, 16th. August 1851.

Through the speed and ingenuity of the erection process the Crystal Palace was largely ready for handing over to the Commissioners of the exhibition in February 1851. The excited press coverage of the works in the Hyde Park – a marketing opportunity which Fox Henderson exploited to the full – came to a head with the opening of the exhibition three months later; a building which was miraculous in its making and dazzling in its final effect – 'fairy-like' were the words most often used. The exhibition juries had no hesitation in awarding one of their medals to the building, stressing in their citation the contribution of Fox Henderson: "By fortunate coincidence the execution of the design was... undertaken by parties well fitted to do it justice".[44] Amidst all this euphoria there was less emphasis on the fact that the firm had significantly underpriced for the project. Their original contract price was £79, 800 (entitling them to retain the materials at the end of the exhibition), and subsidiary contracts covering additions to the brief brought that to £107,780. Their plea that this had proved wholly inadequate because of the resources they had to commit to it fell on sympathetic ears, resulting in an additional payment of £35,000 in November 1851.[45] No doubt Fox was right in claiming that the building was procured in the most effective way, and it was indeed a project on an unprecedented scale, but this was an early indication that the firm was vulnerable to overreaching itself.

Such was the popularity of the Crystal Palace that its removal from Hyde Park once the Great Exhibition had closed was fiercely opposed. Paxton envisaged its reuse as a "Winter Park and Garden under glass"; others proposed a combination of uses, including a permanent display of trades and manufactures and a sculpture gallery.[46] In addition to the question of its adaptability and the earlier undertaking that Hyde Park would be returned to its original state there was the underlying issue of how its continued use would be financed. As it became obvious that the idea of a permanent Government commitment was ebbing away a business alternative, entirely characteristic of the railway, joint stock age, sprang into being. By the time Parliament resolved that the building had to be removed from the park a company was being set up to buy it for £70,000. The intention was to rebuild it at Sydenham in south London as a commercial enterprise, a kind of public Versailles dedicated to wholesome recreation and cultural improvement.[47]

The Crystal Palace Company, incorporated in May 1852, had its roots in railway enterprise. Francis Fuller, in whose name the building was purchased, was the surveyor and land agent to the London Brighton & South Coast Railway and the first Chairman of the company was also Chairman of that line. They saw the project as a golden opportunity to generate recreational traffic from London and further afield. The overall design of this new attraction was in the hands of the old Hyde Park team, led by Joseph Paxton as 'Director of Winter Garden, Park and Conservatory', working with Matthew Digby Wyatt and Owen Jones and with Fox Henderson as contractors (Fox was also a Director of the Crystal Palace Company). The detailed planning for recreating the original building, transformed to meet a radically different brief, was the responsibility of John Henderson (belying his portrayal by Conder as mainly an office manager), supported by John Cochrane as site supervisor, the same role he had played at Hyde Park. C. H. Wild also made a reappearance, now as engineer acting for Fox Henderson on the project. It was in his name that drawings were submitted to the metropolitan authority in November 1852 for the necessary building permissions. Rowland M. Ordish, Bernhard Schmidt and other old Hyde Park hands were also brought on board.[48]

Alongside the need to turn a temporary exhibition building into a permanent, year-round facility was a desire on everyone's part to improve on the lessons of the Crystal Palace. Firstly, on the structural front doubts had been cast on the original building's stability, in particular the performance of the frame connections. More generally, once the initial excitement had worn off, the building was felt to be tiringly monotonous. It was not just disgruntled architects, offended at being bypassed in its design, who pointed to its lack of spatial interest and detail. The chance now came to demonstrate that, starting from the same modular principles, something of consistent architectural quality could be created. The new circumstances also helped promote a fundamental revision of the design. Paxton visualised the recreated structure on its new hilltop site at Sydenham as the keynote to a large new park, to which it was to be linked by broad terraces. And it was now to be a multi-functional attraction, with heating and more sophisticated temperature control, allowing the creation of varied environments for different purposes.[49]

Because it was now a laudable but less patriotic project, run by a commercial company, there was less week by week press interest in the rebuilding of the Crystal Palace and the people involved. Paxton, as the company's master-planner, established the overall strategy, particularly for the layout of the park and its associated waterworks. As regards the building, aspects of its design such as the ridge and furrow roofing – now reconfigured with hipped ends – were recognisably still his. But the new structure, including the reuse of components brought from Hyde Park, bore all the hallmarks of a Fox Henderson project, one for which they made the detailed design, orchestrated the supply of materials, and supervised construction. The new building was raised on brick foundations incorporating the underground heating boilers and pipes. The structure as a whole was ten bays shorter than its Hyde Park predecessor and had a much more modelled appearance. Instead of just one central transept there were now three transepts, the central one 276ft (86m) high plus one at either end of the building 172ft (53.7m) high. All three transepts had arched roofs made up of pairs of wrought iron lattice ribs connected by purlins and strengthened by diagonal bracing. The nave roof, also similarly arched, was of the same height as the lower transepts. The use of arched vaults throughout helped answer the accusation of tedious rectangularity made of the Hyde Park building as well as aiding the ventilation system. Beneath their springing line the arched ribs, and the galleries below, were carried on clusters of cast iron columns, pairs of which projected into the nave and transepts. Although many of these columns were recycled from the first building, they were now part of a structure of much greater architectural effect (Fig.9).

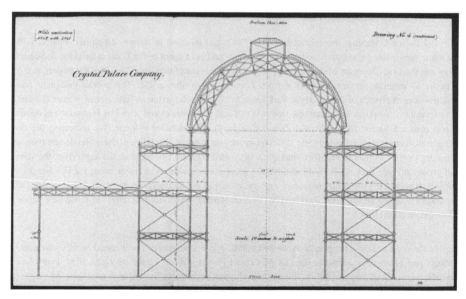

Fig. 9 Sydenham Crystal Palace. Sectional elevation through end of central transept, 1852. City of London Corporation London Metropolitan Archives MBO 512.

The fundamental difference between the two versions of the Crystal Palace was that in the original building the logistics of its construction took priority, whereas at Sydenham the requirement that it should have a greater architectural character and provide a permanent, serviced environment meant that its construction was far more complex. In Hyde Park, as the press never tired of pointing out, the building was its own scaffold but in the erection of the new version there were many parts where special scaffolding was needed. The design of the scaffolding was in itself challenging, as was apparent from accidents which occurred as the works progressed.[50] One of these in August 1853, involving the scaffold for the central transept, resulted in the deaths of thirteen men. The evidence at the subsequent inquest showed that the scaffold consisted of a series of two-tier trusses erected at gallery level, on which the roof ribs were to be constructed. Three of the lower-level trusses gave way, perhaps because their tie bars and connections were put under excessive torsional strain when the trusses were being moved. An engineering witness, Charles Vignoles, testified, "I do not consider it injudicious to have attempted to carry the truss across a span of 128 feet, at a height of 100 feet", but this was clearly an instance when the Fox Henderson team had underestimated the demands of the construction sequence.[51]

Because of its structural complexity and the time needed to finish the interiors, the Sydenham Crystal Palace took two years to complete, 1852–54. It is unclear exactly how much Fox Henderson were paid for their work because on many aspects of the project their contribution merged with that of other contractors working on the roads, landscaping and fitting out of the building. It had offered to re-erect it on the new site for £120,000, but by March 1854 the main building alone has cost the Crystal Palace Company £135,000, excluding the cost of buying the Hyde Park materials, professional fees and interior fittings.[52]

Auguries of Failure

Fox Henderson's seemingly miraculous performance in building and subsequently removing the Hyde Park Crystal Palace consolidated the firm's reputation as masters of iron construction. Within weeks of its opening in May 1851 they completed a station for the Buckinghamshire Railway in Oxford based on a similar structural system and using many of the same castings.[53] In the same year their roof for Sheffield Victoria Station was completed and design work began on the great bow string trusses of Birmingham New Street Station, the largest of 212ft (66.2m) span (Fig.10). The testing of these trusses took place at Smethwick late in 1852.[54] At Portsmouth Dockyard their Smithery for 80–90 forges "somewhat after the style of the Crystal Palace" was completed in 1852–54.[55] In bridge construction, to their bow string designs they added a Warren Truss type, notably at Joseph Cubitt's Newark Dyke Bridge for the Great Northern Railway, for which C. H. Wild made the structural analysis.[56] Plans for other Crystal Palaces were in the offing, for instance one proposed for Sydney Gardens, Bath.[57]

Fig. 10 Birmingham New Street Station. Photograph c.1900. John Wybrow Collection.

Not surprisingly, in the midst of all this activity, there were signs that the firm was over stretched. When the Mayor of Newcastle-on-Tyne visited Smethwick in February 1853 to discuss building a new covered market they had to admit that they couldn't take on such a commission.[58] More shamingly, on two high-profile projects involving no less an engineer than I. K. Brunel, the quality of their work was called in question. The first of these concerned the two water towers at the Sydenham Crystal Palace, which were intended to supply the fountains and other features in the park laid out by Joseph Paxton and also functioned as the chimneys for the palace's heating system. In October 1853 Paxton consulted Brunel about these towers, which were being built by Fox Henderson to the design of C. H. Wild. Brunel was highly critical of many aspects of Wild's design, specifically the tanks, the bracing of tower structures and the foundations. The work which had already been completed was demolished and Brunel proceeded to produce his own design for the towers. Yet despite this turnaround he still recommended that Fox Henderson should be awarded the contract for the new scheme. As he wrote to Paxton, "With all their faults, and no man I believe has had much greater experience than I have of the faults of Messrs. Fox Henderson as contractors, yet I am bound to state that if properly looked after they have the ability and desire to execute excellent work, and that the work of the towers which were pulled down confirms exactly this opinion".[59] Fox Henderson were appointed in 1854 and were indeed "properly looked after" by Brunel, who was quick to find fault in much of what they did. The towers were finally brought into use two years later.

Brunel's impression of Fox Henderson had been deeply coloured by their lack-lustre performance on the building of Paddington Station. As Steven Brindle makes clear in his history of the station, as a member of the Building Committee for the Great Exhibition Brunel had been impressed by Fox Henderson's abilities. Indeed, despite his involvement with the committee's own design for the exhibition building he had advised Charles Fox on how to tender for the project. So it is not surprising that when the decision was made in 1850 to build a new Great Western terminus at Paddington, Fox Henderson was the only firm that was asked to tender for the work.[60] Brunel produced numerous initial sketches of the station and its roof, but as on other railway projects it was Fox

Henderson that produced the detailed drawings. The design process overlapped with the completion of the Hyde Park Crystal Palace, learning from that experience but also advancing the language of iron construction. This was especially true in the design of the wrought iron arched ribs of the trainshed and the bracing between them. However, the overlap between projects which informed the design also had the contrary effect of delaying what Fox Henderson were also famous for, the efficiency of the production and assembly process. By May 1851 the Great Western Board was so perturbed by the lack of progress that they threatened to place the contract in other hands. Later that year they vented their frustration by refusing to pay Fox Henderson for work which had been certified for payment. In November Fox Henderson's excuse for their slowness – that Brunel's office had not yet sent certain drawings – was easily countered by Brunel when he pointed out that the drawings they referred to were unnecessary for the completion of their work.[61] Yet despite all this the firm was awarded a second contract for the completion of the trainshed in 1852, based on the same prices as the first contract.[62] Although given that security, delays in the supply of ironwork continued plus a further stream of excuses, leading the Board to threaten in April 1853 that they would take the project into their own hands. The station did not finally open until 1854.

As well as riding on the reputation that the Crystal Palace gave the firm, Fox Henderson also thirsted after the opportunity to repeat the same achievement. At the height of the Crimean War – the advance on Sevastopol started in September 1854 – it seemed that such a chance had come. With the army demanding the production of 100 Lancaster shells per day John Anderson, Superintendent of Machinery at Woolwich Arsenal, decided that a new shell factory was urgently needed. He, like Paxton at the Crystal Palace, knew essentially what was needed and Charles Fox produced plans and estimates within twenty-four hours, undertaking to complete the building within a month.[63] The Royal Engineers, who were normally responsible for building works at the Arsenal, were naturally aggrieved at being bypassed but acquiesced in December 1854. In the event, working through a severe winter, it took Fox Henderson twice as long to finish the building, which was to house forges, seven steam hammers and four steam engines beneath a corrugated iron roof. Even with its delays this should have been a project which resounded to their credit but in fact it turned sour. The Royal Engineers had their revenge by reporting on its inferior materials and workmanship, the correspondence about it being laid before Parliament.[64]

The same promise to produce a building at breakneck speed was made when the Theatre Royal Covent Garden was destroyed by fire in 1856. The *Illustrated London News* reported that it was "positively affirmed" that Fox Henderson had won the contract to rebuild it, with the promise that it would be completed in six months.[65] That news, perhaps fed to the papers prematurely, turned out to be wrong. The contract for E. M. Barry's new building on the site went to Lucas Brothers, and the theatre was not completed until 1858.

For a multi-faceted firm such as Fox Henderson, the building world was not nearly as propitious in the early 1850s as it had been previously. In particular there was a sharp decline in railway construction of the 1850, following the boom years 1845–50.[66] This helps explain the interest they began to take in foreign railways, inaugurated by the contract for the Western of France Railway which took Charles-Samuel Stokes to Paris in 1851. They later became involved in the Frankfurt, Wiesbaden and Köln Railway and, from 1853, in the line which ultimately led to the firm's downfall, the Zealand Railway from Roskilde to Korsor.[67] But the long delays on the Paddington project and the criticisms made of their performance in building the Lancaster Shell Factory at Woolwich suggest that, on top of the decline of railway work in Britain, the firm was also increasingly vulnerable because of internal weaknesses.

The Rise and Fall of Fox Henderson 1840-1856

Fox Henderson rode to fame because they combined engineering expertise with production and project management, and they were never shy about marketing their skills. Inevitably problems began to arise if one or more elements of their success began to be called in question. If F. R. Conder's recollections are to be trusted, the efficiency and prudent management of the firm in the years immediately before the completion of the Hyde Park Crystal Palace can partly be attributed to Stokes, in which case his move to Paris undermined its performance. Perhaps even more important was the loss of some of the firm's engineering talent, on which its reputation for innovative structural thinking had depended. Edward A. Cowper was the first to go, departing to set up as a consultant mechanical engineer in 1851 before work on the fabrication of his New Street Station had begun. C. H. Wild, who led the design team for the Sydenham Crystal Palace and whose water towers had been faulted by Brunel, began in about 1853 to succumb to the illness from which he died in 1857. Also in 1853 William Dempsey, who had worked on the Crystal Palace at both Hyde Park and Sydenham, left to be a structural consultant. John Cochrane, who was the resident engineer on the same two projects and also for the Lancaster Shell Factory at Woolwich, went in 1855 to join his brother in running the Woodside Ironworks near Dudley.[68] This succession of departures meant that Charles Fox had to carry more of the firm's reputation for structural know-how on his shoulders.

In the early 1850s Fox Henderson was little more than ten years old: apart from Bramah, it was still headed by its original partners. If it began to falter this was not because of a problem of succession in the partnership or, if it had been a family firm, its being passed to a more complacent second or third generation. Instead it seems to have been more the victim of an over-ambitious start in life which could not be sustained under less favourable circumstances. Railway work at home was diminishing, the role of engineering consultants made design-build contracting more difficult, and it has less capacity for innovative experiment. Though more effective management might have seen it through its difficulties, the other ingredients of its initial success had gradually faded away.

Profits		**Losses**	
East Kent Railway contract	£12,000	Crystal Palace Company	£4,000
Wiesbaden Railway	£2,250	Cork and Brandon Railway Company	£6,031
Berlin Waterworks	£8,000	Quarantine Bridge, Paris-Lyon Railway	£6,500
Commissions on Lyons-Geneva Railway	£16,300	Quarantine Bridge, Paris-Lyon Railway	£6,500
English and Irish Magnetic Telegraph	£2,250	Magon Bridge, Lyons-Geneva Railway	£3,000
Ruhwort Mines share	£8,000	Zealand Railway	£74,131
Portadown-Dungannon Railway contract	£15,906		
Sundries	£15,546		

Table 2. Specific profits and losses for Fox Henderson, June 1855-February 1857, from Staffs. Advertiser, 25th. April 1857.

Collapse

The end, when it came, was sudden. Fox Henderson ceased trading in October 1856 mainly because of a loss of £74,000 incurred in building the Zealand Railway. In their contract for that project they had woefully underestimated the amount of excavation required.[69] Their debts, it was said, "were a mere bagatelle" compared with the work they had on their books, though as well as the Zealand Railway they had incurred losses on three other railway projects and the Crystal Palace at Sydenham (Table 2).[70] Of their total debts of £320,000 almost half were unsecured. It was hoped that the firm could carry on – a month later no-one had been discharged – but in February 1857 it was declared bankrupt and 2,000 men were thrown out of work. The surviving materials and equipment, including the patterns for the cast iron components for the Crystal Palace, were auctioned in September 1858, followed by the sale of the works itself. The Smethwick site eventually became the nut and bolt factory of Guest, Keen and Nettlefolds.[71]

Of the two partners, John Henderson was the more severely affected by the firm's failure. He died in January 1858, leaving his wife and daughter destitute. A committee was formed to raise funds to support them, headed by some of the best-known engineers and contractors of the time – Thomas Brassey, Thomas Jackson and Henry Grissell.[72] Charles Fox (who was not listed as a supporter of that fund for Henderson's dependents) went on to establish himself as a consulting engineer in London, joined by his sons Douglas and Francis. In his lifetime (he died in 1874) they completed the widening of the railway bridge across the Thames at Victoria with the complex approach lines to it, and served as consultants for railways in South Africa, Canada and India. Perhaps indeed Fox had long realised that consultancy was the best way forward, rather than trying to run a firm on a much broader front. Though the company which he had helped establish had failed it provided him with a secure stepping-stone to a new kind of professional life.

References

[1] Tom F. Peters, *Building the Nineteenth Century,* Cambridge Mass. and London: MIT Press, 1996, pp. 226-54; John McKean, *Crystal Palace Joseph Paxton and Charles Fox,* London: Phaidon Press, 1994, pp. 18, 21-22; Kate Colquhoun, *A Thing in Disguise. The Visionary Life of Joseph Paxton,* London and NY: Fourth Estate, pp. 168-9, 175-6.

[2] Eric Roll, *An Early Experiment in Industrial Management,* London: Longmans, 1930; Sidney Pollard, *The Genesis of Modern Management,* London: Edward Arnold, 1965, pp. 78-79.

[3] A Civil Engineer, *Personal Recollections of English Engineers,* London: Hodder and Stoughton, 1868, reprinted as F.R. Conder, *The Men Who Built Railways,* London: Thomas Telford, 1963.

[4] *Birmingham Journal,* 16 January 1858, p. 3.

[5] Peter Cross-Rudkin and Mike Chrimes, *Biographical Dictionary of Civil Engineers,* Vol. 2 (1830-1890), London: Thomas Telford, 2008, pp. 310-15. Fox's letter of 3 December 1838 resigning from the London and Birmingham Railway is at The National Archives (hereafter TNA) RAIL 1008/100/254. Fox was living in Bellefield, a suburb of Birmingham, in 1841: see London Metropolitan Archives (hereafter LMA), Sun Insurance Registers, 26 July 1841.

[6] *Staffs.* Advertiser, 9 November 1850, p .3.

[7] Eric Roll (Note 2); David Walker, *Iron Men,* London: Anthem Press, 2016, pp. 107-8. Another well-known example of a partnership is Fairbairn & Lillie, the Manchester engineering firm, where William Fairbairn provided the entrepreneurial and engineering skills while Lillie took responsibility for the workshop.

[8] James Sutherland, 'Iron Railway Bridges', in Michael R. Bailey, ed., *Robert Stephenson- the Eminent Engineer*, Aldershot, Hants: Ashgate, 2003, pp. 243,307; Bennet Woodcroft, *Alphabetical Index of Patentees of Invention*, London, 1854, new impression, NY: Augustus Kelley, 1969, p. 199.

[9] Michael Robbins, 'From R.B. Dockray's Diary', *Journal of Transport History*, Vol. 7, No. 2, November 1965, p. 111. The diary entry is for January 1850.

[10] A Civil Engineer (Note 3), pp. 215-25; *Aris's Birmingham Gazette*, 22 May 1854, p. 1; *Building News*, 2 April 1858, p. 357.

[11] *The Expositor*, Vol.1, 28 June 1851, p. 146; *Leisure Hour*, 13 January 1853, pp. 39-41.

[12] R. A. Church, *The Great Victorian Boom*, London: Economic History Society, 1975, p. 32.

[13] Capt. *Henry Goodwyn, Memoir on Wrought Iron Roofing*, Calcutta: G.H. Huttmann, 1844, pp.10-11; George Dow, *The First Railway in Norfolk*, London: LNER, 2nd. edn. 1947, pp. 10-11.

[14] *Times*, 13 April 1844, p. 7; *Illustrated London News*, 13 April 1844, p.231; *Civil Engineer and Architect's Journal*, Vol. 7, 1846, p. 177.

[15] *Civil Engineer and Architect's Journal*, Vol. 16, 1853, pp. 56-7; *Transactions of the Royal Scottish Society of Arts*, Vol. 4, 1856, pp. 94-7.

[16] Rowland Macdonald Stephenson, *Railways: an Introductory Sketch*, Part 1, London: Weale, 1850, pp. 31-33.

[17] William Humber, *A Practical Treatise on Wrought Iron Bridges and Girders*, London: E. & F. N. Spon, 1857, pp. 15-21.

[18] *Mechanics' Magazine*, 16 September 1848, pp. 285-6; *Civil Engineer and Architect's Journal*, Vol. 11, 1848, pp. 300-1; *Illustrated London News*, 6 January 1849, p. 13; *Bow-String Bridge Ribs. A Description of Ribs Prepared for a Bridge over the Regent's Canal, London for the Blackwall Extension Railway*, Smethwick, London Works, 1849. E.A. Cowper, who was involved in the design of these bridges, commented on their robustness: *Minutes of the Proceedings of the Institution of Civil Engineers* (hereafter MPICE), Vol. 65, 1881, p. 118.

[19] *William Humber, A Complete Treatise on Cast and Wrought Iron Bridge Construction*, London: Lockwood and Co., 2nd edn. 1864, Vol. 1, p. 229; Vol. 2 (Plates), pp. 73-77.`

[20] R. J. M. Sutherland, 'Shipbuilding and the Long-Span Roof', *Transactions of the Newcomen Society*, Vol. 60, pp. 107-26; See also Jonathan Coad, *Support for the Fleet: Architecture and Engineering of the Royal Navy's Bases 1700-1914*, Swindon, Wilts., English Heritage, 2013, pp. 188-89; Duncan Hawkins and Caroline Butler, 'The Iron Slip Cover Roofs of Deptford and Woolwich Royal Dockyards 1844-1855', *London's Industrial Archaeology*, Vol. 13, 2015, pp. 42-61.

[21] Capt. (M) Williams, RE, 'Description of Wrought Iron Roofs Erected Over Two Building Slips in the Royal Dockyard at Pembroke, South Wales', *Professional Papers of the Corps of Royal Engineers*, Vol. 9, 1847, p. 51.

[22] Sutherland, 'Shipbuilding' (Note 20), pp. 120-21; Peter Guillery, ed., *Survey of London Vol. 48 Woolwich*, New Haven and London: Yale University Press, 2012, pp. 105-7.

[23] W. D., 'An Account of an Experiment on the Strength of the Principals of a Wrought Iron Roof of 62 feet 4 inches Span', *Professional Papers of the Corps of Royal Engineers*, Vol. 7, 1844, pp. 225-26.

[24] *Staffs. Advertiser*, 9 November 1850, p. 3.

[25] M. D. Wyatt, 'On the Construction of the Building for the Exhibition of the Works of Industry of all Nations', *MPICE*, Vol. 10 (1851), p. 159.

[26] *Staffs. Advertiser*, 9 November 1850, p. 3.

[27] Herbert Spencer, *An Autobiography*, London: Williams and Norgate, 1904, Vol. 1, pp. 278-81; William Pole, *The Life of Sir William Siemens*, London: John Murray, 1888, pp. 71-90.

[28] William Pole, p. 71.

[29] *Bow-String Bridge Ribs* (Note 18). The publicity letters are preserved in a copy of this booklet held at the Tower Hamlets Local History Library. Pedro Guedes emphasises the marketing strategies of Fox Henderson

in 'Iron in Building: 1750-1855. Innovation and Cultural Resistance' (PhD Thesis, University of Queensland, 2008), Vol. 1, p. 238; Vol. 2, pp. 03-036.

[30] A Civil Engineer (Note 3), pp. 226-41.

[31] *Staffs. Advertiser,* 9 November 1850, p. 3; *Annales des Ponts et Chausees. Lois, Décrees, Arrêtes...,* 1851, pp. 209-36.

[32] A Civil Engineer (Note 3), pp. 227, 241.

[33] *Illustrated London News,* 5 July 1851, p. 21.

[34] 'Helix', (pseud. William Bridges Adams), 'The Industrial Exhibition of 1851', *Westminster Review,* Vol. 53, April 1850, p. 51.

[35] John McKean (Note 1), pp. 14-32; George F. Chadwick, *The Works of Sir Joseph Paxton,* London: The Architectural Press, 1961, p. 51.

[36] *Journal of Design and Manufactures,* Vol. 3, August 1850, p. 191.

[37] *Illustrated London News,* 5 July 1851, p. 22.

[38] *Ibid.,* p. 22.

[39] *Illustrated Exhibitor,* 28 June 1851, pp. 64-66; 16 August 1851, p. 186.

[40] Charles Downes and Charles Cowper, *The Building Erected in Hyde Park for the Great Exhibition of the Works of Industry of all Nations,* London: John Weale, 1852.

[41] *Year-Book of Facts in the Great Exhibition of 1851,* London, 1851, p. 40.

[42] M. D. Wyatt (Note 25), p. 159.

[43] *Illustrated Exhibitor,* 19 July 1851, p. 114; 16 August 1851, p. 187; 23 August 1851, pp. 215, 217.

[44] *Exhibition of the Works of Industry of All Nations: Reports by the Juries,* London: William Clowes & Son, 1852, p. 206.

[45] *Builder,* 15 November 1851, p. 725; 'First Report of the Commissioners for the Exhibition of 1851', *Parlimentary Papers,* 1852, Vol. XXVI (1485), p. 156. Despite the additional payment, Fox Henderson were still financially embarrassed and had to assign the building to the London and County Bank in January 1852: see Hermione Hobhouse, *The Crystal Palace and Great Exhibition,* London: Athlone Press, 2002, p. 78.

[46] Joseph Paxton, *What is to Become of the Crystal Palace?* London: Bradbury and Evans, 1851, p. 4.

[47] *Times,* 30 April 1852, p. 5; Jan Piggott, *The Crystal Palace at Sydenham,* London: Hurst & Company, 2004, pp. 31-35.

[48] George F. Chadwick (Note 35), pp. 144-45; *Times,* 14 September 1852, p. 5.; LMA, MBO512, November 1852- September 1853.

[49] Henrik Schoenefeldt, 'Adapting Glasshouses for Human Use: Environmental Experimentation in Paxton's Designs for the 1851 Great Exhibition Building and the Crystal Palace, Sydenham', *Architectural History,* Vol. 54, 2011, pp. 250-55.

[50] There were four collapses, three of which could be attributed to the design and organisation of the works.

[51] *Builder,* 20 August 1853, pp. 529-30; 27 August 1853, p. 546; *Times,* 17 August 1853, p. 8; 18 August 1853, p. 5; *Civil Engineer and Architect's Journal,* Vol.16, July 1853, pp. 355-8.

[52] *Builder,* 4 March 1854, p. 117; George F. Chadwick (Note 35), p. 145.

[53] R. J. M. Sutherland, 'Oxford Midland Station and the Crystal Palace', *Structural Engineer,* Vol. 53, No. 2, February 1975, pp. 69-72.

[54] *Builder,* 27 September 1851, p. 609; Joseph Phillips, 'Description of the Iron Roof, in one Span, over the Joint Railway Station, New Street, Birmingham', *MPICE,* Vol. 14, 1854-5, pp. 251-72; W. Cawthorne Unwin, *Wrought Iron Bridges and Roofs,* London: E & F. N. Spon, 1869, pp. 119, 125-6; *Leisure Hour,* 13 January 1853, p. 39.

[55] *Artizan,* Vol. 14, 1 January 1856, p. 9; David Evans, *Building the Steam Navy,* London: Conway Maritime Press, 2004, pp. 114-17.

[56] Joseph Cubitt, 'A Description of the Newark Dyke Bridge, on the Great Northern Railway', *MPICE,* Vol. 12, 1852-53, pp. 601-12.

[57] *Staffs. Advertiser,* 14 August 1852, p. 5.

[58] *Ibid.,* 12 February 1853, p. 4.

[59] I. K. Brunel to Joseph Paxton, 4 August 1854, Brunel Private Letterbooks No.10, pp. 20-24, quoted in Angus Buchanan, Stephen K. Jones and Ken Kiss, 'Brunel and the Crystal Palace', *Industrial Archaeology Review,* Vol. 17, Autumn 1994, p. 15.

[60] Steven Brindle, *Paddington Station. Its History and Architecture,* Swindon Wilts: English Heritage, 2013, pp. 37-39.

[61] TNA RAIL 250/5, GWR Minutes of the Board of Directors, 28 May 1851; 6 November 1851; 27 November 1851.

[62] TNA RAIL 250/6, GWR Minutes of the Board of Directors, 1 July 1852; RAIL 252/780, Contract and Specification for Iron Roof at Paddington Station, 8 November 1852.

[63] TNA WO44/298, Lancaster Shell Factory Correspondence 1854-55, 2 December 1854; *Aris's Birmingham Gazette,* 30 July 1855, p. 4.

[64] TNA WO44/298 (Note 63), 16 April 1855-14 May 1855; WO33/4A, General Statement of the Past and Present Condition of the Several Manufacturing Branches of the War Department, 1857; *Parliamentary Papers,* 1854-55, Vol. XXXII (396).

[65] *Illustrated London News,* 28 June 1856, p. 707. The proprietor of the Theatre Royal, Frederick Gye, makes only one reference to Sir Charles Fox in his diaries for 1856 (Royal Opera House Archives).

[66] Harold Pollins, *Britain's Railways. An Industrial History,* Newton Abbot: David and Charles, 1971, p. 40.

[67] Ministeriet for Offentlige Arbejder de Danske Statsbaner, *Rothes Archiv,* Copenhagen, 1962, pp. 103-16, 118, 120, 123, 181, 185.

[68] Peter Cross-Rudkin and Mike Chrimes (Note 5), pp. 183, 200-1, 230, 835-6.

[69] *Staffs. Advertiser,* 1 November 1856, p. 5; D. Morier Evans, *The History of the Commercial Crisis 1857-58,* London: Groombridge, 1859, Appendix pp. xciii-xcvi.

[70] *Staffs. Advertiser,* 25 April 1857, p .6; 1 August 1857, p. 7.

[71] *Aris's Birmingham Gazette,* 28 September 1857, p. 2; 16 November 1857, p. 2.

[72] *Birmingham Journal,* 16 January 1858, p. 3; *Building News,* 2 April 1858, p. 357.

Military reports about the walls and fortification projects in Havana, 19th century

Ignacio-Javier Gil-Crespo

Research Center "José Joaquín de Mora"-Cárdenas Foundation, Spain

The bay of Havana in Cuba was one of the most important harbours in America during the Spanish Empire. Its defence was always under review and progressively increased. The access tothe bay was defended by several forts: San Sebastián de la Punta, la Real Fuerza, El Morro and, after the English attack in the 18th century, San Carlos de la Cabaña. However, the west side of the city towards the interior was a weak point. For this reason, from the 16th century, governors and engineers designed a strong wall from the open sea to the bay, enclosing the city. Nevertheless, in the late 18th and early 19th centuries, the population increased, and many people lived outside the walls, so that governors were afraid of a raid. So, in 1815 a debate about its utility as defence began. Between 1817 and 1861, several defence systems were designed to replace the wall with forts and entrenched fields. Each fortification design developed new defence theories. In the middle of the 19th century warfare was highly improved and fortified systems had to be adapted. The designs of 1817, 1855 and 1861 show perfectly the evolution of warfare and fortification in this epoch. The final result was in 1863 the walls were demolished and forts were not built.

The city walls of Havana (1558-1740) and the fortification of the west side (1763-1779)

The history of construction of the city walls of Havana is well known. After the French pirate Jacques Sores' attack (1555) the governors were afraid of more attacks in this important harbour where the Spanish army and trade ships arrived from the Spain Mainland towards America and vice versa. So, in 1558 they decided to build a wall to protect the city. Between 1572 and 1582, a provisional enclosure made with wood, earth and campaign works amongst the walls of the houses was made. At the end of the 16th century a layout of a wall was designed, but in 1603 the engineer Cristóbal de Roda designed a new, strong wall (Fig. 1). The lack of money and the apathy of the Crown delayed the works. Meanwhile, new projects were proposed, such as that of excavating a channel-ditch between the sea and the bay, turning the city into an island. Finally, in 1674 the works of the wall began, under the supervision of the engineer Juan de Síscara, who had worked on the repairs of the fortifications in Santiago de Cuba after an English attack.

Even without finishing the enclosure, the population of Havana had spread beyond the walls. In 1734 the shipyard was placed near the south bastion of La Tenaza, and a new gate was opened. The workers began to build their houses nearby. In spite of this, in 1740 the work of the walls was completed; that is 182 years! However, the excavation of the ditch and the covered way had to wait until 1797 to be finished.[1]

Due to the quick growth of the population, in 1746, a new layout of city walls was proposed by the engineers Antonio Arredondo and Bruno Caballero. This new wall had six larger bastions with ravelins, ditch, covered way and glacis. The new wall would have had more artillery than the older: five cannons in each facade of each bastion, three in the *gorge* (the interior side or entrance of a bastion or other outwork, which is usually the interval between the two flanks of the work) and ten in the curtains. The castle of La Punta would be buried in the glacis of the new fortification. But it never was built.

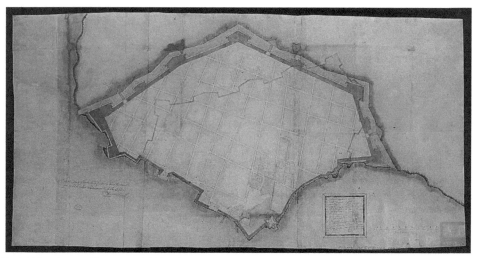

Fig 1. Urban layout of Havana in 1603 with the layout of the cerca vieja (old walls) and cerca nueva (new walls), designed by Cristóbal de Roda (AGI, MP-SD-20)

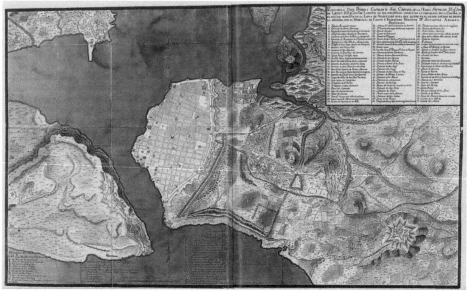

Fig 2. Plan of the new fortifications in Havana after the English attack, drawn by Luis Huet (1776) (AGI, MP-SD-412)

After the occupation by the English in 1762 and the restoration to Spain in 1763, the governor Ambrosio Funes de Villalpando brought the engineer Silvestre Abarca to study and improve the fortifications of Havana. The English army had attacked the city from the hill near the Morro Castle on the other side of the entrance of the bay. At this point, Abarca proposed to build a big fort: San Carlos de la Cabaña (built in 1763-1774). The preoccupation of the governor and the engineer was the west side, also called "landward". As the city had grown beyond the walls, Abarca designed and built two more forts in this area: the castle of Atarés (1763-1767) and the castle of Príncipe (1767-1779). With these three new castles, Havana was surrounded by fortifications which allowed crossed fire between them (Fig. 2).

The debate about the functionality and reports about the condition of the walls (1815-1850)

As well as this military preoccupation, the civil authorities were developing new social and recreational spaces in the glacis. The military space in front of the walls had to be 1,500 yards wide, without any building or vegetation. In this wide space, new avenues were projected in the beginning of the 19th century, and also beyond the walls near the bay.

Between 1811 and 1819 there were several riots in Santo Domingo-Haiti and Florida. The slaves and "colour-castes" rebelled. The harbour of Havana got weak in opposition to the naval power of the United States. The obsession of the military governors was the protection of the city from the west. The population beyond the walls had increased a lot and there were more people outside than in the enclosed Havana. They were afraid of an hypothetical uprising of the "colour-castes". In the meantime, the civil population ignored these problems and used the glacis and the walls as recreational spaces. So, the civil authorities asked the army for the use of the plots and spaces where the walls were.

In February 1815 the engineer Germán Montaña wrote a report about the repairs the fortifications needed and the cost for doing them. As he explained in this report, the wall was ruined on the bay-side and on the sea-front, the Malecón. It was necessary to demolish and re-build it with ashlar and masonry. The report said that the main failing was the lack of foundations, and also some holes and breaches. Montaña valued the cost of the repairs at 100.000 *pesos*.[2]

In August 1817 a new report was written by the engineer Antonio Ventura Bocarro.[3] This report said that the wall had no defensive function due its ruined state. Nevertheless, Bocarro's main complaint was about the neighbours who built houses and other buildings alongside the wall, so that the covered way and the ditch became useless.

Hence, Bocarro proposed to demolish the old wall, build a new wall with the stones of the old wall, and sell the plots of land where the wall had been. The Treasury could earn 300.000 *pesos* with which the new wall could be built and even have some money over. Bocarro revised the idea of building a channel-ditch. The project was approved and a Royal Order on 30th December 1817 ordered the General Captain of the Island of Cuba to think about how to do this "so transcendental project which so many advantages could provide".[4]

On 5th February 1839, the Marshal Narciso López submitted a letter to the Mainland Government in which, after exalting his patriotism ("the luck and happiness of the homeland have been the first and constant aim of my own desire and sleeplessness") and the importance of the city, he wrote about the uselessness of the walls.[5] The objective of this report was to show the financial benefit of demolishing the walls. López made them an offer they would not be able to refuse: 40.000.000 *reales* gained without any risk (that is 2.000.000 *pesos*; seven times more than the estimation of Bocarro in 1817!).

This quantity seduced the Government through the Minister of Finance. López's report arrived to Madrid on 26th February 1839. Four days after, on 2nd March, the Cabinet of Ministers issued a Royal Order with the authorization for the sale of the walls and the closer plots of land. The Royal Order said that half of the profit had to be reserved to improve the fortifications and to build new ones, and the other half had to be remitted to the Royal Treasury. When the Minister of War heard about this order, he reported to Her Majesty and on 18th April a new Royal Order was issued, voiding the sale. A conflict between the two contradictory Royal Orders arose. The military authorities in Cuba argued that first of all a new fortification had to be built before the sale and demolition of the old walls. On 31th May 1841 the situation was resolved by stating that the sale could be "untimely and dangerous".

From then on, the city council would have to ask the Crown for any of the plots that the city walls occupied, if they wanted public spaces for the city. This problem was arisen several times until their demolition in 1863.

The Director Sub-Inspector of Engineers, Mariano Carrillo, wrote a report on 27th February 1842 about the condition of the fortifications of Havana.[6] The complaint of the engineer was that "while we are arguing [about demolition or not], neither the new wall is being built, nor the old is repaired . . . and this will cost 1,500,000 *pesos*, but only for bad trenches". Carrillo exposed the damage to the walls: the sea side was ruined and the part closer to the entrance to the harbour was in very bad condition. Parapets, platforms, the floors of the turrets, gunpowder-stores required immediate repairations. The walls were not ready for the new and more powerful artillery, whose vibrations had caused several damages.

New fortification projects (1852-1861)

These types of reports continued along the years, without almost anything being done. However, there was an event which obliged to the military authorities to think about the conditions of fortifications and the defensive system of Havana. In 1850 Narciso López commanded a raid against the Governor of the island. López, finally, was arrested and executed in the castle of Atarés.[7]

In 1852, a Commission of the Board of Generals issued a new report in which there were descriptions of the island, the inhabitants by departments and "castes", the communications, the fortifications of the ports and the military buildings. Of each fortification, it offered a description of its problems and proposed solutions. The report said that "in spite of the patent vices of the old wall, it must be preserved by arranging its embankments and pits". The new project proposed to make use of the castles of Príncipe and Atarés and build two new ones in the hills of Ánimas and Jesuitas, all of them communicated by a smaller but defensive wall with gun-loops for rifles.[8]

The project of Ramón y Carbonell, Álvares de Sotomayor y Zaragoza (1855)

In February 1855, Colonel Juan de Ramón y Carbonell, Commander Juan Álvares de Sotomayor and Captain Francisco Javier de Zaragoza presented a project for a continuous enclosure with redoubts, defensive barracks, caponiers and a powerful wall with escarpments and gates that would enclose, with a complex and heavily armed wall, the new neighbourhoods that had emerged outside Havana's walls from the cove of San Lazaro to the castle of Atarés.

The new fortification would have a continuous artillery system. Six large bastions were proposed; a semi-bastion and a tenaille, with demi-lunes and advanced traverses. Behind the bastions were buildings and defences. Behind the bastions numbers 2, 3 and 5, three large barracks would be located. They were designed for 1,000 infantrymen, with pavilions for officers, attached dependents and a defensive corridor with casemates for artillery and rifles. On the *gorge* of the bulwarks numbers 1, 4 and 7, redoubts with casemates were placed. On the fronts of the curtains of greater length, there would also be casemates. The whole curtain would be a great artillery front with escarpment, moat, covered road, counterscarp and glacis (Fig. 3).

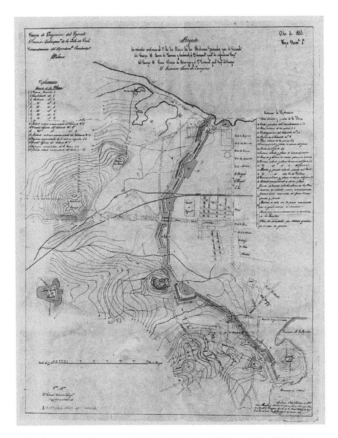

Fig 3. General plan of fortification of Havana, 1855 (AGMM, box 2810, subfile 171-3-1)

The redoubts were fortifications in the shape of a "T" with a forward curved body of about 60 m in length with seven casemates in two floors: in each one there were a gun-loop for cannons on the first floor and three loopholes for rifles on the ground floor. Behind this body, a caponier was inserted into the wall with six casemates on two floors. All concrete construction was protected from impacts by a layer approximately 150 cm thick (Fig. 4).

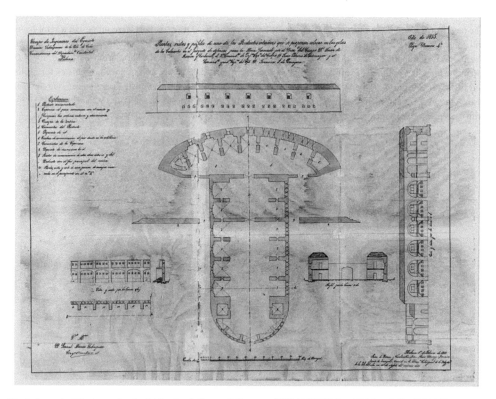

Fig 4. Layout of the type of redoubt for the defence of Havana, 1855 (AGMM, box 2810, subfile 171-3-3)

This great fortification had a front of 3,500 m and was complemented by exterior works such as the battery of Santa Clara, the battery of San Nazario, the castle of the Prince built by Abarca in 1767, the fort in the Alto de los Jesuitas that had already been proposed in other previous projects, in addition to other advanced and campaign works.

The general concept of this fortification was still to enclose Havana with a wall, adapted in its design and construction to the new artillery and the extensive use of the rifle. This idea again placed an impediment to the further growth of the city and required a large clear field on its entire front.

The project of Nicolás Valdés (1861)

The great advances in artillery that were developing throughout the 19th century (with greater power of shot and range) forced fortifications to adapt to the new techniques and fortification theory evolved.

From 1858 (by Royal Order of 29th November, 1858), the use of rifled artillery was adopted in Spain. In 1859, the first rifled cannons were manufactured, which meant that the old type of spherical projectile had to become an elongated one. In parallel, gunpowder was modified so that its reaction was slower and more progressive. The ranges increased from 2,000-3,000 m to 5,000-6,000 m, reaching 7,500 m during the Paris seige of 1870-71 by the Prussians.[9] This new artillery development forced the development, and changed the concept, of fortifications towards the strong polygonal form, heavily armed with big gun batteries[10] to resist direct artillery attack from long distances, and provide the defence of flanks from caponiers and the opening of walls embrasures for a large number of rifles.

On 12th August, 1861 another proposal of greater breadth and complexity for the defence of the land part of Havana was presented in Madrid, signed by the Colonel Engineer Nicolás Valdés, who had signed in the Cuban capital in July of that year.[11] This engineer, renowned for his hazardous and travelled life and knowledge,[12] developed a project consisting of several forts and redoubts that would enclose the extension of the new neighbourhoods that were growing to the west of the old wall (Fig. 5).

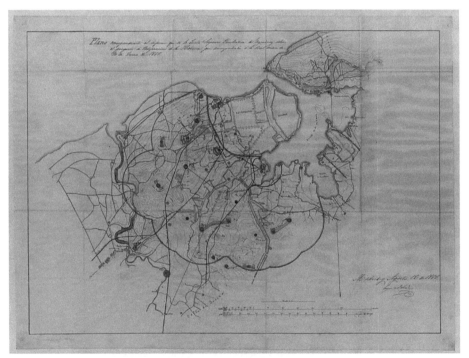

Fig 5. General plan of fortification of Havana, by Nicolás Valdés, 1861 (AGMM, box 2810, plan 02)

Valdés' project was of a much larger scope than that of 1855 and would give defences to a much larger area. The proposal, more modern, was the construction a series of forts erected on the hills that rise west and south of Havana and set so that their fires would cross. At the same time, the forts would have barracks for a large number of infantry troops. They wouild be strategically located defending steps and communications, including those of the railroad. On the opposite side of the bay, the fort of La Cabaña would be reinforced with three more forts and four batteries. All the forts would be equipped with underground cisterns, with a capacity for 100 days, at a ration of 20 litres per soldier per day. Six new forts were proposed (Fig. 6):

1. Fort of Jesuitas, for 500 soldiers and 84 pieces of artillery (33 small calibre)

2. Fort of Rosa de Aldecoa, for 600-700 soldiers and 100 pieces of artillery

3. Fort of Nuestra Señora de los Dolores, for 550 men and 100 pieces of artillery

4. Fort of Chaple, for 550 men and 102 pieces of artillery

5. Fort of Cocal, for 500 soldiers and 82 pieces of artillery

6. Fort of e Las Palmas, for 500-600 men and 94 pieces of artillery

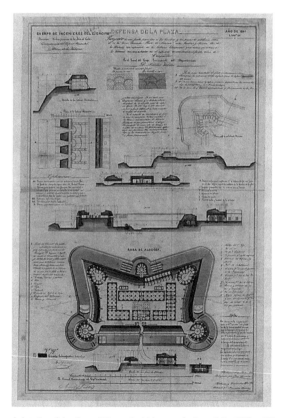

Fig 6. Layout, sections and details of the fort of Rosa de Aldecoa, designed for 550 soldiers and 100 cannons (AGMM, box 2810, plan 07)

Fort Atarés underwent considerable changes in this project. Surrounding the ancient castle in three sides, a new embankment and open parapet for 50 pieces of powerful artillery were designed. There would be a new moat with flanking caponiers in which there would be 14 and 16 casemates. Finally, in the part that overlooks the bay and relegated to a rear position, a barracks for 500 men was projected with pavilions, warehouses and other associated facilities (Fig. 7).

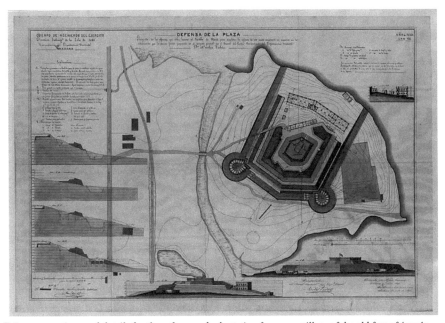

Fig 7. Layout, sections and details for the reform and adaptation for new artillery of the old fort of Atarés, designed for 500 soldiers and about 80 new cannons (AGMM, box 2810, plan 04)

These forts would be complemented by two batteries south of Chaple Fort, in addition to those of Reina, Santa Clara and San Nazario. In consideratin of their expected use, the construction of various campaign works that would reinforce them was foreseen, mainly in the hill of Jesus del Monte (three forts).

The proposal carefully studied the profiles of the batteries, pits and heights to calculate the reach and the shoot-range. The engineer suggested the constructive part and outlined some details. The construction would be done with thick walls and concrete vaults, 1 m thick. A damping layer of up to 3 m of earth would be laid over the vaults. The batteries would be shielded with metal trusses covered by a layer of earth 140 cm thick. The escarpments and slopes, as exposed parts, would be covered. Valdés offered two solutions for this cover: either with stone or with brick. In either cases, design was for a series of superimposed discharge arcs that allow that in case of impact the entire wall does not crumble and it could be quickly repaired.

The demolition of the walls of Havana (1863)

A Royal Order of 22nd May, 1863, extended on 11th June, decreed the demolition of the walls. Without having built any of these proposed fortifications and defences of the west part of Havana, the end of the history of the walls of Havana started on 8th August, 1863 when, with a solemn public feast, popular merrymaking, ecclesiastical blessing and military concern, the demolition began. The then Governor Domingo Dulce y Garay,

Marquis of Castel-Florit (1862-1866) saw this as an opening up of the city and an opportunity for growth and urban beautification, not without its dose of speculation with the sale of plots of land (Fig. 8).

Fig 8. The ceremony of the demolition of the walls, drawn in the satirical newspaper Don Junípero (9th August 1863)

Fig 9. Remaining parts of the walls in 1901, while the space before occupied by the defence was being built.

Fig 10. Photo of the current remains of the walls of Havana, in Belgium Avenue (photo: author)

The process of demolition began by breeching the walls where they met the streets of the intramural Havana, to give those streets continuity beyond the walls. Gradually the sections in front of the blocks were demolished. The process of demolition continued during the rest of Spanish colonization on Cuba, even during the Republic after the independence of 1898(Figs. 9-10).[13]

At the end of the 19th century, during the war against USA and the independence raids in the island, the defence projects of the west part of Havana were abandoned. The new defence projects changed in their theory and idea. An enemy was no longer expected to advance by land. A new plan was designed (in reality, several successive plans and, as usual, lost in bureaucracy and opinions) to defend the island from the coast. A naval attack with its subsequent disembarkation of troops was expected. The improvement of the range and the precision of the weapons as well as the use of submarine torpedoes evolved, once again, the concept of fortification to finish building a series of shore coast batteries with Krupp and Ordóñez cannons that were sent from the Peninsula.

Abbreviations

AGI: Archivo General de Indias (West-Indias General Archive, Seville)
AGMM: Archivo General Militar de Madrid (Military General Archive of Madrid)

Military reports about the walls and fortification projects in Havana, 19th century

References

[1] J.M.F Arrate, *Llave del nuevo mundo, antemural de las Indias occidentales. La Habana descripta: noticias de su fundación, aumentos y estado,* México DF, Fondo de Cultura Económica, 1949, p. 59-60; E. Roig de Leuchsenring, *Los monumentos nacionales de la República de Cuba, vol. 3 (Fortalezas coloniales de La Habana),* La Habana, Junta Nacional de Arqueología y Etnología, 1960; J.E. Weiss, "Arquitectura colonial cubana", La Habana-Sevilla: Letras Cubanas, Agencia Española de Cooperación Internacional, Junta de Andalucía, [1972] 2002.

[2] AGMM, box 2816, subfile 174-1.

[3] AGMM, box 2816, subfile 174-1.

[4] AGMM, box 2816, subfile 174-1.

[5] AGMM, box 2810, subfile 171-1-3, 5-2-1839/12-9-1843.

[6] AGMM box 2810, subfile 171-1-2. Defensas.

[7] Weiss, *Arquitectura colonial,* p. 336-337.

[8] AGMM, box 2810, subfile 172-1.

[9] P. Sailhan, *La fortification. Histoire et dictionnaire,* París, Tallandier, 1991, p. 179-180; J. Vigón, *Historia de la artillería española.* 3 vols Madrid, Consejo Superior de Investigaciones Científicas. Instituto Jerónimo Zurita, 1947; I. Hogg, *The History of Fortification,* Nueva York, St. Martin's Press, 1981, p. 142,171

[10] Sailhan, *Fortification,* p. 181; J.-J. Rapin, *L'esprit des fortifications.* Vol. Presses polytechniques et universitaires romandesLausanne, 2010, p. 40-43

[11] AGMM, box 2810, planos 01-09

[12] Valdés researched about materials strength in Philipines, Santo Domingo and Cuba and wrote about it. Its famous work *Manual del ingeniero* (1869) was a reference book in Engineering and Architecture Schools in Spain along time.

[13] E. Roig de Leuchsenring, *La Habana, apuntes históricos,* La Habana, Consejo Nacional de Cultura, 1963. (Roig 1963, 133, Weiss 2002, 366)

From the drawing to the wall: the operational chain of building stone on the restoration worksite of St. Martin's church in Liège during the nineteenth century

Antoine Baudry

Faculty of Architecture, University of Liège, Belgium

Introduction

The collegiate church of St Martin in Liege (Fig. 1-2) was founded shortly before 965 by the bishop Eraclus, at the summit of a promontory called "Publémont", located to the west of the historical centre of the city [1]. Rebuilt several times over the years, the current gothic church features an imposing fourteenth-century western tower, a nave with four spans and side chapels, a non-salient transept and a choir loft composed of three straight spans and a seven-sided apse, structures that were built in the sixteenth century [2]. At the end of the eighteenth century, the building was requisitioned by the French revolutionaries and converted into stables. In the time leading up to the re-establishment of the parochial ministry following the concordat of 1801, much damage was done to the building: the sacristy was pillaged, windows and stained-glass windows were broken, the marble was stolen, and finally, the lead and eaves gutters were torn off to be melted down, causing the infiltration of rainwater in several places [3]. For a period of around thirty years, the church council tried to carry out the most urgent repairs to keep the monument afloat by renewing the roof. The task was all the more delicate to manage as the economic fortunes of the institution had been greatly dented by the revolutionary seizures and no financial support was offered by the successive French and Dutch governments (1795-1815; 1815-1830) [4]. This precarious situation lasted until 1839, the year in which the administrative body in charge of the restoration and preservation of monuments in the young Kingdom of Belgium was set in motion [5].

Although the general history of restoration work on the church of St Martin after 1839 was clearly signposted by an article specifically dedicated to this subject [6], it should be noted that no elaborate study has yet been dedicated to the restoration work and its many different logistical, material, technical economic or human aspects. The documentation linked to this significant episode in the life of the monument is far from lacking. Indeed, the Fabric of the church preserved an extremely rich and under-used archive group that contains, among other things, precise details about the supply of materials for the construction and the workforce used during the work.

The present article focusses on the use of building stone during the first interventions carried out on the site, which involved the reconstruction of much of the masonry and buttresses of the choir loft and transept. The observations made here concern the years 1839-1845, the period for which the documentation is by far the most varied and abundant: debates and surveys by architects, building specifications, contracts, general accounting, yardage, receipts, invoices, orders etc., although some details are sadly lacking – including the architects' plans. The material remains of this period also allow archaeological observations *in situ*. This wealth of documents makes it possible to recreate, with a high level of certainty, the operational chain of the materials used during the

From the drawing to the wall: the operational chain of building stone on the restoration worksite of St. Martin's church in Liège during the nineteenth century

first years of one the most prestigious and earliest building works carried out in the city of Liege and on a broader scale, the Kingdom of Belgium.

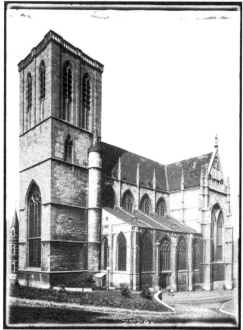

Fig 1. The church of Saint-Martin in Liège.
© *KIK-IRPA, Bruxelles.*

Fig 2. The church of Saint-Martin in Liège.
© *KIK-IRPA, Bruxelles.*

The history of surveys and operations

In September 1839, a delegation from the Royal Commission for Monuments, during a visit to Liege, inspected the church of Saint Martin (Fig. 3) and observed that the external masonry of the edifice was so degraded that it could soon constitute a danger to public safety. The institution promptly sent a report to the Minister of the Interior, the minister responsible, and also to the Governor of the Province outlining its fears and recommended an urgent intervention while at the same time praising the artistic merits of the monument [7].

In December, the architect Jean-Noël Chevron (1790-1867), on the request of the church wardens, compiled an exhaustive report on the state of the building. His conclusion was grim: the external masonry was cracked in several places, many facings had shattered from the effects of frost, some of the walls were worryingly bulging, fragments of masonry had fallen to the floor of the building, and finally, some of the pinnacles crowning the buttresses showed an overhang. The architect identified the weaknesses to the buttresses for the choir loft and transept and recommended a partial reconstruction of several of them, particularly to the upper sections[8]. Following several requests by the communal administration, an estimate for the external work was drawn up in June of the following year. In this seventeen-page document, the architect estimated the cost of each operation to replace a cubic metre of stone: price of material at the quarry, cladding, transport, shaping and placement of new stones, restoration of old stonework, installation of anchoring rods, removal of rubble [9].

Fig 3. The church of Saint-Martin in Liège in 1830. Watercolour by Joseph Fussell. © Musée Wittert – Collections artistiques ULiège.

Although the urgency of the work was pointed out by the *Commission royale des Monuments*, no restoration was initiated during the following years even though the situation only worsened, and several reminders were sent to the higher authorities.[10] This lethargy was explained by the low-income levels of the Church Council which did not have the means to finance costly initiatives. The institution approached different agencies to negotiate precious subsidies for the future of the monument: The City of Liege, the Province of Liege and the Minister for Justice via the Administration of Religious Affairs. This inactivity persisted until April 1843, following the decision of the City Council to grant a sum of 10,000 francs for the restoration work [11]. Financing the restoration work remained a thorny problem during the coming years and affected the smooth running of operations on more than one occasion [12].

The *Commission royale des Monuments* gave priority to the renewal of masonry and two buttresses of the Northern arm of the transept [13]. After referring to the recommendations of the architect [14], the City of Liege advised the Church Council not to appoint the future contractor by public tender as was the custom, because this delicate work *"required a suitably experienced workforce…, good workers, and continuous supervision by an intelligent foreman"*[15]. On the other hand, it authorised this *modus operandi* to choose the stone supplier[16]. The Church Council drew up detailed specifications, which were finalised on November 26th 1843 [17]. An appeal was then launched in three daily newspapers: *Journal de Liège et de la Province, La Tribune* and *Gazette de Liège* [18].

From the drawing to the wall: the operational chain of building stone on the restoration worksite of St. Martin's church in Liège during the nineteenth century

The specifications comprised four articles concerning the stones to be used. The first stated that the volume necessary to restore the parts mentioned above was around 40 cubic metres. The second stipulated that the stones should be *"the same sort"* [19] that had been used in the original construction and should be extracted *"from the hardest layers of the quarries between Samson and Namur and the quarries of the Ourthe and Ambleve"* [20]. They should also be homogenous and free of *"imperfections that could harm the solidity or the neatness of the work"* [21]. The third article mentioned that the stones should be cut with a sharp chisel on their visible surfaces in order to obtain a flat face, and rough-hewn with a large cutting edge on their undersides. They should have sharp edges and a non-thinned tail. Finally, the fourth article indicates the layout of stretchers and bondstones, while stating clearly that the medieval way of arranging stone layers must be complied with in order to be able to reuse all the stones that were in good condition and harmonise the two works[22].

The seven bidders for the project were judged on the price they offered per running metre of hood moulds, per cubic metre of archstone and parallelepipedal blocks. In competition with Philippe Fincoeur, Dieudonné Carpentier and Jean Joseph Lhoneux in Liège, A. P. Legrand and Tonglet in Huy, Jean-Louis Lambermont in Esneux and Antoine Joseph Lejeune in Lille, it was the master quarryman Henri Mention in Tilff who was entrusted with the work [23]. He had worked on several quarries including one with *"petit granit"* at Comblain-au -Pont which was to supply most of the stones necessary for the operations. The village is located around fifteen kilometres south of Liege and is watered by the Ourthe, a tributary of the Meuse, two waterways by means of which the stones would be transported (cf. *infra;* Fig. 4).

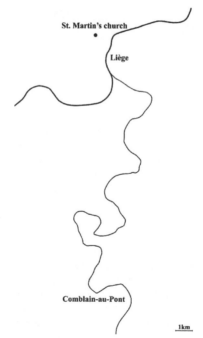

Fig 4. Liège, Comblain- au -Pont and their current hydrographic network.

416

Here we will mention the materials in question. The stone used in medieval construction was a limestone from the Visean ground of the Lower Carboniferous, commonly known as *"limestone of the Meuse"* or *"bluestone"*. It is found in quarries located along the river, between Namur and Engis. The *"petit granit"* used by Henri Mention is not granite in the geological sense of the term. In reality, it is a crinoidal limestone from the Tournaisian soils of the Lower Carboniferous. These two varieties of stone present essentially similar characteristics: a white-grey patina, a good resistance to compression and atmospheric pollution in addition to an excellent cuttability facilitating fine sculpture polishing. The *"small granit"* offers the advantage of being frost-proof, unlike the *"Meuse limestone"* [24].

In the contract he signed on December 13th 1843, Henri Mention committed to lodging 500 francs to the *Banque liégeoise* by way of a guarantee for the construction, and also presented two solvent guarantors, Pierre Charlier and Maximilien Delbart, owners in Tilff [25]. The document specified that the materials would be delivered into the garden next to the church at the cost of the entrepreneur. Before unloading, the stones would be inspected by a delegated individual from the Church Council, which would have the right to reject them if they failed to meet the standards required by the specifications. Any stone that was rejected would have to be replaced within fifteen days under penalty of a fine. If the deliveries exceeded the deadline, the Church Council could demand a payment of 25 Francs per day of delay and purchase the stones from another supplier of its choice at the expense of the contractor. The payment would be made in two instalments, one on delivery and the other six months later [26].

Having established the rules of the game, it was now necessary to choose a project creator. The restoration was entrusted to the architect Jean-Charles Delsaux (1821-1893), who was believed to have a bright future ahead of him as he was due to become the provincial architect the following year and would likely be entrusted with important projects in the Liege region [27]. The work began in April 1844, with the complete reconstruction of the wall of the transept [28]. On May 1st and 13th, the architects of the City and Province of Liege, in the persons of Julien-Étienne Rémont (1800-1883) and Isidore Jamolet (? -?), inspected the church and observed that the two north-west buttresses needed not to be partially reconstructed, but completely reconstructed, which had an impact on the predicted yardage [29].

Convinced that these buttresses had been altered by *"repairs randomly done or in a spirit of saving money"* [30], Jean-Charles Delsaux intended to restore them in their ancient style, using their counterparts on the southern arm of the transept, which were crowned with pinnacles, as a model. He justified this addition by means of two arguments: to strengthen the buttresses to enable them to resist the thrust of the vaults and increase the beauty of the monument which was visible from many locations within the city (Fig. 5) [31]. The presence of analogous adornments in the Church of Saint Jacques in Liege, a contemporary of the Church of Saint Martin, convinced the City of Liege and the *Commission royale des Monuments* [32].

The drawings of Jean-Charles Delsaux were unfortunately not preserved. This can be explained by the fact that there was no legal obligation to submit plans before the year 1862, resulting in the loss of precious documents[33]. The administrative correspondence does give us some information on these elements, however. Therefore, the stones were standardised and numbered in accordance with their dimensions, from "A" to "Z" and "a" to "h", resulting in some thirty different formats for courses, vault stones and pinnacles [34]. This diversity was justified by the desire to respect the heights of irregular medieval courses, and bond the stones by aligning the vertical joints one course in two, although such a characteristic was nothing like primitive building. This conception had a double objective: on one hand, rationalizing the construction to optimise the technical gestures, the work time and therefore result in saving money; on the other hand, presenting a structure in harmony with the medieval building but of a quality that was adjudged to be superior.

From the drawing to the wall: the operational chain of building stone on the restoration worksite of St. Martin's church in Liège during the nineteenth century

Fig 5. The church of Saint-Martin in Liège around 1880. Photograph by W. Damry. © Musée Wittert – Collections artistiques ULiège.

The demolition of the two buttresses was completed at the beginning of August. Julien-Étienne Rémont, Jean-Charles Delsaux, the master mason Libert Bayet and the master stone cutter Ferdinand Barbier were subsequently given directives for their reconstruction: preserve the medieval foundations, staple each new stone and, finally, bind the constructions by cutting the walls of the transept to anchor the buttresses to it [35].

A visit by Julien-Étienne Rémont on October 7th informs us that, on this date, the buttresses were newly reconstructed up to the creation of the vaults [36]. Another visit on November 12th by a delegation of the *Commission royale des Monuments*, indicated that the work planned for that year had ended [37]. The stones were nonetheless delivered until late in the year to give work to the stonecutters workshop during the winter (cf. *infra*) [38].

On March 31st 1845, Julien-Étienne Rémont and Isidore Jamolet inspected the restoration work and observed that, on one hand, the work completed the previous year was satisfactory, and on the other hand, the efforts during that year should focus on the buttresses of the apse so as not to place the vault of the sanctuary in danger [39]. Due to a lack of funding, only one of these buttresses was restored that year [40].

Supply of materials to the site

While the plans, estimates and yardages enabled the master quarryman to know in advance the exact volume of stone to be extracted [41], the orders were only made progressively, in accordance with the needs of the building project, the workload of the stone-cutters and the available financial resources. Seven to eight days passed between the order and the delivery. After this deadline, the Church Council called the master-quarryman to order [42].

The cargoes of rough-hewn blocks whose dimensions exceeded by a few centimetres those of the stones to be used in the building [43], were transported by various boatmen who followed the course of the Ourthe and the Meuse, or by haulage. The blocks were unloaded on a quay situated near the Pont de la Boverie, which is demolished today, around two kilometres as the crow flies from the church (Figs. 6-7) [44]. They were then brought by carriers to the garden of the Church Council where they were checked and later rejected if they had even the tiniest flaw [45]. At least during the first delivery or during a delivery of samples, Julien-Étienne Rémont was delegated to carry out these checks, which then fell to a member of the Church Council, probably assisted by the director of works (cf. *infra*) [46].

Fig 6. Evocation of the banks of the Meuse in Liège in the middle of the 19th century. Lithography by Henri Borremans. © Musée Wittert – Collections artistiques ULiège.

From the drawing to the wall: the operational chain of building stone on the restoration worksite of St. Martin's church in Liège during the nineteenth century

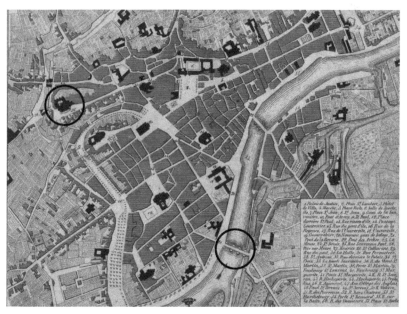

Fig 7. Situation of the pont de la Boverie and the Church of Saint-Martin in Liège, second third of the 19th century. Plan by Cremetti. © Musée Wittert – Collections artistiques ULiège.

Various receipts give us a clear picture of the supply of *petit granit* to the site between May 23rd and December 3rd 1844. During that period, 51 deliveries were carried out, totalling 509 blocks, for a volume of 107,268 cubic metres. The cargoes contained between 1 and 20 blocks, even though some journeys showed 36, 37 and 49, for a maximum value of 5,922 cubic metres [47]. This data suggests that the boatmen delivered the stone to other sites because it is difficult to imagine that the journeys would have taken place for such small volumes, or single stones [48]. There was no shortage of examples at that time : Sainte-Croix, Saint-Paul, Saint-Jacques, to name only the few best-known ones [49].

The stones came mainly from the quarries of Henri Mention, although some were delivered after September 10th by the master quarryman François Dehan who also exploited a quarry at Comblain-au-Pont (40 and 11 deliveries respectively). The intervention of this second master quarryman can be explained by certain complaints the Church Council made to Henri Mention during the previous month. Indeed, the institution was very displeased by the frequent delays in deliveries and the flaws in certain stones. The latter were rejected, which delayed the execution of the work [50]. Henri Mention mostly used the boatman Henri Ledent, while François Dehan worked with his colleague Léonard Coulon. The boatman Joseph Pahaut is only mentioned once in the records [51].

In 1845, the orders for delivery were still being made regularly, in restricted lots and under the same conditions as those mentioned previously [52]. According to the receipts kept, 39 deliveries were made between January 12th and July 31st, totalling 377 blocks, for a volume of 82,153 cubic metres. The stones now came from the quarries "Dehan Mention & Compagnie", which suggests that an agreement had been reached between the two master quarrymen. Here too, the cargoes included between 2 and 23 blocks, with an exceptional journey of 36 blocks, for a maximum volume of 4,488 cubic metres. While Henri Ledent and Léonard Coulon are still the most used boatmen, Joseph Pahaut, Louis Hanson, Jaques Lagasse or a certain Malo also appear in the archives [53].

The workforce in the workplace

The master mason Libert Bayet was named director and supervisor of the work by the Church Council on April 22nd 1844 [54]. This choice can probably be explained by the fact that a member of his family, the master mason Simon Hairs-Bayet, had already been employed by the Church Council between 1833 and 1842 [55]. The latter probably wanted to hire people who had proved worthy and competent in the past. The stone cutters were directly employed by the master quarryman Henri Mention and directed in the workplace by the master stone cutter Ferdinand Barbier [56]. The repair to their tools was incumbent on the Church Council who hired the locksmith P. J. Warnand [57]. The latter also manufactured the lewis tools used for lifting the blocks [58]. To this effect, ropes, pulleys and a double-wheeled winch were purchased at the start of the project [59]. They were all paid bi-weekly [60].

The general accounts give the names of the team leaders but unfortunately not their composition. The teams must have been well-supported, and the site must have resembled a human ant hill. In 1845, during a period of financial difficulty, the Church Council informed the Minister for Justice that it would have to let go the 90 workers on the site if subsidies were not granted [61]. This number included workers belonging to specific occupations that are not dealt with in the context of this article: carpenters, joiners, plumbers, slate workers, painters and ironmongers [62]. During the winter of 1844-1845, a team composed of 13 to14 stone cutters was kept on in the project's workshop in order to prepare the stones for the following season (cf. *infra*) [63]. It is to be noted that P. J. Warnand also worked, during the same period, on the restoration project for the Sainte-Croix Church, located a few hundred metres from Saint Martin. For the year 1846, he was paid 43.84 francs for having "re-sharpened" 2,923 tools at a cost of 1.5 francs per 100. At that time, the team of stone cutters working at Sainte-Croix was composed, on average, of five to eight weekly workers. They worked the same stone, but also the tufa of Maastricht, which was a lot softer. This comparison suggests, more than proves, the consequent and crucial work accomplished by P. J. Warnand on the Saint-Martin site. It is not possible, however, to extrapolate the figures present in the general accounts based on the prices suggested by the worker, because, this one, as well as repairing the stone cutters' tools, also forged lewis tools, staples, supplies pulleys, etc. He didn't do the job alone because the locksmiths Larose and Marnette also worked at making staples and "various irons"[64].

The rubble from the demolition of the buttresses and the scraps from the block-shaping were removed by cart by the carrier Noël Simon, without anyone knowing their final destination or the frequency of these operations [65].

The material remains

Observation of the monument confirms compliance with the specifications. Therefore, the facings were cut with a fine chisel, the impact of which, around $35/dm^2$, are perpendicular to the upper and lower faces of the stone (Fig. 8). They are, moreover, so regular that it is difficult to identify the width of the cutting. A carving of around 5 to 6 cm borders the edges of the side faces. The result is in stark contrast to primitive stone masonry, some were cut with chisels but more freely and less systematically. This new aesthetic is part of this desire to "do better", already mentioned. The joints, of around 0.5 cm in thickness, present a neat and regular implementation. It should be pointed out that the lime supplied by Henri Mention and the master mason Libert Bayet [66], was prepared by unskilled workers but also by women whose presence during the work is often underestimated [67].

From the drawing to the wall: the operational chain of building stone on the restoration worksite of St. Martin's church in Liège during the nineteenth century

Fig 8. Facing restored in 1840's.

Conclusion

This study, based on archival holdings that have been largely under-used up to the present, sheds some light on the systems for supply of materials to the restoration by lithic materials in Liege during a period when an intense policy of restoration and conservation of historical monuments, directly correlated to the independence of the Kingdom of Belgium in 1830. Several approaches could be undertaken to complete this first attempt. On one hand, the study of the restoration work of the old collegiate Church Saint-Martin must be completed by an approach involving other materials of construction, themselves also abundantly documented by the historical and archaeological sources: lead, iron, softwood, etc. On the other hand, a comparative analysis of the major restoration projects in the province of Liege during the 19th century will make it easier to understand the strategies of the supply of construction materials and their evolution in a region and country which is in full industrial expansion.

Acknowledgements

For their help with this study, we would like to thank Enda Breen, Monique Merland, Martine Rowier, Stéphanie Reynders and Francis Tourneur.

References

[1] J.-L. Kupper, 'Les origines de la collégiale Saint-Martin', M. Laffineur-Crépin (dir.), *Saint-Martin. Mémoire de Liège,* Alleur: éditions du Perron, 1990, pp. 15-22.
[2] P. Paquet, 'L'architecture', ibid., p. 123.
[3] Archives of the curate of Saint-Martin, file VII.A.3, letters of December 21st and 23rd 1839.

[4] Ibid., files II.A.1 to II.A.11 (many mentions).

[5] Ibid., file VII.A.3, letters of September 23rd and October 7th 1839; Archives of the *Commission royale des Monuments, Sites et Fouilles,* file Liège 1.9, letter of September 23rd 1839.

[6] F. Di Campli, '1839-1939. Cent ans de restauration', M. Laffineur-Crépin (dir.), *Saint-Martin. Mémoire de Liège,* Alleur: éditions du Perron, 1990, pp. 259-270.

[7] Archives of the *Commission royale des Monuments, Sites et Fouilles,* file Liège 1.9, letter of September 23rd 1839; Archives of the curate of Saint-Martin, file VII.A.3, letter of October 7th 1839.

[8] Archives of the curate of Saint-Martin, file VII.A.3, report of December 21st 1839.

[9] Ibid., file VII.A.3, estimate of June 6th 1840.

[10] Archives of the *Commission royale des Monuments, Sites et Fouilles,* file Liège 1.9, letters of March 11th, May 8th, June 4th and August 6th 1840, Mai 24th, June 5th and September 28th 1841.

[11] Archives of the curate of Saint-Martin, file VII.A.3, letter of July 1st 1843.

[12] Ibid., files VII.A.2 and VII.A.3 (many letters); Archives of the *Commission royale des Monuments, Sites et Fouilles,* file Liège 1.9, note of April 30th 1846.

[13] Archives of the curate of Saint-Martin, file VII.A.2, contract of December 13th 1843; Archives of the *Commission royale des Monuments, Sites et Fouilles,* file Liège 1.9, letters of December 20th 1842 and October 21st 1843 (documents not very explicit, however).

[14] Archives of the curate of Saint-Martin, file VII.A.3, report of December 21st 1839.

[15] Ibid., file VII.A.3, letter of June 7th 1843.

[16] Ibid.

[17] Ibid., file VII.A.2, contract of December 13th 1843.

[18] Ibid., file VII.A.2, invoice of November 28th, December 5th and 9th 1843.

[19] Ibid., file VII.A.2, contract of December 13th 1843.

[20] Ibid.

[21] Ibid.

[22] Ibid.

[23] Ibid.

[24] S. De Jonghe, H. Gehot, L. F. Genicot, F. Tourneur and P. Weber, *Pierres à bâtir traditionnelles de la Wallonie. Manuel de Terrain,* Jambes: Ministère de la Région wallonne, 1996, pp. 188-191; F. Doperé, P. Hoffsummer, M. Piavaux and F. Tourneur, 'Églises liégeoises en chantier au XIIIe et au XIVe siècle', B. Van den Bossche (dir.), *La cathédrale gothique Saint-Lambert à Liège. Une église et son contexte,* Liège: Université de Liège, 2005, p. 102.

[25] We do not know what connects these individuals.

[26] Archives of the curate of Saint-Martin, file VII.A.2, contract of December 13th 1843.

[27] F. Di Campli, *Jean-Charles Delsaux (1821-1893). Architecte provincial,* Herstal : Administration communale de Herstal, 1988, p. 8 (Collection Documents Herstaliens, 8).

[28] Archives of the *Commission royale des Monuments, Sites et Fouilles,* file Liège 1.9, letter of October 15th 1844.

[29] Archives of the curate of Saint-Martin, file VII.A.3, letter of July 1st 1844.

[30] Archives of the curate of Saint-Martin, file VII.A.3, letter of May 17th 1844.

[31] Ibid.

[32] Ibid., file VII.A.3, letters of May 17th, June 26th and July 8th 1844.

[33] *Bulletin des Commissions royales d'Art et d'Archéologie,* t.1, Bruxelles: De Bols-Wittouck, 1862, pp. 238-239.

[34] Archives of the curate of Saint-Martin, file VII.A.2, stones supplied for the buttress of the choir loft in 1845.

[35] Ibid., file VII.A.3, notes of August 7th 1844.

[36] Ibid., file VII.A.3, letter of October 7th 1844.

[37] Archives of the *Commission royale des Monuments, Sites et Fouilles,* file Liège 1.9, letter of November 5th 1844.

[38] Ibid., letter of December 2nd 1844.

[39] Archives of the curate of Saint-Martin, file VII.A.3, letter of April 10th 1845.

[40] Archives of the *Commission royale des Monuments, Sites et Fouilles,* file Liège 1.9, letter of March 25th 1846.

[41] Archives of the curate of Saint-Martin, file VII.A.2, letter of August 1st 1845.

[42] Ibid., file VII.A.2, letters of May 23rd, June 12th, July 9th, August 2nd, 9th, 14th, 19th, 20th and 22nd, October 1st and 9th 1844.

[43] Ibid., file VII.A.2, note of May 17th 1844.

[44] Ibid., file VII.A.2, receipt of September 28th 1844.

[45] Ibid., file VII.A.2, letter of June 12th 1844.

[46] Ibid., file VII.A.3, letter of April 28th 1844.

[47] Ibid., file VII.A.2, receipts of May 23rd and December 3rd 1844.

[48] Archives of other restoration projects are in the course of being stripped.

[49] Archives of the *Commission royale des Monuments, Sites et Fouilles,* files Liège 1.2, 1.4 and 1.11.

[50] Archives of the curate of Saint-Martin, file VII.A.2, letters of August 14th and 30th 1844.

[51] Ibid., file VII.A.2, receipts from May 23rd to December 3rd 1844.

[52] Ibid., file VII.A.2, letters of February 11th, April 8th, May 26th and 27th, June 12th, August 1st, 5th, 8th, 14th and 27th 1845.

[53] Ibid., file VII.A.2, receipts from January 12th to July 23rd 1845.

[54] Ibid., file VII.A.2, note of April 22nd 1844.

[55] Ibid., files II.A.11 and II.A.12, notes of February 12th, December 31st 1836, 1837, 1839, 1840, 1841 and 1842. These mentions concern supplies, deliveries and working days for the church and the presbytery.

[56] Ibid., file VII.A.2, note of April 22nd 1844.

[57] Ibid., file VII.A.2, note of April 22nd 1844; files II.A.12 and II.A.14, notes of June 15th, July 27th, August 24th, September 21st, October 19th, November 16th and December 14th 1844, January 11th, February 8th, March 8th, April 5th, May 3rd and 31st, June 28th, July 26th, August 30th, September 6th, October 2nd, 4th, 18th and 31st, November 15th and 29th, December 9th 1845.

[58] Ibid., file II.A.12, note of May 15th 1844.

[59] Ibid., files II.A.12 and II.A.14, notes of April 28th, June 15th and July 30th 1844; May 31st, June 7th, July 24th and August 23rd 1845.

[60] Ibid., files II.A.12 et II.A.14 (many notes).

[61] Ibid., file VII.A.3, letter of November 18th 1845.

[62] Ibid., files II.A.12 et II.A.14 (many notes).

[63] Ibid., file VII.A.3, letter of May 5th 1845.

[64] Ibid., files II.A.12 and II.A.14, notes of May 1st, November 20th and December 31st 1844, December 23rd and 31st 1845.

[65] Ibid., file II.A.12, note of December 31st 1844.

[66] Ibid., file II.A.14, note of November 2nd 1844; file II.A.15, note of September 6th 1845.

[67] Ibid., file VII.A.2, note of April 22nd 1844.

Twentieth Century

Matthijs Degraeve, Frederik Vandyck, Inge Bertels,
Heidi Deneweth and Stephanie Van de Voorde

Spatial analysis of timber construction SMEs in Brussels (1880-1980)

Matthijs Degraeve, Frederik Vandyck, Inge Bertels, Heidi Deneweth and Stephanie Van de Voorde

Vrije Universiteit Brussel, Belgium

Introduction

Despite frequent innovations in the building process, timber has been persistently used as a construction material, from pre-industrial times until today.[1] The activity of enterprises that were involved in timber construction, such as carpenters, joiners, cabinetmakers, sawyers and merchants, was therefore continuously indispensable. This was also the case in Brussels, where new building styles that required refined woodwork were abundantly adopted.[2] Timber was not only used for the furnishing of buildings, but also for their structure, even during the age of iron engineering.[3]

Although much historical research has been done on timber constructions in Brussels, both from pre-industrial and modern times,[4] the many small and medium-sized enterprises (SMEs) that were involved in realising these constructions remain largely unexplored. In researching actors in the building process, the focus of attention within construction history has namely often been directed towards the few large and prominent enterprises. Nonetheless, the high labour intensity and the high degree of specialisation in the construction process generally obstructed economies of scale, which compelled most construction enterprises to organise their production on a small scale.[5] There is a high need for profound knowledge on this multitude of small contractors, craftsmen and material suppliers that have persistently formed the backbone of the (timber) construction industry.[6]

From the late nineteenth century on, a strong demographical growth caused a boom in construction activity in Brussels. The previously rural outskirts around the city centre rapidly developed into genuine suburbs.[7] A substantial part of the construction labour market was formed by carpenters, joiners and other woodworkers. According to the Belgian industry census of 1896, nearly 12,000 people were professionally involved in the timber industry in all municipalities of the current-day Brussels-Capital Region. They were dispersed over little more than 3,000 enterprises, employing on average four people – making most of them proper timber-SMEs. By 1910, a 50 per cent increase in only fourteen years had taken place, amounting up to slightly less than 18,000 people employed in the sector. This average was strongly surpassed in most Brussels suburbs that were rapidly developing at the time, such as Ixelles (from 1,040 to 1,700 timber workers, or a 63 per cent increase) and Schaerbeek (from 855 to 1,615 timber workers, an 89 per cent increase). Conversely, in the old city of Brussels a decrease of 13 per cent in timber employment took place (Fig. 1).[8]

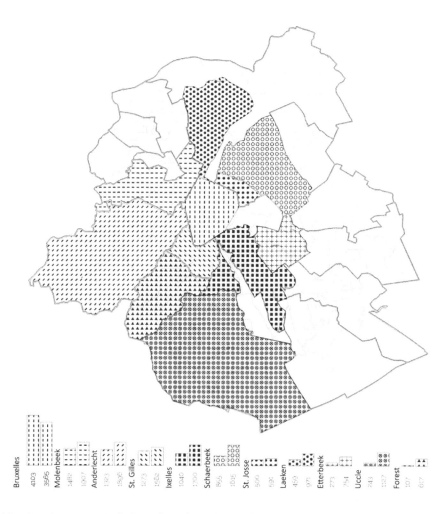

Fig. 1 Total employment rate in the Brussels' timber industry: 1896 (left bar) and 1910 (right bar)

This study's objective is to obtain new insights into the evolution of the organisational flexibility and activities of these small actors in the timber construction industry. This can benefit not only business historical insights within construction history, but also historical research into timber constructions.[9] The paper focuses on the spatial management of the timber-SMEs in Brussels by analysing their economic-geographical logics (the location where they settled) as well as their architectural logics (the building types they used). In this way, we can assess how they were able or unable to spatially maintain their business activities in the urban fabric, precisely during the period when their embeddedness was challenged by comprehensive urban developments (such as functional zoning policies and rising real estate prices) that eventually drove many of them out of the city after the Second World War. The scope of the research starts well before these developments initiated (1880) and ends when their consequences had become clear (1980).

428

Matthijs Degraeve, Frederik Vandyck, Inge Bertels,
Heidi Deneweth and Stephanie Van de Voorde

Methodology

The industrial patrimony used by the Brussels' timber-SMEs between 1880 and 1980 functions as the interdisciplinary point of departure for the spatial analysis. The location of the remaining industrial buildings informs us about the economic-geographical logics, and their architectural typology about the infrastructural logics. Since the aim is not to map every single timber-SME, the fact whether a timber-SME's infrastructure is still there today (regardless of the survival of the enterprise itself) functions as a convenient parameter to scale down the large number of enterprises to a practicable sample, which is however still sufficiently extensive to allow for statements on the spatial characteristics of the entire industry.

To trace a substantial amount of buildings that accommodated timber-SMEs, we used an existing inventory of Brussels' industrial patrimony, the *Inventaire visuel de l'architecture industrielle*, composed in the early 1980s (therefore the *terminus ante quem* of our research). Multiple researchers of the Brussels' *Archives de l'Architecture Moderne* (AAM) then roamed the streets of the Brussels-Capital Region in search of industrial buildings they deemed worthy of inventorying, dating from 1940 or older, for their architectural and/or historical value. Although the inventorisation of buildings was not always based on profound historical argumentation (due to a lack of archives) and the approach was rather unsystematic on a regional scale, it is with over 1600 records the most efficient instrument to trace a multitude of historical industrial buildings in Brussels. Buildings that had accommodated a timber construction activity (whether as their original, successive or actual (1980s) function) were filtered out by searching for keywords related to the timber industry and commerce. This resulted in a database of 157 buildings. 80 of these buildings still exist today, upon which we based the spatial analysis in this paper.

Analysing the data provided by the *Inventaire visuel* produced some basic information on the timber-SMEs: their location, activity (carpenters, joiners, cabinetmakers, sawyers, merchants...) and the period in which they were active (admittedly sometimes quite roughly estimated by the inventorisers). Furthermore, we investigated the infrastructural needs of the timber-SMEs by morphologically analysing the 80 buildings that are still present today. To grasp this multitude and complexity of industrial buildings, a systemic research methodology can be found in the extensive discourse on *type* and *typology*.[10] Not surprisingly, the authors of the *Inventaire visuel* suggest its use for *"the architectural historian engaged with the emerging study on industrial typology"*.[11] According to the Neo-Rationalists' understanding of typology, the proliferation of 'types of buildings' in both space and time embodies certain strongholds under a multitude of cultural, political and economic influences.[12] Interested in the logical construction of the built environment, this research methodology takes basic forms, or types, as the preferred knowledge instrument for researching the city.[13] The type is defined as the abstraction of buildings with inherent similarities, albeit functional or formal, programmatic or stylistic. Even though it serves as the rule for proliferated artefacts, it can only be recognised *a posteriori*.[14] By serially ordering these artefacts, it becomes possible to unveil and define such categories, or types of buildings.[15] The typological study of the timber-SMEs' buildings commenced with analysing the 80 still existing buildings we extracted from the *Inventaire visuel*. From an iterative process between the abstracting parameters and the abstracted object, 25 morphological parameters (of which a selection is presented in Fig. 2) were generated, informed by cadastral data, figure ground maps, building permits and aerial imagery. The parameters resulted in eight categories, or types, to which 90% of the 80 studied buildings attributed. We will present six of the eight categories. This selection is pragmatically based on the availability of data gathered via research of building permits, on-site investigations and the scope of this paper.

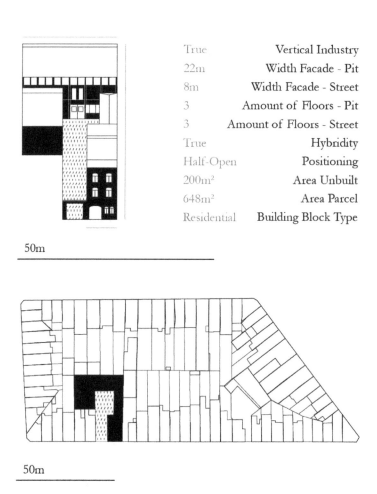

True	Vertical Industry
22m	Width Facade - Pit
8m	Width Facade - Street
3	Amount of Floors - Pit
3	Amount of Floors - Street
True	Hybridity
Half-Open	Positioning
200m²	Area Unbuilt
648m²	Area Parcel
Residential	Building Block Type

50m

50m

Fig. 2 Graphical representation of morphological parameters for Rue Marie- Henriette 52,1050 Ixelles.

Confronting the different parameters on the timber-SMEs' buildings (location, activity, period and building type) with each other, allowed for a spatial analysis of the subsector on a macro scale, both economic-geographically (by spatial GIS-mapping) and architecturally. To provide qualitative evidence for this macro analysis, we also investigated a selection of timber-SMEs and their buildings as case studies. These were selected based on the building types (either some similar cases that validated a type, or exemplary cases from different types), the availability of sources, and on-site accessibility. Both the buildings and the timber-SMEs they accommodated were submitted to an in-depth historical investigation by means of business historical sources such as commercial almanacs, fiscal registers and building permits.

430

Matthijs Degraeve, Frederik Vandyck, Inge Bertels,
Heidi Deneweth and Stephanie Van de Voorde

The location of timber construction SMEs

GIS-mapping

By mapping the buildings that accommodated a timber-SME between 1880 and 1980 on an actual cadastral map (Fig. 3), as well as by mapping other parameters on the timber-SMEs, we can draw some economic-geographical conclusions on the subsector in Brussels.

Two main clusters become apparent. The first is situated along the Canal Antwerp-Brussels-Charleroi, more specifically in the municipalities of Schaerbeek, Molenbeek and Anderlecht (the Canal-cluster). The second cluster is located on the south-eastern side of the city centre, mainly in the municipality of Ixelles (the Ixelles-cluster). To interpret the main economic-geographical features of the industry, we focus on these two clusters by confronting them with the specific timber construction activities executed on these locations (Fig. 4) and with the periodisation of the clusters' growth and decline (Figs 5-6).

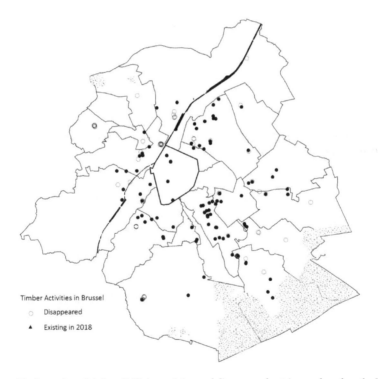

Fig. 3 Geographical mapping of timber-SMEs' remaining and disappeared patrimony, based on the Inventaire Visuel. Created by authors with the use of GIS-software and Brussels' cadastral maps.

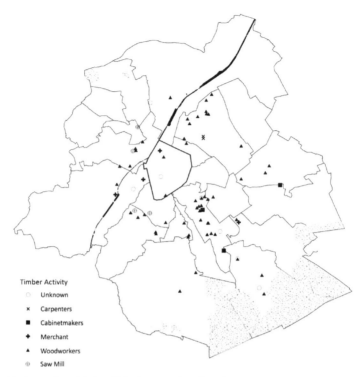

Fig. 4 Geographical mapping of timber-SMEs' activity, based on the Inventaire Visuel. Created by authors with the use of GIS-software and Brussels' cadastral maps.

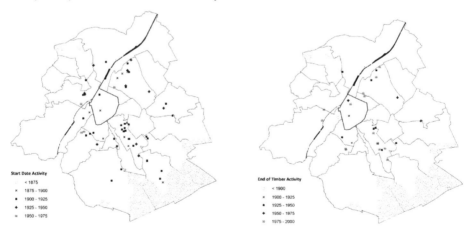

Fig. 5 Geographical mapping of timber-SMEs' activity's starting date, based on the Inventaire Visuel. Made by authors with the use of GIS-software and Brussels' cadastral maps.

Fig. 6 Geographical mapping of timber-SMEs' activity's ending date, based on the Inventaire Visuel. Made by authors with the use of GIS-software and Brussels' cadastral maps.

Matthijs Degraeve, Frederik Vandyck, Inge Bertels,
Heidi Deneweth and Stephanie Van de Voorde

The Ixelles-cluster mainly consisted of joiners and cabinetmakers. Lumber mills and timber merchants were on the other hand nearly exclusively located in the Canal-cluster. Concerning the periodisation, the mapping only shows some slight indications. It seems that the Canal-cluster hosted timber-SMEs for a longer period than the Ixelles-cluster. New enterprises were established throughout the entire period near the Canal, whereas in Ixelles this was mostly the case between 1893 and 1945. In both clusters, many timber activities disappeared after 1945.

In the following paragraphs we analyse why the two clusters developed on these locations, both by using theoretical frameworks and by zooming in on a few case enterprises that illustrate the general trends.

The Canal-cluster

For over a century, the Brussels' Canal was the city's main economic lifeline. From 1832 onwards, it connected the capital city of the brand-new Belgian nation with the southern coal-mining area around Charleroi. Until the Second World War, it attracted various industrial activities in Brussels and caused an enormous growth of the urban economy. Especially after 1860, a large-scale industrial development took place alongside the Canal. The *least cost theory*, formulated in 1909 by the German economist Alfred Weber, forms a logical explanatory framework for this development.[16] It stipulates that industries tend to settle where transportation costs can be minimized. If the production process entails a considerable loss of weight, then the transportation costs to deliver raw materials into the factory are higher than those to deliver the finished products to the clients. Firms executing weight-losing industrial processes therefore settle as close as possible to their suppliers, or at least to the main supply transport channel. Weight-gaining industries on the other hand settle closer to the consuming market.[17]

The *least cost theory* explains why most lumber mills and timber merchants settled in the Canal-cluster. Their industrial process was by definition weight-losing: large timber logs were brought to the factory, where they were sawn and processed into smaller, cheaper conveyable boards. Their settlement near the Canal in turn attracted other enterprises, such as joineries, that depended on their supplies.

An important timber merchant enterprise in the Canal-cluster was established by Jean-Mathieu Lochten in 1882. After a few temporary sites, he settled in 1890 in the Rue des Coteaux in Schaerbeek. It was an excellent location for a timber merchant. Supplies could directly be transported from the Canal via the straight Avenue Rogier (approx. 1.7 km) whereas a train station next to the Rue des Coteaux gave additional transportation opportunities. After Jean-Mathieu Lochten's death in 1908, his son Edmond took over the company. While Edmond's business was continued by his son Henri Lochten after his death in 1932, his two other sons started a timber merchant enterprise of their own. François Lochten settled in 1923 on the other side of the street, in the Avenue Rogier, where this business is still present today. Louis Lochten moved in 1935 to the Rue d'Ostende in Molenbeek, only 750m from the Canal. Louis' enterprise existed until the 1980s.[18] In 1968, Jean-Mathieu Lochten took over the original Lochten company from his father Henri. It remained a family business until 1994, when an employee took over.[19] The firm left the Rue des Coteaux in 2011, settling in an industrial zone in Forest. Today, it is through the enterprise founded by François Lochten that the name is still present in the same neighbourhood in Schaerbeek where Jean-Mathieu Lochten arrived nearly 130 years ago. It indicates the importance of another decisive economic-geographical factor: the strong long-term connection a firm can develop with a specific neighbourhood.

Spatial analysis of timber construction SMEs in Brussels (1880-1980)

The Ixelles-cluster

From the second half of the nineteenth century onwards, a large-scale urban development took place beyond Brussels' pre-industrial city ramparts. The wealthy urban elites settled in large numbers in the eastern uptown districts. The south-eastern suburb of Ixelles attracted many of them between 1880 and 1910. The number of inhabitants more than doubled during this period, from 36,000 to 73,000. It quickly became a densely built municipality. From the GIS-mapping it appears that, from 1893 on, also quite a lot of timber-SMEs, especially joiners and cabinetmakers, settled in this area.

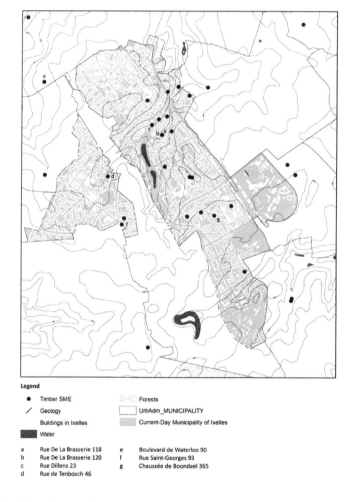

Legend

●   Timber SME   ▨   Forests

╱   Geology   ▢   UrbAdm_MUNICIPALITY

     Buildings in Ixelles   ▨   Current-Day Municipality of Ixelles

■   Water

a   Rue De La Brasserie 118   e   Boulevard de Waterloo 90
b   Rue De La Brasserie 120   f   Rue Saint-Georges 93
c   Rue Dillens 23   g   Chaussée de Boondael 365
d   Rue de Tenbosch 46

Fig. 7 Geographical map showing the contours of the municipality of Ixelles and its timber-SMEs' patrimony. Image created by authors by the use of GIS-software and cadastral maps.

Matthijs Degraeve, Frederik Vandyck, Inge Bertels,
Heidi Deneweth and Stephanie Van de Voorde

Transportation costs to deliver raw materials were also for the timber-SMEs in the Ixelles-cluster an important locational factor. Most of them settled in the valley of the Maalbeek (so-called 'low -Ixelles', Fig. 7). As steep inclinations were nearly insurmountable for heavy-fraught horse-drawn carriages, this valley developed as an industrial axis for SMEs in Ixelles.[20] There were probably even some pre-industrial antecedents of supply transportation costs as cause for the emergence of the Ixelles-cluster. Back then, the nearby Sonian Forest was still a timber resource for the city. Timber suppliers mostly settled in Ixelles, the city's peripheral village closest to the forest.[21] The age-old presence of the timber industry in Ixelles likely facilitated the local continuity of the subsector.

Nonetheless, supply transportation costs can only partly explain the emergence of the Ixelles-cluster. As the *least cost theory* states, the construction process is in the first place *weight-gaining*, since it results in an immovable structure. The furniture-making and other finishing woodwork labour in the workshops of joiners and cabinetmakers had to take place as close as possible to the construction sites, in order to diminish transportation costs for delivering the finished products. As many of the wealthy elites (who had a large demand for woodwork) built their houses in and around Ixelles, the settlement of many timber-SMEs in the same district was a logical consequence.

Locating near clients in a dense residential urban fabric is generally not that easy for the often large-scale weight-gaining industries. However, since the industrial activity of these joiners and cabinetmakers was so small-scale (*cfr. infra*), their settlement in this dense fabric was not at all problematic. In this way, the timber-SMEs could economic-geographically behave not only as weight-gaining *industries*, but also as *retail* businesses. According to Walter Christaller's *central place theory*, retail businesses usually settle where customer accessibility is maximised, according to their products' threshold (the minimum market needed to make it profitable) and range (the maximum distance consumers are prepard to travel to acquire it).[22] Both theories (*least cost* and *central place*) therefore explain the emergence of the Ixelles-cluster. The cluster consisted of timber-SMEs that were able to spatially focus on the demand side. It confirms the observations of similar developments in other regions and periods of construction (finishing) labourers settling where construction activity boomed.[23]

After the settlement of multiple 'pioneer' timber-SMEs in the late nineteenth century, the Ixelles-cluster was consolidated in the first half of the twentieth century, even when construction activity slowed down. Knowledge transfers, settlements of apprentices near their masters, the proximity of local supply distributors and mechanised sawyers, and other agglomeration forces are likely to have continued the long-term local embeddedness of the industry in Ixelles. Just like the Lochten enterprise, many joiners in Ixelles maintained their business on the same location or in the same neighbourhood during their whole professional career. A suitable location was sometimes even handed over to the next generation, so some places eventually hosted timber-SMEs for over a century, as some examples may clarify.

In 1894, joiner Pierre De Groef settled in the Rue Dillens 23 in Ixelles. In 1930, joiner Charles Edrich took over his business and installed a mechanical sawmill, thus providing valuable services for the many not yet mechanised joineries in the neighbourhood.[24] After the war, joiner Vander Velde took over, but quickly left the enterprise to his son, who still runs it on the same location today.[25]

Joiner Alfred Hulet initiated his business in 1897 in the Rue Washington in Ixelles's brand new Ten Bosch neighbourhood.[26] In 1902 he resettled in an adjacent street, the Rue de Tenbosch 46. His firm existed on this very spot until 1968.[27]

The cabinetmaking firm Wallaert forms a contrast with the long-term local embeddedness of many timber-SMEs, at least during the nineteenth century. Its foundation by Louis Wallaert dates to 1818. It was situated in the Rue de la Montagne, one of the most popular shopping streets of Brussels' city centre at the time,[28] indicating the early importance of customer accessibility for timber-SMEs. In 1827, he moved to a larger workshop around the corner.[29] His son Louis E. Wallaert relocated the firm in 1856 to the eastern urban extensions, a brand-new district that attracted many wealthy citizens. In 1868 and 1870 he relocated again to keep up with the urban developments.[30] His brother Hector Wallaert continued this habit after he took over in 1882.[31] He settled along the boulevard surrounding the old city centre, near the Avenue Louise which was the late nineteenth century attraction pole for the wealthy elites. Hector's son Jules Wallaert established the final relocation in 1894 by moving across the street to the Boulevard de Waterloo 90.[32] His son Hector Wallaert continued the firm on the same location from 1916 until 1975, when the then nearly 160 years old family enterprise ceased to exist.[33] Whereas the nineteenth century saw frequent relocations to keep up with the rapid spatial shifts in demand, the firm was able to establish a local embeddedness during the twentieth century, just like several joiners in Ixelles did.

Through this economic-geographical analysis, a contrast became clear between timber-SMEs in the Canal-cluster and those in the Ixelles-cluster. Whereas the former were spatially more focused on the supply side, the latter were focused on the demand side. In both clusters there were nevertheless firms that developed a long-term connection with a specific neighbourhood. A lot of sites were used by an enterprise for many decades, but they also frequently relocated to new sites in the immediate surroundings, according to their evolving infrastructural needs.[34] By evaluating the timber-SMEs' infrastructure, we can therefore explore and explain the contrasting spatial needs of the enterprises in both clusters more in depth.

The architecture of timber construction SMEs' workspaces

The study of the morphological embeddedness of the industrial patrimony unveils a considerable distinction between building blocks of *residential* and *industrial* nature. The patrimony located in residential building blocks largely exceeds other surrounding buildings in terms of horizontal building depth (2,5), built-unbuilt ratio (1-5), parcel width (4,5) and deviates in terms of volumetric composition (1,2). On the other hand, the patrimony in industrial building blocks is surrounded by similarly large structures. What follows is an overview of the studied types and their paragon examples.

Matthijs Degraeve, Frederik Vandyck, Inge Bertels,
Heidi Deneweth and Stephanie Van de Voorde

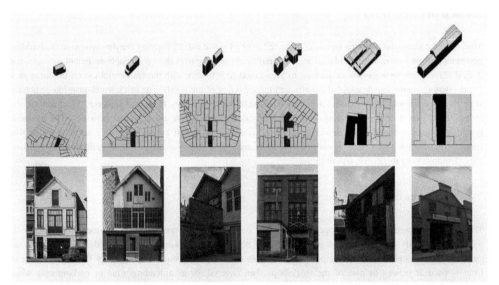

Fig. 8 Representation of case studies for industrial types by means of 3D GIS-date, cadastral maps and images from the Inventaire visual (©AAM / Fondation CIV A Stichting, Brussel). From left to right: (1) Rue Saint-Georges 93 Ixelles, (2) Rue de Tenbosch 46 Ixelles, (3) Rue de la Brasserie 118 Ixelles, (4) Chaussée de Boondael 365 Ixelles, (5) Avenue Rogier 116 Schaerbeek and (6) Rue de Birmingham 58 Molenbeek.

The industrial hall (6)

The 'industrial hall' is conceived as a *plan-libre* with load bearing walls, few columns and high roof structures to be as generic as possible to altering uses. As built/unbuilt ratios are large (up to 100%), the plan entirely depends on the shape of the parcel. Few cases, however, are constituted of multiple industrial halls with intermediate courts accommodating trucks to load and unload goods. Strikingly, none of the industrial halls from the *Inventaire visuel* was originally constructed for a timber-SME, yet they accommodated a wide scope of timber activities: carpentry firms, saw mills and timber merchants. The industrial hall can therefore be regarded as 'generic' and indifferent to its use. As elaborated above, these buildings and activities are mainly found in the Canal zone (Fig. 9), in industrial enclaves and alongside transportation infrastructure – indicating the importance of transportation costs for the enterprises accommodated by these industrial halls. Exemplary is the joinery Thumas (Fig. 8.6) that occupied an industrial hall between 1960 and the 1980s in the Rue de Birmingham in Molenbeek, located next to the Canal, which previously had accommodated different metal construction companies from the early twentieth century on.[35]

Contrary to the industrial halls, most of the remaining industrial building types were embedded in residential building blocks. The hypothesis for further research is that these structures, due to their persistence in time, hold insights on the qualitative co-existence with other (mainly residential) uses. It concerns buildings of older ages, mainly constructed around the turn of the twentieth century. To further categorise these buildings, a distinction is made concerning the volumetric infill of the parcel in three main categories: the monolith building, the main volume withdrawn towards the back, and the gated terraced house with industrial activity in the back.

437

Spatial analysis of timber construction SMEs in Brussels (1880-1980)

The monolith building (1)

Much like the industrial hall, this type is constructed over its entire parcel, copying the dimensions to the building perimeter and providing an open plan. The 100% built ratio of the parcel does not enable sufficient daylight, nor does it leave room for a garden, or parking to accommodate hybridity with the residential use on the same plot. Large openings in the façade enabled the efficient manoeuvring of the goods. The brick warehouse-like structures were not used for storing wood, but accommodated saw mills, carpentry firms and joineries. Contrarily to the industrial hall, most of these buildings were originally designed for their use in timber activities. The monolith typology is mainly found in Ixelles (Fig. 9). Rue Saint-Georges 93 in Ixelles (Fig. 8.1) accommodated five consecutive small woodworking firms between 1928 and 1969. Afterwards there were multiple non-industrial uses, demonstrating its generic nature.[36]

Volume withdrawn towards the back (2)

This type is characterised by its specific volumetric composition: the main (and sometimes only) volume is withdrawn towards the back of the parcel and thus neglects the alignment of its neighbours, making it an eye-catching element in the streetscape. The main volume is used for multi-storey joinery firms. The space in front is used as offices or part of the workshop when covered, or as unloading zone or parking area when uncovered. All cases are multi-storey joineries that were originally constructed for their specific use. None of them was hybrid with a residential use within one parcel. Striking is the short period (1900-1920) during which these wooden buildings were constructed. They are found in Brussels' south-eastern suburbs amidst a dense residential fabric (Fig. 9). Rue de Tenbosch 46 in Ixelles was constructed in 1902 by joiner Alfred Hulet. He altered the building twice. In 1912, the first building at the back of the parcel was enlarged with a cellared, wooden building that is still present today (Fig. 8.2). In 1924, the workshop was again enlarged towards the front, replacing the office space that was relocated to the Rue du Mail, 350m away.[37]

Gated row house with industry in the back (3,4)

The largest populated type has the setup of a row house in the front and industrial activity in the back. A two-meter-wide gate usually enables access to an open court between the front and back building(s). Typologically, a division is made regarding the width of the industrial building in the back: it either equals the front house's width (3) or largely exceeds it (4).

In the Rue de la Brasserie in Ixelles, two adjacent buildings of type (3) accommodated two joiners: Noël Levêque and J. Van Eyck. Before they decided to construct their workshops next to each other in 1903, they already lived nearby, 600m from this new location. It is unclear if they had a contractual collaboration. Van Eyck's enterprise existed on this location until 1925. Levêque's until 1921. Apart from minor stylistic aspects, both backyard workshops are identical (Fig. 8.3). The ground and first floors are constructed in brick walls and load bearing beams, the attic and roof structure in wood. Over the past eighty years, the buildings were used by a printing shop, an accountant and other non-productive functions.[38]

In contrast to type (3), Chaussée de Boondael 365 in Ixelles is constructed on annexed parts from adjacent parcels, making its width largely exceed that of the gated front house. Joiner Théophile Delay built his brick workshop in 1927 in the back of the multi-family row house he inhabited (Fig. 8.4). In 1931 he enlarged it towards the back with another workshop, courtyard and drying room for the wood.[39]

438

Matthijs Degraeve, Frederik Vandyck, Inge Bertels,
Heidi Deneweth and Stephanie Van de Voorde

Types (3) and (4) are constructed with similar logics. The cases reveal that the front house is older than the industrial building in the back, of which 80 per cent was originally constructed for a timber-SME (joinery or cabinetmaking enterprise). These buildings are predominant in the Ixelles-cluster, but also strongly present in the northern suburb of Schaerbeek (Fig. 9). Most of them were constructed between 1900-1925 for type 3, and between 1890-1910 for type 4.

Industrial enclave in residential fabric (5)

The final type is the industrial enclave embedded in dense residential building blocks. These complexes exist of multiple buildings, constructed at once over large-scale parcels. Logically, they were designed for their original use, mainly large saw mills, timber trade and carpentry firms. In 1923, François Lochten constructed a complex of timber, open structures, surrounded by a brick wall, to store and sell tropical woods (Fig. 8.5).[40] His patrimony in the Avenue Rogier in Schaerbeek served the same activities over the course of the past 95 years.

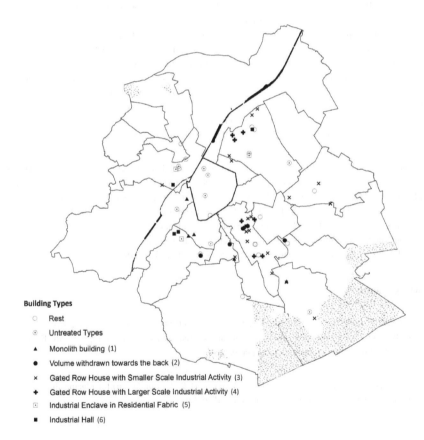

Building Types

○   Rest

◉   Untreated Types

▲   Monolith building (1)

●   Volume withdrawn towards the back (2)

×   Gated Row House with Smaller Scale Industrial Activity (3)

✦   Gated Row House with Larger Scale Industrial Activity (4)

▣   Industrial Enclave in Residential Fabric (5)

■   Industrial Hall (6)

Fig. 9 Geographical mapping of the typology of timber-SMEs' patrimony, based on the Inventaire Visuel. Created by authors with the use of GIS-software and Brussels' cadastral maps.

Conclusion

The *Inventaire visuel de l'architecture industrielle* proved useful to trace industrial patrimony from a certain sector – in this case the timber construction industry – in the Brussels-Capital Region. It enabled us to list 80 still-existing buildings used by a timber-SME between 1880 and 1980. The spatial analysis of these timber-SMEs demonstrated that the economic-geographical level and the architectural level are strongly interrelated, providing insight in the way timber-SMEs spatially organised their activity to partake in the production of the urban space.

By mapping the building types and other parameters we extracted from the *Inventaire visuel*, two industrial clusters appeared, one along the Canal and the other in Ixelles. The Canal-cluster was characterised by large industrial complexes (types 5-6), accommodating enterprises such as lumber mills and timber merchants. In the logic of Weber's *least cost theory*, transportation costs were decisive in their locational decision-making. Since they executed a *weight-losing* industrial process, they were spatially focused on the supply side and settled near the Canal, the main supply transport channel. The Ixelles-cluster on the other hand was characterised by smaller buildings (types 1-4), mainly for joiners and cabinetmakers who executed a *weight-gaining* process. It compelled them to spatially focus on the demand side, as retail businesses did, in accordance with Christaller's *central place theory*. Their limited spatial needs enabled a fluent embeddedness of their industrial activity in the dense residential urban fabric of Ixelles, where around 1900 the demand for their refined woodwork was at the highest. Some timber merchants and others with more spatial (storage) needs (type 5) settled in a dense urban fabric as well, for instance in the northern suburb of Schaerbeek. The buildings in a residential urban fabric (types 1-5) demonstrate an *activity-based* functionality. They were originally built for timber-SMEs, were used by these enterprises for a long period, and were frequently morphologically adapted to their evolving spatial needs. In contrast, the larger industrial halls of type 6 demonstrate a *generic* functionality, accommodating multiple activities over time, among which those of timber-SMEs, for which they were rarely originally built.

Many timber-SMEs preserved a long-term presence in specific neighbourhoods in Ixelles and Schaerbeek, many of them also in the same building for a long period. It indicates that their resilience was facilitated by their small scale and consequent local embeddedness. This seems to contradict Christopher Powell's research on the lifespan of nineteenth-century building firms in Bristol. Only ten per cent existed for more than 35 years, and especially carpenters' firms were prone to early termination.[41] A comparable general business historical analysis on Brussels' construction enterprises is still to be executed. It will shed more light on the relation of the building-SMEs' resilience with their spatial management and local embeddedness.

Acknowledgements

This paper proceeds from the ongoing interdisciplinary research project (IRP) 'Building Brussels' at the Vrije Universiteit Brussel. It investigates small and medium-sized construction enterprises in Brussels from a locational, architectural and business historical perspective.

We thank the Brussels' *Archives de l'Architecture Moderne* (CIVA Foundation) for placing the *Inventaire visuel de l'architecture industrielle* and its photographs at our disposal.

Matthijs Degraeve, Frederik Vandyck, Inge Bertels,
Heidi Deneweth and Stephanie Van de Voorde

Notes and references

[1] W. Addis, *Building: 3000 years of design, engineering and construction,* London: Phaidon, 2007, p. 507.

[2] E. Hennaut and M. Demanet, *Hout en metaal in de Brusselse huisgevel, 1850-1940,* Brussels: Koning Boudewijnstichting, 1997; J. Bertrand, 'Hout in de Brusselse gevels' in *Erfgoed en Ambachten,* Sprimont: Mardaga, 2001.

[3] L. Vandenabeele, I. Bertels and I. Wouters, 'Designing timber trusses in Belgium during the age of iron engineering' pp.612-619 in K. Van Balen and E. Verstrynge, (Eds), *Proceedings of the 10th International Conference on Structural Analysis of Historical Constructions: Anamnesis, diagnosis, therapy, controls,* Leiden: CRC Press, 2016.

[4] Ph. Sosnowska, *De briques et de bois. Contribution à l'histoire de l'architecture à Bruxelles. Étude archéologique, technique et historique des matériaux de construction (XIIIe-XVIIIe s.)* (Ph.D. thesis, Université Libre de Bruxelles, 2013); L. Vandenabeele, I. Bertels and I. Wouters, 'Baltic shipping marks on nineteenth-century timber: Their deciphering and a proposal for classifying old timber', *Construction History,* vol.31, no.2, 2016, pp. 157-175; A. Weitz, P. Charruadas, P. Fraiture and P. Hoffsummer, 'Roof frames in the built heritage of Brussels (Belgium): the contribution of dendrochronology and written sources', *Trace,* vol.14, 2016, pp. 14-22; Ph. Sosnowska, P. Fraiture and S. Crémer, 'Contribution to the history of Brussels floorings, Belgium (16th-19th centuries): Initial results of an archaeological and dendrochronological investigation' in P. Fraiture et al. (Eds) *Between Carpentry and Joinery. Wood finishing work in European Medieval and Modern architecture,* Brussels: Royal Institute for Cultural Heritage, 2017.

[5] E. Buyst, *An Economic history of residential building in Belgium between 1890 and 1961,* Leuven: UP Leuven, 1992.

[6] I. Bertels, H. Deneweth, B. Horemans and S. Van de Voorde, 'Pour une historiographie de l'entrepreneur du bâtiment (1400-2000)' pp.1989-1999 in F. Fleury et al., (Ed.) *Les temps de la construction. Processus, acteurs, matériaux,* Paris: Picard, 2016.

[7] B. Zitouni, *Agglomérer. Une anatomie de l'extension Bruxelloise,* Brussels: VUB Press, 2010.

[8] *Recensement général des industries et des métiers (31 octobre 1896),* Brussels, 1900-02, 18 vol; *Recensement de l'industrie et du commerce (31 décembre 1910),* Brussels, 1913-21, 8 vol.

[9] Paulo Charruadas, P. Fraiture, P. Gautier, M. Piavaux and Ph. Sosnowska, 'Introduction: Wood finishing work, a promising area of research?' in P. Fraiture et al. (Eds) *Between Carpentry and Joinery. Wood finishing work in European Medieval and Modern architecture,* Scientia Artis 12, Brussels: Royal Institute for Cultural Heritage, 2017, pp.7–23.

[10] R. Moneo, 'On Typology', *Oppositions,* no. 13, Boston: MIT Press, 1978, 22-45.

[11] M. Culot (Ed.), *L'inventaire visuel de l'architecture industrielle à Bruxelles* (18 vols), Brussels: AAM, 1980-85.

[12] G. Grassi, *The Logical Construction of Architecture,* Padua: Marsilio Editori, 1967; M. Tafuri, 'The case of Aldo Rossi', *History of Italian Architecture,* Cambridge Massachusetts: MIT Press, 1989, pp.135–139.

[13] G. Caniggia and G. L. Maffei, 'Introduction: motives and propositions', in *Interpreting Basic Building,* Alinea Editrice: Firenze, 1979, pp.51–55.

[14] G. C. Argan, 'On the typology of architecture', *Architectural Design,* vol.33, no.12, 1963, pp.564–565.

[15] G. Grassi, *The Logical Construction of Architecture,* Padua: Marsilio Editori, 1967.

[16] S. De Caigny, 'New Economic Geography als bedrijfshistorische invalshoek: de transformatie van de kanaalzone ten noorden van Brussel tot een industriegebied in het interbellum', *Belgisch Tijdschrift voor Nieuwste Geschiedenis,* vol.33, no.3-4, 2003, pp. 535-575.

[17] A. Weber, *Über den Standort der Industrien,* Tübingen: Mohr, 1909.

[18] BCA (Brussels City Archives), *Almanachs du commerce et de l'industrie* (almanacs).

[19] M. Jacquemin, C. Six and C. Vancoppenolle, *Guide Des Archives d'Associations Professionnelles et D'entreprises En Région Bruxelloise. Gidsen 51,* Brussel: Algemeen Rijksarchief en Rijksarchief in de Provinciën, 2001, pp.293-294.

[20] M. de Beule, B. Périlleux, M. Silvestre and E. Wauty, *Brussel, geplande geschiedenis. Stedenbouw in de 19de en 20ste eeuw,* Brussels: Mardaga, 2017, p.212; M. Culot (Ed.), *L'inventaire visuel,* vol.9 (Ixelles), pp.17-20.

[21] M. Culot (Ed.), *L'inventaire visuel,* vol.9 (Ixelles), p.16.

[22] C. Lesger, *Het winkellandschap van Amsterdam. Stedelijke structuur en winkelbedrijf in de vroegmoderne en moderne tijd, 1550-2000,* Hilversum: Verloren, 2013.

[23] J.E. Abrahamse, H. Deneweth, M. Kosian and E. Schmitz, 'Gouden Kansen? Vastgoedstrategieën van bouwondernemers in de stadsuitleg van Amsterdam in de Gouden Eeuw', *Bulletin KNOB,* vol.114, no.4, 2015, pp.229-267; M. Martini, *Bâtiment en famille: migrations et petite entreprise en banlieue parisienne au XXe siècle,* Paris: CNRS, 2016.

[24] BCA (Brussels City Archives), almanacs.

[25] Interview with joiner Christian Vander Velden (December 15, 2017).

[26] M. de Beule et al., *Brussel, geplande geschiedenis,* pp.210-221.

[27] BCA, almanacs.

[28] E. Debackere, 'Winkelhouden in een hoofdstad. De vestigingsplaatsen van Brusselse winkeliers aan het begin van de negentiende eeuw', *Stadsgeschiedenis,* 2013, pp.19-37.

[29] BCA, patent registers 1818-1827, section 5.

[30] BCA, almanacs.

[31] *Journal de Bruxelles* (29 November 1882), p.4.

[32] BCA, almanacs; BCA, TP 24921.

[33] BCA, TP 105562.

[34] A relocation to a larger terrain in the same neighbourhood was for instance observed for the large Brussels contracting enterprise of Louis De Waele in 1890: M. Degraeve, J. Dobbels, I. Bertels, H. Deneweth and S. Van de Voorde, 'Spatial management of contractors. An analysis of the industrial sites of the Louis De Waele enterprise in Brussels (1867-1988)', *Proceedings of the Sixth International Congress on Construction History, Brussels 2018* (forthcoming, 2018).

[35] BCA, almanacs.

[36] BCA, almanacs.

[37] IMA (Ixelles Municipal Archives), TP 285-46.

[38] BCA, almanacs; IMA, TP 46-118 and TP 46-120-122.

[39] IMA, TP 41-365.

[40] BCA, almanacs.

[41] C. Powell, 'He that runs against time: life expectancy of building firms in nineteenth century Bristol', *Construction History,* vol.2, 1986, pp.61-67.

'Once Hard Men Were Heroes': Masculinity, Cultural Heroism and Performative Irishness in the Post-war British Construction Industry

Michael Mulvey

Department of History, Maynooth University, Ireland

Recruiting Irish labour to resource British engineering and construction projects was by no means a post-war phenomenon, particularly as the Act of Union of 1800 made Ireland part of the United Kingdom. Irish navvies were present in big numbers throughout the nineteenth-century industrial landscape and helped construct the canal and railway networks and most of the great infrastructure tunnel, bridge and dock projects of the Victorian era. Contrary to popular cultural perception, however, they were not dominant in terms of numbers and were equally matched - if not often outnumbered - by indigenous English navvies together with plentiful numbers of Scots and Europeans.[1] In the interwar period, despite the cultural and political tensions created by the Irish War of Independence of 1919-21 which gave rise to the Irish Free State, Irish labour was again called upon in large numbers to resource major UK infrastructural and hydro-electric projects in England and Scotland [2] and such significant London projects as the original Wembley Stadium and the Craven 'A' Factory in Mornington Crescent. Notably many of these jobs were undertaken by leading British contractor, Sir Robert McAlpine Ltd, which -certainly up to the mid-twentieth century – was the prime recruiter and employer of Irish labour to the British construction industry.

During World War Two, the depletion of indigenous male labour through military service fuelled new demand in Britain for wartime agricultural, engineering and construction labour and this led to the systemic recruitment of somewhere in the region of 130-230,000 Irish men and women between 1940 and 1946.[3] These migrants were 'conditionally landed' on temporary Travel Permits and consequently intended as temporary workers.[4] However, in many cases, they stayed and became permanent or semi-permanent residents, albeit with a somewhat dubious legal status as citizens, at least throughout the 1950s. After the war, when wartime travel permit restrictions were lifted and the 'common travel area' reinstated, the chain migration flow which the war had initiated became a deluge. The economic miracle spurred in western Europe and Britain by the Marshall Plan and the corresponding post-war slump in the Irish economy, saw the exponential increase of annual migration throughout the decades following the war. By the early 1970s, Irish migration to Britain, and in particular, London, had reached proportions last seen in the decades following the Great Famine of 1845-50, as can be seen from Table 1:

'Once Hard Men Were Heroes': Masculinity, Cultural Heroism and Performative Irishness in the Post-war British Construction Industry

Table 1- Irish-born residents in Britain, 1931-91

Census of Population, Britain

Census Year	Born in RoI	Born in NI	Total
1931	367,424	137,961	505,385
1941		**WW2**	
1951	537,709	178,319	716,028
1961	726,121	224,857	950,978
1971 *	709,235	248,595	957,830
1981	607,428	242,969	850,397
1991	608,836	228,628	837,464

* Peak of Post-War migration

Sources: 1931-1981: P.J. Drury [Ed.], *Irish Studies 5: Ireland and Britain since 1922*, (Cambridge, 1986), Table 6.3, Irish-born residents in Britain, 1931-1981, p.114

1991: Patrick J. Bracken & Patrick O'Sullivan (2001) The Invisibility of Irish Migrants in *British Health Research, Irish Studies Review*, 9:1, 41-51 citing Mary Hickman and Bronwen Walter, *Discrimination and the Irish Community in Britain* (Commission for Racial Equality, June 1997), pp. 18, 20

The post-war migrant Irish builders and engineers who dominated the British construction industry by the mid-1960s, brought with them cultural, social and emotional baggage which often shaped their modes of conduct within British industrial society and defined them as a specific socio-ethnic sub-group within the post-war industrial proletariat. The foremost workplace credential of the post-war Irish male migrant was masculinity manifested through physical prowess and endurance; qualities which might be said to be encapsulated into a single phrase often used by these men themselves – '*hardiness*'. As a young man I would often hear Irish builders refer to their fellow as a 'hardy man' or a 'hardy stick' when commending their capacity for physical work. In terms of cultural representation the canonical metanarrative of the Irish migrants' working life depicts the experiences of Irish builders as exceptionally tough and dangerous. Indeed one author described them, rather melodramatically, as "inured to hardship and able to survive on a level unimaginable to anyone who has never lived rough". [5] Academic Enda Delaney quotes a migrant's recollection of his encounter with Irish 'tunnel tigers' in the pubs of post-war Glasgow, where "They would explain, *to let us know the hardy breed of men they were*, about the terrible conditions they endured...And it was mostly true" (Emphasis added).[6]   Industrial masculinities have been the subject of extensive research and the importance of manual labour and the requisite physicality needed for its productive efficiency throughout most of the Industrial age is well-established. The 'labouring man' is a trope which is deeply embedded in conceptions of class and culture in late modernity through literature, folksong and oral tradition. Nowhere is this obsession with masculine work identity and the ethics of labouring more visceral than in the ethnic Irish who settled in Britain during and after the Second World War.

444

The title quote of this paper is taken from the folk-song *Murphy Can Never Go Home*,[7] a relatively contemporary version of the 'forgotten Irish' navvy trope in which the omniscient narrator bemoans the rise of the technological age in the line; "Building the blocks of the twenty-first century / What use are they to the labouring man", going on to argue that "Once hard men were heroes / Now they are fools". In many ways this line gives voice to a wider transnational cultural lamentation which continues to unfold in the post-industrial age. Signs of this phenomenon can be seen in the recent industrial decline in mid-America's 'rustbelt' which so effectively propelled the Trump campaign and in Britain's former industrial heartlands where the Brexit vote was so significant; an elegy for the end of physical wage-labour as the dominant resource in industrial capitalism. The ostensible dominance of Irish labour in wartime and post-war reconstruction is reflected anecdotally through the lived working experiences of that part of the Irish diaspora nicknamed the 'mailboat generation'; [8] those - overwhelmingly male - migrants who came to work in construction and engineering predominantly from the early 1940s up until roughly the mid-1980s. It is mainly on the oral histories of the mailboat generation that this paper draws.

As Clair Wills pointedly observed in her recent book The Best are Leaving, "for male migrants in particular, building work and the landscape of reconstruction were not [just] the background to personal stories, but the [very] fabric of their lives. Construction sites were, at once, their workplace and one of the locations of their community". [9] The relationships between migrant Irish construction labour and the raffish, heroic and romanticised iconography of navvy folklore shaped individual and collective ethnic identity amongst the post-war Irish builders. Leitmotifs such as McAlpine's Fusiliers, Murphy's Rangers, Pincher Laddies and Long-distance men forged an urban mythology of masculine Irishness, and the semi-mythical 'characters' of the reconstruction period; men like 'Darkie' Finn, 'Pincher Mac', 'Horse McGurk' and the 'Elephant John' grew out of the burgeoning urban myth of Irish pub-culture. The resulting caricatures imposed performative expectations on the Irish male migrant both within the work environment and the insular social-life of the migrant builder.

The visceral fear of the newly-arrived migrant adolescent male plunged into a world of hegemonic masculinity and the constant necessity to prove one's physical capabilities and toughness is a repeated theme in the cultural representations of Irish builders and this is an area of representation which does tend to reflect the realities of site life for the Irish. However, context, yet again, is a crucial ingredient often missing from fictional depictions. The socio-cultural influences of hegemonic masculinity, physical toughness and reckless endangerment had subsisted in the British construction industry long before the Irish migrants pervaded the post-war rebuilding programme. However, what was exceptional in the Irish case was that these influences were amplified by inherited nationalist and Gaelic ethnic articulations of manhood and masculinity – strong-man narratives drawn from Celtic mythology, particularly the *Cuchulainn* myths resurrected during the late nineteenth-century Celtic revival [10] and remediations of Irish revolutionary heroics and masculinities - which empowered migrant builders within an urban Irish male ethnic enclave, whilst simultaneously corralling them from integration into the wider carapace of capitalist British industry. As late as the 1990s, interviews with Irish migrants in Britain cited Irish nationalism as "a potentially powerful political mobilising force in imagining an heroic (male) subject position within a nation for whom the normal mode of citizenship is that of emigrant status, social exclusion and subordinated and dislocated masculinity".[11] Particularly in the case of literary representations of the Irish builder, drawing as they did from the 1960s Irish revivalist folk-song and urban oral folklore traditions, this myth of a virtuous physical prowess became a trope.

The most powerful example of this trope is to be found in the award-winning photographic novel *I Could Read the Sky*, where one of the workers, PJ, laments the news that their friend Roscoe was found dead inside a concrete sewer pipe where he had been living, unbeknown to all, as he couldn't get digs on the job in Brighton. He intones:

> "We are the immortals...we have one name and we have one body. We are always in our prime and we are always fit for work. We dig tunnels, lay the rails and build the roads and the buildings. But we leave no other sign behind us. We are unknown and unrecorded. We have many names and none are our own. Whenever the stiffness and pain come in and the work gets harder...we change again into our younger selves. On and on we go. We are like the bottle that never empties. We are immortal". [12]

Whilst this fictional passage might again seem at face value to be a somewhat melodramatic and mythologised representation of reality, such rhetoric tends to align with oral interviews with, amongst others, Irish tunnel tigers from the 1960s. For example Con Curtin, a well-known traditional musician and character in post-war London, originally from Brosna, County Kerry, who worked on the Victoria Line in the 1960s summed up the prevailing attitude of bravado and swagger amongst such men in an interview with RTE in 2009:

> "I was on the Victoria Tunnel...I done all that. You couldn't talk when you'd go down. When you'd come up you're decompressed...and you'd get your badge...oh great money...great money but dangerous work...when you were underneath the ground the stars never leave the sky...when you'd go down, you'd look up, stop, as much as to say "will I ever come up here again alive?"...I didn't give a damn...for I was on good money. And I was married that time but I was a tyrant...mad for money..." [13]

Another recollection of the inherent dangers of heavy construction came from Tommy Harvey from Doonbeg, Co Clare, another man who helped to dig the Victoria Line tunnels. Tommy went to London in 1958 at nineteen years of age, and after initially working on the buildings, he became a tunnel miner on the Victoria Line project, which ran overall from 1962-71. His descriptions of the dangers of working in compressed air accord very accurately with the other accounts given:

> "Oh the money was good. That's why we went down there. We weren't there for the craic, we were there for the money. Especially given that we were working with compressed air. You had to be in good health to go down there. You had to be fit and your body had to be right. It was dangerous work". [14]

The virtual invisibility of Irish migrant workers by comparison to their British-born counterparts was also a consequence of the Lump system: casual working, informal subcontracting arrangements, false names and ethnic clustering meant that often accidents –occasionally even fatal ones – went unreported or lacked proper enquiry and consequential follow-up. The Health and Safety Executive and its predecessor, the Factories Inspectorate, "under-recorded prevalence amongst the most vulnerable, casualized, least secure, poorest paid workers in small companies or working with subcontractors" [15] and Irish construction workers fell into all these categories in one way or another. Moreover it became, over time, part of the 'code of honour' amongst Irish migrant builders to respect each other's anonymity. The reporting and formalising of any kind of compensation culture for occupational injury became anathema to these men. Tommy Harvey's recollection of two such deaths on the Victoria Line project serve to highlight this problem:

> "People died there alright... I knew one fella who got killed one night in the pit bottom. He put his hand on a live cable and it blackened him to death. He was a Galway man and he wasn't down under his proper name. His mother came into the morgue and she took down the wrong name and put his correct name up. He was a young man. A man

about 25 or 26 years of age. …Another friend of mine, a Kerry man, who was as young as me, was in a pit bottom on Christmas Eve and they were sending down big timbers. One of them came off the sling and killed him dead. It was very sad".[16]

At the more prosaic level of day-to-day construction and building work, the culture of casual labour hire made commonplace by the development of Lump labour subcontracting in the 1950s and 60s lent itself to the degradation of manual labour to a mere unit of production; the commonplace terminology for working men throughout the Irish pub circuit during the post-war period was 'Skins'. The late John McGahern, considered now by many Irish literary critics to be a worthy successor to Joyce, penned several short stories about his days 'on the buildings' in London. In one, *Hearts of Oak and Bellies of Brass*, a more realist depiction of the casualized work culture of the 1960s reflects the way in which masculine physicality was commodified in the hiring process:

"They'd said to roll my jacket in the gutter before I went in, and when I got on the site to ask for the shout. 'Who has the shout here?' I asked. They pointed Barney out. 'Any chance of a start?' I asked.…

His eyes went over me – shoulders, arms, thighs. I remembered my father's cattle I had stood for sale in the Shambles once, walking stick along the backbone to gauge the rump, lips pulled back to read the teeth; but now I was offering to shovel for certain shillings an hour".[17]

Donall MacAmhlaigh, whose autobiography, *An Irish Navvy: The Diary of an Exile* was written originally in his native Gaelic, is one of the few – and earliest – written factual accounts of the life of post-war Irish builders in Britain, encapsulates this visceral sense of performative masculine expectation early on in his navvy days:

"I worked better after that and I tried hard because I didn't want to have any of the lads saying: *'What kind of a man is this that can't work like a proper navvy?'*. We worked away and when first break came at ten o'clock I had blisters on my hands and my back felt as if somebody had been laying about it with a stick. We got our tea out of a big bucket and every minute of the ten-minute rest was like heaven. When the whistle blew to call us back to work, it was as if a judge was sentencing me to death".[18]

(Emphasis added)

Original Interviews collected as part of my doctoral research confirm this sense of masculine exceptionalism amongst the post-war Irish migrants and the extent to which this self-consciousness persisted down through the generations of migrant Irish workers until well into the 1990s. Paddy B, a Mayo man who went to London in the early 1950s recalled working with Irish gangs on the Harlow newtown project in Essex in the late 1950s:

"Well everybody in our van was Irish, and the biggest part of them was Irish, everybody was Irish out there, very few English…And we had Northern Ireland chaps and all; we had some good brick layers from Northern Ireland there…And there was a few blokes from Kerry and a couple of Mayo blokes and they were putting in the main sewer …there was 4 of them there, some of them digging and another bloke behind shovelling up the loose stuff and another two coming behind that again digging and they were just…*they just walked across that field, you'd think a JCB wouldn't keep up with them…I tell you they were some diggers*".[19]

(Emphasis added)

447

'Once Hard Men Were Heroes': Masculinity, Cultural Heroism and Performative Irishness in the Post-war British Construction Industry

A Marxist reading of these narratives suggests that this seemingly acquiescent culture of inevitable danger and risk amongst the migrant Irish is rooted in the performance of a kind of heroic Stakhanovite masculinity. These kinds of cultural heroisms played into the industrial capitalist tendency to dehumanise manual labour and helped subordinate the economic value of that labour to the capitalist world system because, as Christine Wall has argued, British "construction employers frequently conceived of labour [simply] as a variable input to the construction process, something to be bought when necessary and not intrinsic to the production process itself".[20]

As Mac an Ghaill and others explained, Irish builders of the post-war decades "assembled a migrant masculine identity by inventing a place, a language and a new sensibility of urban industrial life".[21] This urban Irish male sensibility:

> "Valorised manual work, with an accompanying vocabulary of masculinity marked by: hard physical labour, strength, reputation, pride and solidarity. Much of their world was highly gendered, taking place within all-male environments. Versions of masculinity were spatially shaped and lived out within male workplaces, community pubs and clubs, and at Gaelic games. A specific, ethnic, gendered regime was culturally constructed, underpinned by an infrastructure of a male-dominated, hierarchical Catholic Church and an Irish nationalist politics that displayed a wide range of cultural signifiers of masculinity". [22]

The primary identity of post-war Irish migrant builders was thus economically and culturally "anchored in paid labour" – mostly construction labour. As a result of the sub-contract system and the "casualized, deregulated and relatively non-unionised nature of the construction industry, the workplace helped to produce a subordinated masculinity operating in dangerous conditions that resulted in high rates of injury and early death among work colleagues". [23]

There were other important consequences arising from this culture of performative masculinity, in addition to those outlined above, which I contend impacted upon the work-life trajectories of many of these young Irish migrants in the post-war period. The various masculinities inherent in manual labour– martial, hegemonic, temperate and useful – blended with the mythologised heroics of navvy culture and:

- Acted as a mode of post-colonial resistance to full assimilation into the host community, and as a consequence helped manoeuvre social and cultural solutions to the migration question in the UK towards notions of multiculturalism.

- Helped internationalise Irish labour by exposing it to one of the largest industrial labour markets which "rendered Ireland central to the process of core formation in the world economy" by appropriating isolated pockets of rural Ireland – as emigrant nurseries - into the capitalist world economy.[24]

In conclusion, for the migrant Irish engaged in the overtly hegemonic, intemperate and aggressive world of manual labouring, these various outward performances of Irishness also reflected extrinsic shaping influences borne of the social, cultural and political environments in which most of these migrants were born and raised. Most came from the west of Ireland – particularly the counties of Mayo, Donegal, Sligo, Leitrim. Kerry and Cork; areas where rural fundamentalism instilled in these young men a predisposition to an individualist bourgeois-capitalist work ethic as opposed to a proletarianised, unionised workplace culture. Add to this an inherent distrust of Britain on historical grounds (bearing in mind most of these men were born to parents, and schooled by teachers, who had lived through – and in many cases been belligerents in - the Irish War of Independence against Britain and the subsequent Civil War that spanned 1919 to 1923 and had also endured the hardships of deValera's Anglo-Irish Trade War during the 1930s). These factors combined with a deeply entrenched adherence to Catholic dogma, and Irish Gaelic cultural nationalism saw the development in Britain of networks of Catholic Social Clubs and Irish Societies, GAA sports clubs and leagues and cultural organisations such as the Gaelic League, *Comhaltas Ceoltori Eireann* and *Cumman na nGael*. These all had a profound effect on the way in which migrants negotiated the transition to urban working conditions in the construction industry and the kinds of employment practices which they engaged in, with often predictably negative and sometimes tragic results.

Looking forward, given the transformation in construction technologies, automation and artificial intelligence which are facing this current post-Industrial age, one might speculate that the influence of masculinities and conceptions of male physicality will disappear in the construction industry in the UK, especially as the mailboat generation dies out. Whilst the importance of physical and manual prowess has certainly waned under the influence of mechanisation and technological advancement, the latent and pernicious influences of masculine aggression, cavalier attitudes to the importance of personal and collective safety at work, adversarial attitudes to problem-solving and dispute resolution and a pervasive scepticism towards gender balance and progressive change will, I suspect, take some decades yet to work their way out of the underlying culture of the construction industry.

References

[] Terry Coleman, *The Railway Navvies,* (Harmondsworth, 1981), pp. 20-25.

[2] Projects such as Stretford, Radford, Barton and Preston coal-fired power stations, Lochaber Power Scheme, 1944, Galloway Hydro-electric Scheme, 1931-1936, and Risley Munitions Factory, 1935-1938. See Ultan Cowley, *The Men Who Built Britain: A History of the Irish Navvy*, (Dublin, 2001), pp.103-108; and James Miller, *The Dam Builders: Power from the Glens*, (e-book, 2012), p. 4.

[3] Estimates of migration to Britain during World War Two are controversial, since the two primary sources of data conflict. The Irish *Oireachtas Commission on Emigration*, Reports, table 96, p128; NAUK, Doc Ref: Lab 8/1528, AV Judges, *Irish labour in Great Britain*, 1939-45, Table 4, p. 78 gives a total of new Irish Travel Permit Cards issued 1940-1946 as 228,041, whereas the British Ministry of Labour and National Service, Report for Years, 1939-1946, p.55, 1947, XII, 459; NAUK, LAB 8/1487, recruitment of Group Labour in Eire: number of persons who travelled in 1946 shows recruitment of 132,114 for approximately the same period. Delaney points out that according to British civil servants involved in the recruitment of Irish labour in this period, "there was a substantial difference in numerical terms between those who received permits and those who actually travelled [and]…In addition a considerable amount of movement occurred to and from Ireland during the later years of the war and the immediate post-war period, which these statistics do not take into account." (See Enda Delaney, infra, note 4).

[4] Enda Delaney, *Demography, State and Society: Irish Migration to Britain*, 1921-1971, (Montreal, 2000), p128.

[5] Cowley, *The Men Who Built Britain*, (Note 2), p.139.

[6] Enda Delaney, *The Irish in Post-war Britain*, (Oxford, 2007), p.114-115.

[7] Mick Curry, 'Murphy Can Never Go Home', in Frank Harte and Donal Lunny - *There's Gangs of Them Digging – Songs of Irish labour*, (Daisy DLCD022), available at The Living Tradition (http://www.folkmusic.net/htmfiles/webrevs/dlcd022.htm, accessed 18 March, 2015)

[8] Tony Murray, *London Irish Fictions: Narrative, Diaspora and Identity*, (Liverpool, 2012), pp.39-96.

'Once Hard Men Were Heroes': Masculinity, Cultural Heroism and Performative Irishness in the Post-war British Construction Industry

[9] Clair Wills, *The Best are Leaving: Emigration and Post-war Irish Culture*, (Cambridge, 2015), p.111

[10] Murray, *London Irish Fictions*, (Note 8), pp.43-44.

[1] Ibid., p. 43.

[2] Timothy O'Grady & Steve Pyke, *I Could Read the Sky*, (London, 1997), p69.

[3] 'The Balloon in Brosna', Irish radio documentary from RTÉ Radio 1, Ireland - *Documentary on One* - the home of Irish radio documentaries available at http://www.rte.ie/radio1/doconone/2009/0521/645978-the_ballon_in_brosna2/

[4] 'Last of the navvies: Irishman who dug all-night tube line' in *The Irish Times*, Aug 19, 2016, available online at http://www.irishtimes.com/lifeandstyle/people/lastofthenavviesirishmanwhodugallnighttubeline1.2762215(accessed 13 Jun, 2017)

[5] C. Wolkowitz, Bodies at Work, (London, 2006), pp.102-103.

[6] The Irish Times, Aug 19, 2016, (Note 14).

[7] John McGahern, 'Hearts of Oak and Bellies of Brass' in Creatures of the Earth, (London, 1992), p.28-29.

[8] Donall MacAmhlaigh, An Irish Navvy: The Diary of an Exile. Translated from Irish by Valentin Iremonger, (Cork, 2004), p.27.

[9] Michael Mulvey, 'Digging For Gold': Irish Builders In Post-War London – Representation And Reality, Unpublished PhD Thesis, Appendix A, OI#14, p.16.

[20] Christine Wall, An Architecture of Parts: Architects, Building Workers and Industrialisation in Britain. 1940–1970, (Abingdon, 2013), p.33.

[2] Liviu Popoviciu , Chris Haywood & Máirtín Mac an Ghaill, 'Migrating Masculinities' in Irish Studies *Review*, 14:2, (2006), pp.169-187, p.176.

[22] Ibid., p.177, citing R. Connell, *Masculinities*, (Sydney, 1995).

[23] Ibid., p.176.

[24] Jim Mac Laughlin, *Ireland: The Emigrant Nursery and the World Economy*, (Cork, 1994), p.2.

The riding arena in St. Moritz and the locomotive depot in Bern – a comparative study of early glulam construction in Switzerland

Mario Rinke and Roshanak Haddadi

Department of Architecture, Swiss Federal Institute of Technology (ETH), Switzerland

Introduction

Glulam construction technology arrived in Switzerland only a few years after Hetzer's technological invention of robust, industrially fabricated, glued laminated timber elements, in Germany in 1906. The Swiss engineers Bernhard Terner (1875-1960) and Charles Chopard (1879-1954) acquired the patent and the exclusive right in Switzerland in 1909. During the following 24 years, they developed many extraordinary glulam timber structures, which have been acknowledged internationally and belong to the most distinguished architectural examples in timber construction of that time. Among those are many halls for cultural and sports activities, but particularly for industrial and infrastructural purposes.[1]

Outstanding examples of such different applications of this "new material" are the riding arena in St. Moritz (1910) and the locomotive depot in Bern (1912), both still existing almost unaltered. While the public use and, consequently, the representative character of the riding arena led to a more specific arrangement and shaping of the timber components in St. Moritz, the depot in Bern as the first infrastructural use of glulam demonstrated the robustness, economic fabrication and construction with repetitive components.

This paper examines the development of both structures in the context of early glulam technology in Switzerland. In the first part, the design history will be traced considering the context and the boundary conditions respectively followed by a second part focussing on the models used and decisions made to determine relevant construction details such as component shapes and connections. A few years after completion, the early glulam structures sometimes saw unexpected damages, which will be discussed at the end of the paper together with the methods undertaken for the repairing works. One important goal of this study is to understand the construction culture in the design and fabrication of the early glulam structures and, in particular, its relation to common construction principles of popular building typologies and materials at that time.

The invention of Otto Hetzer claimed a new way of producing "skeleton frames, which, with covering material, form roofs or entire buildings made from building elements composed of layers of wood". These glue-laminated elements have been regularly used for larger spans since they allowed fabrication in virtually unlimited sizes bringing larger cross-sections and longer components.[2] More importantly, their fabrication method allowed the modified timber to be used in different typologies than usually associated with it, e.g. arches and frame girders. Curved elements could replace traditional combinations of linear components such as from roof framework using rafters, beams and posts. Such curved roofs offer "less obstruction to the pressure of snow and wind and affording a clear vaulted interior useful space".[3]

The riding arena in St. Moritz and the locomotive depot in Bern – a comparative study of early glulam construction in Switzerland

Terner and Chopard often made use of the new timber technology to enable big spaces, with curved elements unifying traditional columns and beams similar to arch and frame typologies known from steel and reinforced concrete applications. Therefore, the curved glue-laminated elements were specifically shaped with a custom overall form but also with a precisely defined varying depth.

The riding arena in St. Moritz (1910)

One of the earliest examples of glulam construction in Switzerland, and also one of the finest architectural applications,[4] is the riding hall in St. Moritz which was designed by the well-known local architect Nicolaus Hartmann. Terner and Chopard were responsible for the design of the timber structure. In 1910, the Reithalle-Gesellschaft (Riding Arena Association) of St. Moritz signed a contract with Hartmann to design a riding hall on the west shore of the St. Moritz Lake. Hartmann, founding member of the Swiss Heritage Society' regional section, and well known for his preference of the so called regional style using traditional local architectural features, had just finished several museums and the representative head quarter of the Rhaetian Railways in Chur.[5]

Fig 1. Riding arena, St. Moritz. Architect, N. Hartmann, 1911. Entrance, stables and the riding arena. Photo: Schweizerische Bauzeitung, 57/58(1911).

The riding hall consists of a main building and an annex containing the horse stables and storage rooms. Hartmann developed a traditional form with hipped roofs for both buildings and double curved roof areas (Fig. 1). A series of glulam arches make the structure of the 34.5 m long hall spanning 19.8 m, which are designed according to the roof shape as a segment of a circle (Fig. 2). Due to the shape of the riding arena, Terner and Chopard designed two categories of glulam arches slightly different in their geometry: The central area is spanned by four semi circularly shaped arches with a spacing of 4.9 m, while the half hip arches span 14 m and have a semi oval shape (Fig. 2). Every central glulam arch consists of two symmetrical components. All glulam arches feature an I-shape cross section and their depth varies from 45 cm at the basis going to 90 cm at the haunch and arriving at 40 cm at the vertex. Their flanges are 18 cm wide and their webs 9 cm.

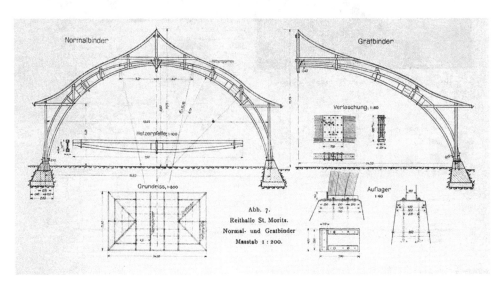

Fig 2. Riding arena, St. Moritz. Engineers, B. Terner and Ch. Chopard, 1911. Photo: Schweizerische Bauzeitung, 57/58(1911).

While the overall structural layout of the arches seems to be a straight forward arrangement and the shape of the arches reflects the nature of the 'new' timber, the connections of the components do not appear to be based on a consistent design practice. At the apex the two arch halves are connected through a vertical timber post, fastened with bolts and suspended at the lower end from both ends of the arch halves. The upper end of the post forms the support of the ridge of the curved roof. Four more support points in the form of purlins are placed on each arch side right on the top of the glulam components. The foot of the arches is placed on a concrete base and is received by an iron shoe made of L-shaped steel beams (Fig. 2). As each half arch consists of two components a site joint is placed near the middle of the half consisting of a lapped scarf joint of the glulam components together with additional strapping using steel plates on both sides making for a stiff connection of the components (Fig. 3).

However, the arches are not the only structural glulam components of the building. While all purlins on the arches span 4.9 m at the most, they exceed that span in the corners of the buildings due to the geometrical distortion. Here 7.5m long curved glulam purlins are used featuring an I-section of varying depth of max 50 cm in the middle (Figs 2-3). Also, the rafters, making the double curved shape of the roof, are glulam beams.

The riding arena in St. Moritz and the locomotive depot in Bern – a comparative study of early glulam construction in Switzerland

Fig 3. Riding arena, St. Moritz, 1911. Interior space. Photo: Municipality of St. Moritz

Constructed in 1910, this building is an interesting example of representing two different, and in some way, opposing attitudes towards timber constructions in the early twentieth century. On the one hand, in the dominant *Heimatstil (regional revival picturesque style)* – of which Nicolaus Hartmann is one of the main representatives[6] – the buildings are characterised by, *inter alia*, carved beams, projecting roofs and wooden façades. Wood, in this context, plays an important role in the picturesque aspect of the regional style of Swiss historic architecture, making reference to the long tradition of timber construction. Therefore, the use of timber opposes the 'banal' image of 'modern' constructions formed by the contemporary use of concrete and steel. In this context, custom-made glulam elements are available in basically any shape and dimension to meet the design of the architect. On the other hand, there is a 'modern' understanding of timber construction based on forms derived from engineering design processes which already gave rational form conceptions to concrete and steel. The engineers Terner and Chopard are the pioneers of modern timber engineering in Switzerland and provided Hartmann with adequate means to enable both an open space for the riding hall and the consistent use of timber for the preferred architectural style.

The locomotive depot in Bern (1912)

To increase the capacity for the storage of locomotives in Bern, the Swiss Federal Railways (SBB) decided to build a new depot near the main station in the Muesmatt district at Depotstrasse. Terner and Chopard designed the entire timber structure for the building which was finished in September 1912. The depot comprises four parallel halls whose structure consists of massive frame girders with spacings of 5 m, three of which spanning 21.2 and one 24.4 m (Figs 4-5). In total, 56 glulam frame girders have been used covering a surface of 780 m².

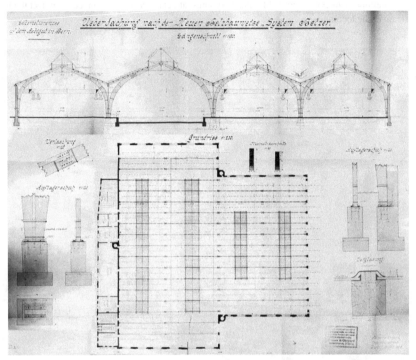

Fig 4. Locomotive depot, Bern. Engineers, B. Terner and Ch. Chopard, 1912. Project proposed in 1910, based on the "new timber construction method: Hetzer system". Photo: SBB Archives, GD-BAU-SBBBAU1-107-13.

Analogously to the arches in the riding hall in Bern, every glulam frame girder consists of two symmetrical parts forming a structural system similar to a three-hinged arch. Like for the arches there, the typical hinged connection at the vertex and the base are very different: At the vertex a traditional jointing technique [7] is used where the two halves of the frame are put against a timber post, which is at its bottom standing on a collar tie connecting the frame parts. The upper part of the post extends into a skylight structure above the vertex. At the base, the frame girders are placed directly on the concrete footing and held by means of iron shoes made of L-shaped steel beams (Fig. 4). Like in Bern, every glulam component, i.e. both halves of the frame girder, consists of two segments meeting in a lapped scarf joint connected through bolts and steel plates on both sides of the girder making for a continuous stiffness of the glulam part. This joint could be related to transportation constraints since a full-length half-girder would have rendered a reasonable transport from fabrication to the construction site impossible. The choice of the location of the joint in the girder has been made during the structural calculations. The engineers have chosen the intersection point of the frame girder with the compression line where there is the lowest bending moment in the structural element.

The rectangular cross section of the frame girders varies throughout their length and has been specifically arranged. They are 20 cm wide and their depth starts from 30 cm at the basis going to 100 cm at the haunch and arriving again at 30 cm at the vertex. The foundations originally were set to start just above the floor level where they received the lower ends of the frame girders. At this point, the timber elements were wrapped in metal sheets of one to two millimeter thickness. Probably, this very unusual detail has been arranged to protect the foot points from the steam of the locomotives.

Fig 5. Locomotive depot, Bern, 1912. Interior space. Photo: Brauen Wälchli Architectes, 1998.

Just at the time of the construction of the depot in Bern the SBB advertised the use of timber for such infrastructural buildings.[8] At that time, steel structures have still been the standard system while reinforced concrete was on the rise as a new robust form of construction. The question can be raised why the Bern depot was a timber structure at all and why SBB favoured timber over the other more common materials.

The histories of timber construction and railways are interwoven in many ways. In the second half of the 19th century, steel and cast iron structures replaced the wooden ones, especially when it came to large span structures such as new bridges and railway stations. Wood seemed to present an old-fashioned appearance. The striking feature of it, though, was its resistance to the smoke of the locomotive engines, the lack of the danger of corrosion and thus lower costs for maintenance. Since 1910 to the end of the steam age, wood was the preferred material for depots and railway halls because of its advantageous resistance against smoke.

In this context, it is interesting to look into the design history of the depot since, as usual, several material and construction options have been discussed. The very first step of planning a locomotive depot in Bern was taken in 1904 when the general management of SBB decided upon a railway layout following the pattern of the Stuttgart main station.[9] The design process of the building began in 1910. Four projects were proposed; three of them followed the common systems of their time: 1) a reinforced concrete roof on steel columns following the Manheim station model;[10] 2) a wooden truss placed on reinforced concrete columns like in a depot in Lausanne. 3) another, rather innovative project was proposed by Terner and Chopard who used glue laminated girders as the main structural components while 4) the last project proposed a combination of wooden trusses as a standard system together with Hetzer girders for the largest span. The type of construction, whether iron, reinforced concrete, wood or glulam, has been decided in favour of the latter. After many discussions and consultations, the SBB chose the Terner and Chopard project proposing Hetzer girders for all spans. The two major criteria for rejecting the other projects were "smoke and heat" and "costs": the concrete, although resistant to smoke, was considered the most expensive solution,[11] as for the steel the major disadvantage was the corrosion problem. For this reason, the Hetzer construction had to be revised omitting the iron drawbars which were initially proposed by Terner and Chopard. According to the request of SBB, an inquiry was to be made into the Hetzer Company to ascertainwhether there had been any German application of glue laminated timber structures for railway sheds. The negative answer revealed that until that date, iron has always been preferred over wood for almost all the larger locomotive depots for German railways "probably for reasons of higher fire safety".[12] However, major fire disasters and practical fire tests have demonstrated the very high danger of iron in cases of fire. Combining its smoke resistance with the better fire protection thanks to its compact volume and the easier and cheaper application of a plaster envelope[13], glue laminated timber was the choice for the project. Moreover, SBB advised all its subdivisions to use timber instead of steel for halls and sheds.

The depot in Bern was the first SBB project where glulam was used. By the time of the construction of the depot, there was neither a timber code nor any other technical specification for the use of glulam. Although a few glulam structures had already been successfully finished in Switzerland at that time,[14] SBB required Terner and Chopard to carry out loading tests with the proposed frame girder geometry prior to the construction of the depot. The main reasons were to learn about the behaviour of the new material and to check the accordance with the theoretical predication of the engineers. In May 1912 two Hetzer girders of 7 m span, scale models of one third of the actual size, were subject to a load test. The vertex sagged by 72 mm under a load 5 times higher than the normal charge without showing any signs of breakage. The glue joints have proven to be very good as all cracks occurred in the wood and not in the joints.[15] Eventually, by the end of 1912 the glulam frame girders were erected and the construction completed. The result received great recognition in Swiss, French and German engineering milieus.[16] The building was used for about ten years (1912-1922) as a depot for steam engines and subsequently it housed electric locomotives.

The design practice of early glulam

Considering the different nature of the newly introduced building material and the immediate use for large span structures, it seems to be interesting to look into the early design practice of glulam structures. There are two design levels which should be considered when examining the early applications of glulam technology. Both levels relate practical decisions during the development of the structures to models and conceptual frameworks that might have been used at that time and should be taken into account as a standard practice of design. While the first level should comprise the structural concept and model behind the design of the components, the second should focus on the constructional details of the parts, i.e. how the determined form is physically produced in the chosen material and how the components are connected.

The riding arena in St. Moritz and the locomotive depot in Bern – a comparative study of early glulam construction in Switzerland

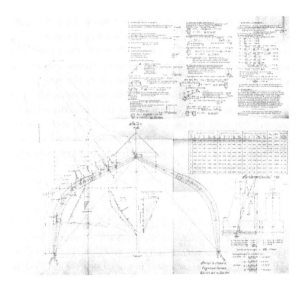

Fig 6. Locomotive depot, Bern. Engineers, B. Terner and Ch. Chopard, static calculations, 1911. Photo: SBB Archives, GD-BAU-SBBBAU1-107-13.

Reflecting the design procedure of both the riding hall and the depot, it can be stated that the structural system used was independent from the new material. In both cases, a three-hinged arch was chosen as a basic model to determine the necessary resistance for regular points of the system according to the assumed standard loads (Fig. 6). No additional assumptions or conditions regarding the new material have been noted in the context of the use of the structural model. Given certain early assumptions and experiences of the limits of resistance for glulam,[17] the structural depth of the respective points was then determined and the final component shape developed. With the help of this model the exact location of the site joints was determined, bringing together the estimated zone of minimum bending moments and suitable split of the structural part for transportation and assembling purposes. In addition to the determination of the site joints, later adjustments to the structural functionality were set after an analysis based on this model. For the riding hall, for instance, the frame girders were equipped with a tension rod to reduce deflections. Therefore, the effect of the location was checked in a bending moment diagram to ensure its effectiveness and to determine the resulting stresses. It can thus be noticed that the model for the structural design of the overall system and its components is similar to a standard modern engineering approach which discusses the structure regardless of the intended building material. This clearly reflects the design practice based on industrial building materials such as steel and reinforced concrete.

Regarding the second layer, the constructional design decisions which were made for the components can now be considered. Both the glulam members of the riding hall and the depot were designed and fabricated as curved parts with varying depth according the required resistance and with joints pragmatically arranged to comply transportation and assembling constrains. However, the cross section is different: While for the depot a compact form is chosen to allow for a minimal surface and easy plastering for fire protection, the glulam arches of the riding hall have a double -T beam section, apparently for the reduction of self-weight. The particular component shape, its varying depth and its specific cross section reflect the capacity of glulam as a new building material which allows to arrange the material purposefully where needed according to a higher understanding of the structural necessity, just as it was known from the typical steel design at that time.

Another important aspect of constructional design is the connection of the components. It has been found during the detailed examination of the details of the two buildings in the earlier sections, that the connections of the components are not based on a consistent design practice. If the structural modelling and the design of the overall system and the shape of its components can be linked to industrial materials like steel, what do the connections refer to? For both buildings the connection of the two glulam parts at the apex is part of traditional carpentry where the timber components run against another timber piece and the interfaces are specifically shaped to receive each other. The design of the girder frame footing hints to a concept outside timber construction. Here, the member is placed directly on the foundation clasped by an iron shoe which holds it in place. This decision refers to standard steel details of that time where a steel plate was attached at the end of the member and then placed on the concrete foundation (Fig. 7). It was the simplest constructional form of a foot hinge; while allowing for a certain degree of rotation it also avoids stress concentrations by placing the full depth of the member on the ground. The detailing of the site joint also reflects a constructional thinking between the materials: while the two segments meet in a lapped scarf joint, a typical timber connection detail, they are actually connected and fixed through bolts and steel plates on both sides of the girder, representing a standard steel connection which was adopted early in the increasingly industrial timber construction during the second half of the nineteenth century.

It can be summarized that the design practice for both the overall structural and the specific constructional development is dominated by models and standards typical for industrial building materials such as steel.

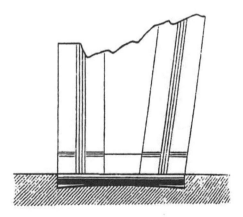

Fig 7. Detail of a steel column foot on a concrete foundation by means of a slightly curved metal sheet to reproduce the hinge effect. Photo: O. Königer, Die Konstruktionen in Eisen, Hannover: Th. Schäfer, 1993, p. 167.

The riding arena in St. Moritz and the locomotive depot in Bern – a comparative study of early glulam construction in Switzerland

Damages and repairs

A few years after completion, the early glulam structures sometimes saw unexpected damages which required extensive repairing works. Theses damages give an insight into the performance of the models used for the design of the early glulam structures and, more generally, make visible the difference of what was expected from the new material and how it turned out to operate. This could be related either to the performance of the material itself or the functioning of the structure in general.

The riding hall in St. Moritz showed several damages in its early years. During the spring of 1916 heavy snow put the roof at risk of collapse. It was found that the snow load has been underestimated in the static calculation (180 kg/cm^2). In addition, the meltwater absorbed by the underlying masses of sludge considerably increased the snow load which resulted in the deformation of the girders. Due to the large deformations, Terner and Chopard reinforced the central glulam arches in 1917 by inserting tie rods (with a diameter of 32 mm) at the height of 6 m. Later on, in 1928, another major damage appeared: the foots of the arches on one side of the arena, near the annex where the horse stables are located, were found to be subject to decay. From the beginning, when the building was finished in 1910, there were light timber fences covering all foots of the arches. It has been suggested that the decay was caused by the poorly ventilated space[18] between the interior fence and the wall next to the stables which might have contributed to an unfavorable humidity level. Terner and Chopard proposed to cut away the damaged pieces of the arch foots and to replace them with steel beams (U profiles) filled with concrete, following the original form of the girders (Fig. 8).

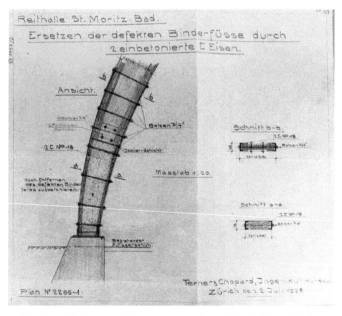

Fig 8. Riding arena, St. Moritz. Engineers, B. Terner and Ch. Chopard, 1911. Base of girders, replacement of decayed sections by steel U profiles filled with concrete in 1928. Photo: Cantonal Archives of Grisons.

In this context, it should also be mentioned that the glue used in early glulam construction was casein glue which is not resistant to moisture. Direct contact with water or high humidity might, therefore, cause a delamination effect and although the renewed dry strength of the glue comes close to the original, the glue joint never closes tightly.[19]

In 1918, the same problem occurred in Bern to the glulam structure of the locomotive depot. Just six years after the opening of the building, there was decay detected at the foots of the girders. Here, however, the glulam members were not trapped in closed spaces, but as mentioned before, were wrapped with metal sheets. In this case, Terner and Chopard proposed to cut off the affected parts and to rise the concrete foundations by that height. The surface of the extended foundation incorporated the steel shoe by clasping the foot of the arch (Fig. 9).

Fig 9. Locomotive depot, Bern. State of the base of one girder after the removal of the decayed section and its replacement by the concrete foundations. Photo: Roshanak Haddadi, 2017.

Conclusion

In this paper, two early applications of glulam in Switzerland have been discussed, the riding hall in St. Moritz (1910) and the locomotive depot from the Swiss Federal Railways in Bern (1912). Both structures revealed an extraordinary use of glulam technology and have been discussed in Switzerland and abroad. A few years after completion, the early glulam structures saw unexpected damages in the form of decay due to high humidity or rain water leaking through the roof. Repairing works sought to replace the damaged parts with other materials and they have been in this state since then.

A close look at the models used and the structural and constructional design decisions derived from them brought insights into references to contemporary design procedures. It has been shown that the studied early glulam structures feature construction details, such as component shapes and connections, which are similar to the design culture of steel and, altogether, they show a hybrid use of traditional and modern timber construction. In general,

461

The riding arena in St. Moritz and the locomotive depot in Bern – a comparative study of early glulam construction in Switzerland

it can be stated that the formally flexible glulam brings timber into line with the design thinking coming from the industrial building materials such as steel and reinforced concrete. The two examples give a good understanding of the capability of glulam at that time and how it was implemented in the existing design practice.

Acknowledgements

This research project is funded by the Swiss National Science Foundation (SNSF).

References

[1] See M. Rinke, 'Terner & Chopard and the new timber. Early Technological Development and Application of Laminated Timber in Switzerland', pp.197-204, *Proceedings of the 5th International Conference on Construction History, Chicago, 2015.* Chicago: Construction History Society of America, 2015.

[2] See M. Rinke, 'Konstruktive Metamorphosen. Holz als immer während es Surrogat', In: M. Rinke & J. Schwartz (Eds.): *Holz: Stoff oder Form: Transformation einer Konstruktionslogik,* Sulgen: Niggli. 2014, pp. 263-277.

[3] Otto Hetzer, UK Patent No 20684, Apr.1907, pp.1-2.

[4] K. Hartmann, *Baumeister in Graubünden, drei Generationen Nicolaus Hartmann, 1850-1950,* Chur: Desertina, 2015, p. 102.

[5] *Historisches Lexikon der Schweiz,* http://hls-dhs-dss.ch/textes/f/F19862.php, consulted on 3 Jan. 2017.

[6] E. Crettaz-Stürzel, *Heimatstil, reformarchitektur in der Schweiz 1896-1914,* Frauenfeld: Huber, 2005, p. 313.

[7] In his hand book, *Lehrbuch der Hochbau-Konstruktionen,* published in 1882, Rudolph Gottgetreu, german architect and university professor, documented and classified the timber connections of the time.

[8] SBB Historic Archives, GD-BAU-SBBBAU1-108-05, SBB Oberingenieur, 10 Nov. 1911.

[9] ibid., GD-BAU-SBBBAU1-107, SBB Obermaschineningenieur, 8 Feb. 1904.

[10] ibid., GD-BAU-SBBBAU1-108-05, SBB Kreisdirektion II, 2 Sep. 1910.

[11] Cost estimation for the projects in reinforced concrete: 910,000, in glulam: 800,000, in glulam and wooden truss: 860,000 francs, (ibid., GD-BAU-SBBBAU1-107-13, 20 Mar. 1911).

[12] ibid, GD-BAU-SBBBAU1-108-05, Ch. Chopard, 12 Sep. 1910.

[13] Chopard also confirms that in the case of Hetzer constructions with their simple arrangements and the almost complete elimination of trusses of all kinds in glulam girders, it is possible to achieve a complete fire safety by means of a fireproof plaster, which had already been applied by the Hetzer Company on many occasions. This could also eventually justify the preference of Terner and Chopard to use the simple rectangular cross sections over I-shaped ones.

[14] Among them in Lausanne, 1909: provisional footbridge bridge and Hotel Beauregard's roof; in Geneva, 1910: skating ring; in Zurich, 1910: Krematorium Sihlfeld and Aeschbssacher furniture factory.

[15] Schweizerische Bauzeitung, „Die neue Lokomotiv-Remise der S.B.B. auf dem Aebigut in Bern", 61/62 (1913), p. 290.

[16] ibid., GD-BAU-SBBBAU1-108-05, Schweiz. A.-G. für Hetzer'sche .Holzbauweisen, 15 Nov. 1913.

[17] Schweizerische Bauzeitung, Die Hetzersche Holzbauweise", 57/58 (1911), p. 217.

[18] See Ch. Mueller, *Entwicklung des Holzleimbaues unter besonderer Berücksichtigung der Erfindungen von Otto Hetzer,* Dissertation, 2003, p. 106.

[19] ibid.

Armstrong Huts in the Great War (1914-1918)

Karey L. Draper and James W. P. Campbell

Queens' College, University of Cambridge, UK

Introduction

Despite the large number of books and research into nearly every facet of the First World War, there is a distinct lack of literature on the design and construction of temporary military buildings that were shipped and used during this period. The Crimean War in the nineteenth century had seen a shift from tented accommodation to the introductory use of huts (temporary buildings) on campaign during wartime. The twentieth century saw increasing experimentation in design leading to a huge expansion of types.[1] Not surprisingly wartimes proved to be particularly intense periods of development and production as the escalating demands of war created huge pressure to solve problems and provide the armed forces with whatever was necessary to win. With the outbreak of the First World War, the need to provide better accommodation for troops, especially in winter, was a driving force in new designs. Initially, this requirement of accommodation was only a consideration for the Home Front in Britain during the build up of forces. With the assumption that the war would be short-lived, there was an expectation that troops in France would live in tents, billets, empty buildings, open fields or in trenches. As it became clear that victory would not be secured so quickly, it was recognised that better accommodation in France needed to be provided. This would require huts that could not only be easily and quickly constructed, as in Britain, but also have an element of portability, packaged compactly, allowing them to be easily shipped across the English Channel and transported to selected sites, and to be moved again if or when the front moved.

August 1914: Declaration of War and a New Building Programme

On 3 August 1914, the day before Britain entered the First World War, Lord Herbert Kitchener was boarding a ship from England to his posting in Egypt, when a message reached him to immediately return to London and meet with Prime Minister Herbert Asquith. Kitchener was a career Army soldier, a Royal Engineer and a distinguished hero of the Boer Wars. Asquith asked him to stay in England and take up the role of Secretary of State for War.[2] It is said that Kitchener is one of the few who recognised this war would last more than a few months, and that it would require a vast investment of manpower. Britain's standing peacetime force was 247,798 men.[3] With this in mind, Kitchener immediately issued a call to arms across Britain, a recruitment campaign that saw over 100,000 men enlist within the first few weeks, with that figure rising exponentially during the following months. By the end of 1915, nearly two and a half million civilian men had volunteered to join the British Army.

This massive surge in the Army population quickly necessitated discussions on how to best accommodate and train the new soldiers. Peacetime military accommodation at the various military camps around the country could take 174,800 men, providing 600 cu ft (or about 60 sq ft) per man.[4] Necessity required fresh measures to be taken to properly support Kitchener's New Army. It is important to understand that the need extended beyond sleeping quarters to everything essential to an actively operating army, including hospitals, stables for their horses, veterinary hospitals, dining halls, kitchens, bathhouses, training facilities, and warehouses for stores. To begin to meet these needs, the War Office reduced space allocation to 400 cu ft per person, (or about 40 sq ft), so more men could be assigned to each building, then eliminated the provision of married quarters for military families.[5] These actions instantly increased accommodation capacity by 87,000 men, but was still far short of the requirement.[6] Bell tents, which had once been standard surplus accommodation for British army camps, were sufficient to provide short-term relief, but only as a temporary measure in fair weather, as they were not suitable for winter use.[7] Obviously, a larger-scale solution was needed urgently. Hutted accommodation that could be erected quickly, survive winter gales and provide warm, dry conditions for men needed to be developed.

Despite good intentions, "the problem of hutting" as Major General George Scott-Moncrieff, Director of Fortifications and Works (1911-1918), referred to it, was a continuous issue. Just before his death, he wrote a first-hand account for the Royal Engineers Journal in 1924, elucidating the extreme difficulty the War Office had faced throughout the war in supplying enough accommodation.[8] This article provides rare insight from a key source and will be utilised in this paper as one of the main references for understanding hutting during the First World War. It is important to note that the initial quote of accommodation was planned for 490,000 men but it eventually became clear this would be far too few. By the winter of 1914-15, the numbers of enlisted men had surged to over a million.[9] Thus, the issue of accommodation was immense and required a whole new way of building.

Major B. H. O. Armstrong and his Hutted Battalion Camp Plan

Initially, the remit of hut design fell to the Royal Engineers and to one engineer in particular, Major Bertie Harold Olivier Armstrong (1873-1950).[10] Armstrong, a Canadian by birth, was a Royal Engineer and staff captain in the War Office. Of his personal history, we know very little. What is known is that on 12 August 1914 he received orders to design a set of hutted buildings that could be constructed across England to support Kitchener's growing army. In just two days, working around the clock with the help of his chief assistant, J.D. Michel, and a small group of draughtsmen, Armstrong produced a complete set of working drawings for a:

> [T]ypical hutted camp of a battalion of infantry at war strength, including 17 different designs (i.e. men's huts, recreation rooms, lavatories, cooking huts, officers' quarters and mess, sergeants' mess, etc.).[11]

Scott-Moncrieff, who was Armstrong's direct superior at this time, deemed this endeavor a remarkable feat:

> [F]or it not only involved the completion, in every detail, of a large number of plans, but it meant the settlement of several very important sanitary and administrative problems, such as the provision of baths, the supply of water, the nature and amount of artificial light, and of interior space and ventilation, the arrangements for messing and cooking, and many other such matters. Indeed, so thoroughly was this done that the result was considered by Lord Kitchener to be unnecessarily good, and after the first camps were far advanced he gave orders to curtail a good deal of what he thought was unwarrantable luxury, in the shape of dining rooms and drying-rooms, etc. Baths, however, were admitted to be a necessity always, both in this country and in the field, and this in itself was a matter of great sanitary importance and a new departure in military administration.[12]

These first designs by Armstrong consisted of timber frames covered in corrugated iron with an asbestos lining. The huts measured 20 ft wide by 60 ft in length by 10 ft in height. (Fig. 1) Each was heated by at least one small stove, with front and rear entry points and six-light windows along the length of each hut, the top panels opening on a louver to allow fresh air.[13]

Figure 1 Belton Park Camp, Lincolnshire. The first parkland to be offered by a country house owner in wartime, became the training grounds for the Machine Gunnery Corps in 1914. These huts are examples of Armstrong's first set of designs, constructed with a timber frame and covered with corrugated iron sheeting. (Lincolnshire Archives, Ref: Pointer 10.1)

Scott-Moncrieff said they were originally intended to house only twenty-four soldiers and one non-commissioned officer-in-charge per hut in order to better enforce discipline, however it seems these specifications became somewhat fluid depending on the demand.[14] Some reports estimate that more than forty men at a time inhabited one hut, perhaps in desire for better shelter in wet conditions, but overcrowding later became the chief cause of outbreaks of disease and sickness.[15] The intended space allotment per soldier in accommodation was intentionally set, to allow for proper ventilation and prevent the spread of infection, but these were probably discarded out of necessity. The second design was slightly larger with a twenty-eight foot span and was used for support structures such as offices and cookhouses. As Scott-Moncrieff commented:

> This was the quickest and probably best form for a limited number of huts, and if only the first 100,000 men had been all that needed accommodation, no other sort would have been necessary. When however, the numbers rose by hundreds of thousands, until the demands amounted to about a million, some other material was required.[16]

However, at least initially, Armstrong's designs for seventeen building types were hugely successful. They were used to expand existing camps and establish new sites across England. The estimated cost of a hutted camp for one thousand men was £15,000.[17] This would provide forty huts at a cost of roughly £375 per hut, or £15 per soldier. With the additional cost of supplemental services such as water, lighting and roads, the total cost was estimated at £20 per soldier. Cost was a factor and Kitchener ordered the elimination of anything that could possibly be considered a luxury. Camps were often established without dining halls and other auxiliary buildings, rather than the full cadre of 17 designs, which Armstrong initially envisioned.[18]

Armstrong Huts in the Great War (1914-1918)

The success of Armstrong's battalion camp designs is that they were adaptable whilst being specialised to purpose. For instance, sleeping huts for the soldiers were deliberately designed to be small, when compared to large barracks of the period. It was felt that smaller huts had much to recommend them above larger designs. Scott-Moncrieff said the decision to keep these sleeping huts small allowed them to more easily conform to local ground conditions: they could be arranged more easily on a hillside or in woods.[19] Smaller numbers of men encouraged discipline, whilst also ensuring better fire safety precautions. Finally, the smaller hut size was more conducive to further adaptability, if and when the building was required for a different purpose, a common occurrence throughout the war.[20]

The Armstrong Hut Debate

Armstrong's initial designs for the War Office were the first to be widely applied during the First World War. These were more permanent structures, made of timber and clad in corrugated metal, or whatever materials were readily on hand. However, there is evidence that Armstrong also designed at least three other huts, which has created some confusion amongst researchers as to what exactly constitutes an "Armstrong Hut." Whilst it is likely that many would agree that the first designs he made for the War Office represent what is most commonly known as the Armstrong Hut, there are several others from the war that carry the same name. Two have timber frames, covered in canvas, and were possibly collapsible to allow for portability. (Fig. 2) Another is called Armstrong Hut Number Four, with the plan published in *Work of the Royal Engineers in the European War* (1924), and differs slightly from the other huts.[21] (Figs 3-4) The name alone supports the theory that Armstrong had several hut designs. The mystery is not helped by the fact that in September 1940, a bomb was dropped on the War Office Record Store on Arnside Street, London destroying the records.[22] Thus, much of what we know necessarily relies on the few remaining primary sources still in existence and these are not altogether clear on the subject.

Figure 2 An Armstrong Hut? Soldiers from the 4th Battalion Yorkshire Regiment referred to this canvas shelter as an Armstrong Hut. (Great War Forum)

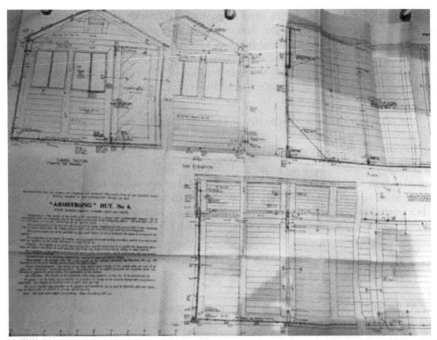

Figure 3 Plans for Armstrong Hut, No. 4.   Plate XLVI, from Work of the Royal Engineers in the European War, published in 1924

Figure 4 Possibly an example of Armstrong's Hut No. 4. Image labeled: 'Men from the King's Own Regiment constructing an Armstrong Hut.' Wareham, August 1915. (Image courtesy of the King's Own Royal Regiment Museum, Accession No. KO1769/01-114)

Armstrong Huts in the Great War (1914-1918)

Several authors on the subject have made incorrect and misleading statements. Mallory and Ottar, in *Architecture of Aggression* (1973), for instance, says that Armstrong Huts were provided in two sizes and constructed of timber and canvas,[23] while Mornement and Holloway's *Corrugated Iron* (2007) claims that Armstrong only deployed Aylwin Huts (timber and canvas construction) to France.[24] It is likely they were misled in their research by a biography of Peter Nissen, *Nissen of the Huts* (1997), written by Fred McCosh, which they referenced frequently in their works.[25] McCosh's narrative is unclear, and often inaccurate. He claims:

> War with Germany was declared on the night of 4th August 1914 and by August 12th Armstrong had issued orders for the construction of hutted camps with the then official Aylwin huts…One hut type followed another, the Aylwin gave way to the Armstrong, the Tarrant, the Liddell and finally, late in 1918, the Weblee.[26]

Too eager to promote his hero, he claims that it is quite likely that Nissen was the first person to suggest hutting, apparently unaware that hutting had been in circulation since the Gloucester Huts of the Crimean War sixty years earlier. In contrast, John Schofield's 2006 study of Army camps for English Heritage attributes Armstrong's hut to his original type plans in August 1914, describing them not with canvas but as having a framework of:

> [R]ed fir scantlings… the cladding was not specified, but corrugated iron was almost certainly the preferred medium…The lining was matchboard and 3 ply; asbestos sheeting was tried at first but found to be too brittle.[27]

He adds that originally, these huts had brick foundations, but shortages in bricks and bricklayers resulted in creosoted wooden piles being used instead.[28] Somewhat confusingly, Schofield mentions later that many Armstrong Huts were dispatched to France.[29] These came in two sizes, completely different from the War Office Type Plan designs, so it is clear these were a different variety than Armstrong's first huts. Schofield concludes, "they were weatherly, but very cold in winter. It is extremely unlikely that any were employed at home."[30] It is possible Schofield is referring to Armstrong's timber and canvas huts. These published works serve to highlight just how wide the gap in knowledge is about huts, and how this paper contributes to a greater understanding of their history and development.

Based on available evidence from primary and secondary sources, this paper puts forth the argument that Armstrong designed at least four different hut types during the wartime period. The first were those constructed of timber and corrugated iron sheeting, or entirely of timber, depending on availability of materials. This paper will refer to these as Armstrong's "Type Plan Huts." He then proceeded to design hospital huts, which were employed both in England and in France. It is probable that Armstrong then turned his mind to designing a hut that could be more portable in the field than his Type Plan Hut, which was heavy and not easily transported. This resulted in a canvas and timber hut that was an amalgamation of both his War Office "Type Plan" design and a tent, one that would perhaps be more practical in the field. This timber and canvas hut, which is what is commonly known as the Armstrong Hut, came in two sizes, as mentioned by Schofield, with the smaller size more common.[31] The Imperial War Museum archive holds an image that, while unconfirmed, may possibly be an example of the larger sized of design. (Fig. 5)

Fortunately, clues to untangling the Armstrong Hut debate is provided by Scott-Moncrieff. He writes:

> Thus it happened that when Major Armstrong got the word to produce hut designs in August 1914, he did not lose a moment. Later on he produced the well-known "Armstrong hut" which, constructed in sections, was made in workshops and sent out ready made to any proposed site and rapidly erected. But, at first there was no necessity for

this, and indeed there was considerable advantage in utilizing local materials and labour. The huts were at first built of a wooden framework with corrugated iron on roofs and external sides, and with asbestos lining inside ... The reason why a type plan of a battalion hutment was so important is that it furnished a guide to any class of unit ... The same types of huts were used in all cases, and it is a tribute to Major Armstrong's foresight that practically the same types were used during the whole war, though details were frequently improved as a result of experience, and materials differed with local circumstances.[32]

Figure 5 Royal Engineers move a hut during the Battle of the Somme, Sept. 1916. It is possible this is an example of one of Armstrong's canvas and timber huts. (© IWM Q1204)

Several times in the article, Scott-Moncrieff describes these first designs as Armstrong's "type plans." Officially, it seems they were also referred to as War Office Type Plan BD85A/14. These were the standardised hut plans used to establish camps all over England, described by Scott-Moncrieff, as well as by researchers such as Schofield, Crawford, and others. Huts of this type were constructed near Alnwick Castle in the autumn of 1914.[33] (Fig. 6) Timber was used for the cladding and corrugated sheeting for the roof. It is worth noting however that these are different from what later was commonly referred to as the Armstrong Hut, which was a lighter weight model possibly adapted to be more appropriate to conditions on the frontlines.

Figure 6 Alnwick Camp was completed in December 1914 and seems to make use of Armstrong's type plan designs. (Image courtesy of Bailiffgate Museum)

To further illustrate the variety of Armstrong's hut designs, Scott-Moncrieff reported that by the middle of October 1914, Armstrong had released a set of type plans for hutted hospitals.[34] Those erected in England were capable of caring for up to 600 patients at a time, while those in France were much larger, with enough wards to provide 1300 beds. These were built in England and France and involved wards, administrative blocks, operating theatres and quarters for medical staff along with mess rooms.[35] Each ward was designed to hold twenty-five beds, a nurse's duty room and store, along with bathrooms and lavatories. Each ward was connected by covered passageways to the administrative and operating huts. The walls were lined with asbestos plaster, often painted.

> The effect in the appearance of the wards, especially when these were brightened with flowers and the tasteful care of the nursing sisters, was charming and would compare favourably with any hospitals in the land. Yet the cost of these hutted hospitals was not great, only some £80 per bed, and it is probable that for practical purposes they were as efficient as the permanent "palaces of pain" which, in civil life (before the war), cost as much, in some cases, as £1,000 per bed.[36]

Presumably, once the Army's camps and hospitals were established with his plans, Armstrong turned his attention towards better accommodation for soldiers fighting abroad. Whilst his type plan huts were well-suited for temporary camps in Britain, they were not intended to be portable. Nor were they manufactured in sections for ease of transport. A prefabricated, lightweight design, which could be easily shipped abroad and quickly erected would have been a likely concept. It is possible this was the Armstrong hut of timber and canvas construction mentioned by soldiers. Unfortunately, unlike his previous type plans, the canvas hut was not hugely successful. There are reports that they were "heavy and awkward to construct and transport ... It also proved extremely cold for the occupants."[37] It would seem likely that this is when Armstrong's Hut No. 4 was devised. It was more solid than the canvas Armstrong Hut, but was packaged in bundles and thus, more portable. An essential piece to understand from these developments was that it was this continued necessity for a portable hut that drove contributions from other builders and inventors throughout the war.

470

Materials shortage

The immense quantities of building materials, especially galvanised corrugated steel sheets, timber and asbestos, required for constructing camps across Britain meant a real possibility of shortages if pre-war manufacturing methods and exporting practices were not revised. Foreseeing this risk, and hoping to neutralize it, the Directorate of Works and Buildings asked the War Office's Contract Office to consider putting these materials under government control.[38] To some extent, at least initially, the plan seemed to work. Timber was in such plentiful supply, its control was not deemed immediately necessary by the Director of Contracts.[39] Asbestos was approved for control so it could be stockpiled for wartime building, and British manufacturers who exported corrugated steel out of the country were temporarily halted.[40] It was this control that chafed the worst, as the growing colonies were their main markets for selling corrugated sheets.[41] However, eventually a deal was struck between the steel manufacturers and the government, wherein they were allowed to continue exporting but only to British colonies, and in return they offered to supply the government with corrugated steel sheets, but at a discounted rate. Scott-Moncrieff noted this was accepted and said everything went smoothly until "suddenly galvanized sheets became unobtainable."[42] Apparently, what was not generally realised until after the first few months of the war was that Germany had control of the world's zinc market, a necessary element in preventing the corrosion of thin corrugated steel.[43] The dipping of steel sheets into molten zinc quickly and efficiently made it more resistant to corrosion. This was a massive setback for the Works Directorate, which realised it would have to either source a different material for the hut walls and roofs or they would have to find extra men to apply coatings of protective paint over the metal sheets, a ridiculously time intensive process.[44] It would appear a combination of the two options was ultimately decided. Armstrong's Type Plan Huts, which initially were constructed clad entirely using the remaining stocks of galvanized corrugated sheets (such as at Belton Park), were later constructed almost entirely of timber weatherboarding (such as at Alnwick).[45]

It is important to note that the predominant designs being employed during this early period of the war were Armstrong's War Office Type Plans and the Aylwin Hut, which many referred to as a hut-tent. These were the most prevalently used during the first year of the war.[46] It was not until 1916 that the Works Directorate in France was able to meet winter hutting needs with other fresh designs, like the *Adrian, Tarrant, Somerville*, as well as the *Nissen Hut*, which was specifically considered to be "ready-made."[47] These could be sent from England, or were constructed in the many workshops set up in France.[48] One notable case was that of the British builder, Tarrant and Co., which established its own workshop in a camp three miles from Calais during the war and avoided labour concerns by staffing it with British female carpenters. These women were responsible for the inspiring feat of constructing 37,000 Tarrant Huts by the end of the war.[49]

Conclusion: The Armstrong Huts

Thus, it seems to be that the name Armstrong Hut likely referred to any of several designs by Major B. H. O. Armstrong. Unlike other huts of the wartime period, none appear to have ever been patented. There were five main types:

1. **War Office Type Plan Hut.** Possibly also known as Type Plan BD85A/14, which were authorised by ArmyCouncil Instruction 352 of September 1914.[50] These were extensively used across England and in France from the onset of war in August 1914. Originally, these consisted of a timber frame clad in corrugated metal sheeting with a corrugated roof, however as material shortages ensued, it became predominantly clad in timber. Originally, the accommodation hut design was supplied in two widths: 20 ft and 30 ft at any length. These were later redesigned into a sectional version of 15 ft and 28 ft, in sections of

10 ft. "This width of section is rather large for transport and handling, but otherwise these huts answered well."[51] Sizes: A. 20/30 ft by 60 ft by 10 ft in height. B. Later redesigned to be narrower at 15/28 ft by 60 ft by 10 ft. The first layout (A) accommodated 30 men each with four feet of wall space per bed. The doors were at either end, and there was a central aisle for tables. When the camp had a dining room, the tables were removed to accommodate more men. It was heated by two stoves, also located in the middle aisle. The later redesigned hut (B) accommodated 22 men each, and were manufactured in ten foot sections. The stoves were placed against the walls, taking the space of two beds.[52] Generally these sleeping huts were: "arranged in rows with ablution rooms and latrines in blocks between every pair of rows." The dining room plan was initially designed at a standard width of 30 feet, but the later sectional huts were narrowed slightly to 28 feet. Schofield incorrectly says the sectional huts were constructed in England and despatched at the beginning of the war,[53] however, Scott-Moncrieff says the sectional design did not come until much later.[54]

2. **Armstrong Hutted Hospital.** Extensively used in England and France from October 1914. A larger version of the Type Plan.

3. **Armstrong Hut.** Two sizes. 15 ft by 24 ft and 9 ft 3 in. by 12 ft. The smaller huts were more commonly used.[55] Timber frame covered in canvas.

4. **Armstrong Hut Tent.** Light timber A-frame covered in canvas (possibly shown in Fig. 3). Very little is yet known.

5. **Armstrong Hut No. 4.** Introduced in early 1916. Brigadier General Baker Brown refers to ordering "1,000 small wooden huts of a new type just evolved by Col. Armstrong." He also said that the other huts were supplemented by a "very light hut made of flat boards, which was very useful for small detachments."[56] These measured 9 ft 2.75 in. by 12 ft 2 in. Linen was used in place of window glazing, which would have made sense if employed close to the front lines where explosions would have made traditional glass windows dangerous. The entire hut was shipped as a series of bundles.

The Armstrong Huts were perhaps the most successful temporary wartime buildings of the First World War. They were only outshined by the introduction of the more convenient, but perhaps less aesthetically pleasing Nissen Hut in 1916. However, for the first years of the war, Armstrong succeeded in creating huts that were easily adapted to any unit and he did it in the space of two days, an incredible feat. They were intended to be temporary, but their longevity is evident in the sheer number of Armstrong Huts that were purchased from the War Office by local communities and served as public buildings from the 1920s through to the present day. As this paper has shown however the Armstrong Hut is not one Hut but a small family of closely related designs, each a clear demonstration of how close attention to detail and innovation in methods of construction were key to solving the problems involved.

References

[1] The contents of this paper are the result of research undertaken by K. Draper, 'Wartime Huts: The Development, Typology and Identification of Temporary Military Buildings in Britain 1914-1945' (PhD thesis, University of Cambridge, 2017), pp. 33-62, supervised by Dr. J.W.P. Campbell. This paper is largely Dr. Draper's work with guidance on format and discussion of content from Dr. Campbell.

[2] C. Messenger, *Call to Arms: The British Army 1914-18*. London: Weidenfelt and Nicolson, 2005, p. 20.

[3] Ibid.

[4] J. Schofield, *Army Camps: History and Development, 1858-2000*. Swindon: English Heritage, 2006, p. 5. See also, W. B. Brown, 'Notes by a Chief Engineer During the Great War of 1914-1918', *Royal Engineers Journal*, (December 1926), 422-436 (p. 423). Regarding the use of cubic feet shifting to square feet measurements, Baker Brown said, 'It was early decided that the ordinary wooden hut without ceiling might be considered as having a cross section equivalent to an average height of 10 feet, so that in practice the cube might be neglected and we could make all our calculations in terms of floor space.'

[5] Schofield, *Army Camps*, p. 5, and Brown, 'Notes', (Note 4), p. 423.

[6] Schofield, *Army Camps*, (Note 4), p. 5.

[7] G. Scott-Moncrieff, 'The Hutting Problem in the War', *Royal Engineers Journal*, (September 1924), 361-380 (p. 366).

[8] Ibid.

[9] Ibid, p. 364.

[10] Ibid.

[11] Ibid, p. 361.

[12] Ibid, p. 362.

[13] Brown, 'Notes', (Note 4), p. 423, says that two stoves were supplied and also tables for meals. Further observations were made by the author from reviewing historic photographs and visiting an original Armstrong Type Plan Hut in Girton, Cambridgeshire, June 2017.

[14] Scott-Moncrieff, 'The Hutting Problem', p. 365. Brown, 'Notes', (Note 4), p. 423, said these huts could accommodate 30 men each with 4 feet of wall space per bed.

[15] J.A. Glover, 'Observations on the Meningococcus Carrier-Rate in Relation to Density of Population in Sleeping Quarters', *The Journal of Hygiene*, 17, No. 4, (October 1918), 367-379, (p. 368).

[16] Scott-Moncrieff, 'The Hutting Problem', (Note 7), p. 364.

[17] Ibid, p. 368.

[18] Ibid, p. 362.

[19] Ibid, p. 365.

[20] Ibid.

[21] Institution of Royal Engineers, *Work of the Royal Engineers in the European War, 1914-1919: Work Under the Director of Works (France)* (Chatham: MacKay and Co., 1924).

[22] The National Archives, WO 363. See online reference http://discovery. nationalarchives.gov.uk/details/r/C4567 [Accessed 17 September 2017]

[23] K. Mallory and A. Ottar, *Architecture of Aggression*. Hampshire: Architectural Press, 1973, p. 77.

[24] A. Mornement and S. Holloway, *Corrugated Iron: Building on the Frontier*. London: W.W. Norton & Co., 2007, p. 112.

[25] Ibid, p. 219.

[26] Fred McCosh, *Nissen of the Huts: A Biography of Lt. Col. Peter Nissen, DSO*. Bourne End: B D Publishing, 1997, p. 87.

[27] Schofield, *Army Camps*, (Note 4), p. 5.

[28] Ibid.

[29] Ibid, p. 7.

[30] Ibid.

[31] Ibid.

[32] Scott-Moncrieff, 'The Hutting Problem', (Note 7), pp. 364-365.

[33] Ibid, p. 377.

[34] Ibid, p. 374.

[35] Ibid.

[36] Ibid, p. 375.

[37] Mallory and Ottar, (Note 23), p. 77.

[38] Scott-Moncrieff, 'The Hutting Problem', (Note 7), p. 370.

[39] Ibid.

[40] Ibid.

[41] Ibid.

[42] Ibid.

[43] Ibid.

[44] Ibid.

[45] Ibid, p. 374. Schofield adds that whilst corrugated iron cladding was preferred it was dependent on local availability. See Schofield, *Army Camps*, (Note 4), p. 5.

[46] Ibid, pp. 7, 9.

[47] Draper, 'Wartime Huts', (Note 1), pp. 33-62.

[48] Mavis Swenarton, 'W. G. Tarrant: Master Builder and Developer', *Monograph 24*, Walton and Weybridge Historical Society, 1993.

[49] Imperial War Museum, Q 2467, http://www.iwm.org.uk/collections/item/object/205078807 [Accessed 17 September 2017]

[50] National Archives, WO 293/1. See John Sheen, *Tyneside Scottish*. Barnsley: Pen and Sword, 2014, p. 48.

[51] Brown, 'Notes', (Note 4), p. 425.

[52] Ibid, p. 423.

[53] Schofield, *Army Camps*, (Note 4), p. 7.

[54] Scott-Moncrieff, 'The Hutting Problem', (Note 7), p. 362.

[55] Schofield, *Army Camps*, (Note 4), p. 7.

[56] Brown, 'Notes', (Note 4), p. 425.

The Unpublished Carpentry Archives of Cecil Hewett (1926-1998):

A survey of his letters and drawings in the Essex Record Office in Chelmsford

Ming Shan Ng[1] and James W.P. Campbell[2]

1. Independent scholar; 2. Faculty of Architecture, University of Cambridge, UK

Introduction

When one thinks of historic carpentry two names come immediately to mind: the Englishman Cecil Hewett (1926-1998) and the Frenchman Henri Deneux (1864-1969). Deneux was an architect working for Historical Monuments Service in France who published a volume entitled *L'Evolution des Charpentes du XIè au XVIIè Siècle* in July 1927.[1] Deneux was a highly successful conservation architect and his copious meticulously produced drawings and models of historic French roofs are still preserved in the archives of Service. Many of his previously unpublished drawings have been published in series of books since his death [2].

Cecil Hewett's background could not have been more different. He was son of a woodworker and he started looking at timber framed buildings as a teenager growing up in Essex. After National Service he trained in cabinetry and silversmithing at Chelmsford School of Art and University College, Swansea, becoming a school teacher in Essex, a calling he pursued for 19 years. During this time he began drawing timber buildings and structures as a hobby.[3] His first publication *Development of Carpentry* (1969)[4] established his reputation as a researcher and led to his change of career. He joined the Greater London Council (GLC) Historic Buildings Division in 1972, and then moved to Essex County Council's Historic Buildings Section in 1974 where he remained for the rest of his working life.[5] Hewett's major publications included *Development of Carpentry* (1969)[6], *English Cathedral Carpentry* (1974)[7], *Church Carpentry* (1974)[8], *English Historic Carpentry* (1980)[9] and *English Cathedral and Monastic Carpentry* (1985) [10]. He also contributed to several television programmes, most notably 'In Search of the Master Carpenters'.[11]

Hewett's richly illustrated publications proved highly popular and they remain hugely influential. As well as providing the first clear descriptions of roof structures in England, he proposed sequences of typological developments that could be identified in historic carpentry. Many of his ideas have been since proved by carbon 14 and dendrochronology. Hewett himself did not normally use scientific dating and indeed worked before the major breakthroughs in dendrochronology that have made the process cheaper and more accurate. Instead he relied entirely on observation, examining medieval timber-framed buildings and dating them by comparing the detailing and arranging what he called evolutionary sequences.

Hewett's work is controversial because it is frequently inaccurate. While Deneux was an architect and took painstaking measurements of all the buildings he surveyed, Hewett's drawings were often done entirely by eye (albeit an extremely good eye). As long as this is known by the reader then the limitations of the drawing can be clearly understood, but Hewett never discussed his methods and this led to subsequent completely justified questions about their reliability and usefulness, still much debated today. His works are still often the only easily accessible published records of particular historic roof structures, but they are not dimensionally accurate and historians need to treat them with caution. They have misled those that are unaware of his methods, but they can still be immensely useful. Hewett published only a fraction of his output and on his death in 1988 the remainder was deposited at Essex Country Record Office. It is these records, which have never been examined, that form the subject of this paper.

Hewett's Papers in the Essex Record Office

Hewett's writings, sketches, drawings and photographs are held in the Essex Record Office in Chelmsford. They are divided into four sections:

Reference A10549 - listed as 'Letters and correspondence on the publication of relating to the editing of his book "English Cathedral and Monastic Carpentry"' is unfortunately unaccessible.

Reference T/P 541/1- listed as 'Photocopies of letters and photographs relating to Wynter's Armourie, Magdalen Lever' contains hand-written and typed letters, photocopies of photographs produced by Hewett mainly in 1954. It i not particularly illuminating from the construction history point of view.

Reference C/DP 2/6/2 - listed as 'The Barn at Grange Farm, Coggeshall: historical and architectural guide', contains a bound book written by Hewett, named 'The Barn at Grange Farm Coggeshall Hall' and three A5 sized booklets, titled 'Origins of Harwich', 'Stock Tower Mill' and 'Mountnessing Windmill: its history and its restoration and how it works', published by Essex County Council in the 90s. These are already in the public domain.

Reference A12039- listed as the 'Papers of CECIL HEWETT (d.1998), historian of timber framed buildings, comprising illustrations of joints and construction of timber framed buildings for his published works, life drawings, draft of Historic English Doors with photographs, and drawings of mills, ploughs, waggons etc.' is by far the most interesting and forms the bulk of the discussion of the remainder of the paper. It contains six accession boxes of Hewett's works. These boxes are numbered 1-6. Inside each of these boxes, the documents are stored in folders, some are assigned according to the documents inside and named with descriptions. Most are drawings, but photographs, notes, work and personal letters and postcards are also kept in these boxes. Some of the work in the boxes has been published in Hewett's books and articles, but most of them have not been published. Some of it is work-in-progress and some of them are drafts for his articles and illustrations. There are also many identical copies of each drawing, showing how Hewett did several drafts before producing the final set of drawings for publication. This reference includes three manuscripts of unpublished books: 'Tree-ring analysis of timbers from the Coggeshall Barn', 'Historic English Doors' and 'Post-Medieval Architecture'; there is also a completed article 'Hammerwork: raising, planshing, stretching and sinking'. Although these were never published, the contents and individual illustrations were often used in other publications. APPENDIX 1 shows a complete analysis of the works and APPENDIX 2 shows a draft catalogue of the published and unpublished contents under this reference. [12] The contents can be divided into a number of categories: drawings of timber frames, drawings of belfries, drawings of doors, drawings of joints, drawings of ornaments, drawings showing the construction process, machinery, silversmithing and letters and documents. Each will now be considered in turn.

Drawings of Timber Frames

There are more than 200 drawings of timber frames stored mainly in Boxes 1, 2, 3 and 4, including frames for barns, churches and cottages. Some of them were published in Hewett's books, primarily in *Development of Carpentry* (1969) and *English Historic Carpentry* (1980). The drawings include Mott's Cottage in Aldham, Little Chesterford Manor House, Southchurch Hall, Priory Place in Little Dunmow, Woodpack Inn at Coggeshall, a house in Stebbing, Prior's Chamber in Prittlewell, the Swan Inn and the old Manor House in Braintree, the Dolphin of Bradwell-juxta-Coggeshall, Tipswain in Asheldham, Houchin's Farmhouse, Barn in Ladylands in Good Easter, the Cock and Bell in High Easter. Maldon, the Monk's Bank in Netteswellbury, the Church of St. Peter and St. Paul in West Mersea, Kennington's in Aveley in Essex, the Red Lion and Powers Hall in Witham, Horham Hall in Thaxted,Jacob's Hall in Brightlingsea, Queen's Elizabeth Hunting Lounge in Chingford, Aylott's Farmhouse in Sattron Walden, Doe's Farmhouse in Toothill, Harlowbury, Braxted Hall, the capella-extra-muros at Little Coggeshall Abbey, nave roofs at Little Braxted, White Roding, Dabury, Great Sampord, Foxearch, Hockley, Pattswick, Godhanger, High Roding, Doddinghurst, Dovercourt, Ulting, Little Burstead, Gosfield, Middleton, Cressing, Margaretting, Birdbrook, Chipping Ongar, Wethersfield, Magdalen Laver, Little Leighs,[13] Paycocke's House and 39 West Street in Coggeshall, Doddinghurst Church in Essex, Thatched Cottage in Elmstead, Jenkyn's Farmhouse, Cobham Oak Cottages in Feering, Grange Farm in Little Dunmow, Pear tree Cottage in Gallows Green in Dunmow, Weaver's Cottage in Pebmarsh, Meadowview Cottage, Eastbridge Hospital, St. Clere's Hall, St. Osyth, Old Sun Inn in Saffron Walden, the Chantry in Stebbing and the Waltham Abbey. Some unpublished drawings are sketches for recording and some are drafts or his publications. Hewett sometimes used tracing paper to draw parts of buildings and later assembled them to form a complete drawing. He also used white paint to make corrections on the drawings which would not be evident in reproduction. The majority of the frame drawings are roof structures. He detailed the posts, beams and columns connections by mainly cross-sections and perspective drawings. He also liked to capture ornaments on the roof frames with black-and-white illustrations. He captured dates on ornaments on frame structures, which helped him to date the buildings. He also drew the jetties of the frames and connections between columns and walls. He investigated the frame structures and dated them by comparing them with other dated structures. He also tried to understand the loading of each post while sketching the frame, and imagine the construction process of lifting columns and beams into place. Some of the frame drawings also have a blown-up drawings of the associated joints. Joint drawings will be further discussed below.

There are also line drawings with typed texts stored in the boxes. Hewett and his team, whose names sometimes appear on the drawings, also produced diagrammatic drawings to show the structural ideas behind the construction of the frame. Fig.1 shows a set of floor plan and cross sectional diagram of Barley Barn at Coggeshall, it is stored in Box 1, file called 'File Acc A12039 Cressing, Barley Barn, Wheat Barn, Granary'. This file includes a lot of recording sketches from his time working on houses in Cressing.

Hewett explored not only the medieval carpentry of timber frame structures but also how he imagined the house had operated in daily use. He produced sketches of the ventilation of timber houses. In the perspective of the framing of a Weaver's Cottage, he also drew how the smoke escaped out of the house from the very top of the pitched roof.

The Unpublished Carpentry Archives of Cecil Hewett (1926-1998):
A survey of his letters and drawings in the Essex Record Office in Chelmsford

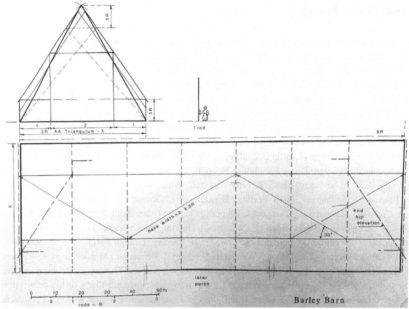

Figure 1. Drawings (plans and cross-sections) of Barley Barn at Coggeshall.(from Box1 File Acc Cressing, Barley Barn, Wheat Barn, Granary)

Drawings of Belfries

There are almost 100 drawings and sketches of frames of belfries and spires (mainly in Boxes 1 and 2). They are mostly perspective drawings showing structure of the entire tower, from the base to the top structure. Some of these drawings were published in *Development of Carpentry* (1969), *English Historic Carpentry* (1980) and *Church Carpentry* (1981). The published drawings include the Navestock Church, Laindon church, Church of St. Lawrence in Upminster, St. Mary in Stifford, the Belfry in Blackmore, Rhenish helm at Sompting with free tenon insert, the Wells Cathedral, Wethersfield church, Aythorpe Roding church, Badwell-juxta-Coggeshall, belfry at Standford Rivers, belfry at Little Clacton, belfry at White Notley and the tower at Little Totham.[14] The shapes of the base structure were rectangular, hexagonal and even octagonal. For example, a rectangular base can be found in the Church of St.Peter & St.Paul in Horndon-on-the-Hill and St. Lawrence in Upminster; a hexagonal base can be found in St. Thomas the Apostle Church Navestock; an octagonal base can be found in the Laindon Church. He illustrated the base frame shapes on sectional plans to show the profile of the frames cut at various levels.

Hewett was particularly interested in joints. In the belfry structures, he captured the details of mortise and tenon joints of the timber connections and investigated the sequence of installation. His sketches and notes show his dating method in action. Fig.2 shows a perspective drawing of the Belfry in West Bergholt, He marked the dimensions of the footprint of structural frame (but no vertical dimensions) and drew the disposition of the timber elements, as well as the sequence of the erection. The drawings include a hand-sketched beam connection joint,he form of which leads Hewett to conclude that the beams were built c.1000 while the support came later, around 1330. It is this sort of analysis that was typical of Hewett.

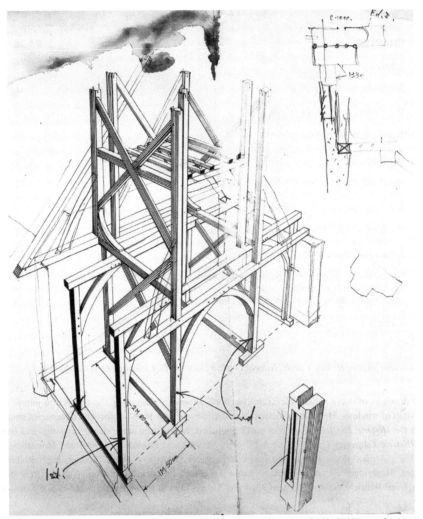

Figure 2. Perspective drawing of the Belfry in West Bergholt, Essex. (from Box 2 File Belfries and spires)

Drawings of Doors

Around 100 drawings of doors can be found in Boxes 1, 2, 3 and 4 together with a full draft of his unpublished book *Historic English Doors* in Box 3. Working notes for the book can be found in a file named 'working notes for Historic English Doors' in the same box.

The draft *Historic English Doors* was typeset in 182 pages, with104 illustrations and photos. TABLE 1 shows the content page of his draft. There is also a draft list of illustrations in APPENDIX 3 (compiled and edited by MSN for this paper).

The Unpublished Carpentry Archives of Cecil Hewett (1926-1998):
A survey of his letters and drawings in the Essex Record Office in Chelmsford

Table 1. Content page of Hewett's draft Historic English Doors in Box 3 (edited by the author)

Hewett's drawings of doors include elevations, sections, axonometric showing the connection joints. There are also drawings of windows. He included details of ornaments and door jambs, some with dimensions and captions. Although the *Historic English Doors* was never published, he included some of the drawings and contents in *English Historic Carpentry* (1980), *Church Carpentry* (1981) and *English Cathedral* and *Monastic Carpentry* (1985). The published doors include the doors at Hadstock, Buttsbury, White Roding, High Roding, Castle Hedingham, Heybridge, Eastwood, Ashen, Little Leighs, Navestock, Belchamp Walter, Great Sampford, Tendring, Great Bardfield, Shalford, Greensted, Selby Abbey, Ely Cathedral, Waltham Abbey and Norwich.[15]

Drawings of Joints

There are more than 200 drawings of joints scattered throughout Boxes 1, 2, 3, 4 and 5. Most of the drawings were published in his books, often in the appendix chapters. The collection includes scarf joints and mortice and tenon joints in Fairstead Hall, Houchin's Farmhouse, Blackmore, Red Lion Inn at Colchester, Dedham, Jacob's Hall and farmhouse at Stebbing and Old Manor House at Braintree.[16] Hewett used perspectives, cross-sections to illustrate different components of the joints, including the mortices, tenons, pegs and keys. Some of them were drawn as details, others as part of larger structures, such as beams, connected to each other. He also drew exploded assembly drawings with dotted lines to show how the pieces were put together.

For example, he sketched in two-dimensions a scarf joint at Dormer Cottage at Petham in Canterbury. He drew the joints and dimensioned them in inches showing the holes for pegs and tenons. Using his typical methods and deep knowledge of joints he assigned it to the thirteenth century. Fig.3 shows his hand sketches for a couple of joints at Bolton. They sketch axonometric drawings with a few key dimensions to show how the carpenters prepared and assembled the joints. There is also another drawing shows a beam from Old St. Mary's Church at West Bergholt, Hewett drew all four sides of the beam on one piece of paper having sketched them on separate sheets.

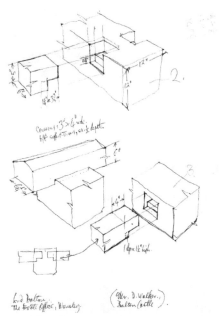

Figure 3. Hand sketches of joints at Bolton (from Box 3 File Rough notes, working sketches)

Drawings of Columns and Ornaments

This category contains sketches and drawings of columns, timber elements such as beams and joists, architectural ornaments and mouldings. These drawings can be found in Boxes 1 and 2 mainly, and many of them are identical. Some of these drawings in the boxes were printed in his books *The development of Carpentry 1200-1700* (1969) and *English Historic Carpentry* (1980). The published drawings include ornaments he investigated in Belfries in Navestocks, Priory Place in Little Dunmow, Prittlewell Priory, Fressingfield in Suffolk, St. Clere's Hall at St. Osyth's Essex and Durham House.[17] Hewett sketched cross-sections, elevations and axonometric sections with notes and dimensions, to illustrate all the faces of the columns and the ornaments, using black and white to show shadow and projecting profile of columns and mouldings. There are also a lot of photographs of beams and columns.

Hewett recorded ornaments on site with rough sketches and worked up more precise drawings at home. Fig.4 shows a pair of his drawings of ornaments from Castle House in Church Street in Saffron Walden. This shows the hand sketch drawn on site next to the carefully crafted presentation drawing.

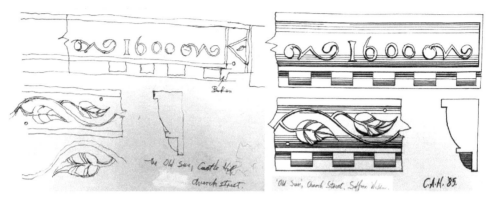

Figure 4. Hewett's hand sketches and drawings of ornaments at Church Street in Saffron Walden. (from Box 2 File S)

Drawings illustrating the process of construction

Among all the other drawings of standing structures, Hewett produced a series of didactic drawings, no doubt intended for an introduction for one of his books illustrating the process of construction. Three of them are found in Box 1 in the file called 'Acc Cressing Barley Barn, Wheat Barn, Granary'. Two are virtually identical. One of the drawing is shown on Fig.5.

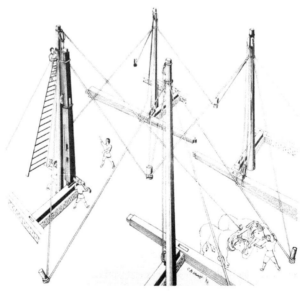

Figure 5. Hewett illustrated construction technique of timber structures in the past. (from Box 1 File Acc Cressing, Barley Barn, Wheat Barn, Granary)

Drawings of Machinery

Two folders in Box 2 contain drawings of machinery, entitled 'Mills' and 'Mills, Carts, Ploughs, Waggons'. There are many 'mechanical' detail drawings, done in 1973 showing the fixing and structure of the machinery. These include a sack hoist, waterwheel with wooden shroud and floats, sluice-gate winch-gear, the 1776 house mill structure, bridge-tree and toe-pot, pit-wheel, shaft and journal, wallower, up-and-down shaft and toe-pot, clock mill mechanical and wheel details, hand-sketch of the Spur-wheel of watermill at Springfield in Essex etc. Fig.6 shows one of a drawing of a cogpit of a house mill. This box also includes an axonometric drawing of the framing and carcass of the House Mill in Bromley-by-Bow[18] and a draft of an article about various timber structures and details of medieval post-mills, including the Aythorpe Roding post-mill and the Billerieay post-mill, with corrections The article describes and illustrates the joint details and their functions.

The folders also contain many drawings that were not done by Hewett but were presumably collected by him as reference material. There is a detailed drawing of elevations and sections of the Morton Mill in Essex, drawn in August 1950 by P. Brown. There is an axonometric section of House Mill in Three Mill Lane in Bromley-By-Bow in Newham, drawn in December 1973, which might be one of the illustrations in Hewett's publication. There is another drawing of Fryering Post-mill by Andre Meikle, built in 1770 and there is a set of drawings of plans, sections and elevations of Danzey Green Windmill in the Avoncroft Museum drawn by Mike Pitkin at Birmingham School of Architecture dated 1981.

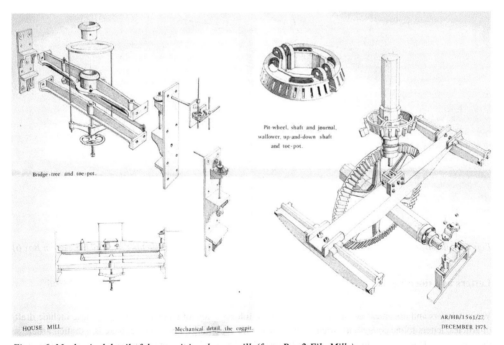

Figure 6. Machanical detail of the cogpit in a house mill. (from Box 2 File Mills)

The Unpublished Carpentry Archives of Cecil Hewett (1926-1998):
A survey of his letters and drawings in the Essex Record Office in Chelmsford

Drawings of Silversmithing

Box 6, which is marked 'Illustration and rough texts for article on silversmith work', contains drawings and a draft unpublished article in silversmithing. The draft article, entitled 'Hammerwork: raising, planshing, stretching and sinking', contains a page of synopsis of contents and ten pages of writings with markups. In it Hewett describes vividly the process of silversmithing and suggested ways to make the silverwork better. For example, he says:

> 'it is best to keep the hammering elbow closely located against one's waist, and to keep the head quite still in order that the polish imparted by each hammer blow may be seen, and the vessel revolved precisely that distance to the right.'[19]

The numbered drawings to accompany the article are stored in the same box (Fig.7).

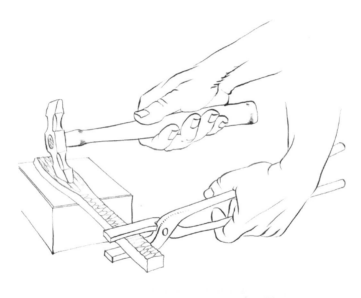

Figure 7. Illustration of Hewett's article 'Hammerwork: raising, planishing, stretching and sinking'. (from Box 6)

Letters and documents

Various letters and document are spread throughout the folders. Most of them are in Box 1. These include drafts of articles, letters to the councillors, friends and notes of his recordings. For instance, there is a drafted article on the old Manor House in Little Square, where he recorded the condition of the building and a description of the structure; there is also a letter to Blair Lees, Stourbank Cottage in Nayland, talking about a late fourteenth-century linen-fold Priest's door in the South Wall of the Chancel in which Hewett speculates on the source of a mark of a name on the outside face of the door. There is a letter is from Mrs. John Buck from Colchester, written in April

1979, talking about a spur for a brace on Little Hall in Lavenham for temporary scaffolding. There is also a note on calibration of Rochford, South Street sent by the Laboratory Manager in Isotope Measurements Laborator in March 1984 and a letter to Hewett for alteration to 17 South Street in Rochford in May 1984. In Box 2, there is particularly interesting a letter sent from the famous Medievalist John Harvey in June 1979 in which Harvey describes the dating system in England between eleventh century to sixteenth century. Part of this text was published in Hewett's book *English Historic Carpentry* (1980).[20] There is also a note describing and dating the service wing in Tiptoft's Hall in Wimbish ascribing it to early thirteenth century. In Box 3 contains a document sent by the Essex County Council to Hewett with a tree ring analysis of timbers from the Coggeshall Barn done by the University of Sheffield in June 1984. The document includes a table of analysis with numbers of rings, dimension with radius and sketch of cross-section profile of the timber structural elements. There are also some newspaper articles about Essex historic timber buildings, photographs of site visit to Summer's Farm in Doddinghurst and some personal postcards.

Summary

This paper was written to give an overview of Hewett's work currently stored in the Essex Recording Office. The catalogues on APPENDIX 1 & 2 and the content above in each category will hopefully help historians in giving them a sense of what is in the archive. The limitations of Hewett's drawings have already been discussed in detail, however he left behind him a wealth of material. Many of the buildings he surveyed were under threat at the time he surveyed them and have since been lost. Much remains unpublished.

Hewett's work in the boxes are however unsorted and not well protected. They are delicate. When they were deposited they were pinned together using metal paper clips, sometimes with a note telling us on what page can we find the images on Hewett's publications. However, some of the paper clips have already left marks. Before the papers were deposited they were clearly not stored properly and Hewett drew on acid paper which has gone yellow and soft. Digitisation of the images is essential as they will inevitably degrade with time and they need to be properly catalogued. Since the publication of this paper an additional set of 474 drawings have been deposited at the archives, found in the council offices. A list of these is published in the catalogue to accompany the exhibition of some of the drawings at this conference. These were digitised before deposit. It is unclear how many more drawings remain to be deposited. What is clear is that Hewett left many hundreds of drawings at his death providing a fascinating insight into his methods and an invaluable archive.

What this paper has hopefully highlighted is how important this collection is and how large it is in scope. Hewett's collection would make an excellent subject for a PhD and certainly requires serious scholarly attention.

Acknowledgement

We would like to thank the staff at the Essex Record Office for their kindness and patience and supporting this research.

References

[1] Henri Deneux, *L'Evolution des Charpentes du XIè au XVIIè Siècle* (Kadar: Paris, 1927).
[2] See the publications of Editions Du Patrimoine, Centre des Monuments Nationaux.
[3] A, Gibson and D. Andrews, 'Obituary: Cecil Hewett', *Independent*, Tuesday 29 September 1998

[4] C. A. Hewett, *The Development of Carpentry, 1200-1700: An Essex Study* (David & Charles: Newton Abbot Ltd., 1969)

[5] Obituary.

[6] see note 4 above.

[7] C.A. Hewett, *English Cathedral Carpentry* (Wayland: London, 1974)

[8] C.A. Hewett, *Church Carpentry: a study Based on Essex Examples* (Phillimore: London, 1974, 2nd edition 1982)

[9] C.A. Hewett, *English Historic Carpentry* (Phillimore: London, 1980)

[10] C.A. Hewett, *English Cathedral and Monastic Carpentry* (Phillimore: London, 1985)

[11] First aired on Friday 18 May 1972 on BBC 2 at 20.10

[12] The appendices will be published in the catalogue of drawings as there was insufficient space in these proceedings. They will also be published in the online version of these proceedings.

[13] Hewett, C. A*., The Development of Carpentry, 1200-1700: An Essex Study* (David & Charles: Newton Abbot Ltd., 1969), pp.39, 65, 67, 76, 80, 82, 88, 104, 107, 144, 146, 149-150, 163-4, 215, 219. *Historic Carpentry*, pp.38, 48, 94, 103, 196, 200, 206-207, 209, 222-3, 299-300; Hewett, C. A., *Church Carpentry: A study based on Essex examples*, (Phillimore & Co. Ltd., London and Chichester, 1974), pp. 11-39, 81-85.

[14] *Development*, pp.17, 34-5, 49, 64, 143; *Historic Carpentry*, pp. 14, 14, 52, 78, 83, 86, 98; *Church Carpentry*, pp. 80-91.

[15] *Historic Carpentry*, pp. 7, 66-8, 94-6, 117, 192-4, 210; *Church Carpentry*, pp. 96-113, 12, 139, 161; *Monastic Carpentry*, pp.157-170.

[16] *Development*, pp.172-210. *Historic Carpentry*, pp.219, 264-82.

[17] *Development*, pp.213-220. *Historic Carpentry*, p.179.

[18] *Historic Carpentry*, p.255.

[19] Hewett, Cecil, unpublished article 'Hammerwork: raising, planishing, stretching and sinking', p.4.

[20] *Historic Carpentry*, p.1.

Immediate Housing Construction following the 1963 Skopje Earthquake

Vladimir B. Ladinski

School of Architecture and Design, University American College Skopje, Republic of Macedonia

Introduction

On Friday 26th July 1963 a magnitude 6[1] and intensity IX MCS[2] earthquake devastated Skopje, the capital of the Republic of Macedonia (than constituent republic of the former Socialist Federal Republic of Yugoslavia), killing 1,070 and injuring 3,300 people[3]. The level of destruction was severe: 80.7 per cent of the total buildings floor area including 75.1 per cent of the dwellings floor area or 67.4 per cent of the dwellings in the city were either destroyed or severely damaged, thus leaving 75.5 per cent of the 200,000 population homeless[4]. It is considered that the level of casualties could have been higher if the earthquake had occurred outside the summer holiday season. The level of destruction and damage was reflected in the earthquake direct losses estimated at over one billion US dollars[5] that was equivalent to 15[6] per cent of the Gross National Product or nearly equivalent to the entire[7] national budget of former Yugoslavia for that year. Therefore, the local, state and federal authorities were facing a major challenge on how to deal with the humanitarian crisis and respond to the consequences of the disaster.

Emergency shelter was provided for 40,000 families during August and September 1963[8] through the supply of 5,000 tents and 1,711 huts[9]. This in combination with evacuation of 140,000 people, mainly mothers with children under the age of 18 and those over 60, for a period between three to nine months[10] allowed the authorities to focus their efforts on damage assessment and post disaster planning activities. Following the completion of the damage assessment, the authorities decided to repair 16,000 damaged dwellings and provide some 14,095 new dwellings[11]. The latter one was for intermediate housing with an expected life span of 20 to 30 years which was to contribute towards meeting much needed housing needs whilst the planning, design and construction of the permanent housing was taking place. The significant post-earthquake recovery and reconstruction efforts were characterised by the high international profile and assistance at the time underpinned by the United Nations declaration to rebuild Skopje as a gesture of international solidarity.

This paper examines the post-earthquake housing reconstruction efforts covering the period between 1963 and 1964 through analysis of the housing development activities related to the construction of the 18 new intermediate housing estates. Building on the review of the literature available on the subject and research, this study contributes to the growing interest in pre-transition architecture and housing construction in the territories of the former Socialist Federal Republic of Yugoslavia, as well as to the area of post disaster intermediate housing provision.

The 1963 Skopje earthquake and the subsequent reconstruction resulted in a wider research interest both following the actual event and more recently, especially among those interested in looking into the legacy and the lessons learned from this event. Since the earthquake occurred some fifty five years ago, there are limited resources that are available online or in a digital format. Majority of the post-earthquake reconstruction related information has been kept by organisations that no longer exist due to their demise through the transition period commencing in 1991 with the declaration of independence and shift to democracy. Probably one of the best known collections of documents related to 1963 Skopje Earthquake is the one within the Institute of Town Planning and Architecture – (ITPA) in Skopje (*Zavod za urbanizam i arhitektura na grad Skopje*). This Institute was established after the earthquake and was responsible for some of the key post-earthquake planning activities. Unfortunately it ceased trading during the transition period. On Friday 21st April 2017 a pre-fabricated building of this organisation was destroyed in a fire. Allegedly the affected building still contained some post 1963 earthquake related documentation. So far it is not clear whether a unique set of documents has been lost or whether the key documents related to the earthquake were already moved some time ago to the National or the City Archive[12]. Nevertheless, due to the closure of the Institute, the access to their collection has not been available for some time now. However, additional key sources of published information on the post 1963 Skopje earthquake have been identified and analysed[13].

Post 1963 Skopje Earthquake Intermediate Housing

Once the damage assessment was completed, the authorities decided to repair 16,000 damaged dwellings and construct 14,095 new dwellings with a view to accommodate up to 50,000 and 70,000 people respectively.[14] Work was able to commence in August 1963. To facilitate this, a significant task force was assembled comprising of 150 construction companies with over 25,000 workers,[15] this allowed most of the 18 new housing estates with prefabricated housing to be completed by May 1964 and the majority of the building repairs to be carried out. Each of the six republics of former Yugoslavia financed and constructed a settlement for up to 15,000 people which meant that 82 per cent of the newly constructed dwellings were produced within the former federation[16]. The reminder of the dwellings originated from other countries, with the former Soviet Union donating a factory for the manufacture of prefabricated blocks of flats.

Even half a century after the 1963 Skopje Earthquake, despite consulting publicly available sources, it is difficult to establish a precise picture relating to the construction of the intermediate housing. These findings have been summarised within Table 1 which attempts to capture, where available, the name of the settlement, the number of dwellings constructed, the country of donation or the origin of the dwellings, as well as the country of origin of the construction company.

Table 1 still contains a number of empty fields, and the number of the settlements on the list is greater than the 18 originally stated settlements. This figure tends to be quoted in publications like *Skopje Resurgent*[17] in English, and Skopje: *Catastrophe – Reconstruction - Experinece* [18] in Macedonian. Both are considered to be based on reliable resources since the former was authored by the United Nations Development Programme (UNDP) and the later by Mr Kole Jordanovski who was the than Director of the General Directorate for the Reconstruction and Redevelopment of Skopje, established after the earthquake to direct and oversee the post-earthquake reconstruction and redevelopment of the city. The poster[19] showing the new settlements in Skopje indicates only 14 new settlements, whilst Jordanovski[20] lists 18 (those for which the actual number of dwellings are identified). It is likely the discrepancy arises due to the use of slightly different names for the settlements like Dolno Vodno and Vodno, whereby the former one refers to a smaller area of a larger district. Equally, settlements like Butel and Gjorche Petrov are listed individually in the poster[21] whilst the Jordanovski[22] lists them by their subdivisions I and II. Similarly, the poster[23] lists the settlement Kisela Voda, which is not included by Jordanovski[24]; however settlements like 11 Oktomvri and Przhino are part of the district known as

Kisela Voda. Therefore, the above explanation may assist with resolving some of the discrepancies related to the names of the new settlements constructed after the earthquake for *intermediate* housing.

*Table 1. List of new settlements with prefabricated intermediate housing built between 1963 and 1964 in Skopje following the 1963 Skopje earthquake (compiled by the Author). Abbreviation: N/A - data not available; * - data information differs between various resources.*

No	Settlement[25][26]	Number of Dwellings[27]	Country of Donation[28][29]	Country of Construction Company[30]
1	11 Oktomvri	341	N/A	N/A
2	Acetilenka	156	N/A	N/A
3	Aerodrom	1,306	N/A	Yugoslav Army
4	Butel I	1,136	UK	Bosnia and Herzegovina
5	Butel II	772	UK?	R. Macedonia
6	Chair (*Čair*)		UK	N/A
7	Dolno Vodno		N/A	N/A
8	Drachevo (*Dračevo*)	1,965	France [Serbia]*	Serbia
9	Gjorche Petrov I (*Ǵorče Petrov I*)	140	Sweden, Germany, UK	R. Macedonia
10	Gjorche Petrov II (*Ǵorče Petrov II*)	700	N/A	R. Macedonia
11	Karposh (*Karpoš*)		N/A	N/A
12	Kisela Voda		Bulgaria	N/A
13	Kozle	1,052	France, World Council of Churches	Serbia
14	Lisiche (*Lisiče*)	1,022	N/A	Montenegro
15	Madzhari (*Madžari*)	1,801	UK	Croatia
16	Przhino (*Pržino*)	256	N/A	N/A
17	Sinngjelikj (*Sinǵeliḱ*) now Metodija Antonov-Chento (*Metodija Antonov Čento*)		Denmark, UK	N/A
18	Shuto Orizari (*Šuto Orizari*)	268	USA	N/A
19	Taftalidzhe (*Taftalidže*)	1,169	Czechoslovakia, Poland, USA Mexico, France, Norway, Switzerland	R. Macedonia, Croatia
20	Vlae	1,001	N/A	Slovenia
21	Vodno	208	N/A	N/A
22	Zhelzara (*Železara*)	491	[Croatia]*	Croatia
23	Other Locations	320	N/A	N/A

According to UNDP[31], 82 per cent of the about 14,000 dwelling units for intermediate housing were produced within former Yugoslavia, whilst 11.5 per cent were ordered and imported from abroad. On the other hand the poster[32] indicated the number of units received as assistance from various countries including 125 from the

World Council of Churches. Unfortunately, the quality of the image is such that is not quite possible to record the numbers with a sufficient level of confidence. Because of the way in which the available information is presented it is difficult to establish the actual number of units contributed by various countries on each of the 18 settlements.

In absence of actual figures, but through a visual survey of these 18 settlements, one can only speculate that the majority of these dwellings may still be in use. Thus, some of the individual houses or semi-detached houses are still in their original form; but the majority have undergone various improvements, either through the addition of an external masonry leaf or render to improve their longevity, or through side or top (with added floor) extensions. Some of them have been replaced with new houses. The different approaches are most likely a reflection of the differences in the economic abilities of the property owners over the years.

Figures 1 to 10 show examples of prefabricated houses from the Taftalidze settlement as they are today. The first three examples (Figures 1 to 3) are examples of the prefabricated houses that have retained most of their original state. The next two examples (Figures 4 and 5) illustrate prefabricated houses which have had an upgrade of the façade to extend the building life. Examples of prefabricated houses with combination of single storey side extensions and single storey with basement extension are shown on Figures 6 and Figures 7 to 9 respectively. Finally, Figure10 contains a top extension where an additional floor has been added to the house. The majority of the images (Figures 1, 4, 5 and 10) show in the background examples of neighbouring sites, where the original prefabricated houses have been replaced with new houses, as was the original intention.

Figure 1. Example of Prefabricated House in Taftalidze, Skopje. Architect, No information. Current state, 2017. Photo: Vladimir Ladinski. Private Archives of Vladimir Ladinski.

Figure 2. Example of Prefabricated House in Taftalidze, Skopje. Architect, No information. Current state, 2017. Photo: Vladimir Ladinski. Private Archives of Vladimir Ladinski.

Figure 3. Example of Prefabricated House in Taftalidze, Skopje. Architect, No information. Current state, 2017. Photo: Vladimir Ladinski. Private Archives of Vladimir Ladinski.

Figure 4. Example of Prefabricated House with New Facade in Taftalidze, Skopje. Architect, No information. Current state, 2017. Photo: Vladimir Ladinski. Private Archives of Vladimir Ladinski.

Figure 5. Example of Prefabricated House with New Façade in Taftalidze, Skopje. Architect, No information. Current state, 2017. Photo: Vladimir Ladinski. Private Archives of Vladimir Ladinski.

Figure 6.   Example of Prefabricated House with Side Extension in Taftalidze, Skopje. Architect, No information. Current state, 2017. Photo: Vladimir Ladinski. Private Archives of Vladimir Ladinski.

Figure 7.   Example of Prefabricated House with Side Extension in Taftalidze, Skopje. Architect, No information. Current state, 2017. Photo: Vladimir Ladinski. Private Archives of Vladimir Ladinski.

Figure 8. Example of Prefabricated House with Side Extension in Taftalidze, Skopje. Architect, No information. Current state, 2017. Photo: Vladimir Ladinski. Private Archives of Vladimir Ladinski.

Figure 9. Example of Prefabricated House with Side Extension in Taftalidze, Skopje. Architect, No information. Current state, 2017. Photo: Vladimir Ladinski. Private Archives of Vladimir Ladinski.

Figure 10. Example of Prefabricated House with Added Floor in Taftalidze, Skopje. Architect, No information. Current state, 2017. Photo: Vladimir Ladinski. Private Archives of Vladimir Ladinski.

Conclusions

The 1963 Skopje earthquake destroyed or severely damaged over three quarters of the housing floor area in the city, leading to a notable programme of recovery and reconstruction with support from the international community. The authorities approached the humanitarian crisis and the homelessness with a three-stage action plan:

i.   Provision of shelter in combination with temporary mass evacuation;

ii.   Construction of prefabricated intermediate housing aimed to provide accommodation for the next twenty to thirty years period in combination with repairs to the existing building stock that could be brought back to use;

iii. Construction of permanent housing.

This paper is focused on the construction of the prefabricated housing for intermediate use. The research has shown that the local, state and federal authorities of former Socialist Federal Republic of Yugoslavia, with assistance from the international community, were able to execute the planning, design and construction of 18 new settlements with 14,095 new prefabricated dwellings between August 1963 and May 1964, thus providing accommodation for up to 70,000 people. These were to provide intermediate housing for the next twenty to thirty years. To achieve this and to reinstate the damaged but repairable building stock, 150 construction companies with over 25,000 construction workers from all of the former 6 republics were engaged. 82 per cent of the dwelling units were manufactured within former Yugoslavia and 11.5 per cent ordered and imported from abroad. 6.5% percent of the dwellings are unaccounted for, but to date it has not been possible to establish whether or not they are related to the dwelling units donated from abroad. The decision to build intermediate dwellings not only provided much needed housing but also moved the construction works outside the city centre. The latter was in support of the authorities' decision for the initial phases of the reconstruction to concentrate on areas outside the city centre in order to allow for the city centre's Master Plan to be completed by 1966 before its reconstruction commenced. The provision of the intermediate housing has contributed towards the improvement of the housing living standards in the city, as some of the lost housing from the older housing stock was fairly basic. Based on the above, it is understandable why the post 1963 Skopje earthquake reconstruction efforts have been acknowledged for the efficiency of the relief operations,[33] the ability to make long term decisions[34] as well as to incorporate fundamental seismic safety features.[35]

The provision of the intermediate housing, the post-earthquake reconstruction and the rebuilding efforts have not been without criticism. For example, the decision to locate the new housing settlements on predominantly green field sites,[36] and the appropriateness and scale of some of the new developments have been questioned,[37] as well as the disruption of local social structures and the destruction of neighbourhood cohesiveness[38]. The lack of public participation and the creation of dwellings that are not always responsive to the cultural needs of the population have been highlighted as issues that probably remain open today[39].

References

[1] According to the United States Geological Survey list of Earthquakes with 1,000 or more deaths 1900-2014, https://earthquake.usgs.gov/earthquakes/world/world_deaths.php (Consulted on 14.01.2017).

[2] J. T. Petrovski, 'Damaging Effects of July 26, 1963 Skopje Earthquake', in *SE40-EEE, 14th European Conference on Earthquake Engineering*, 30 August – 03 September, Ohrid, Skopje: Macedonian Association of Earthquake Engineering (MAEE), 2010 (CD Proceedings).

[3] K. Jordanovski, *Skopje: Catastrophe - Reconstruction - Experience, (in Macedonian)*, Skopje: Matica Makedonska, 1993.

[4] Z. Milutinovic, G. Trendafiloski and T. Olumceva, *Disaster Preparedness: Planning for Small and Medium Size Hospitals Based on Structural, Nonstructural and Functional Vulnerability Assessment*, Report IZIIS 95-68, Skopje: Institute of Earthquake Engineering and Engineering Seismology, University St.Cyril and Methodius, Skopje and Copenhagen: World Health Organisation, Regional Office for Europe, Copenhagen: Skopje, 1995.

[5] Jordanovski, (Note 3).

[6] J. Petrovski and Z. Milutinovic, 'Earthquake Vulnerability and Risk Assessment for Physical and Urban Planning', *Edilizia Popolare*, No. 187, 1985. pp. 18-25.

[7] P. Verney, *The Earthquake Handbook*, New York: Paddington Press Ltd., 1979.

[8] Jordanovski, (Note 3).

[9] A. Alexander, *Natural Disasters*, London: UCL Press, 1995.

[10] Milutinovic et al. (Note 4).

[11] Jordanovski, (Note 3).

[12] Globus, 'How we constantly losing our Kenzo Tange?' (In Macedonian), Globus Magazin, No. 520, May 5th,2017http://www.globusmagazin.com.mk/?ItemID=5BF24AB1CBD1214EB5A5EB72ACAC9E83 (Consulted on 14.01.2018).

[13] V. Ladinski, 'Residential Construction following the 1963 Skopje Earthquake' pp. 435-446, in J.W.P Campbell, N. Baker, M. Driver, M. Heaton, Y. Pan, T. Roseman and D. Yeomans (Eds.). *Building Histories: The Proceedings of the Fourth Conference of the Construction History Society, Queens College, Cambridge, 7th-9th April*, Cambridge: Construction History Society (CHS), 2017.

[14] Jordanovski, (Note 3).

[15] Jordanovski, (Note 3).

[16] I. Davis, 'Skopje Rebuilt - Reconstruction Following the 1963 Earthquake', *Architectural Design*, No. 11, 1979, pp. 660-663.

[17] UNDP - United Nations Development Programme, *Skopje Resurgent: The Story of a United Nations Special Fund Town Planning Project*, New York: United Nations, 1970.

[18] Jordanovski, (Note 3)

[19] Image of a poster showing New Settlements in Skopje, https://en.wikipedia.org/wiki/1963_Skoje_earthquake #/media/File:Skopie_earthquake_1963_new_settlements.JPG(Consulted on 31st December 2017)

[20] Jordanovski, (Note 3)

[21] Image of a poster showing New Settlements in Skopje, (Note 19).

[22] Jordanovski, (Note 3)

[23] Image of a poster showing New Settlements in Skopje, (Note 19).

[24] Jordanovski, (Note 3)

[25] Jordanovski, (Note 3).

[26] Image of a poster showing New Settlements in Skopje, (Note 19).

[27] Jordanovski, (Note 3).

[28] Image of a poster showing New Settlements in Skopje, (Note 19).

[29] UNDP, (Note 17).

[30] Jordanovski, (Note 3).

[31] UNDP, (Note 17).

[32] Image of a poster showing New Settlements in Skopje, (Note 19).

[33] Davis, (Note 16).

[34] M. R.Greene, 'Skopje, Yugoslavia: Seismic Concerns and Land Use Issues During the First Twenty Years of Reconstruction Following a Devastating Earthquake', *Earthquake Spectra*, No. 1, 1987. pp.103-117.

[35] H. J. Lagorio, *Earthquakes: An Architect's Guide to Nonstructural Seismic Hazards*, New York: John Wiley and Sons, 1990.

[36] Davis, (Note 16).

[37] Lagorio, (Note 35).

[38] A. Coburn and R. Spence, *Earthquake Protection*, Chichester: John Wiley and Sons, 1992.

[39] R. Home, 'Reconstructing Skopje after the 1963 earthquake: The Master Plan forty years on', *Planning History*, Vol. 28, No. 2 & 3. 2006. pp. 17-24.

History of Early Twentieth Century Anglo-Caribbean Wooden Houses in Chetumal City, Quintana Roo, Mexico

Joel F. Audefroy

Escuela Superior de Ingeniería y Arquitectura (ESIA), Instituto Politécnico Nacional, Mexico

Introduction

Chetumal's architectural heritage is a historical legacy that unfolded throughout the twentieth century, as of the city's foundation as Payo Obispo in 1898. What makes Chetumal particularly interesting is its unique Anglo-Caribbean-style wooden architecture that does not appear in any other coastal town on the Peninsula of Yucatán.

Interestingly, some Victorian-style houses can be found in Chetumal. The Victorian era began in 1837 when Queen Victoria came to the British throne, and ended in 1901. During that period of industrialization, there were many innovations in architecture, as well as other areas. Britain exported the Victorian style to other countries. This artistic expression was adopted and assimilated in the United States and the Caribbean between 1870 and 1920.

Some authors claim that the Anglo-Caribbean house results from a blend of several components, such as the African hut, the balloon-frame structure and the English bungalow. In fact, the wooden houses in Chetumal and Belize do not use the balloon-frame system that is found in the United States and Northern Baja California, but rather the tongue-and-groove board system.

One or two story houses were built in different styles like the Victorian or the English Bungalow style. These Anglo-Caribbean houses took root through a historical process that came with the imposition of the British colonial exploitation model in what was then British Honduras (Belize) and that influenced part of the present day Quintana Roo State. This influence spread as a result of the Mexican migration to Belize, during the Caste War (1847-1901). Once the conflict ended, the Mexican migrants returned to Payo Obispo with models of Anglo-Caribbean houses.

Wooden houses are in danger of disappearing due to several factors, such as the strong pressure to urbanize land, the lack of interest in conservation, the lack of complete documentation and records, the lack of research for their restoration, as well as their gradual deterioration due to hydro-meteorological events, such as tropical rains and hurricanes. These wooden houses bear historic witness to the city's development and could well become emblematic of Chetumal. There still exist around 140 wooden houses, but only 27 are in good condition. In addition, alterations have been made to the houses (which have been extended, abandoned, or reconstructed) that should be identified in order to have a classification that is closer to the current reality. The problem lies in the condition of the houses that are on the verge of disappearing not only for lack of maintenance, but also because of hurricanes. Janet, the last hurricane to hit Chetumal in 1955, destroyed a significant part of this heritage.

History of Early Twentieth Century Anglo-Caribbean Wooden Houses in Chetumal City, Quintana Roo, Mexico

History of Payo Obispo (Chetumal)

The uniqueness of Payo Obispo lies in the fact that it was founded in the midst of mangrove swamps in 1898. On January 22, 1898, a pontoon boat called "Pontón Chetumal" arrived at the Chetumal Bay, anchoring some three hundred meters from the coast. It was Othón Blanco, a commander in the Mexican Navy, who traveled to that region in order to set up a customs office at the mouth of the Hondo River, a natural border with Belize (then called British Honduras), to put an end to the smuggling of tropical wood in that area. At the same time, he assisted as intermediary, "pacifying" the Maya rebels active on both sides of the Hondo River. The renowned "Caste War" that had started in 1847 came to an end with a final confrontation between federal troops and Maya rebels in 1901. In 1904, the Caste War officially terminated [1].

During the nineteenth century, the Mexican government sought to establish a control centre on the border between Mexico and British Honduras (then a British colony). This led to the idea of creating a settlement on the coast of Chetumal Bay where the Hondo River flows into the sea, a natural border with present-day Belize. This is how Payo Obispo was founded [11].

In those days, the first settlers lacked services and supplies. Life was extremely precarious. Indispensable consumer goods, like clothing, shoe ware, and grain came from the closest town, Corozal, British Honduras. Communication with the rest of Mexico was possible via mail sent by small boats through ports in Guatemala, Honduras, or the city of Progreso in Yucatán State. Since the very beginning, imported goods from British Honduras influenced Payo Obispo.

In 1900, Xcalak port was founded as an additional strategy to control the border with British Honduras. Xcalak is located on the extreme tip of the Payo Obispo Bay. Since the foundation of Xcalak, a port was constructed, the first shipyard in the Mexican Caribbean. Its purpose was to support the military occupation campaign in the area in order to stop the supply of weapons to the Maya rebels during the Caste War [1].

From 1902 to 1922, Payo Obispo's street layout was comprised of five South-North streets and seven East-West streets, as can be seen in Figure 1.

Figure 1: Payo Obispo in 1902 (Source: Quintana Roo State General Archive)

The first houses were made of Paurotis palm (*Acoelorrhaphe*) with roofs made of Palmetto palm (*Sabal japa*), and later of wood with zinc plate roofs. Local history claims that this kind of architecture, of British origin, called "Anglo-Caribbean style" was prominent along the city's main streets in the early days. Local history mentions that "*Valeriano Córdova, a tailor who was only 20 years old, the son of Manuela A. de Córdova, from Corozal, around 1901 brought a disassembled wooden house from Sarteneja, British Honduras, the first wooden house to be raised on the corner of 22 de Marzo Street (currently Carmen Ochoa de Merino Street) with Héroes Street*" [7] [3]. This kind of housing was typically made with tongue-and-groove planks (a system of assembled boards with grooved edges) and was covered with zinc plating. Ignacio Herrera Muñoz, the city chronicler, [6] notes that the wooden houses were constructed between 1898 and 1970. The first neighborhood known as "Casitas" (i.e., "little houses," now known as Venustiano Carranza) had 250 tongue-and-groove wooden houses with zinc roofing.

For twenty years, Payo Obispo did not grow significantly, which can be explained by the fact that the Federal government made the territory of Quintana Roo "disappear" officially, only to later on reinstate it [10].

The political and social conditions prevailing in Mexico were aggravated with the assassination of President Francisco I. Madero and Vice President José María Pino Suarez in February 1913. This was followed by the armed uprising of the army led by Venustiano Carranza. These events generated unfavorable conditions for Quintana Roo, above all for the large-scale landowners whose interests were threatened and were able to influence the central government so that it would decree the restitution of the territory of Quintana Roo. After several events, President Carranza revoked the decree in 1913, issuing new legislation defining that Quintana Roo should again become a federal territory. Finally, towards 1915, Payo Obispo was named the capital city of the territory of Quintana Roo, replacing Santa Cruz de Bravo.

From then on, the population started to grow and its development was accompanied by new economic activities, in addition to the traditional activities, such as the exploitation of trees producing a gummy latex called *chicle*, used for making chewing gum. Import activities ensued.

However, as of 1910, the number of inhabitants started to drop. This population decrease might have been related to Quintana Roo's temporary change of status. It should be noted that in spite of the numerous *chicle* gum camps along the bank of the Hondo River, Payo Obispo's urban grid did not grow for a long time. Inhabitants did not have pure drinking water and lived in unsanitary conditions that favored the proliferation of tropical diseases like malaria. For this reason, its inhabitants started to make what were called *curvatos*, "arcuate barrels," made of wood to harvest rainwater from the roofs at ground level.

The last *chicle* gum and forestry boom in the area (Othon P. Blanco Municipality) took place between 1930 and 1950, and was accompanied by population growth, which increased from 2,790 inhabitants in 1930 to 7,247 in 1950. This growth continued in a sustained way until after 1974, the year in which Quintana Roo was declared a free and sovereign state.

Until 1940, Chetumal's west side had been growing slowly with the addition of new streets and avenues (Figure 2).

History of Early Twentieth Century Anglo-Caribbean Wooden Houses in Chetumal City, Quintana Roo, Mexico

Figure 2: Héroes Avenue circa 1936 (Source: General Photographic Archive of Quintana Roo State).

After Chetumal was hit by hurricane Janet in 1955, it was virtually destroyed. It suffered precarious conditions and its economy went into crisis due to the fact that forest production decreased as a result of woodland devastation in the south due to the hurricane. Since large segments of the population were left practically unemployed, the disaster forced many to migrate. The state's infrastructure was practically non-existent. With the disaster, construction materials like cement blocks and concrete started to be used, thus contributing to the disappearance of the Anglo-Caribbean wooden houses.

In the 1970s, a state-promoted colonization process was set up to encourage migration to Chetumal. This settlement plan was based on an agroindustrial project to be implemented along the riverbank in conjunction with the Álvaro Obregón community. New agricultural communal lands and infrastructure were developed.

In 1972, a Presidential Order transformed Chetumal's trade activity. Arguing that economic activity required the free importation of goods in order to promote natural resource exploitation, specifically for the fishing and tourist industries, a permit was issued for Chetumal to become a free-trade zone. Today, only a small duty-free zone remains on the border with Belize.

In 1974, another Presidential Order decreed Quintana Roo as a new state of the Mexican Federation, with Chetumal as the capital city. Almost simultaneously, a tourism development project was created in Cancún, placing this city as an international tourism destination and the state's economic capital.

Since the 1970s, Chetumal experienced significant population growth, increasing from 23,685 inhabitants in 1970 to 56,709 inhabitants in 1980. In order to protect against eventual flooding caused by hurricanes, the city grew more in the northern section, which is higher than the central section that is close to the bay. In spite of supply scarcity and its geographic isolation from the large-scale regional and national supply centres, the combination of its administrative activities as a state capital with economic activities derived from the free-trade zone, enabled increasing development.

Hurricane Impact on Chetumal

From June to November, hurricanes are a threat for the inhabitants of the coast of Quintana Roo who have learned to be vigilant in order to prevent potential disaster. They have learned to safeguard their belongings and to rely on shelter-based evacuation strategies in case a tropical storm warning becomes a hurricane alert. Hurricane trajectories are unpredictable since they vary from one year to the next. They usually form in the summer in the Eastern Atlantic and the Caribbean Sea. Hurricanes Janet (1955), Carmen (1974), Roxana (1995), and Dean (2007) have had the greatest impact on Chetumal City, leading to flooding and swamping, thus forcing the evacuation of the people in the city's lower lands.

Hurricanes are recurrent in Quintana Roo and form part of Chetumal's cyclone history. It can be observed that for almost a century, from 1916 to 2014, hurricanes and tropical storms have on several occasions hit the land in Chetumal and its Othón P. Blanco Municipality.

The first hurricane recorded in Quintana Roo was unnamed. It took place in 1916 and produced disastrous consequences in Xcalak and Payo Obispo to the extent of destroying the Banco Chinchorro lighthouse [1]. For several decades, there were no significant hurricanes until 1955 when two hurricanes, Hilda and Janet, hit Quintana Roo. Janet, in particular, partly destroyed Chetumal City.

Hurricane Janet hit Chetumal and the Quintana Roo coast directly. On September 26, 1955, Janet was a category 4 hurricane with winds of over 220 km/h (140 mph) and 20 metre (over 65 foot) storm surges. When it hit the land in Xcalak, the wind force had surpassed 275 km/h (170 mph), reaching category 5 with an atmospheric pressure of 914 millibars in the eye of the hurricane. Janet hit Chetumal at 9 pm, causing 90 deaths. Only 3 per cent of the houses were left standing. 300,000 m3 of woodland were devastated and copra production in the south of Quintana Roo State was destroyed.

In order to understand Janet's destructive effect, it helps to know that Chetumal is a coastal city located along Chetumal Bay. The 275-km/h winds flooded the downtown area with water from the bay, devastating the houses. The destruction was aggravated when the water withdrew with uncontainable force. Downtown Chetumal is located in a low area that is practically at sea level. By penetrating seven blocks into the city, the water swept away everything it met whether it was wooden houses, shops, vehicles or infrastructure, as well as people. In the lowest sections of town, the water level reached over two metres.

Figure 3: Hurricane Janet's devastating effects in 1955 (Source: Casa de la Crónica, Chetumal)

History of Early Twentieth Century Anglo-Caribbean Wooden Houses in Chetumal City,
Quintana Roo, Mexico

The passage of Hurricane Janet marked Chetumal's life (Figure 3). Its regional history is divided into before and after. Reconstruction began in its wake. The aid that was sent was mismanaged. There was also deep disagreement between the Quintana Roo government and the victims. The survivors decided to reconstruct the city against the state government's insistence on burning down the downtown section and repopulating the higher areas.

On September 16, 1967, hurricane Beulah hit Cozumel and tilted the Puerto Morelos lighthouse. Hurricane Carmen hit Chetumal on September 2, 1974. It did not have the strength of hurricane Janet. Since there were fewer wooden houses, fewer homes were damaged. The bay water did not flood the downtown blocks, and no lives were lost. Hurricane Carmen was the third hurricane that season. It had a force of 160 km/h (99 mph) (category 2). There was only considerable damage in an area that had been reconstructed 19 years earlier as a result of hurricane Janet. Ignacio Herrera Muñoz, the city chronicler, notes that, "in spite of the fact that the cyclone penetrated inland through a place called "Punta Gavilán," which is about fifty kilometres (31 miles) north of the city, the hurricane gusts started to be felt at 4 am and did not cease until 10 am. The cyclone's greatest fury, as tends to happen in these kinds of cases, was received by Chetumal for between six to seven hours of this terribly devastating day. The rain continued in brief intervals throughout the day" (*Nuevo Siglo*, September 15, 2003) [6].

In spite of its relatively mildness (category 2), hurricane Carmen damaged several houses and public services, knocked down trees and buildings, such as the community centre "Casa del Pueblo", the "Leona Vicario" cinema, the healthcare centre, the airport control tower, and the stores' roller doors warped. A wooden house located on a corner of Barrio Nuevo was totally destroyed.

Anglo-Caribbean House Typology: Chetumal's Cultural Heritage

Housing architecture in the Caribbean has varied considerably since the first Spanish settlements in Cuba, Hispaniola (the Dominican Republic), the French settlements in Haiti, the Dutch settlements on smaller islands, and the British settlements in British Honduras (Belize). The first architectural styles are found in the Dominican Republic with Romanesque, Gothic and Plateresque styles, as well as the Baroque style that can also be found in the Greater Antilles. The British introduced the Georgian and Victorian styles, whereas the French and the Dutch imported architectural elements from their countries of origin. What this diversity of styles have in common is that they are made of wood, which the first settlers found in the Caribbean islands.

Interestingly, Victorian-style houses can be found in Chetumal. The Victorian era started in 1837 when Queen Victoria came to the British throne, and ended in 1901. During that period of industrialization, there were many innovations in architecture, as well as other areas. The British Empire exported the Victorian style. This artistic expression was adopted and assimilated by the United States and the Caribbean, where it was incorporated between 1870 and 1920 (see Figure 4).

Some authors [4] have claimed that the Anglo-Caribbean house is a blend of various components: the African hut, balloon-frame structures, and the British bungalow. In fact, the houses found in Chetumal and Belize do not use the balloon-frame system used in the United States and Northern Baja California. Instead, they use the tongue-and-groove board system.

Figure 4: Victorian-style houses in Chetumal (photos by the author, 2017)

Decree N°127 (issued in October 1995) that led to the approval of the Quintana Roo State Historical, Cultural and Artistic Heritage Protection, Conservation and Restoration Act clearly describes the characteristics of Anglo-Caribbean houses in Chetumal, in particular, in Article 22 of Chapter II:

The wooden houses and buildings of a colonial Anglo-Caribbean architecture prototype constructed between 1898 and 1970 are comprised of five or more of the following characteristics:

- *Roofs made up of one or more gables with galvanized metal roofing, weatherproofed in terra cotta color;*

- *Facade with a wooden porch with or without a corridor, a wooden floor and handrail, with ornamental details typical of this style;*

- *Wooden doors and shuttered windows;*

- *Wooden access stairs and railings, steps and banisters specific to this style;*

- *Balconies or terraces made of wood, including railings and handrails, grooved flooring, and a shed or gabled roof;*

- *Walls made of tongue-and-groove boards laid horizontally; and*

- *A foundation of hard wood support columns buried on firm ground that sustain the flooring or columns the height of the building.*

A front gallery should be added to the description. The gallery is usually, but not always, repeated toward the yard or sides. Some still conserve the *curvato*, a water-capturing container to store rainwater. The flooring is made of grooved or tongue-and-groove floorboards. The pilotis-based foundations buried into the ground allow for appropriate ventilation beneath the flooring and prevents the wood from becoming insect-infested, at the same time, cooling the house.

As noted by Checa Artasu [2], the characteristics of wooden architecture present a stylistic and structural architectural gradient dependent on the dwellers' socioeconomic condition and cultural background. All of this is expressed in the use of materials, the design of inner spaces, and the style expressed by the facade. It seems that the way these wooden houses were constructed in Chetumal was neither by means of self-construction or local programs, but rather through the commercialization of wooden houses, as mentioned by Checa Artasu [2]: "The construction of these houses is based on a blueprint drawn from the catalogues of companies devoted to the commercialization of wood for dwellings or even complete houses [9] [4]. Although whole houses might have been purchased and imported by one of the many companies devoted to that business, it seems more plausible to assume that the plan and the aforementioned catalogues were a first resort which, placed in the hands of local carpenters, or furniture-makers, served to build the houses".

Throughout colonial times, the bungalow model was initially purchased and immediately readapted according to a wide diversity of parametres, socioeconomic levels, cultural backgrounds, organizational capacity, knowledge about construction or availability of a construction specialist. It is a process that took place throughout the British colonies. According to King [9], it was since the end of the 1870s that a housing model that was aimed to improve the living conditions of Europeans in tropical regions became extensive. The bungalow played a relevant role in this expansion.

Differently styled one or two-story houses, such as the Victorian or English cottage were thus constructed. The Anglo-Caribbean houses emerged through a historic process that originated with the imposition of the British colonial exploitation model on what was then known as British Honduras (now Belize), which influenced what is now Quintana Roo State. This influence was transmitted through the migration of Mexicans to Belize, due to the Caste War (1847-1901), who once the conflict was over returned to Payo Obispo bringing these Anglo-Caribbean house models with them.

Most of the wooden houses are built on top of hardwood pilotis (Jamaican dogwood) 2 to 3 metres long and 15 to 20 centimetres in diameter sunk into the earth. The pilotis leave a 40 to 80 centimetre space between the ground and the flooring. On top of these pilotis, beams are placed in a grid to form a rigid framework to support the house. The flooring is made of hardwood-grooved floorboards [5]. Nonetheless, not all the wooden houses had a 40 to 80 centimetre space above ground level. We were able to confirm that some of these houses are at ground level, and are therefore more vulnerable to flooding.

The walls are made of hardwood-grooved boards and are reinforced with wooden posts nailed to the house grid. The door and window frames are based on the same principle as the upright framing.

The windows close with louver doors that can be opened and shut. The dividing walls are usually made of insulation boards or plywood with wooden frames, and in some cases with assembled wooden grooved boards (see Figure 5).

The ceilings are made of paneling or plywood, and in some cases grooved wood boards. The roofing is made up of one to two gables with a sloping wood beam structure covered by 24 gauge galvanized zinc plating. Gabled roofs have vents on the highest part of the walls for air circulation. Hipped roofs are based on balconies that produce lofts or attics made with the tongue-and-groove board system.

The houses' perimetral area has a porch with flat or rounded banisters and handrails joined to a frame. The facades have constructive or ornamental details, such as wooden latticework panels, lintels, friezes that are straight, curved, or mixed that sustain the half-moon galvanized gutters to collect rainwater. This water is stored in a curvato barrel, which were originally made with tongue-and-groove boards in a conical shape and a flat wooden bottom (see Figure 6).

Figure 5: Dividing wall made of grooved boards (photo by the author, 2017)

Figure 6: Anglo-Caribbean house with a curvato barrel in Chetumal (photo by the author, 2017)

The plots upon which the houses stand measure 25 x 50 metres on average (1,250 m2). The total number of plots per block in the downtown area is between 8 and 10, depending on the size of the house. Although the house surface originally depended on the number of inhabitants per family, it was 100 m2 on average.

Conservation

In 2004, the Quintana Roo Cultural Institute (Instituto Quintanarroense de Cultura), coordinating with the Department of Urban Development and the Environment (Secretaría de Desarrollo Urbano y Medio Ambiente), initiated a project to restore the wooden houses, implemented under the concept of a "Master Plan to Restore the Historical Centre of Chetumal City." The plan consisted of restoring some wooden houses and reconstructing others in the downtown area. Work was carried out in an area comprised of 14 blocks and 38 wooden houses, some of which were restored and others reconstructed. Only 27 houses of the existing 140 that were in regular or bad shape were rehabilitated.

The 2004 rehabilitation program did not take into account the vulnerability of the wooden houses to hydro-meteorological risks like hurricanes and floods. The program only consisted of changing the damaged wood and paintwork. No architectural programs were developed to strengthen the roofs' resistance to hurricane gusts. Carpenters were not trained either.

Unfortunately, the city's tourist attraction is at risk of disappearing gradually, as the abandoned houses in bad condition collapse or catch fire. Several houses were found to be in a highly deteriorated state (see Figure 7).

Figure 7: Highly deteriorated house on the corner of Calle 22 de Enero and Francisco I. Madero Streets (photo by the author, 2017)

It is not enough to recognize the city's historical heritage through legislation, unless the law is accompanied by sustainable policies and programs. The Quintana Roo State Historical, Cultural and Artistic Heritage Protection, Conservation and Restoration Act has no implementation decrees that would allow sustainable plans and programs to be carried out.

The rehabilitation of wooden houses has not been included among the Quintana Roo State's future development plans. The Risk Atlas for Chetumal City does not address the existence of particularly vulnerable wooden houses.

Conclusions

The wooden houses in Chetumal City, and, in general, in the Othón P. Blanco Municipality have a very high level of vulnerability. According to the National Institute of Statistics and Geography (INEGI) [8], there are a total of 30,920 wooden houses, 25.7 percent of which have cardboard roofs, 42.7 percent have metal sheet roofing, and 31.6 percent are thatched. INEGI does not mention the state of conservation of these houses.

These wooden houses are at the most a century old, and most of them were constructed or reconstructed after hurricane Janet hit Chetumal in 1955. The records existing at the Quintana Roo State Department of Culture show that of the existing 235 Anglo-Caribbean houses, 51 are in a state of deterioration. The houses' problematic conditions, however, remain unclassified [5].

Except for the 34 houses that were restored in 2004, the other houses, except for a few, have not received appropriate maintenance. We have registered around 60 houses, many of which present heavy deterioration.

Hydro-meteorological events produce several types of impacts, particularly on wooden houses that have not received maintenance. The main kind of damage these houses present are of abiotic origin, since atmospheric or meteorological agents degrade the wood surface without affecting its mechanical properties. Wood quickly absorbs rainwater, causing a difference in moisture between the surface that tends to swell, and the inner layer, thus altering the wood, producing curvatures, warps, or splitting (see Figure 8).

Solar radiation also degrades wood surface via ultraviolet rays which with the passing of time separate macromolecules, forming smaller and more soluble molecules that are more easily attacked by atmospheric agents, above all if the wood's protective layer (either paint or varnish) has lost its coherence and its adhesion to the wood.

We have come across cases of abandoned houses where plants have covered walls and roofing. The lack of maintenance has caused damage through biotic agents, such as mildew, expressed as brown-colored stains. Moisture induced cotton-like formations can also be observed on the wood's surface. In some cases in Chetumal and Xcalak, some houses have been totally abandoned, and only the structural parts remain (see Figure 9).

Figure 8: House deteriorated by the action of meteorological agents(photo by the author, 2017)

Figure 9: An abandoned house in Xcalak (photo by the author, 2017)

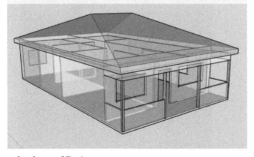

Figure 10: The Chetumal wooden house 3D view

History of Early Twentieth Century Anglo-Caribbean Wooden Houses in Chetumal City,
Quintana Roo, Mexico

Acknowledgments

This piece of research was carried out with funding provided by *Secretaría de Investigación y Posgrado*/SIP), pertaining to the *Instituto Politécnico Nacional* of México. Research Project N° 20171563

References

[1] L. Careaga Viliesid, A. Higuera Bonfil, 2010, Quintana Roo, Mexico, FCE, 292p.

[2] M. Checa Artasu, 2011, "Morfología y representatividad de la vivienda histórica en la frontera México-Belice:algunas notas", *Cuadernos de vivienda y urbanismo*, Vol. 4, No. 8, July-December, 2011: pp. 248-27.

[3] M. Checa Artasu, 2012, "Aproximación turístico cultural para un patrimonio en vías de extinción: la arquitectura histórica en madera de Chetumal, Quintana Roo". In: *El Periplo Sustentable*, No. 23, July-December, 2012, pp. 49-78, Universidad Autónoma del Estado de México, Toluca, Mexico.

[4] M. Checa Artasu, 2008, "La vivienda popular como representación de un proceso histórico: el caso de la frontera Belice-México", *Boletín AFEHC* N°38, published on October 04, 2008. Available at: http://afehc-historia-centroamericana.org/index.php?action=fi_aff&id=2025

[5] A. Daffry Puc, M. A. Gómez Cerón, 2014, Patologías en las casas de maderas anglo-caribeñas. In: *Tecnohistoria, ⌐objetos y artefactos de piedra caliza, madera y otros materiales*, Manuel A. Román Kalisch and Raúl Ernesto Canto Cetina, Coordinators and editors. Universidad Autónoma de Yucatán, Mérida.

[6] I. Herrera Muñoz, 2003, *Crónicas citadinas II*, Chetumal, 347p.

[7] I. Herrera Muñoz, 2006, "Casa de madera... con personaje e historia". In: *Crónica Citadina*. August 31, 2006. [On-line article]. Available at: http:// periodistasquintanaroo.com/opiniones/100706/casanach.html

[8] Instituto Nacional de Estadística y Geografía INEGI (México), Anuario estadístico y geográfico de Quintana Roo 2015 / Instituto Nacional de Estadística y Geografía, Mexico: INEGI, 2015.

[9] A. D. King, 1984, *The Bungalow: The Production of a Global Culture*. London: Routledge & Kegan Paul.

[10] R. I. Romero Mayo, J. Benítez López, 2014, "El proceso histórico de conformación de la antigua Payo Obispo (hoy Chetumal) como espacio urbano fronterizo durante la etapa de Quintana Roo como territorio federal", *Revista Península*, Vol. IX, No. 1 January-June 2014, Mérida, pp. 125-140.

[11] Although the origin of the city's name, Payo Obispo, is uncertain, there are various hypotheses about its origin. However, the most widespread hypothesis is that the city was named after friar Payo Enríquez, Bishop of Guatemala, and later viceroy of New Spain, who visited this area in colonial times. This is at least one of the most widely accepted versions.

The Montreal Stock Exchange Tower by Luigi Moretti and Pier Luigi Nervi (1961-1965)

Roberta Lucente and Laura Greco

Department of Civil Engineering, University of Calabria, Italy

Introduction

The Stock Exchange Tower complex was the result of the investment program promoted and managed by the St. James Place Victoria Real Estate Co. Inc. which was established in 1960 and consisted of a group of investors such as the Mercantile Bank of Canada and Società Generale Immobiliare of Rome (SGI), as well as other Italian investors. Luigi Moretti (1906-73) and Pier Luigi Nervi (1891-1979) received a commission to design the Stock Exchange Tower complex from the SGI of Rome in March 1961. The partnership continued until 1965, when the construction of the single tower was completed.[1] A Canadian project management group flanked the two Italian master builders. The architectural office Greenspoon, Freedlander & Dunne, and the engineers D'Alemagne & Barbacki belonged to this group. The first project hypothesis, developed by Moretti and Nervi between February and July 1961, concerned the construction of a complex consisting of three towers with 51 floors connected by a low building. The initial plan was revised in favour of a solution with two towers and a common platform, but only one was built. After an intensive two-year design process, the building site opened on 14 June 1963. The structures were completed on 27 July 1964 and the tower was inaugurated in the spring of 1965. With a height of 190 meters it was, at that time, the highest skyscraper with a reinforced concrete structure in the world.

This paper, considers the studies developed overall by Italian scholars involved in Moretti's work, investigates the genesis of the Stock Exchange Tower, with reference to the combination of Moretti's morphological research and Nervi's construction system and optimization process. According to the authors' hypothesis, the tower contributed to the links between architectural design and structural engineering in the Italian scenario abroad. In fact, the authors consider the relationship between the architectural space and the structural system as a key topic of their study. Moretti and Nervi shared this concept in their design approach, merging the Italian cultural background in the Canadian experience, then offering an original interpretation of the skyscraper design. The investigation, developed through archival documents and mainstream literature on the building, assumes this perspective of examination, aiming to verify the influence of the Italian background in the general design approach, highlighting the impact of this experience on both Nervi's and Moretti's subsequent works.

General description

The complex finally built consisted of a five-storey building at the base, on which the tower was built with 42 floors above ground, three mechanical floors and a penthouse. Four basements completed the scheme. In the lower part of the complex the headquarters of Montreal stock exchange, one of the largest in the world at the time of construction, were settled. The typical floor of the tower provided for approximately 2,000 square meters of rentable area for offices.

The Montreal Stock Exchange Tower by Luigi Moretti and Pier Luigi Nervi (1961-1965)

The total surface was 135,796 square meters. Staircases and services were concentrated in the core, while the rest of the typical floor surface was freely available through mobile partitions, being free from structural elements.

Figure 1. Stock Exchange Tower,Montreal.Project: L.Moretti,P.L.Nervi,1961-65. Source: MAXXI Museo nazionable delle arti del XXI secolo, Roma. Collection MAXXI Architettura. Archive Pier Luigi Nervi.

Moretti, after the inauguration of the complex, described the Canadian tower thus:

> "The great tower is conceived in an unusual way, according to an architectural scheme that enhances the structural strength of the building, concentrating its expression in the four corner pillars, which constitute in fact the main structure of the building... The awareness of the construction, which is at the bottom of the emotion that gives a work of architecture, is here brought to the maximum diapason with these four pylons which, planted on a granite base, raise their elegant silhouette... The entire building, including the four corner columns, is tapered upwards, thus taking on an unusual and yet classic form that finally repels the prismatic skyscrapers, with the same dimensions, and rejects, so, that construction abstractness that deprive it of the sense of the weight and the effort of matter which, moreover, is the basis of the architectural emotion. For the first time, the curtain wall surface was not conceived flat and rigid, but with a central swelling for each part, as if the four supports with their force compressed the space of the tower".[2]

A reinforced concrete giant

Luigi Moretti and Pierluigi Nervi were, at the time of the SGI commission, already well known. Luigi Moretti was the trusted architect of the Company and he had already encountered Pierluigi Nervi in a project for offices and a residential complex in Catania (1957-60), already commissioned by SGI. In 1950s the Italian architect having invited Nervi to publish some of his works in Spazio, the sophisticated review of art and architecture founded and directed by Moretti.

We can certainly affirm that the architect and the engineer had been chosen for both their affordability and to ensure a high level result.

In 1961, when starting the project, Nervi was a master builder already accomplished in the international context, thanks to the success of his work for the Roman Olympics of 1960 and the *Palazzo del Lavoro* (1959-64) built in Turin to celebrate the centenary of Unification of Italy.

At the same time, some main US projects were under construction, such as the New York George Washington Bridge passenger bus centre (1959-62) and the Dartmouth College Field House in Hanover (1959-64). Moreover the University of Harvard invited him to give the Norton Lectures (1961-62), encouraging the definition of Nervi's international status. Which, along with Riccardo Morandi, were both icons of Italian structural engineering, admired throughout the world.[3]

In these years Nervi abandoned the exclusive experimentation of the technical procedures meticulously designed and applied with the family company Nervi and Bartoli, and decided to "export the Nervi brand" beyond national borders. In the form of structural awareness and construction experience to be put into the service of the great design processes current at the time, in which the Italian engineer, while not controlling the whole building chain, could transfer his way of building.[4]

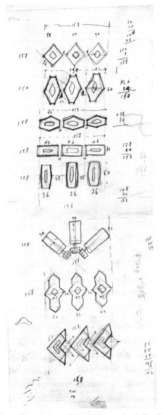

Figure 2. Moretti's preliminary sketches. Source: Archivio Centrale dello Stato, Luigi Moretti Collection, Rome. Courtesy Ministero per i beni e le attività culturali, Rome.(ACS)

The Montreal Stock Exchange Tower by Luigi Moretti and Pier Luigi Nervi (1961-1965)

Luigi Moretti, after the modern masterpieces realized under the fascist regime and the years of professional success in Milan and Rome with his own company Cofimprese, had just started to conquer that international profile that would characterize the final phase of his work, thanks in part to SGI which at the time had committed him to the Watergate complex in Washington (1960-65).

Therefore, Moretti and Nervi were different, yet also similar due to their undoubtable professional capacity and their innovative approach, thus among the aspects of interest in this experience, from a historical viewpoint, we can emphasise the way in which these two master builders interacted.

Moretti was aware of the importance of the structural role in such a building, approached for the very first time. Moreover, throughout his career, he showed a certain sensitivity for structural complexity, but always sought to reach formal and expressive results, which was his real prior objective. In effect, from an analysis of his works, it may be stated that the architect looked for intrepid structural solutions, but without truly considering their concrete expression [5] as, for example, he had done during the 1930s with the system of steel cantilevers masked behind a white ceiling in the Casa delle Armi in Rome (1933-36), one of his best known masterpieces.[6] A natural attitude at realizing the structural solutions necessary to his architectural intentions surely helped him in the relationship with Nervi, this in fact, was defined by direct witnesses as an "affable and fruitful" one.[7]

Figure 3. Moretti's preliminary sketches concerning the first solution, with three towers. Source: ACS

Nevertheless, the very first solutions designed by Moretti, probably in autonomy, reveal an approach totally oriented towards formal aspects, as demonstrated by an abacus of eight different planning solutions. The lack of dates on most of Moretti's drawings, does not allow us to be precise in reconstructing their correct sequence. What seems to be clear, is that Moretti, since the beginning, was involved in the urban insertion of the complex, in the general idea of the five-storey building shared between more than one tower, originally three, and especially in the possible shape of these two components – the five-storey building, its basement and the complex of the three towers – together. This latter was just the main focus of these very first Moretti drawings, even before

Nervi's first structural proposals, that in any case would be referred just to the tower volume, without any reference either to the urban insertion nor to the architectural connection with the lower volume.

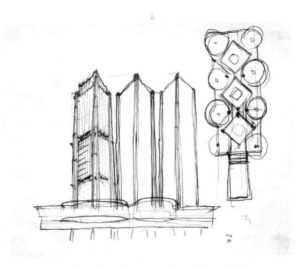

Figure 4. Moretti's preliminary sketches with three volumes lined up diagonally. Source: ACS

From his hand, in fact, Pierluigi Nervi in The Montreal project created an occasion to return to the topic of the high-rise building after the structural project of the Pirelli skyscraper designed by Gio Ponti (1955-58).

The Milanese tower, which at that time was the highest European building, represented the avant-garde of a group of concrete giants – besides the same Montreal Exchange Tower (1961-65) – such as the Australia Square skyscraper in Sydney (1962-67), Parcel 8 in Boston (1964-65), Taunusanlage in Frankfurt (1965-68) and the MLC Center in Sydney (1970-77), in whose projects Nervi was always involved as either designer or structural consultant.

Nervi's experience was supported by research developed on the skyscraper typology in the 1950's by some Italian architects and engineers.[8] In Milan during that decade the skyscraper in Piazza della Repubblica (117 meters, Luigi Mattioni and others with Arturo Danusso, 1950-55), the Velasca tower (99 meters, BBPR with Arturo Danusso, 1950-57), the Galfa Tower (103 meters, Melchiorre Bega, 1956-59), as well as the afore mentioned Pirelli skyscraper (113 meters, Gio Ponti and others with Arturo Danusso and Pier Luigi Nervi, 1955-58) were built. In all these buildings, the towers had a reinforced concrete structure and Arturo Danusso's (1880-1968) structural consultancy was recurrent, shared in the Pirelli project with Pier Luigi Nervi. Referring to this context, on one hand we can affirm that the familiarity of Italian designers and builders with this technique was so well-established that it was favoured to the steel frames for both technical and economic reasons. On the other hand, we can observe that this condition allowed a research on formal systems strongly characterized by the structural design, and then independent, apart from the Galfa tower, from the mainstream of the international skyscrapers catalogue (as affirmed by the same Moretti).

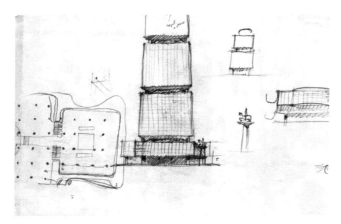

Figure 5. Detail of the tower divided in different parts by the means of intermediate storeys, but without corner pillars. Source: ACS

In the project of the Montreal Stock Exchange Tower the influence of this approach was present, and fortified by the architectural contribution of Luigi Moretti. As noted by some scholars, this Italian method, symbolically represented in the international scenario by the Pirelli headquarters, promoted a figurative strategy that affected the main structural elements, considering the skyscraper design each time as a unique experience signed by original aesthetical features despite the industrialized components and techniques that were currently used in the international steel structures repertoire.[9]

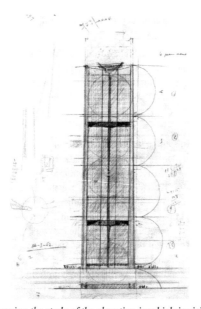

Figure 6. Moretti's drawing concerning the study of the elevation in which is visible the elimination of six floors. 26 March 1962. Source:ACS

Although based on very different cultural premises, Nervi and Moretti shared this idea, arriving at identifying the structural parts of the Stock Exchange Tower as exposed figurative elements, highlighted by their size and form, or underlined by textures of shadows and lights, such as the tapered corner pillars separated from the curtain wall surface, or the technical floors beams set back from the façade plane. This structural repertoire symbolized the Canadian tower as well as the corner reinforced concrete trees that outlined the silhouette of the Pirelli headquarters.

As is well known, the use of reinforced concrete solutions in international skyscrapers projects was very rare, considering the hegemony of steel structures. The CBS Building in New York designed by Eero Sarinen (1960-65) and the Brunswick Building in Chicago designed by Skidmore, Owings and Merril (1960-65) were more significant exceptions. Compared to these two cases, we can moreover underline that the originality of the Stock Exchange tower solution was the use of an innovative structural scheme, that inaugurated an alternative way to solve the stability of the buildings and to oppose the horizontal actions affecting skyscrapers. That is why considering the fundamental role of the reinforced concrete apparatus in the genesis of the tower project, it is useful to recall the fundamental steps of the structural design process, once again seeking to state the contribution of each one of the two designers.

The structural design process of the Montreal complex started at the beginning of 1961.[10] After the February-March drawings, in which Nervi identified and compared different solutions, the first structural calculation of the tower, elaborated by the Roman engineering office in May 1961, followed. It was then updated with the July versions and hence with three work phases developed in April, June and July of the following year.

In 1961, when Nervi began the project of the Stock Exchange Tower he worked from the early phases on the project of a square-plan building, as confirmed by a drawing of the 15 of February 1961.[11] Moretti's abacus system drawings were, on the contrary, characterized by different shape hypothesis: stretched hexagons, slim rhombus or dynamic arrow shaped plans, and thus may well be antecedent to Nervi's square-plan building drawing (Fig. 2). Some of Moretti's sketches seem to reveal even a possible reference to the same form as the Pirelli tower.[12] Moretti's clear interest for formal genesis is confirmed by his working approach to the shape of the five-storey building, in some of the drawings of which we can find curbs and organic morphologies which recurred in the Roman architect's work as testified by projects such as Villa La Saracena (1954-57), Villa La Califfa (1964-67) and Villa La Moresca (1967-81) in Santa Marinella. Some other perspectives, probably of the same period, confirm the great interest, in Moretti's approach, for exploring the volumetric potential of a system of three tower buildings, with powerful and massive results, so as to gain a dramatic effect.

The first Moretti's drawings in which a typical square floor for the tower appears, are those ones with the sequence of three volumes lined up diagonally *vis-à-vis* the two lateral main streets and with the edges nearly in contact among them (Figs 3-4). A beautiful three-dimensional drawing together with some sketches confirm the presence, in this phase, of the four angular pillars.

Nervi and his Roman office had developed a scheme with four corner reinforced concrete supports tapered upward and four columns arranged on the edges of a central core reserved for stairs and elevators. A regular system of windows was organized along the external walls. This solution is documented by a drawing whose date is 15 February 1961. Soon after, on 7 June 1961, an important letter sent from Nervi to his son Antonio, allows us to establish the precise moment in which the solution of the four corner pillars was definitively stated.[13]

The Montreal Stock Exchange Tower by Luigi Moretti and Pier Luigi Nervi (1961-1965)

This consideration concluded a design process started, in the spring of the same year, when Nervi and his collaborators fit on each side of the tower a couple of intermediate pillars, and then introduced diagonal beams that bring the loads from the core on the corner shafts, thus abandoning the previous scheme.[14] The solution was presented on the technical report dated July 1961, that described a system consisting of a central X-shaped reinforced concrete core with variable section, and four variable-section angular piers and eight intermediate columns of constant-section arranged on sides of the façade.

In this scheme, the horizontal elements of the structure were concentrated in the mechanical floors and consisted of six lattice-beams: two arranged according to the diagonals of the plan and four others on the perimeter of the central core, parallel to the sides of the building. Four wall-beams (thickness 50 cm) arranged along the outer perimeter of the tower were also provided in correspondence of each mechanical level. The lattice section of the beams allowed the integration of the ducts. Technical floors had reinforced concrete slabs, while cross ribbed floors of the typical levels had concrete ribs about 40 cm high arranged at about 2 meters, connected by a concrete slab 9 cm thick. The main beams supporting the floors were 75 cm high.[15]

On September 1961, the project was presented in Montreal to the press with a version that was very similar to that studied before the summer. The solution allowed the use of reinforced concrete frames without rigid connections and, therefore, reducing the sections of beams and columns. The structural scheme considered vertical loads, wind and earthquake, taking into account the high seismic vulnerability of the Montreal area.[16]

In March 1962, the height of the tower was reduced, as confirmed by the structural report, dated July 1962 and by a Moretti drawing concerning the study of the elevation dated 26 March 1962 in which the elimination of six floors is visible (Fig.6).

The structural report developed in July was the most complete one and referred to a building consisting of 42 rentable levels, three mechanical floors, the penthouse and four basements.

The idea developed by Nervi, after about a year of study, maintained many elements of the version described in the report of July 1961. The structural solution was based on a clear hierarchy of components. A primary system guaranteed the stability of the tower and opposition to the action of horizontal forces, while a secondary system was used to absorb the loads of floors.[17] The central core composed of reinforced concrete X-shaped sheer walls combined with the corner pillars formed the first system. These vertical structures were associated, to stiffen the scheme and counteract horizontal forces acting on the tower, to large diagonal beams, positioned in correspondence with the three mechanical floors of the building (placed at 5 °, 19 ° and 32 ° level) and monolithically connected to the corner supports. These beams transferred the loads to the corner columns. Four pairs of intermediate pillars, each arranged on one side of the tower and useful to the organization of the floors, formed the secondary system of the structural apparatus defined by the Italian designer.[18] Finally, the skyscraper used only 12 columns without intermediate supports, guaranteeing the flexible use of interior spaces. Nervi's genius combined structural efficiency with real estate market requirements, suggesting a different way to solve the problem of resistance to horizontal actions in high-rise buildings (Figs 7-8).

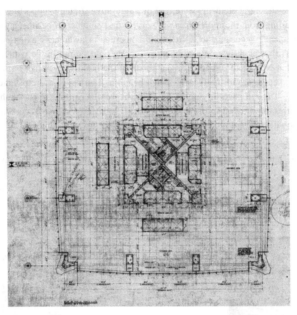

Figure 7. Typical floor plan (7°-17° level). 11 July 1963. Source: MAXXI (Detail)

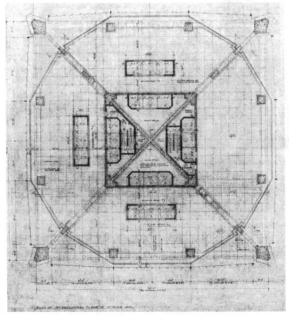

Figure 8. Plan of 19° mechanical floor. 26 July 1963. Source: MAXXI (Detail)

The Montreal Stock Exchange Tower by Luigi Moretti and Pier Luigi Nervi (1961-1965)

As previously stated, the structural elements were part of a figurative strategy supporting the aesthetical research of Italian designers. Starting from these premises, in Nervi's first studies, all perimeter structures were exposed reinforced concrete elements, according to a structural-construction awareness extensively manifested by the Italian master builder. A first modification to this early hypothesis occurred in the winter of 1962. The pairs of intermediate supports that Nervi had provided on each side of the building were set back from the curtain wall. This corresponded to the curvature of the facade, which began to assume, in Moretti's architectural elaboration, the definitive geometry. These had to be one of the main aspects according to the architect's final vision, as demonstrated by a series of drawings, little sketches and perspectives, maybe previous, dealing with the possibility of working on the forward projection of some parts of the tower volumes.

One of the less clear, but also most interesting passages, about this idea is that one illustrated by some perspectives (as always with no dates) which show a volume divided in four parts by the means of some intermediate storeys set back compared to the lower and upper ones – just like the technical floors were in the final version –, but without corner pillars.

Figure 9. The tower under construction. Source: MAXXI   *Figure 10. The cladding panels of the corner pillars. Source: ACE*

These documents seem to testify that this suggestion, later very important from a technical point of view, could have been introduced by Moretti (Fig. 5). We have in fact to notice that in the above mentioned Nervi's plan, the very first with the four corner pillars, the diagonal lattice beams solution and technical floors have not yet introduced. While the critics have never dealt with this passage, we can from another hand agree with those that underline the importance of Moretti's contribution in some detailed aspects, such as the slight reduction of the technical floors height and the very brief inclination of the curtain wall plane, both in favour of the vision from below.[19] These little but significant design choices, go in the direction of defining an Italian version of the high-rise building, so different also in the curtain wall treatment. What Moretti declared, at the end of the construction, in the mentioned sentence, leaves no doubts about the architectural aims of these sophisticated details.

This experiment on a not undifferentiated use of the curtain wall, in Moretti's experience continued later in the Esso building (1960-66) and in the same SGI offices (1960-66) in Rome and in the office complex in piazzale Flaminio (1972-75).

Some other important changes continued in the same direction, also when related to functional and technical necessities. During the design process, also the exposed four corner columns were subject to modifications. They were protected from the freezing climate of Montreal. Strong thermal excursions could cause cyclic deformations of the supports and hence transfer the tension to the diagonal beams and to the central core to which they were connected in correspondence of the three mechanical floors. The cladding was made of precast concrete panels mounted at a distance so as to allow a maintenance path. The circulation of the air in the cavity was useful for heating the panels and limiting their deformation due to thermal action.[20]

Panels were mounted considering the tapered section of the columns and supported by concrete brackets connected to the pillars section (Figs 9-10). The Italian-Canadian design team debated the form and the finish of the corner piers until the opening of the building site, which took place on 14 June 1963. In fact, in February Jack Barbacki tried to change the section of the pillars, simplifying it for economic reasons.[21] The proposal was decidedly rejected by the Italian designers, especially by Moretti, who emphasized the aesthetic and structural value of the chosen section.[22]

Conclusions

The Montreal tower represented abroad an aspect of the Italian structural engineering research, defining a fundamental evolution of the high-rise buildings structural schemes that was based on reinforced concrete solutions. This result was guaranteed by Nervi's genius, whose experience and construction awareness contributed to the development of Moretti's architectural research.

The value of this experimentation on the reinforced concrete structures is proved by the influence that the project had on Nervi's subsequent skyscraper projects. While inaugurating the Montreal complex, Nervi began work on the project of the Parcel 8 office tower in Boston (1964-65) as design consultant.

The structure of the US building consisted of four main facade piers and of a central core, rigidly connected by lattice beams placed in correspondence of the three technical floors. A second order of intermediate facade pillars was supported by the perimeter beams of the mechanical levels, in turn supported by the main columns and by the lattice beams. This scheme reduced the number of structural elements to the ground floor, consisting only of the main pillars and of the core.

Finally, the new structural vision proposed in the Canadian complex affected the subsequent skyscraper generation based on the so-called outrigger schemes, suggesting an alternative point of view despite the current steel framed structures, characterized by the reduction of the intermediate and perimeter supports, and then encouraging a flexible use of the plan and an evolutionary approach to the curtain wall systems. The expressive results of this innovative approach, conquered together with Moretti in the Montreal tower, still remain today as demonstrative of the effectiveness of such a kind of research, also in the historical and critical perspective.

Notes and References

[1] C. Rostagni, 'Luigi Moretti. Forma come struttura o struttura come forma? La torre della Borsa di Montreal' in G. Bianchino, (Eds), *Cantiere Nervi: la costruzione di un'identità*. Milan: Skira, 2012. p. 291.

[2] Archivio Centrale dello Stato, Rome (ACS), Luigi Moretti Collection, Place Victoria Project, Folder no. 40, "Description Watergate and Place Victoria", 1964.

[3] For more on this topic information see A. Bologna, *Pier Luigi Nervi negli Stati Uniti. 1952-1979: master builder of the Modern Age*, Florence: Firenze University Press, 2013.

[4] For more on this topic information see S. Poretti, 'Nervi che visse tre volte', in T. Iori, (Eds), *Pier Luigi Nervi:l'Ambasciata d'Italia a Brasilia*, Milan: Electa, 2008. p. 8-49 and T. Iori, 'Il sistema Nervi', in G. Bianchino, *Cantiere Nervi*, (Note 1) p. 51-54.

[5] S. Poretti, G. Capurso, 'Trasfigurazioni di strutture', in B. Reichlin, (Eds), *Luigi Moretti: razionalismo e trasgressività tra barocco e informale*, Milan: Mondadori Electa, 2010. p. 375-386, and S. Poretti, 'Luigi Moretti's Ideal Structure' in S. Poretti (Ed.), *Italian Modernisms: architecture and construction in the twentieth century*, Rome: Gangemi editore, 2013. p. 270-283.

[6] R. Lucente, *La Casa delle Armi al Foro Italico*, Turin: Testo&Immagine, 2002.

[7] A. Shepard, 'Place Victoria: il simbolo della collaborazione tra architetto e ingegnere' in B. Reichlin, *Luigi Moretti*, (Note 5), p. 341-352.

[8] For more on this topic information see L. Greco, S. Mornati, *La torre Galfa di Melchiorre Bega: architettura e costruzione*. Rome: Gangemi editore, 2012. p. 20-29 and p. 37-39.

[9] S. Poretti, G. Capurso, *Trasfigurazioni di strutture*, (Note 5), p. 378.

[10] O. Lanzarini, 'Moretti e Nervi: alcune considerazioni sul disegno della Stock Exchange Tower a Montreal (1960-1965)', in P. Desideri, (Eds), *La concezione strutturale: Architettura e ingegneria in Italia negli anni cinquanta e sessanta*. Turin: Umberto Allemandi & C, 2013. p. 94.

[11] See Centro Studi e Archivio della Comunicazione (CSAC), Parma, Pier Luigi Nervi Collection, Project Place Victoria Montreal, "Plan and elevation of the tower", 15 Feb. 1961.

[12] Lanzarini, *Moretti*, (Note 10), p. 92.

[13] ibid. p. 94.

[14] ibid.

[15] MAXXI Museo nazionale delle arti del XXI secolo, Roma. MAXXI Architettura Collection (MAXXI), Pier Luigi Nervi Collection, Project Place Victoria Montreal, Folder no. P43/2 I, "Technical Report Place Victoria Montreal. Gruppo grattacieli Sol. A", Roma 14 July 1961. For more on this topic information see M.M. Leoni, G. Neri, 'La struttura come forma. Pier Luigi Nervi e Luigi Moretti (1950-1965)', in S. Pace (Ed.), *Pier Luigi Nervi. Torino, la committenza industriale, le culture architettoniche e politecniche italiane*. Cinisello Balsamo: Silvana Editoriale, 2011. pp. 105-111.

[16] MAXXI, Pier Luigi Nervi Collection, Project Place Victoria Montreal, Folder no. P39, "Structural report", Roma 16 July 1962.

[17] Shepard, *Place Victoria*, (Note 7), p. 343.

[18] R. Legault, 'La risposta di Moretti al paradigma miesiano' in B. Reichlin, (Note 4) p. 329-340.

[19] S. Poretti, G. Capurso, *Trasfigurazioni di strutture*, (Note 5).

[20] A. Bouchet, 'La tour de la bourse: construction antisismique de 47 étages', *La technique des travaux*, no.7-8, 1966, p. 433-438.

[21] MAXXI, Pier Luigi Nervi Collection, Project Place Victoria Montreal, Folder no. P43/3, Typed memorandum, 18 Feb 1943, p.1. For more on this topic information see Lanzarini, *Moretti*, (Note 10) and Shepard, *Place Victoria*, (Note 7).

[22] MAXXI, Pier Luigi Nervi Collection, Project Place Victoria Montreal, Folder P43/3, Letter, 4 March 1963. For more on this topic see Lanzarini, *Moretti*, (Note 10).

Twenty-First Century

The Italian engineering contribution in the technical development of the new Hertziana Library by Juan Navarro Baldeweg

Luciano Cardellicchio

University of Kent, UK

Introduction

Between 2003 and 2012, the New Bibliotheca Hertziana (Max-Planck Institute for the Art History) was built on the site of the garden of Federico Zuccari's sixteenth-century house in the historic urban fabric of Rome. The project aimed to demolish a 1960s building in the centre of Rome keeping its facades and constructing between them a more efficient, safer and more spacious building. The non-standard development of this conservation project led to the invention of several bespoke technical solutions and advanced conservation procedures. This innovative and bold construction process was developed by a pioneering engineering approach. The outcome of this experimental case study extends the building itself, having an impact on new developments in historical environments constrained by archaeological remains.

Despite the foreign origin of the architect, the structural development of this building was entirely carried on by Italian engineers who relied on the ability of crafting the construction process as a unique case study. The structural engineers involved in this project were: Alberto Parducci, Alfredo Marimpietri, Marco Mezzi e Sergio Oliviero. Despite the ambition of the project, they were able to collaborate with the architect at the 'technical design development' stage, delivering a complete new structural design without interfering with the aesthetics of the scheme, which remained untouched.

The archaeological and historical constraints, together with the complexity of demolishing and rebuilding in the centre of Rome, forced the engineers to adapt the idea of a post-tensed ribbed concrete bridge as a major building support for preserving the archaeological ruins scattered underneath the building. The structural invention allows the new building to fly over the ancient ruins without resting on the archaeological remains.

This paper aims to retrospectively discuss the contribution of the structural engineers in delivering this challenging conservation project in central Rome, analysing how the new structural systems was developed, and how it was built. The ultimate aim is to disseminate an untold story, which can unlock the potential impact of this case study for similar constructions. This case study is generally unknown. The author of this paper delivers the major research contributions on the subject[1].

The research environment

This paper stems from the research project entitled 'New building strategies for contemporary development on archaeological sites'. This project started with implementing the PhD thesis 'The New Hertziana Library: the

The Italian engineering contribution in the technical development of the new Hertziana Library by Juan Navarro Baldeweg

design proposal and its construction' (Cardellicchio, 2007) awarded at the Faculty of Engineering of University of Rome Tor Vergata. During the early 1990s, substantial public investment was budgeted to modernise the cultural offer, the business assets and sport infrastructures in the city of Rome. This decision led to a glorious season marked with several architectural competitions aiming to provide Rome with new spaces to house innovative cultural offers, thriving new businesses and international sporting events. This strategy, politically developed and coordinated at both national and city level, gave Rome new contemporary structures such as the auditorium 'Parco della Musica' by Renzo Piano and the MAXXI museum by Zaha Hadid. Following this strategy, a great number of construction sites opened for erecting buildings designed by the famous foreign architects who worked in the eternal city for the very first time.

Between 1999 and 2009, during this new era of contemporary development, the PhD programme 'Architecture and Construction' of the School of Engineering at University Tor Vergata, started to instruct a new series of PhD research projects based on monitoring the construction process of these new city assets. The programme's board comprised the famous architectural historian prof. Claudia Conforti,[2]designer and academic prof. Vittorio De Feo,[3] and was led by ERC award winning prof. Sergio Poretti.[4] The aims of these research projects were (Fig. 1):

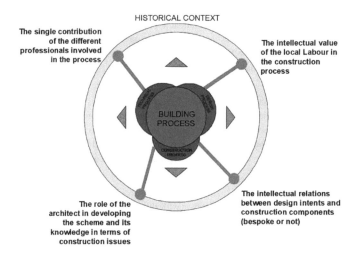

Figure 1. Diagram showing the purposes and methodology for research projects on monitoring contemporary contructions. (Author: L.Cardellicchio)

- To investigate the unique technical development of these buildings distinguished by cutting-edge design solutions;
- To critically evaluate the technical understanding of the designers and assess qualitatively their modus operandi on site;
- To measure the contributions of the different professionals such as the structural and construction engineers to the final aesthetics of the building;
- To understand the degree of adaptability of the local labour (skilled and non-skilled) asked to construct non-standard design requirements;

- To record the knowledge created during the technical development and the construction process of these buildings such as new techniques, new policies, new materials and new components;
- To investigate the intellectual value of the building process of each building mapping the design modifications during the whole process stage after stage, from the first sketch to the completion of the buildings.

The degree of accomplishment of these PhD theses depended on the positive willingness of the architects, engineers and general contractors in making data available. In the case of thePhD thesis about the new Hertziana Library, the client (Max Planck Institute in Munich) and all the professionals involved fully supported the research project.

Methodology

The methodology developed and refined for this research project is based on the following steps:

a) Correlative Analysis between Technical Annotations (TA) and Aesthetic Architectural Components (AACs) in the early sketches, physical study models and competition drawings of the project for the new Hertziana Library to assess the quality and the quantity of technical information delivered by the architect and identify the starting point of the technical design process;

b) Comparative Analysis of drawings submitted at different work stages: to identify the changes occurred to the AACs after the technical development; to define the immovable and changeable characteristics of the design throughout the process. Categorising the changes occurred to the scheme by cause;

c) Interviews with key professional figures who contributed to the development of these buildings, such as Enrico Da Gai (project lead, Rome team), Fernando Pinos (project lead, Madrid team), structural engineers Alberto Parducci, Alfredo Marimpietri and construction manager Gennaro Esposito.

d) Historical analysis of the construction process through archival investigations of pictures from the building site, minutes from meetings and technical reports;

e) Empirical observation to collect data for mapping the type of labour used and the quality of the information flow between architects, engineers and builders;

The accessibility of the data was possible thanks to the generosity of all the professionals involved in the process and of the client, the Max Planck Institute in Rome, which strongly supported this research project.

The reason of the intervention

The Hertziana Library is the Rome-based Italian art history research branch of the Max Planck organisation for the promotion of science in Munich. It is located in the urban peninsula of the sixteenth-century district between via Sistina and via Gregoriana, abutting Trinità dei Monti, near Piazza di Spagna and the Spanish Steps. The institution houses a sequence of three buildings side by side: Palazzo Zuccari, the *Neubau* and Palazzo Stroganoff. Palazzo Zuccari was designed by the famous painter Federico Zuccari for his workshop and residence and it was expanded and remodelled many times over the centuries. Following that, the *Neubau* (New Building) is an offspring of the old garden of Palazzo Zuccari following continuous, uncontrolled additions that took place in the last century to increase the storage space for bookshelves. The urban peninsula terminates with the nineteenth-century Palazzo Stroganoff. While the two historic buildings are used to house research workstations and offices, the *Neubau* contains the library, which contains 270,000 volumes. This substantial number of books is the result of the general growth of research activities of the Bibliotheca during the second half of the twentieth century, where a general climate of economic expansion was appreciated.

The first physical expansion of the library occurred between 1962 and 1966, when the small old buildings erected within the former garden of Palazzo Zuccari were demolished, to be replaced by a modern building providing additional storage room for books and new reading rooms. Designed by architect Silvio Galizia, the project of this modern building aimed to unify the scattered blocks built inside the original garden into a new structure called (for that reason) *Neubau*. During the construction of this building, important archaeological remains were found underneath the site. They consisted of a series of roman retaining walls dated between the first century BC and the first century AD. The archaeological investigation highlighted that these walls were occupying, in fact, the whole footprint of the former garden of the Palazzo Zuccari, extending up to the point where the Spanish Steps is today.[5]

In 1984, the first fire prevention regulations came into force in Italy. Following these new standards the library showed its complete inadequacy with storage areas entirely opened to the only internal staircase of the building. In 1990, the Max Planck Institute commissioned a feasibility study to upgrade the building in compliance with the fire safety legislation.

Unfortunately, the upgrading project would have resulted in a substantial loss of storage space for books, which would have jeopardised the library's long-term feasibility. The complete inadequacy of the building complex, from the viewpoint of fire safety, was confirmed in the mid-1990s when the Fire Department threatened to close the institutions; furthermore, the impossibility of increasing its long-term book capacity eventually sounded the death knell of the building in 1994.

Hans F. Zacher (General Director of Max-Planck Estates Department) with the recommendation of Professor Christoph Luitpold Frommel (Executive Director of the Bibliotheca) decided upon a different programme of refurbishment. Zacher and Frommel called for the demolition of the *Neubau* except for the historic facades, and the commission, through a limited design competition, of a new project that would ensure compliance with modern safety standards as well as enhanced library capacity. The winner of the competition was the Spanish architect Juan Navarro Baldeweg.[6]

The difficult path towards the construction

Immediately after the announcement of the winner, the institute faced two major problems which delayed the start of the construction for almost eight years. The first issue was legislative; the second one was archaeological. One year after the competition, nothing happened. The director of the Institute, Frommel, had to struggle tenaciously and stubbornly against the juridical lack of the City Council in terms of specific procedures that allowed the reconfiguration of the Hertziana Library. No building policy was in place to approve the demolition and reconstruction of a building (erected mainly during the 1960s) in the middle of the historic centre of the city, in violation of the specifications of the General Zoning Plan which provides only 'conservation, restoration or refurbishment' for new development in that area. The Building Commission would have never approved a project based on the total demolition of a building just a few metres from Piazza di Spagna and its reconstruction, in line with a project that did not yet have the detailed drawings required to comply with current building regulations. The legislative issue was solved with the assistance of the Roman architect Enrico Da Gai, appointed by the Max-Planck Institute to untie the bureaucratic knots for approval of the project. The procedure agreed with the

Council was a 'Urban Restoration Plan' that, signed jointly by Da Gai for the Bibliotheca Hertziana and architect Paolo Riccetti for the City of Rome, allowed the demolitions of the buildings erected in the former garden of Palazzo Zuccari.

Following approval of the planning matters, the institute had to deal with the second issues related to the technical development of the project: the presence of substantial archaeological remains underneath the whole footprint of the *Neubau*.

To allow the construction of the new library and preserve the archeological ruins in compliance with the Italian law of archeological conservation a groundbreaking structural project was conceived. The team of engineers in charge of the structural development included Prof Alberto Parducci, at that time full Professor of Structural Engineering at the University of Perugia, Marco Mezzi, Associate Professor of Structural Engineering at the University of Perugia, Sergio Oliviero, full Professor of Geotechnical Engineering at the University of La Sapienza and Alfredo Marimpietri, structural engineer with an extensive experience on-site. Da Gai who, after achieving the right of demolition for the old building, was appointed project leader and technical designer for the whole development process of the library, managed the coordination between the team of engineers and the main architectural office in Madrid (Juan Navarro Baldeweg Asociados).[7]

This coordination between the technical team and the main designer led to a solution where the project submitted at the competition stage remained unaltered. The new structural project only modified the three underground floors, which were redesigned to permit the installation of a large structural device conceived by Da Gai, designed, and developed by Parducci and Marinpietri. The project was to support the new building with a bridge system able to span for 26 metres over the archeological ruins, resting only on two narrow strips of land (1.5 metres wide) outside the historical facades (Fig. 2).

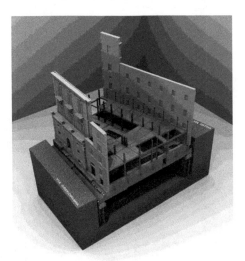

Figure 2. The New Hertziana Library, Rome. Architect, Juan Navarro Baldeweg. 3D digital model of the new structural system with the concrete platform spanning over the archelogical remains.   (Author: Luciano Cardellicchio)

529

The Italian engineering contribution in the technical development of the new Hertziana Library by Juan Navarro Baldeweg

The major component of this bridge system is a three metres deep ribbed platform in reinforced concrete, shaped with pre-stressed concrete ribs aligned along the primary way of spanning, between via Sistina and via Gregoriana. Along the historic facades, two long series of piles were then designed to support the platform and transfer the substantial gravitational and lateral loads to the ground. On top of this platform a steel frame structure was considered the most feasible to overcome the inaccessibility of the site area restricted by its surrounding historic urban fabric.

In order to meet the design requirement, the platform was carefully shaped to support the building without modifying the position of the load-bearing columns decided at the competition stage.[8] The result of this approach led to a structural component entirely bespoke and not geometrically rationalized where the ribs were aligned in different directions to meet the scattered columns of the frame above. The platform, which consists in two floor slabs and the concrete walls between them, was conceived with hybrid building techniques to turn this structural object into a direct instrument to investigate the archeological ruins within the building footprint. The slabs were designed with special slots to allow the removal of the soil used initially to support the formwork of the platform. The slots were designed to permit, at the same time, a meticulous stratigraphic archaeological investigation underneath the platform and the assembly of the metal structure above it (Fig. 3). Following the archeological campaign the slots were closed with the use of metal deck finished with a layer of reinforced concrete. This system allowed the slow archeological investigations without interfering with the assembly of the metal frame. This new building strategy will have an impact on future development in historic areas.[9]

Figure 3. New Hertziana Library, Rome. An archelogist underneath the structural platform flying over the remains. (Photo: Luciano Cardellicchio)

The Construction: a craft approach

Since the beginning of the demolition phase of the old building, it had been evident to the building contractor that the technical requirements of the project would justify the deployment of unconventional construction methods led by a craft approach. The low level of mechanization, the small degree of standardization, and prefabrication of the building components and the use of intense labour for the majority of the work, are the key elements of this construction process.

The main problem faced by the builder was the inaccessibility of the site area, which was restricted by two adjacent historic buildings (Palazzo Zuccari and Palazzo Stroganoff) and by the historical facades. All material – such as debris from demolition, or the casting of concrete for the foundation system, or the metal components for the new structural skeleton, or the glass panel of the glass facade – was put in place with a precise and strict sequence of crane moves. No gap wide enough on the facade was available to provide a quick connection between the interior of the building to the small loading area located outside along via Gregoriana (Fig. 4). Overall, in order to better understand the logistics involved in the construction, it is important to note that during the demolition and reconstruction, different kinds of structures were in place within the original void of the Zuccari garden at the same time. For several years the structure of the old building, the provisional elements that braced the facades during the demolition phases, and portions of the new structure, were all located within the narrow site. One of the aims, for instance, was to use the skeleton of the *Neubau* to brace a portion of the historical facade, and in so doing reduce the impact of provisional elements (Fig. 5). The phases of execution did not follow each other in a systematic sequence such a 'demolition before construction', but overlapped chronologically. This means that during the period of construction, some parts of the *Neubau* contributed substantially to the construction of the new one.

Figure 4. New Hertziana Library, Rome. The removal of a portion of the concrete roof of the old library. (Photo: Luciano Cardellicchio)

The Italian engineering contribution in the technical development of the new Hertziana Library by Juan Navarro Baldeweg

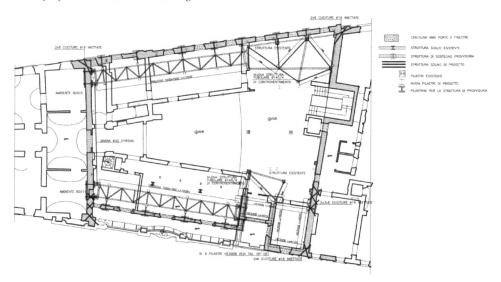

Figure 5. New Hertziana Library, Rome. The layout for the provisional elements used to brace the historic facades. Parts of the steel frame of the old library are used as bracing system. (Drawing: Enrico Da Gai)

The whole construction process featured many innovations led by solutions to unexpected issues occurred on site. The first detail successfully accomplished on site was the injection-valve for the steel pipe used to reinforce each micro-pile. Due to a very incoherent stratigraphy on via Gregoriana scattered pockets of gravel interrupt the layers of lime. The gravel compromised the first attempts of cement injections by blocking the holes.

This caused many failing piles, which were used as tests. With an improved return-limiting valve and a new drilling procedure developed by washing the surface of each hole, the construction of the piles along via Gregoriana was completed in six months (Fig. 6).

Figure 6. New Hertziana Library, Rome. The return-limiting valve system designed on site for the piles along via Gregoriana. (Photo: Luciano Cardellicchio)

The most complex phase was the construction of the massive base/bridge in pre-stressed concrete. The construction of this large ribbed slab was managed in two different times: at first workers casted the two supporting wings outside of the building, along both via Gregoriana and via Sistina, while the demolition of the old library was still running. Secondly, the concrete ribs and floors of the platform were built. (Figs 7-8).

Figure 7. New Hertziana Library, Rome. The first portion of formwork for the ribbed platform. (Photo: Luciano Cardellicchio)

Figure 8. New Hertziana Library, Rome. Reinforcement bars for the pre-stressed concrete ribs of the supporting platform. (Photo: Luciano Cardellicchio)

The Italian engineering contribution in the technical development of the new Hertziana Library by Juan Navarro Baldeweg

Only a craft approach from the builder could guarantee high quality standards when assembling the massive wooden formwork. As noted above, no portions of the structure were precast. The carpenters first assembled the rails, which would hold pre-stressed ribs three metres high; within a month, the entire footprint of the future buildings had been covered by this unique and non-standard formwork. Iron bars were then put in place to erect the thick cages that would reinforce the ribs before casting the material. In order to construct the ribbed slab, the 'craftsmen' of the construction firm were required to extricate themselves from tight spaces, bend bars into dense tangles, assemble timber work in various alignments, and ensure the concrete filled every single space of the formwork, all the while respecting the highest standards of safety. The casting of all the concrete was conducted by transporting small quantities of concrete from the mixer parked on Via Gregoriana, within the construction site, and only through a collecting basket hanging on the crane. To make this phase even slower all the casting must have scheduled during the early hours of the morning before the traffic of the historic centre became a further obstacle for the mixer in order to reach the loading area.

Conclusion

A decade passed from the beginning of the construction until the opening of the library. The archaeological problems were the main cause of this substantial delay. A continuous succession of difficulties and unexpected events marked the construction of the new Hertziana Library. The environmental constraints of the area; the severe lack of space for vehicles and construction machinery; a construction sequence marked by the progressive removal of old parts to supply room for the new structure; and the complex logistics of storing materials were the most challenging issues faced during these ten years. The works was not conducted on a time schedule composed of a regular succession of phases: in fact, the construction management of the site was based on the simultaneous interaction of a number of processes.

References

[1] L.Cardellicchio, *La Nuova Bibliotheca Hertziana. L'architettura e la sua costruzione*. Ariccia: Aracne, 2015.

[2] C.Conforti, *Giorgio Vasari Architetto*. Milan: Electa, 1993.

[3] C.Conforti, F.Dal Co, *Vittorio De Feo. Opere e progetti*, Milan: Electa, 1987.

[4] S. Poretti, *Italian Modernisms. Architecture and construction in the twentieth century*. Rome: Gangemi, 2013.

[5] G. Kaster, *Die Gärten des Lucullus. Entwicklung und Bedeutung der Bebauung des Pincio-Hügels* in Rom, Master dissertation discussed at Technische Universitat München. Supervisors: Prof. G. Gruben, H. Weirmann.

[6] F.Dal Co, J.J.Lahuerta, A.G. Garcia, *Juan Navarro Baldeweg, le opere, gli scritti, la critica*, Milan: Electa, 2012.

[7] M.M. Segarra Lagunes (Ed.) *Proceedings of the Forth National Conference ArcCo*. Rome: Gangemi 2001. E. Da Gai, *Il progetto di restauro e di recupero della Bibliotheca Hertziana a Roma*, Vol. I, , pp.87-100.

[8] The design report submitted for the competition is fully published in: J.N. Baldeweg, *Ristrutturazione della Bibliotheca Hertziana*, 'Zodiac', n.17, Milan: Editrice Abitare Segesta, 1997.

[9] L. Cardelicchio, *Method for a contemporary archeology*, 'D'Architettura', 33, Milan: Motta Editore, 2008, pp. 66-79.